Cases on Social Media and Entrepreneurship

Syed Far Abid Hossain
BRAC Business School, BRAC University, Dhaka, Bangladesh

IGI Global
PUBLISHER of TIMELY KNOWLEDGE

A volume in the Advances in E-Business Research (AEBR) Book Series

Published in the United States of America by
IGI Global
Information Science Reference (an imprint of IGI Global)
701 E. Chocolate Avenue
Hershey PA, USA 17033
Tel: 717-533-8845
Fax: 717-533-8661
E-mail: cust@igi-global.com
Web site: http://www.igi-global.com

Library of Congress Cataloging-in-Publication Data

Names: Hossain, Syed Far Abid, 1982- editor.
Title: Cases on social media and entrepreneurship / edited by Syed Far Abid Hossain.
Description: Hershey, PA : Information Science Reference, [2024] | Includes bibliographical references and index. | Summary: "The book will explore the role of social media entrepreneurship in the contemporary era with a special focus on women entrepreneurship development"-- Provided by publisher.
Identifiers: LCCN 2023058615 (print) | LCCN 2023058616 (ebook) | ISBN 9798369317815 (hardcover) | ISBN 9798369317822 (ebook)
Subjects: LCSH: Social media--Management. | Businesswomen.
Classification: LCC HM851 .C3684 2024 (print) | LCC HM851 (ebook) | DDC 302.23/1--dc23/eng/20240226
LC record available at https://lccn.loc.gov/2023058615
LC ebook record available at https://lccn.loc.gov/2023058616

This book is published in the IGI Global book series Advances in E-Business Research (AEBR) (ISSN: 1935-2700; eISSN: 1935-2719)

British Cataloguing in Publication Data
A Cataloguing in Publication record for this book is available from the British Library.

All work contributed to this book is new, previously-unpublished material. The views expressed in this book are those of the authors, but not necessarily of the publisher.

For electronic access to this publication, please contact: eresources@igi-global.com.

Advances in E-Business Research (AEBR) Book Series

In Lee
Western Illinois University, USA

ISSN:1935-2700
EISSN:1935-2719

Mission

Technology has played a vital role in the emergence of e-business and its applications incorporate strategies. These processes have aided in the use of electronic transactions via telecommunications networks for collaborating with business partners, buying and selling of goods and services, and customer service. Research in this field continues to develop into a wide range of topics, including marketing, psychology, information systems, accounting, economics, and computer science.

The **Advances in E-Business Research (AEBR) Book Series** provides multidisciplinary references for researchers and practitioners in this area. Instructors, researchers, and professionals interested in the most up-to-date research on the concepts, issues, applications, and trends in the e-business field will find this collection, or individual books, extremely useful. This collection contains the highest quality academic books that advance understanding of e-business and addresses the challenges faced by researchers and practitioners.

Coverage

- E-business systems integration
- E-Marketing
- Virtual Collaboration
- Virtual organization
- Web Service-Based Business Systems
- Web 2.0
- Global e-business
- Outsourcing and e-business technologies
- Sustainable E-business
- E-procurement methods

IGI Global is currently accepting manuscripts for publication within this series. To submit a proposal for a volume in this series, please contact our Acquisition Editors at Acquisitions@igi-global.com or visit: http://www.igi-global.com/publish/.

The Advances in E-Business Research (AEBR) Book Series (ISSN 1935-2700) is published by IGI Global, 701 E. Chocolate Avenue, Hershey, PA 17033-1240, USA, www.igi-global.com. This series is composed of titles available for purchase individually; each title is edited to be contextually exclusive from any other title within the series. For pricing and ordering information please visit http://www.igi-global.com/book-series/advances-business-research/37144. Postmaster: Send all address changes to above address.

Titles in this Series

For a list of additional titles in this series, please visit: http://www.igi-global.com/book-series/advances-business-research/37144

Digital Business and Optimizing Operating Strategies
Gökhan Akel (Antalya Belek University, Turkey) and Mustafa Atahan Yılmaz (Pamukkale University, Turkey)
Business Science Reference • copyright 2024 • 313pp • H/C (ISBN: 9798369304280) • US $250.00 (our price)

Building Smart and Sustainable Businesses With Transformative Technologies
Hamed Nozari (Department of Management, Azad University of the Emirates, Dubai, UAE)
Business Science Reference • copyright 2024 • 306pp • H/C (ISBN: 9798369302101) • US $250.00 (our price)

Metaverse Applications for New Business Models and Disruptive Innovation
Muhammad Anshari (Universiti Brunei Darussalam, Brunei) Muhammad Syafrudin (Sejong University, South Korea) and Ganjar Alfian (Universitas Gadjah Mada, Indonesia)
Business Science Reference • copyright 2023 • 265pp • H/C (ISBN: 9781668460979) • US $250.00 (our price)

Digital Technologies for Entrepreneurship in Industry 4.0
Elena G. Popkova (MGIMO University, Russia)
Business Science Reference • copyright 2022 • 270pp • H/C (ISBN: 9781668442654) • US $250.00 (our price)

Driving Transformative Change in E-Business Through Applied Intelligence and Emerging Technologies
Hamed Taherdoost (University Canada West, Canada)
Business Science Reference • copyright 2022 • 307pp • H/C (ISBN: 9781668452356) • US $250.00 (our price)

Virtual Technologies and E-Collaboration for the Future of Global Business
Jingyuan Zhao (University of Toronto, Canada) and Joseph Richards (California State University, Sacramento, USA)
Business Science Reference • copyright 2022 • 273pp • H/C (ISBN: 9781668450277) • US $250.00 (our price)

Navigating Digital Communication and Challenges for Organizations
José Gabriel Andrade (University of Minho, Portugal) and Teresa Ruão (CECS, Universidade do Minho, Portugal)
Business Science Reference • copyright 2022 • 325pp • H/C (ISBN: 9781799897903) • US $230.00 (our price)

Handbook of Research on Smart Management for Digital Transformation
Belem Barbosa (University of Porto, Portugal) Sandra Filipe (University of Aveiro, Portugal) and Claudia Amaral Santos (University of Aveiro, Portugal)
Business Science Reference • copyright 2022 • 614pp • H/C (ISBN: 9781799890089) • US $325.00 (our price)

IGI Global
PUBLISHER of TIMELY KNOWLEDGE

701 East Chocolate Avenue, Hershey, PA 17033, USA
Tel: 717-533-8845 x100 • Fax: 717-533-8661
E-Mail: cust@igi-global.com • www.igi-global.com

Editorial Advisory Board

Table of Contents

Detailed Table of Contents

Social media and social media marketing (SMM) are essential to increase the performance of MSMEs. MSMEs are providing jobs to the youth population and helping to increase social welfare. Past studies could not explain a reliable view on how social media and SMM are useful to enhance the progress of MSMEs in the case of developing countries like India. Therefore, this chapter measures the MSMEs affecting factors as giving more focus on social media and SMM as per the existing studies. It recognizes the contribution of social media in the MSMEs of India. It provides practical policy recommendations to improve the practices of social media and SMM in MSMEs of India. It proposed that social media is useful to increase profits, sales, customers, efficiency, and production of MSMEs. The new entrepreneurs should increase the practice of social media to achieve various targets in SMEs.

The social media advertising market is anticipated to witness a surge in ad spending; projections indicate an annual growth rate (CAGR 2023-2028) of 4.31%, leading to a forecasted market volume of US$255.8 billion by the year 2028. AI algorithms can analyze vast amounts of user data to identify patterns and preferences. This study aims to explore the prospects and challenges of using AI-driven algorithms for optimizing social media advertising and also the functions and benefits of five algorithms prominently used in optimizing social media advertising, namely recommendation algorithms, lookalike audience algorithms, A/B testing algorithms, bid optimization algorithms, and ad fraud detection algorithms. The study also aims at analyzing the challenges associated with AI-driven algorithms from the perspective of customer experience.

Bangladesh is embracing the modern dimensions of today's global economy, and aiding in this quest are the many budding start-ups that join the country's economy every year. The case details the journey of one such prospective start-up, Azoka, an online e-commerce website specializing in the selling of imported food products. However, in such a competitive market, Azoka has to put in more effort to survive and win the race towards success. This case invites students to look into the problems brewing in the existing operations of Azoka and recommend strategies for the company to revive its business.

This case will allow students to have insight about how transformative HR is leveraging employee data to make evidence-based strategic decisions. Berger, striving to increase turnover every four years, faced HR challenges with manual processes and disconnected data across departments. HR functions were hindered by the lack of integration. To address this, Berger implemented SAP SuccessFactors, automating data collection and analysis across departments. The system provides a unified platform for evaluating performance, streamlining recruitment, and aligning employee goals with company strategy. This HR transformation enhances efficiency, eliminates manual updates, and ensures consistency in tracking employees. The move reflects a strategic response to increased customer demand while maintaining product and service quality, offering valuable insights for undergraduate and postgraduate human resource management courses. This study will showcase how HR is gradually shifting to the world of data-centric solutions and facilitating productivity and effectiveness of the firm.

Despite the favorable market conditions, the motorcycle business in Bangladesh faces unique and difficult obstacles that must be met efficiently. These difficulties include intense rivalry, shifting customer preferences, legislative restraints, and infrastructure limitations. This case study will highlight some of the critical difficulties encountered by TVS Auto Bangladesh Ltd as well as potential solutions. By doing so, the company may increase its market presence and strengthen and achieve long-term growth in the dynamic motorcycle industry. TVS Auto Bangladesh Ltd is a subsidiary of TVS Motor, a prominent two-wheeler manufacturer in India. It operates in the motorbike sector in Bangladesh, where it faces numerous hurdles. Due to increased consumer demand, urbanization, and road infrastructure, the motorcycle industry has grown significantly in recent years. As a result, several well-known businesses, including TVS Auto Bangladesh Ltd, have entered the market to profit from the expanding potential.

The hotel and hospitality industry is a type of industry that has a lot of potential if the business model is unique. Otherwise, it is a very competitive industry to operate in. Based on the changing market trends, businesses adapt and evolve over time. New businesses launch religiously, which makes the industry and market very competitive. It is an identified challenge for entrepreneurs or leaders who belong to this industry. This case is based on a similar business that belongs to this sector, which despite being a newcomer to the industry, became a trendsetter. Waffle Up has adapted similar strategies like proactive innovation, willingness to change, resource leverage, etc. Keeping customers engaged in a business is extremely effortful. This case identifies the prioritized factors and the reasonings behind their choice. The case also focused on the downsides of this industry and explored the factors that can lead to the downfall of a business.

A burning question in this 21st century comes in the form of the development of AI (artificial intelligence). The uses of AI, their strengths, their misuses, and the most pressing question: Does AI eliminate jobs? As the authors dive deep into the depths of knowledge and salvage what they find, they bring about the pressing matter whether artificial intelligence should be given supervision or not. Artificial intelligence helps in many ways, but ultimately, the credibility lies on whether artificial intelligence creates scopes for jobs or takes away certain employment scopes.

This chapter primarily focuses on the significant contributions of female entrepreneurs to Bangladesh's economy in the light of technology/IT as a medium. Its primary objective is to present a comprehensive overview of the experiences of female entrepreneurs, including the support they have received, the obstacles they have had to overcome, and other related aspects and the involvement of technology to carry out their day-to-day activity. The central aim of this study is to explore the role of the digital marketplace in empowering women in Bangladesh's entrepreneurial endeavors. The findings of the study reveal that most women in Bangladesh initiate their businesses to attain self-sufficiency and financial independence. They face significant challenges such as social barriers, family constraints, limited resources, and labor shortages. Many of these female entrepreneurs were students, homemakers, or teachers before venturing into business.

The purpose of this study was to delineate the importance of green leadership in strategic brand management. However, by applying the theory of coevolution and multi-level perspective, the authors have developed a model with dependent and independent variables and explained the causal relationship between green leadership and strategic brand management in Unilever. Moreover, they have used the qualitative data collection method to conduct the research because the factors which are related to green leadership are not possible to measure by number, i.e., not quantifiable. The findings of the study conclude that Unilever is the number 1 company that has been following green leadership for a very long time and also moving forward for more innovations.

This chapter assesses the importance and challenges of digital learning in HEIs during COVID-19 in Uttarakhand. It conducted an online survey of 500 students studying in various programmes of HEIs. Quantitative and qualitative data are collected from the students. A total of 396 respondents recorded their responses on various questions related to study. The descriptive results claimed that the skills and learning capacity of most of the students were adversely affected due to online teaching during COVID-19 in HEIs. Teachers and students have faced several challenges to accomplish their objectives related to teaching and learning in online mode. Content-based analysis was applied to explore the impact of digital platforms on skills and learning of students. It inferred that digital platforms possess a negative impact on HEIs. HEIs, therefore, should create appropriate ICT infrastructure and e-platform to increase skills of the students and teachers during online learning.

The emergence of globalization has changed the entire direction of entrepreneurship and business structure. In today's world, technology has become a significant part of our everyday lives, which is impacting various sectors and education. However, this advantage has caused an emerging, challenging, set of constraints and obstacles that future entrepreneurs must navigate. The significance of this proposal is to outlay the content and scope of the chapter, which will help to explore all the significant limitations and challenges faced by social media entrepreneurship, which are AI-driven. This chapter will also portray the impact of these challenges and constraints on the business strategies and success of AI-powered social media entrepreneurship. It primarily targets educators, policymakers concerned with ethical and legal issues related to AI in social media, students of e-business, and anyone interested in technology and entrepreneurship. Alongside this, all the ethical concerns related to Al in social media and the recommendations to mitigate these limitations are discussed.

This research explores how social media transforms women's entrepreneurship, examining its impact on networking, information gathering, and crowdfunding. Assessing advantages, disadvantages, and global potential, it addresses challenges and growth strategies. Acknowledging rapid social media growth, especially on platforms like Facebook and Instagram, the study delves into technology's role, emphasizing underdeveloped countries. It investigates challenges for rural women, proposing strategies

Preface

Welcome to *Cases on Social Media and Entrepreneurship*, a carefully curated collection of insights and analyses that delve into the dynamic intersection of social media and entrepreneurship. In this era of rapid technological advancements, where social media has become an integral part of our daily lives, understanding its profound impact on entrepreneurship is crucial for navigating the ever-evolving business landscape.

This book, authored by Dr. Syed Far Abid Hossain, Asst. Professor, BRAC University, Bangladesh, explores the multifaceted role of social media entrepreneurship, with a distinctive emphasis on women's entrepreneurship development. The contemporary business environment is heavily influenced by social media, playing a pivotal role in shaping, forecasting, and influencing business strategies. To navigate this challenging landscape, entrepreneurs must possess a comprehensive understanding of the social media entrepreneurship system.

The case studies presented in this volume offer a deep dive into real-world industry scenarios, revealing a spectrum of issues faced by entrepreneurs. Through these cases, readers can enhance their entrepreneurial knowledge and skills, gaining valuable insights into problem-solving and strategy development. The solutions proposed in the case studies empower stakeholders to proactively address challenges and broaden their expertise.

The primary audience for this book includes entrepreneurs, investors, relevant stakeholders, government officials, and policymakers. However, its relevance extends to anyone in the business industry seeking to analyze problems and explore potential solutions in the dynamic realm of social media entrepreneurship.

The thematic chapters cover a range of pertinent topics, including the challenges and historical perspectives of social media entrepreneurship, the integration of AI into social media entrepreneurship systems, the impact on business strategy development, and the role of social media entrepreneurship in poverty alleviation. Each chapter is designed to provide valuable insights, fostering a comprehensive understanding of the complexities and opportunities inherent in the marriage of social media and entrepreneurship.

As you delve into the chapters, you will explore critical themes such as the future of social media entrepreneurship, the power of AI-driven strategies, the potential reduction in advertising costs, and the impact of AI on social media entrepreneurs. The collection concludes with a section on key concepts, paradigms, and best practices, providing a comprehensive overview of the subject.

We hope that this book serves as a valuable resource for individuals and organizations seeking to harness the power of social media entrepreneurship for sustainable development and business success. May the insights shared here inspire innovation, strategic thinking, and a deeper understanding of the transformative potential that social media holds for entrepreneurs in the 21st century.

Chapter 1: Modelling Factors Influencing Consumer Behaviour Towards the Brand Equity of Coffee Machines in Malaysia

Authored by Loo Peng and Wong Hoo, this chapter utilizes Aaker's Brand Equity Model to examine consumer behavior in the coffee machine market in Penang, Malaysia. The study identifies brand loyalty, perceived quality, brand awareness, and brand association as influencing factors on brand equity for coffee machine brands. With data collected from 438 respondents, the chapter provides insights into the dynamics of consumer behavior in the Malaysian coffee machine market.

Chapter 2: Development of Social Networks Entrepreneurship in Ukraine

Authored by Nadezhda Lebedeva, this chapter explores the development of social networks entrepreneurship in Ukraine. It investigates the impact of social networks on business, analyzes alternative social networks, and outlines business models within the context of companies and individual users. The chapter reflects on the economic effects created by companies that own social networks, contributing to a broader understanding of the role of social networks in entrepreneurship within the Ukrainian business landscape.

Chapter 3: A Literature Review for the Association of Social Media With Micro and Small Enterprises in India

Authored by Ajay Kumar Singh, Santosh Singh, and Meenakshi Gupta, this chapter critically examines the impact of social media and social media marketing (SMM) on Micro and Small Enterprises (MSMEs) in India. Focusing on the lack of a comprehensive understanding in past studies, the authors explore factors influencing MSMEs and provide practical policy recommendations to enhance the utilization of social media and SMM. The chapter emphasizes the positive contribution of social media in areas such as profits, sales, customer engagement, and overall efficiency, offering valuable insights for new entrepreneurs in the SME sector.

Chapter 4: AI-Driven Algorithms for Optimizing Social Media Advertising: Prospects and Challenges

Written by Amaresh Jha, this chapter delves into the dynamic landscape of Social Media Advertising, projecting its substantial growth. The study explores the applications and challenges of AI-driven algorithms, specifically focusing on five prominent algorithms: recommendation algorithms, Lookalike audience algorithms, A/B Testing algorithms, Bid optimization algorithms, and Ad fraud detection algorithms. It aims to provide a comprehensive understanding of the prospects and challenges associated with integrating AI into social media advertising, offering valuable insights for marketers and advertisers.

Chapter 5: Azoka.com.bd: Amazing Revival Story of Azoka!

Authored by Rahma Akhter, Proma Quadir, Tazrian Ansar, and Nuzhat Tanisha, this chapter presents a captivating case study of Azoka, an online e-commerce website in Bangladesh specializing in imported food products. The narrative unfolds the challenges faced by Azoka in a competitive market and invites readers to analyze existing operational problems while recommending strategies for the company's revival. This chapter provides valuable insights for students, entrepreneurs, and business professionals interested in the dynamics of the e-commerce sector.

Chapter 6: Transformation of HR Roles Through People Analytics: A Case Study on Implementation of SAP Success Factor by Berger Paint Bangladesh

Authored by Marufa Mizan, this case study explores the transformative impact of People Analytics on HR roles, focusing on the implementation of SAP SuccessFactors by Berger Paint Bangladesh. The study showcases how leveraging employee data can lead to evidence-based strategic decisions, streamlining HR functions and enhancing efficiency. The case study offers valuable insights for undergraduate and postgraduate Human Resource Management courses, showcasing the shift towards data-centric solutions in HR.

Chapter 7: Challenges in the Motorbike Industry (TVS Auto Bangladesh Ltd): A Case Study: TVS Auto Bangladesh Ltd: Navigating Challenges in a Growing Market

Written by Rawnak Jahan, this chapter focuses on the unique challenges faced by TVS Auto Bangladesh Ltd in the motorcycle industry despite favorable market conditions. The case study highlights intense competition, shifting customer preferences, legislative constraints, and infrastructure limitations. It aims to provide insights into potential solutions for the company to enhance its market presence, achieve long-term growth, and navigate challenges in the dynamic motorcycle industry.

Chapter 8: Waffle-Up: From Overcoming Challenges to Being the Trendsetter in the Street Food Business of Bangladesh

Written by Tahsin Mallik and Zeun Nova, this case study revolves around Waffle-Up, a newcomer in the competitive hotel and hospitality industry of Bangladesh. Despite challenges in the market, Waffle-Up became a trendsetter by adopting proactive innovation, willingness to change, and effective resource leverage. The case study provides insights into the factors contributing to the success of a business in the challenging industry, offering lessons for entrepreneurs and business leaders in the food sector.

Chapter 9: Is AI a Threat for Social Media Entrepreneurs?

Written by Khaled Arafat, Rusana Rubain, Sifat Swapnil, and Anika Chowdhury, this chapter addresses the evolving role of Artificial Intelligence (AI) in social media entrepreneurship. The authors explore the strengths, misuses, and potential impact of AI on employment in the 21st century. The chapter poses the crucial question of whether AI poses a threat to social media entrepreneurs and navigates the ethical and practical implications of AI in this context.

Chapter 10: Enabling Women Entrepreneurs in Bangladesh Analysis of the Impact of Technology Adoption: Women Entrepreneurship and Technology in Bangladesh

Written by Faiza Ahsan, this chapter sheds light on the significant contributions of female entrepreneurs in Bangladesh, specifically focusing on the role of technology in their endeavors. The study explores the challenges faced by women entrepreneurs, their motivations, and the impact of technology adoption on their businesses. This chapter provides insights into the experiences of female entrepreneurs, offering valuable lessons for those interested in understanding the intersection of gender, technology, and entrepreneurship.

Chapter 11: Green Leadership in Strategic Brand Management

Authored by Sarika Faisal, this chapter explores the importance of Green Leadership in strategic brand management, focusing on Unilever as a case study. Applying the theory of coevolution and multi-level perspective, the chapter develops a model to explain the causal relationship between green leadership and strategic brand management. The study highlights Unilever as a pioneer in green leadership, setting an example for sustainable brand management.

Chapter 12: Importance and Challenges of Online-Learning in Higher Educational Institutions During COVID-19 in Uttarakhand State of India

Authored by Ajay Kumar Singh, Santosh Singh, and Sandeep Sharma, this chapter assesses the importance and challenges of online learning in Higher Educational Institutions (HEIs) during the COVID-19 pandemic in Uttarakhand, India. The study conducts an online survey of 500 students, revealing the adverse effects on skills and learning capacity due to online teaching. The chapter emphasizes the need for appropriate ICT infrastructure and e-platforms to enhance the skills of students and teachers during online learning.

Chapter 13: The Constraints and Obstacles of Social Media Entrepreneurship Powered by AI

Written by Sheneen Hossain, this chapter explores the emerging challenges and constraints faced by social media entrepreneurship in the era of Artificial Intelligence (AI). Focusing on the globalization of entrepreneurship and business structure, the chapter outlines the impact of AI-driven social media entrepreneurship on business strategies and success. It provides valuable insights for educators, policymakers, students, and anyone interested in the intersection of technology and entrepreneurship.

Chapter 14: The Future of Social Media Entrepreneurship in Business for Women Entrepreneurs

Authored by Shafiqua Nawar, Marzia Zaman, Tasnim Zahir, MD Shadman Khan, and Md Sajid Shariar, this research chapter explores the transformative role of social media in women's entrepreneurship. The study examines the impact of social media on networking, information gathering, and crowdfunding for female entrepreneurs. It addresses challenges, growth strategies, and the global potential of women in social media entrepreneurship, offering practical applications and insights for female entrepreneurs and organizations promoting women in business.

Chapter 15: The Role of Social Media Entrepreneurship in Overcoming Possible Obstacles

Written by Rezuana Tabassum, Sayada Mollika, Md. Ahsanul Saqlain, Md. Ikramul Haque, Abdullah Fahim, and Amreen Azam, this systematic literature review chapter provides a comprehensive overview of recent advancements in social media entrepreneurship. Each section, authored by different researchers, contributes to the collective understanding of brand recognition, promotional tactics, customer engagement, and the use of social media for generating prospects. The chapter aims to pave the way for further innovative developments in the field.

Chapter 16: How Social Media Entrepreneurship Can Boost Business in the Future

Written by Mithila Priasa, Rashidul Mahim, Jotirmoyee Prodhan, Tanzila Akther, Tanzid Morshed, and Fatima Juhana, this chapter conducts a thorough study on the revolutionary power of social media in business. The authors explore the impact of social media on business strategies, supported by a comprehensive literature review. The chapter discusses the future implications for both business and social media creators, backed by relevant data and figures.

Cases on Social Media and Entrepreneurship stands as a rich tapestry woven with insights, experiences, and analyses, offering readers a comprehensive understanding of the intricate relationship between social media and entrepreneurship. Authored by Syed Far Abid Hossain and a cohort of esteemed contributors, this collection not only captures the pulse of contemporary business but also addresses the unique challenges and opportunities that arise in the digital age.

The case studies presented within these pages serve as invaluable tools for entrepreneurs, investors, policymakers, and academics, providing real-world scenarios that bridge the gap between theory and practice. Through an exploration of diverse topics such as the impact of social media on micro and small enterprises, the integration of AI into advertising, the revival story of e-commerce ventures, and the transformative role of technology in women's entrepreneurship, readers are offered a panoramic view of the ever-evolving entrepreneurial landscape.

As we delve into the nuances of social media entrepreneurship, the chapters encapsulate not only the challenges but also the resilience and innovation that define the entrepreneurial spirit. From the intricacies of brand management to the transformative power of People Analytics and the emerging challenges posed by AI-driven social media entrepreneurship, the collection serves as a compass, guiding stakeholders through uncharted territories.

We extend our sincere gratitude to the contributors who have shared their expertise, experiences, and research findings, contributing to the richness of this book. It is our hope that this compilation serves as a catalyst for innovation, strategic thinking, and deeper insights into the transformative potential that social media holds for entrepreneurs in the 21st century.

May the knowledge imparted within these pages inspire future endeavors, foster sustainable development, and empower entrepreneurs to navigate the dynamic landscape of social media entrepreneurship with confidence and ingenuity.

Syed Far Abid Hossain
BRAC Business School, BRAC University, Dhaka, Bangladesh

Chapter 1
Modelling Factors Influencing Consumer Behaviour Towards the Brand Equity of Coffee Machines in Malaysia

Loo Soo Peng
Inti International University, Malaysia

Wong Chee Hoo
https://orcid.org/0000-0003-0691-4463
Inti International University, Malaysia

EXECUTIVE SUMMARY

The goals of this chapter are to examine the application of a customer-based brand equity model based on Aaker's brand equity framework from the viewpoint of consumer behaviour in the coffee machine market in Penang, Malaysia. The theoretical framework of this study is derived from Aaker, namely brand equity model. Brand equity includes four dimensions: brand loyalty, perceived quality, brand awareness, and brand association. Customers or users who possess a coffee machine for home or business usage and are 21 or older are sought as respondents in this research. The chapter uses a structured online questionnaire containing a series of statements based on a 5-point Likert scale. Using convenience sampling, data were successfully collected from a total of 438 respondents. Brand loyalty, perceived quality, brand awareness, and brand association were shown to have a positive and significant influence on brand equity for coffee machine brands in Penang, Malaysia.

INTRODUCTION

In recent years, espresso makers that are intended solely for use in the home have evolved in order to meet the needs of individuals who consume coffee in their homes. Coffee has become ingrained in the routines of many people in the morning. Home brewing coffee, whether it be espresso, filter coffee,

DOI: 10.4018/979-8-3693-1781-5.ch001

or mocha, is something that a lot of people like doing on a regular basis. Automatic coffee machines are able to produce a wide range of flavours and brew a diverse selection of coffees, making them extremely versatile. (Adhi & Yunus, 2021) An increasing number of consumers are interested in purchasing a device that can reproduce the high-quality beverages served in cafes at their own residences. This is because there has been a growth in the popularity of the "home barista." According to Zoe (2021), the vast majority of the big corporations that compete in the international market for automatic coffee machines place a high importance on market expansion, product diversity and quality, as well as the development of ecologically friendly products. In response to the growing demand from customers for customised products that are adapted to the specific needs of consumers in various nations (Danya, 2021), manufacturers offer a broad assortment of coffee manufacturing equipment and solutions. This is done in order to meet the growing demand for such products. According to Mordor Intelligence (2022), the market for coffee machines was predicted to be worth 5.11 billion US dollars in 2020 and would climb to 6.36 billion US dollars by 2027, indicating a CAGR of roughly 4.5%. This growth would be driven by an increase in the number of people purchasing coffee machines. Although COVID-19 has caused some damage to the industry as a consequence of manufacturing and supply chain constraints, manufacture of coffee machines has been halted in the United States, Europe, and Asia as a result of a lockdown in China (Wang & Majerison, 2019). This is despite the fact that COVID-19 has caused some of the market's problems in the first place. This is due to the fact that firms in these areas are being pressured to temporarily ship out a significant quantity of their input materials. In spite of the pandemic, investment of commercial infrastructure and office space has ensured continued growth, particularly in Southeast Asia (Adhi & Yunus, 2021). According to Pappu, Quester, and Cooksey (2007), the subject is fascinating to research because to the increased exposure and awareness of consumers. This makes the topic particularly interesting. Given that Malaysia has to do research on the connection between brand equity and customer loyalty, this concept needs to be examined. We will use Aaker's model of brand equity to disentangle the interconnected parts (brand loyalty, perceived quality, brand awareness, and brand association) and analyse the effect that these factors have on coffee machines in Penang, Malaysia from the perspective of the end-user in order to fill the knowledge gap that has been created as a result of the absence of this knowledge. This knowledge gap was created as a result of the absence of this knowledge. This study will not only help us better understand brand equity by completing some of the gaps in our knowledge, but it will also increase our knowledge in areas where other studies have fallen short. Both professionals in the business world and academics might find value in the findings of this study. On the other hand, there was a dearth of study on the subject of how customer-based brand equity (CBBE) effects coffee machine brands, in particular in the city of Penang in Malaysia. For this reason, it is essential that marketers lay a strong emphasis on the branding of individual stores. There has been a lot of study done on brand equity, including its drivers, models, measurement, and definition (Burt, 2000), however there hasn't been any research done on coffee machines as brands. As a result, the purpose of this research is to deconstruct the components of the well-known customer-based brand equity model that was provided by Aaker (1991) and explore the model's effect and influence on the brand equity of coffee machines in Penang, Malaysia. Aaker's model was proposed because Aaker believed that customers were the most important factor in determining a company's brand equity. The purpose of this study is to provide an answer to the question, "Does brand loyalty, perceived quality, brand association, and brand awareness significantly effect the brand equity of coffee machines in Penang, Malaysia?" This will be accomplished by analysing these factors in relation to sales of coffee machines in the region. The results of this study ought to assist in providing an answer to this question.

Table 1. Operational definitions of study

No	Key Term	Definition
1	Brand Equity	Brand equity represents the value (to a consumer) of a product, above that which would result for an otherwise identical product without the brand's name (Leuthesser, 1995). It refers to the total value of the brand as a distinct asset. It can be rendered as the aggregate of assets and liabilities that are associated with the brand name and symbol which brings about the relationship customers tend to create with the brand. Brand equity is reflected in a way how consumers think, feel, and act towards a particular brand (Aaker, 1991).
2	Brand loyalty	Brand loyalty is defined as the extent of consumer faithfulness towards a specific brand and this faithfulness is expressed through repeat purchases and other positive behaviours such as word of mouth advocacy, irrespective of the marketing pressures generated by the other competing brands (Kotler & Keller, 2006; Kotler, et.al., 2008). Brand loyalty also reflects the likelihood that a consumer might switch to a different brand, more so when that brand makes an alteration, either in terms of its price or its product characteristics (Shariq, 2018)
2	Perceived Quality	Perceived Quality is the impression of excellence that a customer experiences about a product, brand or business, derived through sight, sound, touch, and scent. It is the customer's perception of a product's reliability and robustness, the impression of care and craftsmanship invested in its manufacture, the sense of richness and strength of the materials used, the evident fine attention to detail, and the feeling of the depth of engineering behind the design (Nguyen and Luu, 2018).
3	Brand Awareness	Brand Awareness is defined as the likelihood as to how aware a customer is about a brand, product, or service. It refers to whether consumers can recall or recognise a brand, or simply is the first thing on their mind which is top of the mind brand (Xu et.al, 2020).
4	Brand Association	A brand association is a mental connection a customer makes between your brand and a concept, image, emotion, experience, person, interest, or activity. This association can be immediately positive or negative and it heavily influences purchase decisions (Kotler and Keller, 2006).
5	Coffee Machine	The latest coffee machines for home barista that are easy-to-use and easy-to-clean, with coffee capsules allowing the user to easily make a cup of coffee without having to play around with the machine. The models are fully or semi-automatic, contain built-in milk frothers and boast self-cleaning functions, so all user has to do is turn the coffee machine on, pick a setting and let it do its thing (Nayak, 2022).

LITERATURE REVIEW

Figure 1 shows that the Asian coffee machine market is worth US$16 Bn and is predicted to grow 1.6X by 2030. (NCA, 2022). Particularly, capsule coffee machine use has increased. 62% of Americans drink coffee everyday and love preparing it at home, according to the National Coffee Association(NCA). In 2019, Europe has one of the highest coffee consumptions worldwide. Thus, the market size justify the need to research into brand equity of coffee machines.

Brand Equity

This buzzword does not adequately describe customer-based brand equity. Yusoff, Wahab, and Latiff (2018) state that Keller's CBBE pyramid places an emphasis on feelings, whereas Aaker's pyramid is more straightforward and places an emphasis on recognition. According to Xu et al.(2020) research, the reason that Disney's Mickey Mouse is such a successful brand is that it elicits emotional recognition in the brain's split-second purchasing decisions. According to Aaker (1996), brand equity consists of three components: awareness, associations, and loyalty. These things raise the value of a brand. According to Gartner and Ruzzier (2021), the Aaker Model is used to develop a brand strategy that consists of a number of different components that differentiate a brand from its rivals and move it forward.

Figure 1. Asia coffee machine market forecast
Source: States National Coffee Association (NCA), 2022

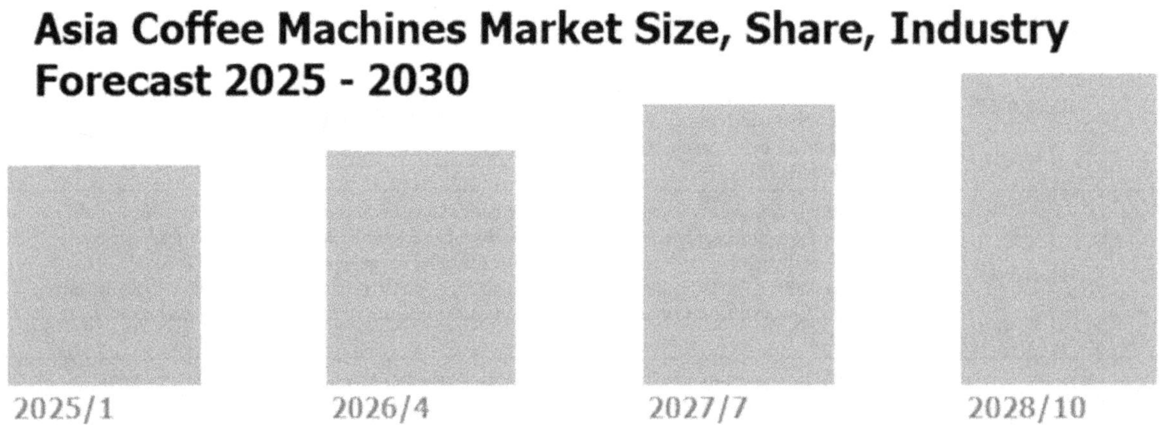

Aaker (1996) identifies five different factors that control brand equity. A product that has higher data scores is likely to have greater brand equity, which encompasses aspects such as customer loyalty, the perception of the product's quality, brand awareness, and the associations consumers have with the brand. According to Xu et al. (2020), when these components are run through the appropriate platforms, they reveal areas in which brand equity could be improved. To achieve this level of recognition, branding must be present at every point of contact with the customer (Kamran, 2022). After that, data can be collected at various stages of marketing in order to inform and increase customer brand loyalty as well as show the uniqueness of the brand in comparison to its competitors (Bilgihan, 2019; Xu et al., 2020).

For the purpose of this investigation, the Aaker Brand Equity Model was utilised. According to Aaker (1996) definition of brand equity, it consists of four different dimensions: brand loyalty, perceived quality, brand awareness, and brand association. Proprietary assets, which are not relevant to this investigation, are also included in this definition of brand equity. The CBBE model developed by Aaker is the most suitable instrument for measuring and analysing the level of brand equity possessed by various manufacturers of coffee machines. This model is the study's dependable factor. According to Sierra et al. (2019), if a brand is successful in achieving resonance, it can identify and capitalise on the loyalty and feelings of customers, whether those feelings are positive or negative. CBBE can be broken down into Keller's four stages, which gives insight into what consumers want before they make a purchase. CBBE can also be broken down into Keller's five stages. Recent research by Prasad et al. (2022) examined the impact of augmented reality technology as a tool for experiential marketing on brand equity.

Brand Loyalty

Yusoff et al. (2022) study the customer-brand relationship using a model that incorporates brand loyalty dimensions that have been shown to have a major impact on brand equity and guides far above brand equity. These brand loyalty dimensions have been shown to have a major impact on brand equity and have been shown to have a major impact on brand equity. They came to the conclusion that brand loyalty contributes to increased brand equity. According to Anas, Sohail, and Farhan (2021), brand loyalty can be defined as a buyer's willingness to repurchase a product despite the availability of alternative options. According to Xu et al (2020), different civilizations have social orders that are more mindful, which results in different levels of customer satisfaction. According to Antra and Yulia (2022), product loyalty is the mind of brand equity, while brand loyalty refers to a strong desire to buy or use a product or service again in the near future. According to Abdul and Ahmed (2022), brand loyalty has an effect on the purchase of comparable products.

In this study, the relationship between brand loyalty and brand equity will be analysed with regard to coffee machines. According to Rungsrisawat and Sirinapatpokin (2019), loyalty is beneficial to both the growth of a product and its long-term outlook. Heuristics make it possible for consumers to restrict their purchases to well-known brands. Loyalty to a brand can result in an increase in market share, the acquisition of new customers, the maintenance of brand expansions, a reduction in promotion rates, and the encouragement of bold brand risks. Yohanes et al. (2022) found a correlation between ideal self-congruence and customer love of brand, ideal self-congruence and customer loyalty to brand, and customer love of brand was found to have a correlation with customer loyalty to brand.

Perceived Quality

According to Aaker (1993), Sumardi (2018), and Marques et al. (2020), perceived brand quality is a consumer's evaluation of a brand's overall excellence or superiority for its intended purpose in comparison to other available options. According to Keller (2003), an increase in a brand's perceived quality can boost its equity. According to Tareq et al. (2022), a satisfied customer base is a direct result of a product or service's perceived level of quality.

Nguyen, Luu, and Hang (2018) reported Return On Investment (ROI) is impacted by a company's perceived quality for the vast majority of major brands. According to Jin et al.'s research from 2020, it is reasonable to assume that a person will consider a product to be the solution to all of their problems if they stop to pick it up and put it in their cart without giving it much thought. The perception of quality is frequently personal. With sufficient empirical evidence, a brand is able to boast about the quality of its products. According to Oliver et al. (2019), the company has no grounds for complaint if a customer quickly chooses an alternative product that may or may not be of a lower quality.

Yulia and Dmitry (2022) mentioned an accurate assessment of a consumer's opinion of a product's quality cannot be made using published research. Brands are benefitted by their perceived quality. The subjective quality is much more important than the objective quality. According to Mehmet and Mohamed (2022), the factors that influence a consumer's perception of quality include their disposition, personality, random conditions, and other elements. The findings of Tareq et al. (2019), companies are able to instantly change the quality of their products from red to green. Customers' perceptions of the brand could shift as a result of activities involving the brand. It seems counterintuitive, but upscale manufacturers of soft drink products use thicker plastic for the bottles of their products. According to Roy, Battacharya, and Mukherjee's research from 2020, brands can sway consumers into making a purchase decision by providing superior customer service, an increase in available information, superior products, or more alluring pricing. According to Yoo and Naveen's research (2021), limited-time price reductions, warranty extensions for automobiles and electronic goods, and savings on after-purchase services such as maintenance and product servicing can have a significant impact on customers' perceptions of the product's quality. Another study by Harun et al.(2022) found quality were found to be a critical determinant of intention to purchase energy efficient appliances.

Brand Awareness

Customers need to be familiar with a brand before they can form a favourable opinion of it. According to Aaker (1991), "awareness" of a brand is defined as the likelihood that a consumer will recognise it as belonging to a particular category of goods or services. According to Sozer and Civelek (2018), having consumers be aware of a brand is one of the prerequisites for building brand equity. This is because consumers need to be aware of the brand before they can form any positive associations with it. According to Wright et al. (2019), the development of brand equity occurs when consumers have a high level of knowledge and familiarity with a brand, which results in positive and unique connections with the brand.

Because it acts as a consumer's "mind storage compartment" where many associations can be stored, through fostering familiarity, signalling the devotion of customers, and prompting consideration of a particular brand at any given time (Aaker, 1991), customer-based brand equity is significantly influenced by brand awareness. This is because brand awareness serves as a consumer's "mind storage compartment" where many associations can be stored. According to Yusoff et al. (2022), the logo of the company is the single most important factor in getting the company's name out there. Since the introduction of sophisticated brand awareness as a factor in consumer brand consideration, the level of brand awareness of a company's products or services has become an increasingly important component of final purchasing decisions made by consumers.

According to the findings of a study conducted by Azzam and Rania (2021) in the Chinese banking industry, advertising had a significant impact on the propensity of customers to make a purchase. According to the findings of the study, customer satisfaction can be increased through increased brand familiarity through advertising's promotion. According to the studies that were discussed earlier, brand awareness is a recognised construct in consumer-based brand equity across industries. Furthermore, it is possible that brand awareness has interconnections with the other sub-dimensions of brand equity.

Brand Association

When considering a company's brand image, it is less important how many people are familiar with the brand's name than how customers feel about the company. According to Aaker (1991), "anything that is related in memory to a certain brand" is the definition of brand associations. Aaker also claims that positive brand associations lead to a positive brand image, which in turn improves brand equity. Similar to how Keller and Lehmann (2006) described brand memories, one way to think of brand connections is as the thoughts that come to mind when you think about the brand. According to Keller (1993), these associations are the primary factor that determine the prestige of a brand. Kotler and Keller (2006) expand the concept of "brand association" to include not only "ideas, perceptions, and emotions associated with the brand," but also "brand-related" colours, music, pictures, smells, beliefs, attitudes, and experiences. (Aaker, 1997).

Keller (1993) contends that the memories and experiences that customers associate with a brand name are the primary contributors to the brand's value. Hossein (2022) used the example of Ronald McDonald to demonstrate how the power of association can be used to associate positive feelings with the McDonald's brand. Establishing yourself as the undisputed leader in your product category when it comes to a distinguishing feature (such as service backup or technological superiority) is one of the most effective ways to protect your brand from competitors. This can be accomplished by establishing yourself as the undisputed leader in your product category. According to the findings of Chan's (2022) research, the presence of a brand in the name of a destination can play a role in determining whether or not tourists choose to visit that location.

Numerous studies (Filieri et al., 2019, Xu et al., 2020; Roosken, 2022; Tareq et al., 2022), among others, have demonstrated the significance of brand association on consumers' buying intent and willingness to pay (Filieri et al., 2019, Xu et al., 2020). Indirectly, businesses benefit from this situation because it results in fewer price-sensitive customers, as well as increased sales and profits. Previous studies have shown that there is a direct correlation between a positive relationship with a brand and increased levels of customer satisfaction (Seo and Park, 2018; Roy, Battacharya and Mukherjee, 2020; Antra and Yulia, 2022). These findings were published in Seo and Park (2018); Roy, Battacharya and Mukherjee (2020); and Antra and Yulia (2022). This, in turn, increases the amount of positive word-of-mouth regarding the brand, which in turn increases the value of the brand overall (Guliyev, 2022). Research conducted in a variety of industries has shown that brand associations have a direct impact on brand equity (Khadim et al., 2018; Sharma, 2019; Yang et al.2019 and Jin et al., 2022). These findings have been published in a number of academic journals.

Underpinning Concepts

We develop a conceptual framework, which is depicted in Figure 2, in order to investigate the hypothesised connection between the enabling aspects that affect the brands' equity in the coffee machines. This allows us to answer the central question of the study. This study places a focus on brand loyalty, perceived quality, brand awareness, and brand association as the four most important components of consumer-based brand equity. The research framework for this study was developed by Aaker (1991). Numerous studies, approaching brand equity from a wide range of theoretical and methodological vantage points, have been conducted using the elements in question. According to the research that was conducted previously and the studies that were cited above, these four aspects appear to play a significant part in determining the value of a brand. Among consumers of coffee machines in Penang, Malaysia, brand loyalty, perceived quality, brand awareness, and brand association were investigated as independent variables in the course of this study.

To answer the research question, the research model is conceptualized in order to understand the proposed relationship between enabling factors influence the brand equity of coffee machine brands shown Figure 2. Based on Aaker's (1991) approach, this study adopts the consumer-based brand equity constructs that consists of four main factors: brand loyalty, perceived quality, brand awareness and brand association. These dimensions of brand equity are widely acknowledged and has been applied to a variety of research in different industries and framework variations. In existing literature mentioned above, it is shown that these 4 factors are considered important factors which affect brand equity. For this study's framework, the dependent variable (DV) is brand equity of coffee machine in Penang, Malaysia while the independent variables (IV) consist of brand loyalty, perceived quality, brand awareness and brand association.

Figure 2. The conceptual framework of success factors influencing the brand equity of coffee machine brands in Penang, Malaysia
Source: Prepared by the authors (2023).

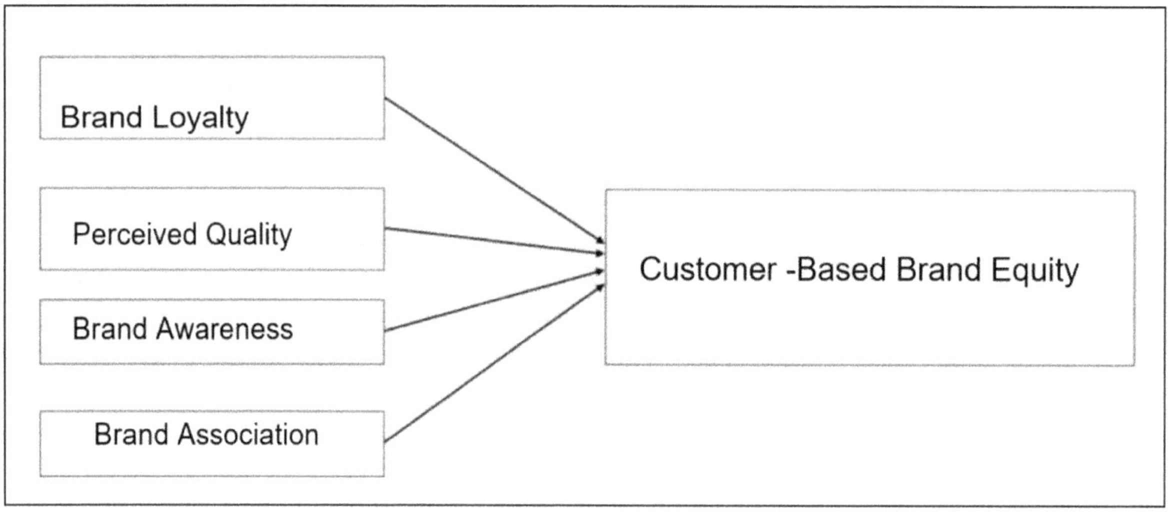

MATERIALS AND METHODS

Research design is the overall approach which has been assimilated by the researcher to integrate various components of the research in a systematic and logical method to effectively address the research questions (Schindler, 2018).

The nature of this research is causal research, the purpose of this research is to identify, determine, and indicate the cause-and-effect relationships between independent variables and dependent variables. To be specific, this research is being conducted to investigate the relationship of Aaker's (1991) brand equity dimensions (brand loyalty, perceived quality, brand awareness, and brand association) towards overall coffee machine brand equity that leads to the selection of the coffee machine in the market. Therefore, this study determines to find out the strength of these relationships and how great the influence is to a consumer. This research will be carried out using survey method by distributing questionnaires to the targeted respondents. Besides that, the study is also based on reviewing previous research and theoretical models. As results, four hypotheses are developed.

Deductive approach is appropriate to apply in this study. This study collects empirical data (primary data) by conducting questionnaire in order to test the existing theory. From this perspective, deductive approach is supported and fulfils the requirement. Quantitative research is chosen as the approach for this study due to the fact that quantification in the data collection and data analysis is involved. Moreover, instead of gaining in-depth insights of the subject matter, the main focus of this study is to test the hypotheses derived from the theoretical model. The relationship between brand equity dimensions and overall coffee machine equity will be determined in this study. Based on these justifications, quantitative approach is more suitable.

The current study examines the brand equity and its dimensions of different success factors for the coffee machine in Penang, Malaysia. As the brand equity and its constructs are the perception of the consumers, the unit of analysis for this study are individuals who are the customers or users of the coffee machine. These individuals are the respondents to the questionnaires for data collection to test the hypotheses in the study. In other words, in aligned with the purpose of this study, the population is the individual of consumers, and it is focused on determining the significance level in the aspect of relationship between independent variables and dependent variable in the study. Furthermore, the questionnaire that designed online is being distributing out to individuals in order to collect data just once time and it will not be extended over a period of time.

Besides, Saunders (2015) supported that the cross-section study will be using when the data is collected at a single point of time. This study is a cross-section study because the research method is distributed the questionnaire via online and it is distributed to the target respondents at one time only and is not repeated answering by the same respondent. More precisely, the target respondents are the customers or users who are 21 years old and above own a coffee machine for residential or commercial use. The research's unit of analysis refers to individual of consumers who are Penang residents.

In the course of this investigation, an online survey in the form of a questionnaire was developed. This gives respondents the opportunity to select from the available options rather than providing them with new ones. This method of inquiry can be finished in a shorter amount of time and with less effort. As a result, it guarantees that the study is relevant and makes the data collection process easier. After the construct measurement is complete, we will collect demographic information so that participants can maintain their anonymity. We chose to sample at convenient times. The researcher decided to go with this method of data collection because it is both quick and efficient. Questions posed through an online "Google Form" are distributed to prospective respondents through e-mail, Facebook, and Whatsapp. In the end, there were 384 respondents who were able to finish the survey successfully. The people who took part in the study are representative of Malaysian society as a whole and include family, friends, and coworkers. (Hinton, McMurray, and Brownlow, 2014) reported that the analysis of the data was completed with the help of the well-known data analysis programme IBM SPSS (Statistical Package for the Social Sciences).

In this study, the determinant-choice questionnaire was developed and used. This allows the respondents to choose the existing alternatives instead of providing new opinions. The advantage of having this type of questionnaire is respondents spend less time to answer and also feel easier to answer. In this way, it ensures the relevance of the study easy compilation of data analysis thereafter. In addition, the demographic information will be gathered after the constructs measurement in order to avoid embarrassment or feel of threat to respondents. The constructs measurement is started from independent variables (brand loyalty, perceived quality, brand awareness and brand association) and followed by dependant variable (overall coffee machine brand equity).

Measurement for all the variables was designed in five-point Likert scale from 1 to 5, with 1=strongly disagree to 5 = strongly agree. The full questionnaire can be found in Appendix 1. The questions items in the survey are adapted from respective sources. By adapting from previous studies, it increases the possibility of reliability and validity of the questions in this study as these questions have been tested in previous research.

RESULTS AND DISCUSSION

Questionnaires were sent out through different social media platforms and an online Google form. There were 384 finished and completed the survey.

Respondents' Demographic Profile

According to Table 2, females made up 53.3% of customers who used coffee machines. Within the sample were 46.7% males. Both men and women have equal purchasing power when it comes to coffee machines. Male customers are more likely to skip surveys than female respondents, which results in a lower response rate from male customers. There were 67.6% Chinese people and 16.8% Malay people. This could be due to the fact that the majority of respondents were either Chinese coworkers or friends of the researcher.

Respondents' ages. The age group of 21 to 30 years old made up 37.3% of the total population. 36.8% are 31-40. This may be an indication that Generation Y, which is currently the largest consumer group, places a high value on lifestyle and experiences, such as purchasing a coffee machine so that they can make their own coffee at home. There was a wide range of marital statuses among the respondents, which suggests that they are either single or married. The respondents' educational backgrounds are listed above. According to table above, the majority of respondents held a bachelor's degree. The remaining individuals have either an SPM or a Diploma. 9.2% of the population holds a PhD.

According to the findings, 87.4% of consumers purchase coffee makers for use in their homes, while only 12.6% purchase them for use in their businesses. The distribution of the respondents' monthly income. 27.1% of respondents make between 4,000 and 6,000 Malaysian Ringgit (MYR) each month, while 25.8% make more than 8,000 MYR each month. Coffee is consumed on more than 10 occasions per month by 45.6% of the respondents. Every person who owns a coffee machine is passionate about coffee and aspires to become their own barista. Finally, the market share leader is the Nescafe Dolce Gusto coffee machine brand from Malaysia with 23.8%, followed by Nespresso and De Longhi with 22.1% each. The discovery demonstrates that competition has increased in the market for coffee machines in Malaysia. The reliability was determined by the fact that each variable had a Cronbach Alpha score that was higher than 0.7.

Table 3 shows that the F values for all independent variables are large and significant at the p0.05 level, hence all hypotheses may be accepted. According to R2, brand loyalty is the single most important driver of brand equity, accounting for 61.9% of the total.

To conclude this chapter, the data analyses are completed by the findings obtained as provided above. In this chapter, the researcher first conducted the pilot test before the full scale distribution to check the data suitability. The data was sequentially tested by factor analysis, reliability test and correlation test to be ensure the adapted items are appropriate and relevant for this study. Researcher then used separately preliminary test and multiple regression to test the hypotheses and obtain the required findings. Next chapter will further explore the discussion of the findings shown in this chapter, and to generate managerial recommendations as well as implications to support the findings obtained.

CONCLUSION

The findings of Marques et al. (2020), which say that consumer loyalty to a brand delivers the largest increase to a company's equity, are given credence by this study, which lends credibility to those conclusions. Because of this, maintaining a consistent level of customer loyalty is essential for every business. Coffee makers place a high value on the continued patronage of their products. According to the conclusions of the survey, loyal clients are what ensures the continued existence of firms. In addition to

Table 2. The frequencies of respondents' demographic profiles

Demographic Profile			Number of Respondents	Percentage
1	Gender	Male	179	46.7%
		Female	205	53.3%
2	Ethnicity	Malay	65	16.8%
		Chinese	260	67.6%
		Indian	59	15.6%
		Others	-	
3	Age	Less than 21 years	18	4.7%
		21 to 30 years	143	34.3%
		31 to 40 years	141	36.8%
		More than 41 years	82	21.2%
4	Marital Status	Single	200	52.2%
		Married	184	47.8%
5	Highest Education Level	SPM or below	35	9.2%
		Diploma	88	23.0%
		Bachelor's degree	215	56.1%
		Master/ PhD	45	11.7%
6	Occupation	Student	34	8.9%
		Self-employed	66	17.2%
		Café Owner		6.0%
		Others		11.2%
		Gov	47	12.2%
		Private Sector	237	61.7%
7	Monthly Income	<MYR 2,000	47	12.3%
		MYR 2,001- 4,000	68	17.6%
		MYR 4001- 6000	104	27.1%
		MYR 6001- 8000	65	17.1%
		>MYR 8,001	100	25.8%
8	Purpose of Purchasing a	Home Use	336	87.4%
	Coffee Machine	Commercial Purpose	48	12.6%
9	Frequency of Coffee	1-5 times / monthly	55	14.3%
	Intake	6-10 times / monthly	136	35.3%
		>10 times / monthly	175	45.6%
		<1 time / bi-monthly (Very less)	18	6.9%
10	Preferred Brand	Breville	68	17.7%
		De'Longhi	85	22.1%
		Nescafe Dolce Gusto	91	23.8%
Nespresso Smeg Others			85 40 15	22.1% 10.5% 3.8%

Source: Prepared by the authors (2023).

Table 3. Hypothesis testing summary

Hypothesis	R2	ANOVA (Regression)		Results
		F	Sig.	
H1: Brand loyalty and brand equity	0.619	700.8	.000	Accepted
H2: Perceived quality and brand equity	0.547	432.4	.000	Accepted
H3: Brand awarenes and brand equity	0.396	279.6	.000	Accepted
H4: Brand association and brand equity	0.571	485.2	.000	Accepted

Source: Prepared by the authors (2023).

this, there was found to be a favourable association between the perceived quality of coffee machines and their brand equity. An rise in brand equity was found to be connected with an increase in perceived quality in four different studies: Foroudi et al. (2018), Sozer and Civelek (2009), Hossein (2022), and Rehan (2022). The trustworthiness of the firm has a direct and immediate influence on the standard of the product or service that is delivered to the customer as well as their estimation of the value of the brand. This study provides support for the research that Hussam and Omar 2022 conducted on the relationship between customer brand views and brand awareness as well as brand equity. According to the conclusions of the study, there are a number of factors that contribute to brand equity. These factors include brand relationships, brand loyalty, and brand image. The brand managers of these companies were able to boost their equity with the help of these research. The findings lend credibility to Keller's (2013) assertion that "attracting consumers is one of the most challenging components of running a business; maintaining them is much more difficult." Keller states that "attracting consumers is one of the most challenging components of running a business." "It is essential to provide outstanding service to one's customers, but doing so is no longer sufficient," said the speaker.

According to Aaker (1991), the term "perceived quality" refers to a customer's overall evaluation of the quality of a product in relation to its intended purpose and other available options. This study lends support to the hypothesis that brand association has a positive impact on coffee machine brand equity. Research conducted by Wright et al. (2019), Zollo et al. (2020), and Yulia and Dmitry (2022) found that there is a positive correlation between brand association and brand equity in all market segments. Therefore, a reputable brand has a better chance of dominating and increasing sales. According to Vita (2022), positive brand associations are recommended. Because people have emotional connections to brands, customers may experience happiness as a result of their associations with those brands. According to the findings of the study, 82% of investors make purchasing decisions based on the reputation of the brand. According to Aaker (1991), it is essential for every branding to encourage strong connections between brands.

The concept of brand equity developed by Aaker for coffee machines was shown to be valid by the study. In this research, factors such as brand loyalty, perceived quality, awareness, and affiliation all played significant roles. The management should work to increase the value of the brand here. The most essential element of any successful brand marketing strategy is devoted customers. According to Wright et al.'s research from 2019, modern consumers are subjected to an overwhelming amount of marketing and are more aware than ever before of deceptive value claims. An authentic brand must reflect the values and norms of its founders or the organisation as a whole in order to keep customers and build relationships that last over time. A strong customer loyalty programme can increase the value of a company's product or service, as well as encourage customers to make additional purchases and recommend the business to others. (ICO, 2022) The coffee machine business in Malaysia is the most rapidly expanding in all of Southeast Asia, and it has consumer-based brand equity. Through the development of customer brand equity, this research will assist marketers of coffee machines in gaining market share as well as revenue. In order to expand their income and their share of the market, coffee machine Marketers are required to evaluate the brand equity of customers.

Due to time restrictions, this investigation relied on a method of non-probability sampling referred to as "convenience sampling." Convenience sampling, on the other hand, does not provide each respondent an equal chance of being selected, in contrast to sample methods that are based on probability. It is possible that as a consequence of this, respondents will offer responses that are in no way pertinent to the topics that are being asked in the research. Because of this, there is a greater chance of receiving data that is erroneous or that leads to the wrong conclusion. In order to acquire a result that is more thorough, specific, and decisive, it is strongly advised that this study be conducted out in other states of Malaysia. It is likely that in the not too distant future, researchers will decide that they wish to focus their studies on more than one location by looking at a wider range of age groups and geographic areas. Because of this, we will be able to generalise with more precision. If, on the other hand, there were more samples to choose from, putting the hypotheses to the test in the event that this research is done again in the future would be a lot less difficult.

REFERENCES

Aaker, D. A. (1991). *Managing Brand Equity: Capitalizing on the value of a brand name*. The Free Press.

AlWahashi & Medjedel. (2022). Impact of CSR on brand equity in the wake of Covid-19 Pandemic: Special Reference To The STC Saudi Arabia. *International Journal of Management & IT A Refereed Research, 13*(2), 15-27. Available at: https://www.globusjournal.com/wp-content/uploads/2022/05/GMIT-132-JJ22-Abdulwahab- Saleh-AlWahashi.pdf

Adhi, R., & Yunus, U. (2021). The Meaning of Coffee for Barista in Speciality Coffee Shop in Indonesia. *Journal of Creative Communications*, *17*(1), 097325862110058. doi:10.1177/09732586211005880

Ali, H., & Omar, M. A. A. (2022). The effects of influencer marketing on overall brand equity through brand awareness and customer brand engagement. *International Journal of Data and Network Science*, *6*(6), 651–658. doi:10.5267/j.ijdns.2022.4.007

Anastasya, Misjedi, Gunawan, Leo, & Tunjungsari. (2022). The Impact of Storytelling Marketing on Brand Equity and Purchase Decisions on Shopee During Pandemic Covid-19. Advances in Social Science, Education and Humanities Research, 4-21.

Bilgihan, Ö., Öztürk, Y., Okumus, F. & Surcu, A. (2019). Brand awareness, image, physical quality and employee behavior as building blocks of customer-based brand equity (CBBE): Consequences in the hotel context. *Journal of Hospitality and Tourism Management, 40*, 114–124. doi:10.1016/j.jhtm.2019.07.002

Burt, S. (2000). The strategic role of retail brands in British grocery retailing. *European Journal of Marketing*, *34*(8), 875–890. doi:10.1108/03090560010331351

Chan, A., Suryadipura, D., & Novel, N. J. A. (2022). Brand Element: Exploring the Effect on City Branding. *International Journal of Professional Business Review*, *7*(4), e0750. doi:10.26668/business-review/2022.v7i4.e750

FACT MR. (2022). *Coffee Machine Market Outlook*. Available at: https://www.factmr.com/report/2452/coffee-machine-market

Filieri, L., Lin, S., Antone, E., & Chatzopoulou, P. (2019). 'Cultural approach to brand equity: The role of brand mianzi and brand popularity in China'. *Journal of Brand Management*, *26*(4), 376–394. doi:10.1057/s41262-018-0137-x

Foroudi, P., Jin, Z., Gupta, S., Foroudi, M. M., & Kitchen, P. J. (2018). Perceptional components of brand equity: Configuring the Symmetrical and Asymmetrical Paths to brand loyalty and brand purchase intention. *Journal of Business Research, 89*, 462–474. doi:10.1016/j.jbusres.2018.01.031

Gartner, W. I., & Ruzzier, M. K. (2021). 'Tourism destination brand equity dimensions: Renewal versus repeat market'. *Journal of Travel Research*, *50*(5), 471–481. doi:10.1177/0047287510379157

Guliyev Seymur, M. (2022). Factors Influencing Brand Equity of Food Componies in Azerbaijan'. Marketing. *Advertising and Branding Journal*, *15*(1), 16–30.

Harun, S. A., Fauzi, M. A., Kasim, N. M., & Wider, W. (2022). Determinants of Energy Efficient Appliances among Malaysian Households: Roles of Theory of Planned Behavior, Social Interaction and Appliance Quality. *Asian Economic and Financial Review*, *12*(3), 212–226. doi:10.55493/5002.v12i3.4463

Hinton, P. R., McMurray, I., & Brownlow, C. (2014). *SPSS explained (2nd ed.)*. Routledge. doi:10.4324/9781315797298

Husain, R., Ahmad, A., Khan, B. M., & Khalil, O. (2022). The role of status consumption and brand equity: A comparative study of the marketing of Indian luxury brands by traditional and social-media. *Journal of Management and Sustainability*, *16*(4), 67–80.

ICO. (2022). *Monthly Coffee Market Report (2021/22)*. Available at: https://www.ico.org/Market-Report-21-22-e.asp

Intelligence, M. (2022). *Coffee machine market - growth, trends, covid-19 impact, and forecasts (2022 - 2027)*. Available at: https://www.mordorintelligence.com/industry-reports/global-coffee-machine-market

Jin, D., Melewar, T.C., Foroudi, P., & Zhong, Z.Y. (2020). An assessment of brand experience knowledge literature: using bibliometric data to identify future research direction. *International Journal of Management Reviews, 22*(3), 287-317.

Julius, Z. (2021). *At home barista experience was one of the key coffee culture trends in 2021*. International Communicafe. Available at: https://www.comunicaffe.com/at-home-barista- experience-one-of-the-key-coffee-trends-of-2021/

Keller, K. L. (1993). Conceptualizing, Measuring and Managing Customer Based Brand Equity. *Journal of Marketing*, *57*(1), 1–22. doi:10.1177/002224299305700101

Keller, K. L. (2003). Brand synthesis: The multidimensionality of brand knowledge. *The Journal of Consumer Research*, *29*(4), 595–600. doi:10.1086/346254

Keller, K. L., & Lehman, D. R. (2006). Brands and Branding: Research Findings and Future Priorities. *Marketing Science*, *25*(6), 740–759. doi:10.1287/mksc.1050.0153

Khadim, R. A., Hanan, M., Arshad, A., Saleem, N., & Khadim, N. (2018). Revisiting antecedents of brand loyalty: Impact of perceived social media communication with brand trust and brand equity as mediators. *Academy of Strategic Management Journal*, *17*(1), 1–14.

Kotler, P., & Keller, K. L. (2006). *Marketing Management (12th ed.)*. Prentice-Hall.

Lee, J. E., Goh, M. L., & Noor, M. N. B. M. (2019). Understanding purchase intention of university students towards skin care products. *PSU Research Review.*, *3*(3), 161–178. doi:10.1108/PRR-11-2018-0031

Marques, C., Silva, R. V., Davcik, N. S., & Faria, R. T. (2020). The role of brand equity in a new rebranding strategy of a private label brand. *Journal of Business Research*, *117*, 497–507. doi:10.1016/j.jbusres.2020.06.022

Mehmet, S., & Mohamed, Y. C. (2022). An Examination of the Effect of Social Media Marketing on Customer Based Brand Equity. *Journal of Business Research*, *69*(12), 5833–5841.

Miliue, D. (2021). *How is the home espresso machine market evolving?* Coffee Roasters and Plant. Available at: https://perfectdailygrind.com/2022/04/home-espresso-machine-evolution/

NCA. (2022). *The National Coffee Data Trends Market Research Series - the "Atlas of American Coffee"*. Retrieved from: https://www.ncausa.org/Research-Trends/Market-Research/NCDT

Nguyen, C. Q., Luu, C., & Hang, T. D. (2018). Factors affecting consumer-based brand equity of Vietnamese pharmaceutical companies. *Dalat University Journal of Science.*, *8*(1S, 1s), 145–157. doi:10.37569/DalatUniversity.8.1S.432(2018)

Oliver, D., Lara-Rodríguez, K., Rojas Contreras, G., & Duque, E. J. (2019). Discovering emerging research topics for brand personality: A bibliometric analysis. *Australasian Marketing Journal*, *27*(4), 261–272. doi:10.1016/j.ausmj.2019.06.002

Pangesti, V. N. (2022). Credible Online Reviews of Skincare Products on Brand Equity and Its Impact on Purchase Intention. *International Conference on Industrial and Systems Engineering, Technology, Innovation, and Management (ICISETIM),* 20-29.

Pappu, R., Quester, P., & Cooksey, R. (2005). Consumer-based brand equity: Improving the measurement empirical evidence. *Journal of Product and Brand Management*, *14*(3), 143–154. doi:10.1108/10610420510601012

Prasad, K., Tomar, A. S., De, T., & Soni, H. (2022). A Conceptual Model for Building the Relationship Between Augmented Reality, Experiential Marketing & Brand Equity. *International Journal of Professional Business Review*, *7*(6), e01030. doi:10.26668/businessreview/2022.v7i6.1030

Rifi, A., & Mostafa, R. B. (2021). Brand credibility and customer-based brand equity: A service recovery perspective. *Journal of Financial Services Marketing*, *27*(1), 1–16. doi:10.1057/s41264-021-00097-x

Roskosa, A., & Stukalina, Y. (2022). *Exploring Brand Equity-Related Factors in Higher Education.* Rural Environment, Education and Personality. Available at https://llufb.llu.lv/conference/REEP/2022/Latvia_REEP_2022_proceedings_No15_online-27- 34.pdf doi:10.22616/REEP.2022.15.003

Roy, D. G., Battacharya, S., & Mukherjee, S. (2020). Qualitative explorations into customer-based brand equity (CBBE) for medical tourism in India. *The Qualitative Report*, *23*(10), 2422–2452.

Rungsrisawat, S., & Sirinapatpokin, S. (2019). Impact of brand equity on consumer purchase intent. *Utopía y Praxis Latinoamericana*, *24*(6), 360–369.

Seo, E. J., & Park, J. W. (2019). A study on the effects of social media marketing activities on brand equity and customer response in the airline industry. *Journal of Air Transport Management*, *6*(6), 36–41.

Sharma, R. (2019). Consumer-Based Brand Equity: Does Country of Origin (COO) Matter to Generation Z Consumers? *South Asian Journal of Management*, *26*(1), 136–150.

Siddiqui, K. (2022). *Celebrity Endorsement, Brand Equity, and Green Cosmetics Purchase Intention Among Chinese Youth.* Academic Press.

Sierra, K., Markovic, S., Singh, J. V., & Iglesias, O. (2019). Do customer perceptions of corporate services brand ethicality improve brand equity? Considering the roles of brand heritage, brand image, and recognition benefits. *Journal of Business Ethics*, *154*(2), 441–459. doi:10.1007/s10551-017-3455-0

Sozer, E. G., & Civelek, M. E. (2018). The Effect of Perceived Benefit on Consumer Based Brand Equity in Online Shopping Context. *Ege Academic Review*, *18*(4), 711–725.

Stukalina, Y., & Pavlyuk, D. (2021). Using customer-based brand equity model in the higher education context: simulating the current university's brand. *Business, Management and Economics Engineering*, *2*(11), 278-288.

Sumardi, A. (2018). Brand Equity: Anticedents Consumer Responses. *Media Riset Bisnis & Manajemen.*, *18*(2), 100–110. doi:10.25105/mrbm.v18i2.5002

Tannady, H. (2022). Ideal Self-Congruence: Its Impacts on Customer Love and Loyalty to Luxury Brands in Indonesia. *International Journal of Professional Business Review*, *7*(6), e0769. doi:10.26668/businessreview/2022.v7i6.e769

Tareq, Homsi, Said, & Frehait. (2021). Role of Big Data in Increasing Brand Equity within Pharmaceutical Industry. *Academy of Entrepreneurship Journal*, *28*(1), 7–13.

Wang, Z. R., & Marjerison, R. K. (2019). Factors Influencing Consumers' Purchase Intentions Towards Made to-Order Tea Drinks in China. *International Journal of Food and Beverage Manufacturing and Business Models.*, *4*(2), 29–52. doi:10.4018/IJFBMBM.2019070103

Wright, L. T., Robin, R., Stone, M., & Aravopoulou, D. E. (2019). Adoption of big data technology for innovation in B2B marketing. *Journal of Business-To-Business Marketing*, *26*(3-4), 281–293. doi:10.1080/1051712X.2019.1611082

Xu, L.Q., Wang, K.Y., Ma, C.G., & Zhang, X.F. (2020). Business intelligence in online customer textual reviews: Understanding consumer perceptions and influential factors. *International Journal of Information Management, 37*(6), 673-683.

Yang, D., Sonmez, M., Gonzalez, M., Liu, Y., & Yoder, C. Y. (2019). Consumer-based brand equity and consumer-based brand performance: Evidence from smartphone brands in the USA. *Journal of Brand Management*, *26*(6), 717–732. doi:10.1057/s41262-019-00154-w

Yoo, B., & Donthu, N. (2021). Developing a Scale to Measure the Perceived Quality of an Online Shopping Mall. *Quarterly Journal of Electronic Commerce*, *2*(1), 31–47.

Zeithaml, V. A. (1988). Consumer Perceptions of Price, Quality and Value: A Means-End Model and Synthesis of Evidence. *Journal of Marketing, 52*(3), 2-22. Available at: https://www.lucintel.com/Malaysia/opportunities-for-the-coffee-maker.aspx

Zhai, Al Mamun, Hayat, Salamah, Low, & Ali. (2022). Brand equity trend analysis for fashion brands (2001-2021). *The Journal of Psychology*, *13*(1), 238–255.

Zia, Younus, & Mirza. (2021). Investigating the Impact of Brand Image and Brand Loyalty on Brand Equity: the Mediating Role of Brand Awareness. *International Journal of Innovation, Creativity and Change, 15*(2), 91–106.

Zollo, L., Filieri, R., Rialti, R., & Yoon, S. (2020). Unpacking the relationship between social media marketing and brand equity: The mediating role of consumers' benefits and experience. *Journal of Business Research*, *11*(7), 256–267. doi:10.1016/j.jbusres.2020.05.001

Chapter 2
Development of Social Network Entrepreneurship in Ukraine

Nadezhda Anatolievna Lebedeva
https://orcid.org/0000-0003-4095-2631
International Personnel Academy, Germany

EXECUTIVE SUMMARY

Social networks are some large segments of internet business with their models of development and existence. Social networks as social and economic phenomenon are considered by researchers of various scientific fields. The basis for such research in modern works is the information technology sector as a platform for the functioning of social networks. Economic disciplines have their place in the structure of scientific areas dealing with social networks. Thus, marketing and management, personnel management, and entrepreneurship reflect modern economic trends related to this issue. In modern conditions, the companies that own social networks allow users to become their business partners, thereby creating completely new economic effects. The main tasks of the research are the determination of the impact of social networks on business, determination of approaches and functions of creation in Ukraine, means of existence of alternative social networks, and outline of business models of alternative social networks in terms of companies and individual users.

INTRODUCTION

In our rapidly developing century, it is difficult to imagine life without the Internet. Practically all spheres of human life are somehow connected with the World Wide Web.

The Internet had a tremendous impact on how businesses were held and developed in the tourism sector and also represented a major support for their expansion. The Digital World became more powerful each day and forced businesses to be present in the virtual space to remain competitive and make online business transactions. (Surugiu et al., 2015, p. 3)

DOI: 10.4018/979-8-3693-1781-5.ch002

As a result of human communication, social networks appeared which began to play a huge role in our lives. Thanks to them, distances have disappeared, certain standards are being created, and even businesses strive to exert a certain influence on their clients with the help of social networks, to gain recognition from as many users as possible. As a result of the above-mentioned processes, the topic of entrepreneurship development in social networks is becoming more and more relevant. The rapid development of Internet technologies and the emergence of artificial intelligence tools require detailed scientific researchers, extensive literary images and deep thinkers with a future perspective. All this can become the basis of business transformation, especially entrepreneurship.

Social networks have become a kind of centre for coordinating human relations with the function of regulating communication processes in the virtual space. Indeed, promoting products and services using social media is a relatively inexpensive way of marketing and advertising, allowing companies to have direct contact with customers and potential consumers. Of course, creating the image of a company or enterprise (even a small one), as well as sales tools, depends on the goals. In a broad understanding of entrepreneurship in social networks, the concept of social capital should be touched upon, since it underlies the interest of entrepreneurship. Ukrainian scientists Shpykulyak and Hrytsaenko (2019) derived a definition of this concept, which can be considered basic when studying the social activities of people. By their definition, social capital is a set of income-generating connections and socio-economic relations that arise in a certain social network based on existing norms and trust. Social capital is formed based on relationships within groups of people who are united by common interests and maintain informal contacts for mutual benefit and assistance. Social capital is inextricably linked with institutional formations, literally formed thanks to them. We believe that social capital plays a leading role in the development of entrepreneurship (Shpykulyak and Hrytsaenko, 2019, p. 192).

Another problem that contributes to the relevance of research on entrepreneurship in social networks is the war in Ukraine. What is the role of such a business to save the country's economy? Perhaps for states that find themselves in similar conditions, the work and experience of Ukrainian exercises will become very useful and interesting. The author of this chapter sees this as a novelty in the context of international scientific cooperation.

The purpose of this chapter is to take a comprehensive look at the development of entrepreneurship in social networks in Ukraine based on scientific literature. The novelty of this study lies in the generalization of the scientific works of Ukrainian scientists taking into account the experience of advanced foreign researchers. During the research, the author used general scientific methods: synthesis, analysis, complex approach, philosophical and theoretical justification and generalization.

BACKGROUND

According to Smal, & Kokot, (2017), the category "social entrepreneurship" is often used in a very broad sense and for a diverse range of initiatives. For many, social entrepreneurship is associated only with the activities of non-profit organizations that have started commercial activities, earning funds to realize their goals. Others use the term to refer to anyone who has started a non-profit organization. This term is often used to describe business owners who integrate social responsibility into their business activities. It is quite difficult to explain in a few words such a multifaceted sphere of human activity as social entrepreneurship and the entire range of its interpretations" (Smal, & Kokot, 2017).

According to Khan's (2022) opinion:

Social media marketing uses online platforms to persuade consumers to go shopping for goods or services. The technique is effective both for individuals and corporates. However, marketers must understand several strategies they can deploy to achieve positive outcomes from this type of marketing. Some include choosing the right social media platforms to communicate the correct information. Also, several preparations are required, such as creating a social media team to manage the posts and ensure they are published consistently. Retailers must keep a healthy relationship with their customers through conversing. The Web adds value to the discussions by allowing people to alter the information on social sites. Resultantly, communication is always getting more and more valuable. Additionally, it will enable people to create and retrieve data. Therefore, businesses and customers get to know each other better since they can effectively find the necessary information, they require about each other. (Khan, 2022, p. 29)

Cesaroni, F. M., Demartini, P., & Paoloni, P. (2017) dedicated their scientific work to women in business and social media. Researchers reviewed the literature on women in business and social media to understand the current state of the art and whether and to what extent research has been conducted to date on these questions: "How and why do women entrepreneurs and managers use social media? Do they use social media for marketing, networking or personal purposes?" (Cesaroni, et al., 2017). The article is based on a literature review on women entrepreneurs/managers and social networks. To this end, the researchers conducted an extensive literature review in Scopus using a set of selected keywords. The selected articles were reviewed and classified in an attempt to identify the main findings resulting from the research and analysis conducted to date. Thus, the result was an extensive body of scholarship on women in business research and a new perspective on social media. What was surprising was that none of the documentation on how and why women in business use social media comes from developed economies. A common feature of the Scopus literature reviewed was that they focused on women entrepreneurs in emerging economies: Kenya, Indonesia, Nigeria, Egypt and South Africa. "In these countries, social media can open up new opportunities for women entrepreneurs and encourage the creation of new women-run businesses due to their flexibility and qualities. The main contribution is to advance knowledge and practice on gender in the management and use of social media, with a focus on empirical research, theoretical development, practice and current issues. The benefits are related to a better understanding of discussions on gender and management topics by redefining networking activities on social networks" (Cesaroni, et al., 2017, p. 316).

The work turned out to be similar in gender themes Sukumar, Arun, Jafari-Sadeghi, Vahid and Xu, Zimu (2021). Their research provides a first-hand data analysis on the influence of social media on entrepreneurship in China with a particular focus on the current young generation (mainly aged 20 and 30). The results have demonstrated that social media has indeed been an integral part of the lives of today's young generation where nearly 80% of the participants reportedly use social media at least once a day. In comparison with popular Western social media sites, Weibo and WeChat are the two dominant sites that have been adopted in China. Results have also shown that social media plays an important role in marketing as well as in the process of information collection. The features of Weibo and WeChat have also resulted in differences in how people utilize them. However, there are also challenges in using social media, such as the existence of false information. The firewall imposed by the Chinese government has also had implications on how businesses use social media in China. The research is not without its limitations. Firstly, the sample selected was small and made it difficult to generalize the results for the whole population. Secondly, data was collected from a Shanghai-based university, the sample needs to be expanded to include further institutions to provide more concrete evidence of the influence of social media on start-ups (Sukumar, et. al., 2021). This study is interesting to the author of this chapter because of the experience of using WeChat in Ukraine, which is described from a pedagogical point of view (Lebiedieva, 2023).

According to Emmanuel, C. P and colleagues (2022): «Facebook, the most popular social media network, exceeded 2.93 billion active monthly users in early 2022, followed by YouTube (2.6 billion), WhatsApp (2.44 billion), and WeChat (1.29 billion), according to Statista» (Emmanuel, et al., 2022). This research paper aims to explore the entrepreneurship opportunities for young female students in emerging nations. Adopting the technology acceptance model paradigm, the authors attempt to understand the moderating effects of perceived usefulness on social media behaviour. The authors conducted a person-administered survey on female students with entrepreneurship intentions. The survey is analyzed using structural equation modelling (Amos). According to the findings, the variables such as social influence, perceived ease of use, perceived enjoyment, perceived usefulness, attitude toward social media and social-media behaviours have a significant relationship, indicating tremendous entrepreneurial opportunities, especially social-media-based, for young women in emerging nations. Results also show that social media attracts women entrepreneurs positively in emerging countries. Since the data was collected only in a single Asian nation, the results may not be generalizable. The study has a significant impact on social media and entrepreneurial development (Emmanuel, et al., 2022, p. 241).

Çiçek, B. (2018) developed a model for an entrepreneur in social networks since the scientist defined a social network entrepreneur as a person who strives for the opportunity to make a profit through social networks, as well as one who initiates and manages a business in these social networks. Such entrepreneurs sell products or services on social networks, and platforms, and earn money through content production. In a structural sense, Çiçek, B. (2018) noted that such people have a different environment than established entrepreneurs.

This environment represents an area where borders disappeared, in the name of doing business. If need be, a street, an office, a room in a house, or any corner in nature, can be a place where a social media entrepreneur can produce content, conduct business and earn money, as well as any user anywhere in the world can be his/her target audience, in fact even his partner, investor, shareholder of the business he/she is about to run. (Çiçek, 2018, p. 13)

The model proposed by Çiçek, B. (2018) includes three basic stages.

The first stage is the learning process. According to this, an entrepreneur who is considering to do business in social media should first determine the limits of the business to be conducted, be an expert at what he/she is going to do, know how to learn from others, learn that there is not a shortcut of doing business and earning money and that he/she should never give up. The second stage is the preparation phase. In the preparation phase, the entrepreneur must have a vision, be innovative, and not be afraid to lose and try again. The final stage is the action-taking phase. The most important thing at this stage is that he/she should not try to do everything on his/her own. He/she needs to be able to get help from others when necessary and in that sense, he/she should be flexible. (Çiçek, 2018, p. 14-15)

Ugolkova (2021) investigated the state and features of digital marketing in modern times business conditions. An important aspect of the work is the analysis of the role of social networks as one of the most important marketing tools. It is highlighted in her work features of using such social networks as

Facebook and Instagram for brand support and development of the base of potential customers. Found to be the most effective way to use social networks as a marketing tool. Ugolkova (2021) also characterized the main trends and innovations in the use of social networks that will be most significant for marketers in 2021 and 2022 given the development of digital technologies.

LITERATURE REVIEW

A fairly large number of scientific literature studies covering completely different areas of economic and human activity are devoted to entrepreneurship in social networks. Works are sometimes completely unexpected on the subject of research. However, all of them are quite relevant in terms of generalization and determination of further strategies for the development of entrepreneurship. For example, Md Jiyon Khan (2022) thesis reflects on "using social media as a marketing strategy for businesses and describes significant ways a company can benefit from social media marketing. It provides insights into social media users, including their ages and how frequently they use social platforms. In addition, it explains how they can utilize the platform, especially through two-way conversation, to maintain cohesion with the consumers. This paper also shows how businesses can use social media not only for marketing commodities but also for maintaining a cohesive relationship with customers. In addition, it has elaborated on tips that can be utilised to integrate customer engagement and run effective social media campaigns. The paper explores tips that can be used to boost social media marketing to increase audience size and sales. For these tips, the top social media platforms have been discussed and specific recommendations elaborated for each. The platforms include Facebook, Twitter, Instagram, and Snapchat" (Khan, 2022, p. 6). Agusiady and his colleagues (Agusiady et al., 2024) considered the influence of social media communication on consumer perceptions of brands and purchase intentions in the pandemic and post-pandemic era. They conducted an analytical study. Very useful research about the responsibility of social media in times of societal and political manipulation is done by Reisach, U. (2021). Interesting and informative article is about potential used of social media/mobile phone to support promotion and marketing in the rural tourism destination is written by Adi, S. and collegues (Adi et al., 2021). Social media and e-mail marketing campaigns are considered in the work by Păvăloaia and other scientists (Păvăloaia et. al., 2020; Allam, 2020; Buljan, & Miočić, 2021).

An unexpected subject of research is presented in a scientific work by Scott Wallsten and Corwin Rhyan (2014) which shows the wide range of the phenomenon under consideration. Their article analyzes the usefulness of social media tools for food truck operators.

The author of this chapter takes a comprehensive approach to studying the problem of entrepreneurship through social networks in Ukraine, paying attention to both social entrepreneurship and the experience of small enterprises that are serious about promoting their products using social networks. Therefore, the literature on the topic was collected differently, but relevant and useful for this theoretical work. Thus, Gritsaenko (2017) studied social capital in the formation of the entrepreneurial network of the agrarian sphere of Ukraine. Yarmolyuk, Fisun and Shapovalova (2020) considered social networks as a modern promotion tool. Galushka (2013) described the phenomenon of social entrepreneurship, the very concept and prospects for development in Ukraine. Kazak (2021) studied the factor assessment of the influence of social networks on the economic efficiency of entrepreneurial activity. Demydchuk and Sapozhnyk (2021) devoted their scientific work to the influence of social networks on the development of entrepreneurial activity. Romanyshyn & Greskiv (2015) studied the peculiarities of marketing

Figure 1. Main characteristics that define social entrepreneurship (summarized by the author of the chapter)

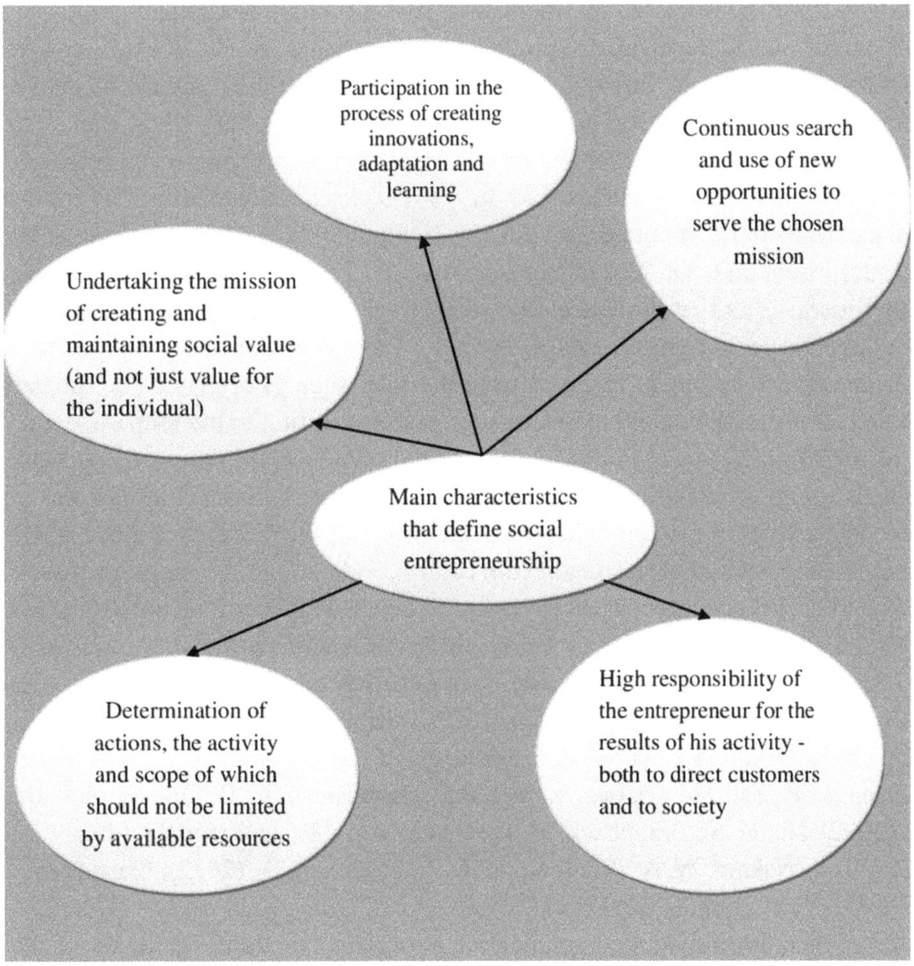

activities in social networks. An interesting study by Kornetskyi and Ishakov (2016) is about alternative social networks, their business model and entrepreneurship. Khymytsia & Sekanova, (2018) provided practical experience of a Ukrainian enterprise thanks to advertising and informational representation in social networks. Ugolkova (2021) described digital marketing and social networks in her scientific work. Influence marketing as a communication tool for product promotion in social Internet networks was investigated by Zhurylo (2020). The actual problem of the use of objects of intellectual property rights during the implementation of entrepreneurial activities in social networks is described by Mihailina & Bevzyuk (2020) and Ognevyuk, (2016). The article by Heiko (2020) is devoted to the priorities of the development of entrepreneurship in Ukraine in the conditions of the COVID-19 pandemic and the post-quarantine period. According to Smal, & Kokot, (2017), the author of this chapter summarized and compiled a diagram of five features that define social entrepreneurship:

Yuskiv (2021) investigated the legal issues of e-commerce in social networks. The influence of digital marketing on the development of entrepreneurship in the conditions of war is devoted to the research of Vytvytska, Suvorova & Koryugin, (2022). The scientific work Mangushev & Pikhtin, (2021) is devoted to the application of digital marketing tools to increase the efficiency of business activity. Electronic technologies and the development of entrepreneurship were studied by Kulikova, (2022), Korotich, Orel & Ryabichko (2010), Kozlovskyi & Tanasienko, (2019), Kornukh & Makhanko (2014). Information systems and technologies in the insurance protection of agrarian entrepreneurship were investigated by Gudz, G. O. (2016). Datskevich, (2016) paid attention to the dialectic of interaction between the social responsibility of entrepreneurship and the social capital of society. In turn, Hrytsaenko (2020) outlines the role of social capital in the development of self-regulation of entrepreneurial activity. "In Ukraine, an attempt was made to legalize social business. In 2011, Oleksandr Feldman, an MP from one of Ukrainian political parties faction, submitted two draft laws to the Verkhovna Rada Committee on Tax Policy: "On Social Enterprises" and "On Amendments to Article 154 of the Tax Code of Ukraine on Support of Social Enterprises." The first introduced the concept of "social enterprise" and defined the criteria by which an enterprise could be recognized as "social". The second draft law proposed to exempt social enterprises from taxation of profits received from the sale (supply) of goods and the performance of social works and services. Oleksandr Feldman also suggested creating an Interdepartmental Commission on Support of Social Enterprises, which would determine the "social" status of a particular enterprise and its compliance with the conditions for receiving tax benefits. The first draft law was rejected at the stage of its consideration by the Committee on Tax Policy of the Verkhovna Rada of Ukraine. After that, Oleksandr Feldman withdrew his second bill from consideration. The adoption of such a law would be premature, and the introduction of preferences and the need to determine the degree of sociality hid the danger of abuse both by traditional business and by the Interdepartmental Commission" (Smal, & Kokot, 2017, p. 16). As for global studies, the work experience has become valuable (Olanrewaju, A. S. T., Hossain, M. A., Whiteside, N., & Mercieca, P. (2020), Secundo, G., Del Vecchio, P., & Mele, G. (2021), Schjoedt, L., Brännback, M. E., & Carsrud, A. L. (2020), Kadam, A., & Ayarekar, S. (2014), Troise, C., Dana, L. P., Tani, M., & Lee, K. Y. (2022), Emmanuel, C. P., Qin, S., Hossain, S. F. A., & Hussain, K. (2022), Nikou, S., Brännback, M. E., Orrensalo, T. P., & Widén, G. (2020), Wallsten, S. J., & Rhyan, C. (2014), Nakara, W. A., Benmoussa, F. Z., & Jaouen, A. (2012), Gustafsson, V., & Khan, M. S. (2017), Wu, Y., & Song, D. (2019)).

All mentioned literature provides comprehensive information on the development of social networks and entrepreneurship in various industries and countries, outlining a strategy for Ukrainian entrepreneurship using the Internet.

RESULTS AND DISCUSSIONS

In almost every country, every person spends at least an hour a day on social networks. According to estimates by Boyko, V., Osadchiy, A., & Boyko, L. (2021), the daily audience of subscribers is 22 million people. Moreover, if previously the main part of it consisted of young people aged 15 to 30 years, now we can safely talk about the popularity of the Internet among children and the user audience of 60 years and above. The range of interests is quite wide: games, educational sites that contain homework for pupils and students, all kinds of stores, and professionally oriented sites. Almost everyone in Ukraine has their website Instagram or Facebook. When a person logs into a social network, he or she can spend a huge amount of time on it: a user looks at one thing, follows a link, and now you're reading new content that directs you somewhere else of interest. Links are even more captivating when friends like them. Sometimes it turns out that the information is not so important, and you can do without the product. However consumer feelings are too strong in modern society, so almost every user has the desire to start a business on social networks. Well-known brands and companies also have their social pages, thanks to which they constantly increase the audience of their fans. Pages on social networks have become a positive and necessary attribute, since they can be shared with friends, recommended to friends around the world, and the like. This is especially useful for the advertising business and brings considerable success to those companies that use it on social networks, receiving almost instant feedback from consumers of goods and services.

The Advantages of Maintaining a Business Account

"Promotion of the brand or business should be considered on such social platforms as Facebook and Instagram. When a potential client sees a live profile of a company on Facebook or Instagram, he understands that the company has been working for a long time and values its reputation. Increasing the level of trust in the brand increases the level of sales. Social networks allow the entrepreneur to do this publicly, the user can count on a faster response, as well as receive additional information from other buyers. Advertising through social networks allows drawing attention to the brand every moment, and quickly informing about new promotions, events and products in the assortment. There is no need to wait for users to go to the site and read the news; people can notify all interested parties through social networks. Everyone chooses the social network in which it will be more profitable and comfortable for him to develop because regardless of the choice of platform, it can be found by the audience" (Boyko et al., 2021, p. 181). There are advantages of conducting an Internet business, which the author of this chapter grouped in a picture:

Scientists also note the advantages of Instagram, where they highlight: - quite detailed statistics. There is an opportunity to analyze and develop a further strategy; - detailed information about the company or brand for customers; - presence of promotion through other social networks; - the possibility of direct communication with the audience; - ability to conduct various types of audience surveys for further analysis; - availability of a wide range of opportunities for information dissemination; - the number of active users of a fairly young age category (18-29 years old); - the existence of real examples of business accounts (Boyko et al., 2021, p.181).

YouTube is a powerful social media tool, being related to the idea of uploading and viewing video files. There are a lot of materials related to heritage tourism on this platform, and anyone interested can easily access information and movies about heritage tourism destinations, such as various museums, castles, churches, and so on. Also, the YouTube advantage offered to the visitors is related to the possibility of uploading a movie of the visited asset, displaying own experiences on the platform, also with own thoughts and positive or negative reviews. Consequently, not only a business from a tourism heritage area can make a movie and post it, but also any visitor who can share experiences, thoughts, personal perspectives. (Surugiu et al., 2015, p. 6)

Features of the Commercial Process

Advertising plays a leading role in promoting goods and services through social networks. According to Ukrainian scientists Roman Borovets, and Yuri Kit (2018), many methods and techniques are commonly used for advertising on social networks. These include traditional promotion through the creation

Figure 2. The advantages of maintaining a business account, for example on Facebook (summarized by the author of the chapter)

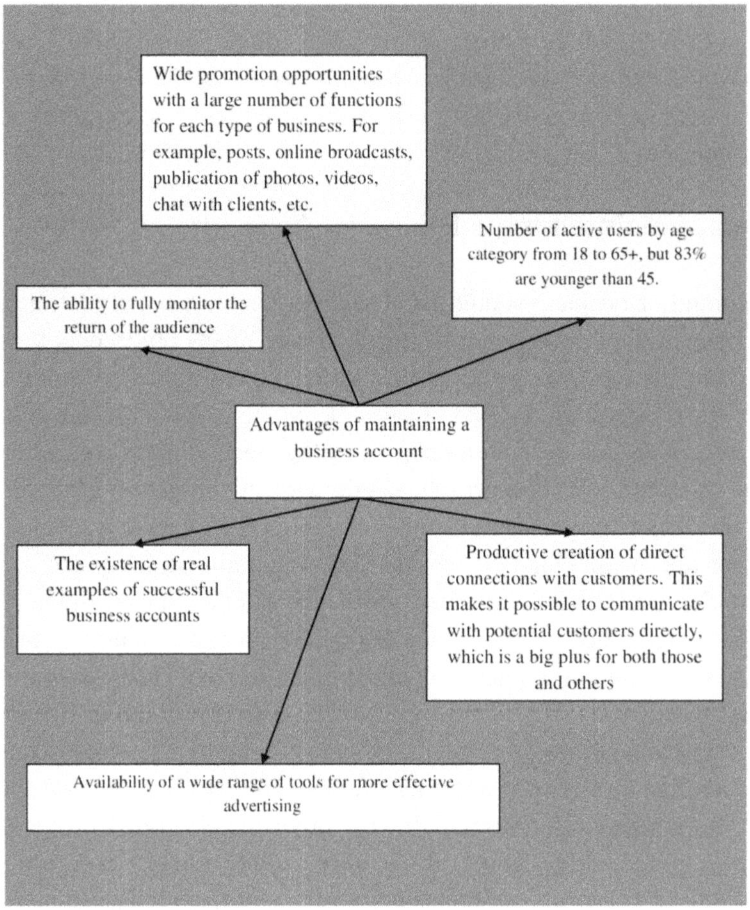

of own groups or public pages, "holding various prize draws or contests, advertising publications in popular communities or on public pages, and placing advertising links in comments or discussions, etc. Recently, advertising on forums and blogs has become one of the most effective marketing tools. This type of advertising helps to solve a wide variety of tasks and competently promote products and services. The main advantage of such a tool as promoting on forums is that the information published on them is posted for a very long time (that is, as long as the site exists, the information will be posted there). Thousands of people will be able to see it during this time. Specialized advertising sites gather a narrow audience that meets the needs of the advertiser. This is an effective way of advertising to promote services and products of a narrower focus" (Borovets, Keith, 2018, p. 56). According to Romanyshyn, & Greskiv (2015), marketing in social networks, like any other type of advertising or way to remind or declare oneself, has certain advantages and disadvantages, positive and negative effects that can affect not only the product that is advertised, but also for the entire enterprise in general. "On the one hand, conducting business using the capabilities of social networks makes it possible to attract a significant number of buyers, thereby increasing the company's profit. On the other hand, in social networks there is an opportunity to quickly share one's impressions, so as soon as one of the users discovers that the advertised product or service has serious flaws, a large circle of people will learn about it. In this case, the promotion of the product may provoke an effect opposite to the expected one. Therefore, when deciding on the involvement of social networks in the implementation of marketing policy, the company's marketers should thoroughly approach this issue and carry out the most detailed analysis of the situation that has arisen or may arise during the implementation of such activities, since the effects of the implementation of marketing activities at two enterprises will be different and the result will always depend on several factors: the field of activity of the enterprise, the product or service and their features, the target audience, etc." (Romanyshyn, & Greskiv, 2015, p. 188). Boyko, V., Osadchiy, A., & Boyko, L. (2021) consider several stages of advertising analysis to obtain profit through a social network: monitoring, analysis, content creation, and advertising placement.

"Monitoring. Information about the potential consumer is collected: age, hobbies, location, social status and other details. It is necessary to understand which social networks he uses, which sites he visits, when, and so on. The more data, the better, because you need to target a certain group of users. Analysis. At this stage, all collected information is analyzed. Based on the data, it is possible to understand how the client can act, where he will receive an advertising message, his advantages and other nuances, which will then help in setting up the campaign. Content creation. Now, based on the analyzed information, you can create a personalized message that will interest the target audience or its segment. Advertising targeting on the Internet should be perceived by a person as if the ad was created just for him. Advertising placement. With information about where people spend their time, advertising channels are selected. These can be search engines (Coor1e Адwords, Yandex Direct and social networks (Facebook, Instagram and others))" (Boiko et al., 2021, p.182). Scientists also provide advice on maintaining social pages if a businessperson expects a large number of customers. It should be an additional team with an administrator, editor, moderator, advertiser and analyst, people who ensure the delivery of goods to consumers. As Romanishyn, S. B., & Greskiv, I. R. (2015) note, representatives of big business were among the first to realize the potential of social networks and began to actively use them for their promotion. "Through social networks, large businesses usually solve strategic long-term marketing tasks: branding, raising awareness of the target audience, increasing loyalty and trust in brand products, tracking thoughts and attitudes among the target audience; determining what the support system will be" (Romanyshyn, & Greskiv, 2015, p. 188).

Romanyshin & Greskiv (2015) also noted that representatives of the following business areas are highly active in social networks: 1) developers and builders; 2) manufacturers; 3) banks and other financial structures; 4) film studios; 5) network service operators; 6) trade networks. In recent years, barriers to entry have fallen dramatically, and the mass influx of small and medium-sized businesses into social networks continues to this day. For the most part, tools are more relevant for them, which enable them to quickly solve tactical tasks: increasing sales, announcing discount promotions, and encouraging users to make repeat purchases. The following types of projects occur more often than others in social networks: – online stores; – online services; – online startups; – and discount aggregators (Romanyshyn, & Greskiv, 2015, p. 189).

Boyko et al., (2021, p.182) note that when an entrepreneur has his online store, there is no need to target different age groups and all people: it is better to focus on a group of people of a certain age, they will most likely have the same interests, so it will be more convenient for the owner to add his product, it will be in the same field and there will be a lot of it, and this is better than a little bit of each, so there will be something to choose from. Also, under each product, they need to indicate why a customer needs to buy it. In some cases, a good feature of the product will encourage a purchase. An important component is the person who will answer the messages or calls, a lot depends on this person. The user can repel any desire to buy something with his behavior, or, on the contrary. A person can advertise the product so well that you will want to buy something else in this store. An online store - even if it is just a store page - is a daily job: forgetting about the page even for a few days, a businessperson can lose some regular customers and not get additional new ones. These are constant responses to comments or messages. The scientists also noted that the majority of purchases on the Internet are made by women, "although, according to various data, female buyers make up 55%, and men – 45%, but it cannot be claimed that these are still accurate calculations. The owners of business pages do not need to neglect the fact that "women love with their eyes", so the Internet page should be properly formed, approximately in the same style, with beautiful and high-quality photos and a clear description of the product (Boyko et al., 2021, p.182).

Taxation

Another relevant issue for Ukraine regarding conducting business in social networks is taxation. Ukrainian scientist Harkusha, (2020) conducted a thorough study of this problem. "Persons who offer custom-made cakes and pies, clothes and knitted items, toys of their production, as well as other similar products on Instagram and other Internet resources should be prepared for the fact that they will need to pay taxes or there will be prosecuted for illegal entrepreneurship. The tax office does not know for sure that this seller of custom-made cakes does not pay taxes. This needs to be checked and proven" (Harkusha, 2020, p. 341).

Such entrepreneurs maintain pages on the social network, post photos of cakes and post price lists. But nothing comes into the budget from the sale of these cakes. E-commerce offers businesses great opportunities to capitalize on the wave of demand from consumers who are interested in shopping online. A large number of participants in social networks create groups of users and try to constantly saturate them with interesting and unique content for the growth of the group's audience to earn money from advertising or direct sales of goods. Hundreds of thousands of Ukrainians have already appreciated the advantages of remote work using social networks, but the state may be concerned about this situation. The fact is that people who provide certain types of services at home and advertise these services on social networks, in most cases, do not register with the state tax service as entrepreneurs. "This means for the budget the loss of not only taxes but also insurance contributions, which the state is forced to compensate from its own "pocket". Moreover, over time, the situation will become more complicated, since the number of illegal self-employed citizens is only increasing. A mandatory condition for increasing tax revenues is to stimulate the economic activity of economic agents both with the help of methods and tools of tax regulation and to strengthen control over the full and timely receipt of taxes to the budgets of all levels. One of the tasks of the state tax service is to search for non-payers. For this, they have many tools: tracking bank accounts - the tax office can request information from the bank and notice that money regularly comes to the card, but there are no taxes on it; denunciations - other people can denounce the non-payer, the tax office will check this statement; search for accounts in social networks, if any. For example, the tax office can find the confectioner's Instagram, make sure that he does not pay taxes, control "buy" the cake, and then force him to pay taxes and a fine" (Harkusha, 2020, p. 341). Having someone's own business is a very good thing. It can be very difficult at the beginning. Self-organization is required for more responsibility than in a hired job. From time to time some difficulties need to be solved. But the advantages that such kind of business gives still prevail. This is financial well-being, this is practically unlimited freedom of action.

"Conducting economic activity without state registration as a business entity or without submitting a notice of commencement of the economic activity, if the obligation to submit such notice is provided for by law, or without obtaining a license to conduct a type of economic activity that is subject to licensing by the law, or during the period of suspension of the license, if the legislation does not provide for the conditions for carrying out licensed activities during the period of suspension of the license, or without obtaining a document of a permissive nature if its receipt is provided for by law (except in cases of application of the principle of tacit consent), – entails the imposition of a fine, with or without confiscation of manufactured products, production tools, raw materials and money received as a result of the commission of this administrative offence. Actions provided for in Part 1 of Art. 164 of the Code of Civil Procedure, committed by a person who was subject to administrative fines for the same offence during the year, or related to the receipt of large amounts of income, entail the imposition of a fine from 2,000 to 5,000 tax-free minimum incomes of citizens with confiscation of manufactured products, production tools, raw materials and money received as a result of committing this administrative offence. The receipt of income in large amounts takes place when its amount exceeds the tax-free minimum income of citizens by a thousand or more times" (Harkusha, 2020, p. 342). Individual entrepreneurs can use the simplified system of income taxation for taxation of activities in social networks. The simplified system of taxation, accounting and reporting is a special mechanism for dealing with taxes and fees, which replaces the payment of separate taxes and fees with the payment of a single tax in the manner and under the conditions specified by the Tax Code of Ukraine (PKU), with simultaneous maintenance of simplified accounting and reporting (Harkusha, 2020, p. 342).

Kazak, and Goncharenko (2021) offer such an algorithm for conducting business activities in social networks. To create a page in a social network, a person needs to: 1. Determine the target audience. The most important thing is to prepare well and think carefully about the strategy, and what well-known companies do in social networks. To build trust relations with customers, an entrepreneur need to know their preferences and desires. By dividing potential audiences into groups based on interests, age or profession, he can create three basic promotional text messages for each group and find out which social network he likes to use audience, and this needs to be emphasized. After all, every social network is unique in its structure and purpose. 2. Coordination of work. All profiles on different social networks should have the same purpose and be involved in work. There is a main site with their products combined. This is the basis of the brand. 3. Start. Working on social networks takes at least an hour to create posts and textual content that will be enjoyable and help readers solve their problems. 4. Observation. It is important to look at people's opinions about products, and to respond to their comments, even if they are negative. 5. Use of advertising in social networks. Using paid advertising, the entrepreneur can attract a more targeted audience, he can run targeted advertising that is aimed at the display itself target audience. 6. Analysis. It is important to constantly evaluate the results, determine those actions that are performed and those that are not performed properly and monitor the development and results of people's activities. Many social networks are possible to use for monitoring and evaluation of activities. Today it is impossible to do without a public exhibition of business, as this is one way to increase the number of visible products. A healthy company profile helps to create a positive image of the business, increase its reputation, and promote, and increase the level of trust, which affects business profitability (Kozak and Honcharenko, 2021, p. 15–16).

Boyko et al. (2021) singled out the two most popular networks: Facebook and Instagram. "Instagram is intended for an audience aged 14 and over, people under 25 rarely use Facebook, if they do, it is only for work or study, and they choose Instagram for free time. Facebook is a social network for older people, it is more convenient for them and there are branded stores, the products of which are aimed at an older audience. Constant development, improvement of person's habits, and continuous learning – this is what can improve the business account and lead to a large number of buyers. The entrepreneur should never stand still and think that a thousand subscribers are good and will be enough for business development. There are no online stores with little demand, there are online stores with bad advertising and imperfect page management. The matter is only in the hands of the owner, and it is his desire and passion for this business that can have the highest reward - a large number of consumers" (Boyko et al., 2021, p.186).

Dynamics of Ukrainian Entrepreneurship

Vytvytska, O., Suvorova, S., & Koryugin, A. (2022) examine the challenges of war that affect the economic activity of domestic businesses. "Part of the problems of working in crisis conditions were solved during the COVID-19 quarantine when a large number of enterprises switched from a traditional form of marketing to a digital one. However, the situation has become even more complicated: now the business operates in conditions of a rapid decrease in the solvency of the population, unstable tax legislation, a complete reformation of the labour market, and threats of complete or partial loss of property. It is necessary to adapt to all these conditions and ensure relatively stable activity in the conditions of a completely unstable market" (Vytvytska et al., 2022, p.1). Scientists note that the war of 2022 led to the fact that half of Ukrainian enterprises were completely closed. Those that remain afloat are operating well below their capacity. Business owners are forced to look for new opportunities for their development while taking into account the needs of consumers, which were also changed by the war. Despite the military actions, there is a rapid increase in Internet users in Ukraine. At the beginning of 2021, their number increased to 29 million Ukrainians (Vytvytska et al., 2022, p.1). An increase in the share of users aged 12 to 65 living in cities with a population of 50,000 or more was noted. With the beginning of the war in Ukraine, this indicator is increasing, because for the sake of their safety, people are forced to make online purchases. Internet shopping is often the only way to get a product or service in times of war. However, war is not the main reason for the growth of the Internet audience. In particular, the increase in the number of Internet users is recorded all over the world" (Vytvytska et al., 2022, p.1). The scientists (Vytvytska et al., 2022) consider the use of digital marketing to be the most optimal in war conditions. Thanks to it, it becomes possible to promote goods on the market and develop partnership relationships in the void due to market changes in the niche. Scientists prove that in the conditions of war, digital marketing is built on the following principles: 1. Variability of the target audience. That is, changing the gender, age, geographical location, and lifestyle of potential buyers. This should be taken into account for specific proposals. 2. New progressive marketing techniques. New marketing methods based on patriotism, support of the army, etc. appeared in Ukraine. Many Ukrainian companies transfer part of the income from the sale of goods and services to the needs of the army, which receives the support of a patriotic audience.

3. Confirmation of business reliability. "The work of the enterprise during the war is a sign of its reliability, because if the enterprise can organize reliable service and quality services or goods during the war, then even after the end of hostilities, it will cope with this task. For many young enterprises, working in war conditions allows them to earn a good reputation among their audience" (Vytvytska, et al., 2022, p.2). 4. Development of innovativeness. Difficult situations require new solutions, therefore crises contribute to the emergence of new and progressive marketing techniques. 5. Support and loyalty of Ukrainian businesses. "Competent marketing strategy of the enterprise allows entering the world

market. This is facilitated by a loyal attitude towards the Ukrainian products caused by the difficult situation in Ukraine. The use of digital marketing principles allows enterprises to achieve marketing goals in wartime conditions, which, despite market changes and economic decline, leads to a significant increase in sales volumes" (Vytvytska et al., 2022, p. 3).

War does not always create critical threats to the development of entrepreneurial activity. If we talk about digital technologies of business and marketing in particular, then this state of crisis it is necessary to use it with benefit, taking advantage of the opportunities that arise. In particular, today the whole world supports Ukraine and the development of business, because it understands how important it is to ensure victory in the war. If we talk about digital marketing, then the most relevant offer is the platform for business development from Meta. Thanks to the Meta Blueprint global educational program, Ukrainian companies can gain new knowledge and skills in the field of digital marketing. After training and attending seminars, you can get a certificate confirming advanced training in this area. Business representatives get the opportunity to master advanced digital marketing technologies. They learn to work with advertising and implement their own creative strategies. It is worth noting that access to the educational content of the platform is free. (Vytvytska, et al., 2022, p. 6)

To calmly engage in business development on the Internet, it is necessary to comply with the requirements of Ukrainian legislation, which are grouped by Harkusha (2020), because the transition of business to the Internet and cashless payments will make it easier to identify tax evaders, and it will not be possible to hide for long. "The fact that a person spend all the profit on consumables or plan to officially register later will not save you from fines. No one will specifically check you at the time of registration. If you work illegally, you risk more" (Harkusha, 2020, p. 344). According to the scientist, it is the third group of the exempted taxation system that is most suitable for taxation of activities in social networks, since both natural and legal entities can be on it. This group is beneficial for those who need to work with income taxpayers and/or be a registered taxpayer. The interest rates of the single tax for the third group of single tax payers are established by Clause 3 of Article 293 of the Tax Code of Ukraine. Income is determined based on accounting data, which is kept by Article 296 of the Tax Code of Ukraine (Harkusha, 2020, p. 344). He also advises asking for help from a specialist in the field of taxation to make all the calculations correctly. Therefore, it is recommended to either hire an accountant (at least outsourced) or use services similar to those offered by the specialists of Juscutum and "League: Law" –"Taxes and reports in Telegram – ReporTax" (Harkusha, 2020, p. 344).

Having studied scientific papers, as well as open statistical data (Derkach, 2023; Kapustina, 2020; Omelchuk, 2020), the author of this chapter has compiled the following diagram (Figure 3), which demonstrates the growth dynamics of the topic considered in this chapter.

The positive dynamics of the increase in e-commerce in Ukraine over the past 10 years demonstrates the tightening of competition on the Internet as a whole and on social networks. And just as in a regular market, being the only seller, it is easy to get consumers out of special financial and time costs, since the consumer has no choice. With the appearance of an increasing number of competitors, it is necessary to implement strict measures to attract and retain consumers and increase costs. So on the Internet with the appearance of an increasing number of competitors, attracting consumers becomes more and more complex and costly. It is necessary to constantly analyze the demand and supply of competitors in order to develop an interesting offer for consumers.

Figure 3. Dynamics of Ukrainian entrepreneurship (summarized by the author of the chapter)

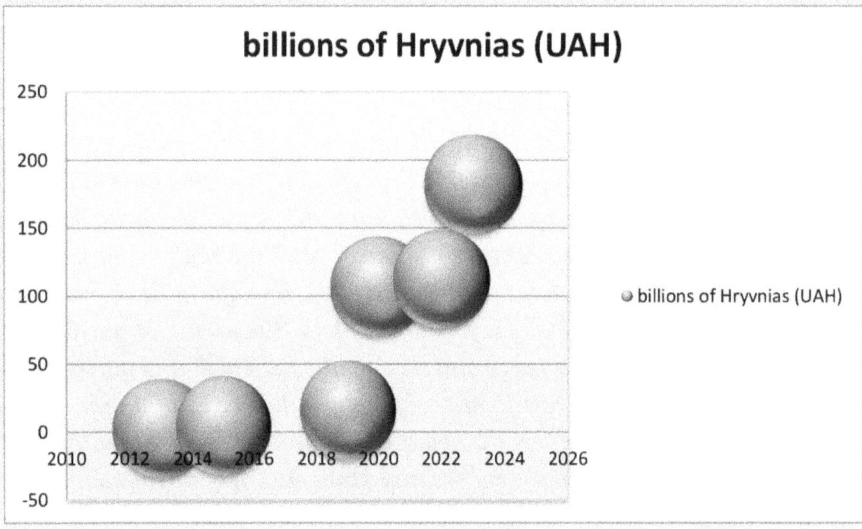

From the above diagram, it can be seen that the coronavirus has spurred the development of online commerce in Ukraine. Ukrainians spent UAH 107 billion on online purchases in 2020. It's about buying both goods and services. The amount spent is much higher than in 2019 (Kapustina, 2020; Omelchuk, 2020). In addition, the number of online payments has also increased. As a result of all this, a huge percentage of all purchases in Ukraine take place online, including on social networks. In 2023 more and more purchases in the country also take place online (Derkach, 2023).

The level of entrepreneurship in social networks is growing because the level of involvement of the Ukrainian population in social networks on the Internet is increasing. Even in a result of the combat actions, there was an increase in Internet commerce in 2022 and 2023. Thus, the dynamics are increasing and entrepreneurship in social networks is growing.

CONCLUSION

Based on the studied sources, the author of this chapter comes to the following conclusions. Social networks have become the centre of people's communication not only in terms of human communication but also in business relations. Their influence is so great that even successful companies maintain their social pages to increase sales and attract customers. Entrepreneurship in social networks is devoted to a fairly large amount of scientific literature, covering completely different spheres of economic and human activity. The works are sometimes completely unexpected in terms of the research subject. However, all of them are quite relevant in terms of summarizing and determining the further strategy of business development. For successful sales, it is necessary to have a sufficiently large number of subscribers. An entrepreneur can attract them independently or with the help of advertising. If the person uses the page of social networks correctly, observing all the rules and requirements, so can make a significant profit, and even during the war. There are several stages of advertising analysis in Ukraine: monitoring, analysis, content creation, and advertising placement. In Ukraine, the following types of projects are most often seen in social networks: online stores, online services, online startups, and discount aggregators. More purchases on the Internet are made by women, so the entrepreneur needs to indicate in the product description why exactly this item can be useful to them and why it is necessary to buy this product from him. There is a certain algorithm for creating an entrepreneur's page on a social network, as well as a tax recommendation for a smooth business, which are described in detail in this chapter.

The level of entrepreneurship in social networks is growing because the level of involvement of the Ukrainian population in social networks on the Internet is raising, which provokes not only an increase in the number of companies and private entrepreneurs, but also tougher competition. When consumers have a lot of choice, the rules in the market begin to be dictated not by manufacturers, but by consumers, because all activities should be aimed at meeting their needs and matching their preferences.

Even, as a result of the fighting, there is an increase in Internet commerce in 2022 and 2023. Thus, the dynamics of entrepreneurship in social networks is growing.

ACKNOWLEDGMENT

This research received no grant from any organization.

REFERENCES

Adi, S., Heripracoyo, S., & Simamora, B. H. (2021). Potential used of social media/mobile phone to support promotion and marketing in the rural tourism destination. *Proc Int Conf Ind Eng Oper Manag,* 3370-3379. 10.46254/AN11.20210609

Agusiady, R., Saepudin, D., & Aripin, Z. (2024). The Influence of Social Media Communication on Consumer Perceptions of Brands and Purchase Intentions in the Pandemic and Post-Pandemic Era: An Analytical Study. *Journal of Economics, Accounting, Business, Management, Engineering and Society*, *2*(1), 16–30.

Allam, Z., & Allam, Z. (2020). Digital urban networks and social media. *Cities and the digital revolution: Aligning technology and humanity*, 61-83.

Atamanchuk, Z. A. (2019). Digital transformations in international tourism as a factor of economic. *Strategic priorities of the transformation of the economy in conditions of digitalization: Materials of the International Scientific and Practical Conference, Zaporizhzhia.* Zaporizhia Polytechnic National University.

Borovets, R., & Kit, Y. (2018). Advertising of the company's activities via the Internet. *Information, communication, society: Materials of the 7th International Scientific Conference ICS-2018.* Lviv: Publishing House of Lviv Polytechnic.

Boyko, V., Osadchiy, A., & Boyko, L. (2021). Social networks are a promising direction of business promotion in entrepreneurial activity. *KhNTU Bulletin, 2*(77), 178-185.

Buljan, B., & Miočić, B. K. (2021, June). Youth Entrepreneurship in Rural Areas–Reflection on Croatia. *Proceedings of FEB Zagreb International Odyssey Conference on Economics and Business*, 3, 196-212.

Cesaroni, F. M., Demartini, P., & Paoloni, P. (2017). Women in business and social media: Implications for female entrepreneurship in emerging countries. *African Journal of Business Management, 11*(14), 316–326. doi:10.5897/AJBM2017.8281

Çiçek, B. (2018). Social Media Entrepreneurship. *İçtimaiyat Sosyal Bilimler Dergisi, 2*(1), 10-17.

Datskevich, N. O. (2016). The dialectic of interaction between the social responsibility of entrepreneurship and the social capital of society. *Efficient Economy,* (7), 1-4.

Demydchuk, L. B., & Sapozhnyk, D. I. (2021). Influence of social networks on business development. Academic Press.

Derkach, N. (2023). How much Ukrainians spent on online purchases in 2023. *PAYSPACE.* https://psm7.com/ru/e-commerce/skolko-ukraincy-potratili-na-online-pokupki-v-2023-godu.html

Eachempati, P., Srivastava, P. R., & Zhang, Z. J. (2021). Gauging opinions about the COVID-19: A multi-channel social media approach. *Enterprise Information Systems, 15*(6), 794–828. doi:10.1080/17517575.2020.1856418

Emmanuel, C. P., Qin, S., Hossain, S. F. A., & Hussain, K. (2022). Factors influencing social-media-based entrepreneurship prospect among female students in China. *Heliyon, 8*(12), e12041. doi:10.1016/j.heliyon.2022.e12041 PMID:36483305

Galushka, Z. (2013). The phenomenon of social entrepreneurship: Concepts and prospects for development in Ukraine. *Bulletin of Taras Shevchenko Kyiv National University Economics*, (148), 15–17.

Gudz, G. O. (2016). Information systems and technologies in insurance protection of agrarian entrepreneurship. *Accounting and Finance*, (2), 95–103.

Gustafsson, V., & Khan, M. S. (2017). Monetising blogs: Enterprising behaviour, co-creation of opportunities and social media entrepreneurship. *Journal of Business Venturing Insights, 7*, 26–31. doi:10.1016/j.jbvi.2017.01.002

Harkusha, S. A. (2020). Taxation of activities in social networks. *Eastern Europe: Economics. Business and Management.*, *2*(25), 340–345.

Heiko, T. (2020). Priorities for the development of entrepreneurship in Ukraine in the conditions of the COVID-19 pandemic and in the post-quarantine period. *Bulletin of Socio-Economic Research, 2*(73), 62-71.

Hrytsaenko, M. I. (2017). Social capital in the formation of the entrepreneurial network of the agrarian sphere of Ukraine. *Economy of Agro-Industrial Complex, 5,* 58-64.

Hrytsaenko, M. I. (2020). The place of social capital in the development of self-regulation of entrepreneurial activity. Academic Press.

Improving the level of SEO in Ukraine. (2016). https://seosolution.ua/blog/infographics/internet-trade.html

Kadam, A., & Ayarekar, S. (2014). Impact of Social Media on Entrepreneurship and Entrepreneurial Performance: Special Reference to Small and Medium Scale Enterprises. *SIES Journal of Management, 10*(1).

Kapustina, K. (2020, December 29). The corona virus has spurred the development of online commerce in Ukraine. *Today*. https://economics.segodnya.ua/economics/business/cifra-dnya-ukraincy-podseli-na-internet-shoping-skolko-tratim-v-seti-1497960.html

Kazak, A. S. (2021). Factor assessment of the influence of social networks on the economic efficiency of entrepreneurial activity. Academic Press.

Khan, M. J. (2022). *Social media marketing* [Master's thesis]. Centria University of Applied Sciences. https://www.theseus.fi/handle/10024/780131

Khymitsa, N., & Sekanova, A. (2018). Advertising and information presentation of PJSC "Myronivskyi Hliboprodukt" in social networks. *Information Communication and Society*, *1*, 77.

Kornetsky, A. O., & Ishakov, E. Sh. (2016). Alternative social networks: Business model and entrepreneurship. *Scientific Bulletin of Kherson State University. Ser. Economic Sciences*, 19(1), 95–99.

Kornukh, O. V., & Makhanko, L. V. (2014). Startup as a progressive form of innovative entrepreneurship. *Investments: Practice and Experience*, (23), 26-30.

Korotich, O. B., Orel, Yu. L., & Ryabichko, O. V. (2010). Entrepreneurship as a socio-economic phenomenon. *Theory and Practice of Public Administration*, (4), 211-216.

Kozlovskyi, S. V., & Tanasienko, O. I. (2019). The paradigm of social entrepreneurship. Academic Press.

Kulikova, N. O. (2022). *Electronic technologies and development of entrepreneurship*. Symi.

Lebiedieva, Z. (2023). *ESP Writing as a Practical Mean of Cultural Communication Between Ukrainian Music Teachers and Chinese Students. In Cases on Error Analysis in Foreign Language Technical Writing*. IGI Global. doi:10.4018/978-1-6684-6222-5.ch008

Mangushev, D. V., & Pikhtin, A. V. (2021). Application of digital marketing tools to increase the efficiency of business activities. *Modern Economics.*, *30*, 147–152. doi:10.31521/modecon.V30(2021)-23

Martín-Rojas, R., Garrido-Moreno, A., & García-Morales, V. J. (2020). Fostering Corporate Entrepreneurship with the use of social media tools. *Journal of Business Research*, *112*, 396–412. doi:10.1016/j.jbusres.2019.11.072

Mihailina, T., & Bevzyuk, K. (2019). Problems of using objects of inttllectual property rights during business activities in social networks. Economic and Law Paradigm of Modern Society, 81.

Nakara, W. A., Benmoussa, F. Z., & Jaouen, A. (2012). Entrepreneurship and social media marketing: Evidence from French small business. *International Journal of Entrepreneurship and Small Business, 16*(4), 386–405. doi:10.1504/IJESB.2012.047608

Nikou, S., Brännback, M. E., Orrensalo, T. P., & Widén, G. (2020). Social media and entrepreneurship: exploring the role of digital source selection and information literacy. *Understanding Social Media and Entrepreneurship*, 29-46.

Ognevyuk, G. (2016). Peculiarities of using intellectual property objects in social networks. *Entrepreneurship, Economy and Law,* (7), 21-25.

Olanrewaju, A. S. T., Hossain, M. A., Whiteside, N., & Mercieca, P. (2020). Social media and entrepreneurship research: A literature review. *International Journal of Information Management*, *50*, 90–110. doi:10.1016/j.ijinfomgt.2019.05.011

Omelchuk, N. (2020). How much Ukrainians spent on online purchases. *PAYSPACE.* https://psm7.com/ru/e-commerce/itogi-goda-skolko-potratili-ukraincy-na-pokupki-v-internete-v-2020.html

Păvăloaia, V. D., Anastasiei, I. D., & Fotache, D. (2020). Social media and e-mail marketing campaigns: Symmetry versus convergence. *Symmetry*, *12*(12), 1940. doi:10.3390/sym12121940

Reisach, U. (2021). The responsibility of social media in times of societal and political manipulation. *European Journal of Operational Research*, *291*(3), 906–917. doi:10.1016/j.ejor.2020.09.020 PMID:32982027

Romanyshyn, S. B., & Greskiv, I. R. (2015). Peculiarities of marketing activities in social networks. *Bulletin of the Lviv Polytechnic National University,* (819), 183-188.

Schjoedt, L., Brännback, M. E., & Carsrud, A. L. (2020). *Understanding Social Media and Entrepreneurship*. Springer. doi:10.1007/978-3-030-43453-3

Secundo, G., Del Vecchio, P., & Mele, G. (2021). Social media for entrepreneurship: Myth or reality? A structured literature review and a future research agenda. *International Journal of Entrepreneurial Behaviour & Research*, *27*(1), 149–177. doi:10.1108/IJEBR-07-2020-0453

Shpykulyak, O. G., & Hrytsaenko, M. I. (2019). Intellectual model of social capital: concepts of institutionalization. *Cooperation,* 186-196.

Smal, V., & Kokot, V. (2017). What you should know about social entrepreneurship [Guide]. Academic Press.

Sukumar, A., Jafari-Sadeghi, V., & Xu, Z. (2021). The influences of social media on Chinese start-up stage entrepreneurship. *World Review of Entrepreneurship, Management and Sustainable Development*, *17*(5), 559–578. doi:10.1504/WREMSD.2021.117442

Surugiu, M. R., & Surugiu, C. (2015). Heritage tourism entrepreneurship and social media: Opportunities and challenges. *Procedia: Social and Behavioral Sciences*, *188*, 74–81. doi:10.1016/j.sbspro.2015.03.340

Troise, C., Dana, L. P., Tani, M., & Lee, K. Y. (2022). Social media and entrepreneurship: Exploring the impact of social media use of start-ups on their entrepreneurial orientation and opportunities. *Journal of Small Business and Enterprise Development*, *29*(1), 47–73. doi:10.1108/JSBED-01-2021-0041

Ugolkova, O. Z. (2021). Digital marketing and social networks. *Management and Entrepreneurship in Ukraine: Stages of Formation and Development Problems, 3*(1), 146-152.

Vytvytska, O., Suvorova, S., & Koryugin, A. (2022). The influence of digital marketing on the development of entrepreneurship in the conditions of war. *Economy and Society*, (40), 1–7.

Wallsten, S. J., & Rhyan, C. (2014). Social media and entrepreneurship: The case of food trucks. *Technology Policy Institute: Selected Works*, *1*, 1–12.

Wu, Y., & Song, D. (2019). Gratifications for social media use in entrepreneurship courses: Learners' perspective. *Frontiers in Psychology*, *10*, 1270. doi:10.3389/fpsyg.2019.01270 PMID:31214081

Yarmolyuk, O. Ya., Fisun, Yu. V., & Shapovalova, A. A. (2020). Social networks as a modern promotion tool. *Entrepreneurship and Innovation, 11*(2), 62-65. doi:10.37320/2415-3583/11.28

Yuskiv, N. O. (2021). Legal problems of electronic commerce in social. *European integration changes in the legislation of Ukraine*, 127.

Zhurylo, V. V. (2020). Influence marketing as a communication tool for product promotion in social Internet networks. *Entrepreneurship and Innovation*, *11*(2), 29-36.

Chapter 3
A Literature Review for the Association of Social Media With Micro and Small Enterprises in India

Ajay Kumar Singh
https://orcid.org/0000-0003-0429-0925
Department of Humanities and Social Sciences, Graphic Era University (Deemed), Dehradun, India

Santosh Singh
https://orcid.org/0000-0003-2448-4794
School of Liberal Arts and Management, DIT University, Dehradun, India

Meenakshi Gupta
https://orcid.org/0000-0002-7866-4961
School of Economics, Shri Mata Vaishno Devi University, India

EXECUTIVE SUMMARY

Social media and social media marketing (SMM) are essential to increase the performance of MSMEs. MSMEs are providing jobs to the youth population and helping to increase social welfare. Past studies could not explain a reliable view on how social media and SMM are useful to enhance the progress of MSMEs in the case of developing countries like India. Therefore, this chapter measures the MSMEs affecting factors as giving more focus on social media and SMM as per the existing studies. It recognizes the contribution of social media in the MSMEs of India. It provides practical policy recommendations to improve the practices of social media and SMM in MSMEs of India. It proposed that social media is useful to increase profits, sales, customers, efficiency, and production of MSMEs. The new entrepreneurs should increase the practice of social media to achieve various targets in SMEs.

DOI: 10.4018/979-8-3693-1781-5.ch003

1. BACKGROUND

At present social-economic development cannot be achieved without micro and small enterprises (MSEs) due to is significant contribution in social, economic and technological development related activities (Patnaik & Satyaprakash, 2015). Nowadays, it considered as a worthy engine of economic growth. MSEs create jobs for skilled and unskilled workers; contribute to industrial production; increase foreign trade, money flow, and increase national income (Singh & Jyoti, 2020). MSEs are crucial sources of capital formation and infrastructure development (Mitra et al., 2016). MSEs are helpful to increase industrial development that is beneficial to increase infrastructural and technological development (Singh & Kumar, 2021). MSEs are also considered as engines of economic growth due to multiple reasons like it nurture a conducive ecosystem for industrial development, it creates extensive jobs, absorb more people, enhance income of the people, and use new technology and innovation develop by research organization (Singh & Kumar, 2022b; Alam et al., 2023). While social and economic factors, financial development, trade openness, science & technological related indicators, government inactivates and intellectual property rights (IPRs) regime also enhance progress of MSEs and entrepreneurship ecosystem (Singh et al., 2020; Emmanuel et al., 2022; Alam et al., 2023; Madumithaa et al., 2023; Singh & Jyoti,2023a).

Technological development and innovation are also favourable to create a conducive ecosystem for sustainability of micro, small and medium enterprises (MSMEs) (Singh et al., 2019a). Singh et al. (2020) also noted that growth of the manufacturing sector depends on IPRs and technological development. Thereupon, social media is also working as an effective player to enhance production and performance of MSMEs (Alam et al., 2023). Social media helps to increase the promotion of a specific firm. Society also creates a favourable environment for MSMEs to increase the exports and imports across countries. Consequently, social media is supportive to increase foreign trade. Social media is also a driver to increasing foreign direct investment (FDI) from one country to another. Consequently, at present the usage of social media in small-scale enterprises has emerged as a key driver to increase the growth of MSMEs.

Social media also builds a foundation for marketing and to sustain an operative relationship between businessmen and customers in MSEs (Srinivasan et al., 2016). Alam et al. (2023) suggested that social media is useful to increase the performance of SMEs directly and indirectly. Recently, the contribution of social media in the creation of new business opportunities has become a central key agenda in most developing economies (Kumarasamy & Srinivasan, 2017; Hassan & Shahzad, 2022). Social media is a platform that expansively increase the use of internet and information technology (IT) in social communication and exchange of e-content in the business and social sectors (Kaplan & Haenlein, 2010; Neti, 2011; Srinivasan et al., 2016; Lakshmi et al., 2017). Social media brings multiple opportunities for marketing of new products in MSMEs (Suariedewi et al., 2022).

Social media essentially uses digital technology, digital infrastructure, mobile and IT for exchanging knowledge and ideas among the large group of communities (Neti, 2011; Hossain et al., 2021; Oyewobi et al., 2023; Singh & Jyoti,2023b; Madumithaa et al., 2023). Social media, therefore, provides a platform to share and disseminate information among the peoples across regions (Apenteng & Doe, 2014; Amoah et al., 2023). Henceforth, it is an online platform for disseminating the information among the large group of communities (Neti, 2011). Social media is also a revolution and technological innovation to increase the transfer of knowledge, research & development (R&D), and technological development in R&D fields (Ihsaniyati et al., 2023). Social media also creates a favourable ecosystem to increase the quality of the education system. Therefore, it is an effective driver to increase the learning capacity and skills of people. Social media also facilitates the online platform for sharing the ideas and knowledge to improve networking among the economic agents (Lakshmi et al., 2017).

Social media is based on networking that promotes trust among the more than two parties who are involved in social interaction and business communication (Neti, 2011; Madumithaa et al., 2023). Thus, social media is vital to increase communication development and make social change (Ihsaniyati et al., 2023). Social media, therefore, assists to increase customer's relationships with producers, and their collaboration in the long-term (Amoah et al., 2023). Generally, it is an inclusion of media and social. Media create a conducive ecosystem to improve the advertisement and spread the ideas and information through several online platforms. While social media enhances the interaction of communities across regions or countries (Neti, 2011). Social media also works as democratization of material, altering people from content readers into content publishers (Neti, 2011). Social media is a medium to socialize the peoples across the community.

MSMEs is the crucial part of the Indian manufacturing sector (Singh et al., 2019a). MSMEs is defined as: An enterprise can be considered micro enterprise when its turn over exceeds twenty-five lakh rupees, and an enterprise can be considered as small enterprise when its turn over lies between 25 lakh rupees to 5 crore rupees in a year under manufacturing sector (Aruna, 2015; Lakshmi et al., 2017). Medium enterprise has a limit of annual turnover of more than 5 – 10 crore rupees in the manufacturing sector (Aruna, 2015; Lakshmi et al., 2017). In the service sector, micro enterprises have turnover around ten lakh rupees, while small enterprises have turn over between ten lakh rupees to two crore rupees in a year (Aruna, 2015; Lakshmi et al., 2017).

In the Indian economy, small scale industries (SSIs) have an important position to boost economic growth (Patnaik & Satyaprakash, 2015). Small-scale enterprises (SSEs) could generate new employment opportunities, and exports of goods and services, therefore it could also reduce regional imbalance in growth patterns across Indian states (Patnaik & Satyaprakash, 2015; Kumar & Ayedee, 2018). SSEs are also helpful to boost large-scale industries that enhance manufacturing activities in India (Patnaik & Satyaprakash, 2015). Then, SSIs is also increased the participation of industrial delegates in the R&D sector (Patnaik & Satyaprakash, 2015). In India, MSEs, social media and social networks are supportive to maintain the company-customer relationship and to increase the viable value of MSMEs (Basri, 2016). Social media is also helpful to increase the success of MSMEs in India (Madumithaa et al., 2023).

India as an emerging economy that has a large population size, therefore in India social media would be positive to create an entrepreneurship ecosystem. Also, MSMEs are providing jobs to the youth population in India. Although, existing researchers could not estimate how social media is useful in Indian MSMEs? The present chapter, therefore, is intended to address the answer of following research questions:

- What are the key components of social media and social marketing that are useful for social and economic development?
- How social media and social media marketing are effective and conducive to create MSMEs?
- Which types of firms in MSMEs can be created through social media in India?
- How can entrepreneurs increase the usability of social media and social marketing in their business activities?

2. THEORETICAL REVIEW ON THE INTERLINKAGES OF SOCIAL MEDIA WITH MSMES

Social media is a significant way for businessmen who wish to extent their business and attract more consumers who review the goods and services produced by MSMEs through social media (i.e., online or web survey) (Apenteng & Doe, 2014; Kumarasamy & Srinivasan, 2017). For instance, online purchasing of goods and services for the students could be easy due to social media during covid-19 (Aboulilah et al., 2022). It has the potential to increase the connections of customers with new markets, and increase the revenue of MSMEs (Madumithaa et al., 2023). Social media also enables to increase the association of customers and companies (Madumithaa et al., 2023). Consequently, millions of customers provide review comments on available products that are supplied by the enterprises using social media. Social media has a viability to increase the development of SMEs (Apenteng & Doe, 2014; Kumarasamy & Srinivasan, 2017). Sendawula et al. (2022) reported that social media is helpful to increase the sustainable growth of MSEs in Uganda. Social media also contributes to increasing the sustainability of firms in SMEs (Amoah et al., 2023; Bruce et al., 2023). Earlier studies empirically and theoretically proved that social media is essential to create social networks which are helpful for SMEs in several ways (Lakshmi et al., 2017). Furthermore, entrepreneurs can use social media as crucial tools for marketing of new products introduced by SMEs (Hossain et al., 2020). For example, social media could provide extensive benefits to MSEs in the European economies. Moreover, around 61% of the MSEs are using social media to promote marketing, and to increase advertising, brand management and customer relationships in Europe. Social media also brings a revolution to increase the performance and growth of SMEs and entrepreneurship ecosystem in India. Furthermore, the new start-up or venture needs marketing and publicity that can be easily promoted through social media (Hossain et al., 2023). Social media, therefore, is also supportive to create start-ups. Social media is also a revolution to increase environmental sustainability as it reduces wastage in most production activities (Padhi & Sharma, 2022). Environmental sustainability is a core component of sustainable development. Henceforth, usages of social media in MSEs and other production sectors may be positive to increase sustainable development. Social media is also providing greater advantages to MSEs in most industrial economies like the United Kingdom, Nederland and Latvia (Kumar & Ayedee, 2018). Social media is providing a platform to promote, advertising and marketing activities in MSEs of Belgium (Srinivasan et al., 2016). Consequently, social media have a significant influence on economic, social, business, environment and political transformation (Vatanasakdakul et al., 2020).

Internal and external factors of SMEs are useful to enhance growth and performance of SMEs. Most scholars estimated the technical efficiency of different firms in the Indian manufacturing sector and other countries (Singh et al., 2019a). Accordingly, most researchers examined the impact of internal and external variables on technical efficiency of firms. Few studies assessed the impact of R&D intensity, globalization and trade openness on firm's performance in terms of profits, sales, revenue, employment generation, foreign collaboration, foreign trade, foreign direct investment and exports capability on the performance of SMEs in India (Singh & Kumar, 2021; Singh & Jyoti, 2020). Thereupon, several studies also observed the implications of social media and marketing, and other control variables on the performance and sustainability of SMEs. Accordingly, numerous studies provided empirical evidence that social media and social media marketing are crucial drivers to boost the performance of MSEs.

The brief summary of past studies that examine the association of social media and social media marketing with MSMEs in India and other countries is given in Table: 1. Al-Mommani et al. (2015); Kanth et al. (2023) pointed out that MSMEs can increase their benefits using and improving social media marketing. Social media and social media marketing are innovative tools that enhance the business and marketing of MSMEs (Rasheed & Nafiz, 2022). Social media marketing is essential to increase the business communication and production operation (Chatterjee et al., 2021). Ainin et al. (2015) measured the SMEs influencing factors in Malaysia. Financial performance of MSEs could be increased due to use of Facebook. There is found a positive impact of Facebook users on consumer services and consumer relations, and information accessibility in SMEs.

Social media is helpful for SMEs to increase the branding of their products and reduce their costs significantly, and enhance customer relations (Oyewobi et al., 2023; Alam et al., 2023). Social media also enhances the product promotion of SMEs at greater scale (Hassan & Shahzad, 2022). Most studies empirically verified that social media helps to enhance the sustainability of SMEs (Bruce et al., 2023). Social media is also positive to increase the sales and cost advantages of MSEs (Gümüş & Kütahyali, 2017). Suariedewi et al. (2022) also noticed a significant impact of social media marketing on sustainability of MSMEs in Indonesia. Social media marketing is essential to increase collaboration of customers with entrepreneurs (Hossain et al., 2020; Rasheed & Nafiz, 2022). The findings of Lakshmi et al. (2017) also highlighted that growth of small and medium sized enterprises significantly get influenced due to social media in Arabian countries.

This section also describes the results of earlier studies that projected the association of social media and social media marketing with MSEs in India. There is appeared a positive and significant association of social media with MSEs in India. Srinivasan et al. (2016) measured the role of social media in the marketing process of MSEs in the Indian manufacturing sector using correlation techniques. Social media has a great contribution to increase the branding of new products and trust of customers in MSEs (Srinivasan et al., 2016). Furthermore, social media is also beneficial to increase customer acquisition and customer retention in MSMEs. Chatterjee and Das (2016) estimated the economic performance of micro-enterprises in Jharkhand (Bihar). Information and communication technology (ICT) creates a conducive platform for social media. Therefore, total factor productivity of Indian manufacturing firms could be increased due to application of social media in SMEs (Mitra et al., 2016).

Basri (2016) observed that social media is significantly associated with social, political, cultural and economic domains in the Arab World. Kumarasamy and Srinivasan (2017) noticed that social media provides a crucial opportunity to transform the way of business for entrepreneurs in India. The entrepreneurs can reduce the monetary cost, and increase the production and sale operation of new ventures by adopting social media or social platforms (Hassan & Shahzad, 2022; Hossain et al., 2023). Social media also seemed effective for the business community to achieve various targets on time with minimum costs (Emmanuel et al., 2022). Kumar and Ayedee (2018) observed the significance of social media in MSMEs of India. Singh et al. (2019a) also explained the significance of social media in Indian MSMEs.

Chatterjee and Kar (2020) examined the significance of factors leading the social media marketing in SMEs in India. Social media marketing helps to increase the business outcome in SMEs. Using a few proxy variables such as telephone subscribers and internet users for social media, Singh and Ashraf (2020) described a crucial impact of social media on the entrepreneurship ecosystem. However, Padhi and Sharma (2022) found positive and negative impacts of social media marketing on SMEs in India. Madumithaa et al. (2023) did a primary survey of companies and customers to analyse the role of social media and socio-economic indicators in MSMEs of India. It also reported a significant role of social media in MSMEs of India.

Table 1. Summary for association of social media with MSMEs in India and other countries

Author(s)	Country	Objectives	Method	Findings
Meske and Stieglitz (2013)	Germany	Observe the adoption, usage and benefits of social media in SMEs	Descriptive data analysis	Social media helps to increase internal communication and collaboration among customers and entrepreneurs in SMEs
Neti (2011)	India	Provide the concept of social media and marketing in context of firms	Conceptual and descriptive analysis	Social media cannot be separated from the online world
Ainin et al. (2015)	Malaysia	Assess the role of Facebook on performance of SMEs	PLS method	Financial performance of SMEs increases as Facebook users increase
Al-Mommani et al. (2015)	-	Analysis the role of social media and networking on competitive values of MSMEs	Review of literature	SMM strategies help to increase benefits and competitive values in MSMEs
Basri (2016)	Arab world	Estimate the impact of social media on SMEs	Review of literature	Social media has multiple positive impacts on SMEs
Srinivasan et al. (2016)	India	Explain the role of social media marketing (SMM) in MSMEs	Exploratory research analysis	Social media is useful to increase brand awareness and brand trust in MSMEs
Lakshmi et al. (2017)	Arab world	Observe the significance of social media in SMEs	Using literature review	It noticed a unique association between social media and SMEs
Gümüş and Kütahyali (2017)	Turkey	Examine the perception of social media users in SMEs	Descriptive analysis	Social media is an active player to increase marketing in SMEs
Kumarasamy and & Srinivasan (2017)	India	Examine the impact of social media on small business entrepreneurs	Literature review	Social media provide perfect benefits to the entrepreneurs
Kumar & Ayedee (2018)	India	Explain the summary on the usages of social media business expansion, promotion and marketing of SMEs	Previous literature	Social media play a positive role in business activities of SMEs
Ahmad et al. (2019)	UAE	Identify the indicator that increase the intention of SMEs to use social media	PLS-SEM Method	Social media adoption does not show a significant impact on performance of SMEs
Chatterjee and Kar (2020)	India	Examine the factors that increase the perception to adopt SMM in SMEs	PLS-SEM Method	Social media is helpful to increase benefits in SMEs
Vatanasakdakul et al. (2020)	Indonesia	Assessing the factors influencing to adopt social media in SMEs	Structural equation modelling (SEM)	Social media is positive to increase price value in micro enterprises
Singh et al. (2020)	Across countries	Examine the impact of social media on gross value added of manufacturing sector	Log-linear regression model	Social media is positive to enhance the growth of manufacturing sector
Chatterjee et al. (2021)	India	Assess the significance of SMM for sustainable growth of MSEs	Structural equation modelling	SMM showed a significant impact on sustainable growth of SMEs
Sendawula et al. (2022)	Uganda	Perceive the impact of social media on sustainable growth of MSEs	Exploratory factor analysis	Social media is appeared to increase the sustainable growth of MSEs
Padhi and Sharma (2022)	India	Identify the role of SMM on sustainability of SMEs	Descriptive analysis	It found positive and negative impact of SMM on SMEs

Table 1. Continued

Author(s)	Country	Objectives	Method	Findings
Hassan and Shahzad (2022)	Malaysia	Assess the impact of social media on social commerce performance	PLS-SEM technique	Social commerce performance is significantly improved as use of social media increases
Suariedewi et al. (2022)	Indonesia	Examine the indicators that use SMM in MSMEs	SEM-PLS model	SMS showed a positive impact on MSMEs
Rasheed and Nafiz (2022)	Maldives	Examine the social media marketing affecting indicators in MSMEs	Correlation and regression analysis	Performance of MSMEs increases as practices of social media increases
Amoah et al. (2023)	Ghana	Examine factors affecting social media and their influence on sustainability of firms	PLS-SEM technique	Social media adoption has a significant influence on sustainability of firms
Madumithaa et al. (2023)	India	Investigate the impact of social media on SMEs	Using literature survey	Success of SMEs depend on social media
Bruce et al. (2023)	Ghana	Assess the performance and sustainability of SMEs	PLS-SEM technique	Social medial is positively correlated with sustainability of SMEs
Alam et al. (2023)	-	Examine the benefits of social media in SMEs	Systematic literature review	Acceptance of social media has a positive impact on performance of SMEs
Ihsaniyati et al. (2023)	-	Examine the role of social media in knowledge sharing	Literature review	Social media is a useful determinant of knowledge sharing
Kanth et al. (2023)	-	Examine the implications of SMM in MSMEs	Systematic literature review	SMM is beneficial to increase the profits of MSMEs
Oyewobi et al. (2023)	Nigeria	Investigate the impact of social media adoption on performance of SMEs	PLS-SEM model	Use of social media has a positive impact on knowledge accessibility and customer relations in SMEs

Source: Author's compilation as per the existing studies.

3. BRIEF OVERVIEW OF DATA SOURCES AND METHODOLOGY

This chapter uses existing literature that includes the view of existing researchers on social media and social marketing, and their contribution in MSEs of India. Global data on social media is derived from: https://www.statista.com/. Furthermore, it also provides the overview and strength of MSMEs and importance of social media and social marketing in MSEs of India. Therefore, required data for Indian states are also taken from the Ministry of Micro, Small and Medium Enterprises (Government of India); and published research articles and reports.

4. IMPORTANCE OF MSMES IN INDIA

MSEs can be considered as an engine of economic growth in India due to multiple reasons (Singh et al., 2019a). MSMEs help to create jobs for skilled and unskilled people, absorb agricultural labour, and create demand for products. It is also supportive to increase per capita income and national income of a country. It is also beneficial to increase the foreign trade and global value chain. It is also a significant driver to increase the transfer of technology from one nation to another nation. The growth of MSMEs also attracts the FDI inflows that further create physical infrastructure and business opportunities. Therefore, it is positive to increase money supply in the domestic market and maintain the economic value of local currency in the international market. Hence, it indicates that MSMEs are supportive to enhance economic and social development of peoples at larger scale in India (Srinivasan et al., 2016; Chatterjee & Kar, 2020; Padhi & Sharma, 2022). The sector is highly helpful to reduce poverty and income inequality in India (Singh & Kumar, 2022b). MSMEs provide jobs for a large segment of the population in India (Ali & Husain, 2014). Therefore, MSMEs sector is dominant due to its significant contribution in the GDP of India (Padhi & Sharma, 2022). MSMEs sector contributes manufacturing output and employment creation in India (Srinivasan et al., 2016). It also prepares a suitable path for further development of the entrepreneurship ecosystem (Hossain et al., 2020; Padhi & Sharma, 2022; Singh & Ashraf, 2020). There are around 46 million MSMEs which provide jobs to approximately 106 million people in India (Kumar & Ayedee, 2018). Whereas around 40% of Indian workforce engaged in SMEs which contributes around 6.11% share in manufacturing sector and 24.63% share in India's service sector's GDP (Kumar & Ayedee, 2018).

Moreover, SMEs are a backbone of the Indian economy as the employment opportunities in this sector consistently increased in the last decade (Kumar & Ayedee, 2018). Most importantly, this sector contributes around 40% of India's total exports, 45% of India's manufacturing output (Ali & Husain, 2014). The Indian MSMEs sector produces around 6000 products and it contributes around 8% share in India's GDP (Ali & Husain, 2014; Srinivasan et al., 2016). Furthermore, MSMEs are fostering the entrepreneurship ecosystem in the country. India has around 633.92 Lakh MSMEs, while 4000 were large enterprises. India has around 630.52 Lakh Micro enterprises that counts more than 99% of the total number of MSMEs. While small and medium sectors contribute around 0.52% and 0.01% share in total MSMEs in India. The distribution of MSMEs in various categories of enterprises is given in Figure: 1. The MSMEs are playing a significant role to create a conducive business environment in India. Available data on MSMEs and its contribution in the Indian economy during 2012 -2015 is presented in Figure: 2. The MSMEs contribute around 29% share in India's GDP (Figure: 3).

To provide the comprehensive information on the MSMEs sector of India, the data of MSMEs is derived from MSMEs Census (2006-07) and NSS 73rd Round (2015-16). The data infers a significant

Figure 1. Percentage distribution of enterprises by male/female owners in SMEs of India
Source: Ministry of Micro, Small and Medium Enterprises (Government of India, 2017-18).

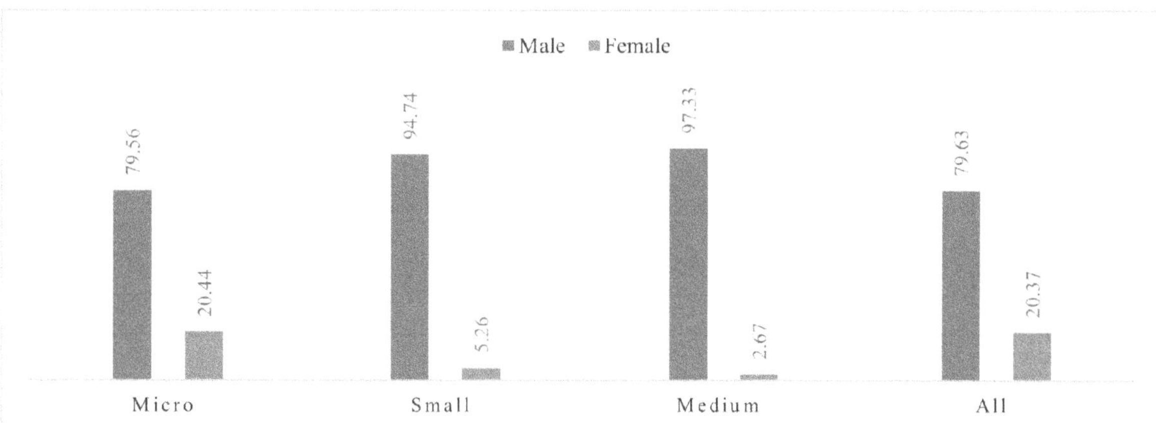

Figure 2. Contribution of MSMEs in India (in Rs. Crores adjusted for FISIM at current prices)
Source: Central Statistics Office (CSO), Ministry of Statistics & Programme Implementation and (Ministry of Micro, Small and Medium Enterprises, Government of India, 2017-18).

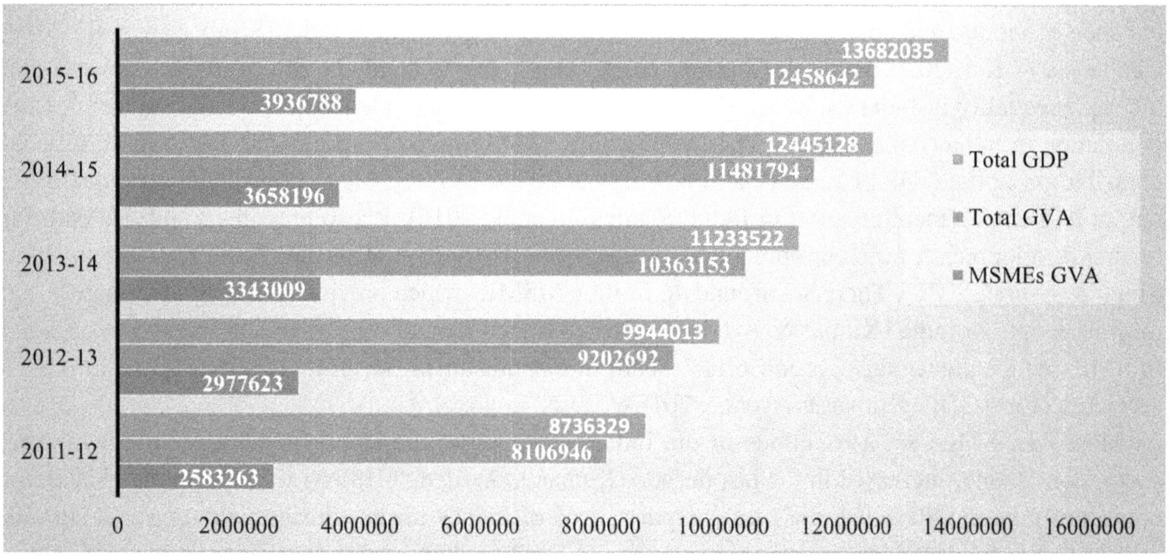

Figure 3. Growth and share of MSMEs in GVA and share of MSMEs in GDP of India
Source: Central Statistics Office (CSO), Ministry of Statistics & Programme Implementation and (Ministry of Micro, Small and Medium Enterprises, Government of India, 2017-18).

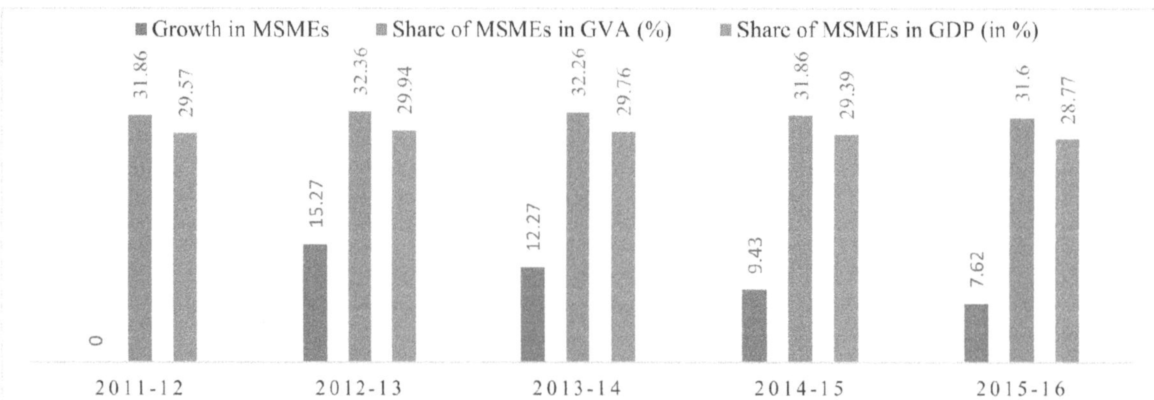

Table 2. Number of MSMEs (in Lakh) in India

Parameters	NSS 73rd Round (2015-16)	Fourth All India Census of MSMEs (2006-07)	Annual Compound Growth Rate (in %)
No. of MSMEs	**633.88**	**361.76**	**6.43**
Manufacturing	196.65	115.00	6.14
Services	437.23	246.76	3.63
Employment	**1109.89**	**805.24**	**3.63**
Manufacturing	360.42	320.03	1.33
Services	749.47	485.21	4.95

Source: Ministry of Micro, Small and Medium Enterprises (Government of India, 2017-18).

Figure 4. Category-wise distribution of enterprises (numbers in Lakh) in India
Source: Ministry of Micro, Small and Medium Enterprises (Government of India, 2017-18).

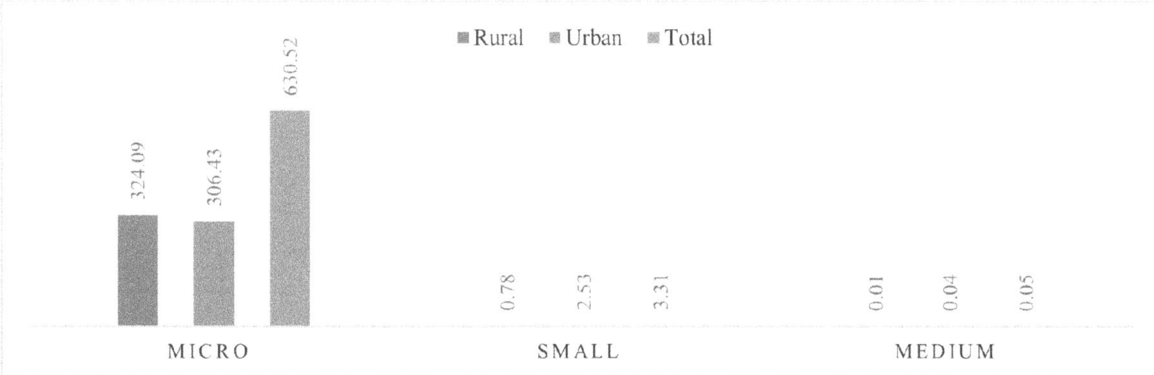

increment in the various sectors of MSMEs (i.e., manufacturing and service sectors) in India during 2006-07 to 2015-16. MSMEs sector provides employment to around 1109.89 Lakh Indian population (Table: 2).

Figure 4 provides the distribution of MSMEs sector in rural and urban India. It says that rural areas have the largest number of micro enterprises, while rural area contribute only 0.78 and 0.01 Lakh small and medium enterprises respectively. India has around 633.88 lakh enterprises that includes 630.52 Lakh medium enterprises, 3.31 small enterprises and 0.05 medium enterprises. While, rural India has a larger number of micro enterprises (Padhi & Sharma, 2022).

The state-wise distribution of MSMEs is given in Figure: 5. Uttar Pradesh has the largest number of MSMEs with a share of 14.20% in the total MSMEs of India. West Bengal has the second largest number which contributes around 14% share in Indian MSMEs (Ministry of Micro, Small and Medium Enterprises, Government of India, 2017-18). Remaining 10 states of India count around 74.05% share in MSMEs of India (Ministry of Micro, Small and Medium Enterprises, Government of India, 2017-18). Bihar, Andhra Pradesh, Gujarat, Rajasthan and Madhya Pradesh have less than 5% contribution in MSMEs of India. Table 3 shows the state-wise distribution of the estimated number of MSMEs in India. It refers that Uttar Pradesh, West Bengal, Tamil Nadu, Maharashtra, Karnataka, Bihar, Andhra Pradesh, and Gujarat have the greater number of MSMEs in India.

MSMEs is also providing jobs to large populations in Uttar Pradesh, West Bengal, Tamil Nadu; Maharashtra, Karnataka, Bihar, Andhra Pradesh and Gujarat states of India. However, Micro enterprises are providing more jobs to the population as compared to small and medium enterprises (Refer to Table: 4).

5. PROBLEMS AND FACTORS AFFECTING MSMES IN INDIA

Earlier studies already identified several factors in various categories at firm's level. Firm's current yearly turnover, quality certification of firms, labour productivity of firms, age and size of the firms, availability of finance for modernization of firms, firm's annual salary, wage rate, firm's export products, availability of raw material of firms, building capacity and quality of suppliers of firms, and social media and networking are found significant to maintain the sustainability of MSEs in India. Also, most

Table 3. State-wise distribution of estimated number of MSMEs (2015-16) in India

State/UT	Estimated Number of Enterprise (Number in Lakh)			
	Micro	Small	Medium	MSMEs
Uttar Pradesh	89.64	0.36	0.00	89.99
West Bengal	88.41	0.26	0.01	88.67
Tamil Nadu	49.27	0.21	0.00	49.48
Maharashtra	47.60	0.17	0.00	47.78
Karnataka	38.25	0.09	0.00	38.34
Bihar	34.41	0.04	0.00	34.46
Andhra Pradesh	33.74	0.13	0.00	33.87
Gujarat	32.67	0.50	0.00	33.26
Rajasthan	26.66	0.20	0.01	26.87
Madhya Pradesh	26.42	0.31	0.01	26.74
Telangana	25.94	0.10	0.01	26.05
Kerala	23.58	0.21	0.00	23.79
Odisha	19.80	0.04	0.00	19.84
Jharkhand	15.78	0.10	0.00	15.88
Punjab	14.56	0.09	0.00	14.65
Assam	12.10	0.04	0.00	12.14
Haryana	9.53	0.17	0.00	9.70
Delhi	9.25	0.11	0.00	9.36
Chhattisgarh	8.45	0.03	0.00	9.36
Jammu & Kashmir	7.06	0.03	0.00	7.09
Uttarakhand	4.14	0.02	0.00	4.17
Himachal Pradesh	3.86	0.06	0.00	3.92
Tripura	2.10	0.01	0.00	2.11
Puducherry	0.96	0.00	0.00	0.96
Nagaland	0.91	0.00	0.00	0.91
Goa	0.70	0.00	0.00	0.70
Chandigarh	0.56	0.00	0.00	0.56
Mizoram	0.35	0.00	0.00	0.35
Sikkim	0.26	0.00	0.00	0.26
Arunachal Pradesh	0.22	0.00	0.00	0.23
A & N Islands	0.19	0.00	0.00	0.19

Source: Ministry of Micro, Small and Medium Enterprises (Government of India, 2017-18).

studies given focus on external factors like firm's collaboration with foreign firms and technological development support of firms, and linkages with academic institutions of firms to increase the growth of SMEs. ICT for management (ERP, supply chain, inventory etc.), waste management and equipment maintenance capabilities of firms is also a significant driver to increase the progress of MSEs (Singh et

Table 4. State-wise estimated number of employees (2015-16) in Indian MSMEs

State/UT	Employment (Number in Lakh)		
	Female	**Male**	**Total**
Uttar Pradesh	27.27	137.92	165.26
West Bengal	43.51	91.95	135.52
Maharashtra	17.97	72.77	90.77
Tamil Nadu	32.27	64.45	96.73
Karnataka	19.73	51.11	70.84
Bihar	4.78	48.26	53.07
Gujarat	13.71	47.44	61.16
Madhya Pradesh	10.13	38.61	48.80
Rajasthan	8.01	38.31	46.33
Andhra Pradesh	21.01	34.98	55.99
Kerala	13.77	30.86	44.64
Telangana	15.24	24.91	40.16
Odisha	8.37	24.87	33.26
Delhi	2.41	20.59	23.00
Punjab	4.24	20.55	24.80
Jharkhand	5.57	19.34	24.91
Assam	1.78	16.37	18.15
Haryana	2.78	16.27	19.06
Chhattisgarh	4.07	12.79	16.86
Jammu & Kashmir	1.50	9.37	10.88
Uttarakhand	0.69	5.91	6.60
Himachal Pradesh	1.13	5.29	6.43
Tripura	0.44	2.51	2.95
Manipur	1.40	1.52	2.92
Puducherry	0.57	1.27	1.84
Goa	0.41	1.20	1.60
Meghalaya	0.72	1.19	1.91
Nagaland	0.59	1.18	1.77
Chandigarh	0.12	1.17	1.29
Mizoram	0.28	0.34	0.62
Sikkim	0.14	0.31	0.45
Arunachal Pradesh	0.11	0.29	0.41
A & N Islands	0.10	0.29	0.39

Source: Ministry of Micro, Small and Medium Enterprises (Government of India, 2017-18).

Figure 5. State-wise distribution of enterprises in India
Source: Ministry of Micro, Small and Medium Enterprises (Government of India, 2017-18).

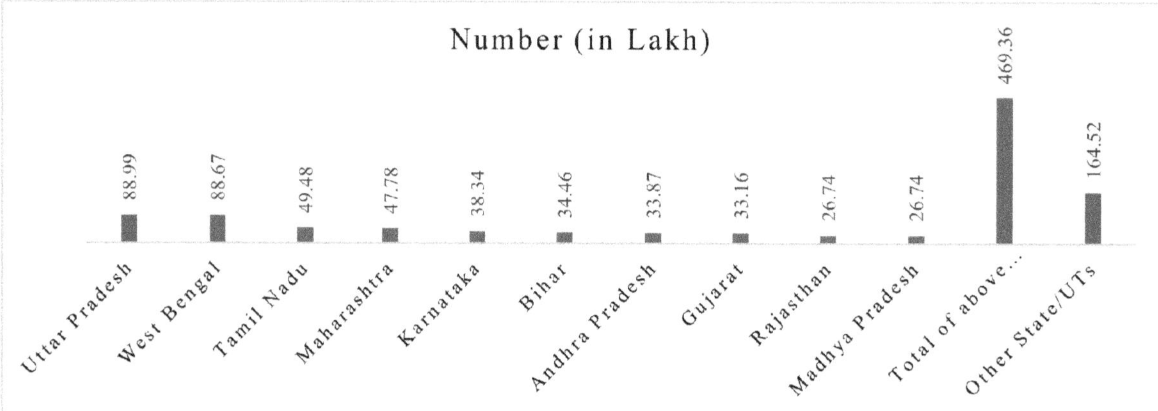

al., 2019a; Chatterjee & Kar, 2020). The brief summary of micro and small enterprises affecting factors is given in Table: 5.

Furthermore, skilled (scientists, engineers) and unskilled manpower are also found as crucial factors to increase the benefits in MSEs. The contribution of science and technological development cannot be avoided in creation of MSEs (Chatterjee & Kar, 2020), therefore earlier studies observed that R&D expenditure, production technology upgradation by firms, number of process innovations of firms, new products introduced by firms, appropriateness of technology of firms, and knowhow of updating/ acquiring latest technological development of firms are seemed significant driver in MSEs. The Indian manufacturing sector has low scope for unskilled workers; therefore, the sector could not create extensive jobs (Singh et al., 2020).

The Indian MSMEs are facing several problems such as financial problems, low quality of raw materials, low skilled workers, low R&D capacity, low number of researchers, inappropriate knowledge of intellectual property rights, low technology transfer, ineffective government policies, low utilization of social media in marketing, etc. Lack of finance is a root cause for low productivity of MSMEs in India (Ali & Husain, 2014; Aruna, 2015). Most industries are in poor positions due to low credit facilities (Ali & Husain, 2014). It is also observed that most MSEs receive around 15% funds from internal sources, 25% from financial organizations (e.g., Banks and other organizations), and 10% from financial markets. Also, there is a high rate of interest in the Indian financial market, therefore MSEs could not receive financial support from the banking sector. Lack of raw material is also an important problem for MSEs in India. MSEs are also facing problems due to scarcity and poor quality of raw material (Ali & Husain, 2014; Aruna, 2015; Singh et al., 2020). Hence, MSEs are facing the problem of quantity, quality and regulatory of the supply of raw material in India (Aruna, 2015). Also, MSEs have the problem of machinery & equipment and inadequate infrastructure in India (Ali & Husain, 2014; Aruna, 2015).

Most MSEs produce goods and services using low quality raw materials. Therefore, MSEs cannot meet the requirements of local and international consumers. Also, SMEs are unable to maintain global standards in the international market. Hence, lack of raw material has emerged as a key challenge for Indian MSEs. Inappropriate marketing is another problem for MSEs in India (Ali & Husain, 2014; Aruna, 2015). Low social marketing networks are also creating barriers for SMEs (Aruna, 2015). Small

Table 5. Brief summary of micro and small enterprises affecting factors

Variables	References
Firm's current yearly turnover	Faruq and Yi (2010); Alvarez and Crespi (2011); Akpan et al. (2012); Mazanai and Fatoki (2012); Ali and Husain (2014); Apenteng and Doe (2014); Sahu and Narayanan (2015); Sahu (2015); Ainin et al. (2015); Sahu and Narayanan (2015); Vu (2016); Chen et al. (2016); Kumar and Sharma (2016); Vu (2016); Chaudhuri (2016); Srinivasan et al. (2016); Basri (2016); Chatterjee and Das (2016); Kumarasamy and Srinivasan (2017); Rajesh (2017); Gümüş and Kütahyali (2017); Kumar and Ayedee (2018)
Labour productivity of firms	
Age and size of the firms	
Firm's Annual salary and/or wages	
Skilled (scientists, engineers) and unskilled manpower	
Percentage of turnover is spent on R&D	
Production technological development upgradation by firms	
Firm's export products	
Availability of raw material of firms	
Firm's collaboration with foreign firms	
Firm have quality certification	
Firm introduce any product/ process innovations	
Linkages with academic institutions of firms	
Appropriateness of technology of Firms	
Knowhow updating capacity of firms	
Acquiring latest technological development of firms	
ICT for design and improved products (prototyping, simulations) by firms	
Equipment maintenance capabilities of firms	
Building capacity and quality of suppliers of firms	
ICT for management (ERP, Supply Chain, Inventory etc.) by firms	
Availability of finance for modernization of firms	
Social Media and networking	

Source: Author's compilation as per the existing studies.

Figure 6. Number of social network users in India from 2015 to 2023 (in millions)
Source: www.statista.com.

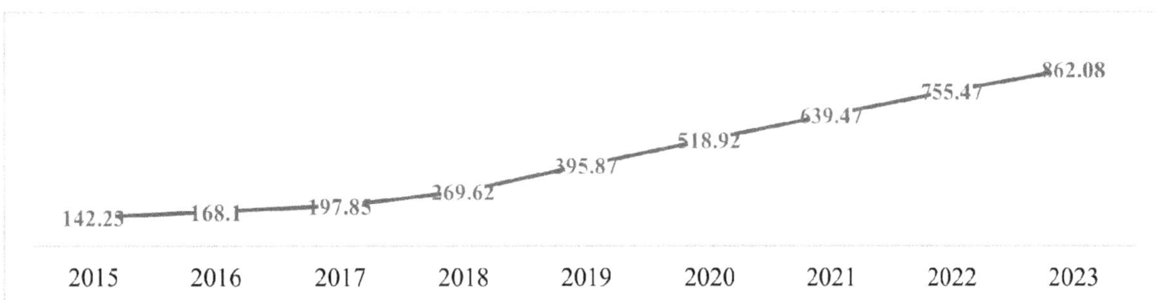

Figure 7. Social network user penetration in India from 2018 to 2023 (in %)
Source: www.statista.com.

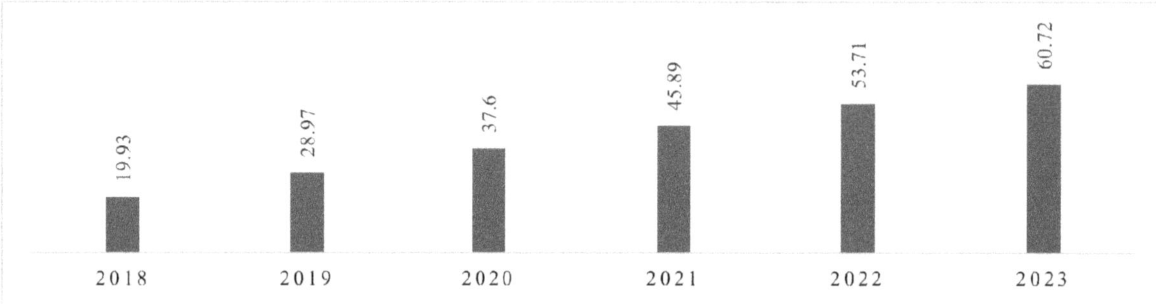

units of business enterprises have low financial capacity; therefore, these cannot spend more money on marketing of goods and services (Singh et al., 2019b). Also, high cost of funding is caused to reduce profitability of MSEs in India (Aruna, 2015). The Indian financial market has poor cash flow due to greater dependency of MSEs on financial support (Aruna, 2015). Acute power shortage is also a critical problem for industrial units in India (Aruna, 2015).

Indian labourers are also having low skills to increase their contribution in SMEs (Aruna, 2015). India also has low contribution in research & development (R&D) and development of products; therefore, India firms have low competitiveness. Furthermore, scarcity of competent manpower, inadequacy of financial support, lack of innovation temperament and lack of seed funding are creating barriers in Indian SMEs. Higher educational institutions and research universities have low focus on innovative research projects for developing competitive goods and services in the product market (Jyoti & Singh, 2023). Therefore, there is a low rate of commercialization of research that is also unable to increase technology transfer from research organization to industrial fields in India (Singh & Kumar, 2022a). It is also essential for industries to provide equipment, machines and funds to research organizations. Therefore, the Indian MSMEs sector has a low level of technological development capacity (Ali & Husain, 2014; Aruna, 2015). Lack of managerial skills of micro and small entrepreneurs is also a vital problem for small scale enterprises and entrepreneurship ecosystems in India (Aruna, 2015; Singh, 2023).

Research and development (R&D) plays a crucial role to improve competitiveness, while India has a very position in R&D (Singh & Kumar, 2022a). Hence, it is suggested there must be a special fund to promote technological development. SMEs also need to create a research and development team at industry level. India has very little contribution to create the additional skills in population due to lack of training centres. Hence, it is essential to create more training centres across Indian states. Furthermore, there is a need to encourage employees to upgrade skills by providing incentives.

6. SOCIAL MEDIA AND MSMES IN INDIA

The role of social media in various forms is increasing in India. India has the top position in usages of social networking in the world (Lakshmi et al., 2017). Recently, the number of social media users has increased unprecedentedly in rural and urban India. Number of social network users in India from 2015 to 2020 (in Millions) is given in the Figure: 6. Figure 7 provides the social network user penetration in

Figure 8. Number of Facebook users in India from 2017 to 2023 (in millions)
Source: www.statista.com.

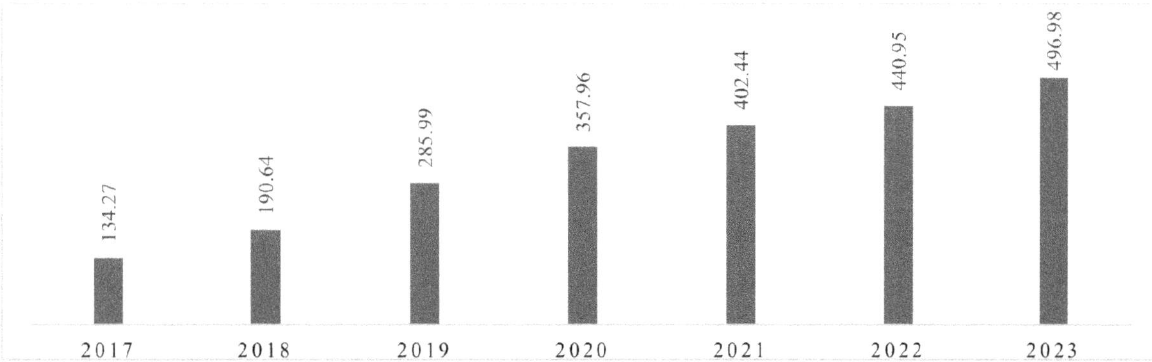

India from 2018 to 2023 (in %). Around 80% of micro and small companies depend on social media to expand their business, advertisement, publicity and attract more customers in India (Madumithaa et al., 2023). Probably, India is among the few countries which adopted social media as a marketing tool (Neti, 2011; Srinivasan et al., 2016). For instance, social media is helpful to create venture capital in the firms (Hossain et al., 2023).

Traditional techniques of media were newspaper, magazine, TV, and radio and social media (Basri, 2016). At present the uses of social media emerged in several ways i.e., YouTube (for video sharing), Facebook, shopping cart, LinkedIn, e-brochure, E-Commerce, Google Plus (for social networking); Twitter (for micro blogging service); Bookmarking (videos) Digg, MySpace, StumbleUpon, Delecious, Scribd, Flickr (Neti, 2011; Apenteng & Doe, 2014; Al-Mommani et al., 2015; Basri, 2016; Kumar & Ayedee, 2018; Emmanuel et al., 2022). Facebook, Instagram; WhatsApp and Twitter. Above-mentioned social platforms are providing extensive opportunities for MSEs to expand their business and attract more customers (Madumithaa et al., 2023). There are around 487.5 million WhatsApp users in India.

Moreover, the number of Facebook users will consistently increase in India during 2017 – 2023 (Figure: 8). There are around 32.8% active social media penetration in India. India has 2nd largest online market after China in the world. The Internet creates the platform for social media. Therefore, the use of social media increases as the number of internet users increases. The progress of India in the number of internet users is given in the Figure: 9. Internet and online infrastructure make a significant change in e-commerce in India. India has around 76.7% active e-commerce penetration. Also, India has the fastest growing mobile internet market in the world.

Social media is working as an effective marketing technological tool for MSEs in India (Neti, 2011; Lakshmi et al., 2017; Kumar & Ayedee, 2018). Around 92% of micro and small businessmen are using social media for marketing purposes in India (Lakshmi et al., 2017). It also attracts new customers and also increases the engagement of existing customers in the marketing (Al-Mommani et al., 2015; Kumarasamy & Srinivasan, 2017). Therefore, new entrepreneurs can connect new consumers with their business using social media (Hassan & Shahzad, 2022). Furthermore, social media may be useful to increase the sales and cost advantages of SMEs (Al-Mommani et al., 2015; Basri, 2016; Gümüş & Kütahyali, 2017; Emmanuel et al., 2022). Social media is also creative to meet the customers, and enhance sales volume, reduce transaction costs in MSMEs (Rasheed & Nafiz, 2022). Many companies use social media as a profitable marketing tool in India and other countries (Lakshmi et al., 2017; Hossain et al., 2021).

Figure 9. Number of internet users in India from 2010 to 2023 (in millions)
Source: www.statista.com.

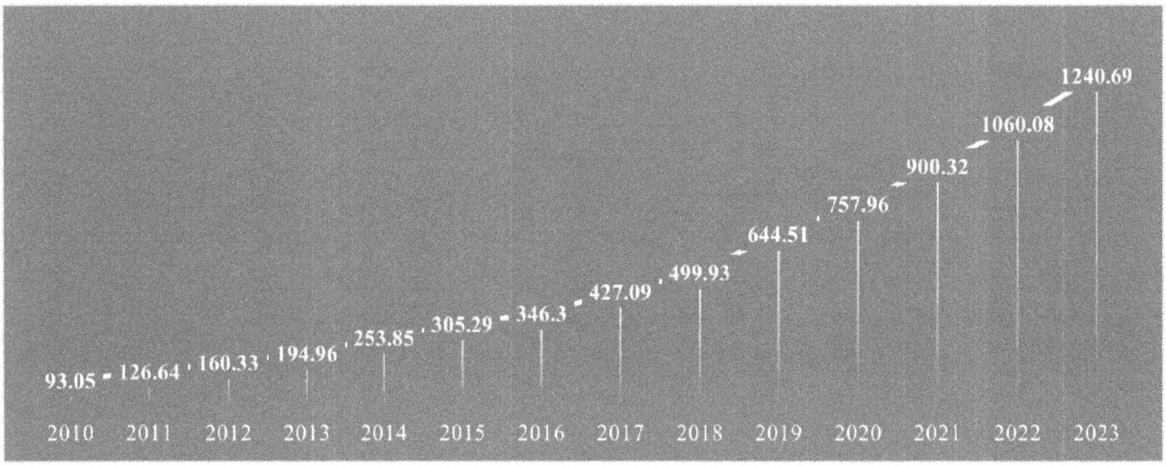

Social media also provides a real-time resource regarding market trends and consumer needs (Srinivasan et al., 2016). Hence, social media also creates an appropriate platform for communication and exchange of information between the entrepreneurs in MSMEs and consumers (Kaplan & Haenlein, 2010; Al-Mommani et al., 2015; Basri, 2016; Singh & Ashraf, 2020). Social media is a driver to sustain the competition across firms in MSMEs (Madumithaa et al., 2023; Bruce et al., 2023). It also creates an appropriate platform to attract the attention of new customers and engage existing customers (Lakshmi et al., 2017). MSMEs help to reduce the marketing costs with improving consumer service through social media, which provide the competitive advantages to MSMEs (Basri, 2016; Bruce et al., 2023). Therefore, social media may be useful to increase revenues for the business community (Neti, 2011). Social media also maintains the social networks that are used as a marketing and monitoring tools for new firms (Neti, 2011; Basri, 2016; Srinivasan et al., 2016). Products and service quality of enterprises also get significant benefits through social media (Al-Mommani et al., 2015).

Social media also attracts new clients in MSEs (Lakshmi et al., 2017; Gümüş & Kütahyali, 2017). It is also observed that social media is assisted to firms to maintain their engagement with customers (Kumar & Ayedee, 2018). Furthermore, social media is also creating a new strategy to increase the communication with entrepreneurs and consumers in national and global markets (Al-Mommani et al., 2015). Global competitions also increased due to use of social media across firms in India (Neti, 2011; Al-Mommani et al., 2015). Social media is also useful to make friends and provide educational materials for people and listen to music (Apenteng & Doe, 2014). The government also gets a platform to know the public opinion on various policies and their progress in a specific region (Apenteng & Doe, 2014).

Social media is also a prime source to create extensive jobs and make individual effective decision makers in social, economic, business and political areas. Accordingly, it is contributing toward the growth of growth of SMEs in India (Kumar & Ayedee, 2018). In short, business community and SMEs can get following benefits from social media: (i) Share their expertise and knowledge of new goods and service launched by SMEs, (ii) Provide freedom to their consumers, (iii) Direct connection of customers with owner of the firms, (iv) Engage prospects through customer evangelism (Neti, 2011), (v) Online information to the consumers (Aboulilah et al., 2022). Social media works as a medium of marketing between business community and customer (Srinivasan et al., 2016; Aboulilah et al., 2022). For small businesses, networking is crucial tools to maintain the long-term relationship between service providers and service receivers. Hence, social media would play an effective role to create the multiple opportunities for small entrepreneurs in terms of cost benefits, publicity of new goods and services, and transfer of knowledge of new products across regions under the national boundary of the country.

7. CONCLUSION

India has around 633.88 lakh enterprises which includes 630.52 Lakh medium enterprises, 3.31 small enterprises and 0.05 medium enterprises. While rural India has a larger number of micro enterprises. Hence, there is a need to increase the use of social media to increase the number of MSES in India. Hence, it is recommended that the Indian government should make effective efforts to utilize social media to create more MSEs. MSMEs is also providing jobs to large populations in Uttar Pradesh, West Bengal, Tamil Nadu; Maharashtra, Karnataka, Bihar, Andhra Pradesh and Gujarat states of India. However, Micro enterprises are providing more jobs to the population as compared to small and medium enterprises. Additionally, Uttar Pradesh, West Bengal, Tamil Nadu, Maharashtra, Karnataka, Bihar, Andhra Pradesh, and Gujarat have the greater number of MSMEs in India.

This study also observed internal and external factors that help to boost the performance of MSMEs in India. Firm's current yearly turnover; labour productivity of firms, firm's annual salary and/or wages, firm's export products, availability of raw material of firms, building capacity and quality of suppliers of firms, and social media and networking are found as internal factors of SMEs in India. Also, the growth of MSEs are significantly associated with several external factors like firm's collaboration with foreign firms, linkages of firms with public R&D institutions, linkages with private R&D and technology support of firms, linkages with academic institutions of firms, appropriate marketing strategies and entrepreneurial skills and training of people. Skilled (scientists, engineers) and unskilled manpower are also found as crucial factors to increase the benefits of MSEs. R&D expenditure, production technology upgradation, number of product and process innovations of firms, firm introduce any product/ process innovations, appropriateness of technology of firms, knowhow of updating/acquiring latest technology of firms are also seemed significant driver for MSEs and entrepreneurship ecosystem in India (Singh, 2023).

Social media and social media marketing (SMM) are found to be crucial tools in SMEs to sustain business expansion and promotion of SMEs (Kumar & Ayedee, 2018). Promotion, advertising, marketing, and customer relation would be effective through social media (Neti, 2011; Aruna, 2015; Srinivasan et al., 2016; Kumar & Ayedee, 2018). Therefore, India has a better opportunity to increase the number of SMEs through social media (Kumar & Ayedee, 2018). It is also noticed that the progress of social media has significantly increased in India in the last decade. For instance, the number of intended users, Facebook users and social network users will consistently increase in India during 2015 – 2023. Despite that India needs to adopt policies that are adopted by Malaysia, Belgium, China and other countries to increase the growth of SMEs through social media and social media marketing. India requires social media as crucial tools to create small and micro scale enterprises (Srinivasan et al., 2016). Waste management and equipment maintenance capabilities of firms is also a significant driver to increase the progress of MSEs. Social media would facilitate the development of online social networks by designing and connecting a user's-based profile in India and other countries (Lakshmi et al., 2017; Aboulilah et al., 2022).

8. POLICY SUGGESTIONS

The chapter describes the contribution of social media and social media marketing in the MSMEs of India as per the existing literature. It also provides the crucial indicators that are useful to increase the growth of the Indian manufacturing sector. Accordingly, it could produce the following suggestions to increase the growth of entrepreneurship ecosystem and MSMEs in India: In the era of technological development and digitalization, social media could be helpful to increase growth, production, productivity, efficiency, profits, outputs and new customers of SMEs in India (Singh & Jyoti,2023b). Also, the SMEs could also improve their financial transaction due to application of social media and SMM. Therefore, it is suggested that Indian entrepreneurs should apply social media to achieve their task in SMEs. Social media needs appropriate digital and ICT infrastructure, active ecosystem (Singh & Jyoti,2023b). Thus, India should create digital infrastructure to increase the practicability of social media and SMM in SMEs.

Most entrepreneurs are unable to use social media due to their digital illiteracy and low skills ability. Furthermore, most entrepreneurs especially in rural India are unable to use social media due to low ICT infrastructure and internet speed. Hence, the Government of India should develop appropriate ICT infrastructure in rural areas to enhance the practicability of social media and SMM in small-scale enterprises. There is a requirement to increase the collaboration between research academia and SMEs in India. Furthermore, social media would be positive to create new business opportunities for the working population in India. Social media would also create the entrepreneurial skills, technological skills and knowledge among the youth population in India. It would also nurture an innovative ecosystem in higher educational institutions and research universities in India. Therefore, it is essential for the Government of India to provide vocational training to skilled and unskilled workforce to increase their involvement in small scale enterprises (Ali & Husain, 2014).

The government should take assistance from social media to increase the attraction of the working population in entrepreneurial activities. Social media should establish more sector-specific technical training and skill development centres for the students and businessmen in India. There must be internship facilities for the students in research organizations as per the current needs of the manufacturing sector. The Government of India needs to provide financial support, electricity with reasonable prices and raw materials to MSMEs (Aruna, 2015). New entrepreneurs should focus on social entrepreneurship to get crucial benefits from social media and SMM (Hassan & Shahzad, 2022). The scientific research community should also discover cheap IT instruments for all people in the society to improve their usability of social media and social marketing the business activities in rural areas of India. The Government of India should give more focus on IPRs regime and technological development to increase the use of social media and SMM in entrepreneurial activities (Singh & Jyoti, 2020; Singh, 2023).

9. LIMITATION OF THIS STUDY AND FURTHER RESEARCH INSTRUCTIONS

This chapter is based on existing literature and provides the significance of social media and SMM to create SMEs in the developing economies as giving relatively more focus on India. This chapter also comes with crucial policy suggestions to increase the usability of social media and growth of SMEs in India. The scientific research community needs to develop an appropriate and viable empirical model to assess the influence of social media on creation of MSEs in India. There is urgency to identify the way of social media to generate more MSEs in India using primary surveys of new firms. Also, existing researchers can undertake research that must include the role of social media in large business and multinational corporations (MNCs) of India. The impact of social media and social media marketing on the performance of firms may vary in India. For instance, India has more than 65 different industries in MSMEs, while social media and social media marketing have diverse impacts on these industries. However, the present chapter could not examine the role of social media in specific firms of India's MSMEs. Moreover, digital infrastructure, and information & communication technology are also supportive to increase the development of social media and SMM (Singh & Jyoti,2023b). Thus, the government should develop appropriate digital and ICT infrastructure to increase the extensive practices of social media in entrepreneurial activities. While digital literacy is necessary to increase the development of digital infrastructure (Ihsaniyati et al., 2023). Hence, existing researchers can also examine the contribution of digitalization and digital infrastructure in the success of MSMEs in India.

Furthermore, social media is useful to increase the progress of government policies, technology transfer and commercialization, entrepreneurship ecosystem, start-up ecosystem, and science & technological development. Social media and social media marketing have positive implications on multiple sectors like education, social change, social communication, technology transfer, commercialization of technology, foreign trade, product value creation, etc. Further study can be considered to examine the factors affecting entrepreneurs' intention to adopt social media in the business activities of India. There is appropriate scope of social media in rural areas of India. However, limited studies could investigate the implications of social media in the entrepreneurship ecosystem of rural India. Hence, it may be another area of study in the further research.

REFERENCES

Aboulilah, H. M. E., Hossian, S. F. A., Vuong, B. N., & Jebril, T. (2022). Exploring the relationship between WeChat usage and e-purchase intention during the COVID-19 pandemic among university students in China. *SAGE Open*, *12*(4), 1–13. doi:10.1177/21582440221139447 PMID:36466966

Ahmad, S. Z., Bakar, A. R., & Ahmad, N. (2019). Social media adoption and its impact on firm performance: The case of the UAE. *International Journal of Entrepreneurial Behaviour & Research*, *25*(1), 84–111. doi:10.1108/IJEBR-08-2017-0299

Ainin, S., Parveen, F., Moghavvemi, S., Jaafar, N. I., & Shuib, N. L. M. (2015). Factors influencing the use of social media by SMEs and its performance outcomes. *Industrial Management & Data Systems*, *115*(3), 570–588. doi:10.1108/IMDS-07-2014-0205

Akpan, S. B., Ukoha, O. O., Onyenweaku, C. E., & Johan, D. E. (2012). Empirical relationship among technical efficiency, macroeconomic variables and industrial policy regimes: A case study of sugar industry in Nigeria. *International Journal of Economics and Management Sciences*, *1*(10), 1-11. https://www.hilarispublisher.com/abstract/empirical-relationship-among-technical-efficiency-macroeconomic-variables-and-industrial-policy-regimes-a-case-study-of--19461.html

Al-Mommani, K., Al-Afifi, A., & Mahfuz, M. A. (2015). The impact of social networks on maximizing the competitive value of micro, small, and medium enterprises. *International Journal of Management Science and Business Administration*, *1*(3), 64–70. doi:10.18775/ijmsba.1849-5664-5419.2014.13.1005

Alam, A. R., Asdar, M., Munizu, M., & Mappanyompa, A. N. B. (2023). The importance of social media in improving SMEs performance. ICAME 2022, AEBMR, 239, 124-131. doi:10.2991/978-94-6463-146-3_13

Ali, A., & Husain, F. (2014). MSME's India: Problems, solutions and prospectus in present scenario. *International Journal of Engineering and Management Sciences*, *5*(2), 109–115. http://www.science-andnature.org/IJEMS/IJEMS-Vol5(2)-Apr2014/IJEMS%20Vol5(2)-8.pdf

Alvarez, R., & Crespi, G. (2011). Determinants of technical efficiency in small firms. *Small Business Economics*, *20*(1), 233–244. https://www.jstor.org/stable/40229263

Amoah, J., Bruce, E., Shurong, Z., Egala, S. B., & Kwarteng, K. (2023). Social media adoption in smes sustainability: Evidence from an emerging economy. *Cogent Business & Management*, *10*(1), 1–28. doi:10.1080/23311975.2023.2183573

Apenteng, S. A., & Doe, N. P. (2014). Social media & business growth: Why small/medium-scale enterprises in developing world should take an advantage of it (A case of the country Ghana). *IOSR Journal of Business and Management*, *16*(5), 76–80. doi:10.9790/487X-16547680

Aruna, N. (2015). Problems faced by micro, small and medium enterprises – A special reference to small entrepreneurs in Visakhapatnam. *IOSR Journal of Business and Management*, *17*(4), 43–49. https://www.iosrjournals.org/iosr-jbm/papers/Vol17-issue4/Version-5/F017454349.pdf

Basri, W. (2016). Social media impact on small and medium enterprise: Case review of businesses in the Arab World. *Arts and Social Sciences Journal*, *7*(6), 1–5. doi:10.4172/2151-6200.1000236

Bruce, E., Keelson, S., Amoah, J., & Egala, S. B. (2023). Social media integration: An opportunity for SMEs sustainability. *Cogent Business & Management*, *10*(1), 1–20. doi:10.1080/23311975.2023.2173859

Chatterjee, N., & Das, N. (2016). A study on the impact of key entrepreneurial skills on business success of Indian micro-entrepreneurs: A case of Jharkhand region. *Global Business Review*, *17*(1), 1–16. doi:10.1177/0972150915610729

Chatterjee, S., Choudhuri, R., Sakka, G., Grandhi, B., Galati, A., Siachou, E., & Vrontis, D. (2021). Adoption of social media marketing for sustainable business growth of SMEs in emerging economies: A moderating role of leadership support. *Sustainability (Basel)*, *13*(21), 1–16. doi:10.3390/su132112134

Chatterjee, S., & Kar, A. K. (2020). Why do small and medium enterprises use social media marketing and what is the impact: Empirical insights from India. *International Journal of Information Management*, *53*(1), 102103. Advance online publication. doi:10.1016/j.ijinfomgt.2020.102103

Chaudhuri, D. D. (2016). Impact of economic liberalization on technical efficiency of firms: Evidence from India's electronics industry. *Theoretical Economics Letters*, *6*(1), 549–560. doi:10.4236/tel.2016.63061

Chen, A., Patton, D., & Kenney, M. (2016). University technology transfer in China: A literature review and taxonomy. *The Journal of Technology Transfer*, *41*(1), 891–929. doi:10.1007/s10961-016-9487-2

Emmanuel, C. P., Qin, S., Hossain, S. F. A., & Hussain, K. (2022). Factors influencing social-media-based entrepreneurship project among female students in China. *Heliyon*, *8*(12), 1–9. doi:10.1016/j.heliyon.2022.e12041 PMID:36483305

Faruq, H. A., & Yi, D. T. (2010). The determinants of technical efficiency of manufacturing firms in Ghana. *Global Economy Journal*, *10*(3). doi:10.2202/1524-5861.1646

Gümüş, N., & Kütahyali, D. N. (2017). Perceptions of social media by small and medium enterprises SMEs in Turkey. *International Journal of Business and Information*, *12*(2), 1–4. doi:10.6702/ijbi.2017.12.2.2

Hassan, S., & Shahzad, A. (2022). The impact of social media usage on small and micro social commerce enterprises in Malaysia. *Pakistan Journal of Commerce and Social Sciences*, *16*(1), 141–166.

Hossain, S. F., Shan, X., Musa, M., & Rahman, P. (2023). Social media and increase venture creation tendency with innovative ideas: The case of female students in Asia. *Research Anthology on Applying Social Networking Strategies to Classrooms and Libraries*, *4*(1), 1716–1731. doi:10.4018/978-1-6684-7123-4.ch093

Hossain, S. F. A., Nurunnabi, M., Hussain, K., & Shan, X. (2020). Smartphone-based m-shopping behavior and innovative entrepreneurial tendency among women in emerging Asia. *International Journal of Gender and Entrepreneurship*, *12*(2), 173–189. doi:10.1108/IJGE-03-2019-0054

Hossain, S. F. A., Shan, X., Nurunnabi, M., Tushar, H., Mohsin, A. K. M., & Ahsan, F. T. (2021). Opportunities and challenges of m-learning during the COVID-19 pandemic: A mixed methodology approach. In E-Collaboration Technologies and Strategies for Competitive Advantage Amid Challenging Times (pp. 210-227). IGI Global. doi:10.4018/978-1-7998-7764-6.ch007

Ihsaniyati, H., Sarwoprasodjo, S., Muljono, P., & Gandasari, D. (2023). The use of social media for development communication and social change: A review. *Sustainability (Basel)*, *15*(3), 1–35. doi:10.3390/su15032283

Jyoti, B., & Singh, A. K. (2023). Does digitalization have a causal relationship with economic development? An experience from a country-wise panel data statistical analysis. In R. Sine Nazlı & G. Sari (Eds.), Handbook of Research on Perspectives on Society and Technology Addiction (pp. 34-61). IGI Global. doi:10.4018/978-1-6684-8397-8.ch003

Kanth, G., & Prasad, R. S. R. (2023). A systematic literature review on social media marketing in small and medium enterprises. *SEDME (Small Enterprises Development, Management & Extension Journal)*, *50*(1), 80-95. doi:10.1177/09708464221129005

Kaplan, A., & Haenlein, M. (2010). Users of the world, unite! The challenges and opportunities of social media. *Business Horizons*, *53*(1), 59–68. doi:10.1016/j.bushor.2009.09.003

Kumar, A., & Ayedee, A. (2018). Social media tools for business growth of SMES. *Journal of Management*, *5*(3), 137–142.

Kumar, S., & Sharma, R. (2016). Patenting and technical efficiency of manufacturing firm in India: Evidence from medium and high technology firms. In N. Siddharthan & K. Narayanan (Eds.), *Technology. India Studies in Business and Economics*. Springer. doi:10.1007/978-981-10-1684-4_3

Kumarasamy, T., & Srinivasan, J. (2017). Impact of social media applications on small and medium business entrepreneurs in India. *International Journal of Commerce and Management Research*, *3*(10), 50–53.

Lakshmi, V., Mahboob, A., & Choudhry, A. (2017). A study on impact of social media on small and medium enterprises. *International Journal of Scientific Development and Research, 2*(11), 64–71.

Madumithaa, N., Mishra, A., Sruthi, S., Sivaperumal, K., & Adhav, S. (2023). Implications of social media and socio-economic activities on micro and small enterprises in India. *International Journal of Professional Business Review, 8*(4), 1–18. doi:10.26668/businessreview/2023.v8i4.1240

Mazanai, M., & Fatoki, O. (2012). Perceptions of start-up small and medium-sized enterprises (SMEs) on the importance of business development services providers (BDS) on improving access to finance in South Africa. *Journal of Social Sciences, 30*(1), 31–41. doi:10.1080/09718923.2012.11892980

Meske, C., & Stieglitz, S. (2013). Adoption and use of social media in small and medium-sized enterprises. In F. Harmsen & H. A. Proper (Eds.), *Practice-Driven Research on Enterprise Transformation. PRET 2013. Lecture Notes in Business Information Processing, 151*. Springer. doi:10.1007/978-3-642-38774-6_5

Mitra, A., Sharma, C., & Véganzonès-Varoudakis, M. A. (2016). Infrastructure, ICT and firms' productivity and efficiency: An application to the Indian manufacturing. In Globalization of Indian Industries, India Studies in Business and Economics. doi:10.1007/978-981-10-0083-6_2

Neti, S. (2011). Social Media and its role in marketing. *International Journal of Enterprises Computing and Business Systems, 1*(2), 1–16. https://www.ijecbs.com/July2011/13.pdf

Oyewobi, L., Adedayo, O. F., Olorunyomi, S. O., & Jimoh, R. A. (2023). Influence of social media adoption on the performance of construction small and medium-sized enterprises (SMEs) in Abuja-Nigeria. *Engineering, Construction, and Architectural Management, 30*(9), 4229–4252. doi:10.1108/ECAM-01-2022-0039

Padhi, A., & Sharma, A. (2022). Analysis the impact of social media marketing on SMEs in India. *International Journal of Public Sciences and Law, 2*(2), 3332–3361. https://ijpsl.in/wp-content/uploads/2022/01/Analysing-the-Impact-of-Social-Media-Marketing-on-SMEs-in-India-merged.pdf

Patnaik, K. S. K., & Satyaprakash, B. (2015). Role of social media in the growth of small scale industries in Coastal Orissa. *IOSR Journal of Business and Management, 17*(11), 1-3. https://www.iosrjournals.org/iosr-jbm/papers/Vol17-issue11/Version-1/A0171110103.pdf

Rajesh, R. S. N. (2007). *Technical efficiency in the informal manufacturing enterprises: Firm level evidence from an Indian state*. MPRA Paper No. 7816. https://mpra.ub.uni-muenchen.de/7816/

Rasheed, A. A., & Nafiz, A. (2022). Factors influencing the adoption of social media marketing by micro, small, and medium-sized enterprises (MSMEs) of the Maldives and its impact on MSME performance. *International Journal of Social Research & Innovation, 6*(1), 47–73. doi:10.55712/ijsri.v6i1.50

Sahu, P. K. (2015). Technical efficiency of domestic and foreign firms in Indian manufacturing: A firm level panel analysis. *Arthshastra Indian Journal of Economic & Research, 4*(2), 7–21. doi:10.17010/aijer/2015/v4i2/65534

Sahu, S. K., & Narayanan, K. (2015). Environmental certification and technical efficiency: A study of manufacturing firms in India. *Journal of Industry, Competition and Trade*, *16*(1), 191–207. doi:10.1007/s10842-015-0213-9

Sendawula, K., Kimuli, S. N. L., Turyakira, P., & Kibanja, G. (2022). Social media perceptions, readiness and usage in fostering sustainable growth of micro and small enterprises in Uganda. *African Journal of Economic and Management Studies*, *13*(4), 598–613. doi:10.1108/AJEMS-08-2021-0378

Singh, A. K. (2023). Relative performance of entrepreneurship ecosystem for selected countries using a composite Z-score technique of index estimation. *Eurasian Journal of Management & Social Sciences*, *4*(2), 1–32. doi:10.23918/ejmss.V4i2p1

Singh, A. K., Acharya, S. R., & Chavda, P. (2017a). Implications of intellectual property rights and socio-economic factors on growth of manufacturing sector in selected cross economies: An empirical assessment. In *Twelfth Biennial Conference on Entrepreneurship Organized by EDII Ahmedabad* (pp. 262-279). Bookwell Publishing House.

Singh, A. K., Arya, A., & Jyoti, B. (2019b). A conceptual review on economic, business, intellectual property rights and science & technology related activities in Asian economies. *JNNCE Journal of Engineering & Management*, *3*(2), 1-22. http://jjem.jnnce.ac.in/article/JJEM030201.pdf

Singh, A. K., & Ashraf, S. N. (2020). Association of entrepreneurship ecosystem with economic growth in selected countries: An empirical exploration. Journal of Entrepreneurship. *Business Economics (Cleveland, Ohio)*, *8*(2), 36–92.

Singh, A. K., Ashraf, S. N., & Acharya, S. R. (2017b). Viability of Bayh Dole Act of USA in the context of India: Critical evidence from review of literature. In *Proceedings of the 12th Biennial Conference on Entrepreneurship Organized by EDII Ahmedabad* (pp. 235-252). Bookwell Publishing House.

Singh, A. K., Ashraf, S. N., & Arya, A. (2019a). Estimating factors affecting technical efficiency in Indian manufacturing sector. *Eurasian Journal of Business and Economics*, *12*(24), 65–86. doi:10.17015/ejbe.2019.024.04

Singh, A. K., & Jyoti, B. (2020). Factors affecting firm's annual turnover in selected manufacturing industries of India: An empirical study. *Business Perspectives and Research*, *2*(3), 33–59. doi:10.38157/business-perspective-review.v2i3.206

Singh, A. K., & Jyoti, B. (2023a). Empirical investigation for assessing the causality of entrepreneurship ecosystem with entrepreneurial behavior and attitudes across countries. In E. Abe & I. Abe (Eds.), *Cases on the Interplay Between Family, Society, and Entrepreneurship* (pp. 315–353). IGI Global. doi:10.4018/978-1-6684-8748-8.ch012

Singh, A. K., & Jyoti, B. (2023b). Empirical evidence from different income group countries on the interdependency between digitalization and economic development. In 5G, Artificial Intelligence, and Next Generation Internet of Things: Digital Innovation for Green and Sustainable Economies (pp. 44-85). IGI Global. doi:10.4018/978-1-6684-8634-4.ch003

Singh, A. K., & Kumar, S. (2021). Assessing the performance and factors affecting industrial development in Indian states: An empirical analysis. *Journal of Social Economics Research*, *8*(2), 135–154. doi:10.18488/journal.35.2021.82.135.154

Singh, A. K., & Kumar, S. (2022a). Expert's perception on technology transfer and commercialization, and intellectual property rights in India: Evidence from selected research organizations. *Journal of Management, Economics, and Industrial Organization*, *6*(1), 1–33. doi:10.31039/jomeino.2022.6.1.1

Singh, A. K., & Kumar, S. (2022b). Measuring the factors affecting annual turnover of the firms: A case study of selected manufacturing industries in India. *International Journal of Business Management and Finance Research*, *5*(2), 33–45. doi:10.53935/26415313.v5i2.211

Singh, A. K., Singh, B. J., & Ashraf, S. N. (2020). Implications of intellectual property protection, and science and technological development in the manufacturing sector in selected economies. *Journal of Advocacy. Research in Education*, *7*(1), 16–35.

Srinivasan, S., Bajaj, R., & Bhanot, S. (2016). Impact of social media marketing strategies used by micro small and medium enterprise (MSMEs) on customer acquisition and retention. *IOSR Journal of Business and Management*, *18*(1), 91–101. https://www.iosrjournals.org/iosr-jbm/papers/Vol18-issue1/Version-3/M0181391101.pdf

Suariedewi, G. A. A. M., Adyatma, W. C., & Wulandari, G. A. A. (2022). The impact of social media marketing for MSMEs sustainability in Covid-19 period. *Journal of Business and Management Review*, *3*(9), 641–655. doi:10.47153/jbmr39.4602022

Vatanasakdakul, S., Aoun, C., & Putra, Y. H. S. (2020). Social media in micro-enterprises: Exploring adoption in the Indonesian retail sector. *Journal of Global Information Management*, *28*(3), 184–203. doi:10.4018/JGIM.2020070110

Vu, H. D. (2016). Technical efficiency of FDI firms in the Vietnamese manufacturing sector. *Review of Economic Perspectives*, *16*(3), 1–13. doi:10.1515/revecp-2016-0013

Chapter 4
AI-Driven Algorithms for Optimizing Social Media Advertising:
Prospects and Challenges

Amaresh Jha
https://orcid.org/0000-0002-6083-1610
University of Petroleum and Energy Studies, India

EXECUTIVE SUMMARY

The social media advertising market is anticipated to witness a surge in ad spending; projections indicate an annual growth rate (CAGR 2023-2028) of 4.31%, leading to a forecasted market volume of US$255.8 billion by the year 2028. AI algorithms can analyze vast amounts of user data to identify patterns and preferences. This study aims to explore the prospects and challenges of using AI-driven algorithms for optimizing social media advertising and also the functions and benefits of five algorithms prominently used in optimizing social media advertising, namely recommendation algorithms, lookalike audience algorithms, A/B testing algorithms, bid optimization algorithms, and ad fraud detection algorithms. The study also aims at analyzing the challenges associated with AI-driven algorithms from the perspective of customer experience.

1. INTRODUCTION

1.1 Background and Significance of the Study

The rapid evolution of digital marketing practices and the transformative impact of artificial intelligence technologies has raised the problem of integration of AI algorithms on Social media platforms (Corrigan, Craciun,& Powell, 2014). This is further an implication of the transitioning of traditional advertising methods into highly personalized and data-driven strategies. While AI-driven algorithms offer unparalleled opportunities for advertisers to optimize targeting precision and content personalization, they also

DOI: 10.4018/979-8-3693-1781-5.ch004

raise significant challenges and concerns. The extensive collection and utilization of user data by these algorithms has sparked debates over privacy infringement and ethical considerations(Stalidis, Karapistolis & Vafeiadis, 2015). As AI technologies become more sophisticated, the potential for algorithmic bias, lack of transparency, and unintended consequences in social media advertising has become a pressing concern, necessitating a comprehensive examination of the prospects and challenges associated with the utilization of AI in this domain. The problem is also rooted in the need for a delicate balance between advertising effectiveness and user trust. While AI-driven algorithms have the capacity to enhance key performance indicators and deliver more relevant content to users, there is a growing recognition that ethical standards and user consent are paramount. Instances of data breaches, concerns about the misuse of personal information, and the opacity of algorithmic decision-making processes have led to a more critical scrutiny of AI-driven social media advertising. Jha & Jha (2022) in their study "Data Encryption Dispute Resolutions under Intermediary Guidelines of Information Technology Act" provide a detailed account of Challenges and Future Framework. Advertisers, social media platforms, and regulatory bodies are grappling with the challenge of fostering an environment where AI technologies can maximize advertising potential while ensuring users' rights.

Understanding how AI-driven algorithms contribute to the optimization of social media advertising is crucial for marketers (Davenport & Ronanki 2018). Insights into targeting precision, content personalization, and overall campaign effectiveness can guide advertisers in leveraging AI technologies to enhance the impact of their campaigns. This knowledge is essential for staying competitive in an increasingly digital and data-driven advertising landscape. This study also aims to shed light on the ethical considerations associated with the implementation of AI in social media advertising. As concerns about user privacy, transparency, and algorithmic bias grow, the study's findings provide a foundation for developing ethical frameworks and best practices. This is vital for ensuring responsible and user-centric advertising practices that align with evolving societal expectations.

The study's exploration of how AI-driven algorithms impact key performance indicators (KPIs) in social media advertising provides valuable benchmarks for assessing campaign success. This knowledge empowers advertisers to make data-driven decisions, allocate resources effectively, and refine strategies for better results. Understanding the comparative advantages over traditional methods is particularly relevant in optimizing advertising budgets. Industry professionals, including marketers, advertisers, and technology developers, can benefit from the study's insights. It equips them with a deeper understanding of the strengths and limitations of AI-driven algorithms, enabling informed decision-making in strategy development, technology adoption, and compliance with ethical standards.

1.2 Research Objectives

- To examine the impact of AI on Social Media Advertising effectiveness.
- To identify and analyze key challenges and ethical considerations.
- To evaluate the impact of AI on Key Performance Indicators (KPIs) in Social Media Advertising.

1.3 Research Questions

- How do AI-driven algorithms contribute to the optimization of social media advertising, particularly in terms of targeting precision, content personalization, and overall campaign effectiveness?

- What are the key challenges and ethical considerations associated with the implementation of AI-driven algorithms in social media advertising, and how do these challenges impact user privacy, transparency, and the potential for algorithmic bias?
- To what extent do AI-driven algorithms enhance key performance indicators (KPIs) in social media advertising, such as click-through rates, conversion rates, and user engagement, and how do these improvements compare to traditional advertising methods?

2. REVIEW OF LITERATURE

2.1 AI in Advertising and Marketing

The landscape of advertising has undergone rapid transformation, marked by a substantial integration of artificial intelligence (AI) and its diverse applications. Despite the presence of AI in advertising literature since the 1990s, recent years have witnessed a surge in research attention and development, opening up multifaceted avenues for future exploration. This evolution, however, lacks a comprehensive understanding, necessitating a state-of-the-art review to propel future research endeavors. To bridge this gap, this review systematically maps the trajectory of AI advertising research by conducting a thorough bibliometric and framework-based analysis of 75 scholarly articles spanning the period from 1990 to 2022. The study's notable findings encompass publication trends in AI advertising, classification using TCCM, and contextual insights derived from bibliographic coupling. Unveiling four prominent themes, the review identifies programmatic advertising and automation, ad planning and engagement, advertising effectiveness, and trust in AI advertising as focal points in contemporary research. Beyond historical analysis, this review furnishes practical guidelines and outlines future research directions, enriching the landscape of AI advertising literature. Furthermore, it extends its implications beyond academia, offering insights for industry practitioners and highlighting the potential of identified themes to shape advertising practices and contribute to the theoretical evolution of the field. In essence, this comprehensive review serves as a valuable compass, navigating the past and charting the course for the future of AI in advertising research.

Agrawal, Gans, & Goldfarb (2020) in their study "How to Win with Machine Learning" published in Harvard Business Review outline strategies for organizations to succeed with machine learning. It provides practical insights into leveraging data effectively and aligning machine learning initiatives with business goals, making it a valuable resource for business leaders and marketers.

Amatulli et al. (2021) in their study "Omnichannel Shopping Experiences for Fast Fashion and Luxury Brands" delve into the realm of omnichannel experiences for fast fashion and luxury brands. It contributes to the understanding of how these brands can optimize their digital presence and customer engagement strategies across multiple channels.

Bessis & Dobre (2014) in their study "Big Data and Internet of Things: A Roadmap for Smart Environments" provide a roadmap for integrating big data and the Internet of Things (IoT) in smart environments. It offers a comprehensive overview of the challenges and opportunities in creating intelligent ecosystems, making it relevant for researchers and practitioners in the field.

Boyd (2010) did research on "How Spotify Recommends Your New Favorite Artist". This Medium article by Boyd sheds light on Spotify's recommendation algorithm. It serves as a case study, offering insights into the application of machine learning in music recommendation systems, a pertinent area in the era of digital streaming.

Beri (2020) in his study "Machine Learning in Marketing: Overview, Learning Strategies, Applications, and Future Developments" provides a comprehensive overview of machine learning in marketing. The paper covers learning strategies, applications, and future trends, making it a valuable resource for researchers and marketers seeking a broad understanding of the field.

Campbell et al. (2020) in their study provide actionable insights into transforming data into strategic decisions and is essential reading for marketing professionals navigating the data-driven landscape. Corbo et al. (2022) in their article "The Evolving Role of Artificial Intelligence in Marketing: A Review and Research Agenda provide a comprehensive overview of the evolving role of AI in marketing. It identifies key trends and proposes a research agenda, making it a valuable resource for scholars and practitioners interested in the future of marketing.

Corrigan et al. (2014) in their case study "Consumer Analytics to Make Marketing Decisions" demonstrated the practical application of consumer analytics in making marketing decisions. It serves as a valuable example for educators and practitioners interested in bridging the gap between theory and real-world implementation.

Cuccurullo et al., (2016) provide a bibliometric analysis of performance management trends over 25 years. While not directly focused on AI, it provides a historical context for the evolution of performance management, which is relevant in the context of AI's impact on marketing metrics.

Davenport & Ronanki (2018) in their article "Artificial Intelligence for the Real-World outline practical applications of artificial intelligence in real-world business scenarios. It emphasizes the need for a strategic approach to AI adoption, making it a must-read for business leaders navigating the AI landscape. Davenport, Dalle Mule, & Lucker (2011) in their article "Know What Your Customers Want Before They Do" Published in Harvard Business Review, explore the concept of anticipatory analytics, emphasizing the importance of understanding customer needs before they articulate them. It provides insights into the proactive use of data in shaping customer experiences.

Davenport et al., 2020 in their study "How Artificial Intelligence Will Change the Future of Marketing" outline the transformative impact of AI on marketing. It offers a forward-looking perspective on how AI will shape the future of customer engagement and strategic decision-making.

de Cosmo, Piper, & Di Vittorio (2021) in their study "The Role of Attitude toward Chatbots and Privacy Concerns in the Relationship between Attitude toward Mobile Advertising and Behavioral Intent to Use Chatbots" explore the intricate relationship between users' attitudes toward chatbots, privacy concerns, mobile advertising, and their behavioral intent to use chatbots. The authors delve into the psychological aspects of user interactions with chatbots, shedding light on the factors that influence user acceptance and engagement. The paper provides valuable insights for marketers and developers aiming to enhance user experiences with chatbots by addressing privacy concerns and aligning with users' attitudes.

De Mauro et al. (2015) in their study "What is Big Data? A Consensual Definition and a Review of Key Research Topics" Published in the AIP Conference Proceedings, offer a consensual definition of big data and provides a comprehensive review of key research topics in the big data domain. The authors contribute to the conceptual clarity of big data, facilitating a better understanding of its applications and implications. The paper is a foundational resource for researchers and practitioners seeking to navigate the multifaceted landscape of big data. In their another study De Mauro et al. (2018) analyzed job roles and skill sets required for professionals in the big data domain. By categorizing the diverse skill sets needed, the authors provide guidance for individuals and organizations navigating the dynamic field of big data. The paper is valuable for both academic and industry audiences, offering insights into the evolving demands of the big data job market. De Mauro, Sestino, & Bacconi (2022) in their study titled "Machine Learning and Artificial Intelligence Use in Marketing: A General Taxonomy" Published in the Italian Journal of Marketing, present a general taxonomy of machine learning and artificial intelligence applications in the marketing domain. The authors categorize and analyze various use cases, providing a structured framework for understanding the diverse applications of AI in marketing. Taxonomy contributes to the clarity and organization of knowledge in the field, making it a valuable resource for researchers and practitioners seeking to navigate the complexities of AI in marketing.

Dedehayir & Steinert (2016) in their study "The Hype Cycle Model: A Review and Future Directions" critically review the hype cycle model and outlines future directions for its application. The authors provide insights into the strengths and limitations of the hype cycle as a conceptual framework for understanding technology adoption. The paper is essential reading for researchers and practitioners interested in the dynamics of technology hype and its implications for decision-making. Duan, Edwards, & Dwivedi (2019) in their study "Artificial focus on the evolution, challenges, and research agenda of artificial intelligence for decision-making in the era of big data. The authors provide a comprehensive overview of the landscape, discussing the evolution of AI, challenges in implementation, and proposing a research agenda to address emerging issues. The paper serves as a valuable resource for scholars and practitioners navigating the intersection of AI and big data in decision-making contexts.

Jha (2023) contributes significantly to the evolving discourse on immersive marketing in the metaverse. By developing metrics for performance analysis and addressing security challenges, the paper offers a well-rounded exploration of this emerging field. Its practical insights and comprehensive approach make it a valuable resource for both academics and industry professionals navigating the intersection of marketing, technology, and virtual environments.

Elliott (2018) in his paper provides a thoughtful exploration of the coding process in qualitative data analysis. The discussion on the nuances of coding, including issues of reliability and reflexivity, makes it a valuable resource for researchers engaged in qualitative studies. The paper encourages a deeper reflection on the coding process, enhancing the rigor and credibility of qualitative research methodologies.

Erevelles et al. (2016) in their study delve into the transformative impact of big data consumer analytics on marketing. By highlighting the evolving landscape, challenges, and opportunities, the authors contribute to the understanding of how big data reshapes marketing strategies. The incorporation of real-world examples and case studies enhances the practical relevance of the paper.

Fleming (2019) explores why robots in organizational studies take a unique perspective by questioning the assumption that robots are designed to replace human jobs. The paper challenges conventional narratives, offering a refreshing viewpoint on the relationship between robots and employment. It encourages a more nuanced understanding of the role of automation in organizational contexts.

Ford et al. (2023) provide an overview and guidelines for AI advertising. By offering insights into the current landscape of AI in advertising and practical guidelines for its implementation, the authors contribute to the growing literature on the intersection of artificial intelligence and marketing. The inclusion of guidelines enhances the applicability of research for industry practitioners.

Flower (2019) in his study brings attention to the ethical implications of emerging technologies. The real-world examples and interviews with stakeholders enrich the narrative, making it an engaging and informative piece. The paper stimulates critical discussions on the balance between security and privacy in the era of smart home devices. French (2018) explores the potential of AI chatbots to engage in meaningful conversations. The paper sheds light on the evolving role of chatbots in customer interactions and the impact on user experience. It serves as a relevant resource for businesses looking to leverage AI chatbots for customer engagement strategies.

Gans et al. (2017) believe that experiments on the impact of AI on strategy offers valuable insights into the transformative potential of artificial intelligence. The paper stimulates strategic thinking by presenting hypothetical scenarios, encouraging readers to envision the implications of AI in various contexts. It provides a conceptual foundation for future research on AI and strategy.

Gaudin (2016) explores how data scientists and AI function as personal stylists at Stitch Fix offers a glimpse into the practical applications of AI in the fashion industry. By showcasing real-world examples, the paper illustrates how AI can enhance personalized recommendations, contributing to a more data-driven and customer-centric approach in retail.

Guda & Subramanian (2019) address the issue of management of on-demand workers in the gig economy. The exploration of surge pricing, forecast communication, and worker incentives provides practical insights for businesses operating in the on-demand service sector. The paper contributes to the understanding of the dynamic and complex nature of managing a flexible workforce.

Haleem et al. (2022) conduct a literature-based study on AI applications in marketing and offer a comprehensive overview of the current state of research in the field. By synthesizing existing literature, the authors provide a valuable resource for scholars and practitioners seeking to understand the diverse applications of AI in marketing. The inclusion of a literature-based approach enhances the paper's credibility and scholarly contribution.

Harriet (2016) provides a detailed account on Lowe's introduction of LoweBot, an autonomous in-store robot, highlighting a practical application of robotics in the retail sector. The case study provides insights into the adoption of automation technologies to enhance customer experiences and operational efficiency. The paper contributes to the discourse on the integration of robots in physical retail environments.

Huang et al. (2021) in their study "A strategic framework for artificial intelligence in marketing" present a strategic framework for the application of artificial intelligence in marketing. By outlining key components and considerations, the authors provide a guide for marketers navigating the integration of AI into their strategies. The strategic framework contributes to a systematic and informed approach to leveraging AI for marketing purposes.

Kohlegger et al. (2009) in their paper "Understanding maturity models: Results of a structured content analysis" provide a comprehensive exploration of maturity models through structured content analysis. By examining various maturity models, the authors contribute to the understanding of the evolution and application of maturity models across different domains. The structured analysis offers valuable insights for researchers and practitioners seeking to leverage maturity models for organizational development.

"Marketing 5.0" by Kotler et al.(2021) introduces a forward-looking perspective on marketing, emphasizing the role of technology in serving humanity. The authors propose a holistic approach that combines technological advancements with human-centric values. This visionary work challenges marketers to align their strategies with the evolving landscape of technology and societal needs.

Kumar et al. (2019) in their paper delve into the critical role of artificial intelligence in personalized engagement marketing. By offering a comprehensive understanding of AI's implications for customer engagement, the authors bridge the gap between theory and practice. The paper provides practical insights for businesses aiming to enhance customer experiences through personalized marketing strategies.

Kurachi et al.(2018) explore the use of AI chatbots to elevate consumer contact points to a new level of sophistication. Focusing on the practical application of AI in enhancing consumer interactions, the paper contributes to the growing literature on AI's role in shaping customer experiences. The insights presented are particularly relevant for industries seeking innovative approaches to customer engagement. Casaló et al(2021). Offer a creative perspective on engaging users on Instagram by promoting positive emotions. By emphasizing the emotional aspect of user engagement, the authors contribute to the understanding of effective social media strategies. The focus on positivity adds a unique dimension to the discourse on social media marketing. Ma and Sun(2020) in their paper provide a bridge between machine learning, AI, and human insights in marketing. The authors emphasize the connection between computing power and human understanding, highlighting the collaborative potential of technology and human expertise. The paper serves as a guide for marketers navigating the integration of machine learning and AI into their decision-making processes.

Mariani and Fosso Wamba (2020) investigate the innovation strategies of consumer goods companies in the digital age, with a specific focus on the role of big data analytics. The paper sheds light on how companies leverage big data analytics to drive innovation, providing valuable insights for businesses aiming to stay competitive in the digital era.

Marr (2016) in his book "Big Data in Practice," offers a practical exploration of how successful companies have leveraged big data analytics to achieve extraordinary results. By featuring real-world case studies, Marr provides actionable insights for businesses looking to harness the power of big data. The book serves as a valuable resource for both practitioners and researchers interested in the practical applications of big data.

Mayring (2008) in his work on qualitative content analysis provides a foundational understanding of this research methodology. The emphasis on systematically analyzing qualitative data enhances the credibility and rigor of qualitative research. Researchers and students can benefit from Mayring's approach, which offers a structured method for extracting meaningful insights from textual data.

Miklosik and Evans(2020) conduct a literature review on the impact of big data and machine learning on digital transformation in marketing. The paper synthesizes existing research, offering a comprehensive overview of the evolving landscape. Researchers and practitioners will find this review valuable for understanding the current state of knowledge in the intersection of big data, machine learning, and digital marketing.

Miklosik et al. (2019) in their paper focus on the adoption of machine learning-based analytical tools in digital marketing. By exploring the factors influencing adoption, the authors contribute to the practical understanding of integrating machine learning into marketing strategies. The insights provided are relevant for marketers looking to capitalize on the analytical capabilities of machine learning in the digital domain.

Nedra et al. (2019), in their paper "Determinants of customers' intentions to use hedonic networks: The case of Instagram", outline the factors influencing customers' intentions to use Instagram, focusing on hedonic aspects. By delving into the realm of hedonic networks, the authors provide valuable insights into user behavior on Instagram. The research is well-grounded and contributes to understanding the motivations behind engagement on visually driven social media platforms.

Nguyen and Simkin (2017) explore the intersection of the Internet of Things (IoT) and marketing, offering a comprehensive overview of the current landscape and future trends. This paper serves as a valuable resource for marketers seeking to understand how IoT technologies can be strategically leveraged to enhance customer experiences and drive innovation in marketing.

Osisanwo et al. (2017) provide a detailed examination and comparison of supervised machine learning algorithms. By focusing on classification techniques, the authors contribute to the understanding of the strengths and limitations of various algorithms. The paper is a valuable resource for researchers and practitioners navigating the landscape of machine learning for classification tasks. Phoemphon et al.(2018) present a hybrid model integrating fuzzy logic and an extreme learning machine for wireless sensor network localization. The paper explores the synergies of different computational approaches, offering a novel solution to a practical problem. Researchers in the field of wireless sensor networks will find this work valuable for its innovative approach to localization.

The case study "How Harley-Davidson used artificial intelligence to increase New York sales leads by 2,930%" by Power (2017) showcases the practical application of artificial intelligence in marketing, detailing how Harley-Davidson utilized predictive analytics to achieve a remarkable increase in sales leads. The real-world example provides valuable insights for businesses looking to harness the power of AI for marketing and sales optimization.

Puntoni et al. (2020) in their work "Consumers and Artificial Intelligence: An Experiential Perspective" offer an experiential perspective on consumers and artificial intelligence. The paper explores how consumers interact with AI, focusing on the experiential aspects of these interactions. The research contributes to the emerging literature on the intersection of consumer behavior and AI, offering nuanced insights into the experiential dimensions of AI adoption.

Sestino and De Mauro (2021) present a comprehensive exploration of the implications, applications, and methods of leveraging artificial intelligence in business. The paper provides a valuable overview for business leaders, managers, and researchers seeking to understand the multifaceted landscape of AI adoption in various business contexts.

Sestino et al. (2020) in the paper "Internet of Things and Big Data as enablers for business digitalization strategies" discuss the synergies between the Internet of Things (IoT) and Big Data as enablers for business digitalization strategies. The authors provide practical insights into how businesses can harness the combined power of IoT and Big Data to drive digital transformation. The work is particularly relevant for industries exploring digitalization strategies.

Shankar (2018) in his paper "How Artificial Intelligence (AI) Is Reshaping Retailing" explores the transformative impact of artificial intelligence on retailing. By providing a strategic overview, the author highlights the evolving role of AI in reshaping the retail landscape. The paper is a valuable resource for retailers and marketers aiming to stay abreast of technological advancements and capitalize on AI for competitive advantage.

Sheth and Kellstadt (2021) in their research examine the challenges and opportunities posed by the data tsunami in the realm of data-driven marketing. The paper calls attention to the need for evolving research techniques to keep pace with the increasing volume and complexity of data. Researchers and practitioners in data-driven marketing will find this work insightful for shaping future research agendas.

Stalidis et al. (2015) contribute to the field of marketing decision support by integrating artificial intelligence and knowledge modeling, with a specific application to tourist destination management. The paper demonstrates the practical implementation of AI in supporting decision-making processes within the tourism industry. Researchers and practitioners in destination management will find this work valuable for its applied approach to AI.

2.2 Cases in AI-Driven Algorithms for Optimizing Social Media Advertising

This section of the chapter presents a comprehensive case study analysis, examining how prominent companies leverage artificial intelligence (AI) algorithms to optimize their social media advertising strategies. The showcased cases span diverse applications of AI, ranging from personalized content recommendations to real-time bidding optimization, highlighting the pivotal role of AI in shaping the contemporary digital marketing landscape.

Netflix, a leading streaming service, exemplifies the integration of AI algorithms to meticulously scrutinize user behavior and preferences. By considering factors such as viewing history, search queries, and user demographics, Netflix tailors its approach to personalized content recommendations. This strategic use of AI enables Netflix to strategically target users with relevant advertisements across various social media platforms. Similarly, Facebook, a prominent social media platform, utilizes AI to predict ad performance through the analysis of historical data and user engagement. Employing intricate algorithms that scrutinize user interactions, including likes, shares, and clicks, Facebook optimizes ad delivery, finely tuning its targeting mechanism to identify audiences more likely to engage with the advertised content.

Nike, a global leader in sportswear, employs AI-powered dynamic ad creatives to adapt in real-time based on user behavior and preferences. For instance, users engaging frequently with running-related content trigger Nike's algorithms to dynamically generate ads showcasing the latest running shoe models. This personalized approach enhances user engagement on social media platforms, creating a more tailored advertising experience. On the other hand, Spotify, a renowned music streaming service, embraces AI-driven A/B testing to dynamically optimize ad creatives and messaging. Through automated testing of different ad variations on social media platforms, algorithms analyze user responses in real-time. This iterative process aims to improve click-through rates and conversion rates, ensuring the efficacy of Spotify's advertising endeavors.

Coca-Cola, a global beverage giant, employs sentiment analysis algorithms to evaluate social media conversations and user comments. By strategically using AI to comprehend the sentiment surrounding its brand, Coca-Cola tailors ad copy and messaging to align with current consumer sentiment, effectively addressing concerns and feedback. In the e-commerce sector, eBay leverages AI algorithms for real-time bidding optimization on social media advertising platforms. These algorithms meticulously analyze user behavior, competitive bidding dynamics, and ad relevance. The outcome is the dynamic adjustment of bid amounts, ensuring optimal placement for eBay ads in real-time scenarios.

Amazon, a global e-commerce, and technology giant, utilizes AI-driven customer segmentation to categorize users based on their preferences, purchase history, and overall behavior on the platform. This segmentation strategy facilitates the creation of highly targeted social media ad campaigns, ensuring users are exposed to products and promotions that resonate with their interests. Finally, in the realm of online advertising, Google Ads incorporates AI algorithms for the detection and prevention of ad fraud. Through pattern recognition and anomaly detection, these algorithms identify irregularities in ad engagement, click patterns, and user behavior, offering a proactive approach to maintaining the integrity of campaigns and mitigating potentially fraudulent activities. Together, these cases underscore the multifaceted applications of AI in optimizing social media advertising, enhancing user experience, and driving more effective digital marketing strategies.

2.3 Research Gap

While existing literature acknowledges the role of AI-driven algorithms in optimizing social media advertising, there is a research gap in providing a comprehensive understanding of their contributions, specifically in terms of targeting precision, content personalization, and overall campaign effectiveness.

Current studies often lack a detailed exploration of the mechanisms through which AI enhances these aspects and the nuanced ways in which advertisers benefit from improved optimization.

The literature review reveals a limited scope in addressing the challenges and ethical considerations associated with the implementation of AI-driven algorithms in social media advertising. There is a need for more in-depth exploration of how these challenges, encompassing user privacy, transparency, and algorithmic bias, manifest in practical applications. The existing body of work often lacks a nuanced examination of the impact of ethical considerations on user trust and the long-term implications for the advertising ecosystem.

Current literature provides insights into the positive impact of AI-driven algorithms on key performance indicators (KPIs) in social media advertising. However, a research gap exists in terms of a comprehensive evaluation of the extent of these enhancements. There is a need for studies that delve deeper into quantitative assessments, comparing improvements in click-through rates, conversion rates, and user engagement facilitated by AI-driven strategies against traditional advertising methods. This would contribute to a more robust understanding of the practical advantages and potential limitations of AI in achieving advertising goals.

2.4 Theoretical Framework for AI in Social Advertising

The theoretical framework below provides a foundation for understanding the interplay between AI and social advertising from various psychological, communication, and ethical perspectives.

Bandura's seminal work, Social Cognitive Theory (1999) emphasizes the role of observational learning and imitation in shaping human actions. In the context of social advertising, this theory becomes instrumental as AI-driven algorithms enable precise targeting and personalization. By analyzing users' behaviors and preferences, these algorithms craft advertisements that serve as models for desirable actions. Social Cognitive Theory, in this context, suggests that individuals are more likely to engage with and be influenced by content that mirrors behaviors observed in their social environment. Consequently, advertisers can leverage AI to create tailored messages that resonate with specific audience segments, fostering a sense of relatability and social connection. The application of Social Cognitive Theory in social advertising not only enhances the potential for message retention but also contributes to the establishment of brand trust and loyalty through a strategically designed, socially resonant approach.

The Elaboration Likelihood Model (ELM), originally proposed by Petty and Cacioppo (1986), finds profound application in the realm of social media advertising, particularly when integrated with artificial intelligence (AI). ELM posits two routes to persuasion: the central route, which involves in-depth cognitive processing, and the peripheral route, which relies on heuristic cues. AI in social media advertising significantly influences both routes by dynamically tailoring content to users. Through the central route, AI algorithms analyze user data to deliver personalized and relevant advertisements, fostering deeper cognitive engagement. Simultaneously, the peripheral route is impacted as AI optimizes visual and emotional elements to trigger heuristic responses. By adapting messages based on individual preferences, attitudes, and online behaviors, AI enhances the persuasive impact of social media advertising, making it more likely to elicit favorable responses from users through both cognitive and affective pathways within the Elaboration Likelihood Model framework.

The Uses and Gratifications Theory, pioneered by Katz, Blumler, and Gurevitch (1973), provides a valuable lens for understanding the audience's motivations and choices in consuming media. In the context of social media advertising, the integration of artificial intelligence (AI) aligns seamlessly with this theoretical framework. AI algorithms analyze user behavior, preferences, and interactions to deliver personalized and gratifying content. By leveraging Uses and Gratifications Theory, social media advertisers can tailor their messages to fulfill specific user needs and desires. AI's capacity to predict and understand user preferences enables the creation of advertisements that not only align with individual interests but also offer a more satisfying and relevant user experience. This symbiotic relationship between Uses and Gratifications Theory and AI in social media advertising leads to a more nuanced understanding of consumer motivations, allowing advertisers to craft content that not only captures attention but also genuinely resonates with the diverse gratifications sought by users in their online interactions.

The Technology Acceptance Model (TAM), developed by Davis (1986), provides a comprehensive framework for understanding users' acceptance and adoption of technology. In the context of social media advertising, the integration of artificial intelligence (AI) aligns with TAM principles. TAM emphasizes perceived usefulness and ease of use as key determinants of technology adoption. AI in social media advertising enhances perceived usefulness by tailoring content based on user preferences, behavior, and demographics. The intuitive nature of AI-driven interfaces contributes to ease of use, making interactions with advertisements more seamless and engaging. By leveraging TAM, advertisers can assess users' attitudes toward AI-driven features, predicting their acceptance and adoption of personalized and algorithmically optimized social media advertising content. The model thus guides advertisers in developing AI-driven strategies that align with user expectations, fostering greater acceptance and engagement in the dynamic landscape of social media advertising.

The Extended Parallel Process Model (EPPM), introduced by Witte (1992), offers valuable insights into how individuals process and respond to fear appeals in communication. In the context of social media advertising, the EPPM can be applied to understand and enhance the effectiveness of messages that incorporate fear-based elements. By strategically integrating artificial intelligence (AI) into social media advertising campaigns, advertisers can tailor content to evoke appropriate levels of fear or concern while providing a viable solution or call to action. The EPPM framework allows advertisers to gauge the potential threat and efficacy of their fear-inducing messages, ensuring that the audience is motivated to take the desired action without succumbing to defensive responses. AI-driven analytics can aid in fine-tuning fear appeals by analyzing user responses and adjusting the intensity of the message, thereby optimizing the persuasive impact of social media advertising campaigns within the parameters outlined by the Extended Parallel Process Model.

The Psychological Reactance Theory, developed by Brehm(1966), offers insights into how individuals respond to perceived threats to their freedom of choice. In the realm of social media advertising, understanding, and mitigating psychological reactance is crucial for crafting persuasive messages. Advertisers can apply this theory by strategically employing artificial intelligence (AI) algorithms to personalize content in a way that maintains a sense of autonomy for users. By avoiding overly aggressive or restrictive messaging, AI-driven social media advertising can reduce the likelihood of triggering psychological reactance. Moreover, AI can analyze user behavior and preferences to tailor content that aligns with individual choices, mitigating resistance and enhancing receptiveness to the advertised message. In essence, the application of Psychological Reactance Theory in social media advertising, particularly when augmented by AI, emphasizes the importance of balancing personalized content delivery with the preservation of user autonomy to optimize the effectiveness of persuasive campaigns.

Csikszentmihalyi's Flow Theory(1990), which explores the concept of optimal experiences and immersion, finds intriguing application in the realm of social media advertising. Advertisers can leverage this theory by incorporating artificial intelligence (AI) to create content that captures users' attention and fosters a state of flow during their online interactions. AI algorithms can analyze user preferences, behavior, and engagement patterns to deliver personalized content that aligns with individual interests, thus enhancing the overall user experience. By optimizing the balance between challenge and skill in the content delivery process, advertisers can create a seamless and engaging flow state for users, increasing the likelihood of extended interaction with the advertised message. In essence, the application of Csikszentmihalyi's Flow Theory in social media advertising, especially when guided by AI, seeks to create an immersive and enjoyable experience that not only captures user attention but also facilitates a deeper connection between the audience and the advertised content.

2.5 AI-Driven Algorithms in Social Media Advertising

2.5.1 Recommendation Algorithms

Recommendation algorithms play a pivotal role in enhancing user experience by providing personalized suggestions tailored to individual preferences. Leveraging machine learning techniques, these algorithms analyze user behavior, historical data, and interactions to predict and recommend products, content, or services. In social media advertising, recommendation algorithms are employed to suggest relevant advertisements to users based on their past engagement, demographics, and interests.

For user cosine Similarity and Pearson Correlation Similarity a simple algorithms is used as below:

Where These formulae represent the essence of collaborative filtering, where r_{ui} is the rating of user u on item i, $\bar{r}_u$ is the mean rating of user u, sim(u,v) is the similarity between users u and v, and N(u) and N(i) are the sets of users and items similar to user u and item i, respectively.

Figure 1.

$$\mathrm{sim}(u,v) = \frac{\sum_i r_{ui} \cdot r_{vi}}{\sqrt{\sum_i r_{ui}^2} \cdot \sqrt{\sum_i r_{vi}^2}}$$

Figure 2.

$$\mathrm{sim}(u,v) = \frac{\mathrm{cov}(u,v)}{\sqrt{\mathrm{var}(u) \cdot \mathrm{var}(v)}}$$

Figure 3.

$$i\colon \hat{r}_{ui} = \bar{r}_u + \frac{\sum_{v \in N(u)} \mathrm{sim}(u,v) \cdot (r_{vi} - \bar{r}_v)}{\sum_{v \in N(u)} |\mathrm{sim}(u,v)|}$$

Figure 4.

$$\text{Similarity Score} = \frac{\sum_{i=1}^{n} \text{Weight}_i \cdot \text{Feature}_i}{\sqrt{\sum_{i=1}^{n} (\text{Weight}_i \cdot \text{Feature}_i)^2}}$$

2.5.2 Lookalike Audience Algorithms

Lookalike audience algorithms are instrumental in expanding the reach of targeted advertising campaigns. Rooted in the principle of identifying similarities, these algorithms analyze the characteristics and behaviors of a source audience and then identify new users who share similar traits. In social media advertising, lookalike audience algorithms enable advertisers to efficiently target individuals who are likely to be interested in their products or services based on the behavior of an existing, well-defined audience. This approach not only optimizes ad targeting precision but also aids in reaching potential customers who may have similar preferences and behaviors.

The formula for Lookalike Audience Algorithms involves identifying individuals who share similar characteristics or behaviors with a source audience. For each individual in the target audience, calculate a similarity score based on their features compared to the features of individuals in the source audience. This score represents how closely the characteristics of the target individual align with those in the source audience.

Feature i represents the i-th feature of an individual (e.g., demographics, purchase history), and Weight i is an optional weight assigned to each feature.

2.5.3 A/B Testing Algorithms

A/B testing algorithms, also known as split testing, are employed to compare and evaluate the performance of different variations of advertisements or marketing strategies. In social media advertising, these algorithms randomly allocate users into different groups, exposing each group to a distinct version of an ad, and then measure key performance indicators such as click-through rates or conversion rates. This systematic approach allows advertisers to empirically assess the impact of changes in ad elements, helping them make data-driven decisions to optimize campaigns for maximum effectiveness.

The formula for evaluating the results of an A/B test typically involves statistical analysis.

Conversion Rate (CR) for Version A

2.5.4. Bid Optimization Algorithms

Bid optimization algorithms are essential in programmatic advertising to determine the optimal bid amount for ad placements in real-time auctions. Employing machine learning and predictive analytics, these algorithms assess various factors, including user data, historical performance, and competition, to automatically adjust bid amounts. In social media advertising, bid optimization algorithms enhance cost efficiency by ensuring advertisers bid appropriately to reach their target audience while adhering to budget constraints. This dynamic and automated bidding process contributes to better ad placement and improved return on investment.

Figure 5.

$$CR_A = \frac{\text{Number of Conversions in A}}{\text{Number of Visitors to A}}$$

Figure 6.

$$Bid_{\text{optimal}} = \text{Second Highest Bid} + \epsilon$$

Figure 7.

$$Bid_{\text{ML}} = \text{ML Model Prediction}$$

In a second-price auction model, the winner pays the second-highest bid amount. The optimal bid is calculated as follows:

Here, ϵ is a small adjustment factor to ensure that the winning bid is just above the second-highest bid. This factor may be based on historical auction data and bidding strategy.

Bid optimization algorithms may leverage machine learning models that consider various features, historical performance, and real-time data to predict the optimal bid. The formula for a machine learning-based bid is determined by the model's output.

Machine learning models can learn complex patterns in bid landscapes and adjust bids dynamically based on changing conditions.

2.5.5. Ad Fraud Detection Algorithms

Ad fraud detection algorithms are crucial for maintaining the integrity and effectiveness of digital advertising ecosystems. These algorithms employ advanced analytics and anomaly detection techniques to identify and mitigate fraudulent activities such as click fraud, impression fraud, or fake traffic. In the context of social media advertising, ad fraud detection algorithms help advertisers and platforms identify and filter out illegitimate interactions, ensuring that advertising budgets are spent on genuine engagements and improving the accuracy of performance metrics. These algorithms contribute to the overall health and reliability of digital advertising environments.

If the click fraud ratio exceeds a predefined threshold, it may trigger further investigation or action.

If the impression fraud ratio surpasses a predetermined threshold, it signals potentially fraudulent activity.

Figure 8.

$$\text{Click Fraud Ratio} = \frac{\text{Illegitimate Clicks}}{\text{Legitimate Clicks} + \text{Illegitimate Clicks}}$$

Figure 9.

$$\text{Impression Fraud Ratio} = \frac{\text{Illegitimate Impressions}}{\text{Legitimate Impressions} + \text{Illegitimate Impressions}}$$

3. RESEARCH METHODOLOGY

The primary objective of this research is to explore and understand the perspectives of industry experts, practitioners, and stakeholders regarding the impact of AI-driven algorithms on social media advertising. Specifically, the study aims to investigate the contributions, challenges, and ethical considerations associated with the implementation of AI in social media advertising, as well as assess the extent to which AI-driven algorithms enhance key performance indicators (KPIs) compared to traditional advertising methods. The sample will consist of professionals directly involved in social media advertising, including marketing executives, data scientists, AI specialists, and individuals with expertise in advertising strategy and analytics. A purposive sampling approach will be employed to ensure the inclusion of diverse perspectives and experiences within the field.

In-depth, semi-structured interviews will be conducted with 45 participants. The semi-structured format allows for flexibility in questioning and encourages participants to elaborate on their responses. The interviews will be conducted virtually or in person based on participant preferences and geographical locations. The interview questions will be designed to address the research objectives, focusing on three main themes: contributions of AI to optimization, challenges and ethical considerations, and the impact on key performance indicators. Open-ended questions will be used to allow participants to express their views freely and provide detailed insights.

The collected data will undergo thematic analysis to identify recurring patterns, themes, and categories related to the research questions. This analysis will be guided by the three main themes: contributions, challenges, and impact on KPIs. Themes will be coded and organized to draw meaningful conclusions. Participants will be provided with detailed information about the study's purpose, the interview process, and their rights. Informed consent will be obtained before conducting interviews. Participants' identities and responses will be kept confidential. All data will be anonymized, and any direct quotations used in the study will be de-identified to protect participants' privacy.

To enhance the reliability of the findings, data triangulation will be employed by cross-referencing insights obtained from interviews with existing literature and industry reports. To ensure validity, participants will be given the opportunity to review and verify the accuracy of their responses, providing an additional layer of validation to the findings. Findings will be reported in a comprehensive manner, using quotes and examples to illustrate key themes. The results will be presented in alignment with the research questions, offering a detailed exploration of the contributions, challenges, and impact of AI-driven algorithms in social media advertising. The study may be limited by the availability and willingness of participants to share their experiences. Additionally, the rapidly evolving nature of technology and advertising practices may result in findings that are context-specific and subject to change over time.

4. FINDINGS

The thematic analysis reflects a consensus among interviewees regarding the substantial positive impact of AI-driven algorithms on social media advertising. However, it also underscores the need for addressing critical challenges related to privacy, transparency, and algorithmic bias. The findings suggest that while AI contributes significantly to campaign optimization and KPI enhancement, responsible implementation and ethical considerations are crucial for sustained success in the dynamic landscape of social media advertising.

4.1 Contributions of AI-Driven Algorithms to Social Media Advertising Optimization

Respondents overwhelmingly acknowledged that AI-driven algorithms significantly contribute to the optimization of social media advertising. The consensus was that AI enhances targeting precision by analyzing user behavior and preferences, enabling advertisers to reach the most relevant audience segments. Content personalization was highlighted as a major strength, with AI algorithms tailoring advertisements based on individual user data. Several respondents emphasized that these personalized ads often lead to higher user engagement, as they align more closely with individual interests. Overall, the majority of respondents believed that AI-driven algorithms enhance campaign effectiveness by maximizing relevance and impact.

Targeting Precision: A recurrent theme among interviewees highlighted the instrumental role of AI-driven algorithms in enhancing targeting precision. Respondents emphasized that these algorithms leverage user data to identify and reach specific audience segments, resulting in more accurate and relevant ad placements.

Content Personalization: Interviewees consistently noted the significant impact of AI algorithms on content personalization. The ability to analyze user behavior enables tailored content delivery, creating a more engaging and personalized experience for users.

Overall Campaign Effectiveness: The majority of respondents agreed that AI-driven algorithms contribute to overall campaign effectiveness. By optimizing targeting and personalization, these algorithms help advertisers achieve better results, increase brand engagement, and drive higher conversion rates.

4.2 Challenges and Ethical Considerations in AI-Driven Social Media Advertising

Privacy Concerns: A recurring theme among respondents was the concern regarding user privacy. Many felt that the extensive data collection required for AI algorithms raised questions about the ethical use of personal information. Several respondents expressed the need for clearer regulations and guidelines to protect user privacy in the context of AI-driven advertising.

Transparency Issues: A notable portion of respondents raised concerns about the lack of transparency in AI algorithms, particularly in terms of how decisions are made. Transparency was seen as critical to establishing trust with users and addressing ethical concerns.

Algorithmic Bias: Respondents acknowledged the potential for algorithmic bias in social media advertising, emphasizing the importance of ongoing efforts to identify and rectify bias issues. There was a consensus that algorithmic bias could impact the inclusivity and fairness of ad targeting.

4.3 Impact on Key Performance Indicators (KPIs) in Social Media Advertising

Positive Impact on KPIs: The majority of respondents reported positive experiences with AI-driven algorithms in improving key performance indicators (KPIs) in social media advertising. Many highlighted enhanced click-through rates, conversion rates, and increased user engagement as direct outcomes of AI optimization. Respondents noted that the ability of AI to analyze and adapt in real-time contributed to the improved efficiency of advertising campaigns.

Comparison with Traditional Methods: Several respondents drew comparisons between AI-driven strategies and traditional advertising methods. While acknowledging the effectiveness of traditional approaches, the consensus was that AI-driven algorithms outperform in terms of precision, personalization, and adaptability.

5. CONCLUSION AND RECOMMENDATION

The insights garnered from the interviews with 45 respondents shed light on the multifaceted impact of artificial intelligence (AI) on social media advertising effectiveness. The first objective, aimed at examining the influence of AI on social media advertising effectiveness, revealed a generally positive correlation. Respondents highlighted the ability of AI algorithms to optimize targeting, personalize content, and enhance overall campaign efficiency. The second objective, focusing on identifying and analyzing key challenges and ethical considerations, uncovered a nuanced landscape. While respondents acknowledged the undeniable benefits of AI, they also expressed concerns about data privacy, algorithmic biases, and the potential for manipulation. Ethical considerations emerged as crucial factors that need careful attention to ensure responsible and transparent use of AI in social media advertising. The third objective, centered around evaluating the impact of AI on Key Performance Indicators (KPIs) in social media advertising, demonstrated a notable improvement in several metrics. From increased click-through rates to enhanced engagement and conversion rates, AI was perceived as a catalyst for elevating KPIs. However, challenges related to accurately measuring and attributing these improvements to AI interventions were also highlighted. The findings underscore the transformative potential of AI in social media advertising, with respondents expressing a mix of enthusiasm and caution. As organizations navigate this evolving landscape, it becomes imperative to strike a balance between leveraging AI for improved performance and addressing ethical considerations. Moving forward, continuous monitoring, adaptability, and a commitment to ethical AI practices will be instrumental in maximizing the benefits of AI while mitigating potential risks in the realm of social media advertising.

Ethical considerations in AI-driven Advertising are paramount as technological advancements continue to shape the landscape of marketing and consumer engagement. One critical concern revolves around user privacy, as AI algorithms often rely on vast datasets to personalize advertisements. Striking a balance between personalization and privacy protection is crucial to avoid infringing upon users' rights. Additionally, addressing algorithmic bias is imperative to ensure fair and equitable representation in targeted advertising. Transparency and Explainability in AI algorithms are ethical imperatives, allowing users to comprehend the logic behind personalized content delivery. Advertisers must navigate the ethical complexities of behavioral prediction, ensuring responsible use of data analytics to avoid manipulative practices. As AI-driven advertising evolves, ethical considerations play a pivotal role in maintaining trust between advertisers and consumers, fostering a responsible and respectful approach to personalized content delivery. Adhering to ethical principles ensures that AI technologies contribute positively to the advertising landscape while respecting user autonomy and societal values.

6. LIMITATIONS

The study on AI-driven algorithms for optimizing social media advertising faces several limitations that should be acknowledged to provide a clear context for interpreting the findings. First, the rapidly evolving nature of technology and the dynamic landscape of social media platforms pose a challenge. The algorithms and advertising strategies in use today may undergo substantial changes in the near future. This temporal limitation may affect the generalizability of the study's conclusions, as the findings may not fully capture emerging technologies or shifts in social media advertising practices. Second, the study's scope may be constrained by the availability and willingness of industry professionals and stakeholders to participate in interviews. The perspectives gathered may not be fully representative of the entire spectrum of experiences within the diverse landscape of social media advertising. Additionally, there might be potential biases in the responses, as participants may provide information that reflects their organizations' interests or may be reluctant to share certain aspects of their experiences.

REFERENCES

Agrawal, A., Gans, J., & Goldfarb, A. (2020). How to win with machine learning. *Harvard Business Review*.

Amatulli, C., De Angelis, M., Sestino, A., & Guido, G. (2021). Omnichannel shopping experiences for fast fashion and luxury brands: An exploratory study. In *Developing Successful Global Strategies for Marketing Luxury Brands* (pp. 22–43). IGI Global. doi:10.4018/978-1-7998-5882-9.ch002

Bandura, A. (1999). A social cognitive theory of personality. In L. Pervin & O. John (Eds.), *Handbook of personality* (2nd ed., pp. 154–196). Guilford Publications.

Bessis, N., & Dobre, C. (Eds.). (2014). *Big data and internet of things: A roadmap for smart environments* (Vol. 546). Springer. doi:10.1007/978-3-319-05029-4

Boyd, C. (2010). *How Spotify Recommends Your New Favorite Artist*. Medium.

Brehm, J. W. (1966). *A theory of psychological reactance*. Academic Press.

Brei, V. A. (2020). Machine learning in marketing: Overview, learning strategies, applications, and future developments. *Foundations and Trends in Marketing*, *14*(3), 173–236. doi:10.1561/1700000065

Campbell, C., Sands, S., Ferraro, C., Tsao, H. Y., & Mavrommatis, A. (2020). From data to action: How marketers can leverage AI. *Business Horizons*, *63*(2), 227–243. doi:10.1016/j.bushor.2019.12.002

Corbo, L., Costa, S., & Dabi, M. (2022). The evolving role of artificial intelligence in marketing: A review and research agenda. *Journal of Business Research, 128*(March), 187–203.

Corrigan, H. B., Craciun, G., & Powell, A. M. (2014). Case study consumer analytics to make marketing decisions. *Marketing Education Review*, *24*(2), 159–165. doi:10.2753/MER1052-8008240206

Csikszentmihalyi, M. (1990). *Flow*. Harper & Row.

Cuccurullo, C., Aria, M., & Sarto, F. (2016). Foundations and trends in performance management. A twenty-five years bibliometric analysis in business and public administration domains. *Scientometrics*, *108*(2), 595–611. doi:10.1007/s11192-016-1948-8

Davenport, T., Guha, A., Grewal, D., & Bressgott, T. (2020). How artificial intelligence will change the future of marketing. *Journal of the Academy of Marketing Science*, *48*(1), 24–42. doi:10.1007/s11747-019-00696-0

Davenport, T. H., Dalle Mule, L., & Lucker, J. (2011). Know what your customers want before they do. *Harvard Business Review*, *89*(12), 84–92.

Davenport, T. H., & Ronanki, R. (2018). Artificial intelligence for the real world. *Harvard Business Review*, *96*(1), 108–116.

Davis, F. D. (1986). *A Technology Acceptance Model for Empirically Testing New End-User Information Systems: Theory and Results*. Sloan School of Management, Massachusetts Institute of Technology.

de Cosmo, L. M., Piper, L., & Di Vittorio, A. (2021). The role of attitude toward chatbots and privacy concerns the relationship between attitude toward mobile advertising and behavioral intent to use chatbots. *Italian Journal of Marketing*, *1*(1-2), 83–102. doi:10.1007/s43039-021-00020-1

De Mauro, A., Greco, M., & Grimaldi, M. (2015, February). What is big data? A consensual definition and a review of key research topics. In AIP conference proceedings (Vol. 1644, No. 1, pp. 97–104). American Institute of Physics.

De Mauro, A., Greco, M., Grimaldi, M., & Ritala, P. (2018). Human resources for Big Data professions: A systematic classification of job roles and required skill sets. *Information Processing & Management*, *54*(5), 807–817. doi:10.1016/j.ipm.2017.05.004

De Mauro, A., Sestino, A., & Bacconi, A. (2022). Machine learning and artificial intelligence use in marketing: A general taxonomy. *Ital. J. Mark.*, *2022*(4), 439–457. doi:10.1007/s43039-022-00057-w

Dedehayir, O., & Steinert, M. (2016). The hype cycle model: A review and future directions. *Technological Forecasting and Social Change*, *108*, 28–41. doi:10.1016/j.techfore.2016.04.005

Duan, Y., Edwards, J. S., & Dwivedi, Y. K. (2019). Artificial intelligence for decision making in the era of Big Data—Evolution, challenges and research agenda. *International Journal of Information Management*, *48*(February), 63–71. doi:10.1016/j.ijinfomgt.2019.01.021

Elliott, V. (2018). Thinking about the coding process in qualitative data analysis. *The Qualitative Report, 23*(11), 2850–2861. doi:10.46743/2160-3715/2018.3560

Erevelles, S., Fukawa, N., & Swayne, L. (2016). Big Data consumer analytics and the transformation of marketing. *Journal of Business Research, 69*(2), 897–904. doi:10.1016/j.jbusres.2015.07.001

Fleming, P. (2019). Robots and organization studies: Why robots might not want to steal your job. *Organization Studies, 40*(1), 23–38. doi:10.1177/0170840618765568

Ford, J., Jain, V., Wadhwani, K., & Gupta, D. G. (2023). *AI advertising: An overview and guidelines.* Retrieved February 11, 2019 from https://www.sltrib.com/news/business/2019/02/01/doorbells-have-eyes/

French, K. (2018). *Your new best friend: AI chatbot.* Retrieved February 13, 2019 from https://futurism.com/ai-chatbot-meaningful-conversation

Gans, J., Agrawal, A., & Goldfarb, A. (2017). How AI will change strategy: A thought experiment. *Harvard Business Review Online.* Retrieved February 11, 2019 from https://hbr.org/product/how-ai-will-change-strategy-a-thought-experiment/H03XDI-PDF-ENG

Gaudin, S. (2016). *At stitch fix, data scientists and a.I. become personal stylists.* Retrieved February 11, 2019 from https://www.computerworld.com/article/3067264/artificial-intelligence/at-stitch-fix-data-scientists-and-ai-become-personal-stylists.html

Guda, H., & Subramanian, U. (2019). Your uber is arriving: Managing on-demand workers through surge pricing, forecast communication, and worker incentives. *Management Science, 65*(5), 1995–2014. doi:10.1287/mnsc.2018.3050

Haleem, A., Javaid, M., Qadri, M. A., Singh, R. P., & Suman, R. (2022). Artificial intelligence (AI) applications for marketing: A literature-based study. *International Journal of Intelligent Networks, 3*, 119–132. doi:10.1016/j.ijin.2022.08.005

Harriet, T. (2016). *Lowe's introduces LoweBot, a new autonomous in-store robot.* CNBC. https://www.statista.com/outlook/dmo/digital-advertising/social-media-advertising/worldwide

Huang, M. H., & Rust, R. T. (2021). A strategic framework for artificial intelligence in marketing. *Journal of the Academy of Marketing Science, 49*(1), 30–50. doi:10.1007/s11747-020-00749-9

Jha, A. (2023). Immersive Marketing on Metaverse: Development of Metrics for Performance Analysis and Security-Related Challenges. In P. Pires, J. Santos, I. Pereira, & A. Torres (Eds.), Confronting Security and Privacy Challenges in Digital Marketing (pp. 267-289). IGI Global. doi:10.4018/978-1-6684-8958-1.ch013

Jha, A., & Jha, A. (2022). Data Encryption Dispute Resolutions under Intermediary Guidelines of Information Technology Act Challenges and Future Framework. *DESIDOC Journal of Library and Information Technology, 42*(3), 201–207. doi:10.14429/djlit.42.3.17869

Jordan, M. I., & Mitchell, T. M. (2015). Machine learning: Trends, perspectives, and prospects. *Science, 349*(6245), 255–260. doi:10.1126/science.aaa8415 PMID:26185243

Katz, E., Blumler, J. G., & Gurevitch, M. (1973). Uses and Gratifications Research. *Public Opinion Quarterly*, *37*(4), 509–523. doi:10.1086/268109

Khokhar, P., & Chitsimran. (2019). Evolution Of Artificial Intelligence In Marketing, Comparison With Traditional Marketing. *Our Heritage*, *67*(5), 375–389.

Kohlegger, M., Maier, R., & Thalmann, S. (2009). Understanding maturity models results of a structured content analysis. *Proceedings of IKNOW '09 and ISEMANTICS '09*, 51–61.

Kotler, P., Kartajaya, H., & Setiawan, I. (2021). *Marketing 5.0: Technology for humanity*. Wiley.

Kumar, V., Rajan, B., Venkatesan, R., & Lecinski, J. (2019). Understanding the role of artificial intelligence in personalized engagement marketing. *California Management Review*, *61*(4), 135–155. doi:10.1177/0008125619859317

Kurachi, Y., Narukawa, S., & Hara, H. (2018). AI chatbot to realize sophistication of consumer contact points. *Fujitsu Scientific and Technical Journal*, *54*(3), 2–8.

Luis, V., Casaló, L. V., Flavián, C., & Ibáñez-Sánchez, S. (2021). Be creative, my friend! Engaging users on Instagram by promoting positive emotions. *Journal of Business Research*, *130*, 416–425. doi:10.1016/j.jbusres.2020.02.014

Ma, L., & Sun, B. (2020). Machine learning and AI in marketing – Connecting computing power to human insights. *International Journal of Research in Marketing*, *37*(3), 481–504. doi:10.1016/j.ijresmar.2020.04.005

Mariani, M., & Fosso Wamba, S. (2020). Exploring how consumer goods companies innovate in the digital age: The role of big data analytics companies. *Journal of Business Research*, *121*, 338–352. doi:10.1016/j.jbusres.2020.09.012

Marr, B. (2016). *Big data in practice: How 45 successful companies used big data analytics to deliver extraordinary results*. Wiley. doi:10.1002/9781119278825

Mayring, P. (2008). *Qualitative Inhaltsanalyse*. Beltz Deutscher Studien Verlag.

Miklosik, A., & Evans, N. (2020). Impact of big data and machine learning on digital transformation in marketing: A literature review. *IEEE Access : Practical Innovations, Open Solutions*, *8*, 101284–101292. doi:10.1109/ACCESS.2020.2998754

Miklosik, A., Kuchta, M., Evans, N., & Zak, S. (2019). Towards the adoption of machine learning-based analytical tools in digital marketing. *IEEE Access : Practical Innovations, Open Solutions*, *7*, 85705–85718. doi:10.1109/ACCESS.2019.2924425

Murgai, A. (2018). Transforming digital marketing with artificial intelligence. *Int J Latest Technol Eng Manag Appl Sci*, *7*(4), 259–262.

Nedra, B. A., Hadhri, W., & Mezrani, M. (2019). Determinants of customers' intentions to use hedonic networks: The case of Instagram. *Journal of Retailing and Consumer Services*, *46*, 21–32. doi:10.1016/j.jretconser.2018.09.001

Nguyen, B., & Simkin, L. (2017). The Internet of Things (IoT) and marketing : The state of play, future trends and the implications for marketing. *Journal of Marketing Management*, *33*(1–2), 1–6. doi:10.1080/0267257X.2016.1257542

Osisanwo, F. Y., Akinsola, J. E. T., Awodele, O., Hinmikaiye, J. O., Olakanmi, O., & Akinjobi, J. (2017). Supervised machine learning algorithms: Classification and comparison. *International Journal of Computer Trends and Technology*, *48*(3), 128–138. doi:10.14445/22312803/IJCTT-V48P126

Petty, R. E., & Cacioppo, J. T. (1986). The Elaboration Likelihood Model of Persuasion. *Advances in Experimental Social Psychology*, *19*, 123–205. doi:10.1016/S0065-2601(08)60214-2

Phoemphon, S., So-In, C., & Niyato, D. T. (2018). A hybrid model using fuzzy logic and an extreme learning machine with vector particle swarm optimization for wireless sensor network localization. *Applied Soft Computing*, *65*, 101–120. doi:10.1016/j.asoc.2018.01.004

Power, B. (2017). How Harley-Davidson used artificial intelligence to increase New York sales leads by 2,930%. *Harvard Business Review*. https://hbr.org/2017/05/how-harley-davidson-used-predictive-analytics-to-increase-new-york-sales-leads-by-2930

Puntoni, S., Reczek, R., Giesler, M., & Botti, S. (2020). Consumers and Artificial Intelligence: An Experiential Perspective. *Journal of Marketing*, *85*(1), 131–151. Advance online publication. doi:10.1177/0022242920953847

Sestino, A., & De Mauro, A. (2021). Leveraging Artificial Intelligence in Business: Implications, Applications and Methods. *Technology Analysis and Strategic Management*, 1–14.

Sestino, A., Prete, M. I., Piper, L., & Guido, G. (2020). Internet of Things and Big Data as enablers for business digitalization strategies. *Technovation*, *98*, 102173. doi:10.1016/j.technovation.2020.102173

Shankar, V. (2018). How Artificial Intelligence (AI) Is Reshaping Retailing. *Journal of Retailing*, *94*(4), 6–9. doi:10.1016/S0022-4359(18)30076-9

Sheth, J., & Kellstadt, C. H. (2021). Next frontiers of research in data driven marketing: Will techniques keep up with data tsunami? *Journal of Business Research*, *125*, 780–784. doi:10.1016/j.jbusres.2020.04.050

Stalidis, G., Karapistolis, D., & Vafeiadis, A. (2015). Marketing Decision Support Using Artificial Intelligence and Knowledge Modeling: Application to Tourist Destination Management. *Procedia: Social and Behavioral Sciences*, *175*, 106–113. doi:10.1016/j.sbspro.2015.01.1180

Witte, K. (1992). Putting the fear back into fear appeals: The extended parallel process model. *Communication Monographs*, *59*(4), 329–349. doi:10.1080/03637759209376276

Chapter 5
Azoka.com.bd: Amazing Revival Story of Azoka!

Rahma Akhter
https://orcid.org/0000-0002-5196-5422
BRAC University, Bangladesh

Proma Quadir
BRAC University, Bangladesh

Tazrian Binte Ansar
BRAC University, Bangladesh

Nuzhat Tanisha
BRAC University, Bangladesh

EXECUTIVE SUMMARY

Bangladesh is embracing the modern dimensions of today's global economy, and aiding in this quest are the many budding start-ups that join the country's economy every year. The case details the journey of one such prospective start-up, Azoka, an online e-commerce website specializing in the selling of imported food products. However, in such a competitive market, Azoka has to put in more effort to survive and win the race towards success. This case invites students to look into the problems brewing in the existing operations of Azoka and recommend strategies for the company to revive its business.

Subject Area

The case enables the students to interact with conventional service marketing, e-commerce and supply chain management inside a management framework.

DOI: 10.4018/979-8-3693-1781-5.ch005

Study Level

The target audience for this case includes graduate, MBA, or higher-level students taking courses in such topics as supply chain management and service marketing.

CASE OVERVIEW

The aspiration to become an entrepreneur always inhabited Mr.X . Having dedicated most of his life working for others, Mr. X wanted to do something himself by working for himself. He was looking for the right opportunity to launch his dream of becoming an entrepreneur. That opportunity came in the form of Azoka.

In March of 2021, the founder of Azoka, an e-commerce platform, recognized the general consumer uncertainty surrounding the availability and quality of foreign products being sold in Bangladesh. Amidst the pandemic that left the state of businesses worldwide in shambles, he realized this huge gap that had appeared in the market and set out to utilize this opportunity to satisfy consumer demand for foreign food products. Distraught at the general absence of authenticity surrounding imported food, he took notice of the compromises that consumers had to make due to an overall lack of convenience provided by traditional retailers. Hence, the founder was inspired by a new-found drive to provide consumers with extensive access to imported and locally-produced food products.

Operating in a highly competitive industry with more than 700 competitors, including industry giants like Daraz and Chaldal, naturally led to Azoka grappling with intense competition and extensive entry barriers (International Trade Administration, 2022). Despite the dire nature of the situation, the company managed to fight its way through fierce rivalry with a comprehensive system of in-house supply chains and brand partnerships that allowed them to offer products at a cheaper cost and more affordable price. Simultaneously, an ardent dedication to offering the best customer experience further triggered the establishment of a user-friendly website, with the inclusion of a broad product portfolio, customer care and feedback, online payment benefits, and a swift 24-hour delivery service for maximum satisfaction.

Due to being a new entrant in the market, Azoka is faced with a myriad of short and long-term strategic decisions for expansion despite managing to push through effectively within the industry. How could the company retain and expand its consumer base in Dhaka? Taking into consideration the upward trend for e-commerce within the country, how could Azoka make itself available nationwide and establish itself as the market leader?

METHODOLOGY

Western culture takes pride in showing how expensive one's purchase is, whereas Asian culture takes utmost joy in showing off how cheap their purchases are. Asians believe that art lies in the skill of being able to save your hard-earned money. This ideology makes Asians the most price-sensitive consumer base amongst all others. Therefore, how is it that businesses around Asia are able to extract a profitable rate from such a consumer base? As a researcher, the objective is to find the answer to this very question and Azoka became the perfect. To get an understanding of the tricks and tips of operating in a challenging market the researchers conducted an interview with the owner of Azoka. Through the interview, the planning and intricacies of running a business in a challenging environment entailed for an entrepreneur were captured.

Azoka and Supply Chain Dilemma

Being surrounded by such intense competition meant Azoka needed to incorporate unique differentiation in its operations in order to run ahead of all others. Mr.X realized the crowded market has used most of the obvious tricks to become different, hence he began looking at other aspects of the business. His answer lay in the business's supply chain structure.

Whereas most retailers haggle with wholesalers on a daily basis to procure their stock, Azoka undertook a different approach to secure their stock more efficiently than competitors. Azoka's in-house supply chain system allows the company to remove the intermediary aspect of wholesaling altogether, resulting in the planning and management of the entire process and networking/communication with suppliers done by the company itself with complete liberty over governing the system. Moreover, procurement of goods directly from manufacturers further eliminates the dependency on third parties due to the general control over and predictability surrounding the whole process (Young Foodies, 2022). Hence, the company is able to reduce costs significantly and hold autonomy not only over the supply chain, but in making creative decisions regarding the customization of product packaging, delivery boxes, and so on.

Regardless of maintaining freedom over its supply chain, Azoka can very easily fall victim to external shocks due to elevated vulnerability. The pandemic further raised difficulties in dealing with complications that would otherwise have been simple to overcome. Successfully importing products was a major challenge due to the global shutdown that came along with the pandemic, leading to shortages in terms of products under foreign brands (Aboulilah, Hossain, Vương, & Jebril, 2022). This abrupt halt to the worldwide trading system implied grave consequences to Azoka's operations. Hence, to keep the business alive and re-establish some amount of control, they had to make a drastic shift towards providing their customer base with locally produced brands only, like Aftab Foods, Golden Harvest, and Khaas Foods.

Azoka and Its Disoriented Website

Bringing changes to the supply chain structure was just the tip of the iceberg. Procuring the goods was step one in their journey, making sure that consumers are aware of the availability of the product was the actual mission. They needed to make sure their revenue channel, its website is able to show the full potential of their inventory.

Azoka's main revenue center is its website. Their website houses both national and international brands. Imported foreign food products stand side by side with premium versions of domestic food brands. Azoka is keen on expanding its categories and hence is constantly adding new products, some of which are entirely new in the market.

Their keenness to expand is shaped by the demand in the market. Although Azoka projects itself as a comprehensive outlet to shop imported grocery items, its offerings largely include food and beverage items and its latest additions also belong to the same category. However, the brand has made an attempt at diversifying its portfolio. Consumers can now shop for baby care products like diapers and accessories from the website. Depending on the demand their next step will be to step into the booming skincare demand in Bangladesh.

Azoka and Its Painstaking Delivery

One of the biggest challenges being an online store in the world's most densely populated city is the delivery of purchases to customers. However, the terrible traffic condition of Dhaka was not an excuse big enough for Mr. X to back down from the challenge.

Azoka Limited has its office, warehouse, and dispatch center situated in Gulshan, an affluent neighborhood in Dhaka with most of its residents belonging to the upper-middle-class to upper-upper-class segment (The Financial Express, 2022). This particular income group is Azoka's target market. Being this close to their target market makes the delivery process to consumers faster and more cost-effective. However, is their target market concentrated in this area only? What about their consumer bases outside this circle? Like Gulshan, there are other posh neighborhoods in Dhaka like Dhanmondi. Dhanmondi is located further away from the firm's dispatch center, complicating the delivery process. Moreover, considering the heavy traffic on the roads of Dhaka the distance gap can delay their service by far.

A study by the World Bank revealed that the average traffic speed in Dhaka is 7 kmph which is a significant drop from the speed of 21 kmph ten years ago. The study also illustrated that in 13 years' time, this average speed will be slower than walking speed (Haider, 2018). To counteract this problem, the firm uses bicycles, which can be easier to navigate and pass through heavy traffic. Currently, they have a team of six delivery men who use bicycles as their mode of transportation in delivering the goods. However, this won't be sustainable as it brings forth new challenges like limiting the company's delivery potential. Cyclists often use the main road due to the lack of proper bicycle lanes risking them of encountering reckless drivers and uncivil pedestrians; with the growing online purchase and demand for the products Azoka Limited has to offer, the team of six delivery men has to be increased so that they can easily expand their delivery territory.

Lastly, Azoka offers frozen food products for its consumers which are delivered using iceboxes. Ice Boxes sometimes cannot bear the heat of Dhaka roads where the average temperature is 34.5 degrees Celsius during summer (Chowdhury, 2021). Furthermore, considering the traffic situation in Bangladesh and the uneven roads coupled with the negligible safety of products in bicycles, bicycles might not be the safest option when it comes to delivering fragile goods, as there are chances of the product shattering with even the slightest jerk. On the other hand, Azoka's competitors use trucks in order to reduce delivery time, and ensure proper preservation of goods, frozen or fragile. As Azoka continues to use vulnerable modes of delivery like a bicycle consumers are left to worry about the safety of their orders and ponder on shopping from alternative sites that assure them of the well-being of their purchase.

Azoka's Current Marketing Strategies

Acquiring consumers is a massive skill required to survive in the cut-throat e-commerce industry of Bangladesh. With hundreds of available options to customers, how can Azoka show its potential to consumers? How can they relegate their amazing offerings? It is through their marketing.

Azoka maintains a comprehensive and active Facebook platform to harness its consumers. Their vigorous engagement through this web platform has allowed their page to accumulate over 65,000 followers and likes. At the beginning of the page, consumers are met with the company's tagline of trusting Azoka to be the consumer's one-stop shop for authentic products. This assurance is followed by a range of posts uploaded by Azoka to inform consumers about their latest offerings.

Azoka believes in forming a connection with its consumers and wants to be a part of their joyous celebrations in life. They are regular in extending their greetings by posting good wishes during important occasions like Eid, Christmas and New Years.

In an effort to further bond with their consumers, they have a review section to acknowledge consumer appreciation and disappointments.

The constant engagement requires expertise and hence Azoka has outsourced its marketing. An outside firm is responsible to maintain the page, navigate advertisements on Facebook and handle consumer feedback and queries coming through the page. The marketing partner has not limited Azoka to Facebook, they also subscribe to Google advertisement services to maintain their market presence. The use of social media is crucial to small businesses like Azoka as research shows consumers are more keen to purchase products from e-commerce platforms if their offerings are integrated with social media (Hossain et al., 2020).

Being a relatively new company with a narrow consumer base, Azoka isn't keen on any other forms of marketing except for digital marketing. Considering their consumer size and nature, online advertisement covers their targeted audience.

The Way Forward

With present challenges such as their website, delivery and stiff competition looming over Mr. X's aspirations, he hasn't ignored the prospects of the future. He realizes that that in order to grow successful an e-commerce brand needs to be comprehensive. Consumers expect an e-commerce retailer to be a one-stop shop for them as it is inconvenient for consumers to keep track of multiple orders from different retailers. Azoka understands this concern of its consumer base and hence they plan on developing themselves into this one-stop shop for their consumers.

At present Azoka's portfolio primarily includes food products with the exception of children's diapers. The brand plans on changing this in the coming future as they want to include personal care, hygiene, beauty and health, cleaning supplies etc. in their portfolio. Such inclusions will truly turn them into the ideal e-commerce retail shop that consumers want to engage with. Apart from introducing new categories the brand also plans on growing its consumer base beyond Dhaka. The company has already taken steps to do this. Azoka has started to accept orders from different parts of Bangladesh. They have started offering their services in Rongpur, Cox's Bazar, Patuakhali, Sylhet and Barisal. The brand won't limit itself to these regions in the future and will add more territories to offering its services.

Azoka realizes that in order to rise above this competitive market it needs to offer its best to the consumers. In the foreseeable future, they plan on not only expanding their operations but also improving their flaws and perfecting themselves to become the only choice for consumers.

As a small business Azoka it is not feasible to simultaneously go through both expansion techniques. They have to make a choice to either diversify their offerings in their current market reach in Dhaka or they can maintain their current offerings and build a consumer base outside Dhaka to project an overall increase in potential revenue.

Theoretical Foundations: Exploring the Underlying Theories

The theories pertinent to the case of AZOKA's business revival primarily fall under the CRM (Customer Relationship Management) category. In terms of e-CRM (electronic Customer Relationship Management), a major theory involves Relationship Marketing Theory, which states the importance of focusing on retaining customers by prioritizing them, rather than on sales through new customers (Berry, 2002). This strategy is vital for the longevity and success of the brand. AZOKA's current operating model would benefit greatly by building relationships with their customers, primarily through improving the user-friendliness of their website and social media platforms, alongside employing customer service focusing on transparency and helpfulness. The Technology Acceptance Model is also relevant, as it states that the customer's capabilities in handling technology have to be considered for the highest efficacy (Adams et al., 1992). If AZOKA is to add features to its website, it has to keep in mind the perceived value it will add to its customer base, and this is a topic that needs to be researched by them. To increase customer satisfaction in transactions with AZOKA, Social Exchange theory is to be considered, where every negotiation has a deeper underlying cost-benefit analysis (Roeckelein, 2006). For the customer to feel that shopping with the brand was in their favor, customer loyalty programs in the form of memberships and personalized deals can be used. Another model is the Information Systems Success Model, which highlights how all parts of a system add up to create something more than its sum. There are six notable factors: information quality, system quality, service quality, system use/usage intentions, user satisfaction, and net system benefits (DeLone & McLean, 1992). These are incredibly valuable analytics for any business, and AZOKA would be able to determine metrics such as customer satisfaction, performance of the business and brand loyalty to steer the company's operations to align with necessary action.

Expected Learning Outcomes

After studying the case, students should be able to

- Evaluate the five dimensions of services quality, namely reliability, responsiveness, assurance, empathy, and tangibles, for an e-commerce platform.
- Understand customer gap in a service industry and analyze the importance of closing the gap by assessing the Gaps Model of Service Quality
- Scrutinize the Perceived Risks, mainly functional, financial, temporal, physical, psychological, social, and sensory risks, in purchasing and using e-commerce services.
- Recommend and formulate a Services Marketing Triangle for an e-commerce service with contingencies and effective strategies for sustainable growth and survivability.

Discussion Question

1. Evaluate the five dimensions of service quality of Azoka.com.bd. How have the different business strategies created an impact on the dimensions?
2. Identify the customer gap for Azoka.com.bd and analyze the Gaps model of Service quality to close the customer gap.
3. Apply the services marketing triangle with respect to Azoka.com.bd. How did an inverted services marketing triangle help Azoka.com.bd overcome the challenges imposed by the non-alignment of the three sides of the services marketing triangle, previously followed by Azoka.com.bd?
4. Assess the perceived risks in purchasing and using Azoka.com.bd. Which of these risks can be minimized and how?

REFERENCES

Aboulilah, H. M. E., Hossain, S. F. A., Vương, B. N., & Jebril, T. (2022). Exploring the Relationship between WeChat Usage and E-purchase Intention During the COVID-19 Pandemic Among University Students in China. *SAGE Open*, *12*(4). doi:10.1177/21582440221139447 PMID:36466966

Adams, D. M., Nelson, R. E., & Todd, P. (1992). Perceived usefulness, ease of use, and usage of information technology: A replication. *Management Information Systems Quarterly*, *16*(2), 227. doi:10.2307/249577

Bangladesh - eCommerce. (n.d.). Retrieved from https://www.trade.gov/country-commercial-guides/bangladesh-ecommerce

Berry, L. L. (2002). Relationship Marketing of Services Perspectives from 1983 and 2000. *Journal of Relationship Marketing*, *1*(1), 59–77. doi:10.1300/J366v01n01_05

Chowdhury, A. R. (2023, June 5). More roads are not the answer to Bangladesh's traffic problem. *The Daily Star*. Retrieved from https://www.thedailystar.net

Chowdhury, M. H., & Chowdhury, M. H. (2021, October 5). *Extreme heat bakes 25 Dhaka neighbourhoods as climate warms up: study*. Retrieved from https://bdnews24.com/environment/extreme-heat-bakes-25-dhaka-neighbourhoods-as-climate-warms-up-study

DeLone, W. H., & McLean, E. R. (1992). Information Systems Success: The quest for the dependent variable. *Information Systems Research*, *3*(1), 60–95. doi:10.1287/isre.3.1.60

Emmanuel, C. P., Su, Q., Hossain, S. F. A., & Hussain, K. (2022). Factors influencing social-media-based entrepreneurship prospect among female students in China. *Heliyon*, *8*(12), e12041. doi:10.1016/j.heliyon.2022.e12041 PMID:36483305

Hossain, S. F. A. (2019). Social networking and its role in media entrepreneurship. *Journal of Media Management and Entrepreneurship*, *1*(1), 73–86. doi:10.4018/JMME.2019010105

Hossain, S. F. A., Nurunnabi, M., Hussain, K., & Saha, S. K. (2019). Effects of variety-seeking intention by mobile phone usage on university students' academic performance. *Cogent Education*, *6*(1), 1574692. doi:10.1080/2331186X.2019.1574692

Hossain, S. F. A., Nurunnabi, M., Hussain, K., & Xu, S. (2020). Smartphone-based m-shopping behavior and innovative entrepreneurial tendency among women in emerging Asia. *International Journal of Gender and Entrepreneurship*, *12*(2), 173–189. doi:10.1108/IJGE-03-2019-0054

Hossain, S. F. A., Xu, S., Musa, M., & Rahman, P. (2022). Social media and Increased venture creation tendency with innovative ideas. In IGI Global eBooks (pp. 1716–1731). doi:10.4018/978-1-6684-7123-4.ch093

Hossain, S. F. A., Xu, S., Nurunnabi, M., Tushar, H., Mohsin, A. K. M., & Ahsan, F. T. (2021). Opportunities and Challenges of M-Learning During the COVID-19 Pandemic. In E-Collaboration Technologies and Strategies for Competitive Advantage Amid Challenging Times (pp. 210–227). doi:10.4018/978-1-7998-7764-6.ch007

Hossain, S. F. A., Zhao, X., Nurunnabi, M., & Hussain, K. (2020). Ubiquitous role of social networking in driving M-Commerce: Evaluating the use of mobile phones for online shopping and payment in the context of trust. *SAGE Open*, *10*(3). doi:10.1177/2158244020939536

Mohsin, A. K. M., Lei, H., & Hossain, S. F. A. (2021). Impact of COVID-19 Pandemic on Consumer Economy: Countermeasures analysis. *SAGE Open*, *11*(2). doi:10.1177/21582440211008875

Roeckelein, J. E. (2006). *Elsevier's Dictionary of Psychological Theories*. Retrieved from http://ci.nii.ac.jp/ncid/BA7675599X

Supply chain outsourcing vs in-house - an honest comparison. (2022, March 9). Young Foodies. https://youngfoodies.co.uk/supply-chain-outsourcing-vs-in-house-an-honest-comparison

The Daily Star. (n.d.). *The Daily Star – Leading English Daily among Bangladesh Newspapers*. Retrieved from https://www.thedailystar.net/

The Financial Express. (2022, March 31). Gulshan, Banani, Baridhara residents to pay increased holding tax from July. *The Financial Express*. Retrieved from https://thefinancialexpress.com.bd

Vương, B. N., Tushar, H., & Hossain, S. F. A. (2022). The effect of social support on job performance through organizational commitment and innovative work behavior: Does innovative climate matter? *Asia-Pacific Journal of Business Administration*. Advance online publication. doi:10.1108/APJBA-06-2021-0256

APPENDIX

Teaching Notes

Case Summary

The numerous burgeoning start-ups that enter the Bangladeshi economy each year help the nation embrace the contemporary aspects of the modern global economy. The case describes the development of one such potential start-up, Azoka, an online retailer that focuses on the sale of imported food items. Azoka, however, must work more than merely being average to survive and triumph in the quest for success in such a fierce environment. Therefore, the strategies and other factors of sustenance and survivability of Azoka remain a realistic subject for detailed studies by business department students in contemplating the suitable service marketing model in the context of e-commerce business in Bangladesh.

Teaching Objectives

The instructional objectives of the case are to:

Analyze the e-commerce platform in Bangladesh, in terms of the five dimensions of service quality, namely reliability, responsiveness, assurance, empathy, and tangibles.
Identify the competitive advantages by analyzing trends of operations, customer gap in a service industry and analyze the importance of closing the gap by assessing the Gaps Model of Service Quality
Relate the impacts of the Perceived Risks, mainly functional, financial, temporal, physical, psychological, social, and sensory risks, in purchasing and using e-commerce services.
Learn to formulate future guidelines for the Services Marketing Triangle for an e-commerce service with contingencies and effective strategies for sustainable growth and survivability.

Teaching Plan and Approach

The case is designed for a 90-minute class session. The suggested teaching plan is as follows:

I. Introduction (5 minutes)
   - Greet participants and introduce the session's objective.
   - The case's importance to the study of the service business and the e-commerce sector should be discussed.
   - Emphasize the relevance of critical thinking and effective communication in real-world scenarios.

II. Case Study Introduction (10 minutes)
   - Present the case study to participants, ensuring everyone has a copy.
   - Provide a brief overview of the background, context, and key players involved.
   - Highlight the main challenges or issues faced by the organization or individuals in the case.
   - Engage students in a discussion about the challenges encountered by online businesses in the dynamic era of e-commerce.

III. Analysis Phase (30 minutes)
   - Divide participants into small groups of 3-4 people.
   - Instruct each group to read and analyze the case study, identifying the key problems or challenges.
   - Encourage participants to consider multiple perspectives and examine the underlying causes of the issues.
   - Circulate among the groups, offering guidance and clarifications as needed.
   - After 20 minutes, reconvene as a whole group and invite each group to share one or two key problems they identified.
   - Facilitate a discussion to consolidate the identified problems and create a collective understanding.
   - Investigate and assess the reliability, responsiveness, assurance, empathy, and tangibles components of service quality for an e-commerce platform.
   - Analyze the relevance of closing the customer gap in the service sector by evaluating the Gaps Model of Service Quality.

IV. Problem-Solving Phase (30 minutes)
   - Explain that participants will now engage in a brainstorming session to generate possible solutions.
   - Ask each group to come up with at least three potential solutions to address the identified problems.
   - Encourage creativity and remind participants to consider both short-term and long-term implications.
   - For 20 minutes, the students will be analyzing the different theories and managerial frameworks the study highlights such as RATER or SERVQUAL models, digital marketing, eCRM, etc.
   - Reassemble the whole group and invite each group to share their most innovative or promising solution.
   - Facilitate a discussion to explore the feasibility and potential outcomes of the proposed solutions.
   - Discuss the effectiveness of the customer's various types of risks including functional, financial, temporal, physical, psychological, social, and sensory risks.
   - Create a Services Marketing Triangle for an e-commerce service with backup plans and successful techniques for long-term success.

V. Evaluation and Selection (15 minutes)
   - Guide participants in evaluating the proposed solutions, considering their advantages, disadvantages, and potential risks.
   - Discuss criteria for selecting the most viable solution, such as feasibility, impact, and alignment with organizational goals.
   - Facilitate a group discussion to arrive at a consensus on the best solution or combination of solutions.
   - Summarize the decision and emphasize the rationale behind the chosen solution.

VI. Conclusion and Reflection (5 minutes)
   - Recap the main points discussed throughout the session.

- Highlight the importance of critical thinking, collaboration, and effective communication in problem-solving.
- Reinforce the importance of E-commerce practices for an online service and minimize the associated risks.
- Encourage students to evaluate the service marketing considerations and difficulties for an online retailer.
- Persuade participants to reflect on their learning and consider how they can apply these skills in their professional and personal lives.

VII. Q&A and Wrap-up (5 minutes)

- Open the floor for any questions or clarifications.
- Provide additional resources or references for further learning, if available.
- Thank participants for their participation and conclude the session.

Suggested Teaching Strategy

An instructor may introduce the case, facilitate group discussions to analyze the case and propose solutions, engage in a whole-class discussion to share insights and explore different perspectives, apply relevant business concepts and theories, incorporate real-world examples, utilize interactive activities, invite guest speakers for expert insights, and assessing students' understanding through assignments and feedback. This comprehensive approach fosters critical thinking, collaboration, and the practical application of knowledge to real-world business challenges.

Suggested Answers to Discussion Questions

1. Evaluate the five dimensions of service quality of Azoka.com.bd. How have the different business strategies created an impact on the dimensions?

The RATER Model application is explained as follows:

Reliability: AZOKA promises to maintain its consistency in providing authentic products to consumers. They have a range of selections on their site for a variety of imported products and work accordingly to deliver only the original goods themselves. Moreover, their ISO certification is further proof of their commitment to quality and credibility. They also plan and manage the entire supply chain process themselves and promise to get goods delivered to customers within 24 hours, thus eliminating any risks that come with depending on third party suppliers.

Assurance: AZOKA has the ISO (International Organization for Standardization) certification as proof of its quality, credibility, and authenticity. The founder established the platform in order to provide foreign imported goods at an affordable price and currently, they manage a delivery team of six men to achieve their promise of prompt delivery within 24 hours. Consumers are also able to communicate directly with staff in real-time via Facebook messages to get their queries answered and complaints addressed. Hence, they provide their customer base with sufficient reliability and assurance.

Tangibles: AZOKA deals with the highly competitive market of e-commerce where more than 700 sites are currently housed in Bangladesh. However, they fail to utilize effective marketing strategies like industry giant competitors such as Chaldal and Daraz. Although they maintain Search Engine Optimization (SEO), they fall short in utilizing the internet and the variety of digital marketing opportunities that it provides. Moreover, their Facebook posts too are very randomized instead of products being offered in a cohesive and informative manner. Thus, people barely know about the platform and its services and opt for more well-known alternatives instead.

Empathy: AZOKA and its staff have the ability to build and maintain positive relationships with consumers. The founder started the platform in the first place to address the market gap of the unavailability of foreign food products within the country. Moreover, due to being an e-commerce site, the staff requires maintaining regular contact with consumers to answer their queries and make sure the products are being delivered on time and in good condition. However, although they are capable of creating customer loyalty, due to e-commerce giants like daraz, chaldal, and other alternatives, AZOKA has been failing to gain enough traction.

Responsiveness: AZOKA maintains relatively decent customer service on its website with a user-friendly platform. They promise a swift delivery process and due to their intentions in providing the best service possible, they have a dedicated option on their website for receiving consumer feedback. Simultaneously, they address and deal with consumer queries via Facebook messages to communicate with and aid them better while aiming to provide a more fulfilling experience.

2. Identify the customer gap for Azoka.com.bd and analyze the Gaps model of Service Quality to close the customer gap.

Usually, customers seek few basic services and supplementary advantages from any grocery store or supermarket. These include convenience and the availability of products, customer service and a friendly staff-body to assist the customers. Customers also expect a variety of products, reasonable prices and quality of the products, a safe environment both in the parking lot and in the store itself, loyalty programs, and membership cards. Some features that are not as common but are newly being adopted include mobile applications, websites, social media presence, online ordering systems, home delivery services, online payments through credit cards or mobile financial services (MFS), and so on.

To analyze whether Azoka is able to fully meet these customer expectations and thereby eliminate its customer gap, the SERVQUAL model or the Gap Model of Service Quality has been implemented.

- **Gap 1:** Does the management's idea of the customer's expectations and the actual expectation of the customer align with each other?

To better know whether Azoka's idea of the customer's expectations and the actual expectation of the customer align with each other or not, the firm can undertake several measures. Azoka could conduct a survey to evaluate the gap or collect feedback or reviews from the customers through their Facebook page or website. They could also utilize inventory management to keep track of the purchases, frequency of the purchases and when or which season or event they are being bought during. Furthermore, they can hire a service quality officer who may be able to help better dissolve the gap.

- **Gap 2:** Are the management's promised service quality specifications able to meet the customers' expectations?

To ensure that the promised service quality specifications are able to meet the customers' expectations, Azoka could increase its inventory and as a result, increase its warehouse space, ensure good management and administration, and make sure the products' price and quality complement each other. Most importantly, it needs to train its customer service representatives and allow them access to inventory and delivery service details, so that they can further assist the customers with their purchases.

- **Gap 3:** Does the service quality specification reflect the actual service?

To solve this problem, Azoka can impose control over operations, increase personnel, implement proper training and maintain a Service Quality Assurance Team.

- **Gap 4:** Does the management's promise reflect the actual service delivered?

In order to reduce the communication gap between Azoka and its customers, they should first know exactly what is being served, — is it convenience or fast delivery or budget-friendly options? It should not create any false impression or fake any information that does not reflect its promise. They should use real information and update their website and social media platforms accordingly. Throughout, Azoka should be honest and maintain the promises or bars it has imposed and ensure that it aligns with its budget.

- **Gap 5:** Does the expected service quality align with the perceived service quality?

Of the aforementioned customer expectations, Azoka is able to meet most of them. However, as compared to its competitors like Chaldaal, Pandamart, and so on, Azoka lacks in terms of product variety. Moreover, they do not have any physical store consumers can visit to purchase, and although they have several MFSs to help consumers complete their online purchases, they do not have the option to pay via bKash. Bangladesh's MFS is led by market leader bKash, which has more than 50 million users and 300 thousand agents all across the country, of which around 98 percent of them reside in Dhaka alone (Ria, 2023, GSMA Mobile and Development Intelligence, 2012). The unavailability of these services may result in Azoka losing a considerable amount of customers as a result of not being able to align expected service quality with perceived service quality.

3. Apply the services marketing triangle with respect to Azoka.com.bd. How did an inverted services marketing triangle help Azoka.com.bd overcome the challenges imposed by the non-alignment of the three sides of the services marketing triangle, previously followed by Azoka.com.bd?

Azoka utilizes the service marketing triangle to overcome the non-alignment of the three sides of the traditional triangle, such that their strategies are developed to promote and deliver their promises or services to generate satisfied customers. The triangle focuses on three vertices, company, employees and customers, and the marketing strategy that enhances their relationship, internal marketing, external marketing and interactive marketing

For Azoka to generate satisfied customers, it used both external and interactive marketing. Through external marketing, the brand directly markets or promotes to its customers, and through interactive marketing, it promotes to its customers through its employees. But to ensure that the latter is effective, they first need to ensure that their employees are satisfied. To do such, they use internal marketing strategies. Here, employees include those directly working under the firm, and those with whom it is indirectly connected, such as their delivery service agent, in-house supply chain, and other partners such as LankaBangla Finance Limited, etc.

Azoka first emphasizes on keeping its employees motivated by having an efficient salary and wages policy, a warm and friendly work environment, and most importantly, good, helpful and considerate supervisors and colleagues. The employees are trained continuously on methods they can use to keep customers satisfied and are repeatedly reminded of the company goals such that they can communicate better both with the company and its customers. Once the employees are motivated and educated enough, only then can they properly serve the customers better based on the firm's interactive marketing strategies. These interactive marketing strategies can be in the form of salespersons selling personally, customer service centers, 24/7 online customer support, service encounters and service scapes.

Azoka also exploits its external marketing scheme by directly communicating with customers about its services and what they promise to them. The firm relies heavily on its social media presence and its user-friendly website to ensure satisfied and loyal customers. They utilize social media marketing and digital marketing to ensure such. Through their platforms, they create awareness, manage price and service expectations and inform customers regarding any necessary news regarding the firm. They also advertise and promote discounts, sales, and offers through these. For example, they promoted an 8% discount if the customers used LankaBangla Finance Limited's credit card. Here, Azoka partnered with LankaBangla Finance Limited to generate a discount for its customers.

4. Assess the perceived risks in purchasing Azoka.com.bd. Which of these risks can be minimized and how?

In this vast pool of e-commerce businesses Azoka has to differentiate in order to survive and the means to survival is acing customer service. Consumer satisfaction is achieved when businesses timely respond to consumer expectations. In pursuance of that Azoka needs to identify the perceived risks in purchasing from them.

Azoka's product catalog mainly consists of imported food and beverages. They have products that are alien to the Bangladeshi consumer base. This generates perceived physical risk. Consumers may feel reluctant to buy these products as they find themselves unaware of the ingredients used in the product. At a physical store, consumers have the liberty to look at the ingredients properly, whereas online they have to make their decision using the picture of the product. Consumers don't face this dilemma with common brands as they have been using them for long enough to understand their suitability. This comfort level isn't felt against imported food and beverage products.

Such unfamiliarity with products also gives rise to perceived financial risks among consumers. Azoka's website offers a wide range of options for different categories of food products. These options include imported versions of known brands as well as introducing new brands. Consumers become more inclined towards known brands and don't develop a habit to try out new ones. The price-sensitive consumer base won't bet their money on a product they feel unsure about. This makes Azoka's entire offering redundant. They want to be a one-stop shop for exclusive items. When consumers aren't willing to experience this exclusivity, Azoka's USP becomes ineffective.

This lack of surety in making a purchasing decision results in perceived time risk. Online purchasing is preferred by consumers due to its convenience. They don't have to get ready and travel to the shop to make a purchase. They can do this from the comfort of their home. This saves their time. Time is an important matter here. When a consumer decides to shop at Azoka they are met with hundreds of options for different products. While this is a good thing about giving consumers the choice, the downside of this approach is consumer decisions. The exclusive products aren't cheap, as a result, consumers will suffer from indecision. Them facing difficulty in taking a judgment call will make the process tedious for them. Eventually, their attention span will run out and they will postpone their shopping. The next time they decide to make a purchase they will likely choose another website as consumers will count their previous experience with Azoka as a waste of time.

Azoka can take certain steps to minimize these risks and improve their consumer experience. Firstly, Azoka needs to include clear pictures of the ingredient list of products alongside the usual product picture. Products also come with allergic reaction warnings on their labels. In order to make it more relevant Azoka should highlight the matter in the description of the product. These actions undertaken by them will ensure that consumers are well aware of what they are about to consume, minimizing the chances of physical risks for them.

Secondly, Azoka needs to bring its exclusive products into the spotlight. This can be done through extensive social media advertising. Their social media pages should promote these new brands more often than popular brands. They can also send PR boxes to social media influencers and make them engage the consumers with these unfamiliar items. This will bridge the information gap and consumers will consider these products worth spending their money on.

Lastly, Azoka can feature an itemized list of items to save time for consumers. Based on purchasing patterns Azoka can organize a list of products that typically appear on a consumer's monthly grocery shopping itinerary. This will save consumers some time by providing them with a pre-made list. Through this method, Azoka can also incorporate its newly launched products. This will provide convenience to consumers as well as help develop an attitude amongst them toward new products. Azoka as a startup in a competitive industry will struggle to attain success. Industry giants are already way ahead of them in management and financial aspects. Then there are also similar-sized small e-commerce brands that are also leaving no stone unturned to accomplish their goals. Therefore, in order to rise above all Azoka needs to become exemplary in customer service.

Reference

https://www.facebook.com/azoka.com.bd/posts/pfbid0cub5B7Txq4poELQE4g2L8oVGAGrS-vDWBXfrcKKnopRgNt7F6kLdtiyWuNmydTvYol https://www.gsma.com/mobilefordevelopment/wp-content/uploads/2013/01/Case_Study_-bKash.pdf https://futurestartup.com/2023/04/27/bkashhistory/#:~:text=Today%2C%20bKash%20is%20the%20leading,300%2C000%20agents%20across%20the%20country.

Chapter 6
Transformation of HR Roles Through People Analytics:
A Case Study on Implementation of SAP Success Factor by Berger Paint Bangladesh

Marufa Mizan
BRAC University, Bangladesh

EXECUTIVE SUMMARY

This case will allow students to have insight about how transformative HR is leveraging employee data to make evidence-based strategic decisions. Berger, striving to increase turnover every four years, faced HR challenges with manual processes and disconnected data across departments. HR functions were hindered by the lack of integration. To address this, Berger implemented SAP SuccessFactors, automating data collection and analysis across departments. The system provides a unified platform for evaluating performance, streamlining recruitment, and aligning employee goals with company strategy. This HR transformation enhances efficiency, eliminates manual updates, and ensures consistency in tracking employees. The move reflects a strategic response to increased customer demand while maintaining product and service quality, offering valuable insights for undergraduate and postgraduate human resource management courses. This study will showcase how HR is gradually shifting to the world of data-centric solutions and facilitating productivity and effectiveness of the firm.

1. INTRODUCTION

In the recent competitive business landscape era organizations are shifting from traditional approach to transformational HR approach. Gradually they are focusing more on building a strong workforce by treating their people as one of the most valuable assets. Because it's only possible for the organization to be one step ahead in their industry when their team constantly comes up with more innovative ideas, and their employees are flexible enough to adapt themselves with the fast forwarding changes as fast as possible. However, building a skilled workforce and retaining them can be a complex process. And

DOI: 10.4018/979-8-3693-1781-5.ch006

there comes the role of people analytics. People analytics is a "data centric" approach that manipulates employee data to get insight about patterns, trends, and correlations by using advanced algorithms, calculations, and logic commands. And SAP successfactors is one of the advanced HR software platforms which operates based on people analytics. This platform extracts and represents data in a meaningful manner and provides insights in a form of report; which enables HR professionals to take data driven decisions on major HR based areas like performance management; talent acquisition; compensation management (Sahoo, 2019). Any firm can address this drastic fast forward change in a proactive manner by incorporating frameworks like Strategic HR and Transformative HR which will be assisted by data driven informed decisions.

Berger Paint Limited is one of the leading organizations in the painting industry of Bangladesh. Lately the company has been witnessing significant organizational growth. However sustaining the growth can also be challenging as involves increased functionality. One of the major challenges they faced during that time was talent acquisition and retention. The study has focused on the challenge a HR personnel might face due to the growth of the firm and what steps they have addressed to get back on the track. The objective of this case study is to showcase how transformative HR approach is becoming significantly vital for today's organizations to make strategic decisions for the organization.

To prepare the case initially primary data have been collected through interviews and surveys. In the finding section; the challenges faced by the company have been broadly discussed and in the analysis section it has been highlighted how they have managed to address the challenges and what was the scenario afterwards they managed to address the challenge.

2. METHODOLOGY

To prepare the case, data have been collected from interviews and surveys. Interview was conducted to get in depth insight about how the organization managed to address their challenges through implementing one of the widely used enterprise software like SAP Success Factor. Therefore, the primary data collected was from a HR personnel who is directly in charge of the directly in charge of the whole process.

However the purpose of the survey was to showcase the reaction of the employee about what they think about their organization's automated HR process. Therefore, instead of focusing on any single department the survey was conducted on the 10 employees who are in different departments of Berger which includes HRM, Sales, IT, and Finance. Basically the survey provided insights on how employees are reacting towards this change.

3. LITERATURE REVIEW

3.1 HR 4.0

The integration of Industry 4.0 in Human Resource Management is referred as HR 4.0. It supports the idea of more technically advanced and data driven approach. It involves the incorporation of artificial intelligence, big data analytics, internet of things, cloud computing. (Sivathanu & Pillai, 2018) This allows the elimination of repetitive workload and automation of HR process. Repetitive task such as payroll processing, leave management, benefit administration can be automated leveraging advanced HR software. Automation not only enhances efficiency but also allows HR professionals to focus more on strategic aspect of human resources such as talent management, employee engagement, and compensation management. (Shamaileh et al., 2023)

3.2 Role of HRIS in Transformative HR

Madhu (2019) stated that in the traditional HR approach the role of the HR department could not be measured and the way other departments prepare sales reports or audit reports HR could not prepare such a data based report. However the emergence of transformative HR has changed the whole scenario. Because now HR follows the evidence based approach where they conduct every HR related function based on the data from sources like appraisal reports or self-assessment surveys. (Obeidat, 2012) This is why previously the contribution of the HR department in making strategic decisions was not taken into consideration but now HR plays the role of equal to the business partner of a firm when it comes to making strategic decisions. Now HR relies on quantifiable data like revenue per employee, operation costs per work team to provide preventive measures and insights to track productivity and efficiency of the firm.

3.3 Post COVID-19 Pandemic and Adoption of HR Tools

The Covid-19 pandemic has significantly accelerated and extended the digital transformation of the organization. In order to ensure the sustainability of the firm and address the challenges brought by Covid 19 lockdown measures, HR professionals relied on various information and communication technologies. According to the World economic Forumis 2020 report, 84% of the responded showcased the rapid acceleration of digitalization of work along with that there will be 50% increase in job automation along with the increase of digital technologies. (Da Silva et al., 2022) Therefore, advanced HR tools like AI, machine learning, and analytics (Saxena et al., 2021) played a crucial role in this context. Enhancing individual's abilities, knowledge, skills, competencies, to effectively employ and understand diverse technologies associated with the fourth industrial revolution (4IR) aligns with the concept of HR4.0 as highlighted by Shamim et al. (2016).

Kumar et al. (2019) noticed a growing demand for technological expertise in HRM due to the rising virtual nature of work. The covid-19 pandemic led to a rise in the use of remote work, remote work, and e -working and different work management platforms to fulfill the demand created by the crisis (Dlamini & Ndzinisa, 2020). Gigauri (2020) noted that electronic working platforms and employees who are working in virtual work arrangements will continue to dominate the future world of work.

In recent years there has been an emergence of HR tools in corporate entities of Bangladesh. Along with SAP Successfactor widely used applications like LinkedIn, PowerBi generates insight based on analytics (Kashive and Khanna, 2022). LinkedIn has a significant impact on hiring preference for Bangladeshi Employers (Nadim Khan, 2021). Previously many research work has been conducted on people analytics however less attention was given on presenting how the corporate world is actually relying on people analytics to conduct HR functions.

3.4 The Concept of People Analytics

In the growing competitive business era it is possible for any organization to imitate the business strategies of their competitors. However, imitating the working style, thinking process of the employee can be pretty much difficult to do. Therefore nowadays, organization who are one step ahead are focusing on building a strong workforce so that imitating their thought process or the way they generate innovative ideas become impossible for the competitors to imitate. (Mohammed, 2019). However, finding a pool of talents and tuning them into a strong workforce can be difficult for any organization. And in order to address this situation organization are implementing people analytics. The terminology people analytics and HR analytics are similar. Both refer back to the process of gathering, sorting and analyzing vast amount employee data and extract meaningful insight to take decision in different HR based functions like manpower forecasting, talent management, compensation management, training and development. With the help of analytical tools HR managers able to get insight about different patterns and trends which allow them take more data centric decisions. HR analytics involves the usage of tools which operates based on different statistical operation, algorithms and different HR metrics like retention rate, cost per hire, employee turnover rate (Levenson 2005).

HR is gradually shifting to the world of data centric solutions, therefore it must leverage its ground in employee advocacy, advancement and understanding. In order to do that they must focus on three actions. Firstly, they can ease into HR analytics by investing more time and attention to retain employee buy-in. Secondly, they need to emphasize the objectivity of data centric decision making processes. Last but not the least, HR professionals also need to act empathetically towards those who are going to be affected by those decisions. (Lipkin, 2015).

3.5 SAP SucessFactors

SAP SucessFactors is one of the product line of renowned enterprise software SAP which is an integrated cloud based human capital management (HCM). This platform enhances collaborative efficiency through its optimized integration system. This system strengthens real- time management, enhancing control capabilities to adapt changing needs. It focuses on controlling labor costs, promoting managerial profitability and optimizing performance management to mitigate operational risks. With six distinct features, including supporting strategic decision making and realizing development plans. It liberates HR management from traditional transactional task, allowing for a more substantial focus on strategic management work. It transcends being merely an HR operating system, evolving into a management platform that elevates enterprise HR management to a strategic level. By facilitating the realization of "human capital" operations which fundamentally enhances enterprise creativity and boosts core competitiveness.

4. FINDINGS: COMPANY AND THE PROBLEM BACKGROUND

Originating from England, Berger Paint started its journey in Bangladesh back in 1970. With experience of around 250 years the company is still thriving in the painting industry. The company's mission is to increase their turnover by 100 percent every 5 years. With around 1000 employees Berger is operating at around 12 different sales depots around the country.

As per the company's mission Berger has succeeded to increase its turnover every four years. However, in order to keep up with the increasing customer demand along with maintaining the products and services quality ; they were looking forward to recruiting more employees from different departments like sales, production, and supply chain. They wanted to improve employee experience both for its new and old employees. Therefore their HR team had to focus on delivering valuable strategic projects. The HR functions of the company were following manual processes which were not connected to other departments. For instance the employee data were not integrated with the other departments like the production or sales department and the HR team always had to keep the current update manually. Additionally there was no consistency in tracking employees which kind of created a challenge for the HR team to evaluate the employee performance and set their goal and objective. The recruitment process of the company was also not organized as it used to take place through mails and paper resumes. The whole process was time consuming and more complex. Also the employee onboarding experience was also not up to the mark.

5. DISCUSSION

5.1 Analysis of Interview

Based on the interview which took place with Assistant Manager X (Appendix 1) states that their entry level recruitment; employee onboarding, goal and objectives are settled in the SAP platform. For recruitment they outlined the required skills for a specific role in the organization. She stated that "I am an HR personnel and definitely my required skill sets will differ from someone who is working in the Finance department. Where I need to be competent enough with communication; maintaining confidentiality or good presentation skill; on the other hand employees from Finance need to be good with numbers and preparing reports". Therefore, the data type for recruitment are job descriptions. The next few phases in recruitment for instance assigning applicants with a task or setting interview schedule are prepared through SAP. Previously which used to take place through mail. About the effectiveness of the SAP Manger X that "For sure SAP has streamlined the whole process. For instance before implementation of SAP I have to manually prepare the interview schedule. And it was so time consuming that I could not contribute myself in any other roles. So as you can say as a resource of my organization SAP has made me more efficient and effective. About setting goals and objectives Manager X claims that SAP has a default setting which consists of some parameters like Financial/ Customer Satisfaction/ Internal Growth. And at the beginning of each year they set those parameters for their organization. The goal and objective of employees are set aligning with the organizational goal. To evaluate those goals and objectives job details like qualifications; skills and responsibilities are given preference just like recruitment. Manager X stated that "During evaluation we follow performance metrics. In the Y axis we give criteria for performance measurement and in the X axis values are given". Employees score themselves and managers score their direct reports in the end of the year. Regarding employee onboarding Manager X mentioned that the employee onboarding experience enhanced a lot right after implementation of SAP. She stated that "Previously new employees had to wait for a long time for their laptop or stationeries. However, now the situation has completely changed. Now the IT team and admin gets notified through SAP as soon as a new employee joins. Thus IT prepares laptop and admin can prepare workstations beforehand. Same goes for those who manage stationeries and other required materials of an employee".

However Ms. also added that onboarding is the newest feature of SAP. Therefore we are facing some technical errors with the software itself. They are communicating with the SAP team to sort it out. SAP is still working on their onboarding's functionality. Regarding the challenges the organization is facing due to the implementation of the software. Manger X conveyed that even though Berger welcoming more fresh minds but a majority of their employees have been working here for around 20/25 years.

Who age around 45 years or more. In contrast SAP is the newest addition to their work and to some extent they are facing difficulties to get along with it. She also added that considering the situation they are trying to keep the process as convenient as possible.

5.2 Analysis of Survey

The survey was conducted to investigate the employee's reaction about the implementation of SAP Successfactor. All the employees were asked for their opinion towards their organization's process of goal and objective setting through a data centric software. Even though half of these responses were positive in terms of effectiveness of this approach, the other half of them agree with the idea that solely relying on data based software might not optimize overall organizational growth. Rather it will be most effective if the whole process is more collaborative where goal and objective setting process will take place; combining SAP and employee's supervisor/team lead and their work mate.

One of the rising debates about data based software is privacy. Therefore the purpose of this section was to figure out what Berger's employees think about this aspect. However, even though a majority of the employees disagreed with the fact that their privacy will be intervened through their employee data, a portion of them think otherwise.

Around 90% of the employees agree with the fact that there is a lack of enough training and support resources for employees to run an advanced software like SAP in Bangladesh. As gradually companies are implementing sap this might affect the long term performance of the company.

Figure 1.

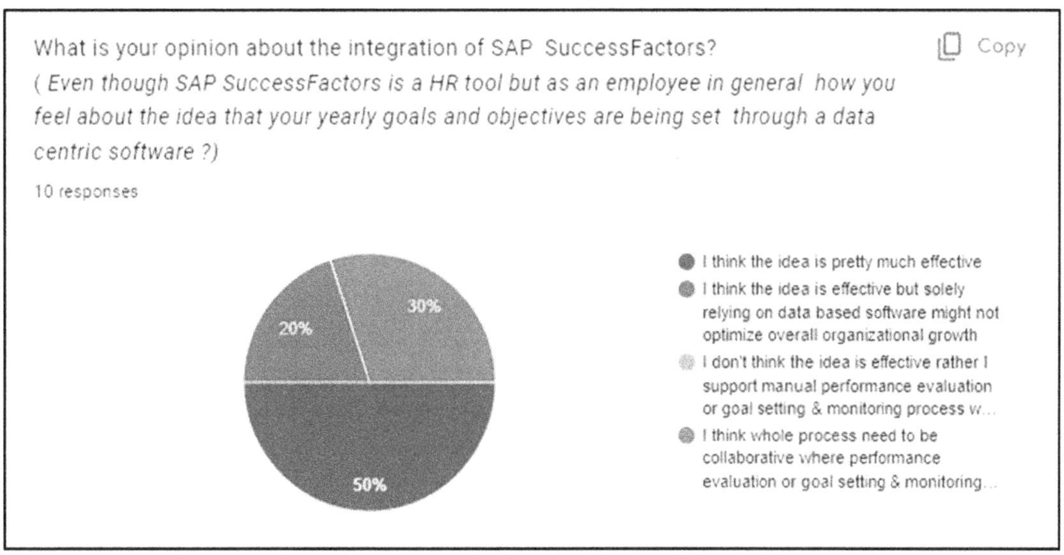

Figure 2.

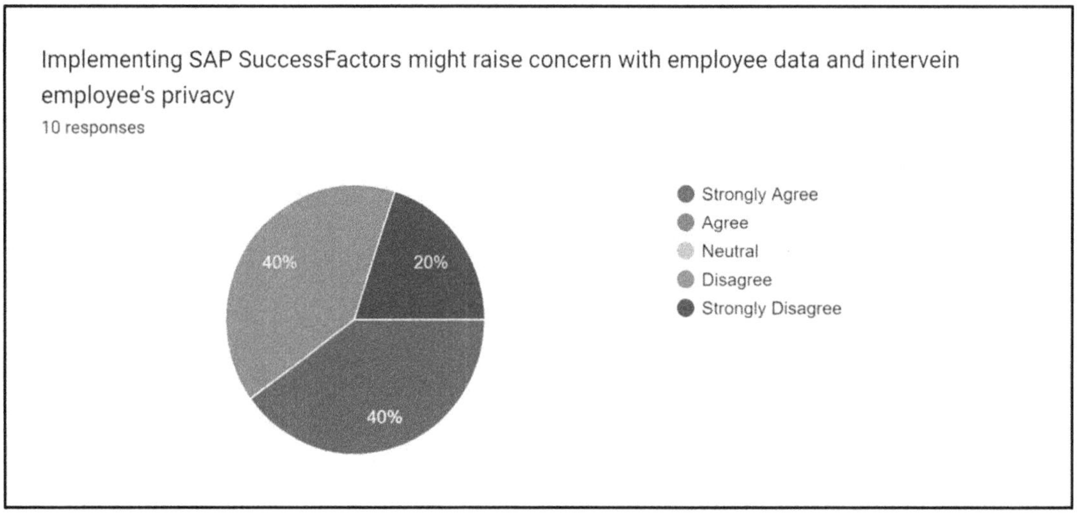

Figure 3.

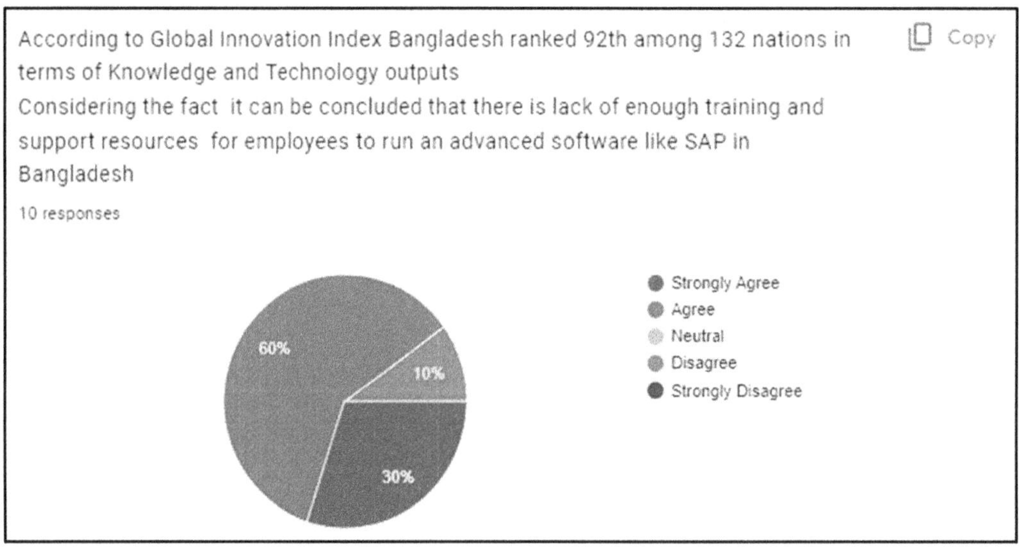

6. RECOMMENDATION

- From survey analysis it is visible that a generous amount of employees still think that their privacy will be intervened because of the employee data. And this might create challenges for the company in the long run. Therefore it is highly suggested that organizations promote more transparency in the whole process. In order to do so, they need to ensure 'Two Way Communication' between the employee and management.

Initiatives like maintaining data privacy policy; controlling the access of data, obtaining employee consent before collecting their personal data will positively influence the whole process.

- Around 90% participants of the total survey agreed with the fact that there is a lack of enough training and support resources for employees to run an advanced software like SAP. Therefore future research would be beneficial if it is able to figure out how to facilitate employee competencies so that they can get along with these organizational software. Additionally, firms like Berger who are incorporating advanced technology like SAP in their operational system, then they must make sure that their employees are equipped with proper skill sets to run the program. If it requires any training and development they have to provide it beforehand by conducting TNA (Training Need Analysis). Additionally the workplace culture needs to build in a way which is more welcoming towards innovation and constant update.
- Software like SAP heavily rely on data to generate any report. Therefore the quality and accuracy of the data need to be maintained for optimal functionality. Any biases and irrational judgements might corrupt the accuracy of data. Therefore, HR must conduct data audits, ensuring data verification and validation in order to ensure an 'Ethical Decision Making' approach in the organization.
- SAP stores business data which can be confidential therefore it is highly suggested to ensure a robust security system in order to avoid any unwanted circumstances like cybersecurity threats, data breach. Hence an individual team for system maintenance is essential to avoid these challenges, who will constantly monitor the overall performance and security strength of the software.

7. LIMITATIONS AND AREAS FOR FUTURE RESEARCH

One of the strength of this paper could also be one of its limitations. The samples used in this research were mostly managers who are directly involved in practicing HR analytics. Undoubtedly, it can be said that the insight gathered from this group is capable of clear understanding about the current state of the applications, where it is stands and what will be the probable state in future. No one can deny the fact that they have in depth idea due to their own experience in the practical field and expertise. However, such sample may be biased to some extent. It would be valuable if the sample could include the experience of business owner who are implementing HR analytical based software to their business. They would be able to provide in depth insight about how this analytical software is enabling their business to expand or grow. Along with that it would also be valuable if the opinion of an IT specialist would be taken. Because, they would be able to provide the understanding on what is happening at the backend of the software and how the whole process supporting business analytics. Therefore it would be possible to showcase the concept on how technology will support the applications of people analytics in future. Therefore in this research it is unclear that how HR analytical based software is influencing the growth of business and what are the possible loopholes in this process in terms of technical aspect. This paper has highlighted how people analytics is being integrated to make strategic decision.

However, there are different aspect of HRM where HR analytics can be integrated. Future research can be conducted on those areas. In order to promote sustainable green HRM practices HR analytics can be integrated. People analytics can help organizations assess the environmental impact of their workforce related activities. By analyzing the environmental impact of their workforce related activities. By analyzing data on employee commuting patterns, travel and energy consumption, HR professional can identify areas for improvement and implement strategies to reduce the carbon footprint associated with these activities. This includes promoting telecommuting, encouraging public transportation use or implementing flexible work schedules to minimizing unnecessary commuting.

Another area where people analytics can be integrated to address the generational shift in any organization. People analytics allow organization to analyze and understand the diverse needs and motivations of various generation, such as Generation X, Millennials and Generation Z. By leveraging data on factors like work preferences, communication styles and career goals, companies can create targeted approaches to talent management, recruitment and employee enjoyment that resonate with each generation . Along with that people analytics enables organizations to support personalized learning and development initiatives. Different generations may have distinct learning preferences and requirements. By analyzing data on training effectiveness and skill development, organization can tailor learning programs to meet the diverse needs of employees across various age groups.

Last but not the least the intersection of cybersecurity an HR analytics can also be considered for future research. Protections of sensitive employee information, ensuring compliance with privacy regulations and implementing secure access controls. Additionally, HR analytics can benefit from cybersecurity measures to safeguard the integrity and confidentiality of the data being analyzed. Collaboration between cybersecurity and HR analytics teams is essential for creating a secure and data driven workplace environment. It involves establishing robust security protocols for HR systems, educating employees on cybersecurity best practices and aligning HR analytics initiatives with privacy and compliance standards. By integrating these two domains effectively, organizations can foster a secure and efficient work environment while leveraging valuable insights from employee data.

Figure 4. The number of publications published on people analytics (Source: Dimensions)

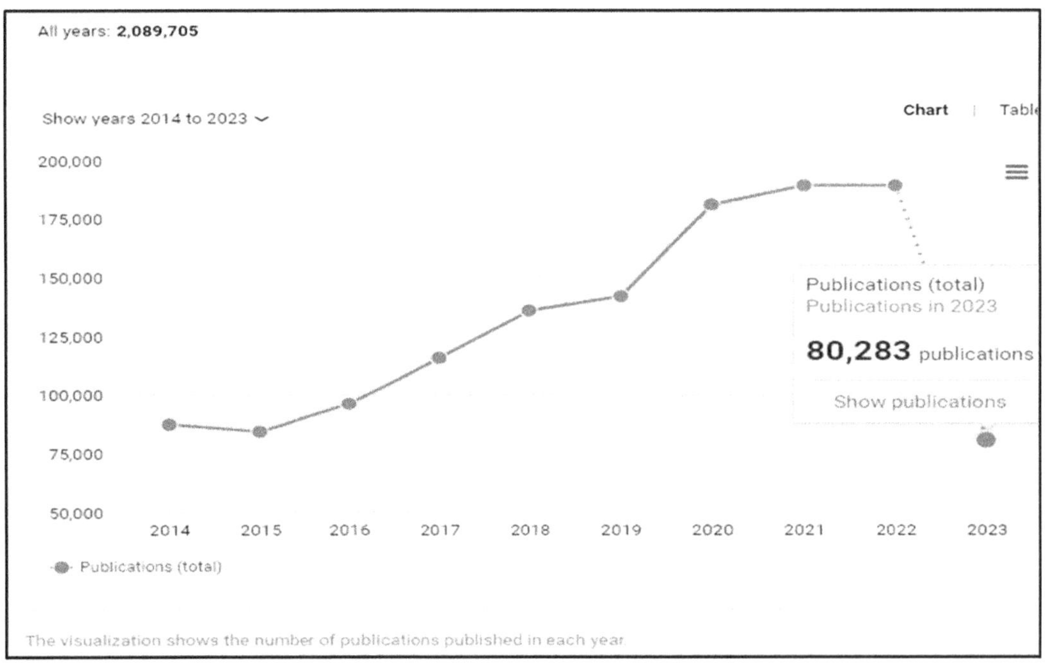

Figure 5. the search interest of last five years in Bangladesh on topics like data analytics, HR analytics, people analytics, employee analytics (Source: Google Trend)

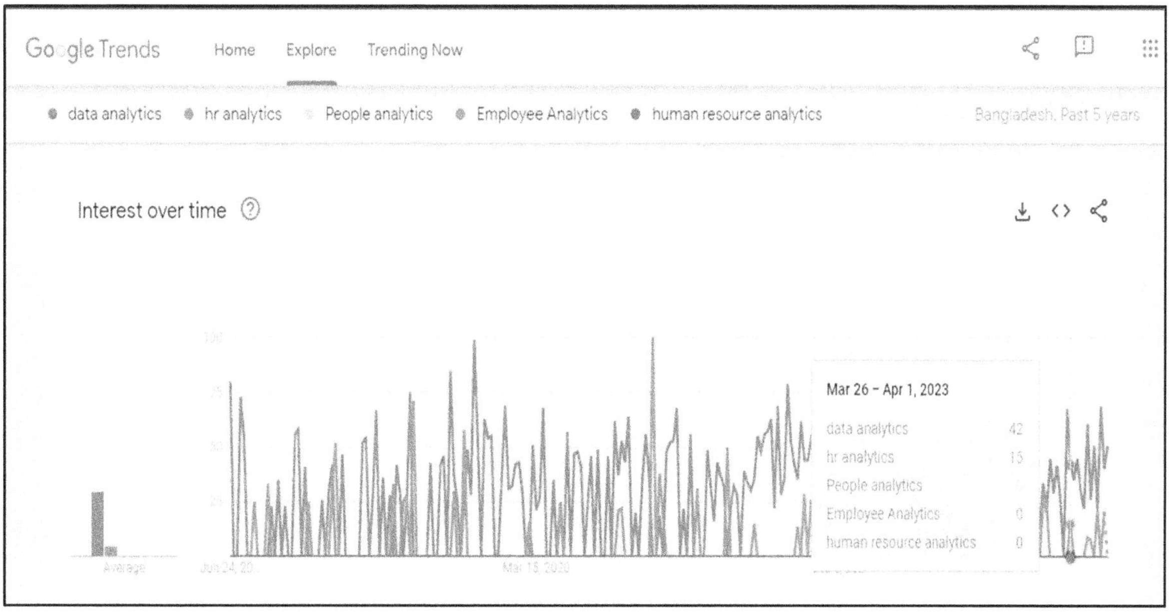

8. CONCLUSION

To focus on long term sustainable growth in the competitive business landscape, relying on HR frameworks like Transformative HR, Strategic HR has been increasing drastically. The collaboration between these HR approaches with appropriate data driven methods will escalate the overall performance of the organization in the most effective and efficient manner.

REFERENCES

Da Silva, L., Soltovski, R., Pontes, J., Treinta, F. T., Leitão, P., Mosconi, E., Resende, L. M., & Yoshino, R. T. (2022). Human resources management 4.0: Literature review and trends. *Computers & Industrial Engineering*, *168*, 108111. doi:10.1016/j.cie.2022.108111

Dlamini, R., & Ndzinisa, R. (2020). Universities trailing behind: Unquestioned epistemological foundations constraining the transition to online instructional delivery and learning. *South African Journal of Higher Education*, *34*(6), 52–64. doi:10.20853/34-6-4073

Gigauri, I. (2020). Effects of Covid-19 on Human Resource Management from the Perspective of Digitalization and Work-life-balance. *International Journal of Innovative Technologies in Economy*, *4*(31), 1–10. doi:10.31435/rsglobal_ijite/30092020/7148

Hossain, S. F. A., Shan, X., Nurunnabi, M., Tushar, H., Mohsin, A. K. M., & Ahsan, F. T. (2021). Opportunities and challenges of m-learning during the COVID-19 pandemic: A mixed methodology approach. *E-Collaboration Technologies and Strategies for Competitive Advantage Amid Challenging Times*, 210-227.

Kashive, N., & Khanna, V. T. (2022). Emerging HR analytics role in a crisis: An analysis of LinkedIn data. *Competitiveness Review*.

Khan, H. M. (2021). The Role of LinkedIn Profile on Hiring Preference: Evidence from Bangladeshi Employers. Asian Journal of Economics. *Business and Accounting*, *21*(18), 42–56.

Lipkin, J. (2015). *Sieving through the data to find the person: HR's imperative for balancing big data with people centricity*. Academic Press.

Obeidat, B. Y. (2012). The Relationship between Human Resource Information System (HRIS) Functions and Human Resource Management (HRM) Functionalities. *Journal of Management Research*, *4*(4). Advance online publication. doi:10.5296/jmr.v4i4.2262

Sahoo, M. B. (2019). People Analytics and Disruptive Technologies are Transforming Human Resources Roles. *Southwestern Business Administration Journal*, *18*(1), 4.

Saxena, M., Bagga, T., & Gupta, S. 2021, January. Hr during covid-19 era: Study on recent HR transformations through technological tools and trends. In *2021 11th International Conference on Cloud Computing, Data Science & Engineering (Confluence)* (pp. 110-113). IEEE.

Shamaileh, N. A., Eldahamsheh, M. M., Alneimat, S., Istaiteyeh, R., Azzam, I. A., & Al-Hawary, S. I. S. (2023). The effects of smart human resources 4.0 on employee job effectiveness: The mediating role of employee job satisfaction. *International Journal of Data and Network Science*, *7*(2), 801–808. doi:10.5267/j.ijdns.2023.1.009

Shamim, S., Cang, S., Yu, H., & Li, Y. (2016). *Management Approaches for Industry 4.0: A human resource management perspective*. IEEE. doi:10.1109/CEC.2016.7748365

Sivathanu, B., & Pillai, R. (2018). Smart HR 4.0 – how industry 4.0 is disrupting HR. *Human Resource Management International Digest*, *26*(4), 7–11. doi:10.1108/HRMID-04-2018-0059

ADDITIONAL READING

Chau, K. Y., Huang, T., Moslehpour, M., Khan, W., Nisar, Q. A., & Haris, M. (2023). Opening a new horizon in green HRM practices with big data analytics and its analogy to circular economy performance: An empirical evidence. *Environment, Development and Sustainability*. Advance online publication. doi:10.1007/s10668-023-03725-9

DiClaudio, M. (2019). People analytics and the rise of HR: How data, analytics and emerging technology can transform human resources (HR) into a profit center. *Strategic HR Review*, *18*(2), 42–46. doi:10.1108/SHR-11-2018-0096

Gattullo, M., Scurati, G. W., Fiorentino, M., Uva, A. E., Ferrise, F., & Bordegoni, M. (2019). Towards augmented reality manuals for industry 4.0: A methodology. *Robotics and Computer-integrated Manufacturing*, *56*, 276–286. doi:10.1016/j.rcim.2018.10.001

Gianecchini, M. (2021). *Sustainable HRM - Gen Z and their different perceptions of typical Sustainable HRM characteristics in the workplace*. https://thesis.unipd.it/handle/20.500.12608/39707

Hameed, Z., Khan, I. U., Islam, T., Sheikh, Z., & Naeem, R. M. (2020). Do green HRM practices influence employees' environmental performance? *International Journal of Manpower*, *41*(7), 1061–1079. doi:10.1108/IJM-08-2019-0407

Kabanda, G. (2021). Performance of machine learning and big data analytics paradigms in cybersecurity and cloud computing platforms. *Global Journal of Computer Science and Technology: G Interdisciplinary, 21*(2), 1-25.

Kovach, K. A., & Cathcart, C. E. Jr. (1999). Human Resource Information Systems (HRIS): Providing Business with Rapid Data Access, Information Exchange and Strategic Advantage. *Public Personnel Management*, *28*(2), 275–282. doi:10.1177/009102609902800208

Mefi, N. P., & Asoba, S. N. (2021). Sustainable human resource practices for organizational competitiveness post the COVID-19 pandemic. *Academy of Entrepreneurship Journal*, *27*(2), 1–7.

Saling, K., & Michael, D. (2020). Leveraging people analytics for an adaptive complex talent management system. *Procedia Computer Science*, *168*, 105–111. doi:10.1016/j.procs.2020.02.269

Verma, A., Bansal, M., & Verma, J. (2020). Industry 4.0: Reshaping the future of HR. *Strategic Direction*, *36*(5), 9–11. doi:10.1108/SD-12-2019-0235

Vương, B. N., Tushar, H., & Hossain, S. F. A. (2022). The effect of social support on job performance through organizational commitment and innovative work behavior: Does innovative climate matter? *Asia-Pacific Journal of Business Administration*. Advance online publication. doi:10.1108/APJBA-06-2021-0256

Xu, J. (2020). Business design of human resource management based on SAP-HR system and Human Resources Management software. *Journal of Physics: Conference Series*, *1578*(1), 012080. doi:10.1088/1742-6596/1578/1/012080

APPENDIX

8. Teaching Notes

Synopsis

This case will allow students to have insight about how transformative HR is leveraging employee data to make evidence based strategic decisions. This case is applicable for an undergraduate and postgraduate program for the Human Resource Management courses which includes courses like strategic human resource management; change management; manpower planning and forecasting, Human Resource Information System .As per the company's mission Berger has succeeded to increase its turnover every four years. However, in order to keep up with the increasing customer demand along with maintaining the products and services quality ; they were looking forward to recruiting more employees from different departments like sales, production, and supply chain. The HR functions of the company were following manual processes which were not connected to other departments. For instance the employee data were not integrated with the other departments like the production or sales department and the HR team always had to keep the current update manually. Additionally there was no consistency in tracking employees which kind of created a challenge for the HR team to evaluate the employee performance and set their goal and objective. The recruitment process of the company was also not organized as it used to take place through mails and paper resumes. The whole process was time consuming and more complex. Also the employee onboarding experience was also not up to the mark. Soon enough Berger realized the need for the HR transformation. They implement SAP success factors. The automated process collects and analyzes employee data from every department and gives a common platform to evaluate employee performance; recruitment and retention and set goals and objectives for each employee aligning with the company strategy.

This study will enable to showcase how HR is gradually shifting to the world of data centric solutions and facilitating productivity and effectiveness of the firm.

Target Audience

- Level- Undergraduate and Postgraduate
- Field Of Study - Human Resource Management, Human Resource Information System, HR Analysis, Change Management.
- Level of difficulty- Moderate Level
- Discipline(s) for which the case is most relevant- Bachelor of Business(BBA), Master of Business Administration(MBA) Major in Human Resource Management and Bachelor in Science(BSc), Master in Masters in Science (MSc) degree in courses includes Human Resource Information System, HR Analytics, Change Management, Business Intelligence

Learning Objectives

1) To learn the significance of data centric decision making approach in Transformative HR
2) To learn the role of HR analytics to address the drastic changes in the business environment.

3) To learn how the HR team of a firm plays a crucial role in the strategic decision making process.

Methods

The case study utilized mixed methodology. To prepare the case initially primary data have been collected through interviews and surveys. Interview was conducted to get in depth insight about how the organization managed to address their challenges through implementing one of the widely used enterprise software like SAP. And a survey was conducted on 10 of the employees from different departments of Berger to get insight about the post implementation scenario of the SAP; which basically showcases how employees are reacting towards this change.

Teaching Plan and Objective

The case in a classroom setup may require around 90 minutes. The first 60 minutes will be allocated for lectures where all the relevant theories and frameworks will be discussed. The last 30 minutes will be allocated for a group discussion. Where all the lecture assignment questions will be discussed to the students. Each group should have 4 -6 students with a group leader.

Every member will have to present a specific section of the case.

The topic discussion of 60 minutes will be divided into following manner-

- First 20 minutes- Detailed discussion about Transformative HR and Strategic HR to give a clear idea about the role of these two approaches to address the recent change in the competitive business landscape.
- Second 20 minutes- Detailed discussion about people/HR analytics to give a brief idea about the role data centric decision making approach in Transformative HR and Strategic HR approach and it optimizes the overall organizational growth.
- Last 20 minutes- Students in class will be given a detailed scenario about how can they incorporate HR frameworks like Transformative HR and Strategic HR in their future workplace, how they should prepare themselves as a HR analyst, what are the challenges they might face while incorporating data centric decision making approach in their future workplace and how can they address those challenges.

After 60 minutes discussion there will be a group task. Students will get 30 minutes for the task. Five different questions have been given and those questions will be discussed for 25 minutes and the last 5 minutes will be allocated for presentation.

Assignments Questions

From the above case study, could you please answer the following questions?

1. What is the role of data centric decision making process in the context of transformative HR?
2. How can enhancing employee experience affect the strategy of the firm?

3. “The HR team of Berger will play a crucial role to align the HR activities with the strategic goal of the organization” - do you agree with the statement? Why or why not?
4. What are the possible challenges an organization might face while incorporating advanced technology like SAP in the operational process? How the HR team can address those challenges.
5. “To address the fast forward changes in the external business environment, organizations must rely on evidence-based HR now more than ever” justify the sentence in the context of Berger Paint Bangladesh with appropriate examples.

Answer to the Question No 1

Transformative HR approach refers to proactive HR practices which focuses on creating a workforce who are more adaptable towards any kind of changes and welcoming towards constant innovation and development. And in order to promote Transformative HR practice in a firm, a data centric decision making process plays one of the most crucial roles .By analyzing vast amounts of data this approach allows HR to make informed decisions. Through constant monitoring it enables us to figure out the areas for improvement. Additionally, by predicating future circumstances it allows HR to take proactive measurements. As a result it optimizes the overall organizational performance by increasing productivity and minimizing cost.

For example, an organization collecting data for a while and through employee data analysis they figured out the best performing managers, and one of the common characteristics among them is communication. Through this ability they are creating a positive environment for their team members. Later on they incorporated their findings into a training program for newly recruited employees of the organization. Later on they witness a significant positive change in their overall organizational performance.

Answer to the Question No 2

Enhancing employee experience refers to the organizational effort to provide a positive work environment which enables employees to become more engaging and committed towards their work place. However enhancing employee experience can be a complex process as it does not include only fulfilling the basic needs of employees, rather it is about their overall employment journey which includes every minor to major requirement of an employee. Factors like recognition of their contribution, opportunities to learn and grow, meaningful work, taking their opinion for making any major decision, and two way communication with upper management, plays a positive role in facilitating the employee experience. And when organizations manage to implement those factors, employees start to consider themselves as a part of the organization rather than just an employee. They become more loyal to the organization and give their best effort to assist the organization to reach their long term strategic goal.

For example an IT company always looks forward to coming up with adding something creative to their product lines. However rather than just imposing any target goal they let their employees come up with their own idea. Here organizations let their employees think out of the box rather than just giving them strict guidelines and this allows employees to think their opinion and idea matters.

Answer to the Question No 3

Yes, I agree with the statement that the HR team of Berger will play a crucial role to align the HR activities with the strategic goal of the organization. Providing my justification below-

In the given case it has been highlighted that Berger Limited is using their HR tool to recruit new employees and setting goals and objectives. And while doing those they are making sure they are recruiting the right people who have required skill sets to assist the firm to achieve their organizational goal. Similarly when they are setting goals and objectives individually they are making sure that those are aligned with the organization's goals and objectives. For instance the mission of the organization is to increase their turnover by 100 percent every 5 years. Therefore they set the goal and objective of each employee which will allow the organization to achieve that long term goal.

Answer to the Question No 4

The possible challenges an organization might face while incorporating advanced technology like SAP in the operational process can be resistance towards change and not having enough technological know-how to run the advanced software. The way they can address those issues are discussed below.

Firstly, employees might not willingly get along with the incorporation of an automated operational process. However in order to address the situation the organization might showcase in front of them, how incorporation of a technology might streamline the whole organizational process. They have to provide relevant data and logical justification which will convince the employee that incorporating the software will positively influence the organizational productivity.

Secondly, the absence of technology might bring insecurity among the employees. They might think the automated process may cause them to lose their job or they are not skilled enough to run the software. Hence, HR needs to make a positive environment which will allow the employee to think otherwise. Constant communication and providing required training will help to address such situations.

Answer to the Question No 5

I agree with the statement that "To address the fast forward changes in the external business environment, organizations must rely on evidence-based HR now more than ever"

Evidence based HR refers to the process of collecting data and analyzing those data to extract meaningful insight and turn them into reports to take informed decisions. Different HR metrics like revenue per employee, cost per hire, turnover rate can be calculated through collecting data and can give significant insight while making any major decisions. Therefore if there demographic, technological, economic change then it is highly suggested for the companies to rely on evidence based approach. Because those changes might influence the organization as well. And if they want to keep up with the changes they have to take proactive measurements by relying on these approach.

For instance, an organization which is witnessing a major demographic change in their workforce. Because most of the generation X people (age between 41-56) are retiring from their workplace. And newly recruited employees are mostly generation Y (age between 25 to 40).

Where in general the expectations of all the generation X employees from their organization was similar. They mostly look forward to job security or work life balance. But generation Y expectations are different. They want remote working facilities, flexible working hours, or newness in their job responsibility. So if the organization does not conduct environment scanning through the evidence based approach and fails to address those changes then they will face challenges in the long run to maintaining employee experience and retention rate.

Suggested Core Reading:

Books:

- Kavanagh, M.J. and Johnson, R.D. eds., 2017. Human resource information systems: Basics, applications, and future directions. Sage Publications.
- Mello, Jeffrey A. (2013-14) Strategic Human Resource Management, 3rd Edition, Cengage Learning
- Caldwell, C. and Anderson, V.A. eds., 2019. Human Resource Management: A Transformative Approach. Nova Science Publishers.

Journals/Articles:

- Hota, J., & Ghosh, D. (2013). Workforce analytics approach: An emerging trend of workforce management. AIMS International Journal, 7(3), 167-179.
- McCartney, S., & Fu, N. (2022). Promise versus reality: a systematic review of the ongoing debates in people analytics. Journal of Organizational Effectiveness: People and Performance, 9(2), 281-311.

APPENDIX: 2 INTERVIEW

Position: Assistant Manager, Culture and Employer Branding Job duration in Berger Paint Bangladesh: 4 years

Gender: Female

Question: 1 For how long Berger has been using SAP?

Answer: Berger has been using SAP for around three years.

Question: 2 The utilization of SAP Successfactor can be really diversified. Can you tell me specifically in which HR activity you are taking assistance from SAP? (e.g.: recruiting management/ compensation management/ succession planning/ manpower forecasting)

Answer: Yes SAP has different modules for these activities however currently we are using SAP for recruitment, onboarding and setting goals and objectives.

Question: 3 As you mentioned you are using SAP for recruitment processing. So there's several phases in recruiting (e.g.: job posting/CV screening/interview/negotiation) and is everything conducted through the software or are there some specific phases?

Answer: Not every phase conducts through the software however a major amount of activities in the requirement process conduct through SAP. Basically for senior level or executive posts we directly appoint someone with the assistance of headhunters but in entry level job positions the recruitment takes place in SAP. Which usually starts with setting up the competency framework. Later on all the applicants need to open an account in SAP. And through the same platform a task assigned to the selective ones. And setting the interview schedules takes place in SAP as well.

Question: 4 What kind of data are being used for goal & objective setting?

Answer: Usually SAP has its own default system. Which consists of some parameters like Financial/ Customer Satisfaction/ Internal Growth. So at the beginning of each year we set those parameters both for our organization and individual employees. Then during evaluation a self- assessment approach is being followed. Where both employees and their supervisor score them in terms of those pre decided parameters.

Question: 5 What were the most noticeable changes after the implementation? Did it actually make the HR process effective and efficient?

Answer: Yes for sure it has streamlined the whole process. For instance before implementation of SAP I have to manually prepare the interview schedule. And it was so time consuming that I could not contribute myself in any other roles. But now the situation has changed completely. Also previously the employee onboarding experience was not quite satisfactory which enhanced a lot with the assistance of SAP.

Question: 6 Is there any challenges your organization is facing due to the implementation of this software?

Answer: Yes there have been some issues we are facing however we are taking measures to address those situations. Most of our employees have been working here for around 20/25 years. Who age around 45 years or more. In contrast SAP is the newest addition to their work and to some extent they are facing difficulties to get along with it. And secondly, onboarding is the newest feature of SAP. Therefore we are facing some technical errors with the software itself.

However we are communicating with them to sort it out. SAP is still working on their onboarding's functionality.

Chapter 7
Challenges in the Motorbike Industry (TVS Auto Bangladesh Ltd): A Case Study

Rawnak Jahan
BRAC University, Bangladesh

EXECUTIVE SUMMARY

Despite the favorable market conditions, the motorcycle business in Bangladesh faces unique and difficult obstacles that must be met efficiently. These difficulties include intense rivalry, shifting customer preferences, legislative restraints, and infrastructure limitations. This case study will highlight some of the critical difficulties encountered by TVS Auto Bangladesh Ltd as well as potential solutions. By doing so, the company may increase its market presence and strengthen and achieve long-term growth in the dynamic motorcycle industry. TVS Auto Bangladesh Ltd is a subsidiary of TVS Motor, a prominent two-wheeler manufacturer in India. It operates in the motorbike sector in Bangladesh, where it faces numerous hurdles. Due to increased consumer demand, urbanization, and road infrastructure, the motorcycle industry has grown significantly in recent years. As a result, several well-known businesses, including TVS Auto Bangladesh Ltd, have entered the market to profit from the expanding potential.

INTRODUCTION

TVS Auto Bangladesh Ltd is a subsidiary of TVS Motor, a prominent two-wheeler manufacturer in India. It operates in the motorbike sector in Bangladesh, where it faces numerous hurdles. This case study will highlight some of the critical difficulties encountered by TVS Auto Bangladesh Ltd, as well as potential solutions .Due to increased consumer demand, urbanization, and advancements in road infrastructure, the motorcycle industry in Bangladesh has grown significantly in recent years. As a result, several well-known businesses, including TVS Auto Bangladesh Ltd, have entered the market in order to profit on the expanding potential.

DOI: 10.4018/979-8-3693-1781-5.ch007

Figure 1. Motorbike interest over time in Bangladesh
Source: Google Trend, 2023

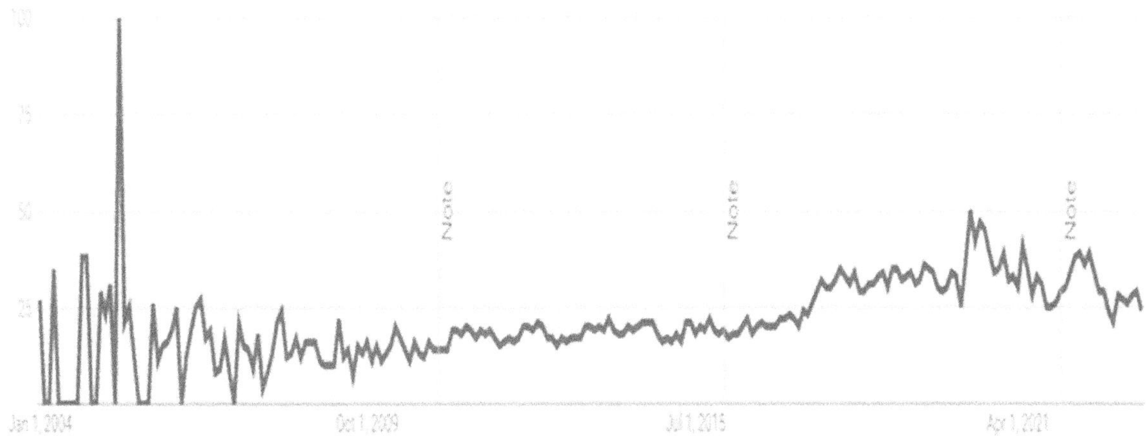

Despite the favorable market conditions, the motorcycle business in Bangladesh faces unique and difficult obstacles that must be met efficiently. These difficulties include intense rivalry, shifting customer preferences, legislative restraints, and infrastructure limitations. TVS Auto Bangladesh Ltd must develop appropriate strategies to navigate these hurdles and maintain its competitive position in the market.In this case paper, we will go over many difficulties in depth and offer feasible solutions to assist TVS Auto Bangladesh Ltd in overcoming them. By doing so, the company may increase its market presence, strengthen its brand, and achieve long-term growth in the dynamic motorcycle industry.

BACKGROUND OF TVS AUTO BANGLADESH LIMITED

TVS Auto Bangladesh Limited first established itself in 2007, In Bangladesh . The company rose to the second-highest seller of two-wheelers in Bangladesh within seven years of starting operations. A joint venture between T V SundramIyenger& Sons Ltd. (an Indian firm) and Rian Motors Ltd. (a Bangladeshi corporation) is TVS Auto Bangladesh Limited. Customer satisfaction is the company's main priority, and they have developed their brand around it. In Tongi, Gazipur, TVS Auto Bangladesh Ltd. has a motorbike production and assembly facility. The constant source of inspiration for TVS is the consumer and his shifting wants. It includes 210+ dealers around the nation, a 3S facility, 10 in-house service centers, 850 Certified Service Points (CSP), and a 120-part stockpile. TVS Motor Company, the third-largest two-wheeler manufacturer in India and one of the top ten worldwide, recorded sales of Rs. 1434.3 crore in the first quarter of 2020–21 as opposed to a total revenue of Rs. 4469.8 crore in the quarter ended June 2019. The key to TVS Motor's success is its considerable research and development, which produces products that lead the industry in terms of innovation. By anticipating customer needs and offering high-quality automobiles at the ideal time and price, we at TVS achieve ultimate customer satisfaction.The plant has a total size of approximately 2,23500 square feet.The monthly production capacity is roughly

Figure 2. Interest by sub-regions
Source: Google Trend, 2023

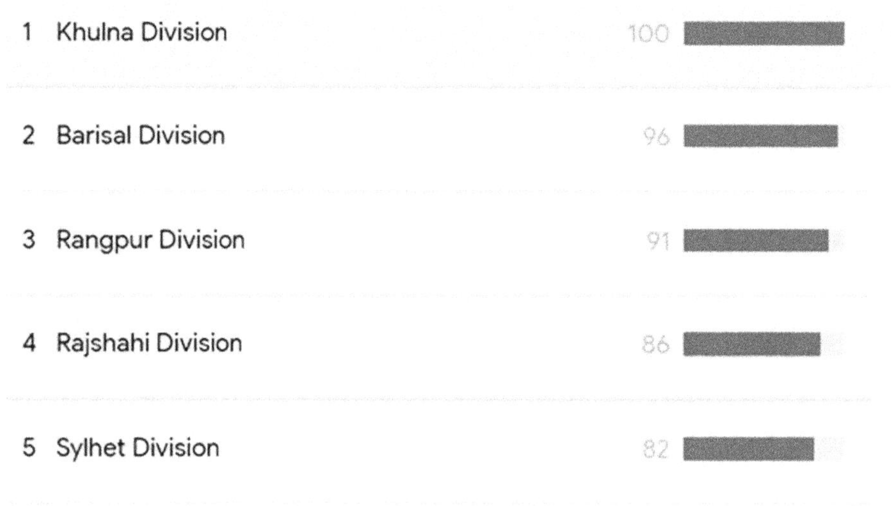

18,000 units.About 11 nodes make up the company's showroom, while 13 nodes make up its service center. Furthermore, TVS products only give you reasons to smile!

RECENT CHALLENGES IN THE MOTORCYCLE INDUSTRY IN BANGLADESH

The motorbike sector in Bangladesh has faced significant challenges as a result of government regulations, a VAT-tax hike, new laws, and traffic rules. This research intends to analyze and explore the effects of these difficulties, as well as potential solutions. Govt. rules, policies and tax rate are the main threats now a day.

Bike Tax Token In Bangladesh By CC:

- 50-100cc bike Tax is BDT 5000-5,750 for 10 years.
- 101-150cc bike Tax is BDT 5750-11,500 for 10 years.
- Over 150cc bike Tax in BDT 12,000 plus.

Bike Import Tax By CC:

- Up to 100cc: 45% tax
- 101cc to 150cc: 61% tax
- 151cc to 200cc: 100-150% tax
- 201cc to 250cc: 200% tax
- Above 250cc: 250% tax
    - **New Regulations:** New regulations from the government, including as mandated helmet wear, licensing requirements, and safety standards, have produced both opportunities and

Table 1.

Traffic rules and fine 2018	Traffic rules and fine 2023
139 – Using hydrolic horn – 100 Tk.	3-month jail or Tk 10,000 fine using horn violating rules .
140 – Disobeying red signal – 500 Tk. (Same as special fine) .	1-month jail or Tk 10,000 fine for traffic signal violation .
155 – Driving without insurance or licence – 750 Tk.	6-month jail or Tk 25,000 fine for driving without insurance or licence .
149 – Driving without safety – 300 Tk.	3-month jail or Tk 10,000 fine for riding motorcycle without helmet .

challenges for the motorcycle industry. These laws have resulted in higher costs for manufacturers and customers, as well as logistical difficulties for distributors and retailers.

- **Traffic Rules:** The government's efforts to improve traffic management have resulted in increasing fines and punishments for traffic offenses, but the absence of strict enforcement and knowledge among motorcycle riders has hampered the effectiveness of these measures. To solve this, a complete approach is required, including stronger enforcement, public awareness efforts, and improved driver training programs.

REASONS FOR INCREASING DEMAND OF MOTORBIKE IN BANGLADESH

- **Affordability**: Motorbikes are generally more affordable compared to cars, making them a popular choice among a large segment of the population with limited financial resources. TVS Auto Company faces the challenge of meeting the diverse price points and affordability expectations of different customer segments.
- **Urbanization and Congestion:** Rapid urbanization and increasing traffic congestion have made motorbikes a convenient and time-efficient mode of transportation, particularly in crowded urban areas.TVS Auto Company needs to address the challenge of designing and marketing motorbikes that are suitable for navigating congested roads and meeting the specific needs of urban commuters.
- **Employment Opportunities:** The growth of e-commerce and delivery services has created a demand for motorbikes as a means of efficient and timely product delivery. This increased demand presents an opportunity for TVS Auto Company to cater to the needs of delivery service providers and optimize their motorbike models for such purposes.
- **Lifestyle Aspirations:** Motorbikes are often associated with a sense of freedom, independence, and an adventurous lifestyle, particularly among the younger generation. TVS Auto Company needs to position its motorbike models to align with the lifestyle aspirations and preferences of this target demographic.
  I. Challenges for TVS Auto Company While the growing demand for motorbikes in Bangladesh presents opportunities, it also brings several challenges for TVS Auto Company. This section discusses the key challenges the company faces in meeting the increasing demand.
  II. Challenge: Production Capacity and Supply Chain Management Meeting the rising demand for motorbikes requires robust production capacity and an efficient supply chain management system. TVS Auto Company faces the challenge of scaling up production, ensuring a stable

Figure 3. Synopsis of last 12 months
Source: Google Trend, 2023

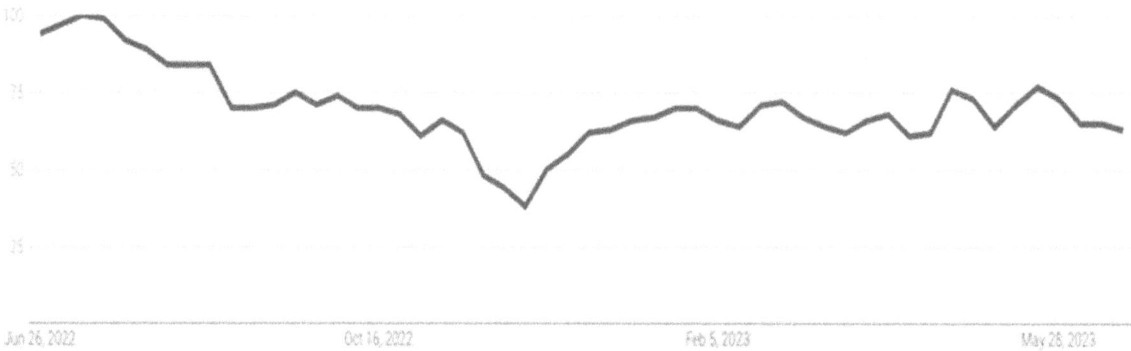

supply of raw materials, and optimizing its distribution network to meet the demand across the country.

III. Challenge: Regulatory Compliance and Market Regulations The motorbike industry in Bangladesh operates within a regulatory framework that includes safety standards, emission norms, and import/export regulations. TVS Auto Company must navigate these regulations effectively to ensure compliance, obtain necessary certifications, and manage any potential barriers to market entry.

IV. Challenge: Competition and Market Share As the demand for motorbikes grows, so does the level of competition in the market. TVS Auto Company faces the challenge of maintaining and expanding its market share in the face of intense competition from both local and inter-

Figure 4. Countries with highest bike popularity (Source: Google Trend, 2023)

Figure 5. Factors contribute to the increasing demand for scooters

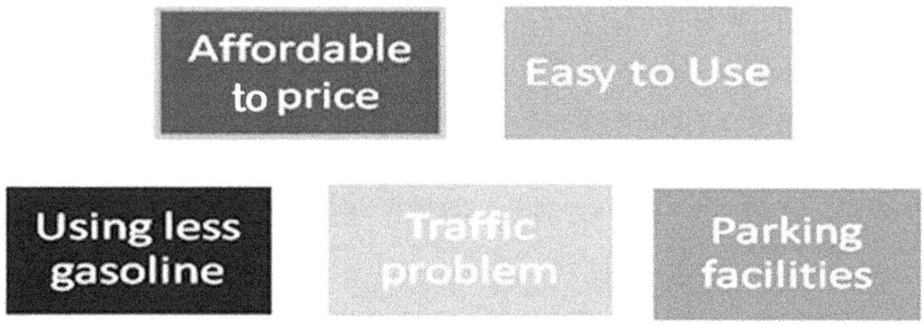

national motorbike brands.This necessitates continuous product innovation, differentiation, and effective marketing strategies.

V. Challenge: Customer Preferences and Changing Trends Understanding customer preferences and staying attuned to changing market trends is crucial for sustaining success in the long run.

GROWING DEMAND OF SCOOTEY

For our case study on this topic we took interview of two scooty users:

Scenario 1

Asuk is a 35-year-old man. He is working for a private company. His office is in Motijheel, but he lives in Narayanganj. He can easily travel because he has his own scooter. He says having a scooter has made his life easier and more affordable.

Scenario 2

Bina is a university student. She needs to go from Wari to Bashundhara every day for his university classes. She was having a lot of trouble taking the bus anymore. Buses didn't always have seats available. Additionally, the journey took a long time as the bus stopped at every station. Moreover, She was always late for class. And it would have been tough to endure a long time in the bus while the weather was hot outside. She purchased a scooter a few weeks ago. Now she can get around fast and simply by riding a scooter, which makes it possible for her to get to the university swiftly. She is no longer facing the same difficulties as before.

So, the growing demand for scooters, particularly among women, signifies a changing trend in modern cities. Scooters provide independence, convenience, affordability, and environmental benefits. They offer women a reliable and autonomous mode of transportation, reducing their reliance on public transport. The lightweight nature and simplicity of operation make scooters popular among boys, while their practicality and cost efficiency attract a broader consumer base. With the increasing costs of living and the need for sustainable transportation solutions, scooters present an appealing option for everyday commuting. As the demand for scooters continues to rise, manufacturers and policy makers should address the specific requirements of this market segment to further enhance the scooter industry's growth and contribution to urban mobility.

MANAGERIAL IMPLICATIONS

To increase sales in the motorbike business in Bangladesh, managers should concentrate on the following managerial implications:

1. Strategic planning and market positioning:
   - Carry out thorough market research to understand consumer demands, trends and preferences.
   - Formulate a clean and clear tactical plan that aligns with market opportunities and competitive dynamics.
   - Determine target market segments and adapt marketing efforts accordingly.
   - Position the products and brand effectively and efficiently to variate from competitors.
   - Constantly monitor the market and adapt strategies accordingly to stay competitive.
2. Product diversification and innovation:
   - Periodically measure market demands and offer new variants of products to cater to various consumer needs and wants.
   - Spend in advancement and research to boost product performance, features and design.
   - Keep up with technological advancements and offer innovative technologies and features in motorbikes.
   - Provide customization options to appeal to individual consumer preferences.
   - Periodically update and upgrade existing product lines to stay relevant in the market.
3. Construct strong consumer relationships:
   - Prioritize splendid consumer service and support to build strong and long-lasting relationships.
   - Train and empower sales and service teams to supply personalized attention and support to customers.
   - Set up reward schemes and loyalty programs to incentivize referrals and repeat purchases.
   - Strongly engage with customers through online forums, events or through social media.
   - Take feedback from customers and implement it to develop products and services.
4. Spending in infrastructure advancement:
   - boost distribution networks and broaden dealership coverage in various regions of Bangladesh.
   - Improve after-sales service infrastructure to provide efficient and repair and maintenance services.
   - Invest in training and advancement programs for dealerships and service centers to assure standard and quality service.
   - Collaborate with various financial institutions to enable easy financing options for customers.
   - Develop a robust supply chain management system to assure timely delivery of motorbikes and spare parts across Bangladesh.
5. Collaboration and creating partnership with business and government stakeholders:
   - Involve in dialogue with government authorities to address regulatory challenges and encourage a favorable business environment.

- ◦ Collaborate with business associations to urge for policies that support the growth of the motorbike business.
- ◦ Work closely with suppliers and manufacturers to ensure the availability of high-quality parts and components at competitive prices.
- ◦ set up partnerships with other business shareholders, such as fuel suppliers and insurance companies to offer bundled services to consumers.
- ◦ Take part in business events and exhibitions to showcase products and build relationships with potential partners and consumers.

By applying these managerial implications, managers in the motorbike business in Bangladesh can boost sales, increase market share, and build a sustainable and strong business.

LITERATURE REVIEW

(1) Hossain, S. F. A., Shan, X., Musa, M., & Rahman, P. (2023). Social media and increased venture creation tendency with innovative ideas: the case of female students in Asia. In Research Anthology on Applying Social Networking Strategies to Classrooms and Libraries (pp. 1716-1731). IGI Global. The author's book chapter focuses on the complex relationship between social media and entrepreneurship creation. Social media is crucial to business and innovation in the current digital era. Social media is an effective tool that allows us to build various chances and connect with people on an individual basis anywhere in the world. Social media is a significant international platform which gives businesses access to a worldwide audience, reduces marketing expenses, builds brand recognition, increases consumer interaction, and speeds up product development and innovation. Because of its large worldwide readership, it gives companies access to a variety of demographics and unexplored development prospects. In addition to facilitating direct consumer connection and problem-solving, social media also promotes transparency and trust. It facilitates informed decision-making and accelerates innovation by helping to test new ideas and obtain market information. Besides, social media presents a number of challenges for launching new businesses, such as time commitment, handling unfavorable reviews, information overload, privacy issues, and ongoing change. For businesses with little funding, managing community management, analytics, and content production may be challenging. Sustaining a favorable brand image and responding to criticism are essential for long-term success. It's also crucial to comprehend your target viewers, provide interesting content, and put strong data security procedures in place. Sustaining engagement and enhancing social media strategies need constant change. People respond to change and effective business growth in this modern day.In the venture development process, social media may be utilized to produce interactive content, collaborate with micro- and influencers, conduct targeted advertising campaigns, hold competitions and giveaways, and provide customer support. These tactics have the potential to increase involvement, get insightful information, and forge closer ties within the community. Adapting plans and enhancing overall efficacy may be achieved by regular monitoring of social media performance and its integration with other marketing channels. Businesses can boost their reach and effectiveness by using analytics, connecting social media with additional advertising campaigns, and offering individualized customer care. (Syed Far Abid Hossain X. S., Social Media and Increased Venture Creation Tendency With Innovative Ideas:The Case of Female Students in Asia)

(2) Aboulilah, H. M. A. E., Hossain, S. F. A., Vuong, B. N., & Jebril, T. (2022). Exploring the Relationship between WeChat Usage and E-purchase Intention During the COVID-19 Pandemic Among University Students in China. Sage Open, 12(4), 21582440221139447. Most of the students were affected by the COVID-19 pandemic, which caused worldwide educational institute closures. Students at universities in China mainly depended on WeChat for their e-commerce needs, even when everything returned to regular. This study investigates consumers' motivations for choosing WeChat, their future plans, and the relationship between their e-shopping habits and the platform. During the COVID-19 outbreak, university students found WeChat, a well-known e-commerce site, to be an invaluable resource. It became the preferred means of payment, communication, and online shopping, with 1.0825 billion active users. Due to its distinctive blend of safe payment methods and social networking, it created a network of vendors that helped people communicate and make part-time money. WeChat's flexibility and reactivity cemented its advantages, even in the face of early shortages in conventional marketplaces. Because of its strength in the market, WeChat may have fewer opportunities for in-person product engagement during the pandemic. Additionally, customers may be dissatisfied with the delivery of their orders and may not have as many options to choose from. As users exchange personal data and conduct financial transactions, privacy and security concerns surface, calling into question the necessity of using a variety of channels. It is possible to enhance the online purchasing experience by investing in privacy and security technology, expanding the variety of e-commerce platforms, and educating consumers on safe online conduct. Collaboration between companies and social media sites like WeChat can help improve crisis management. Trust is a key factor in mitigating the association between market volatility and e-purchasing. A balanced strategy is necessary to improve the e-shopping experience and preserve customer trust in times of crisis, despite the restricted product diversity and privacy issues. This study offers insightful information for managers making decisions (Haitham Medhat Abdelaziz Elsayed Aboulilah, 2022).

(3) Hossain, S. F. A., Shan, X., Nurunnabi, M., Tushar, H., Mohsin, A. K. M., & Ahsan, F. T. (2021). Opportunities and challenges of m-learning during the COVID-19 pandemic: A mixed methodology approach. E-Collaboration Technologies and Strategies for Competitive Advantage Amid Challenging Times, 210-227. This research focuses at the advantages and disadvantages of mobile learning (m-learning) in the context of the COVID-19 pandemic. It indicates a growing propensity to employ mobile devices and smart technologies and apps for online learning. The study used a hybrid technique that combines focus group interviews and surveys with academic staff and students at universities. University students have many chances and emphasize the sustainability of education because to m-learning technology, despite some limitations. With benefits like e-learning and artificial intelligence, m-learning is becoming more and more common in the UK, the Far East, and the USA. Nonetheless, there is a lack of knowledge on the difficulties pupils encounter and obtaining advanced possibilities under dire circumstances. In order to assist education throughout the pandemic, governments and education ministries have deployed software and apps. Additionally, a TV school program has been introduced to enhance students' comprehension of class contents (Syed Far Abid Hossain X. S., 2021).

(4) Emmanuel, C. P., Qin, S., Hossain, S. F. A., & Hussain, K. (2022). Factors influencing social-media-based entrepreneurship prospect among female students in China. Heliyon, 8(12). The research focuses at the possibility of social media platforms for entrepreneurship among young female students in developing countries, especially China. The association between variables and entrepreneurial impulses is examined using the Technology Acceptance Model (TAM). According to the research, there are more chances for entrepreneurship when social media is user-friendly, practical, and enjoyable. Due to its limited sample size and simplistic model, social media entrepreneurship among young women in

developing nations creates challenges for platform developers and business owners. Important information on the potential of social media to assist young female students in impoverished nations in starting their own enterprises. In the future, research might compare user behaviors on other platforms, enhance the technology acceptance model (TAM) model, and enlarge the sample size in order to have a better knowledge of platform-specific opportunities and issues (Factors influencing social-media-based entrepreneurship prospect among female students in China, 2022).

(5) Hossain, S. F. A., Nurunnabi, M., Hussain, K., & Shan, X. (2020). Smartphone-based m-shopping behavior and innovative entrepreneurial tendency among women in emerging Asia. International Journal of Gender and Entrepreneurship, 12(2), 173-189. The research investigates the relationship between women's entrepreneurial impulses and smartphone-based m-shopping in rising Asian countries, emphasizing the possibility for low-barrier entrance and economic empowerment. Social media and m-commerce sites give women more options, less risk and investment, flexibility, and a better work-life balance. By meeting a wide range of client demands, they enable women to run their enterprises in addition to other duties, make use of their current abilities, and foster creativity. For women, this dynamic aspect of internet marketplaces is beneficial. Women's engagement in e-commerce has obstacles due to social and cultural hurdles, competitive online markets, restricted access, and the gap in digital literacy, particularly in rural regions. Marketing plans, financial stability, and entrepreneurial abilities are necessary for internet enterprises to succeed. By giving women in marginalized communities access to inexpensive internet, training in digital literacy, and infrastructure, government programs and private sector collaborations can help close the digital gap. Online networks and the advancement of gender equality can inspire more women to pursue entrepreneurship, while training programs and mentorship can provide women with the tools they need to succeed as business owners. Emerging Asia's smartphone-based m-commerce presents a promising avenue for women's economic emancipation, but it also calls for focused government, corporate, and community initiatives (Syed Far Abid Hossain M. N., 2020).

(6) Vuong, B. N., Tushar, H., & Hossain, S. F. A. (2023). The effect of social support on job performance through organizational commitment and innovative work behavior: does innovative climate matter?. Asia-Pacific Journal of Business Administration, 15(5), 832-854. This research focuses on how social support affects job performance in Vietnamese small and medium-sized enterprises (SMEs), emphasizing the role that creative work practices and organizational dedication have as mediating variables. Through the connection between organizational culture (OC) and innovation (IWB), the research demonstrates a favorable association between social support (SS) and job satisfaction (JP). It emphasizes how crucial an inventive environment is to fortifying this connection. Nevertheless, some of its drawbacks are cross-sectional data, limited generalizability, and inadequate investigation of underlying processes. In order to get deeper insights, future studies should employ qualitative research methodologies, broaden to include new social support elements, employ experimental or longitudinal designs, and spread to different sectors and situations. Through understanding the link between social support, organizational commitment, creative work behavior, and job performance in Vietnamese SMEs, the research helps organizations foster conditions that encourage better performance (AKM Mohsin L. H., 2021).

(7) Mohsin, A. K. M., Hongzhen, L., & Hossain, S. F. A. (2021). Impact of COVID-19 pandemic on consumer economy: Countermeasures analysis. Sage Open, 11(2), 21582440211008875. This article discusses the COVID-19 pandemic's effects on China's consumer economy by drawing comparisons with the SARS epidemic of 2003. Examining both immediate and long-term impacts, it looks at shifts in supply, demand, the regulatory landscape, and possible responses. In comparing the current state of affairs with the SARS pandemic, the paper offers a thorough examination of the macroeconomic land-

scape. Along with highlighting novel business models, it delineates three mechanisms of effect on the retail industry. Its drawbacks include the fact that it is based on SARS epidemic history data and offers no concrete justifications or empirical support for "compensatory consumption" as a potential mitigating factor. The impact of the COVID-19 epidemic on China's consumer economy is analyzed. More empirical data and a more thorough examination of consumer behavior and policy dynamics, however, would be beneficial. Additionally, the investigation may shed light on China's response to public health emergencies, particularly those involving the retail industry. The results might help design more robust and adaptable economic strategies as well as guide strategic decision-making. To confirm projections and investigate the effects of the pandemic on certain businesses, more study is required (AKM Mohsin, 2021).

(8) Hossain, S. F. A., Xi, Z., Nurunnabi, M., & Hussain, K. (2020). Ubiquitous role of social networking in driving M-Commerce: evaluating the use of mobile phones for online shopping and payment in the context of trust. Sage Open, 10(3), 2158244020939536. This study analyzes the connection between social media and mobile commerce, concentrating on the ways in which mobile applications affect consumer payment choices and levels of trust. It seeks to comprehend how mobile applications affect customer behavior and how social media interacts with m-commerce platforms. Online shopping companies may benefit greatly from social media's expanded reach, stronger brand development, better consumer interaction, easy m-commerce platform integration, and influencer marketing. These platforms provide businesses with a way to interact with consumers in real time, develop connections, and connect with a wide range of audiences. But there are drawbacks as well, such as worries about security, the need for internet access, short attention spans, information overload, and the problem of creating a distinctive corporate identity. In order to overcome these obstacles, companies must put strong security measures in place, think about accessibility and coverage for mobile networks, draw users in with interesting content, and handle the competitive environment on social media platforms. In order to improve their tactics and increase return on investment, businesses must also use analytics tools and metrics to evaluate the success of their social media marketing initiatives. Ultimately, even if social media has many advantages, businesses must carefully take these considerations into account when putting their ideas into practice. Boost social media presence with interesting content, work with relevant influencers, and give cybersecurity and data protection a priority if you want to improve M-Commerce through social media (Syed Far Abid Hossain Z. X., 2020).

(9) Hossain, S. F. A. (2019). Social networking and its role in media entrepreneurship: Evaluating the use of mobile phones in the context of online shopping–A review. Journal of Media Management and Entrepreneurship (JMME), 1(1), 73-86. This research focuses on the increasing impact of social media and mobile devices on media entrepreneurship, specifically concentrating on the younger generation's use of mobile phones for online shopping and entrepreneurial aspirations. Due to their daily active users, ability to foster digital entrepreneurship among younger, opportunity-driven generations, and role in the fast rise of social media, mobile devices are essential for entrepreneurship. With 2.53 billion users as of 2018, smartphones provide a variety of features, such as banking, online shopping, and internet access. The investigation of the trajectory of mobile devices towards media entrepreneurship is restricted, and media entrepreneurship remains immature and inadequately studied. One example of how businesses may use these platforms to their advantage is Facebook's success. Future research should examine how mobile devices—such as tablets, iPads, and notebooks—affect media entrepreneurship. Including a variety of sources, such as newspapers, conferences, and books, can add to the study's depth. The conceptual framework for media entrepreneurship spurred by mobile device usage may be validated by a meta-analysis or empirical investigation. The discussion portion must include information about

social media, how mobile phones are used for online shopping, and the variables that influence social networking and online purchasing (Syed Far Abid Hossain S. o., 2019).

(10) Hossain, S. F. A., Nurunnabi, M., Hussain, K., & Saha, S. K. (2019). Effects of variety-seeking intention by mobile phone usage on university students' academic performance. Cogent Education, 6(1), 1574692. This research focuses into how university students' academic performance is affected by using mobile phones, particularly because of the rising use of social networking sites. A relationship that is positive between the use of mobile devices and academic achievement, indicating that students who actively seek out new knowledge may do better. On the other hand, an addiction to mobile use can cause worry and anxiety, which makes it difficult to concentrate in class. This connection can be moderated by variety-seeking intention, enabling students who have a strong propensity for variety-seeking intention to experiment with different applications. Students that find their phones beneficial for studying and academic work are more likely to explore new applications, which is another factor contributing to their purpose to seek diversity. The impact of variety-seeking intention on academic performance in university students. It suggests that understanding this relationship can help create more engaging learning environments, improve app developers' designs, and help students manage their mobile usage more effectively. However, the study's limitations include its focus on mobile phone usage, its limited scope, and its limited understanding of psychological factors. Future research should explore variety-seeking intention, mobile phone usage, and academic performance across different educational contexts and age groups (Syed Far Abid Hossain M. N., 2019).

REFERENCES

Evans, J., O'Brien, J., & Ch Ng, B. (2018). Towards a geography of informal transport: Mobility, infrastructure and urban sustainability from the back of a motorbike. *Transactions of the Institute of British Geographers*, *43*(4), 674–688. doi:10.1111/tran.12239

Google Trend. (2023). *Google trends*. https://trends.google.com/trends/explore?geo=BD&q=uber&hl=en

Haitham Medhat Abdelaziz Elsayed Aboulilah, S. F. (2022). *Exploring the Relationship between WeChat Usage and E-purchase Intention During the COVID-19 Pandemic Among University Students in China*. doi:10.1177/21582440221139447

Hansen, A. (2016). Driving development? The problems and promises of the car in Vietnam. *Journal of Contemporary Asia*, *46*(4), 551–569. doi:10.1080/00472336.2016.1151916

Hossain, S. F. A. M. N. (2019). Effects of variety-seeking intention by mobile phone usage on university students' academic performance. In Cogent Education (Vol. 6, pp. 1-18). Academic Press.

Hossain, S. F. A. X. S. (n.d.). Social Media and Increased Venture Creation Tendency With Innovative Ideas:The Case of Female Students in Asia. In Research Anthology on Applying Social Networking Strategies to Classrooms and Libraries (p. 16). doi:10.4018/978-1-6684-7123-4.ch093

Hossain, S. F. A., Nurunnabi, M., Hussain, K., & Shan, X.SFA. (2020, April 27). M. N. (2020). Smartphone-based m-shopping behavior and innovative entrepreneurial tendency among women in emerging. *International Journal of Gender and Entrepreneurship*, *12*(2), 173–189. Advance online publication. doi:10.1108/IJGE-03-2019-0054

Mohsin, A. K. M. (2021). L. H. In *Impact of COVID-19 Pandemic on Consumer Economy*. Countermeasures Analysis., doi:10.1177/21582440211008875

Mohsin, A. K. M. L. H. (2021). In Impact of COVID-19 Pandemic on Consumer Economy: Countermeasures Analysis. doi:10.1177/21582440211008875

Paulraj, M. P., Majid, M. S. A., Yaacob, S., & Zin, M. Z. M. (2008, December). Motorbike engine faults diagnosing system using neural network. In *2008 International Conference on Electronic Design* (pp. 1-6). IEEE. 10.1109/ICED.2008.4786641

SFA. (2019). Social Networking and Its Role. Journal of Media Management and Entrepreneurship (pp. 73-86). doi:10.4018/JMME.2019010105

SFA. (2020). Z *Ubiquitous Role of Social Networking in Driving M-Commerce*. Evaluating the Use of Mobile Phones for Online Shopping and Payment in the Context of Trust. doi:10.1177/2158244020939536

SFA, X. S. (n.d.). *Opportunities and Challenges of M-Learning During the COVID-19 Pandemic: A Mixed Methodology Approach*. doi:10.4018/978-1-7998-7764-6.ch007

SFA, X. S. (n.d.). *Social Media and Increased Venture Creation Tendency With Innovative Ideas: The Case of Female Students in Asia*. Academic Press.

ADDITIONAL READING

Jain, A. K., & Sullivan, S. (2020). An examination of the relationship between careerism and organizational commitment, satisfaction, and performance. *Personnel Review*, *49*(8), 1553–1571. doi:10.1108/PR-05-2019-0280

Kameswari, M. L., Kumari, A. S., & Reddy, D. R. (2005). Consumer Buying Behaviour in Two-wheeler Industry-with Special Reference to Hero Honda Motorbikes. *Indian. Journal of Marketing*, *35*(10).

Kumar, A., Singh, K., Singh, K., & Jashwara, S. (2023). Quality Enhancement of Motorbike Manufacturing Plant Using Six Sigma DMAIC Methodology. In *Emerging Trends in Mechanical and Industrial Engineering: Select Proceedings of ICETMIE 2022* (pp. 749-758). Singapore: Springer Nature Singapore. 10.1007/978-981-19-6945-4_56

APPENDIX

Teaching Notes

Synopsis

TVS Auto Bangladesh Ltd is a subsidiary of TVS Motor, a prominent two-wheeler manufacturer in India. It operates in the motorbike sector in Bangladesh, where it faces numerous hurdles. This case study will highlight some of the critical difficulties encountered by TVS Auto Bangladesh Ltd, as well as potential solutions. Due to increased consumer demand, urbanization, and advancements in road infrastructure, the motorcycle industry in Bangladesh has grown significantly in recent years. As a result, several well-known businesses, including TVS Auto Bangladesh Ltd, have entered the market in order to profit on the expanding potential. Despite the favorable market conditions, the motorcycle business in Bangladesh faces unique and difficult obstacles that must be met efficiently. These difficulties include intense rivalry, shifting customer preferences, legislative restraints, and infrastructure limitations. TVS Auto Bangladesh Ltd must develop appropriate strategies to navigate these hurdles and maintain its competitive position in the market. In this case paper, we will go over many difficulties in depth and offer feasible solutions to assist TVS Auto Bangladesh Ltd in overcoming them. By doing so, the company may increase its market presence, strengthen its brand, and achieve long-term growth in the dynamic motorcycle industry. TVS Auto Bangladesh Limited first established itself in 2007, In Bangladesh . The company rose to the second-highest seller of two-wheelers in Bangladesh within seven years of starting operations. A joint venture between T V SundramIyenger& Sons Ltd. (an Indian firm) and Rian Motors Ltd. (a Bangladeshi corporation) is TVS Auto Bangladesh Limited. Customer satisfaction is the company's main priority, and they have developed their brand around it. In Tongi, Gazipur, TVS Auto Bangladesh Ltd. has a motorbike production and assembly facility. The constant source of inspiration for TVS is the consumer and his shifting wants. It includes 210+ dealers around the nation, a 3S facility, 10 in-house service centers, 850 Certified Service Points (CSP), and a 120-part stockpile. TVS Motor Company, the third-largest two-wheeler manufacturer in India and one of the top ten worldwide, recorded sales of Rs. 1434.3 crore in the first quarter of 2020–21 as opposed to a total revenue of Rs. 4469.8 crore in the quarter ended June 2019. The key to TVS Motor's success is its considerable research and development, which produces products that lead the industry in terms of innovation. By anticipating customer needs and offering high-quality automobiles at the ideal time and price, we at TVS achieve ultimate customer satisfaction. The plant has a total size of approximately 2,23500 square feet. The monthly production capacity is roughly 18,000 units. About 11 nodes make up the company's showroom, while 13 nodes make up its service center.

Methods

The case utilized secondary data at the beginning followed by some person administered interview over the phone. So, it used mixed methodology approach.

Key discussion points in the class:

1. The recent challenges faced by motorbike industry in Bangladesh
2. The future issues and opportunities

Table 2. An Imaginary Class Design

Topic: Case study on TVS, Bangladesh		**Duration: 80 minutes**
Learning Objectives: End of the session students will be able to: i. Use suitable case study solution about TVS, Bangladesh ii. Know the TVS, Bangladeshcase study in depth		**Number of students: 30–40**
Learning Activity (LA)		**Activity type**
Part 1 (25 + 5 minutes)	LA1. Download sample case study from renowned source Q1. What is case study? Q2. Why should you learn and use case study?	Lecture Group work consists of 6 students in each group
	LA2. Introduction referencing style – APA 6 or any	Independent, referred and practical learning

Study Topic: Learning case solution procedure – step by step		**Duration: 1 hour**
Part 2 (15 +15 minutes)	**LA3. Download 4-5 cases Q1. Know about the key points Q2. Introduce a solution Q3. Brainstorming - TVS, Bangladesh**	**Collective work: Group activity consists of 6 members in each group**
	LA4. Study in groups of 6 people to analyze the cases 1. Group 1: Discuss the objectives of the cases 2. Group 2: Discuss the background 3. Group 3: Analyze the key information 4. Group 4: Identify possible solution	**Collective work: Group activity consists of 6 members in each group**
Part 3 (15 minutes)	LA5. Compile all the tasks from each group 1. A group member from every group will make a presentation for 2 minutes 2. Clarification for other group members if they are not clear about the presentation.	Collective work: Group activity consists of 6 members in each group
Part 4 (10 minutes)	LA6. Exercise time - TVS, Bangladesh	Independent ability to assess the students
	LA7. Complete the exercise and provide feedback	
Post class (5 minutes)	Students' feedback on TVS, Bangladesh Need for a review class on TVS, Bangladesh Miscellaneous - TVS, Bangladesh	Intuitive activity

3. The traffic problem and the bikers
4. Sustainable transportation
5. Alternative solution
6. Road safety and bikers safety issues.

Assignments Questions

From the above case study, could you please answer the following questions?

1. What are the key success factors of bike industry in Bangladesh?
2. How to ensure the bike service effectively or successfully?
3. Is bike industry under threat in Bangladesh?
4. What are the challenges of TVS?
5. Do a competitive analysis of TVS.

Figure 6.

TVS MOTOR COMPANY LIMITED

BUSINESS RESPONSIBILITY AND SUSTAINABILITY REPORT FOR FY 2022-23

SECTION A: GENERAL DISCLOSURES

I. DETAILS

1	Corporate Identity Number (CIN) of the Listed Entity	L35921TN1992PLC022845	
2	Name of the Listed Entity	TVS Motor Company Limited	
3	Year of incorporation	10-06-1992	
4	Registered office address	"Chaitanya", No.12, Khader Nawaz Khan Road, Nungambakkam, Chennai - 600 006	
5	Corporate address	"Chaitanya", No.12, Khader Nawaz Khan Road, Nungambakkam, Chennai - 600 006	
6	E-mail	contactus@tvsmotor.com	
7	Telephone	044-28332115	
8	Website	www.tvsmotor.com	
9	Date of start of Financial Year	**Start Date**	**End Date**
	Financial Year	01-04-2022	31-03-2023
10	Name of the Stock Exchange(s) where shares are listed	BSE Limited, Mumbai and National Stock Exchange of India Limited, Mumbai	
11	Paid-up Capital	₹ 47,50,87,114	
12	Name and contact details (telephone, email address) of the person who may be contacted in case of any queries on the BRSR report		
	Name of Contact Person	K S Srinivasan	
	Contact Number of Contact Person	+91 44 2833 2115	
	Email of Contact Person	srinivasan.ks@tvsmotor.com	

Figure 7.

II. PRODUCTS / SERVICES

14. Details of business activities

S. No.	Description of main activity	Description of business activity	% of turnover
1	Manufacturing	Motor vehicles, trailers, semi trailers and other Transport Vehicles	100

15. Products / Services sold by the entity (accounting for 90% of the entity's Turnover):

S. No.	Product / Service	NIC Code	% of total Turnover contributed
1	Motorcycle, Scooters, Mopeds	30911	81
2	Three-wheelers	30912	8
3	Parts & Accessories	30913	10

III. OPERATIONS

16. Number of locations where plants and / or operations / offices of the entity are situated:

Location	Number of plants	Number of offices	Total
National	3	30	33
International	-	2	2

17. Markets served by the entity:

a. Number of locations

Location	Number
National(No. of States)	28
International(No. of Countries)	80

Figure 8.
Source: TVS official website, 2023

IV. EMPLOYEES

18. Details as at the end of Financial Year:

a. Employees and workers (including differently abled):

S. No	Particulars	Total (A)	Male		Female		Others	
			No. (B)	% (B/A)	No. (C)	% (C/A)	No. (H)	% (H/A)
EMPLOYEES								
1.	Permanent (D)	3,559	3,134	88.06	425	11.94	-	-
2.	Other than Permanent (E)	214	187	87.38	27	12.62	-	-
3.	Total employees (D + E)	3,773	3,321	88.02	452	11.98	-	-
WORKERS								
4.	Permanent (F)	1,900	1,899	99.95	1	0.05	-	-
5.	Other than Permanent (G)	7,234	6,603	91.28	631	8.72	-	-
6.	Total workers (F + G)	9,134	8,502	93.08	632	6.92	-	-

b. Differently abled Employees and workers:

S. No	Particulars	Total (A)	Male		Female		Others	
			No. (B)	% (B/A)	No. (C)	% (C/A)	No. (H)	% (H/A)
DIFFERENTLY ABLED EMPLOYEES								
1.	Permanent (D)	13	10	76.92	3	23.08	-	-
2.	Other than Permanent (E)	-	-	-	-	-	-	-
3.	Total differently abled employees (D + E)	13	10	76.92	3	23.08	-	-
DIFFERENTLY ABLED WORKERS								
4.	Permanent (F)	13	13	100.00	-	-	-	-
5.	Other than Permanent (G)	144	118	81.94	26	18.06	-	-
6.	Total differently abled workers (F + G)	157	131	83.44	26	16.56	-	-

Chapter 8
Waffle-Up:
From Overcoming Challenges to Being the Trendsetter in the Street Food Business of Bangladesh

Tahsin Raysha Mallik
https://orcid.org/0009-0002-3696-3928
BRAC University, Bangladesh

Zeun Tafsir Nova
BRAC University, Bangladesh

EXECUTIVE SUMMARY

The hotel and hospitality industry is a type of industry that has a lot of potential if the business model is unique. Otherwise, it is a very competitive industry to operate in. Based on the changing market trends, businesses adapt and evolve over time. New businesses launch religiously, which makes the industry and market very competitive. It is an identified challenge for entrepreneurs or leaders who belong to this industry. This case is based on a similar business that belongs to this sector, which despite being a newcomer to the industry, became a trendsetter. Waffle Up has adapted similar strategies like proactive innovation, willingness to change, resource leverage, etc. Keeping customers engaged in a business is extremely effortful. This case identifies the prioritized factors and the reasonings behind their choice. The case also focused on the downsides of this industry and explored the factors that can lead to the downfall of a business.

INTRODUCTION

Mohammed Salman, the founder of well-known street joint Waffle-Up located in Bangladesh, has been in the restaurant business for a little over nine years now. Salman has faced some challenges being in this industry for instance mistreatment and under qualified employees. Despite new challenges coming in their way Mohammed Salman's dedication and leadership has made Waffle-Up another favorite street

DOI: 10.4018/979-8-3693-1781-5.ch008

joint amongst others for dessert lovers. The people of Bangladesh are not used to having dessert as a street snack much less waffle for that matter. Waffle itself is a fairly new dessert for Bangladeshi people and was only served in overpriced restaurants. Opening a waffle shop was always an intention for Mohammed Salman but the timing was never accurate. The hotel and hospitality are a fairly competitive industry to operate in Bangladesh as new alternatives are being introduced regularly. Before starting Waffle-Up Salman was operating another restaurant named Treehouse which fought for stability when the pandemic hit. It was one of the major challenges that Mohammed Salman faced before starting Waffle-Up. It was Mohammed Salman's innovative thinking to focus on product development and branding that made Waffle-Up a successful venture which is much appreciated by their customers.

BACKGROUND

Waffle-Up, a dine-in or drive-in street joint, operates in the hotel and hospitality management industry of Bangladesh. Hotel and hospitality industry is a type of industry that has a lot of potential if the business model is unique, otherwise it is a very competitive industry to operate in. In Bangladesh despite having a lot of potential, the people working in the hotel industry are not treated with a lot of respect and dignity. And this is an identified challenge for entrepreneurs or leaders who belong to this industry.

Mohammed Salman who has been operating in this industry also faced this challenge way before starting Waffle-Up. The lack of respect is a type of challenge that is pretty difficult to overcome and the only way to overcome this is for the business to become successful. Due to this reason many young entrepreneurs despite having potential do not want to enter the industry (Hossain, 2023).

Established in late 2021, Waffle-Up is a street dessert joint that only serves waffles. It is known for its square shaped waffles and trendy packaging which majorly attracts young customers. The difference is the shape of the waffle and the packaging that serves waffles in a stick is the unique selling point for Waffle-Up. As the founder Mohammed Salman has been in the hotel and hospitality management industry for the past nine years, knew the advantages and disadvantages of the industry. Keeping all that experience in mind Salman focused on the branding of Waffle-Up. Waffle-Up serves different flavors of Waffles as well as various add ons. The price range of the waffles starts from 160/- and they also charge extra for different add ons on the waffles. The price range is not too low and not too high but some customers feel the price may be high in terms of quantity.

Street food business is a well-established industry in Bangladesh. And the majority of the market offers savory foods to their customers. Bangladeshi people are dessert loving by default and waffles are an emerging dessert that has been introduced in the Bangladesh market of late. And Waffles were served only in expensive restaurants which was out of affordability for a considerable amount of people. But Mohammed Salman saw an opportunity here that others could not decipher. Keeping all of this in mind Waffle-Up started its journey with an emerging dessert item Waffle at a street joint that too at an affordable price. Waffle-Up started its journey with a quick-service restaurant (QSR) in a small roadside store on Road 13 in Banani, Dhaka. From then there is no turning back. Now Waffle-Up has eight operating stores spread-out in different areas in Dhaka and they are planning to launch new stores in Dhaka as well as outside Dhaka. What attracts more to the customers is the edgy packaging as well as yellow themed stores with hot pink LED light strips. The whole outlook of the store along with the delicious waffles gives the customers a fulfilling time. Mohammed Salman's foresight about the market trends helped

Figure 1.
Source: The Business Standard, 2023

him to shape the brand image of Waffle-Up in a way that people remember this place by not only their product but also by their vibrant stores.

LITERATURE REVIEW

Introduction on Street Food

Food and Agricultural Organization defines street food as, "Street foods are ready-to-eat foods and beverages prepared and/or sold by vendors or hawkers especially in the streets and other similar places", (*Food for the Cities: Street Foods*, n.d, para 1). Street foods occupies a significant portion of food that millions if low- and middle-class urban residents consumes on a regular basis. Street foods costs considerably low and are most convenient way of getting a nutritionally balanced meal outside of their homes for many lower income people in terms being able to the correct combination of food. Many underprivileged people rely on the sale and preparation of street food as a reliable income source.

Street Food Vending

In Bangladesh, selling street food is a common and distinguishing aspect of a sizable unorganized economy. Street food vending is significant because it meets an essential requirement for those living in cities and is frequently observed in public areas, (Muzaffar et al., 2009). According to Food and Agricultural Organization, Street food vendors cluster in public spaces, especially those near schools. For their lunch and snacks, the majority of students at these schools rely on the carts. Thus, nutrition, safety, and hygiene become very important concerns, (*The Street Food Initiative in Khulna | Improving Food Safety in Bangladesh | FAO*, n.d.). Due to their growing urbanization and industrialization, low-income nations like Bangladesh are seeing changes in their food consumption patterns. In these countries, restaurants and street food vendors play a significant role in satisfying the demand for food, (Nizame et al., 2019).

Street Food Hygiene

Food handlers plays significant role in maintaining food safety at every stage, including preparation, processing, manufacturing, and retailing. "Poor hand hygiene and food handling put consumers of restaurant and street food at risk of enteric disease, especially in low-income countries", (Nizame et al., 2019. para 1). Because it can be challenging to guarantee that food is prepared and sold in a hygienic manner, street food vendors have been linked to foodborne illnesses among the general public, (Almeida et al., 1996, as cited in (Muyanja et al., 2011)

Size of Hospitality industry in Bangladesh

According to Dhaka Tribune, from 2009 to 2022 hospitality and the restaurants sector encountered with tremendous growth. Approximately 58% restaurant's number has increased. A study done by Bangladesh Bureau of statistics (BBS) tells that, restaurants number in 2009 to 2010 was 2.75 lakh and by the year of 2022 the number increased and now number reached at 4.36 lakh. The number is increasing which is clearly visible. With the growth of restaurants, the contribution to country's GDP also increasing. Moreover, privately owned restaurants are approximately 4.35 lakh and on the other side, approximately 852 restaurants are owned by the government. So, it is evident that, private ownership is dominating this hospitality industry. (Imran Hassan, 2022)

Sweet Food Market Size

According to The Business Standard, sweet food has higher potential demand over worldwide. Sweet food sector holds approximately around 20,000 crore amounts of business. Here, local entrepreneurs from all over country almost two thousand people works behind to make this large amount of money. Green view research firm conducted a research in 2022, according to that Bangladesh had valued $309.98 billion sweet business market size. Furthermore, the size will increase by 2028 and will be valued over $401.54 billion. Although, some issues had raised while obtaining the certificate for sweet exportation. But it was resolved eventually in the clearance process. Despite of being the potentially sweet market could not shine over the year in global market. In global market the size of sweet food slightly increased which is not remarkable (Chowdhury, 2023).

DISCUSSION

Street Food Culture in Bangladesh

Bangladesh's streets are blessed with various kinds of food flavors. Even every particular season has designated street food. Like, for summer streets get filled with Kulfi carts, seasonal fruits juice stalls, Shingara, shamucha. In winter, streets get filled with different pithas including patishapta, Dudhpuli, Shemai pitha, Chitoi pitha and so on. Also, momo carts, soups, kababs and all kinds of fried items. In the rainy season, khichuri, halim, rolls, porota, Bhorta and tea stalls can be found. Fuchka and chotpoti, the most famous street food, are available for the whole year. Each and every food gives comfort according to the weather needs and peoples demand. From spicy, savory items to sweet, each and every flavor of food has a ubiquitous influence in almost every street. As a matter of price, the foods are affordable along with pleasurable taste. These street foods also play a big role in attracting foreigners. Because they got to taste inquisitive foods in the streets. Each and every food complement each other. Moreover, the foods we get in our streets have the essence of different countries. Such as, India, China, Japan, Turkey, and the United States. So, street food is made according to the taste of Bengali people's taste buds with a pinch of exotic touch. Most popular street food in the street is fuchka and chotpoti. These foods are often found together under one street food cart. The fillings inside the fuchka are mashed potatoes and chickpeas and the fuchka shell is made of granulated wheat or white flour. In fuchka often it is made with tamarind chutney and with one take or bite they get popped in the mouth and burst with flavor. The toppings like mint chutney, onion, sliced egg, lime juice, green chili make a wonderful mixture of sweet, spicy, sour and savory flavor. Another one, various flavored grills, kabab, tikka can be found in the cart. These foods make the air fill with spice and heavy aroma which make people come and create an urge to taste those grilled items. Tea is another street food item which can be easily found in every corner of the street. Tea also comes with different flavors and names such as, Malai tea, Milk tea, green tea, Herbal tea, colored tea, Ice tea, Malta flavored tea, Spice tea, Ginger tea and so on. These tea leaves are made by local people who live in the hill tract. These tea carts are called Tong Dokan in Bengali. In the early morning or break time from the office or educational institution people go there just to get a cup of tea so that they can recharge themselves and refresh themselves with tea. Shingara and shamucha is another food which is made with flour. The fillings of shingara are made with vegetables, smashed potatoes or sometimes beef or chicken meat. According to the fillings, the price would be adjusted. Shingara and shamucha is served with different flavorful chutneys such as mint, coriander or tomato chutney. These are deep fried foods which are also eaten with a hot cup of tea.

Moreover, different types of pitha puli are the main focus of the winter season. Usually, they are sweet in taste and some pithas are spicy in taste. Different regions have different sets of pithas with unique designs. One of them is the Nakshi pitha origin district of Narsingdi.In oder to make this, rice flour needs to boil first then by making the dough it gets the desired shape by various molds. After that, those floured pithas are left to dry, then it gets deep fried in oil. Finally, it gets soaked in sugar syrup. This pitha is as hard as toast biscuit. Most of the pithas main ingredients are hard boiled milk and lots of sugar or jaggery powder. Another pitha is patishapta which is made with rice flour, white flour, suji and water. The process is quite simple to follow to make this pitha. By all these things a thick batter needs to form and by using the batter a porota shaped pitha has been made but before making the porota shape filling needs to be there. In this pitha, filling is quite important. For the filling required ingredients are milk, ghee, coconut, jaggery. These ingredients have to cook together and have to settle in a paste form. After that, those fillings are ready to use.

Bangladeshi people's usual habit is to eat something sweet after the main meal. And this habit becomes more enjoyable in the winter. As everyone loves to explore new types of street food, it can be said that Waffles can be a great street food for easily adaptable countries like Bangladesh, (Dhaka's Street Food Odyssey, n.d.)

Challenges Faced by Street Vendors

Mostly street food business owners have low financial capability. Because of that, they could not keep focus on many stuffs. They do not have stable financial situation to start a business. Lack of education sometimes drives them to make food unhealthy where food safety become unsure. Moreover, they do not get proper training or a proper place to start a business. Also, lack of pure water and food waste disposal become very challenging for street vendors. Above all of them, hygiene is the main issue while making foods in a street. But money is the obstacle which becomes hard to conquer. (Khan Redzwan Habib, 2016). While making dessert in streets the difficulty levels become higher. Because some dessert needs store in a fridge or sometimes need special cooling system to make dessert. For example, to make waffle, electricity is an essential tool. Without the electricity waffle cannot be made. Because waffle maker needs electricity to make the waffle. After the waffle maker done its part, waffle needs immediate cooling to get a specific shape. Because of that, electrical fan is another stuff which is required by the vendors. Vendors have to arrange the electricity in streets which needs permission from authority. Sometimes it becomes the barrier not to get the permission from authority.

Sweet Market of Bangladesh

People of Bangladesh mostly assume that, sweet means dessert. According to that, there is no specific dessert market established till now. So, based on sweet market here is some information regarding this booming market.

Sweet market in Bangladesh is worth TK 20,000 crore now. It includes dairy products, confectionery items like, biscuits, cheese. And the demand for sweets is not only increasing locally but also increasing outside Bangladesh. In every festival sweet demand got increased. More specifically, people here consume sweets which are non-branded because of the popularity from ages. Such as Gosh, Gopal. (*Bangladesh's Sweets Businesses Thriving with a Market Worth Tk20,000 Crore*, 2021)

The Execution of Waffle-Up

Waffle-Up is a new trend setter in Bangladesh. It came with the idea of introducing a dessert item as a street food. Mohammed Salman the Co-founder of Waffle-Up made every strategy before going into this startup. When he launched waffles as a street food there were no other alternative stores. Basically, the team of Waffle-Up utilized the first mover advantage which actually created hype from young generation to senior citizens. Moreover, there are lots of other factors that need to be considered such as the demand of this particular item, will it be culturally accepted or not and so on, (Vuong et al., 2022). According to 'Trading economics' consumer spending increased drastically. It was 31189.65 BDT Billion in 2022 and in 2023 it increased to 32840.47 BDT Billion. This spending behavior can assure that consumers of Bangladesh are ready to spend and there is a huge scope for bringing new ventures. From spending behavior to lifestyle change everything brought to us a new path to work on. Where new generations love to spend and want to try out new things to gather experience.

Waffle-Up makes sweet waffles but soon they are planning to make some savory waffles. When people think about waffles a picture comes to their mind automatically that a waffle would be wrapped into Nutella or chocolate which can only be liked by chocolate lovers or those who have a sweet tooth. So, they have thought of going for another taste such as savory. To sustain in this market, they are using the same recipe in each and every outlet. There is an option to use local knowledge about the taste, unique cuisine and ingredients which can be found easily. Mohammed Salman said that they have done R&D over 2 to 3 years to know about the consumer demand. So that they can offer high quality products at a very competitive price. Moreover, they will continuously introduce new flavors, toppings. Also, they can try to introduce new beverage items by maintaining the same quality. Furthermore, they also attracted the audience with a vibrant color approach such as pink color packaging by making some characters which represent and tell their story.

The effective leadership and foresight as a leader and entrepreneur have been the only reason behind the success of Waffle-Up. Being in the industry of hotel and hospitality management has taught Mohammed Salman to differentiate and recognize the change in market. Already a successful restaurateur and the founder of another successful venture Treehouse, Salman wanted to start a waffle shop below Treehouse but due to the inappropriate timing he could not do so. But when pandemic hit, Salman's restaurant Treehouse was facing struggles as the others in the market. But Mohammed Salman saw an opportunity there and started developing the products as well as branding to start Waffle-Up. According to an interview given in The Prestige Global, Mohammed Salman Said, "Before launching Waffle-Up, we had spent nearly two years behind its product development and four months in branding". Here Salman tried to differentiate Waffle-Up by keeping the color of the brand different from the other Waffle Joints in the world. Also, in an attempt to differentiate, Salman gave the product a unique way of serving by serving the Waffles in a stick. Which was a completely new way of serving waffles.

As the hotel industry is very competitive and people tend to replicate new products introduced in the market by either replicating the packaging or by reducing the price. This detail did not go unnoticed by Mohammed Salman and he decided to give their product at the most competitive price that is possible without compromising the quality. Also, their packaging contains illustrations of different characters that are not easily duplicable. Before launching Waffle-Up, Mohammed Salman wanted to make this venture scalable that did not require any chefs as sometimes restaurants' popularity become dependent on the chef. To avoid this problem and make Waffle-Up scalable Salman created a standard secret recipe so that it can be easily replicable amongst different branches of Waffle-Up.

The store design is also another factor that attracts customers. The unique illustrated walls of the store as well as yellow and teal themed colors with hot pink LED light strips. This gives the stores a unique and photogenic look which attracts more youngsters. Also, as the stores are very small to avoid crowds and gatherings, the business model of Waffle-Up was kept different by keeping the joint a quick-service restaurant (QSR) where dine-in and drive-in was offered. All these small details there never went unnoticed by Mohammed Salman who made Waffle-Up the trendsetter in Bangladeshi street food business.

Waffle-Up founder said that they are planning to make as many outlets as possible near to customers in Dhaka city. Eventually, they plan to go internationally to look out for more opportunities. Additionally, Mr. Salman said that they are using foodpanda delivery service where almost 50% of their overall sales are from that platform. As online delivery platforms are rising tremendously, they are using it to grab the main attention of the business. A lot of opportunity created by the blessing of digitalization.

They have a dedicated surveillance team who are continuously monitoring the operation so that they do not have to face any sorts of human errors. Moreover, Waffle-Up is managing their whole operation through their central kitchen so that the customers have the chance to get the same taste every time. To ensure that, they are using a process-oriented business model. Here, they take all the necessary measurements about the quantity and send the materials as per the measurement to make the batter to all the available outlets in Dhaka city. Moreover, Waffle-Up collects the contact number of the customers so they get feedback and reviews so that they can serve their customers better. Their main purpose is to provide best quality service which would be quick as well as affordable.

Challenges Faced Due to Competitors

Every hyped trend has a downside which will actually create more competitors. Waffle-Up also faced the same thing. For example, After the introduction of Waffle-Up a new waffle street food came to light called Waffle time. So, now the customers will have the alternate option to try and to make a difference between these two waffle stores. Here, certainly Waffle-Up has to face comparison with the other stores.

Another such example is, is waffle bae. Waffle bae has their innovative ideas. They offer event facilities for personal functions. Moreover, they take customized orders based on individual preferences. Such as, they even provide vegan waffles as per request. (Ads, 2023). Whereas, waffle up focusing on quality of their waffle and bringing out new flavors for the consumers.

Before launching into the market street food joints that served desserts or sweet items only used to serve items like jilapi, doi which are common sweets in Bangladesh. Also, during winter time various pitha which are a type of sweet snack, for example, bhapa, chitoi, puli etc. can be found in almost every road. So, to divert the customers' mind to accept waffles as any other street food item can be acknowledged as an extraordinary approach.

Also, another considerable factor is practicing sustainability. Most businesses do not consider this factor this early in their business. As it is not possible to be 100% percent sustainable Waffle-Up is trying to make some changes like using bamboo sticks to at least make some impact.

To stay competitive in this market, they must add some new features or value adding services to the consumers so that they can be highlighted. As they already have some competitive strategy, one of them is that their recipe is handled by the co-founder himself and it can't be shared. By this way they are able to provide real and actual taste in every purchase of consumers. To measure the competition, they can consider the online reviews, food groups to check the feedback about the likings and disliking's of their own brand as well as other brands. This way they will have a chance to improvise themselves and that will be easy to monitor the customers' food habits. In addition, if one person can guess the flavor just by taking the smell of the waffle, then she or he can enjoy the waffle for free. Because every customer seeks variety, (Hossain et al., 2019). Waffle-Up can also come up with a competitive pricing strategy. For example, they can make three different sizes of waffles and can price them in such a way so that customers only buy the waffles that actually Waffle-Up wants them to buy. Like, Nutella flavored waffle 150 taka, Nutella and vanilla flavored waffle 180 tk and Nutella, vanilla and ice cream flavored waffle 220 tk. Here, customers will see more benefits in buying the last choice and choose it, rather than buying the previous two. Because here, they are getting a lot from the previous flavors which is also worth the money. By these innovative tactics they can overcome the intense competition. Moreover, nowadays youth are more focused on social media so that can be a really good way to introduce Waffle-Up brands to the younger generations. Obviously, there will be a lot of competition who will battle in the same field. That is where Waffle-Up needs to come with differentiating ideas to tackle this.

Challenges Due to Pandemic

During pandemic every business suffered a lot. Specially the street food business. People were not well adjusted with with m-learning, (Hossain et al., 2021). Because of the hygiene and risk of spreading covid there was restrictions for street food vendors not to serve to customers. But after few months, there were less restrictions in terms of serving the food. Restaurants and street vendors were allowed to open to their shop until 7pm but not for take away. (*Struggles of Dhaka's Street Food Vendors to Survive during Pandemic*, n.d.) They were not allowed to sit and eat in a restaurant or open space, (Aboulilah et al., 2022).

Waffle up to tackle this crisis came up with their own strategies. Due to covid everyone is more active on social media, (Emmanuel et al., 2022). And Salman took the opportunity. They used to get all the orders via online app. They took only 10 minutes to prepare any waffles. They were focusing on fast come and get fast service.

Hygiene Standards and Licensing

As waffle needs to rent a place for their stall for that reason, they need to have trade and food license. Otherwise, they won't be allowed to do business, but waffle up has all the license along with food hygiene certificate, food premises acceptance certificate. Salman said, they serve food by maintaining proper hygiene. Maintaining a hygiene standard in very necessary to gain consumer's trust. They use disposable food prep gloves and caps. All the staff member has to strictly follow the kitchen hygiene rule. And their shops also maintain a regular cleaning schedule so that provide their customer a fresh and homely environment.

Salman's Leadership and Its Challenges

Waffle-Up is redefining the orthodox leadership in terms of Bangladesh's culinary sector with the addition of mouthwatering waffle creations. The unorthodox outlook in leadership and street food aesthetic is as uncommon as their "Death by Nutella" waffle.

When the word leader comes to our mind, we imagine a suited booted person with a polished look who has exceptional foresight when it comes to their leadership. But Mohammad Salman is as casual as it goes. Wearing sneakers and comfortable sweatshirts and having an exceptional vision which does not reside in the boardroom but in the streets of Dhaka, he set the example that if you are an observer of trends and have the vision to try out something new you can shine. When an unconventional attitude of "try-it-and-see" is fueled by consistent innovation, success is bound to come. Salman follows autocratic leadership style where he himself holds all the centralized authority and maintain his leadership all across his waffle up branches. For example, to maintain the original taste of waffle up, he came with exact measurement process. From batter to secret sauce each and every item has been made by following the measurement chart.

When it comes to Waffle-Up their entire team is the main ingredient that shapes the experience, not just a compilation of parts in a machine. Each and every employee of Waffle-Up are empowered on their own and has a creative streak. Here, the managers and leaders are not the only ones to make decisions. Every employee is capable of owning their tasks and taking on the job decisions to run the everyday operation smoothly. It is possible because there is open communication and constructive criticism and flat hierarchies. Because of this reason the work atmosphere is lively and new concepts are coming out every day just like waffles that has turned out to be perfectly crispy.

The phrase "Customer is king" is quietly popular. But when it comes to Waffle-Up the customer is not only the king but also the co-designers. Customers are the taste testers of any newly created recipe. Mohammad Salman has constant engagement with the customers where customers can voice their opinions and reactions through open communication. It is something that Bangladeshi consumers have not seen until very recently. The unique experience that Mohammad Salman is providing to the customers where they are not only the consumers of their products but are also an active participant of the whole process. This foresight of including the customers as a component in the business has made Waffle-Up a success in such a short time.

In recent times, to keep up with the ever-changing trends constant innovation and experimentation is the key. Waffle-Up did not stick with the same old waffle recipes. "Death by Nutella '' and "Bangla Pizza ", the widely popular items of Waffle-Up are the outcome of such experimentations.

Waffle-Up approached the consumers with a lighthearted and a bit playful attitude. The lively, vibrant colored logo, out of the box mascot and quirky social media presence points out the passion for uniqueness and a fun-loving leadership. Social media plays as an entrepreneurial tool in recent times, (Hossain, 2019). The majority of the customers are from the younger generation and respond very well to the quirkiness of Waffle-Up. This makes the brand a favorite street joint of youngsters and the delicious waffles work as the cherry on top.

The downside of having customers that belong to the younger generation is that the shorter attention span. And they are very active online, (Hossain et al., 2020). In today's evolving world, the newness does not stay the same for a long time. As new trends are coming literally every day, the buzz of Waffle-Up is bound to fade at some point. Eventually the novel ideas of Waffle-Up will subside and be copied by the competitors.

Due to the ongoing high inflation rates the USP of Waffle-Up, delicious waffles with different varieties in an affordable way is severely hampered. Because of the present inflation storm the brand is compelled to make difficult decisions to run smooth operations in the market. In this inflation the prices of the raw materials have been the driving force behind making any difficult decisions. As a result of making difficult decisions the brand may face a decline in their profit margin.

Another thing to consider here is maintaining the profit margin in terms of logistical dilemma. During the pandemic food delivery has become insanely popular, (Mohsin et al., 2021; Hossain et al., 2020). Even though it has expanded the customer base for Waffle-Up, logistical difficulties have become an issue. Upholding the quality and guaranteeing a pleasant customer service while delivering the waffles to customers doorsteps have been proven as a challenge.

Challenges Faced During Expansion

The popularity that Waffle-Up presents is mainly centered in Dhaka, the capital of Bangladesh. Even though very recently they have announced the launch of their new branch in Singapore, expansion into new countries or cities requires resource allocation and careful consideration into relevant factors. The positive side of expansion is exploring new horizons and newer customers from different demography. To establish the same brand awareness outside the capital will require the same foresight and dedication to cater to the different taste buds of different regional customers.

Salman mentioned that, in Dhaka in terms of expansion they really did not face any issues. But outside Dhaka, they had a problem to find rental place for their shop. As they just need not more than 150 square feet space for their shop. Moreover, from selling or profit point of view, in Dhaka they can keep their shop open for like 2am because of demand. But outside Dhaka, customers are hard to find after midnight.

By the growing popularity and the increased number of restaurants it has been a huge responsibility for the owners of this business to provide training to the staff. It is a huge thing to accomplish because they are the service provider who will directly serve the customers. As multiple restaurants need to be served and the quality of the food and staff has to have the same level of skills and knowledge. So, in this business this responsibility needs to be addressed carefully to avoid any sorts of problems.

CONCLUSION

Waffle-Up's growth and success has been pumped by the innovative and creative leadership style of Mohammad Salman. But the current state of market indicates that, Waffle-Up's approach and operation style need a bit of change to remain in the industry. As street food industry is one of the fasted expanding industries in Bangladesh, new ventures are launching every other day and that to by introducing even newer and innovative approach. Their further efforts to leave a mark in the culinary world will need an equal balance between the energetic entrepreneurial structure and constant development of sustainable innovation. Because, they need to not only melt the hearts and taste buds of their customers but also beat the competitors.

By time people's taste and trend both will change. So, to keep with the trend entrepreneurs must plan accordingly to fit into new setups. As the founder Mohammad Salman said that they do not only keep themselves restrained in the sweet items, they also want to introduce new flavors. Also, to keep the same taste in every outlet, he centrally monitored the recipe by keeping the method secret. He also added that, "I do not want to depend on any chef or any manpower. "A standardized recipe will be followed in every store without much dependency and the fear of not being able to make the same taste again and again. A business needs to evolve with the fast-growing market. By overcoming the ever-growing inflation rate at the same time keeping up their creative streak. Waffle-Up is also trying to follow the path. Firstly, inside Dhaka city then, they are planning to move outside Dhaka and eventually they have big future plans to expand in United Arab Emirates and Egypt, and being the trendsetter in not only Bangladesh but also overseas.

This case study just touches the surface of Waffle-Up's incredible leadership approach. It will be amazing for us to be the part of Waffle-Up's impactful journey ahead and watch how it unfolds new adventure and opportunities for the brand.

REFERENCES

A Quickbite Trendsetter - The Prestige Magazine. (2023, January 25). https://theprestige.global/a-quickbite-trendsetter

Aboulilah, H. M. A. E., Hossain, S. F. A., Vuong, B. N., & Jebril, T. (2022). Exploring the Relationship between WeChat Usage and E-purchase Intention During the COVID-19 Pandemic Among University Students in China. *SAGE Open*, *12*(4). doi:10.1177/21582440221139447 PMID:36466966

Ads, R. R. (2023, July 22). *Waffle Bae Best Neon Sign Company in Bangladesh*. Best Advertising Agency in Bangladesh. https://redroseadbd.com/best-neon-sign-company-in-bangladesh/

Bangladesh's sweets businesses thriving with a market worth Tk20,000 crore. (2021, June 1). The Business Standard. https://www.tbsnews.net/supplement/bangladeshs-sweets-businesses-thriving-market-worth-tk20000-crore-254023

Chowdhury, J. (2023, August 28). Do our sweets have sweeter potential in the global market? *The Business Standard.* https://www.tbsnews.net/economy/do-our-sweets-have-sweeter-potential-global-market-689978

Dhaka's Street Food Vendors to Survive during Pandemic. (n.d.). Retrieved January 8, 2024, from https://www.changemag-diinsider.com/blog/struggles-of-dhaka-s-street-food-vendors-to-survive-during-pandemic

Emmanuel, C. P., Qin, S., Hossain, S. F. A., & Hussain, K. (2022). Factors influencing social-media-based entrepreneurship prospect among female students in China. *Heliyon*, *8*(12), e12041. doi:10.1016/j.heliyon.2022.e12041 PMID:36483305

Food for the Cities: Street foods. (n.d.). https://www.fao.org/fcit/food-processing/street-foods/en/

Habib, K. R. (2016). Understanding Challenges Faced By Street Food Vendors to Maintain Street Food Hygiene in Dhaka City. *Journal of Food and Nutrition Sciences*, *4*(4), 78–85. doi:10.11648/j.jfns.20160404.11

Hassan, I. (2022, December 7). Hospitality and the restaurant sectors grows 58% in 11 years. *Dhaka Tribune*. https://www.dhakatribune.com/business/279949/hospitality-and-the-restaurant-sectors-grows-58%25

Hossain, S. F. A. (2019). Social Networking and Its Role in Media Entrepreneurship. *Journal of Media Management and Entrepreneurship*, *1*(1), 73–86. doi:10.4018/JMME.2019010105

Hossain, S. F. A., Nurunnabi, M., Hussain, K., Saha, S. K., & Wang, S. (2019). Effects of variety-seeking intention by mobile phone usage on university students' academic performance. *Cogent Education*, *6*(1), 1574692. Advance online publication. doi:10.1080/2331186X.2019.1574692

Hossain, S. F. A., Nurunnabi, M., Hussain, K., & Shan, X. (2020). Smartphone-based m-shopping behavior and innovative entrepreneurial tendency among women in emerging Asia. *International Journal of Gender and Entrepreneurship*, *12*(2), 173–189. doi:10.1108/IJGE-03-2019-0054

Hossain, S. F. A., Shan, X., Musa, M., & Rahman, P. (2023). Social media and increased venture creation tendency with innovative ideas: the case of female students in Asia. In *Research Anthology on Applying Social Networking Strategies to Classrooms and Libraries* (pp. 1716–1731). IGI Global.

Hossain, S. F. A., Shan, X., Nurunnabi, M., Tushar, H., Mohsin, A. K. M., & Ahsan, F. T. (2021). Opportunities and Challenges of M-Learning During the COVID-19 Pandemic. *Advances in Social Networking and Online Communities*, 210–227. doi:10.4018/978-1-7998-7764-6.ch007

Hossain, S. F. A., Xi, Z., Nurunnabi, M., & Hussain, K. (2020). Ubiquitous Role of Social Networking in Driving M-Commerce: Evaluating the Use of Mobile Phones for Online Shopping and Payment in the Context of Trust. *SAGE Open*, *10*(3). doi:10.1177/2158244020939536

Mohsin, A., Hongzhen, L., & Hossain, S. F. A. (2021). Impact of COVID-19 Pandemic on Consumer Economy: Countermeasures Analysis. *SAGE Open*, *11*(2). doi:10.1177/21582440211008875

Muyanja, C., Nayiga, L., Brenda, N., & Nasinyama, G. (2011, October). Practices, knowledge and risk factors of street food vendors in Uganda. *Food Control*, *22*(10), 1551–1558. doi:10.1016/j.foodcont.2011.01.016

Muzaffar, A. T., Huq, I., & Mallik, B. A. (2009, February 18). Entrepreneurs of the Streets: An Analytical Work on the Street Food Vendors of Dhaka City. *International Journal of Business and Management*, *4*(2). Advance online publication. doi:10.5539/ijbm.v4n2p80

Nizame, F. A., Alam, M. U., Masud, A. A., Shoab, A. K., Opel, A., Islam, M. K., Luby, S. P., & Unicomb, L. (2019, September 4). Hygiene in Restaurants and among Street Food Vendors in Bangladesh. *The American Journal of Tropical Medicine and Hygiene*, *101*(3), 566–575. doi:10.4269/ajtmh.18-0896 PMID:31333161

Nyawo, T., Kesa, H., & Onyenweaku, E. (2021, April 30). *Food Safety and Hygiene: Knowledge, Attitude and Practices among Food Handlers*. doi:10.46222/ajhtl.19770720.117

Raidah, N. (2023, July 16). Waffle-Up: worth the fuss? The Daily Star. https://www.thedailystar.net/shout/news/waffle-worth-the-fuss-3193591

Struggles of Dhaka's Street food Vendors to Survive During Pandemic. (n.d.). Retrieved January 8, 2024, from https://www.changemag-diinsider.com/blog/struggles-of-dhaka-s-street-food-vendors-to-survive-during-pandemic

The Street Food Initiative in Khulna | Improving food safety in Bangladesh | FAO. (n.d.). https://www.fao.org/in-action/food-safety-bangladesh/news/detail/en/c/411752/

Tradingeconomics.com. (2019). Available at: https://tradingeconomics.com/bangladesh/consumer-spending

Vuong, B. N., Tushar, H., & Hossain, S. F. A. (2022). The effect of social support on job performance through organizational commitment and innovative work behavior: Does innovative climate matter? *Asia-Pacific Journal of Business Administration*. Advance online publication. doi:10.1108/APJBA-06-2021-0256

Waffle Up: A bistro trendsetter. (n.d.). The Financial Express. https://thefinancialexpress.com.bd/lifestyle/others/waffle-up-a-bistro-trendsetter-1661320894

WaffleUp. Square is the new heart. (2022, June 10). *The Business Standard*. https://www.tbsnews.net/features/food/waffleup-square-new-heart-437010

ADDITIONAL READING

Alfiero, S., Lo Giudice, A., & Bonadonna, A. (2017). Street food and innovation: The food truck phenomenon. *British Food Journal*, *119*(11), 2462–2476. doi:10.1108/BFJ-03-2017-0179

Alimi, B. A. (2016). Risk factors in street food practices in developing countries: A review. *Food Science and Human Wellness*, *5*(3), 141–148. doi:10.1016/j.fshw.2016.05.001

Dawson, R. J., & Canet, C. (1991). International activities in street foods. *Food Control*, *2*(3), 135–139. doi:10.1016/0956-7135(91)90081-7

Dhaka's street food odyssey. (n.d.). *The Financial Express*. Retrieved December 17, 2023, from https://thefinancialexpress.com.bd/lifestyle/food/dhakas-street-food-odyssey

Praesri, S., Meekun, K., Lee, T. J., & Hyun, S. S. (2022). Marketing mix factors and a business development model for street food tourism. *Journal of Hospitality and Tourism Management*, *52*, 123–127. doi:10.1016/j.jhtm.2022.06.007

APPENDIX

Teaching Note

An Imaginary Class Design

Figure 2.

Topic: Waffle-up case study		Duration: 90 minutes
Learning Objectives: End of the session students will be able to: i. Use suitable case study solution ii. Know the case study in depth		Number of students: 30–40
Learning Activity (LA)		Activity type
Part 1 (25 + 5 minutes)	LA1. Download sample case study from renowned source Q1. What is case study? Q2. Why should you learn and use case study?	Lecture Group work consists of 6 students in each group
	LA2. Introduction referencing style	Independent, referred and practical learning

Appendix 1: Part One of Teaching Note

Figure 3.

Study Topic: Learning case solution procedure – step by step		Duration: 1 hour
Part 2 (15 +15 minutes)	LA3. Download 4-5 cases Q1. Know about the key points Q2. Introduce a solution Q3. Brainstorming	Collective work: Group activity consists of 6 members in each group
	LA4. Study in groups of 6 people to analyze the cases 1. Group 1: Discuss the objectives of the cases 2. Group 2: Discuss the background 3. Group 3: Analyze the key information 4. Group 4: Identify possible solution	Collective work: Group activity consists of 6 members in each group
Part 3 (15 minutes)	LA5. Compile all the tasks from each group 1. A group member from every group will make a presentation for 2 minutes 2. Clarification for other group members if they are not clear about the presentation.	Collective work: Group activity consists of 6 members in each group
Part 4 (10 minutes)	LA6. Exercise time	Independent ability to assess the students
	LA7. Complete the exercise and provide feedback	
Post class (5 minutes)	Students' feedback assessment Need for a review class Miscellaneous	Intuitive activity

Learning Outcomes

- Know more about the challenges an entrepreneur and/or leader face before starting a new venture.
- Know more about how to overcome the challenges of the hotel and hospitality management industry in Bangladesh as well as how to remain in the market.
- Know more about how to thrive in a fairly competitive industry and differentiate amongst the competitors.
- Know how an effective and innovative leadership can turn a new venture into a customer favorite joint.

Methods

The case utilized secondary data at the beginning followed by some person administered interview over the phone. So, it used a mixed methodology approach.

Key Discussion Points in the Class

1. The recent challenges faced by street food industry in Bangladesh
2. The future issues and opportunities of by street food industry in Bangladesh
3. The price hike problem and the threats
4. Sustainable consumption possibility
5. Competitive advantage of street food

Assignments Questions

From the above case study, could you please answer the following questions?

Figure 4.

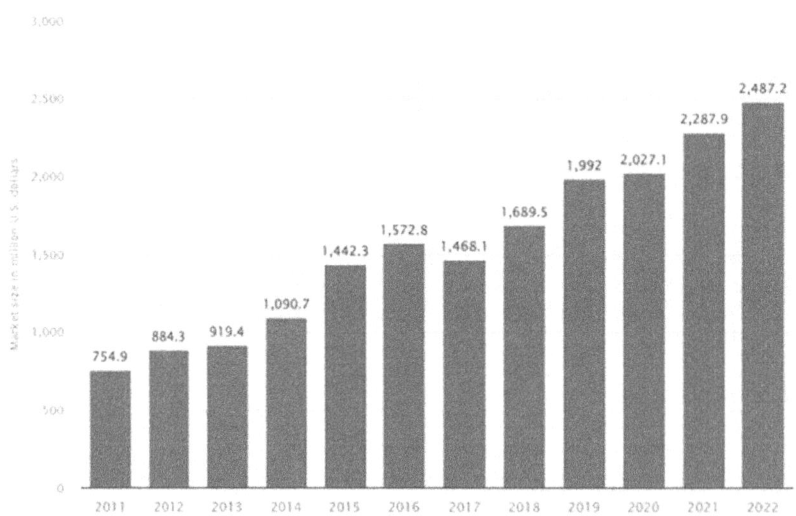

Figure 5.

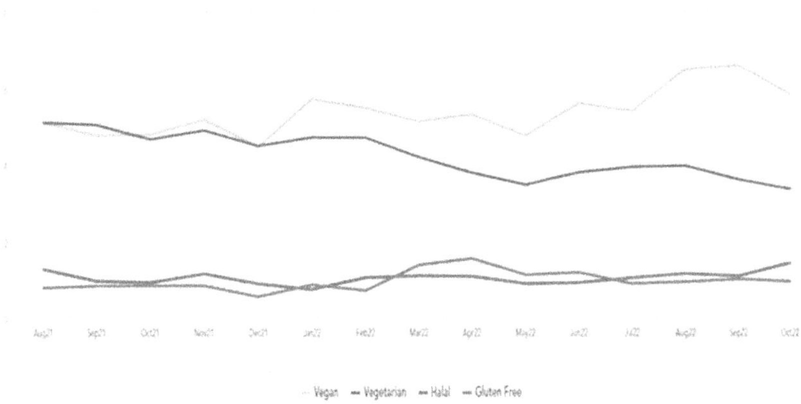

1. What are the key success factors of street food in Bangladesh?
2. How to ensure the street food service effectively or successfully?
3. Is the street food industry under threat in Bangladesh?
4. What are the challenges of the street food industry?
5. Do a competitive analysis of the street food industry?

Us Street food market: growing trend. Source: Statista, 2023
Various food choices. Source: Tastewise, 2023 official website

Chapter 9
Is AI a Threat for Social Media Entrepreneurs?

Khaled Arafat
BRAC University, Bangladesh

Rusana Rubain
BRAC University, Bangladesh

Sifat Jakia Swapnil
BRAC University, Bangladesh

Anika Zarin Chowdhury
BRAC University, Bangladesh

EXECUTIVE SUMMARY

A burning question in this 21st century comes in the form of the development of AI (artificial intelligence). The uses of AI, their strengths, their misuses, and the most pressing question: Does AI eliminate jobs? As the authors dive deep into the depths of knowledge and salvage what they find, they bring about the pressing matter whether artificial intelligence should be given supervision or not. Artificial intelligence helps in many ways, but ultimately, the credibility lies on whether artificial intelligence creates scopes for jobs or takes away certain employment scopes.

INTRODUCTION

"The real problem is not the existential threat of AI. Instead, it is in the development of ethical AI systems."

--Rana El Kaliouby

Artificial intelligence (AI) is a double-edged sword in the world of social media entrepreneurship. While it can spur innovation and growth, there are also worries about possible risks associated with AI deployment. The main goal of artificial intelligence, a branch of computer science, is to imbue machines with human-like intellect and reasoning so they can support people in many ways.

DOI: 10.4018/979-8-3693-1781-5.ch009

"Artificial Intelligence is a tool, not a threat."

--Rodney Brooks

Artificial intelligence (AI) has gradually become more preventive and powerful in a variety of sectors including technology, health sector, production and manufacturing and so on. These developments have all contributed to the enormous change in this field that we are currently seeing. This theory suggests that machines could become intelligent which turns human lives into blessings. Today's world is full of innovation. For the benefit of mechanized knowledge, mass development we are getting the facilities to be updated in every sector, for instance all general and technical sections. Increasingly unavoidable and remarkable figure organizations are essential to the operation of modern coordination frameworks. Due to the advancement of the machinery's capabilities, large databid being analyzed more quickly, broadly and profoundly than at any other moment. Sensors, devices, algorithms, smart devices as well as personnel within these companies are constantly creating new information. Materials handling frameworks and creation planning are efficiently handled by support learning approaches. All the organizations are looking to combine AI principles with traditional Operational Research methodology to solve any business problems in an effort to turn continuous data into meaningful decisions. The development of Artificial intelligence also pays attention for the social media entrepreneurs to spread vastly.

The introduction of artificial intelligence (AI) has significantly changed the social media business environment by providing a multitude of benefits that boost productivity, innovation and overall performance. The noteworthy ways AI has helped social media entrepreneurs tells us how blessing ways has created it for them to spread. For instance, in terms of Personalized Content Exhortation, Netflix uses AI for making history-based movie and TV program recommendations, which enhances customer pleasure and extends platform engagement. Also, in terms of Customer Interaction for Chatbots,for example, Facebook messenger chatbots helps companies become more efficient by helping with reservation management, customer service and answer queries also. Analytics for social media, like Sprout social tracks social media metrics using AI analytics to assist business owners better understand audience engagement and plan their content strategy. Also, in terms of Content Scheduling and Creation, like Hootsuite uses AI to recommend the ideal times to publish content so that it receives the most exposure and interaction of different social media networks. Moreover, Targeted Advertising, for instance, Facebook Ads use AI to target particular demographics, interests, and behaviors, giving users more relevant ads.

Artificial intelligence (AI) integration is becoming both a source of potential concern and a stimulus for innovation in the quickly changing field of social media entrepreneurship. Businesses are opening up new ways for improving analytics; however, the very developments that drive social media companies' growth also bring with them concerns about algorithm biases, privacy, and the changing face of digital engagement.

"Humans should be worried about the threat posed by artificial intelligence."

--Bill Gates

Since these technological breakthroughs bring both possibilities and difficulties to the forefront, it is important to consider whether AI poses a threat to social media entrepreneurs. The focus of this talk will be on how AI is changing the social media entrepreneurial landscape. Examples of how AI fosters innovation as well as growth will be covered, along with situations where its effects could lead to concern about privacy, entrepreneurial process, and morality. Although artificial intelligence (AI) offers social media entrepreneurs a plethora of benefits, it also poses certain challenges that require conscious attention.

In terms of job displacement, an illustration of this would be if social media companies used AI algorithms to filter material instead of hiring human moderators, which would result in job losses. Also, AI has the greatest concern on privacy. AI in data analysis may raise concerns about user privacy. For instance, user data is being collected and analyzed by AI-powered analytics without clear authorization, sparking privacy disputes. Also, in today's world, artificial intelligence plays a great role in spreading misinformation. Like, AI-powered deepfake technologies generate information that appears authentic, yet it is actually fake, possibly deceiving users. We, the whole world, face a loss of human touch in customer interactions, such as AI-driven chatbots that do not meet users' complex wants with general responses.

Again, artificial intelligence-generated threats, like sophisticated phishing attacks, may increase vastly. For example, deep fake or messages are created by AI that are used in social engineering assaults to trick users on social media sites. That becomes a matter of a day-to-day incident which may cause thousands of people's death.

1.2 Research Methodology

The research methodology for inspecting whether or not AI poses any danger to social media entrepreneurs depends on both a secondary and qualitative approach. In this paper, different well-publicized articles are used to discuss distinct modes of Artificial Intelligence applications whose integration will bring business performance enhancement and customer engagement and the areas and individuals who will be a victim of suffering to have a poor quality of life the decision of entrepreneurs to dependent on the technological creations for the competitiveness.

1.2.1 Research Questions

RQ 1. How does artificial intelligence-driven automation influence the versatility and proficiency of social media entrepreneurship?

Social media platforms such as Facebook, Instagram, Snapchat, and LinkedIn leverage AI through advanced machine learning, computer vision, social artificial intelligence, social listening, automation, etc (Ashaolu & Musa, 2021).

RQ 2. What is the impact of algorithms on social media?

Algorithmic work is a sociotechnical rational argument among algorithms and professionals. This course of action and performing algorithmic work comprises, adjusting the openness and closeness of platform operations, changing the actual work operation and performative collaborations as the calculations change, and planning the most proficient method to comprehend and take advantage of the benefits of the algorithmic rationale for the organizational and professional mission (Norström, Islind, & Snis, 2020).

RQ 3. How does the use of AI-driven examination influence the capacity of social media entrepreneurs to comprehend and engage with their target audience?

AI-driven examination reforms social media entrepreneurs' audience understanding by rapidly handling huge amounts of data, offering nuanced experiences into audience ways of behaving, inclinations, and patterns. This works with designated content creation and customized engagement strategies, improving connection and reverberation with the target demographic.

RQ 4. How does AI negatively impact social media entrepreneurs?

AI analyzes the purchasing pattern of the customers to better understand their needs and preferences but sometimes this analyzing power of AI finds out information about customers which are extremely personal. For example, AI can find out an unmarried customer is pregnant by analyzing her buying habits and pattern, preference and browsing style. This is something that many users dislike, thus it hampers a business. Additionally, in many cases the privacy of the customers are at stake. To emphasize, data collected for one purpose can be used for another illegal purpose. Therefore, personal information of any client can get disclosed if the companies do not have a strong security system. Moreover, the AI algorithm isn't coded by humans, rather it is developed by AI itself, through machine learning (Mishra, 2022).

1.2.2 Article Selection and Study Procedure

As the paper is based on secondary literature-based systematic research, the authors scanned multiple databases of journal article's search engines and websites such as Google Scholar, Jstor, Athens, Research Gate, Springer, Sage, Emerald Insights, Science Direct to obtain papers rich in information. In the preliminary stage, we gathered around 40 articles published from 2014 to 2023 using the necessary keywords such as artificial intelligence, social media, entrepreneurship, AI-business, Al-marketing, etc. Secondly, we classified the obtained articles based on the pros and cons of having Al integrated with social media handles for business, eliminating 16 articles. Later on, on the basis of the functionality of the AI-powered applications and software, we had to eliminate 14 more articles, and we obtained ten articles that have been studied in detail to satisfy the chapter's objective.

1.2.3 Data Collection

see table 1.

1.2.4 Result

AI's Effect on Social Media Business Owners--

Artificial Intelligence (AI) in social media entrepreneurship has produced a range of outcomes and significantly changed the field.

Algorithmic Difficulties:

As a result, social media companies use AI algorithms that affect how visible entrepreneurs' material is, making it difficult to maintain steady reach and engagement.

Increased Productivity:

As a result, social media management responsibilities have been made easier by AI-driven solutions, which have automated procedures like scheduling content and engaging audiences.

Customized User Interfaces:

As a result, social media users have more relevant and interesting experiences thanks to AI algorithms that examine user behavior and give personalized information.

Support for Content Creation:

As a result, AI helps with content production by producing text and images quickly and effectively, enabling business owners to create materials of a high caliber.

Advanced Information Analysis:

Table 1.

Articles	Objectives	Methodology	Findings
Giuggioli and Pellegrini (2022)	To discover the consequences of incorporating AI as an enabler for entrepreneurs, considering Industry 4.0 specialized standards.	Systematic literature review of 31 empirical (quantitative), 5 empirical (qualitative), and 24 theoretical papers.	Integration facilitates optimistic prospects, enactment, education, research, and decision-making while endangering medium-skilled employment.
Upadhyay, Upadhyay, and Dwivedi (2021)	To study the possible factors of whether entrepreneurs are inclined to accept the integration of Artificial intelligence or not.	A pilot survey through online channels acquired 476 usable empirical responses measured by Cronbach's alpha and Fornell–Larcker criterion reliability tests for the AIADE model.	Entrepreneurs positively react to the integration of AI in terms of exposure, affordance, and generativity, which makes AI technology a gain-and-retain tool of competitive advantage in digital entrepreneurship.
Lee, Pan, and Hsieh (2021)	To investigate the factors of practical human and artificial intelligence (AI) relationship-building approaches via AI chatbot promotion for brands resulting in consumers' satisfaction with communication, and determine methods to improve consumer buying choice.	Assessed using partial least squares-structural and covariance-based structural equation modeling with 331 samples provided by Microsoft Xiaoice users.	Well-designed AI chatbots with expressive and affectionate sociable assistance can generate satisfactory results in human-AI customer communication, but long-term relationship formation is hampered.
Raneri, Lecron, Hermans, and Fouss (2022)	To conceive and test a predictive benchmark yielding entrepreneurs with a digital infrastructure for automated results to tackle AI-based predictive technologies with the convention of dealing with uncertainties.	Quantitative data extracted from an entrepreneurial project: EasyTips to utilize following the effectuation theory and qualitative data.	In the hybrid practice, entrepreneurs may stumble with the menace and indecisiveness of decision-making, but AI is presumably to practice idiomatic and predictive measures in digital product outcomes.
Yusoff, Anwar, Rahayu, Lajin, and Ridzwan (2023)	Among entrepreneurs, to explore the possible applications and usage of emotion AI with challenges and prospects to enhance SMM campaigns.	Using qualitative data from 17 different articles.	According to the needs of the entrepreneurs to assess and reach the target market, emotion AI is customizable but can also be a risky manipulative tool.
Perifanis and Kitsios (2023)	To study the incorporation of AI with business, IT techniques for digital adaptation, the significance of a dual strategic emphasis on visionary and systematic AI deployment, the requirement for reliable AI governance, and the usefulness of AI to sustain adaptive modification.	162 articles from Scopus, Science Direct, and Web of Science databases were evaluated following the approaches of Webster and Watson's systematic literature review.	Integrating AI resources with business or IT systems can affect organizations and facilitate the alignment of digital conversion and the collegial ambidexterity development of visionary and systematic AI deployment.
Carbonara and Tagliavemti (2023)	To explore the possibilities of AI being an opportunity or a threat in SMEs?	An extensive research taken from different point of views.	In SMEs, AI works as a tool for opportunity. However, amidst the opportunities, the threats are seen to be more effecting.
Scherer (2016)	Regulating AI and assessing the risk involved in it	Accessing AI and implementing them through laws to make it safe for use.	Implementing laws for the safe use of AI
Wach, Duong, Ejdys, Kazlauskaitė, Korzynski, Mazurek, Paliszkiewicz and Ziemba (2023)	Finding out the negative sides of Artificial Intelligence and critically analyzing the controversies and risks imposed by them.	Developing a conceptual framework and studying them	Risks of Generative Artificial Intelligence (GAI) and threats imposed by them in the cyber world.
Ali, Ghouri, Naseem, Soomro, Mansoor, Momani (2022)	Identifying AI as a major threat to individuals and national security through the use of Deepfake Technology (DT)	Analyzing the risk of AI and Deepfake Technology and their mode of misuse.	Wrongfully using DT to scam people and spread misinformation on different grounds and create a chaotic environment.

Consequently, advanced AI-powered analytics that offers thorough insights into user behavior and content success are advantageous to entrepreneurs.

In summary, social media entrepreneurs now benefit from enhanced productivity, customized user experiences, and sophisticated analytics as a result of the incorporation of AI. Even while the outcomes have many benefits, business owners still need to overcome algorithmic obstacles to maintain profitability and exposure in a changing digital environment.

Moreover, Adapting to the AI Era in Social Media Entrepreneurship--

The incorporation of Artificial Intelligence (AI) into social media entrepreneurship has ushered in transformative outcomes, reshaping how entrepreneurs navigate the digital landscape.

Ethical Perspectives and Openness:

As a result of navigating ethical issues pertaining to user privacy and the responsible application of AI, entrepreneurs must pledge to operate transparently.

Ecosystem of Adaptive Entrepreneurship:

An entrepreneurial ecosystem that rewards flexibility is fostered by the AI era. Businesses that use AI technologies and modify their plans appropriately can get a competitive advantage.

The outcome of AI integration in social media entrepreneurship is characterized by increased productivity, evolving skill sets, redefined engagement strategies, ethical considerations, and a need for adaptability. Entrepreneurs navigating this landscape proactively can harness the positive outcomes and position themselves for sustained success in the AI-driven modern era.

2. DISCUSSION

In the unwinding and progressing era of the 21st century, Artificial Intelligence is a man-made predictive and causal tool to enrich human dynamism economically, socially, and personally. For social media entrepreneurs who generate revenue using social media handles, aligning the technology with their business may be fraught with significant prospects and menaces. Artificial Intelligence is competent in gathering analysis data, discovering unexplored ideas and efficacious techniques, and dealing with reasoning, algorithms, and statistics to build goodwill (Obschonka & Audretsch, 2019). Entrepreneurs are often treated as conclusive decision-makers utilizing the outcomes of the data sets. Undoubtedly, the alignment welcomes optimistic results that impact the nature of the day-to-day business operations of social media for entrepreneurs. However, the actions of Artificial intelligence can also be viewed as a mode of being a swindler, manipulator, and many more, resulting in unemployment, rendering negative figures, and loss of goodwill in the target market.

2.1 Reasoning for AI as a Non-Threatening Tool for Social Media Entrepreneurs

2.1.1 Digital Offerings and Transformations

Using distinguishable modes of artificial intelligence (AI) and their integration provides multifarious positive opportunities for digital transformation in entrepreneurial activities. Preliminary studies state that AI enables entrepreneurs to determine whether they should commence the business notion or not and how the creation will influence people's standard of living and quality of life (Giuggioli & Pellegrini, 2022). In addition, the revolutionary measures speed up the emergence of contemporary technologies, opportunities, expansion, and competition, triggering events such as solving problems with artificial intelligence-supported message bots, applications, and virtual intelligence assistance. Digital offerings and transformation furnish the business with a smart operation system that can embark on innovation from diversified categories and clusters, bringing modifications in forming interactive business models, products, and relationships with customers and stakeholders.

Artificial intelligence, reasoned as machines, is constantly compelling and more satisfactory in analyzing enormous volumes of data, whereas humans are more suitable performers with sketchy data sets. In such cases, AI is a mechanism for effectively using time and limited resources. Data clarification assists in the invention, breakdown, and prediction of ongoing trends and decision-making to discharge crucial signals to be processed through social platforms. Digital transformation reduces apprehension and helps forecast prices, sales, and probable business funding channels, motivating an entrepreneur to vigorously and profoundly remain in the shade of the applications and mechanisms associated with artificial intelligence. Automation has facilitated deep learning, self-employment benefits, and modes of specialization of AL supported the solution providing applications, inferior costing with higher efficiency rate, and AI-generated learning content for learners (Giuggioli & Pellegrini, 2022). For such numerous benefits of automation, entrepreneurial activities became revolutionary, a substitute for human labor, and predictive and fostering change in organizational designs.

2.1.2 Artificial Intelligence Promotional Channels

Marketing and promotion for creating awareness of a product or service is crucial for an entrepreneur's target market to generate feasible revenue and keep expenses low and effective. Traditional marketing is used to incur more promotional expenses, limited exposure and sales area, and plenty of middlemen, charging high commissions, contributing to selling the product or service, resulting in minimal profit share. Traditional marketing strategies or offline methods cannot cope with the rapid advancement of technology and digitalization in the competitive market. In contrast, on social media platforms, brand promoters are hyped up for showcasing business products by making small video content for better interactivity with the customer. This shifting to digital marketing using social media platforms is also quite expensive as the brand promoters require training and development sessions (Liu & Li, 2021). Entrepreneurs shifting to fully artificial intelligence-oriented tools can showcase themselves as brand promoters for digital marketing and promotions, eliminating the human brand promoters.

In the current phase, details, purchases, communication through AI ChatBots, payment modes, review of products, etc., are also available on company websites in different languages and currencies. In the Internet of Things (IoT) era, customers can easily access information and develop their modes of purchase power. The dynamism of artificial intelligence can bring innovative and unexplored ideas for enhancing promotional power. Digital marketing through artificial intelligence applications provides the scope of two-way communication; products and services can be customized or modified based on the customers' enthusiastic suggestions. With rapid development, customers are prone to convenience, affordance, openness, and quite unpredictable to hold loyalty towards one specific brand; thus, brand marketers must be more up-to-date and integrate the craftsmanship of technological innovations. AL-Marketing attracts and expands the contemporaneous exemplar for prosperous business and entrepreneurship.

2.2 Reasoning for AI as a Threatening Tool for Social Media Entrepreneurs

2.2.1 Failure of Artificial Intelligence to Understand Emotion

Entrepreneurs use AI Chatbots to connect with customers within a few seconds and initiate conversations. AI Chatbot is designed by combining IQ (intelligence quotient) with EQ (emotional quotient) to build an intelligent reactive and prescient feedback system in a customized, adaptive, flexible, and compassionate manner based on scrutinizing the contemporary and past preferences of a customer (Lee, Pan, & Hsieh, 2021). Many small, medium, and large companies let artificial intelligence software developers design custom-made Chatbots for them, which store limited data and function according to pre-programmed instructions. AI Chatbots such as Siri, Alexa, Drift, Ada, etc., have built-in instructions of what to say when a particular thing is asked, and the response will be provided if and only if the AI can find it in its information store using keywords.

Multiple research state that AI Chatbots can provide informational support to a customer or a user, but an attempt to bring fairness and credibility to the social theory of interactivity with the intent of genuine emotions is insufficient. Emotion AI is still in its preliminary stages; its performance's application and results are questionable as it cannot determine or predict the accuracy of human emotions (Yusoff, Anwar, Rahayu, Lajin, & Ridzwan, 2023). Al-powered tools, software, and applications can detect pre-programmed positive and negative sentiments and are subject to manipulation. AI is an effective tool to manipulate the thoughts and preferences of customers and sometimes might result in negative consequences.

2.2.2 Artificial Intelligence as a Sole Competitive Advantage

Integrating artificial intelligence with social media businesses is a resourceful and ground-breaking technological advancement that ushered productivity, efficiency, and competitiveness to sustain in the long run for both the organization and the individual. The competitive pressure of an Artificial Intelligence oriented business can deploy any technology as well. Indeed, AI tools can redesign business operations in a limited time, utilizing limited resources, and turning the tables and nature of forecasts on multiple market factors may provide a source of further exposure. In such scenarios, entrepreneurs take AI tools and applications as a competitive advantage from the openness, affordance, and generativity perspective (Upadhyay, Upadhyay, & Dwivedi, 2021). Entrepreneurs with massive numbers of competitors tend to gain and retain their competitiveness solely based on AI applications that may eliminate them from the market.

2.2.3 Opportunities or Threats of AI in SMEs (Small and Medium-Sized Enterprises)

AI can impose quite a challenge in both SMEs and entrepreneurship, as well as different factors all over. AI, as stated in the full form, is Artificial Intelligence, a powerful system that analyzes given data and data collected from the surrounding environment and makes decisions based on its findings. One thing is certain, when AI takes a decision, it's the SYSTEM taking the decision, not the human, which leaves a certain room for HUMAN connection. When a human takes a decision, he factors in many emotions, like sensitivity, humility, emotional state, etc., which directly or indirectly affects the decision. When AI comes into the equation, all of the emotions are seen to be invalid. Machines are not programmed to express any emotions; they are programmed to work based on raw data. Which leaves us to the turmoil, can AI be used in all fields? For example, AI can be used in Business Analytics, but can it be used in taking any executive decisions?

For SMEs, Social Media Entrepreneurs can act as a helping hand in both marketing advertisement and boosting sales. SMEs hire these entrepreneurs for the tough of human connection i.e., the very thing AIs lack in. These entrepreneurs know their products, know the audience, know how human emotion works, and so on. If these works are given to a programmed system, the very reason of social entrepreneurship will lose its meaning. Sure, some opportunities are created by AIs, but that doesn't imply the fact that all works will be performed by programmable Artificial Intelligence. Some just need a human touch. Some just need to be perceived from a human's point of view.

2.2.4 Dark Sides of AI and Their Controversies

Let's paint a picture. Imagine an entrepreneur, knowing the ins and outs of social media, knows his audience well, knows how to present a product, brings in maximum engagement, and even gets some attention from potential business investors. Now comes Generative Artificial Intelligence (GAI). Using GAI, scripts are made, ads are made, and even dialogues are created using it. This not only hampers and defeats the very purpose of social entrepreneurs, but it is also seen to be done it in a very poor way. Now comes the dark side. A very modern example of GAI can be cited as ChatGPT3. Significant interest in artificial intelligence has been demonstrated by the chatbot industry, and ChatGPT is a widely recognized example of this. ChatGPT, a generative model built upon the transformer architecture, has attracted significant attention for its capability of generating text that exhibits a natural aesthetic. The OpenAI ChatGPT language model utilizes machine learning and deep learning techniques to produce conversational text-based responses that closely resemble human behavior. OpenAI initiated the development of ChatGPT in the year 2018. The initial version of the GPT algorithm, GPT-1, was trained using unsupervised instructional techniques on a substantial corpus of textual data. In total, 117 million parameters comprising it.GPT-2 and GPT-3, which are comprised of 175 billion and 1.5 billion parameters, respectively, and are regarded as two of the most comprehensive language models ever developed, are then constructed (Radford et al., 2019). Initially, OpenAI refrained from disclosing the complete model to the public out of apprehension regarding the potential for GPT-2 to generate harmful or misleading material (Wach et al.).

Witnessing the misuse of ChatGPT, and how it is mishandled, with no accountability and responsibility mechanism, and ways to abuse it, another problem has risen, promptly leading to Deepfake Technology (DT). With the rise of the 21st century, the top priority of different information all leads back to its authenticity. With DT, it becomes a problem. This is a serious problem for entrepreneurs because this technology can be abused to the fullest. A Deepfake video can be constructed using any famous social entrepreneur's face-structure and can be used to spread false information, or even damage their reputation. This acts as a bad mileage for entrepreneurs, not to mention ruining them and their careers. A famous example can be given in the form of Tom Cruise, a veteran actor in Hollywood. In a released video, he was seen performing a magic trick in a studio. This was back in 2021. Another example of a deep fake video is seen in the form of Indian actress Rashmika Mandana, very recently, where she was spotted entering a public elevator wearing intimate clothes. Both the videos, the people, the environment, were seemingly real, but the fact is it's not real, which shows how dangerous DT is.

2.2.5 Possibility of AI Replacing Jobs

AI has already started its work of replacing many jobs, for example, VR, cars without drivers, assistants who are automated in various sites, etc., the likes of which were mainly human-handled (Bruun & Duka, 2018). The world is where humans work in order to contribute, sustain and survive. AI doing these works is another way of diminishing employment scopes, and if left unchecked, will permanently diminish the need for human touch (Bruun & Duka, 2018). Just like this, in social entrepreneurship, AI will subsequently replace entrepreneurs and their jobs. This will inevitably wipe out future job scopes that social entrepreneurs thrive in.

CONCLUSION AND RECOMMENDATION

In conclusion, the field of social media entrepreneurship as well as artificial intelligence (AI) interact in a complex way which presents both novel possibilities and obstacles. The narrative of AI's life-changing potential, which views the strategic integration of AI technology as a foundation for innovation and competitive advantage, counters the worry that AI could pose a danger to social media entrepreneurs

Indeed, there are important concerns raised by the introduction of AI to the social media space, the most significant of which is the fear of job displacement. The potential for AI to automate duties can simplify some aspects of operations, but it also raises questions about the long-term employment prospects of those performing regular social media management tasks. In order to avoid further deteriorating the employment picture, entrepreneurs should strategically reconsider their approach and prioritize the development of skills that work in tandem with AI technologies.

Beyond some obstacles, though, is a marketing brimming with opportunity for social media companies that are astute enough to leverage artificial intelligence. Automation increases productivity as well as frees up entrepreneurs for concentrating on the strategic features of the businesses instead of doing menial jobs. Moreover, AI algorithms offer individualized user experiences that boost engagement and give firms who employ these technological aspects a competitive advantage. Again, conscious entrepreneurship is based on the belief that artificial intelligence (AI) has the power to transform decision-making via data analytics. As well as with the use of AI-driven analytics, social media entrepreneurs may better understand the behavior of users, develop individualized marketing campaigns, and predict market trends. Because the digital landscape is constantly changing, this data-driven strategy helps to cultivate a culture of responsiveness as well as agility.

When it comes to negotiating the always-changing terrain where social media entrepreneurship and artificial intelligence (AI) collide, being driven and flexible is crucial. Since AI and upskilling are complementary. Social media entrepreneurs should prioritize upskilling as well as reskilling projects. Entrepreneurs can embrace AI as a strategic asset rather than a threat by developing competence in areas like data analytics and AI integration. Another significant aspect is to learn about ethical AI practices, as it is essential to give ethical issues top priority while developing and implementing AI systems. In order to prevent prejudices from being reinforced and to guarantee that AI is used responsibly on social media platforms. Also, entrepreneurs should promote openness and justice.

Essentially, the overall story accepts the difficulties presented by AI while still promoting these all technologies as essential instruments for development and progress. Entrepreneurs in the social media space are at a turning point in their history, wherein the thoughtful application of AI will protect them from possible risks and also usher in a period of unparalleled creativity and influence. Instead of being a threat, the moral and wise use of AI becomes essential for business owners who want to survive and prosper in the fast-paced and cutthroat world of social media in terms of business.

REFERENCES

Aboulilah, H. M. A. E., Hossain, S. F. A., Vuong, B. N., & Jebril, T. (2022). Exploring the Relationship between WeChat Usage and E-purchase Intention During the COVID-19 Pandemic Among University Students in China. *SAGE Open*, *12*(4). doi:10.1177/21582440221139447 PMID:36466966

Ali, A. (2022). Battle of Deep Fakes: Artificial Intelligence Set to Become a Major Threat to the Individual and National Security. *2022 International Conference on Cyber Resilience (ICCR)*, 1–5. 10.1109/ICCR56254.2022.9995821

Bruun, E. P. G., & Duka, A. (2018). Artificial intelligence, jobs and the future of work: Racing with the machines. *Basic Income Studies*, *13*(2). Advance online publication. doi:10.1515/bis-2018-0018

Carbonara, E., & Tagliaventi, M. R. (2023). *Smes in the digital era: Opportunities and challenges of the digital single market*. Edward Elgar Publishing. doi:10.4337/9781803921648

Cyrine, B.-H., Mario, T., Troise, C., & Yablonsky, S. A. (2022). New technologies and entrepreneurship: Exploring entrepreneurial behavior in the digital transformation era. *International Journal of Entrepreneurial Behaviour & Research*, *28*(5), 1129–1137. Advance online publication. doi:10.1108/IJEBR-08-2022-999

Emmanuel, C. P., Qin, S., Hossain, S. F. A., & Hussain, K. (2022). Factors influencing social-media-based entrepreneurship prospect among female students in China. *Heliyon*, *8*(12), e12041. doi:10.1016/j.heliyon.2022.e12041 PMID:36483305

Giuggioli, G., & Pellegrini, M. M. (2022). Artificial intelligence as an enabler for entrepreneurs: A systematic literature review and an agenda for future research. *International Journal of Entrepreneurial Behaviour & Research*, *29*(4), 816–837. doi:10.1108/IJEBR-05-2021-0426

Hossain, S. F. A. (2019). Social networking and its role in media entrepreneurship: Evaluating the use of mobile phones in the context of online shopping–A review. *Journal of Media Management and Entrepreneurship*, *1*(1), 73–86. doi:10.4018/JMME.2019010105

Hossain, S. F. A., Nurunnabi, M., Hussain, K., & Saha, S. K. (2019). Effects of variety-seeking intention by mobile phone usage on university students' academic performance. *Cogent Education*, *6*(1), 1574692. doi:10.1080/2331186X.2019.1574692

Hossain, S. F. A., Nurunnabi, M., Hussain, K., & Shan, X. (2020). Smartphone-based m-shopping behavior and innovative entrepreneurial tendency among women in emerging Asia. *International Journal of Gender and Entrepreneurship*, *12*(2), 173–189. doi:10.1108/IJGE-03-2019-0054

Hossain, S. F. A., Shan, X., Musa, M., & Rahman, P. (2023). Social media and increased venture creation tendency with innovative ideas: the case of female students in Asia. In *Research Anthology on Applying Social Networking Strategies to Classrooms and Libraries* (pp. 1716–1731). IGI Global.

Hossain, S. F. A., Shan, X., Nurunnabi, M., Tushar, H., Mohsin, A. K. M., & Ahsan, F. T. (2021). Opportunities and challenges of m-learning during the COVID-19 pandemic: A mixed methodology approach. *E-Collaboration Technologies and Strategies for Competitive Advantage Amid Challenging Times*, 210-227.

Hossain, S. F. A., Xi, Z., Nurunnabi, M., & Hussain, K. (2020). Ubiquitous role of social networking in driving M-Commerce: Evaluating the use of mobile phones for online shopping and payment in the context of trust. *SAGE Open*, *10*(3). Advance online publication. doi:10.1177/2158244020939536

Lee, C. T., Pan, L., & Hsieh, S. H. (2021). Artificial intelligent chatbots as brand promoters: A two-stage structural equation modeling-artificial neural network approach. *Internet Research*, *32*(4), 1329–1356. doi:10.1108/INTR-01-2021-0030

Liu, Y., & Li, Z. (2021, December 1). *Application analysis of artificial intelligence technology in brand Marketing Strategy*. Retrieved from https://ieeexplore.ieee.org/stamp/stamp.jsp?tp=&arnumber=9759931

MishraA. (2022). Retrieved from https://www.researchgate.net/publication/357705863_Role_of_Artificial_Intelligence_in_Social_Media_Marketing

Mohsin, A. K. M., Hongzhen, L., & Hossain, S. F. A. (2021). Impact of COVID-19 pandemic on consumer economy: Countermeasures analysis. *SAGE Open*, *11*(2). doi:10.1177/21582440211008875

NorströmL.IslindA.SnisU. (2020). Retrieved from https://www.researchgate.net/publication/342421823_Algorithmic_Work_The_Impact_of_Algorithms_on_Work_with_Social_Media

Obschonka, M., & Audretsch, D. B. (2019). Artificial intelligence and big data in entrepreneurship: A new era has begun. *Small Business Economics*, *55*(3), 529–539. doi:10.1007/s11187-019-00202-4

Perifanis, N., & Kitsios, F. (2023). Investigating the Influence of Artificial intelligence on business Value in the digital Era of Strategy: a literature review. *Information, 14*(2), 85. doi:10.3390/info14020085

SadikuM.AshaoluT.MajebiA.MusaS. (2021). Retrieved from https://www.researchgate.net/publication/368060163_Artificial_Intelligence_in_Social_Media

SchererM. U. (2021, March 8). *About*. HeinOnline. https://heinonline.org/HOL/LandingPage?handle=hein.journals%2Fhjlt29&div=15&id=&page=

Upadhyay, N., Upadhyay, S., & Dwivedi, Y. K. (2021). Theorizing artificial intelligence acceptance and digital entrepreneurship model. *International Journal of Entrepreneurial Behaviour & Research*, *28*(5), 1138–1166. doi:10.1108/IJEBR-01-2021-0052

Vuong, B. N., Tushar, H., & Hossain, S. F. A. (2023). The effect of social support on job performance through organizational commitment and innovative work behavior: Does innovative climate matter? *Asia-Pacific Journal of Business Administration*, *15*(5), 832–854. doi:10.1108/APJBA-06-2021-0256

Wach, K., Duong, C. D., Ejdys, J., Kazlauskaitė, R., Korzynski, P., Mazurek, G., Paliszkiewicz, J., & Ziemba, E. (2023, June). 'The Dark Side of Generative Artificial Intelligence: A Critical Analysis of Controversies and Risks of ChatGPT'. *Entrepreneurial Business and Economics Review*, *11*(2), 7–30. eber.uek.krakow.pl. doi:10.15678/EBER.2023.110201

Yusoff, Y. B., Anwar, I. F. B., Rahayu, S. B., Lajin, N. F. B. M., & Ridzwan, M. B. (2023). A Review on Integrating Emotional Intelligence with Artificial Intelligence in Social Media Marketing Among Entrepreneurs. *Journal of Contemporary Social Science and Education Studies*, *3*(2), 44–50. https://www.researchgate.net/publication/373840570_Journal_of_Contemporary_Social_Science_and_Education_Studies_A_Review_on_Integrating_Emotional_Intelligence_with_Artificial_Intelligence_in_Social_Media_Marketing_Among_Entrepreneurs

Chapter 10
Enabling Women Entrepreneurs in Bangladesh:
Analysis of the Impact of Technology Adoption

Faiza Tanaz Ahsan
The University of Nottingham, UK

EXECUTIVE SUMMARY

This chapter primarily focuses on the significant contributions of female entrepreneurs to Bangladesh's economy in the light of technology/IT as a medium. Its primary objective is to present a comprehensive overview of the experiences of female entrepreneurs, including the support they have received, the obstacles they have had to overcome, and other related aspects and the involvement of technology to carry out their day-to-day activity. The central aim of this study is to explore the role of the digital marketplace in empowering women in Bangladesh's entrepreneurial endeavors. The findings of the study reveal that most women in Bangladesh initiate their businesses to attain self-sufficiency and financial independence. They face significant challenges such as social barriers, family constraints, limited resources, and labor shortages. Many of these female entrepreneurs were students, homemakers, or teachers before venturing into business.

Entrepreneurship plays a crucial role in driving a nation's economic progress by generating wealth, reducing unemployment, and alleviating poverty. This chapter primarily focuses on the significant contributions of female entrepreneurs to Bangladesh's economy in the light of technology/IT as a medium. Its primary objective is to present a comprehensive overview of the experiences of female entrepreneurs, including the support they have received, the obstacles they have had to overcome, and other related aspects and the involvement of technology to carry out their day-to-day activity. The central aim of this study is to explore the role of the digital marketplace in empowering women in Bangladesh's entrepreneurial endeavors.

DOI: 10.4018/979-8-3693-1781-5.ch010

The findings of the study reveal that most women in Bangladesh initiate their businesses to attain self-sufficiency and financial independence. They face significant challenges such as social barriers, family constraints, limited resources, and labor shortages. Many of these female entrepreneurs were students, homemakers, or teachers before venturing into business. According to respondents, their products have positively impacted people's quality of life.

Most female entrepreneurs aspire to expand both their online and offline businesses while also providing employment opportunities for unemployed women. The study indicates that a substantial proportion of online entrepreneurs are young women, and a significant number of startups emerged in 2020, suggesting a correlation with the effects of the COVID-19 pandemic. Facebook serves as the primary platform for selling products among these women entrepreneurs. Most of them source their products from wholesalers to secure better deals and benefits, while some opt to produce their goods to ensure authenticity.

The involvement of women in entrepreneurship significantly enhances the economic development and social well-being of their communities, as well as their families' income. The findings underscore the profound impact of female entrepreneurship on both Bangladesh's economic landscape and the lives of these entrepreneurial women.

INTRODUCTION

In recent times, the advancement of women's entrepreneurship within Small and Medium Enterprises (SMEs) in Bangladesh has become a focal point in policymaking aimed at the overall development of the SME sector as a strategy for inclusive growth. The reasons for this focus are evident. On a global scale, despite comprising half of the human population, women are conspicuously absent in terms of owning and managing their own businesses, particularly in developing countries. While acknowledging the significant strides made by women globally and in Bangladesh in various economic activities and professional pursuits, especially since the establishment of the *Beijing Platform of Action* for women, challenges persist on the ground. These challenges are exacerbated by women's trifecta of hardships in Bangladesh—entailing extreme poverty, pervasive discrimination, and inequality, and, significantly, limited participation in the workforce.

Despite constituting half of the population in Bangladesh, women continue to face significant under-representation in the business sector. While the Ready-Made Garments (RMG) industry sees a substantial female presence, comprising nearly 90% of its 5 million workers, their involvement in non-RMG industrial sectors is minimal. This underscores the untapped potential of a substantial female workforce as a valuable source for economic growth and social advancement. To foster a sustainable democratic society marked by inclusive participation, poverty reduction, and overall prosperity, it is imperative to promote the development of women entrepreneurship.

The intersection of social networking and media entrepreneurship with a focus on the role of mobile phone usage in online shopping. Conducted through a systematic literature review without primary data collection, the research examines literature from the last five years (2013-2018). The findings highlight the widespread popularity of social networking, online shopping, and digital media entrepreneurship, facilitated by the accessible and affordable use of mobile phones. Despite the increased popularity of media entrepreneurship, the study suggests that its implementation has been lacking. The research points towards opportunities for improving online shopping experiences, building trust, simplifying decision-making in online purchases, and addressing unemployment issues in emerging and developing nations. While acknowledging limitations, such as inconsistent research papers and limited empirical evidence, the study provides implications and contributions for online shoppers, marketers, policymakers, and entrepreneurs. Ultimately, it recognizes the growing role of social networking in the development of media entrepreneurship, particularly in the context of mobile phone usage for online shopping. (Syed,2019)

In Bangladesh, female entrepreneurs constitute only 10% of the overall entrepreneur population (Chowdhury & Rabbani, 2013), a notably lower figure when compared to the more than 25% seen in advanced market economies (GEM, 2010). The vast majority (97.6%) of Bangladeshi women entrepreneurs operate in micro-enterprises with less than 10 employees, with only 2%, 0.24%, and 0.16% involved in small (10–49 employees), medium (50–99 employees), and large enterprises (100 and above employees) respectively (Uz Zaman & Islam, 2011). The primary sectors for women entrepreneurs are manufacturing (62%), trading (13%), and service (13%), with specific concentrations in handicrafts (70%), home textile (16%), parlor (5%), food processing (4%), agricultural products processing (3%), and printing (2%) businesses (BWCCI, 2008). In the handicrafts sector, women are predominantly viewed as workers, although men are also occasionally employed. Cultural values vary across sectors, with male family members in certain industries expressing concerns about women interacting with non-family males, limiting their freedom of movement. However, in the handicrafts sector, women can operate their businesses from home or nearby, aligning with social norms and expectations. This context makes the handicraft sector a fitting subject for our study on the contextual nature of entrepreneurial orientation (EO) and its impact on business performance, presenting a scenario distinct from that in developed countries. The distinctive features of venture creation, such as creativity, innovation, and original thinking, are crucial for business success. Social media aligns well with entrepreneurial processes, exhibiting traits like autonomy, creativity, risk-taking, star animation, and competitive aggressiveness. Media and companies are encouraged to adopt a risk-taking and innovative entrepreneurial approach.

The goal of social media in venture creation is to establish a bridge between the broader discipline of venture creation and the specificities of the media industry, facilitating the exchange of ideas and practices. Overall, the entrepreneurial orientation of firms, characterized by processes, practices, and decision-making activities, is influenced by the symbiotic relationship between media and venture creation. (Syed et. Al, 2023).

Existing literature highlights that the primary obstacle for women initiating businesses in Bangladesh is the social milieu, encompassing prevailing societal norms, religious values, family expectations, and traditions, which curtail women's mobility and significantly impact their engagement in entrepreneurial endeavors (De Vita et al., 2014; Mozumdar et al., 2017, 2020). Women's participation in entrepreneurial activities in this context is intricately tied to patriarchal structures, where many rely on parents or spouses for initial financial support to commence business ventures, and religious factors play a significant role (Drinkwater, 2009; Mozumdar et al., 2020; Chowdhury & Rabbani, 2013). Given that around 90% of the population adheres to Islam, societal norms influenced by Islamic views often hinder women's involvement in business activities (Drinkwater, 2009; Islam et al., 2009). For example, women observing purdah, the practice of screening women from men using a veil in Muslim communities, encounter difficulties accessing financial institutions, procuring raw materials, and selling products in public spaces where interactions with men are necessary (Mozumdar, 2018).

Moreover, the business landscape in Bangladesh poses various impediments to women's participation in entrepreneurial activities, ranging from physical barriers such as poor infrastructure and technology to institutional barriers like bribery and corruption within complex bureaucratic systems (Mozumdar et al., 2020). These barriers are anticipated to influence business performance, particularly when women are confined to traditional roles, such as mothers or wives, and face challenges in exhibiting innovativeness or proactiveness, particularly in an unsupportive business environment. Understanding how women entrepreneurs navigate these challenges, employing entrepreneurial orientation (EO) to seize opportunities and achieve business performance, is of both theoretical and practical significance. In constrained environments, the dimensions of EO may encounter limitations, yet the impact on business performance could still be positive (Fuentes-Fuentes et al., 2015; Lumpkin & Dess, 1996). The case of Bangladesh and the handicraft sector serves as an ideal context to investigate whether such dynamics hold true for women entrepreneurs operating within environments characterized by social and business constraints.

Extensive research has been conducted on women entrepreneurship for several significant reasons. Firstly, over the past decade, there has been global recognition of women entrepreneurs as a crucial yet untapped resource for fostering economic growth. Secondly, various studies highlight that women entrepreneurs play a substantial role in national economic development by creating employment opportunities for themselves and becoming self-employed. Additionally, they are perceived to contribute innovative solutions to management, organizational, and business challenges, bringing fresh perspectives essential for seizing entrepreneurial opportunities. However, it's worth noting that despite their potential, women entrepreneurs remain a minority, particularly in developing countries.

Gender Perspectives on Entrepreneurship

Are women fundamentally different from men as entrepreneurs, possessing distinct characteristics and traits? No, because both genders are generally assumed to share commonly identified entrepreneurial traits, such as a creative mindset, drive, initiative, a willingness to take risks, and independence, among others. However, the extent of these traits can be influenced by social circumstances and the economic environment, which significantly shape an individual's entry into business and their performance thereafter. To comprehensively understand the differences in the entrepreneurial qualities of men and women, an objective evaluation of the performance of both groups at the firm level post-entry into business is necessary. It's crucial to acknowledge that women's entrepreneurship is intertwined with their societal position and the role of entrepreneurship in the same society. It tends to thrive better in a positive socio-economic and cultural setting, including family circumstances, along with a conducive macro-economic environment. Therefore, under favorable circumstances and applying the general concept of entrepreneurship, women entrepreneurs can be identified simply as women or groups of women initiating, organizing, and managing a business enterprise. A South Korean study, as part of the APEC Regional study on women entrepreneurs in 1999, defines a women entrepreneur as the de facto owner of a business actively involved in its day-to-day operations. Depending on specific country circumstances, various criteria, such as the Government of India's definition, may be used to identify women as entrepreneurs, emphasizing ownership, control, and employment contribution by women in the enterprise.

Factors Influencing Women's Engagement in Entrepreneurship in Bangladesh

According to the conventional textbook perspective, the primary determinant prompting individuals to enter business is profit, with additional motivating factors including economic growth and significant innovation potential within an environment offering promising technological opportunities (Szirmai et al., 2011). Further research by Vivarelli (2012) suggests that, beyond profit expectations and positive factors, various negative factors such as the fear of unemployment, low wages, and a lack of white-collar job opportunities in the formal job market may also influence potential entrepreneurs, conflicting with their personal traits and motivations for entering business.

In addition to external factors, certain internal characteristics of new enterprise founders, such as prior work experience, family traditions, financial status, and personal motivation, serve as driving forces for entrepreneurial initiatives. Likewise, the subsequent performance (including growth and survival) of an entrepreneur appears to be significantly influenced by factors like education level, training, skills, past job experiences, human capital strategies, involvement in innovation-oriented economic sectors (such as technology and knowledge-intensive industries), and the overall economic and business environment. The focus now turns to examining these supply and demand factors that impact the growth of women entrepreneurship in Bangladesh.

Empirical evidence is drawn from two significant studies on women entrepreneurship in Bangladesh, namely SMEF 2009 and BWCCI 2007. The SMEF study, encompassing a sample survey of 1035 women entrepreneurs, provides national coverage across 34 districts, 6 divisions, and 50 upazilas, including respondents from both urban and rural areas. In comparison, the BWCCI study involves a sample survey of 130 entrepreneurs, offering regional coverage.

Regarding the motivating factors leading women to pursue business in Bangladesh, the data indicates that profit earning, often expressed as a willingness to contribute to family incomes, is identified as the most crucial factor at 48%. Subsequently, inspiration from family and friends (20%), a desire for professional independence (24%), financial freedom and security (14%), and the aspiration for self-employment (14%) follow suit. Additionally, other factors such as self-inspiration, higher social status, and the establishment of women's rights are recognized as significant drivers. The BWCCI study underscores the noteworthy influence of women entrepreneurs belonging to families with a business background, where either parents or husbands are involved in business, playing a pivotal role in inspiring them to enter entrepreneurship. The collective evidence from these major studies indicates that, similar to many other developing countries, the primary determinants on the supply side prompting women's entry into entrepreneurship in Bangladesh are profit motives, followed by economic freedom, self-dependence, financial security, and inspiration from family and friends with business backgrounds.

Introduction to the Role of Technology in Contemporary Business Environments in Bangladesh

Artificial intelligence (AI) holds the capacity to bring substantial improvements to businesses in Bangladesh by automating repetitive tasks, streamlining operations, and delivering valuable insights through data analysis (Babu, 2021). For instance, AI can enhance efficiency by overseeing and controlling production processes, identifying defects, and forecasting maintenance needs in the manufacturing sector. Additionally, AI-powered chatbots can be employed for efficient customer service, while AI-based systems contribute to optimizing inventory management and predicting consumer demand in the retail industry.

In the financial sector, AI plays a pivotal role in identifying fraudulent activities and assessing credit risks, as outlined by Singh, Hasan, and Rajendran (2023). Moreover, AI contributes to enhancing healthcare in Bangladesh by analyzing medical images, detecting diseases, and predicting patient outcomes, as evidenced by the research conducted by Uzir et al. (2021). The impact of AI on business practices is evident and has instigated substantial changes. As of 2022, the global artificial intelligence market was valued at USD 136.55 billion. Projections indicate an expected annual growth rate of 37.3% from 2023 to 2030, as reported by Grand View Research in 2022. This underscores the significant and ongoing influence of AI in shaping the landscape of business.

As of 2023, businesses incorporating AI may achieve a 25% improvement in customer satisfaction, as indicated by Zapanta, T. (2023). A table providing a summary of potential AI applications across various industries is available (refer to Table 1). In general, the adoption of AI in business is witnessing widespread growth, and companies in Bangladesh are progressively embracing this technology to enhance their operations and maintain competitiveness in the global market. Although Bangladesh initiated an AI strategy in March 2020, progress in development has been relatively slow since then. Bangladesh possesses the potential to harness its scientific and technical infrastructure for the advantages of AI by establishing dedicated AI research organizations and attracting top talent. The country is capable of initiating AI-based research programs addressing local challenges, including but not limited to Bangla Natural Language Processing (NLP), factory automation, agricultural support, personalized education, and healthcare for underprivileged regions, as highlighted by Sayeed Ahmed in The Daily Star on January 28, 2023.

The Relevance of Intersection of Women Entrepreneurship and AI/Technology

In the 2022 GSMA Mobile Gender Gap report, Bangladesh is identified as having the most significant gender disparity in mobile internet usage among 10 low and middle-income countries. The data reveals that 36% of men use the internet compared to only 19% of women. According to the 2021 Bangladesh Country Gender Assessment by the World Bank, women constitute a mere 14% of all STEM professionals in the country as of 2019. Additionally, only 20% of employees in the IT sector are women, as reported in 2017. Women's representation in leadership roles within the IT industry is notably low, accounting for just 15% of top positions at IT firms. Furthermore, only about 1% of the country's IT companies are led by women, and a mere 2% of Bangladesh's IT entrepreneurs are women. Despite an increased number of girls successfully completing secondary and higher secondary studies in Bangladesh, the statistics indicate that only 8% of them choose to enroll in science departments, with a mere 1.5% pursuing studies in engineering and technology, as of 2019. These figures underscore the existing gender gap and emphasize the urgent need for immediate actions to address this issue. Basic digital literacy is crucial for women, especially considering the significant role it played during the pandemic. In urban areas, a considerable number of online businesses initiated and managed by women emerged, providing crucial support to families during challenging times. However, it's important to note that this trend was predominantly observed in urban settings. In rural areas, only a minimal percentage of women, approximately 4%, have ever utilized a computer, in contrast to the 13% observed in cities. Additionally, ownership of smartphones varies, with 57% of urban women possessing smartphones compared to 42% in rural areas. This discrepancy underscores the importance of addressing digital literacy and access issues, particularly in rural communities, to ensure more inclusive participation in the digital landscape.

To address the technological expertise gap among most women in the country, The World Bank, in collaboration with Women in Digital and UNDP, initiated the 'Digital Innovation Challenge for Women 2023.' This initiative placed a special emphasis on reaching out to girls from rural areas. Launched on International Women's Day (IWD), the competition garnered 132 submissions from girls, forming 58 teams, who presented their proposals to a panel of tech experts and startup companies serving as mentors over a three-month period. Subsequently, 30 teams were shortlisted for the next phase. The challenge concluded with an awards ceremony on May 20, 2023, where three winning teams were selected from the top eight teams after presenting their pitches to the judges.

The organizers commended the innovative ideas and sophisticated models developed by these young women, who had traveled significant distances to participate. Particularly inspiring was their focus on creating solutions for challenges they face in their lives. Examples include an environmentally friendly solar cooking stove, an affordable locally developed model for the ELISA test to detect tuberculosis and other diseases, and eight types of biodegradable sanitary napkins priced between 2-15 BDT and dispensed via a vending machine. The last entry emerged as the overall winner.

Digital innovations wield the transformative power to narrow gaps in mobility, pay, labor force participation, and education. Involvement of women in technology not only contributes to closing these gaps but also sparks the development of innovative solutions that cater to women's specific needs, fostering gender equality. The integration of women in the technological landscape is not only a matter of inclusivity but also a strategic move that leads to more comprehensive and effective solutions for societal challenges related to gender disparities. The digital gender divide goes beyond the shortage of women and girls in STEM, extending to deep-seated social barriers and norms that impede their entry into STEM and ICT sectors. It is imperative to address this challenge through diverse approaches, including mentorship, awareness campaigns, involvement of families and communities in dismantling gender stereotypes, and showcasing successful women role models who have paved the way for thriving careers in these fields. Confronting cultural obstacles requires concerted efforts to eliminate ingrained biases.

Another significant impediment is the prevalence of cyberviolence against women and girls, underscoring the urgent need for awareness initiatives and the implementation of preventive measures, such as technology and cybersecurity training. Effectively addressing these issues is essential to establish an inclusive digital environment that empowers women and girls to actively participate and succeed in the digital era.

A comprehensive strategy that encompasses education, employment, and societal norms is essential to identify and address the barriers hindering gender equality in the technology sector. This multifaceted approach is crucial for unlocking the full potential of the digital realm for women. Initiatives supported by The World Bank, such as *WePower* to increase the representation of female engineers in the energy sector and Women Entrepreneurs Finance Initiative (WEFI) for digital marketing and e-commerce training, showcase efforts to bridge gender gaps. The Bank is also backing projects like Private Investment and Digital Entrepreneurship (PRIDE), offering advanced ICT skills and certification for Bangladeshi women, and Accelerating and Strengthening Skills for Economic Transformation (ASSET), with a goal to involve 350,000 women in skilling and training programs. Through these endeavors, there is a concerted effort to ensure that women can fully leverage the abundant opportunities provided by ICT.

In Bangladesh, The World Bank is making significant investments in skill development, preparing women and girls for the evolving landscape of work. While the mentioned competition may have been modest in scale, it serves as a testament to the readiness of women to embrace and excel in the challenges posed by the digital era.

Empowered Women: Leaving Their Digital Footprints

Women in Bangladesh are achieving success in the technology, startup, and online business sectors through self-confidence, determination, and a resilient commitment to overcoming challenges. Numerous women have established promising startups, led key positions in platforms, and built internet-based enterprises, showcasing their skills and talents. Despite these individual successes, a significant gender gap persists in the tech, startup, and related fields, with most positions occupied by males, posing substantial challenges in achieving equal rights for all genders.

According to articles based on interviews published by The Daily Star, female entrepreneurs in Bangladesh face both challenges and rewards while utilizing information technology and establishing businesses within the expansive e-commerce landscape of the country. Despite significant progress in women's empowerment across various sectors, the representation of women in the tech and startup domains remains less than satisfactory, accounting for less than 20 percent of overall participation in the sector.

The journey of Farhana A Rahman, the first woman Senior Vice-President of the Bangladesh Association of Software and Information Services, was marked by challenges. Having completed post-graduation in nutrition, she underwent IT training in 2003 to pursue freelancing due to the inability to adhere to traditional 9-to-5 office hours for personal reasons. Initially obtaining work through connections abroad, she witnessed her guest room transform into a crowded workspace within a year, leading her to create 10 jobs. In 2005, she founded UY Systems Ltd, specializing in software development and web solutions. Farhana highlights that the acceptance of women in the technology sector was initially low, although the situation has improved. Nonetheless, she notes that many girls lack guidance on becoming entrepreneurs, and there is limited support to nurture them. She points out that families are often hesitant to take similar risks for female members aspiring to be entrepreneurs as they would for males. Additionally, challenges arise when women abruptly quit jobs, and families may not permit them to spend extended hours in the office. Despite these challenges, UY Systems currently exports its services to numerous countries and employs approximately 125 people.

Syeda Khadiza Dina entered the technology sector in 2005, leveraging her master's degree in law to establish business process outsourcing for accounting. As the Managing Director of ZS Solutions Ltd, her firm has evolved to offer a range of IT services, encompassing software and app development for international entities. ZS Solutions Ltd boasts clients such as Robi and *Upay*. Dina notes the challenges of leading a tech firm as a woman, emphasizing the difficulties in gaining the trust of customers. She often faces questions regarding whether she inherited the business from her father or manages a firm owned by her husband. Despite these challenges, her firm has grown, and she currently employs 25 people.

Since the onset of the coronavirus pandemic, women have showcased their capabilities and resilience in a sector known as f-commerce. With physical stores closing due to the health crisis and associated lockdowns, coupled with customer hesitancy to leave their homes, women entrepreneurs stepped up and initiated businesses using Facebook, a platform with over 40 million users in Bangladesh. These women entrepreneurs have taken charge of their families, helping them navigate through the financial challenges brought about by the pandemic. Nasima Akter Nisha, the president of the Women and e-Commerce Forum (WE), highlights that women are actively selling a wide range of products online.

The Women and e-Commerce Forum's Facebook page, with 1.3 million members, serves as a platform for women to showcase and sell their products or services. F-commerce has emerged as a source of employment for approximately four lakh women across the country, highlighting its significant impact on creating opportunities in the workforce.

In a noteworthy trend, highly educated women are choosing to return home after leaving positions at leading global companies, opting to launch their own startups with the aim of addressing societal issues using technology. Maliha M Quadir is one such individual, having worked at prestigious companies like Morgan Stanley, Standard Chartered, and Nokia. In 2014, she founded *Shohoz*, which has now become the largest online ticket destination in Bangladesh. This positive development reflects a growing trend of skilled women leveraging their expertise to contribute to the entrepreneurial landscape and address local challenges through innovative technological solutions.

Ambareen Reza, one of the co-founders of *Food panda* in 2013, served as the managing director and played a crucial role in propelling the firm to the forefront as the leading food delivery platform in Bangladesh. Her journey has been marked by numerous challenges spanning her professional, academic, and personal life. Choosing to venture into entrepreneurship as a woman in Bangladesh, leaving behind her job in Australia, initially faced skepticism from both family and friends. Despite encountering these challenges, Reza's unwavering perseverance served as her guiding force, enabling her to navigate through various obstacles successfully. Opting to become a woman entrepreneur in Bangladesh and leaving her job in Australia was not initially well-received by her family and friends, Ambareen reveals. However, her perseverance became the key factor in overcoming these challenges. Describing herself as a problem solver, she emphasizes her approach of being objective, addressing the immediate issue, and moving forward at every step of her journey. Reflecting on her past, Ambareen believes that confronting and surmounting these challenges has played a crucial role in enhancing her resilience. Currently, she leads multiple operations and initiatives, aiming to enhance the accessibility of online delivery services for customers and ensure a seamless customer experience. Ambareen envisions a future where businesses will increasingly analyze data, utilizing machine learning and artificial intelligence to inform their decision-making processes.

To make strides in the fast-paced professional world, young women should venture into STEM (Science, Technology, Engineering, and Mathematics) and prepare themselves for challenging roles. Sonia Bashir Kabir, after serving as the managing director of Microsoft Bangladesh, Myanmar, Nepal, Bhutan, and Laos, has transitioned into a technology entrepreneur with the founding of *SBK Tech Ventures*. Sonia expresses her dream of empowering women to embrace technology, emphasizing that this is crucial for democratizing technology. She highlights the need for addressing the challenge of women being left behind in Bangladesh, asserting that digital inclusion is a joint responsibility of both men and women, with joint risks associated with exclusion. Sonia advocates for changing the perception that technology is not for women or girls, emphasizing the importance of exposing them to STEM and empowering them as future leaders. She stresses the need to ensure that women play a role in creating technologies that prevent the replication of old gender stereotypes and inequalities in the digital space. Moreover, Sonia underscores the importance of accelerating gender parity and increasing women's economic participation globally. In the evolving digital landscape, female entrepreneurs have the flexibility to start businesses with minimal investment and access global markets. To encourage women entrepreneurs, Sonia emphasizes the need for building an ecosystem where women are inspired, encouraged, and rewarded for leveraging technology and embracing entrepreneurship.

Analysis of the Role of AI/Technology in Women-Led Businesses: A Global Perspective

Throughout the Pacific Islands, women have experienced numerous advantages from digital technology in their businesses. It has facilitated their access to new markets, with instances such as Tongan women utilizing Facebook to sell handmade crafts to the diaspora (FAO and SPC, 2019). Additionally, technology has enabled remote communication, reducing travel costs, facilitating supply orders, and offering calculator functions (GSMA, 2014). The use of mobile banking technology has empowered business owners to maintain records of savings and transactions, enhancing their eligibility for loans to formalize or expand their ventures (UNESCAP, 2020). In places like Kosrae and Yap, Federated States of Micronesia, the increased use of mobile phones and improved boats has made night-fishing with husbands safer for more women (Pacific Community, 2019).

Beyond employment, digital technology brings further empowerment to women. Initiatives like *mWomen*, initially a collaboration between Vodafone and the Ministry of Women, Children, and Poverty Alleviation, have provided free SMS advice on legal rights related to gender-based violence in Fiji (UNESCAP, 2016). Moreover, the use of digital technology can contribute to women's freedom, with mobile phones being perceived as a safety measure for travel (Pacific Community, 2019).

On International Women's Day in 2023, the United Nations organized a workshop titled "*DigitALL: Innovation and Technology for Gender Equality*." This event emphasized that digital entrepreneurship holds significant potential for fostering women's integration into the digital economy, unlocking new business prospects, achieving efficiency gains, and facilitating better access to markets and global value chains.

Although the digital economy is a vast and diverse category, the International Finance Corporation (IFC) projects that women have the potential to contribute over $300 billion to e-commerce markets alone in Africa and Southeast Asia between 2025 and 2030. The IFC highlighted three key advantages that e-commerce presents for women entrepreneurs. First and foremost, it lowers barriers to entry compared to traditional brick-and-mortar businesses. This means that women entrepreneurs can initiate their businesses with lower startup costs and without the necessity for a physical storefront, providing a substantial advantage.

Yvette Uwimpaye, a young entrepreneur hailing from Rwanda, recognized the challenges people faced while navigating multiple markets for their shopping needs. In response to this issue, she conceived Murukali, a streamlined online shopping platform designed to save both time and money. With remarkably low start-up costs amounting to $1,155, she successfully launched this platform, revolutionizing the shopping experience in Rwanda.

Secondly, digital entrepreneurship empowers women to connect with customers globally, enabling them to broaden their customer base and expand their businesses beyond local markets. Birame Sock, an entrepreneur based in Senegal, exemplifies this by founding Kwely, an online B2B wholesale sourcing marketplace specializing in products made in Africa. This digital platform provides buyers worldwide with access to high-quality and distinctive African products that meet international standards.

Furthermore, digital entrepreneurship offers a level of flexibility concerning work hours and location. Women entrepreneurs facing caregiving responsibilities or mobility constraints can derive significant benefits from digital technologies in managing their businesses.

Obstacles in Harnessing Technology: A Closer Look at Challenges

According to a report from the United Nations Economic and Social Commission for Asia and the Pacific's (ESCAP) Catalyzing Women's Entrepreneurship (CWE) program, women entrepreneurs in Bangladesh face significant challenges in using and applying technology to enhance their businesses, particularly those engaged in Social Media-Based Women Entrepreneurs (SMBWE). The report reveals that 49% of respondents felt confident in handling the technology applications required for efficient online business management at the initial stage. However, the remaining 51% encountered challenges related to techno-literacy when starting their businesses, gradually overcoming these hurdles. Despite progress, about 27% of SMBWE continued to struggle with technological issues during the scale-up phase. Common challenges included managing social media pages, promoting products online, lack of information on social media-based business, and creating social media business pages. Qualitative assessments reiterated the variety of technological challenges, emphasizing critical issues such as updating content on social media pages and posting customer updates. Many female entrepreneurs expressed a lack of knowledge and control over the posting process, leading them to hire others for these tasks. SMBWE often face difficulties in understanding which types of posts maximize outreach, what content attracts customer attention, and how to monitor the reach of live videos. Consistency in reaping benefits from online posts remains a challenge, even with additional expenditure. Additionally, low bandwidth emerged as a barrier to running social media-based businesses.

Vuong et al found that strong social support in the workplace has a positive impact on employees' job performance. This relationship is partially explained by the mediating factors of organizational commitment and innovative work behavior. Additionally, the presence of an innovative climate further enhances the positive connection between social support and innovative work behavior.

Pervasive online gender-based abuse emerged as the fourth most significant challenge, with 42% of Social Media-Based Women Entrepreneurs (SMBWE) reporting it at the start-up stage. This issue persists as a prevalent concern affecting women, with 34% of respondents facing significant online abuse during the scale-up phase. Operating businesses primarily on online platforms, promoting products through Facebook live, and presenting personal images make women vulnerable to hate speech, sexually explicit dialogue, and fake information campaigns in a context of gender-based inequities and cultural discrimination. Active SMBWE reported inappropriate, negative, and harmful comments from random men in various online spaces, including social media pages, posts, live sessions, and direct messages. This challenge intensified during the government-imposed COVID-19 lockdown. Alongside aggressive comments, SMBWE experienced the malicious circulation of personal details online ('doxing'), albeit in a small number of cases (2 to 3 percent). Women also highlighted instances where they were ridiculed, with critics suggesting they have nothing better to do than engage in live sessions for product promotion. SMBWE adopted various strategies to address online abuse, such as ignoring negative comments, promoting positive customer reviews, and safeguarding their self-confidence. When faced with relentless perpetrators, women resorted to banning, blocking, or reporting cases of harassment to the authorities. However, they noted a lack of sufficient support from family and society in addressing this challenge and advocated for awareness campaigns through social and mass media to sensitize customers and normalize women in business.

Policy Implication for Women Entrepreneurs in Bangladesh

The government has announced a stimulus package of USD 2.35 billion with a subsidized interest rate for small and medium enterprises. However, the allocation of loans specifically for women-owned small firms has not been determined yet (Rahman, 2023). This paper strongly advocates for the development of the loan policy with a consideration of the gender-specific challenges faced by women business owners. Narrative accounts from some women reveal the possibility of having to close their businesses, with patriarchal experiences playing a significant role. For instance, they may face higher product costs due to the gender-stereotypical attitudes of wholesalers. Recognizing these gendered challenges, policymakers should prioritize providing financial support to women. Additionally, this article emphasizes the severe gendered consequences of business closures for women, especially young, divorced women. Therefore, this group of women should be given priority in accessing loans in this highly patriarchal country.

Further investigation into this topic reveals several problematic areas that demand attention from policymakers. One significant impediment in sustaining businesses for women is associated with the delivery service, highlighting the need for policymakers to implement measures to improve this aspect. Additionally, while the online platform is considered a viable option for some women to operate their businesses (Khan & Newaz, 2020), concerns have been raised by a respondent regarding the challenges in transitioning businesses to the digital platform. Therefore, developing suitable policies to support women business owners in preparing for online commerce is crucial. In summary, by addressing the diverse gender-specific challenges faced by women business owners, as uncovered by the respondents, policymakers in Bangladesh and similar nations can formulate appropriate policies to effectively support women in the context of COVID-19.

Women entrepreneurs across various age groups and educational backgrounds have encountered diverse challenges, emphasizing the necessity for each female entrepreneur to acquire technological skills. Their experiences encompassed learning to utilize technology for crafting new strategies to source raw materials, transform them into finished goods, attract and persuade customers, ensure timely delivery, and handle online transactions. The study's findings underscore the impact of marketing strategy decisions and the adoption of social media on women's business performance, emphasizing the importance of a systematic effort to understand the unique needs of this vulnerable group.

Given the disparity in risk tolerance between women and men, authorities should devise interventions to avert or mitigate adverse effects on disadvantaged groups. Recognizing the pivotal role of technology in contemporary life, strategic investments in technology infrastructure, such as internet coverage, can significantly aid entrepreneurs. Automation in financial institutions and manufacturing industries allows business owners to make marketing decisions remotely, minimizing direct human contact, especially during crises like the COVID-19 outbreak. The experiences highlighted in this study underscore that the lack of essential resources can significantly impede businesses' ability to manage operations effectively. To enhance business performance during crises, women entrepreneurs must enhance their knowledge and skills in technology. Emphasis should be placed on developing solutions that empower women business owners to withstand conditions like pandemics.

Implication of Findings

Besides women who have access to urban entrepreneurship, enhancing the empowerment of rural women involves elevating their self-value, enabling them to make independent choices, and upholding their right to influence societal change for their well-being and that of others. This is closely tied to a fundamental human right, crucial for establishing a more harmonious and prosperous world. The empowerment of women plays a crucial role in the health and social development of families, communities, and nations. Creating a safe, joyful, and productive environment allows women to realize their full potential, contributing to the workforce, fostering the well-being of their children, and promoting sustainable economies that benefit society and humanity as a whole.

A recent study conducted by Rahman et al. in 2023, titled 'The impact of social media entrepreneurship on sustainable development: Evidence from online clothing shops in Bangladesh,' discovered that the involvement of women in social media entrepreneurship has a positive effect on the family income of rural women ($p < 0.05$). This suggests that engaging in social media entrepreneurship enhances the income of rural women, leading to their empowerment. Consequently, women from rural areas, through their participation in social media entrepreneurship, can contribute to both their family's income and the overall economic development of the country. The findings of this research can be applied to other economies sharing similarities with Bangladesh's context, aligning with previous studies. The emergence of social media has provided women with a new platform for communication, self-expression, political organization, and activism. Women across the globe connect through social media, supporting each other in various roles such as professionals, legislators, politicians, and business owners. Undoubtedly, social media has opened opportunities and empowered women in Bangladesh, allowing them to be independent and confident decision-makers. Empowering women translates to giving them a voice in political, economic, and social spheres.

Secondly, the research uncovered a significant positive correlation between women's engagement in social media entrepreneurship and sustainable development ($p < 0.05$). It emphasizes that women's participation in social media entrepreneurship establishes a framework for achieving sustainable development aligned with specific Sustainable Development Goals (SDGs), including SDG 05 (gender equality), SDG 01 (no poverty), and SDG 10 (reduced inequalities), ultimately contributing to women's empowerment. The study notes that SDG 05 and SDG 10 promote the increased utilization of technology, particularly information and communication technology (ICT), to support women and girls globally in realizing their full potential.

Furthermore, the government has initiated a program aimed at supporting the development of rural women entrepreneurs, alongside a project dedicated to fostering the growth of women entrepreneurship in the ICT sector. These initiatives align with the findings of the study and are consistent with previous research. The purpose of social media is to provide a platform for individuals to express themselves online, discussing matters important to them. This freedom of expression is considered integral to personal success and fulfillment. While acknowledging the potential exposure to discrimination and cultural pressures, social media simultaneously helps women maintain their integrity, confidence, and independence.

The active participation of rural women is deemed essential for achieving Sustainable Development Goal 5 (SDG 5), which calls for the elimination of all forms of discrimination against women and girls, ensuring their full and meaningful participation in decision-making across political, economic, and public spheres. SDG 5 also advocates for increased use of technology, particularly ICT, to empower women and girls globally. In alignment with these goals, the ICT department has launched the "She Power Project: Sustainable Development for Women through ICT," with the ambitious objective of enhancing the lives of 10,500 females. The project focuses on three distinct programs: transitioning freelancers to entrepreneurs, supporting IT service providers, and empowering call center representatives.

In conclusion, a noteworthy positive association is observed between the family income of rural women and sustainable development ($p < 0.05$). Social media entrepreneurship emerges as a transformative avenue for income generation, particularly for women, and the additional income generated by rural women contributes significantly to sustainable development. The evolving landscape of social media has played a pivotal role in reshaping the portrayal of women, providing them with new opportunities for business and networking. The surge in women entrepreneurs on social media platforms, especially during the Covid-19 era in Bangladesh, underscores the platform's impact on creating economic opportunities.

Social media not only alters societal perceptions but also enhances women's liberty, freedom, empowerment, independence, and autonomy. It serves as a catalyst for women to explore and experiment, ultimately boosting confidence and economic standing as entrepreneurs. This empowerment has far-reaching effects on personal growth, societal well-being, and overall progress. The study's findings align with previous research, highlighting the positive correlation between social media engagement and women's economic empowerment.

While emphasizing the critical role of women's empowerment in the transition to a knowledge-based society, the study underscores the transformative power of social media in amplifying women's voices, traditionally suppressed and repressed. Beyond empowering women, social media serves as a connecting force for individuals, amplifying diverse voices. The participation of women in online businesses not only contributes to family income but also has broader implications for societal and economic advancement. In essence, the study's outcomes, supported by statistical analysis, suggest that fostering social media entrepreneurship among rural women can be an effective strategy for their empowerment and the promotion of sustainable development.

CONCLUSION

Entrepreneurs are now facing an increasing demand to engage with digital infrastructure and participate in a dynamic digital business and financial landscape. This shift is believed to bring substantial advantages, particularly for women traditionally marginalized in male-dominated entrepreneurial settings. The reduction of entry barriers in entrepreneurship and the extensive information accessibility facilitated by the Internet are anticipated to offer significant benefits. The ongoing digital transformation of both the economy and society is poised to reshape the entrepreneurial landscape by emphasizing alternative sources of finance through Internet-based platforms, such as crowdfunding and peer-to-peer lending. This transformation is creating new market prospects for potential entrepreneurs, including women.

In the past decade, scholarly attention has progressed in understanding the barriers limiting women's access to entrepreneurship. While numerous interventions have aimed to narrow the gap in individual skills between men and women, there has been a lack of policy initiatives addressing structural or institutional impediments (Henry et al., 2017). Given the pivotal role of digitalization in entrepreneurship, it is imperative to reassess existing policies focused on supporting women-owned start-ups and growth-oriented businesses. Initiatives tackling gender-related constraints need to incorporate the potential of digital tools and technologies to truly empower women and achieve the anticipated effects. The challenges ahead are substantial, urging policymakers to embrace novel approaches that thoroughly consider digital aspects in promoting female entrepreneurship. Policy initiatives should factor in the social, economic, and cultural context where female entrepreneurship intersects with digital engagement. Information and communication technologies, as they advance, are expected to offer unforeseen and egalitarian opportunities for marginalized groups like women, if boundary conditions do not limit their impact.

Future studies could explore a set of questions to further our understanding of the relationship between digitalization and gender disparity in entrepreneurship:

1. Digital Levers for Women: What digital tools and strategies can women leverage to overcome gender disparities in entrepreneurship?
2. Impact of Digital Advancements: How do advancements in digital technologies influence women's decisions to enter entrepreneurship?
3. Firm Strategies and Gender Stereotypes: What mechanisms can firms develop and implement to counteract gender stereotypes in entrepreneurship, and how does digitalization play a role in this context?

Additionally, a separate line of research could focus on contextual factors and their impact on the entrepreneurial outcomes of businesses led by women.

REFERENCES

Abdullah, M. (2020, June 12). Bangladesh globally ranks 10th on daily increase in Covid-19 cases. *Dhaka Tribune*. Retrieved from https://www.dhakatribune.com/bangladesh/2020/06/12/bangladesh-ranks-10th-globallyon-daily-increase-in-covid-19-cases

Aboulilah, H. M. A. E., Hossain, S. F. A., Vuong, B. N., & Jebril, T. (2022). Exploring the Relationship between WeChat Usage and E-purchase Intention During the COVID-19 Pandemic Among University Students in China. *SAGE Open, 12*(4). doi:10.1177/21582440221139447

Ahmed, N., Monzur, H., & Iqbal, H. (2017). Women Entrepreneurs in SMEs: Bangladesh Perspective. *Journal of Business and Entrepreneurship, 15*(3), 112–125.

Babu, K. E. K. (2021). Artificial intelligence in Bangladesh, its applications in different sectors and relevant challenges for the government: An analysis. *International Journal of Public Law and Policy, 7*(4), 319–333. doi:10.1504/IJPLAP.2021.118891

Chowdhury, S., & Rabbani, G. (2013). Policies and institutional supports for women entrepreneurship development in Bangladesh: Achievements and challenges. *International Journal of Research in Business and Social Science, 2*(1), 31-39.

De Vita, L., Mari, M., & Poggesi, S. (2014). Women entrepreneurs in and from developing countries: Evidences from the literature. *European Management Journal, 32*(3), 451–460. doi:10.1016/j.emj.2013.07.009

Drinkwater, M. (2009). 'We are also Human': identity and power in gender relations. Rights-based approaches to development: Exploring the potential and pitfalls. Kumarian Press.

Fuentes-Fuentes, M. D. M., Bojica, A. M., & Ruiz-Arroyo, M. (2015). Entrepreneurial orientation and knowledge acquisition: Effects on performance in the specific context of women-owned firms. *The International Entrepreneurship and Management Journal, 11*(3), 695–717. doi:10.1007/s11365-014-0336-1

GSMA. (2022). *GSMA Gender Gap*. Retrieved from: https://www.gsma.com/r/gender-gap/

Hechevarría, D., Bullough, A., Brush, C., & Edelman, L. (2019). High-growth women's entrepreneurship: Fueling social and economic development. *Journal of Small Business Management, 57*(1), 5–13. doi:10.1111/jsbm.12503

Hossain, S. F. A. (2019). Social Networking and Its Role in Media Entrepreneurship: Evaluating the Use of Mobile Phones in the Context of Online Shopping – A Review. *Journal of Media Management and Entrepreneurship, 1*(1), 1–14. doi:10.4018/JMME.2019010105

Hossain, S. F. A., Nurunnabi, M., Hussain, K., & Shan, X. (2020). Smartphone-based m-shopping behavior and innovative entrepreneurial tendency among women in emerging Asia. *International Journal of Gender and Entrepreneurship, 12*(2), 173–189. doi:10.1108/IJGE-03-2019-0054

Hossain, S. F. A., Shan, X., Musa, M., & Rahman, P. (2023). Social media and Increased venture creation tendency with innovative ideas: The case of female students in Asia. In Research Anthology on Applying Social Networking Strategies to Classrooms and Libraries. doi:10.4018/978-1-6684-7123-4.ch093

Hossain, S. F. A., Shan, X., Nurunnabi, M., Tushar, H., Mohsin, A. K. M., & Ahsan, F. T. (2021). Opportunities and Challenges of M-Learning During the COVID-19 Pandemic: A Mixed Methodology Approach. In *E-Collaboration Technologies and Strategies for Competitive Advantage Amid Challenging Times*. doi:10.4018/978-1-7998-7764-6.ch007

IslamN. (2020) Women Empowerment through Entrepreneurship Development in Bangladesh: A Multivariate Analysis. *International Journal of Management, 11*(10). https://ssrn.com/abstract=3734569

Lumpkin, G. T., & Dess, G. G. (1996). Clarifying the entrepreneurial orientation construct and linking it to performance. *Academy of Management Review*, *21*(1), 135–172. doi:10.2307/258632

Mamun, M. Z., & Haq, M. R. (2023). Urban Women Entrepreneurship Development in Bangladesh: Challenges and Preparations. *International Journal of Research and Innovation in Social Science*, *7*(7), 129–149. doi:10.47772/IJRISS.2023.70709

Mozumdar, L., Farid, K. S., & Sarma, P. K. (2017). Relevance of social capital in women s business performance in Bangladesh. *Journal of the Bangladesh Agricultural University*, *15*(1), 87–94. doi:10.3329/jbau.v15i1.33533

Mozumdar, L., Hagelaar, G., van der Velde, G., & Omta, S. W. F. (2020). Determinants of the business performance of women entrepreneurs in the developing world context. *J, 3*(2), 17.

Mozumdar, L., Materia, V. C., Hagelaar, G., Islam, M. A., van der Velde, G., & Omta, S. W. F. (2022). Contextuality of Entrepreneurial Orientation and Business Performance: The Case of Women Entrepreneurs in Bangladesh. *Journal of Entrepreneurship and Innovation in Emerging Economies*, *8*(1), 94–120. doi:10.1177/23939575211062433

Mozumder, N. A. (2018). A multilevel trust-based model of ethical public leadership. *Journal of Business Ethics*, *153*(1), 167–184. doi:10.1007/s10551-016-3341-1

Rahim, S. A., Islam, S. M. S., & Bepari, S. P. (2018). A contextual study on the development of women entrepreneurs in Bangladesh. *Global Journal of Entrepreneurship*, *3*(1). https://link.gale.com/apps/doc/A613341443/AONE?u=anon~b51a2dff&sid=googleScholar&xid=919e2b15

Rahman, M. M., Hasan, M. J., Deb, B. C., Rahman, M. S., & Kabir, A. S. (2023). The effect of social media entrepreneurship on sustainable development: Evidence from online clothing shops in Bangladesh. *Heliyon*, *9*(9), e19397. doi:10.1016/j.heliyon.2023.e19397 PMID:37662716

Rahman, S. (2023). Women Making a Mark in Digital Space. *The Daily Star*. Retrieved from https://www.thedailystar.net/business/economy/news/women-making-mark-digital-space-2977961

Singh, K., Hasan, M., & Rajendran, R. P. (2023). Opportunities and Challenges of AI/ML in Finance. *The Impact of AI Innovation on Financial Sectors in the Era of Industry*, *5*(0), 238–260.

Sirimanne, S. N., & Adhikari, R. (2023, March 8). *How to unlock women's potential in the digital economy*. UNCTAD.

Szirmai, A., Naudé, W., & Goedhuys, M. (Eds.). (2011). *Entrepreneurship, innovation, and economic development*. Oxford University Press. doi:10.1093/acprof:oso/9780199596515.001.0001

Uz Zaman, A. H., & Islam, M. J. (2011). Small and medium enterprises development in Bangladesh: Problems and prospects. *ASA University Review*, *5*(1), 145–160.

Uzir, M. U. H., Al Halbusi, H., Lim, R., Jerin, I., Hamid, A. B. A., Ramayah, T., & Haque, A. (2021). Applied Artificial Intelligence and user satisfaction: Smartwatch usage for healthcare in Bangladesh during COVID-19. *Technology in Society*, *67*, 101780. doi:10.1016/j.techsoc.2021.101780 PMID:34697510

Vivarelli, M. (2012). *Innovation, employment and skills in advanced and developing countries: A survey of the literature*. Academic Press.

Vuong, B. N., Tushar, H., & Hossain, S. F. A. (2023). The effect of social support on job performance through organizational commitment and innovative work behavior: Does innovative climate matter? *Asia-Pacific Journal of Business Administration, 15*(5), 832-854. doi:10.1108/APJBA-06-2021-0256

Zapanta, T. (2023, February 28). *The impact of AI on business*. Microsourcing. Retrieved from https://www.microsourcing.com/learn/blog/the-impact-of-ai-on-business/

Chapter 11
Green Leadership in Strategic Brand Management

Sarika Faisal
BRAC University, Bangladesh

EXECUTIVE SUMMARY

The purpose of this study was to delineate the importance of green leadership in strategic brand management. However, by applying the theory of coevolution and multi-level perspective, the authors have developed a model with dependent and independent variables and explained the causal relationship between green leadership and strategic brand management in Unilever. Moreover, they have used the qualitative data collection method to conduct the research because the factors which are related to green leadership are not possible to measure by number, i.e., not quantifiable. The findings of the study conclude that Unilever is the number 1 company that has been following green leadership for a very long time and also moving forward for more innovations.

1. INTRODUCTION

Green leadership is an emerging concept within the field of brand management. It is a way of thinking that encourages companies to take responsibility for their environmental impact and to make positive internal and external changes to create a sustainable future. Moreover, green leadership focuses on the long-term sustainability of a brand rather than short-term gains, and it can be applied to any organization, regardless of size or industry. This type of leadership incorporates sustainability into every aspect of a company's operations, from product design to marketing and corporate social responsibility. Unilever recently completed an international survey that found that 33% of customers now choose products based on their social and environmental effects. Additionally, there is a potential market worth €966 billion for companies that disclose their ecological credentials (Planteria Group). Green leadership can help organizations become more competitive, improve their brand image, and build customer loyalty by prioritizing sustainability and setting a positive example for other companies.

Green leadership in business is a significant development that changes how organizations run and engage with their environment. It entails using sustainable practices and methods to ensure that compa-

DOI: 10.4018/979-8-3693-1781-5.ch011

nies may lessen their environmental impact while still offering their clients products and services. On the other hand, being a proactive leader in sustainability enhances reputation. It fosters customer trust, which may increase sales and ensure the company's long-term success (Sarah long, 2022). Also, Green leadership is concerned with boosting resource efficiency and effectiveness, environmental performance, and enterprises' social and environmental impact. Although just 60% of firms have a sustainability strategy, 90% of CEOs agree that sustainability is essential (World Economic Forum,2022). Nevertheless, understanding and embracing green leadership is crucial for businesses if they want to sustain their financial viability and competitiveness in the long run.

By integrating sustainability into brand management, a company can ensure that its fundamental principles are represented in its products, services, and operations. In addition to creating sustainable products (goods and services) and implementing social-ecological criteria, companies can promote sustainable lifestyles and behavioral changes, mainly via critical reflection and modifying current norms (Kemper & Ballantine, 2019). There are numerous theoretical approaches to the study of brand sustainability, including one that has yet to be applied very much to look at sustainability tactics from a marketing viewpoint (Voola et al., 2022).

Unilever is a market leader in the production and sale of consumer goods, and its product line spans a variety of markets, including those for food, health, beauty, and personal care. Due to its dedication to sustainability and social responsibility, Unilever has developed a reputation as a trustworthy and forward-thinking business. The mission of Unilever is to improve people's lives and the environment while offering its customers high-quality, ethically sourced goods and services. Unilever's Sustainable Living Plan (USLP) illustrates how a business complies with sustainability requirements (Mutia Khairunnisa, 2021). USLP helps to promote profitable development for its brands, save money, and foster innovation, serving as the company's model for long-term success in an unstable environment. The company has saved over €1 billion by implementing the USLP, partly due to advances in factory water and energy efficiency and the adoption of circular packaging solutions through collaborations with Algramo and Loop (Sustainable Brands, 2020).

Unilever has promised to make all its plastic and packaging 100% reusable, recyclable, or compostable by 2025 and is a founder signatory to the UK Plastics Pact (Esgn Asia, 2019). For packaging to be recognized by recycling plant scanners and processed for recycling, Unilever has invented a new detectable black pigment as part of the multinational's UK and Ireland "Get Plastic Wise" campaign (Lucy Whitehouse,2019). The new approach was created as part of

Unilever UK's dedication to The UK Plastics Pact and its new "Get Plastic Wise" campaign, a five-point plastics strategy that seeks to address plastic waste in the UK (Sustainable Plastics, 2019).

The most recent GlobeScan-SustainAbility study identifies Unilever as the No. 1 business sustainability leader for the eleventh consecutive year. Unilever raised from 14% to 62% of its agricultural raw materials that are obtained sustainably. Moreover, their manufacturing operations worldwide use 100% renewable grid power (Unilever,2020).

Unilever has been recognized as a global leader in corporate sustainability by the international environmental non-profit CDP, earning a spot on its "A-List" for combating climate change, preserving forests, and ensuring the security of water supplies (Unilever, 2020). Their initiatives take place at a time when businesses need to act as responsible global citizens (Matt Miller, 2022).

Research Objectives

1) To determine the relationship between green leadership and sustainability and strategic brand management.
2) To assess what impact green leadership has on strategic brand management. 3) To examine how green leadership and sustainability influence strategic brand management.

2. LITERATURE REVIEW AND HYPOTHESIS DEVELOPMENT

2.1 Literature Review

Every company is trying to acquire green leadership and respond to various environmental changes through new activities which helps to gain a competitive advantage (Jia, J., Liu, H., Chin, T. and Hu, D. (2018).Through the mediating roles of organizational commitment and innovative work behavior, as well as the moderating role of innovative climate, Vuong, Tushar, and Hossain (2022) examine the impact of social support on job performance. Jaime Lerner once said " If you want creativity, take a zero off your budget. If you want sustainability, take off two zeros''. A few factors that made recent environmental challenges like climate change; also have an impact on economic development that leads to green creativity. (Chen, Y.S.; Chang, C.H(2013). But to increase the activities of green leadership involves the cooperation between the firm's strategies and HRM's active participation. However, green resource management is firmly related to green leadership because it highlights the practices of the employees toward the environment, sustainability, and the influence of ecological factors, and how it's aligned with the company's strategy to magnify green creativity by providing green training. (Ren, S.; Tang, G.; Jackson, S.E(2017). Also green leadership can incorporate green pay, green recruitment, and selection, and green performance management to build strategic brand management for the company (Tang, G.; Chen, Y.; Jiang, Y.; Paillé, P.; Jia, J.(2018). Moreover, according to Aboulilah, Hossain, Vuong, and Jebril (2022) state that the study intends to fill a research void in the literature on e-shopping by emphasizing the significance of examining the connection between WeChat usage and e-purchase intention among Chinese university students. The goal of Hossain, Nurunnabi, Hussain, and Saha (2019) is to close this research gap and add to the body of knowledge in the field of IT literature in a few ways. Previously companies were not so concerned about such attributes but now since the competition is too high so it's very important to practice such activities because when a consumer judges a brand they not only judge it by their products or service but also look at the brand ethics, brand management, brand image and also what's the contribution to the society. Moreover, now it's an unavoidable issue because companies are struggling to keep the balance between profitability and sustainability. Instead of going for a short-term strategy now, they have invested more in the long-term strategy. The literature on the function of educational institutions and students in the entrepreneurship arena has been emphasized in a number of ways, according to Cousté, Qin, Hossain, and Hussain (2022).

In a few cases, they are redesigning the packages, ensuring more green products, taking care of waste management in a sustainable way, and trying to incorporate a cradle-to-grave approach in product management (Mittal, S.; Dhar, R.L.(2016).By examining innovativeness in entrepreneurship in relation to smartphone usage and the growing propensity of women to engage in business, this study closes a gap in the existing literature (Hossain, Nurunnabi, Hussain, & Shan, 2020).However, In the next three months, new coronavirus pneumonia will alter China's economic macroenvironment, affecting both total supply and total demand, predict Mohsin, Hongzhen, and Hossain (2021). This includes quantifiable outcomes like the consumer price index's volatility, the slowdown in investment, and the overall retail market's fall (CPI).

Companies also realized that green products are not only good for the environment since it's less harmful. Also, it might help the firm to gain a competitive advantage because many consumers are boycotting products that are harmful to the environment and willing to pay more for green products; considering this issue they might have to redesign their business strategy and model (Xie, Bagozzi, and Grønhaug, 2015). The advent of mobile commerce, enabled by wireless terminals like smartphones, PDAs, or cell phones, in conjunction with network access, is transforming transactional procedures and presenting obstacles to established regulatory structures (Hossain, Xi, & Hussain, 2020).

But it's more despondent to conclude that a lot of companies are unaware of the importance of green leadership in their supply chain and are stuck in the pollution governance product management model. Furthermore, various studies show that green leadership also helps to evaluate one's attitudes and perception towards green values, and also employees most likely prefer a sustainable climate (Zientara and Zamojska, 2016). Another study showed that green intrinsic and extrinsic motivation has a major influence on green leadership also in green creativity that caters to the employee's motivation to come up with more innovative and green products to ensure the company's sustainability (Iglesias, O. and Ind, N. (2020). The rise of mobile commerce, enabled by wireless terminals like smartphones, PDAs, or cell phones, in conjunction with network access, is transforming transactional procedures and presenting obstacles to established regulatory structures (Hossain, Xi, & Hussain, 2020). It's not only consumer preference now but the stakeholders are associated with this new concept and pressurizing the firm to redesign the strategy to gain social, environmental, and economical consequences. Even various scholars have put out emphasis on getting first mover advantage by practicing green leadership in the firm which will also revamp the image as well as the market share of the firm (Chen and Chang, 2013; Packalén, 2010; Yong et al., 2020). To pursue green leadership as a core organizational component, green innovation, and green creativity must be put into the green agenda so that the attitude of the firm toward ecological issues can be changed and encourage green creativity like how to reduce water and paper usage (Jia et al., 2018; Singh et al., 2020). Although employees who are more environmentally concerned, passionate about saving the world, and also aware of the bad outcomes are more likely to fit with the organizational culture and goal-attainable strategy. On the other side of the argument, the concept of brand management has evolved with time. Now it's more about a commitment and responsibility of a brand that also fulfills the demand of the stakeholders; what they perceive about the brand. Few academics suggested that previously brands were more focused on the utilitarian needs of the consumers but then slowly the evaluation takes place. Consumers convert their drive to more quality products and then they started to broaden their horizons by wanting functional and emotional benefits like good customer service, and a strong brand image, brand ethics should align with consumers' perception of the brand only then brand management will be successful because it could create a strong long term bond between the consumers and the brand (Iglesias, O. and Ind, N. (2020). In a recent study, it is stated that by involving in green innovation employees will come up with a strategy that might involve new technologies, management activities to minimize waste, performing corporate social responsibility, and ensuring strategic brand management. (Abbas, J. (2020)

2.2 Hypothesis

The dependent and independent variables are given below:

Dependent Variable: Strategic Brand Management

Independent Variables: Green Leadership, Sustainability.

The relationship between green leadership and sustainability with strategic brand management can be closely compared to "The 3 Pillars of Corporate Sustainability". Among the 3 pillars, the first one is the Environmental Pillar which is related to Green Leadership. On the other hand, the second and third ones are the Social and Economic Pillar which provide more sustainability to the brands. Based on these the hypothesis is being developed.

H1: *Green Leadership impacts Strategic Brand Management positively.*

In an endeavor to accomplish sustainable environmental goals, green leadership can have an effect on interpersonal and organizational relationships. Furthermore, further research needs to be done on some definitions of green leadership (Tan et al., 2011). Green Leadership can lead to a brand with more exposure, more brand image, and more brand equity. But this green leadership can be costly at times which provides us with our second Hypothesis.

H2: *Green Leadership impacts Strategic Brand Management negatively.*

According to Lee et al. (2014) and Crossman (2011), decision-making that is focused on environmental values is also associated with green leadership. Decision Making is a core factor in Strategic Brand Management. A wrong decision while thinking about the environment might cause the brand in many ways which will result negatively.

H3: *Green Leadership impacts Strategic Brand Management negatively.*

Brand equity, sustainable business practices, and consumer green views and preferences are all closely related. Sustainability may give a brand's image a deeper meaning, leading to greater emotional ties and distinction. Green Leadership along with sustainability shapes up the brand image, brand equity, and purchase decision. that there are consumers who are willing to pay higher prices for green brands (Litvine, D. and Wustenhagen, R, 2011), green branding is an important driver of brand equity (Benoit-Moreau, F. and Parguel, B., 2011).

H4: *Green Leadership and sustainability does not have any influence in Strategic Brand Management.*

This is a null hypothesis where the variables are being shown not related towards Strategic Brand Management.

The hypotheses here are interrelated with the 3 pillars of corporate sustainability. The three pillars are Environmental Pillar, Social Pillar and Economic Pillar. The relation between the theory and hypothesis is given below in a diagram.

RESEARCH METHODOLOGY

This research was conducted with a qualitative approach. The data that were being collected and used to conduct the research was mostly about branding, brand management, brand image, green leadership, sustainability etc. This information can not be measured with numbers and so the approach will be a qualitative approach where the factors of green leadership and sustainability will be measured in terms of strategic brand management.

DISCUSSION

Intro to the Discussion Part

Business sustainability & implementing appropriate strategies are crucial for any business regardless of its operating industry. As the strategy leaves its influence on the economical, supply chain, cultural aspect of the business directly as a whole, the importance of proper implementation is absolutely essential. Green & sustainable leadership has been proven to be an integral part of the accumulation of all major aspects of the business discussed earlier in order to maintain the company goal, mission & vision with a view to creating a long-term sustainable value addition for all the stakeholders of the company & society as a whole.

Discussion of Findings

Unilever has been recognised as the no.1 corporate sustainability leader company for 10 years in a row. The plan of Unilever's Sustainable Living Plan includes various ambitious targets such as impact on improving the life & health of 1 billion people worldwide, collecting 100% of agro c

i) Businesses need to rely upon people who understand the sustainability goals.
ii) The business people need to make the sustainability goals personal.
iii) It is crucial for businesses to monitor & regularly measure the sustainability goals.

Colquitt et al. (2011) state that the management and workforce as a whole can be assessed based on personal successes (job outcomes), such as work engagement and job performance or conduct that contributes positively or negatively (organizational performance). Green leadership can affect how individuals and organizations interact in an effort to achieve sustainable environmental goals. Green HRM offers an unbeatable and rewarding opportunity to improve the environmental performance of companies that implement it according to Gutiérrez-Broncano et al. (2022)

Implications for Theory

Co-evolution Theory and Multi-level Perspective, reflecting three directions of theory development, namely 1) shifting from "what" to "how", 2) growing use of interdisciplinary approach, and 3) towards broader systems. Unilever has long been addressing all their vision &

goals from the "what" viewpoint but according to the Co-evolution Theory and Multi-level Perspective, it is high time they shift to addressing as a "how to". Sustainable leadership & strategic management begins with sustainable actions & decision making but it must incorporate value addition across the steps of implementation & value chain of the stakeholders.

Practical Implications

The Corporate Sustainability theory resides on 3 pillars including: Environmental, Social & Economic pillar. The Environmental Segment is concerned with a corporation's pledge to reduce waste products such as carbon emissions. This component oftenly acquires the most attention owing to its immediate impact on the societal and economic pillars. If a product or service has a low carbon footprint, and being ecologically responsible can occasionally be more cost effective and entice new clients.

The Social Pillar is dedicated to assisting the company's business, culture, and personnel. There are several techniques to assisting the social pillar, however they all revolve around workforce well-being. The value chain is one of the most important parts of providing an appropriate working atmosphere for employees. This involves ensuring a safe working environment, fair remuneration, and forbidding the use of child labor to justify the end product.

The Economic Pillar is the company or program's financial aspect. Regrettably, money is the most crucial resource, and in order to be long-term sustainable, a firm must be prosperous. Strategic planning is a factor that pertains to the economic pillar, often referred to as the governance pillar. This is where a firm or project must examine or acknowledge the calculated risk of a certain venture, and determine how it will affect overall financially.

LIMITATIONS AND SUGGESTIONS FOR FUTURE RESEARCH

Despite the fact that this paper produced numerous promising outcomes, we must now acknowledge the limitations of our research paper. Therefore, speaking of the limitations, time limit was a major constraint as we didn't get much time to conduct further research and take interviews of the managers/employees of Unilever and converse with them about the green leadership in their strategic brand management. If we had more time on hand, we could gather more primary data which would have been helpful for our research. As it was a bit challenging to gather enough data for our research and to gain access to the data,this could result in an incomplete conclusion to our research. Furthermore, this data scarcity could be the result of our study's design. The slight hazy, sloppy research outline may cause additional difficulties in interpreting our findings. . A limitation of qualitative research is its lack of validity and reliability. Because qualitative research is conducted in the field, it is extremely difficult to replicate studies. (Wiersma,2018) Limited information resulted in a small sample size which is a reason why our research isn't 100% accurate

Also, we have studied one company in a specific industry, using an explorative, qualitative research method. The findings are based on an analysis of secondary data of company employees and external stakeholders. The results may therefore be more or less idiosyncratic to the company studied, and we should be cautious in interpreting and generalizing the results to other companies and other industries. This paper is constrained by factors that may have an impact on Unilever's strategy. It would be worthwhile to look into other recently explained variables that are not covered in this paper. Despite these obvious limitations, the paper provides novel insight into an emerging field of marketing and management research of Unilever.

We would like to discuss the following limitations and suggestions on the research we conducted:

We advocate for research into which types of leadership styles and corporate cultures promote the development of sustainable and ethical brand management for Unilever. To be more specific:

i) What kind of leadership style best promotes green leadership for the brand?
ii) What kind of corporate culture is best suited to the development of responsible and sustainable brand management?

iii) Does Unilever produce any positive outcomes in terms of employee engagement and/or employer brand attractiveness while ensuring green leadership?

There is a need for academic research that discusses how Unilever in terms of green leadership should define and promote their brand purpose. It is critical to comprehend the potential links between their brand purpose and corporate brand heritage and capabilities. It's suggested that to be more specific these questions could be studied:

i) What is the best way for Unilever to define and embrace a corporate brand purpose ensuring sustainability?
ii) How can Unilever link corporate brand purpose and strategy with their green leadership activities?
    ii) What key performance indicators should the brand develop to assess the degree to which their brand purpose is being met in terms of green leadership?

Empirical research is also required to investigate how the brand can develop a balanced multi-stakeholder perspective in terms of green leadership. Some related research questions are as follows:

i) How can the brand foster a diverse set of stakeholder perspectives in terms of being responsible towards the environment?
ii) What role do various stakeholders (CEOs, investors, employees, and so on) play in encouraging sustainable branding?
iii) How can the brand reconcile potential stakeholder conflicts of interest?

In addition, more research is required to determine how to incorporate a long-term green leadership perspective into strategic decision-making. Among the possible questions are:

i) In their strategic decision-making processes, how can the corporate brand promote a long-term sustainable strategic perspective?
ii) How do they balance short-term and long-term goals regarding sustainability?

However, the limitations of the current study also provide opportunities for future research. The study's main findings indicate that environmental awareness as a CSR activity combined with active leadership has repercussions on the reputation and corporate brand of Unilever. However, these findings should be investigated further in both qualitative and quantitative studies.

Additional case studies of Unilever and companies in similar and other industries may shed more light on how companies integrate environmental awareness into their business strategies, how environmental awareness is embedded in employees' values, and how environmental awareness is communicated to external stakeholders. These processes are poorly understood, and the corporate brand literature would benefit from a better practical and theoretical understanding of these processes. Cross-industry, quantitative studies, on the other hand, can investigate the impact of environmental awareness and CSR in general on the corporate brand, which in this case is Unilever,in comparison to the impact of other factors such as customer loyalty, product variety, product quality, and so on.

Given the increased focus on CSR and environmental issues, there should be plenty of opportunities to conduct both qualitative and quantitative studies on Unilever's green leadership in strategic brand management in the coming years. Future opportunities to gather more data could also lead to answers of the suggested questions mentioned above.

REFERENCES

Abbas, J. (2020). Impact of total quality management on corporate green performance through the mediating role of corporate social responsibility. *Journal of Cleaner Production, 242*, 118458. doi:10.1016/j.jclepro.2019.118458

Aboulilah, H. M. A. E., Hossain, S. F. A., Vuong, B. N., & Jebril, T. (2022). Exploring the Relationship between WeChat Usage and E-purchase Intention During the COVID-19 Pandemic Among University Students in China. *SAGE Open, 12*(4). doi:10.1177/21582440221139447

Anderson, J. (2020, January 13). *What is Your "Green Leadership Style"?* Retrieved from Planteria website: https://www.planteriagroup.com/blog/what-is-your-green-leadership-style/

Benoit-Moreau, F., & Parguel, B. (2011). Building brand equity with environmental communication: An empirical investigation in France. *EuroMed Journal of Business, 6*(1), 100–116. doi:10.1108/14502191111130334

CDP gives Unilever triple "A" for sustainability leadership. (n.d.). Retrieved from Unilever website: https://www.unilever.com/news/news-search/2020/cdp-gives-unilever-triple-a-for-sustainability-le adership/

Chang, R.-D., Zuo, J., Zhao, Z.-Y., Zillante, G., Gan, X.-L., & Soebarto, V. (2017). Evolving theories of sustainability and firms: History, future directions and implications for renewable energy research. *Renewable & Sustainable Energy Reviews, 72*, 48–56. doi:10.1016/j.rser.2017.01.029

Chen, Y. S., & Chang, C. H. (2013). The determinants of green product development performance: Green dynamic capabilities, green transformational leadership, and green creativity. *Journal of Business Ethics, 116*(1), 107–119. doi:10.1007/s10551-012-1452-x

cosmetics design-europe.com. (n.d.). *Unilever's new pigment to help recycling of plastic packaging*. Retrieved from cosmeticsdesign-europe.com website: https://www.cosmeticsdesign-europe.com/Article/2019/05/29/Unilever-s-new-pigment-to-help-re cycling-of-plastic-packaging?utm_source=copyright&utm_medium=OnSite&utm_campaign=co pyright

Cousté, P. E., Qin, S., Hossain, S. F. A., & Hussain, K. (2022). Factors influencing social-media-based entrepreneurship prospects among female students in China. *Heliyon, 8*(12), e12041. doi:10.1016/j.heliyon.2022.e12041 PMID:36483305

Crossman, J. (2011). Environmental and spiritual leadership: Tracing the synergies from an organizational perspective. *Journal of Business Ethics, 103*(4), 553–565. doi:10.1007/s10551-011-0880-3

Global experts rank Unilever No.1 for sustainability leadership. (n.d.). Retrieved December 20, 2022, from Unilever website: https://www.unilever.com/news/news-search/2020/global-experts-rank-unilever-no1-for-sustaina bility-leadership/

Golob, U., Burghausen, M., Kernstock, J., & Davies, M. A. P. (2022). Brand management and sustainability: Exploring potential for the transformative power of brands. *Journal of Brand Management, 29*(6), 513–519. doi:10.1057/s41262-022-00293-7

Hossain, S. F. A., Nurunnabi, M., Hussain, K., & Saha, S. K. (2019). *Effects of variety-seeking intention by mobile phone usage on university students' academic performance*. doi:10.1080/2331186X.2019.1574692

Hossain, S. F. A., Nurunnabi, M., Hussain, K., & Shan, X. (2020). Smartphone-based m-shopping behavior and innovative entrepreneurial tendency among women in emerging Asia. *International Journal of Gender and Entrepreneurship, 12*(2), 173–189. doi:10.1108/IJGE-03-2019-0054

Hossain, S. F. A., Xi, Z., & Hussain, K. (2020). *Ubiquitous role of social networking in driving M-commerce: Evaluating the use of mobile phones for online shopping and payment in the context of trust*. doi:10.1177/2158244020939536

Iglesias, O., & Ind, N. (2020). Towards a theory of conscientious corporate brand co-creation: The next key challenge in brand management. *Journal of Brand Management, 27*(6), 710–720. Advance online publication. doi:10.1057/s41262-020-00205-7

Jia, J., Liu, H., Chin, T., & Hu, D. (2018). The Continuous Mediating Effects of GHRM on Employees' Green Passion via Transformational Leadership and Green Creativity. *Sustainability (Basel), 10*(9), 3237. doi:10.3390/su10093237

Kemper, J. A., & Ballantine, P. W. (2019). What do we mean by sustainability marketing? *Journal of Marketing Management, 35*(3–4), 277–309. doi:10.1080/0267257X.2019.1573845

Khairunisa, M., & Kusuma, N. (2021, July 9). *How Unilever Transforms Its Business with Unilever Sustainable Living Plan.* Retrieved from Green Network Asia website: https://greennetwork.asia/news/how-unilever-transforms-its-business-with-unilever-sustainable-li ving-plan/

Kim, T.-Y., Liden, R. C., Kim, S.-P., & Lee, D.-R. (2015). The interplay between follower core self-evaluation and transformational leadership: Effects on employee outcomes. *Journal of Business and Psychology, 30*(2), 345–355. doi:10.1007/s10869-014-9364-7

Lamach, M. W. (2017, October 27). *How Our Company Connected Our Strategy to Sustainability Goals.* Retrieved from Harvard Business Review website: https://hbr.org/2017/10/how-our-company-connected-our-strategy-to-sustainability-goals

Lee, M. H., Lin, C., Lin, C. K., & Lu, W. Y. (2014). Moderating effect of institutional responsiveness on the relationship between green leadership and green competitiveness. *Social Behavior and Personality, 42*(9), 1483–1494. doi:10.2224/sbp.2014.42.9.1483

Li, W., Bhutto, T. A., Xuhui, W., Maitlo, Q., Zafar, A. U., & Ahmed Bhutto, N. (2020). Unlocking employees' green creativity: The effects of green transformational leadership, green intrinsic, and extrinsic motivation. *Journal of Cleaner Production, 255*, 120229. doi:10.1016/j.jclepro.2020.120229

Lifebuoy, P. (2020, May 7). *Unilever Marks Sustainable Living Plan's 10th Year; New "Compass" to Guide Further Progress*. Retrieved from Sustainable Brands website: https://sustainablebrands.com/read/leadership/unilever-marks-sustainable-living-plan-s-10th-year -new-compass-to-guide-further-progress

Litvine, D., & Wüstenhagen, R. (2011). Helping "light green" consumers walk the talk: Results of a behavioural intervention survey in the Swiss electricity market. *Ecological Economics*, *70*(3), 462–474. doi:10.1016/j.ecolecon.2010.10.005

Long, S. (2022, October 14). *The Benefits of Active Leadership in Sustainability*. Retrieved from Green Business Bureau website: https://greenbusinessbureau.com/topics/green-culture/the-benefits-of-active-leadership-in-sustain ability/

Mittal, S., & Dhar, R. L. (2016). Effect of green transformational leadership on green creativity: A study of tourist hotels. *Tourism Management*, *57*, 18–127. doi:10.1016/j.tourman.2016.05.007

Mohsin, A. K., Hongzhen, L., & Hossain, S. F. A. (2021). *Impact of COVID-19 pandemic on consumer economy: Countermeasures analysis*. doi:10.1177/21582440211008875

Packalén, S. (2010). Culture and sustainability. *Corporate Social Responsibility and Environmental Management*, *17*(2), 118–121. doi:10.1002/csr.236

Rafi, T. (2022, June 9). *Why sustainability is crucial for corporate strategy*. Retrieved from World Economic Forum website: https://www.weforum.org/agenda/2022/06/why-sustainability-is-crucial-for-corporate-strategy/

Ren, S., Tang, G., & Jackson, S. E. (2017). Green human resource management research in emergence: A review and future directions. *Asia Pacific Journal of Management*, *2*, 1–35.

Singh, A., Varghese, L. M., Yadav, R. D., & Mahajan, R. (2020). A pollution reducing enzymatic deinking approach for recycling of mixed office waste paper. *Environmental Science and Pollution Research International*, *27*(36), 45814–45823. doi:10.1007/s11356-020-10440-9 PMID:32803575

Song, W., & Yu, H. (2018). Green innovation strategy and green innovation: The roles of green creativity and green organizational identity. *Corporate Social Responsibility and Environmental Management*, *25*(2), 135–150. doi:10.1002/csr.1445

Tan, B., Pan, S., & Zuo, M. (2011). *Attaining and enacting green leadership: Insights from the green IT initiatives of China Mobile*. Academic Press.

Tang, G., Chen, Y., Jiang, Y., Paillé, P., & Jia, J. (2018). Green human resource management practices: Scale development and validity. *Asia Pacific Journal of Human Resources*, *56*(1), 31–55. doi:10.1111/1744-7941.12147

Unilever. (2020, August 13). *Global experts rank Unilever No.1 for sustainability leadership*. Retrieved from Unilever website: https://www.unilever.com/news/news-search/2020/global-experts-rank-unilever-no1-for-sustainab ility-leadership/

Voola, R., Bandyopadhyay, C., Azmat, F., Ray, S., & Nayak, L. (2022). How are consumer behavior and marketing strategy researchers incorporating the SDGs? A review and opportunities for future research. *Australasian Marketing Journal*, *30*(2), 119–130. doi:10.1177/14413582221079431

Vuong, B. N., Tushar, H., & Hossain, S. F. A. (2022). The effect of social support on job performance through organizational commitment and innovative work behavior: Does innovative climate matter? *Asia-Pacific Journal of Business Administration*, *14*(2), 156–172.

Xie, C., Bagozzi, R. P., & Grønhaug, K. (2015). The role of moral emotions and individual differences in consumer responses to corporate green and non-green actions. *Journal of the Academy of Marketing Science*, *43*(3), 333–356. doi:10.1007/s11747-014-0394-5

Yong, J. Y., Yusliza, M. Y., & Fawehinmi, O. O. (2020). Green human resource management: A systematic literature review from 2007 to 2019. *Benchmarking*, *27*(7), 2005–2027. doi:10.1108/BIJ-12-2018-0438

Yuri, B. (2021). *Transformation of business sustainability strategies of FMCG companies in the 21st century on the examples of Unilever and L'Oréal* [Master's Thesis]. Retrieved from https://dspace.spbu.ru/bitstream/11701/32242/1/MT_Ksenia_Koreneva_GSOM.pdf

Zientara, P., & Zamojska, A. (2016). Green organizational climates and employee pro-environmental behavior in the behavior in the hotel industry. *Journal of Sustainable Tourism*, *1*, 1–18.

Chapter 12
Importance and Challenges of Online Learning in Higher Educational Institutions During COVID-19 in Uttarakhand State of India

Ajay Kumar Singh
https://orcid.org/0000-0003-0429-0925
Department of Humanities and Social Sciences, Graphic Era University (Deemed), Dehradun, India

Santosh Singh
https://orcid.org/0000-0003-2448-4794
Department of English, DIT University, India

Sandeep Kumar Sharma
https://orcid.org/0000-0002-0080-598X
Department of English, DIT University, India

EXECUTIVE SUMMARY

This chapter assesses the importance and challenges of digital learning in HEIs during COVID-19 in Uttarakhand. It conducted an online survey of 500 students studying in various programmes of HEIs. Quantitative and qualitative data are collected from the students. A total of 396 respondents recorded their responses on various questions related to study. The descriptive results claimed that the skills and learning capacity of most of the students were adversely affected due to online teaching during COVID-19 in HEIs. Teachers and students have faced several challenges to accomplish their objectives related to teaching and learning in online mode. Content-based analysis was applied to explore the impact of digital platforms on skills and learning of students. It inferred that digital platforms possess a negative impact on HEIs. HEIs, therefore, should create appropriate ICT infrastructure and e-platform to increase skills of the students and teachers during online learning.

DOI: 10.4018/979-8-3693-1781-5.ch012

1. INTRODUCTION

The higher educational institutions (HEIs) are the important drivers to increase social and economic development in multiple ways (Tadesse & Muluye, 2020; Singh & Kumar, 2022). HEIs are the knowledge and innovative creator organizations that enhance the skills and scientific understanding of the students and make them socially and economically active. HEIs also create an appropriate ecosystem where students are prepared to face the real challenges pertaining to the social and economic problems more efficiently. HEIs also help to generate several innovative ideas in the brain of the students and teachers, thereby they can be economically and socially productive (Ramane et al., 2021). Consequently, the future of the coming generation greatly depends on students' skills and knowledge received through education imparted in various disciplines or programs in HEIs. The HEIs also help to encourage science & technological development that promotes innovation, knowledge, technology know-how and technical devices (Singh & Kumar, 2022). Manufacturing sector creates and discovers new products using the innovation and technology developed by the students in HEIs (Singh & Ashraf, 2019). Consequently, manufacturing firms meet the requirement of new goods and services in the society (Singh et al., 2019). Thereupon, HEIs have a spillover effect on industrial and manufacturing growth (Singh et al., 2019).

HEIs also create a bridge between research organizations and the manufacturing sector (Singh & Kumar, 2022). Manufacturing sector can buy the advanced and innovative technologies from the HEIs and has the greater possibilities to produce new products to satisfy the current needs of the consumers (Singh et al., 2020). Hence, these technologies are also being implemented by manufacturing firms to increase their production, efficiency of inputs and productivity (Singh et al., 2019). Hence, HEIs have a positive contribution to increase the technical and economic efficiencies of the manufacturing and industrial sector. Moreover, the manufacturing sector hires the skilled workforce (i.e., engineers, scientists, designers, etc.) from HEIs (Singh et al., 2019). The growth of the manufacturing sector helps to increase innovation in the market, competition across firms, jobs for workers and infrastructural and industrial development (Singh & Jyoti, 2020). The HEIs also create a favorable ecosystem to increase industrial development and entrepreneurial activities (Singh & Kumar, 2022). Further, the growth of other sectors also depends on advanced technologies developed and discovered by HEIs. For instance, agricultural technologies, appropriate technology, digital technologies and artificial intelligence are beneficial to increase production of the agricultural sector (Ashraf & Singh, 2022; Jyoti et al., 2023). Many studies also provided the significance of digital technology in HEIs, agricultural sector, business activities, financial sector etc. (Singh & Jyoti, 2023c).

Information and communication technology (ICT) is a vital driver of digitalization and it also creates a favorable ecosystem of digital infrastructure (Sreeraj et al., 2021; Singh & Jyoti, 2023 a,b). Online education highly depends on the effectiveness of ICT and appropriate digital platforms in HEIs (Dayal, 2023). While effective implementation of ICT needs extensive training to the students and teachers in HEIs. However, extensive movement of digitalization can create disturbance in the education, health and commerce sector due to many reasons (Kampa, 2023). Despite that, most economic activities are transferring from offline mode to online mode due to application of digital processes across countries (Jyoti & Singh, 2023). Hence, most countries are moving towards the digital economy as increasing their dependency on technologies developed by either HEIs or manufacturing industries (Singh & Jyoti, 2023a). Financial stability and inclusion have already improved due to use of various digital technologies that are invented by HEIs (Singh & Jyoti, 2023c). Thus, HEIs are working as a catalyst to increase the transformation of global countries towards a digital or green economy. The HEIs are prime originators of social thinkers, entrepreneurs, economists, politicians, scientists, medical practitioners and engineers who take initiatives to make social changes, and also contribute towards the economic growth and development (Singh, 2023).

The students and teachers are the two main stakeholders in the HEIs (Joshi et al., 2020). These stakeholders accept the various challenges to meet the current technological and social needs of common people, businessmen, industries, market, society, and government. Furthermore, students and teachers develop an appropriate R&D ecosystem for creation of technological skills, innovation, ideas and knowledge to increase the social and economic development of the society (Singh & Kumar, 2022). R&D ecosystem has a vital contribution to increase the science & technological strength of HEIs. Therefore, contributions of students and teachers are noteworthy to increase the strength of R&D ecosystem and S&T development in HEIs. While the performance and skills of students and teachers depend on various indicators and activities in HEIs. Past studies given significant attention to access the factors affecting academic performance of students and teachers in HEIs across countries.

The all-economic activities were disturbed due to complete lockdown during the Covid-19 across globe (Singh et al., 2022). Therefore, academic activities were transferred from offline mode to online mode in HEIs world-wide. The academic activities of higher educational institutions (HEIs) were fully transferred from classroom teaching to online teaching after COVID -19 across countries. Online learning or e-learning is defined as using electronic and ICT devices in the education system (Duggal, 2022). It is a web-based learning that uses electronic devices, computer, mobile, laptop, internet and electronic media in the education sector (Singh, 2020). E-learning, therefore, is an electronic device that uses social media for video conferencing, email and sharing e-contents in soft copy (Sk, 2021). Online learning or e-learning does not require physical presence of learners and trainers in the education system. Online learning, therefore, brings numerous benefits to the learners and educationist.

Educators or trainers can deliver the online classes for the learners and students from across the globe. Thus, the students can save time, traveling costs and get rid of the compulsion of physical presence in the online system of education. Online learning has cost advantages for the teachers, students and management in the education sector (Sk, 2021). Although, the sudden transition of online learning brought several negative implications on teaching and learning capacity of students during Covid-19 in HEIs (Das, 2021). The students and teachers faced mental and physical health, and fatigue due to online learning (Varyani & Navaneeth, 2022; Kalia et al., 2024). The sudden movement of digital education is also caused to create a panic in the education sector (Ramane et al., 2021). As online learning cannot fully compensate for the loss of students due to their low interaction with the teachers (Sharma, 2021). Also, the students and teachers cannot do open discussion on desired topics during e-learning. Online learning, therefore, may not be supportive to increase the skills of the students and make them better thinkers and competitors in the academic field. Most teachers and teachers were unable to operate the ICT and computer due to lack of skills and technical literacy (Joshi et al., 2020). Furthermore, it was difficult for the teachers to prepare online materials, PPT, and other contents to deliver the online classes (Nambiar, 2020). Therefore, the digital revolution seems unable to maintain social equality and quality among the teachers and students in online learning (Grover & Mathew, 2022). Online learning could not help to increase the quality of discussion among teachers and students (Nambiar, 2020). Teachers could not get significant time to prepare the teaching material to deliver the online classes (Ramane et al., 2021).

Moreover, productivity, efficiency and skills of students were adversely affected due to adoption of online mode of classes in Saudi Arabia (Azmi et al., 2022). It was also difficult for economically poor and marginal students to manage the ICT infrastructure (i.e., computer, laptop, smart mobile and internet) to be involved in online learning in most developing countries (Sk, 2021; Tadesse & Muluye, 2020; Das, 2021). Most developing countries do not have e-educational materials, digital technology and information technology to increase the transformation of their education system into e-learning (Tadesse & Muluye, 2020; Khan et al., 2021; Sreeraj et al., 2021). The developing countries, therefore, were facing more problems to adopt online systems in HEIs as compared to developed countries. The USA, South Korea and the United Kingdom have the best positions to adopt online education effectively in their HEIs (Varyani & Navaneeth, 2022). However, the most developing countries have large populations with relatively low per capita income, inappropriate ICT infrastructure and low technological skills to adopt online learning in HEIs (Rahman, 2021; Jyoti & Singh, 2023). Consequently, skills and learning capacity of students were in a worsen position due to adoption of online platforms of teaching in HEIs of these countries (Jena, 2020). As there was no interaction between teachers and students, thus online learning reduces the interpersonal relationship between them. Online learning, therefore, also increases the physical and psychological disorder among the teachers and students (Ramane et al., 2021). Most specifically, online learning could not be beneficial for practical based subjects in many disciplines like engineering, medical and applied sciences.

India is a developing country and it has a large population. India has a high diversity in per capita income, infrastructural development, ICT infrastructure, internet connectivity and speed, industrial development, geographical area and academic institutions across states (Joshi et al., 2020; Singh, 2020; Nambiar, 2020; Singh & Kumar, 2021; Singh et al., 2022). Sharma (2021) also reported that internet facilities must be available to increase the success of online learning in India. Also, there is a high diversity in the ICT infrastructure in rural and urban areas of India (Goswami et al., 2021; Rahman, 2021). India has low technological skills and digital preparedness (Grover & Mathew, 2022). Furthermore, students belonging to marginal and weaker sections of the society are more vulnerable due to adoption of online platforms in HEIs (Goswami et al., 2021). Most students do not have smart-phones, computers and internet in remote areas of India (Joshi et al., 2020; Sengupta, 2022). Therefore, online classes could not be accessed by poor students in remote areas of India (Sk, 2021; Yadav, 2021), and it enhanced discrimination among the poor and rich students. However, the Government of India introduced Digital India and Skill India programs to increase the digital literacy in India before Covid-19 (Palvia et al., 2018; Bast, 2021). Digital India policy could be useful to increase the application of e-learning in the HEIs of India (Sharma, 2021). However, most students could not adjust themself with online learning during Covid-19 in India (Roy & Brown, 2022). The academic activity of 32 crore students were significantly affected due to Covid-19 in India (Das, 2021). Therefore, the transition of online learning of academic activities increases more vulnerability for most students in HEIs of India. Consequently, the online education system also creates many problems for teachers and students (Dayal, 2023).

India has a dominant position in the number of HEIs in the world (Nambiar, 2020). The HEIs of India are divided in private and public sectors. The HEIs under public and private sectors have significant diversity in terms of funds, human resources, digital infrastructure, technology, government interventions and students in India. HEIs also have a significant diversity in the availability of resources, skills of students and teachers, teaching materials, digital infrastructure, and instruments of online teaching in India. Therefore, most private institutions could not consider the above-mentioned weakness to implement online-classes for the students in India. Therefore, the students could not get significant benefits from online teaching platforms in HEIs of India after COVID-19. Findings of Rahman (2021)'s study indicate that due to low speed of internet and its high cost, the learning capacity of students in online mode of classes in Assam, India. Joshi et al. (2020) also noted that students are not connected with internet facilities, smart phone and ICT infrastructure especially in rural India. Muthuprasad et al. (2021) reported that low broadband connectivity makes it more difficult for the students to adopt online learning in rural India. In the said perspective, several studies addressed the issues of students in HEIs of India using primary surveys.

In India, most institutions are moving towards online learning without considering the student's opinion and their economic capacity to bear the high cost of ICT infrastructure. While previous studies could not include the student's opinion on the diversity in online and offline classes in India (except, Bast, 2021; Khan et al., 2021; Muthuprasad et al., 2021; Rani & Bhattacharya, 2022). Furthermore, most studies addressed the psychological issues of students due to practice of online learning (Bast, 2021; Deka, 2021; Gopal et al., 2021; Khan et al., 2021; Chahal & Rani, 2022). However, prior studies could not give more priority to examine the impact of online learning on memorizing capacity of the students. Earlier studies could also not consider the mistakes of students and teachers due to initiation of online classes in India. It also seemed that existing researchers could not identify the academic integrity due to implementation of online learning in HEIs. Most specifically, no study could explain the future perspective of HEIs due to extensive use of digital technology in India. Also, earlier researchers are incapable of providing practical suggestions to increase the skills of students during online learning in India. This chapter, therefore, is significant different from the previous literature and address following research questions in their investigations:

· How is learning in an online classroom is differ from offline classroom?
· Does the corona pandemic have an effect on the memorizing capacity of the students and teachers?
· Are students and teachers making more mistakes in solving questions in online teaching?
· How academic integrity is hampering due to adoption of online platforms in HEIs?
· How can online platforms of teaching be favorable to increase academic integrity in HEIs?
· What is the adverse impact of online learning on HEIs in India?
· Why is online learning unable to create skills among the students in India?

The present chapter has following objectives:

· To assess the importance and challenges of online learning in HEIs as per the findings of recent literature after Covid-19 in India.
· To examine the impact of online platforms on skills and learning capacity of students in HEIs.
· To provide practical and viable policy suggestions to increase the academic integrity in HEIs of India.

The chapter is used to findings of existing literature to assess the importance and challenges of online learning in HEIs India. While the impact of online learning on skills and learning capacity of the students using an online survey of 500 students studying in various programmes of HEIs in Uttarakhand. It applied descriptive analysis to achieve said objective. While Cronabch's Alpha test is applied to check the scale reliability of collected data. Finally, policy implications are also provided as per previous studies. The current chapter is organized as: The 1st section provides the introduction, research gap, research questions/research hypothesis and research objectives. The review of literature is discussed in the 2nd section. Research methodology is presented in the 3rd section. The 4th section describes the descriptive results. The concluding remark is highlighted in the 5th section. Policy implications are given in the 6th section. Limitations and scope for further research is provided in the 7th section.

2. REVIEW OF LITERATURE

The online system for learning is not a new concept and experiment in the technological and academic fields (Srinidhi et al., 2022). The online platform for learning began after the discovery of the internet and information and communication technology (ICT) in the 1990s. Therefore, technology has a vital impact on the education system (Duggal, 2022). The progress of online education is increasing due to technological change, discovery of new technology, internet and information & communication technology (ICT) at global level (Palvia et al., 2018). However, most teachers have difficulty conducting online classes due to lack of technology and ICT infrastructure at home in most developing countries (Tadesse & Muluye, 2020). As most developed countries adopted online platforms for specific activities in their HEIs and financial institutions after 1991 due to revolution in digital technology and development of the IT sector (Grover & Mathew, 2022). Few developing countries including India were also using online platforms to achieve specific tasks in HEIs (Sengupta, 2022). For instance, most activities like ticket booking of air tickets, railways, money transfer and e-business were completed through an online system before Covid 19 pandemic in India. While most countries fully converted physical class mode to fully virtual mode in the education sector after Covid-19 (Azmi et al., 2022). The online mode of teaching is adopted to avoid the academic losses of students in HEIs across countries. However, the students faced several problems such as physical, social, economic, mental, skills and learning due to initiation of online classes in HEIs of most developing countries.

The impact of online learning on the education system does not seem uniform across countries. Roy and Brown (2022), for instance, explained the impact of e-learning practices are not similar in HEIs. Thers is found a mixed impact of online learning of students on HEIs in different countries. Furthermore, previous studies adopted different dependent and independent variables to explore the impact of online learning on HEIs (Roy & Brown, 2022). Accordingly, several methods like structural equation modeling, descriptive analysis, and content-based analysis etc. are adopted by existing researchers to explain the positive and negative externalities of online learning on HEIs in India (Arora & Srinivasan, 2020; Goswami et al., 2021; Deka, 2021; Acharya et al., 2022; Duggal, 2022; Chahal & Rani, 2022; Bansal, 2023; Kalia et al., 2024). Azmi et al. (2022), for instance, observed the depression level of students in Saudi Arabia. It reported that the level of depression of study increased during Covid-19. The level of depression increased due to boring virtual classes and fear of examination. Therefore, the productivity of students decreased due to practices of online learning in the education sector.

In India, numerous scholars explained the problems of students and teachers due to implementation of online learning in HEIs across regions and states before and after Covid-19. The practice of online learning in HEIs was limited in India before Covid-19. Past studies identified the problems of students and teachers due to initiation of online learning in different disciplines of HEIs in India. Khan et al. (2021) argued that e-learning is properly accepted by students in India. However, Kundu and Kundu (2022) concluded that online education is not comfortable for the students in India. It is observed that the learning capacity of most students were negatively impacted due to adoption of online platforms of classes in HEIs of India. Arora and Srinivasan (2020) determined the benefits and challenges of virtual classes in HEIs of India. Low network of internet, low internet accessibility, lack of training and lack of awareness are significant challenges on online classes in India (Rani & Bhattacharya, 2022). Moreover, less attendance of students and low interaction of students with teachers are also reducing the effectiveness of online classes in India.

Joshi et al. (2020) also suggested that the online model of education creates several challenges for teachers in India. Teachers have low technical facilities, low training and low infrastructure at their home. Therefore, initiation of online teaching creates additional burden for teachers during Covid-19 in India. Rajhans et al. (2020) assessed the impact of online leaning of students in optometry education during Covid-19 in India. The results indicate that the optometry education degree program of students could be completed due to transition of online mode of classes. Jena (2020) explained the importance of online learning in the education sector of India during Covid-19 period. The finding showed that the students can save time, reduce cost, complete the academic syllabus through online learning. However, online learning was not effective for low-income families. Sk (2021) examined the impact of online learning platform on teachers and students in India. It concluded that online learning showed a positive impact on all stakeholder in HEIs of India.

Yadav (2021) examined the impact of online learning on education and health of the students in India. It noticed that around 30% of students were satisfied with online teaching. It also claimed that online learning could increase the addiction level of students under age 14 to extensive use of IT instruments like mobile and laptop. Accordingly, most students suffered from mental sickness and eye problems. Ramane et al. (2021) also analysed the health status of students during online learning in India. Learners' ability is adversely affected due to low internet connectivity, lack of communication with the teachers and their peers during online classes. Nambiar (2020) also recognized that poor internet connectivity, irregularity in electricity, poor broadband network and poor quality of video reduce the involvement of the students in online learning in India during Covid-19. The students and teachers also face different health problems like headache, backache, shoulder pain and neck pain due to online learning (Ramane et al., 2021). Sharma (2021) examined the satisfaction level of students to attend the online classes in Delhi. It reported that online classes were convenient and easily accessible for the students during the lockdown period (Nambiar, 2020). Online mode of education was also suitable to pursue classes as per the convenience of the students (Varyani & Navaneeth, 2022). However, online classes are not interactive and teachers and students do not give proper attention to them. Hence, most students were not happy with online learning and do not wish to continue with it after the Covid-19 (Nambiar, 2020).

Goswami et al. (2021) examined the implications of online learning in HEIs in India using primary survey. It reported the learning capacity of students belonging to SC, OBC and ST were negatively impacted due to digitalization of the education system. High cost of internet, low infrastructure of IT, and poor internet connectivity are observed crucial variables that hamper the learning capacity of students especially in rural areas of India (Lockee, 2022). Furthermore, most students were unable to operate the online platform due to their low digital illiteracy. Most students do not have internet connections, internet speed, electricity and IT infrastructure (Muthuprasad et al., 2021; Lockee, 2022). Digital education could not be improved due to poor school infrastructure and insignificant pedagogical capabilities in India (Martín & Ramos, 2022). The students and teachers bonding are also negatively affected due to online education in India (Ramane et al., 2021; Dayal, 2023).

Rahman (2021) described the implementation process of online learning in HEIs of Assam, India during COVID-19 lockdown. The findings infer the poor internet connectivity, high cost of internet, poor ICT infrastructure and irregular electricity hamper the online learning education in Assam during lockdown period. Dayal (2023) also reported that online education is adversely affected due to poor internet connectivity in Assam. Gopal et al. (2021) examined the factors that increase the satisfaction level of students during online classes in India. It noticed that the quality of instructor, course design and feedback are helpful to increase the satisfaction of the students during online classes. However, findings of Dayal (2023) claimed that online education does not find effective ways to increase the quality of education in India.

Muthuprasad et al. (2021) observed the perception of students towards online learning in the agricultural university of India. The results indicate that most students are desired to attend online classes to complete various curriculum during the Covid – 19. Internet accessibility is a crucial driver to increase the online education system (Dayal, 2023). However, online learning could not provide significant benefits to the students due to low internet connectivity in rural areas of India (Lockee, 2022). Also, online learning seems ineffective in practically oriented subjects. Acharya et al. (2022) observed the effectiveness of online learning in HEIs of India during Covid-19 period. It suggested that the design of online courses and its assessment are beneficial to increase the success of online learning. Although, the online education system increases the financial burden on poor families to arrange IT infrastructure for their children (Kundu & Kundu, 2022).

Navaneeth and Ismail (2022) reported that the online education system could not be successful due to lack of technological resources and socio-economic disparities in India. Duggal (2022) identified the determinants of acceptance of e-learning of students in India. Availability of infrastructure, design of courses, and student's competency to use ICT infrastructure are helpful to increase the perception of students to accept e-learning. Findings of Srinidhi et al. (2022) also inferred that very few students accepted that online education is fruitful and most parents agreed that online education is not good. Online education also showed adverse effects on the health of students in India. Kampa (2023) examined the mobile learning readiness scale and its acceptance level of students in teaching in Odisha, India using primary data. It proposed that mobile-learning may be effective in an online distance learning environment.

Dayal (2023) explained the problems of teachers and their wellbeing due to transition of online education in India during Covid-19. It found that online teaching is responsible for increasing the various mental and physical health issues. Bansal (2023) examined the problems of students due to implementation of online learning in the education sector of India during Covid-19. It reported several challenges like low awareness and attitude of students towards technology and insignificant administrative support in online learning. Kalia et al. (2024) investigated the impact of Covid-19 on different stakeholders in the education sector of India. It reported that the academic activities of key stakeholders were negatively impacted due to mental distress, physical immobility and technological illiteracy.

It is also noted that technological constraint, health issues, instructor's incompetency and low internet speed reduce the success of online learning (Muthuprasad et al., 2021). Quality of education and technological development are useful to increase online learning. Technical efficiency of faculty, low internet speed, data limit, poor learning environment, learner's inefficiency, health issues and lack of monitoring and reduce the success of online learning during Covid-19 in India (Muthuprasad et al., 2021; Rahman, 2021; Varyani & Navaneeth, 2022). Deka (2021) determined the factors affecting effectiveness of online education in India. Involvement of students, learning ecosystem, and administrative support appeared significant indicators to enhance the online learning. Lack of resources like computers, laptop and broadband connection also reduce the intention of the students to be involved in online classes in India (Rajhans et al., 2020; Duggal, 2022).

Previous studies also observed the factors which enhance the perception of students to adopt e-learning in HEIs (Khan et al., 2021; Chahal & Rani, 2022). The quantity and quality of online education is also determined by business, government, law, ICT capacity, internet, technology transfer, income and digital infrastructure (Palvia et al., 2018; Dayal, 2023). Nambiar (2020) explored the perception of students and teachers on online learning in Bangalore city of India. It concluded that online learning can be effective in improving the interaction between teachers and students, quality of lecture, technical literacy, and practical curriculum. Bast (2021) observed the perception of students towards digital education in India. Khan et al. (2021) found positive perception of students towards online learning in India during Covid-19. Chahal and Rani (2022) explored the opinion of students to accept e-learning in HEIs in India. The findings claimed that personal innovativeness, self-efficacy and social factors play a significant role in increasing the involvement of students to be involved in e-learning practices. Therefore, policy makers should give more focus on above-mentioned variables to increase the participation of students in online learning. Duggal (2022) also notified the contribution of technology and ICT to increase the perception to accept e-learning in the education system. Rani and Bhattacharya (2022) identified the perception of students towards online learning and its impact on the education system in India. The study found that 50% of students were not happy with the online learning and most students also accepted that online learning is not fruitful to increase their interaction with the teachers.

The above-mentioned review clearly indicates that the impact of online learning on HEIs in India does not seem uniform (Jena, 2020; Rahman, 2021; Yadav, 2021). Online learning could be helpful for a few programmes in HEIs of India (Nambiar, 2020; Rajhans et al., 2020; Jena, 2020; Sk, 2021; Kampa, 2023). Although, most studies emphasized that online learning could not provide more success to the students due to lack of ICT infrastructure in HEIs and poor economic ability of the students to bear the high cost of ICT tools (Joshi et al., 2020; Muthuprasad et al., 2021; Ramane et al., 2021; Kundu & Kundu, 2022; Navaneeth & Ismail, 2022; Lockee, 2022; Martín & Ramos, 2022; Rani & Bhattacharya, 2022; Dayal, 2023). Furthermore, online learning creates more problems for the students who belong to SC, OBC and ST (Goswami et al., 2021). It is also reported that health status of students and teachers are stressful due to online teaching practices in India (Ramane et al., 2021; Dayal, 2023; Kalia et al., 2024). Although, the previous literature could not examine the perception of students towards online and offline learning. Also, earlier researchers could not consider the impact of online learning on academic integrity in HEIs of India. The earlier academicians could not explain the future perspectives of HEIs due to extensive practice of online learning in HEIs of India. This chapter is an attempt to fill the mentioned research gap in this study.

3. APPLIED METHODOLOGY

3.1. Data Collection Technique

This study used primary data that was collected through an online survey of 500 students studying in different programs in HEIs in Uttarakhand state of India. However, only 396 students could provide the answers on all questions related to this study. Therefore, a sample size of 396 students was used for descriptive analysis. The survey was conducted from January 31, 2022 to March 31, 2022.

3.2. Study Area

The survey area of this study was Uttarakhand state of India. Uttarakhand is a largely hilly area and it has low ICT and digital infrastructure with low internet facility. Thus, the state was facing more difficulty in the adoption of online teaching practices in HEIs. Therefore, this state was considered to understand the implications of online teaching practices on academic fraternity in the randomly selected 20 HEIs.

These HEIs include universities/research institutions and colleges from Uttarakhand. The sample of 500 students were taken from the selected HEIs of this state. These 500 students were randomly selected from 10 private and 10 public institutions in Uttarakhand. Hence, 25 students from each institute/university were considered as respondents in this chapter. As the name of students and educational institutions were confidential, therefore, the authors could not disclose the name of selected institutions and students in the manuscript. While the authors can produce the raw data as per the need of the publisher.

3.3. Format of Questionnaire

The chapter uses well-structured questionnaires that include the qualitative and quantitative information pertinent to this study. Accordingly, it develops a google form to conduct the online survey of the students. The email ID of the students are taken from the top management of the selected institutions and universities. We developed 23 questions that reflect the overall performance of the students.

3.4. Descriptive Analysis

Gopal et al. (2021) developed a structural equation model to extract the satisfaction level of students during online classes. Sharma (2021) used descriptive analysis to identify the satisfaction level of students towards online classes in Delhi, India using Liker scale data. Chahal and Rani (2022) applied technology acceptance model and structural equation model to examine the factors influencing the student's intention to adopt e-learning in HEIs of India. Azmi et al. (2022) applied descriptive and multiple regression analysis to detect the depression level of students due to Covid-19 in Saudi Arabia. Roy and Brown (2022) used quantitative analysis to identify the challenges of students and teachers due to implementation of online teaching practices in HEIs of India. Duggal (2022) developed a structural equation model to examine the perception of students to accept e-learning in HEIs of India. The descriptive statistical techniques are used to explain the performance of primary data (Rajhans et al., 2020). Singh et al. (2023) preferred logit and probit models to examine the indicators enhancing the farmer's perception to adopt adaptation strategies to mitigate the negative impact of climate change in the Indian agricultural sector. Singh and Singh (2024) examine the impact of social-economic characteristics on willingness to pay and ability to acquire drinking water from suppliers in India. Probit and logit models produce the probability of a specific independent variable on output (Singh et al., 2023).

The main objective of this chapter is to explore the impact of online learning on HEIs in India. Therefore, most variables are collected in binary form (i.e., yes or no) in this chapter. Yadav (2021) also used binary data (i.e., yes or no) and Likert scale data to examine the impact of online learning on education and health of students in India. Nambiar (2020) also considered binary data (i.e., agree or disagree) to identify the view of students and teachers on online learning in India. Further, the performance of the students during online class may not be explained by a specific indicator. Thus, it is not easy to decide dependent and independent variables for the empirical investigations. Most collected data were in the form of binary numbers in this research. Therefore, descriptive analysis was used to explore the implication of digital platforms on skills and learning capacity of students. The prime aim of HEIs is to increase the skills of students and make them innovative in multiple ways. Another objective of HEIs is to increase the competitive level of students. Henceforth, increasing skills of the students measure the overall performance of HEIs. Cronbach's alpha test was used to check the internal consistency of

Table 1. Age, gender, location, and academic programme of respondents

Features	Group	Frequency	Percentage
Age (in Years)	17-19	283	71.46
	20-22	104	26.26
	23-25	9	2.27
Gender	Male	227	57.32
	Female	169	42.68
Domicile State	Bihar	55	13.89
	Chhattisgarh	5	1.26
	Delhi	4	1.01
	Gujarat	7	1.77
	Haryana	6	1.52
	Himachal Pradesh	7	1.77
	Jammu and Kashmir	10	2.53
	Jharkhand	4	1.01
	Karnataka	7	1.77
	Madhya Pradesh	8	2.02
	Rajasthan	9	2.27
	Uttar Pradesh	115	29.04
	Uttarakhand	149	37.63
	West Bengal	10	2.53
Academic Programme	B.A. (Hons)	72	18.18
	B.Sc. (All)	85	21.46
	B.Tech. (All)	147	37.12
	BBA	37	9.34
	BCA	55	13.89

Source: Author's observation based on survey.

collected data (Sharma, 2021; Khan et al., 2021; Rajhans et al., 2020; Duggal, 2022). SPSS and STATA statistical software are used to analyze the collected data.

4. DESCRIPTIVE AND EMPIRICAL FINDINGS

The age, gender, domicile state and academic programme is given in Table 1. As most students in the sample were in the age group between 17-19 years. While 57.37% and 42.68% were male and female, respectively in the sample. The majority of students were from Uttarakhand, Uttar Pradesh and Bihar.

The sample has few students from Chhattisgarh, Delhi, Gujarat, Haryana, Himachal Pradesh, Jammu and Kashmir, Jharkhand, Madhya Pradesh, and West Bengal. Furthermore, the sample included the students from B.A. (Hons), B.Sc. (All), B.Tech. (All), BBA, and BCA courses.

The statistical summary of the student's responses on 23 various questions is given in Table: 2. The scale-reliability of collected data is checked using Cronbach's alpha test. The statistical values of Cronbach's alpha test for all variables were more than 0.8 that showed these variables have internal viability and consistency. Furthermore, the descriptive results indicate that 70% of students accepted that online learning is different from online learning. 56% of students admitted that online learning has insignificant scope to increase the interaction between teachers and students. Rani & Bhattacharya (2022); Dayal (2023) also explored that online learning is inefficient to increase the interaction among the teachers and students. Majority of students did not attend online classes seriously and showed their low interest (Nambiar, 2020). Therefore, 61.11% students perceived that their learning, skills, knowledge and innovative ideas were negatively affected due to above-mentioned reasons.

Around 76.77% of students were unable to concentrate on their studies due to online learning. 41.92% students were satisfied with the online learning. Further, only 69.95% students could complete academic tasks on time during online classes. 89.39% students reported that teachers have completed the prescribed syllabus during the online classes. However, 58.08% students claimed that teachers could not monitor the presence of the students during online learning. Therefore, it reduces the presence of students in the online classes. Online classes also increase the actual time of students to solve the questions. As there was no interaction and discussion among the teachers and students in the online classes. Therefore, 64.90% students accepted that they have more doubts during the online learning. Accordingly, 89.39% of students changed their usual time of study during Covid-19. Since survival was the most important thing during Covid-19 pandemic, studies were pushed down the priority list by students. Thus, 73.99% students were reported struggling to keep away from the negative, anxiety-provoking thoughts during Covid-19 pandemic.

Thereupon, 54.29% students were in a position to adapt and adjust themselves to prevent from Covid-19 during the online learning. The online learning practices were implemented in short duration in academics. Thus, most students were not able to arrange ICT infrastructure at their home which eventually affected their familiarity negatively with online learning. Most students could not be present in online classes due to lack of ICT infrastructure and low internet speed. Accordingly, 60.10% students could collect e-materials for their study during the online classes. 71.46% of students received proper content and reading materials from their respective teachers during the online classes. 60.35% students agreed that online learning increases the financial burden to arrange ICT infrastructure at their home to attend online classes. Kundu and Kundu, (2022) also noticed that online learning increased the financial burden for economically poor students to arrange ICT infrastructure.

43.18% and 63.64% could not attend online classes due to poor internet connectivity and irregularity in electricity, respectively. Nambiar (2020); Muthuprasad et al. (2021); Muthuprasad et al., 2021; Rahman (2021); Rani & Bhattacharya (2022); Lockee (2022) also observed that low network of internet and regulatory in electricity created barriers for the students to attend online classes during Covid-19. Accordingly, 72.22% of students were worried about submitting a quiz, assignment and answer sheet of exams during online classes. Online learning was found inappropriate for practical subjects as online 28.28% students could complete the assigned task of practical subjects during the online learning. As most students belong to the low-income group community, 29.80% students reported that they do not have a proper environment at their home to attend the online classes. Most specifically, only 31.82% of students preferred online learning in academics. Thus, the learning capacity of students decreased due to the initiation of online teaching. Furthermore, teachers are also unable to increase the participation of students in online classes.

Table 2. Statistical summary of student's responses on questions

Questions	Response (in %)		Mean	Std. Deviation	Cronbach Alpha Test
	Yes	No			
Does online classroom is different from actual classroom? (Yes =1, No=0)	69.95	30.05	0.6995	0.4591	0.8673
Does student-teacher interaction in online classroom is effective? (Yes =1, No=0)	44.19	55.81	0.4419	0.4972	0.8701
Did online classes improve your learning, skills, knowledge and innovative ideas? (Yes =1, No=0)	38.89	61.11	0.3889	0.4881	0.8745
Do you perceive that your ability to focus/concentration on studies decrease due to online learning? (Yes =1, No=0)	76.77	23.23	0.7677	0.4228	0.8697
Did you complete assigned academic task on time during online classes? (Yes =1, No=0)	69.95	30.05	0.6995	0.4591	0.8673
Did the teachers/instructors do complete the syllabus during online classes? (Yes =1, No=0)	89.39	10.61	0.8939	0.3083	0.8709
Did the teachers/instructors do monitor of your presence in online classes? (Yes =1, No=0)	41.92	58.08	0.4192	0.4941	0.8785
Did you notice that the actual time for solving questions increases in online classes? (Yes =1, No=0)	75.76	24.24	0.7576	0.4291	0.869
Do you have more doubts to solving questions in online classes? (Yes =1, No=0)	64.90	35.10	0.6490	0.4779	0.8672
Did you notice that your usual timing of study changes from pre-corona pandemic time? (Yes =1, No=0)	89.39	10.61	0.8939	0.3083	0.8709
Is it difficult for you to keep away from the negative, anxiety-provoking cue to your studies in online classes? (Yes =1, No=0)	73.99	26.01	0.7399	0.4392	0.8699
Are you unable to adapt and adjust yourself with the current environment of Covid-19? (Yes =1, No=0)	54.29	45.71	0.5429	0.4988	0.8711
Are you satisfying with the online learning? (Yes =1, No=0)	41.92	58.08	0.4192	0.4941	0.8785
Did you collect e-materials for your study yourself in online learning? (Yes =1, No=0)	60.10	39.90	0.6010	0.4903	0.8702
Did teachers/instructors provide you receive proper contents and reading materials during online classes? (Yes =1, No=0)	71.46	28.54	0.7146	0.4522	0.8741
Did you use online learning for your study before COVID-19? (Yes =1, No=0)	88.13	11.87	0.8813	0.3238	0.8711
Did you face any financial restriction to bear the cost of ICT infrastructure (i.e., computer, laptop, smartphone, internet broadband etc.)? (Yes =1, No=0)	60.35	39.65	0.6035	0.4898	0.8800
Did you have proper internet connectivity with high speed for online classes in your location? (Yes =1, No=0)	43.18	56.82	0.4318	0.4960	0.8771
Did you have regular electricity to attend online classes? (Yes =1, No=0)	63.64	36.36	0.6364	0.4817	0.867
Are you worry for submission of quiz, assignment and exam on time during online classes? (Yes =1, No=0)	72.22	27.78	0.7222	0.4485	0.8691
Are you capable to complete the task of your practical subjects during online classes? (Yes =1, No=0)	28.28	71.72	0.2828	0.4509	0.8781
Do you have proper/separate/environment at your home to be regular in the online classes? (Yes =1, No=0)	70.20	29.80	0.7020	0.4579	0.8684
Will you prefer online learning in future? (Yes =1, No=0)	31.82	68.18	0.3182	0.4664	0.8755

Source: Author's observation based on survey.

5. CONCLUDING REMARK

The results of past studies infer that online learning was innovative and revolutionary in the academic sector to avoid the loss of students in HEIs of India and other countries during COVID-19. Online learning was favorable to save time, reduce physical presence of students and teachers, and it also saved travel time (Nambiar, 2020). Online learning seemed useful for the students and teachers to save time, reduce travel cost and complete the academic task during Covid -19 (Sk, 2021). Online learning, therefore, could also provide protection to the students and teachers from the Covid-19 pandemic. Online learning was convenient for the students and teachers during Covid-19 pandemic (Sharma, 2021). In general, online learning is also helpful to the students who do not have time to be physically present in offline classes. There were also observed many benefits of online learning like technological advancement, technology transfer, skills and knowledge transfer in the education sector of developed and developing countries (Kundu & Kundu, 2022). Most developed countries have developed an appropriate ecosystem of online learning in the education sector before Covid-19. Accordingly, many developing countries took the initiative to start online learning in the academic sector before spreading the Covid-19. However, developing countries have poor ICT infrastructure, digital technology, low technological skills, low technological adoption capacity, low technological development and low internet speed. Also, there is a high illiteracy, low technological skills and low per capita income in most developing countries (Bansal, 2023). Moreover, research institutions and universities are not in a position to adopt online classes in these countries. Therefore, online learning could not reflect the desired impact on education systems across countries during Covid-19.

India does not have adequate ICT infrastructure to adopt fully online learning in HEIs (Grover & Mathew, 2022). Therefore, academic institutions of India were not ready to implement online learning for the students before Covid-19. As online learning and course material were not a significant part of the education system of India before Covid-19 (Kundu & Kundu, 2022). The HEIs of India were bound to apply online learning to the student to prevent them from the pandemic and minimize their academic loss during Covid-19 (Nambiar, 2020; Deka, 2021). However, online learning has not seemed appropriate for the students and teachers in long-time. The finding of previous literature that deals with the impact of online learning on HEIs in India provides significant results. Most students were not serious about attending the online classes. The students in remote areas were unable to take online classes effectively due to unavailability of high internet speed and electricity. Furthermore, a large number of students have low efficiency and skills to operate laptops to attend online classes. Faculty were also not able to monitor the progress of students in online mode. At present, therefore, the fully online education system is not feasible in India due to diversity in social, economic, technological, cultural, ICT infrastructure across different locations (Nambiar, 2020; Kundu & Kundu, 2022).

In India, online learning could not provide greater success in education sector due to following reasons: Low network of internet (Nambiar, 2020; Muthuprasad et al., 2021; Rahman, 2021; Rani & Bhattacharya, 2022; Lockee, 2022), low internet accessibility (Ramane et al., 2021; Rani & Bhattacharya, 2022), poor broadband network (Nambiar, 2020), high cost of internet (Rahman, 2021; Lockee, 2022), low ICT infrastructure (Muthuprasad et al., 2021; Rahman, 2021; Duggal, 2022; Lockee, 2022), lack of technological and ICT resources like computer, laptop, broadband connection (Rajhans et al., 2020; Kundu & Kundu, 2022; Duggal, 2022), poor quality of video (Nambiar, 2020), low electricity (Nambiar, 2020; Rahman, 2021; Muthuprasad et al., 2021), lack of awareness of students in online learning (Rani & Bhattacharya, 2022; Kalia et al., 2024), low awareness and attitude of students towards technology

(Bansal, 2023), lack of training of students and faculty (Rani & Bhattacharya, 2022) low digital literacy of the students and teachers (Lockee, 2022), low interaction among the students and teachers (Rani & Bhattacharya, 2022; Dayal, 2023), lack of monitoring of the student's presence in the online class, lack of communication of students with their peers (Joshi et al., 2020; Ramane et al., 2021), low technical facility (Joshi et al., 2020), and instructor's incompetency to operate online platform (Muthuprasad et al., 2021). Therefore, oline learning reduces the satisfaction level of the students (Yadav, 2021). Online learning increased the financial burden for economically poor students to arrange ICT infrastructure in India (Kundu & Kundu, 2022). Hence, the majority of the students and teachers were not like online learning (Nambiar, 2020). Thereafter, online learning creates many health issues like headache, backache, shoulder pain and neck pain for the teachers and students during Covid-19 (Muthuprasad et al., 2021; Ramane et al., 2021; Srinidhi et al., 2022; Dayal, 2023). Mental distress, physical mobility and depression among the students increased due to online learning during Covid-19 in India (Kalia et al., 2024).

The survey results of this chapter also provide a confirmation that online learning could not appear beneficial for the students due to lack of student-teacher interaction on physical mode, limited skilled and technological innovators, issue related concentration, internet connectivity and electricity challenges, and absence of full proof monitoring system. Online mode of learning also seems not a viable option for economically weaker sections due to the high cost of digital tools and internet connections. Additionally, online increased the financial burden to bear the cost of laptop, computer, and internet. Most students registered difficulties in submitting quiz, assignment and exam answer sheets during online classes. Also, online learning was not found useful for practical subjects. Therefore, the findings suggest that the majority of students reported their unwillingness to online learning in the HEIs of India.

6. POLICY IMPLICATIONS

The government of India should increase extensive investment in the IT sector to increase the online platform in HEIs (Goswami et al., 2021). The government should also provide special training to students and teachers to increase their usability of IT infrastructure in online learning and provide IT instruments to the weaker and marginally weaker section of the society. Connectivity is also one major challenge in front of the Government of India, specifically in rural areas. Infrastructural development, availability of electricity, high speed internet connectivity would be positive to increase the effectiveness of online education systems in India (Tadesse & Muluye, 2020; Singh, 2020; Martín & Ramos, 2022; Bansal, 2023). It is also essential to increase the self-efficacy of students to improve their participation in online learning practices in India. The descriptive findings of this chapter are helpful to implement effective policies to increase skills and learning capacity of the students in HEIs in India and other developing countries (Tadesse & Muluye, 2020). The government should provide appropriate online infrastructure and ICTs to the HEIs to increase the academic integrity in India. Thereafter, the initiation of online learning will be more successful in India (Kundu & Kundu, 2022). There is a requirement to provide the special training to the students to increase their involvement in online learning in HEIs (Azmi et al., 2022). The government should also give extensive focus to increase the development of telecommunication infrastructure in India (Palvia et al., 2018). Digital infrastructure in rural and remote area would increase the success of online learning in India (Joshi et al., 2020). The HEIs also create a favorable ICT infrastructure to increase the practicability of students and teachers to use e-learning. Quality of the online education system must be improved in India (Palvia et al., 2018). The HEIs should develop a scientific platform to complete the syllabus of practical subjects through online learning.

7. LIMITATIONS AND SCOPE FOR FURTHER RESEARCH

The findings of this research are based on a sample of 396 students from HEIs of Uttarakhand. Due to limited sample size the findings may not be generalized to draw an appropriate conclusion about online learning across India. Furthermore, the impact of online learning on the quality and skills of students depends on their programme and discipline. For instance, online learning is found unproductive for practical programs like chemistry, physics, engineering, medical sciences, pharmaceuticals, etc. Online learning also seemed ineffective to increase the skills of students in many subjects that need training and laboratory (Kundu & Kundu, 2022). However, this chapter does not consider the above-mentioned issues in the investigation. Hence, the study can examine the impact of online learning of the students in different disciplines of HEIs. The findings of this chapter are based on Indian universities; and could not include the foreign university in the estimation. Therefore, further research can be included to examine the influence of online learning on HEIs in other developed and developing countries to get more policy proposals to increase the quality in the education sector through e-learning. Teachers and other stakeholders also face physical and mental health issues and anxiety to conduct the online classes (Nambiar, 2020; Kalia et al., 2024). The students and teachers have many health issues due to online learning (Rani & Bhattacharya, 2022). Hence, further study can be carried out to examine the impact of the online education system on ability, efficiency, performance, productivity, innovativeness and skills of teachers and students in India. Therefore, online learning must be stress free for teachers and students. Accordingly, it would be effective to sustain the health of educators in India.

REFERENCES

Acharya, A., Mukherjee, S., Bhattacharjee, A. K., Datta, D., & Deyasi, A. (2022). COVID-19: will it be a game changer in higher education in India? *Data Science for COVID-19*, *2*(1), 611-629. doi:10.1016/B978-0-323-90769-9.00034-7

Arora, A. K., & Srinivasan, R. (2020). Impact of pandemic COVID-19 on the teaching – learning process: A study of higher education teachers. *Prabandhan: Indian Journal of Management*, *13*(4), 1–13. doi:10.17010/pijom/2020/v13i4/151825

Ashraf, S. N., & Singh, A. K. (2022). Implications of appropriate technology and farm inputs in the agricultural sector of Gujarat: Empirical analysis based on primary data. *Agricultural Economics Research Review*, *35*(2), 59–77. doi:10.5958/0974-0279.2022.00031.3

Azmi, F. M., Khan, H. N., & Azmi, A. M. (2022). The impact of virtual learning on students' educational behavior and pervasiveness of depression among university students due to the COVID-19 pandemic. *Globalization and Health*, *18*(70), 1–9. doi:10.1186/s12992-022-00863-z PMID:35836278

Bansal, M. (2023). Multidimensional impact of COVID-19 on the Indian education sector. *Management and Labour Studies*, *48*(2), 214–223. doi:10.1177/0258042X211069509

Bast, F. (2021). Perception of online learning among students from India set against the pandemic. *Frontiers in Education*, *6*(1), 1–8. doi:10.3389/feduc.2021.705013

Chahal, J., & Rani, N. (2022). Exploring the acceptance for e-learning among higher education students in India: Combining technology acceptance model with external variables. *Journal of Computing in Higher Education*, *34*(1), 844–867. doi:10.1007/s12528-022-09327-0 PMID:35668837

Das, P. K. (2021). Impact of pandemic Covid-19 on higher education-Indian context. *Universal Journal of Business and Management*, *1*(1), 13–21. doi:10.31586/ujbm.2021.010102

Dayal, S. (2023). Online education and its effects on teachers during COVID-19 – a case study from India. *PLoS One*, *18*(3), 1–15. doi:10.1371/journal.pone.0282287 PMID:36862704

Deka, P. K. (2021). Factors influencing student engagement in online learning during the COVID-19 pandemic period in India. *Journal of Management in Practice*, *6*(1), 1–16.

Duggal, S. (2022). Factors impacting acceptance of e-learning in India: Learners' perspective. *Asian Association of Open University Journal*, *17*(2), 101–119. doi:10.1108/AAOUJ-01-2022-0010

Gopal, R., Singh, V., & Aggarwal, A. (2021). Impact of online classes on the satisfaction and performance of students during the pandemic period of COVID 19. *Education and Information Technologies*, *26*(1), 6923–6947. doi:10.1007/s10639-021-10523-1 PMID:33903795

Goswami, M. P., Thanvi, J., & Padhi, S. R. (2021). Impact of online learning in India: A survey of university students during the COVID-19 crisis. *Asian Journal for Public Opinion Research*, *9*(4), 331–351. doi:10.15206/ajpor.2021.9.4.331

Grover, S., & Mathew, L. (2022). Exploring the digital revolution in education in India during COVID-19 pandemic. *International Journal of Social Quality*, *12*(2), 51–71. doi:10.3167/IJSQ.2022.120204

Jena, P. K. (2020). Online learning during lockdown period for COVID-19 in India. *International Journal of Multidisciplinary Education Research*, *9*(5), 82–91. doi:10.31235/osf.io/qu38b

Joshi, A., Vinay, M., & Bhaskar, P. (2020). Online teaching amidst COVID-19 in India: An outlook. *Asian Journal of Distance Education*, *15*(2), 105–111.

Jyoti, B., & Singh, A. K. (2023). Does digitalization have a causal relationship with economic development? an experience from a country-wise panel data statistical analysis. In R. Sine Nazlı & G. Sari (Eds.), Handbook of Research on Perspectives on Society and Technology Addiction (pp. 34-61). IGI Global. doi:10.4018/978-1-6684-8397-8.ch003

Jyoti, B., Singh, A. K., & Ashraf, S. N. (2023). Appropriate technologies and their implications in the agricultural sector. In P. H. Alex Khang (Ed.), *Advanced Technologies and AI-Equipped IoT Applications in High-Tech Agriculture* (pp. 65–87). IGI Global. doi:10.4018/978-1-6684-9231-4.ch004

Kalia, P., Behal, B., Kaur, K., & Mehta, D. (2024). Impact of COVID-19 on education in India: Stakeholders' voice. *Benchmarking*, *31*(1), 243–264. doi:10.1108/BIJ-11-2021-0665

Kampa, R. K. (2023). Combining technology readiness and acceptance model for investigating the acceptance of m-learning in higher education in India. *Asian Association of Open Universities Journal*, *18*(2), 105–120. doi:10.1108/AAOUJ-10-2022-0149

Khan, M. A., Vivek, V., Nabi, M. K., Khojah, M., & Tahir, M. (2021). Students' perception towards e-learning during COVID-19 pandemic in India: An empirical study. *Sustainability (Basel)*, *13*(1), 1–14. doi:10.3390/su13010057

Kundu, A., & Kundu, S. (2022). Online education in India, an insight into the future: From the students' experience during the lockdown for COVID-19. *Towards Excellence*, *14*(2), 292–305. doi:10.37867/TE140227

Lockee, B. B. (2022). Online education in the post-COVID era. *Nature Electronics*, *4*(1), 5–6. doi:10.1038/s41928-020-00534-0

Martín, A. V. D., & Ramos, J. M. L. (2022). DEIFD framework: Evaluation of digital education deployment in India in the midst of Covid-19 pandemic. *Social Sciences & Humanities Open*, *6*(1), 1–11. doi:10.1016/j.ssaho.2022.100281

Muthuprasad, T., Aiswarya, S., Aditya, K. S., & Jha, G. K. (2021). Students' perception and preference for online education in India during COVID – 19 pandemic. *Social Sciences & Humanities Open*, *3*(1), 1–11. doi:10.1016/j.ssaho.2020.100101 PMID:34173507

Nambiar, D. (2020). The impact of online learning during COVID-19: Students' and teachers' perspective. *International Journal of Indian Psychology*, *8*(2), 783–793. doi:10.25215/0802.094

Navaneeth, M. S., & Ismail, S. (2022). How inclusive is online education in India: Lessons from pandemic. In *Socioeconomic inclusion during an era of online education, Manuel, B. G. (Edt.)* (pp. 135–155). IGI Global. doi:10.4018/978-1-6684-4364-4.ch007

Palvia, S., Aeron, P., Gupta, P., Mahapatra, D., Parida, R., Rosner, R., & Sindhi, S. (2018). Online education: Worldwide status, challenges, trends, and implications. *Journal of Global Information Technology Management*, *21*(4), 233–241. doi:10.1080/1097198X.2018.1542262

Rahman, A. (2021). Using students' experience to derive effectiveness of COVID-19-lockdown-induced emergency online learning at undergraduate level: Evidence from Assam, India. *Higher Education for the Future*, *8*(1), 71–89. doi:10.1177/2347631120980549

Rajhans, V., Memon, U., Patil, V., & Goyal, A. (2020). Impact of COVID – 19 on academic activities and way forward in Indian optometry. *Journal of Optometry*, *13*(1), 216–226. doi:10.1016/j.optom.2020.06.002 PMID:32703749

Ramane, D. V., Devare, U. K., & Kapatkar, M. V. (2021). The impact of online learning on learners' education and health. *The Online Journal of Distance Education and e-Learning : TOJDEL*, *9*(2), 303–309.

Rani, S., & Bhattacharya, S. (2022). A descriptive study to assess the impact and perception of online classes on student community pan India during COVID-19. *The Journal of Communicable Diseases*, *1*(1), 9–14. doi:10.24321/0019.5138.202202

Roy, S., & Brown, S. (2022). Higher education in India in the time of pandemic, sans a learning management system. *AERA Open*, *8*(1), 23–37. doi:10.1177/23328584211069527

Sengupta, S. (2022). Possibilities and challenges of online education in India during the COVDI-19 pandemic. *International Journal of Web-Based Learning and Teaching Technologies*, *17*(4), 1–11. doi:10.4018/IJWLTT.285567

Sharma, B. (2021). Online classes experience among students during lockdown. *The online Journal of Distance and e-Learning*, *9*(2), 247-254.

Singh, A. K. (2023). Relative performance of entrepreneurship ecosystem for selected countries using a composite Z-score technique of index estimation. *Eurasian Journal of Management & Social Sciences*, *4*(2), 1–32. doi:10.23918/ejmss.V4i2p1

Singh, A. K., & Ashraf, S. N. (2019). Viability of Bayh-Dole Act of USA in context of India: critical evidence from review of literature. *JNNCE Journal of Engineering & Management, 3*(1), 7-22. http://jjem.jnnce.ac.in/article/JJEM030102.pdf

Singh, A. K., Ashraf, S. N., & Arya, A. (2019). Estimating factors affecting technical efficiency in Indian manufacturing sector. *Eurasian Journal of Business and Economics*, *12*(24), 65–86. doi:10.17015/ejbe.2019.024.04

Singh, A. K., Ashraf, S. N., Sharma, S. K., & Kumar, S. (2023). Factors affecting farm income and climate adaptation strategies in the farming sector of Gujarat state of India. In B. J. Sadhik, J. Adewole, A. Yeneneh, & L. Abidoye (Eds.), *Opportunities and Challenges in Climate-Friendly Clean Water and Energy Technologies* (pp. 122–147). IGI Global. doi:10.4018/978-1-6684-7303-0.ch006

Singh, A. K., & Jyoti, B. (2020). Factors affecting firm's annual turnover in selected manufacturing industries of India: An empirical study. *Business Perspectives and Research*, *2*(3), 33–59. doi:10.38157/business-perspective-review.v2i3.206

Singh, A. K., & Jyoti, B. (2023a). Empirical evidence from different income group countries on the interdependency between digitalization and economic development. In 5G, Artificial Intelligence, and Next Generation Internet of Things: Digital Innovation for Green and Sustainable Economies (pp. 44-85). IGI Global. doi:10.4018/978-1-6684-8634-4.ch003

Singh, A. K., & Jyoti, B. (2023b). Does digitalization have a bi-directional causal relationship with the entrepreneurship ecosystem? Evidence from a country-wise panel data analysis. In R. Yanamandra & L. Indiran (Eds.), *Handbook of Research on Designing Sustainable Strategies to Develop Entrepreneurial Intention* (pp. 178–172). IGI Global. doi:10.4018/978-1-6684-8781-5.ch007

Singh, A. K., & Jyoti, B. (2023c). *Impact of digitalization on global sustainable development across countries*. Green and Low-carbon Economy. doi:10.47852/bonviewGLCE32021482

Singh, A. K., & Kumar, S. (2021). Assessing the performance and factors affecting industrial development in Indian states: An empirical analysis. *Journal of Social Economics Research*, *8*(2), 135–154. doi:10.18488/journal.35.2021.82.135.154

Singh, A. K., & Kumar, S. (2022). Expert's perception on technology transfer and commercialization, and intellectual property rights in India: Evidence from selected research organizations. *Journal of Management, Economics, and Industrial Organization*, *6*(1), 1–33. doi:10.31039/jomeino.2022.6.1.1

Singh, A. K., Kumar, S., & Jyoti, B. (2022). Impact of the COVID-19 on food security and sustainable development goals in India: Evidence from existing literature. *GNOSI: An Interdisciplinary Journal of Human Theory and Praxis, 5*(2), 94-109. http://gnosijournal.com/index.php/gnosi/article/view/196/225

Singh, A. K., Singh, B., & Ashraf, S. N. (2020). Implications of intellectual property protection, and science and technological development in the manufacturing sector in selected economies. *Journal of Advocacy. Research in Education*, *7*(1), 16–35. https://oaji.net/articles/2021/1704-1615668997.pdf

Singh, A. K., & Singh, S. (2024). A case study from kanpur nagar, uttar pradesh for assessing the economic value of water and its determinants. In A. Karmaoui (Ed.), *Water-Soil-Plant-Animal Nexus in the Era of Climate Change* (pp. 212–242). IGI Global. doi:10.4018/978-1-6684-9838-5.ch010

Singh, S. (2020). An analysis of factors responsible for the rapid growth of e-learning in India. *Palarch's Journal of Archaeology of Egypt/Egyptology*, *17*(12), 1454-1466.

Sk, M. S. (2021). Impact of COVID-19 on e-learning at higher education in India. *Towards Excellence*, *13*(1), 184–191.

Sreeraj, R. N., Joy, S., Lijisha, P. V., & Senthilkumar, T. (2021). A study to assess the impact of online learning among school children in Kerala. *Medicon Medical Sciences*, *1*(2), 29–34.

Srinidhi, S., Vezhaventhan, D., Shoba, J. K. S., Kirubagaran, K., Karthikheyan, T. C., & Gopalan, K. R. (2022). Effect Of Online Education on Elementary Education in India *Journal for Educators. Teachers and Trainers*, *13*(2), 76–88.

Tadesse, S., & Muluye, W. (2020). The impact of COVID-19 pandemic on education system in developing countries: A review. *Open Journal of Social Sciences*, *8*(1), 159–170. doi:10.4236/jss.2020.810011

Varyani, H., & Navaneeth, M. S. (2022). The past, present and future of e-learning: In India. *International Journal of Policy Sciences and Law*, *1*(1), 99–118.

Yadav, A. K. (2021). Impact of online teaching on students' education and health in India during the pandemic of COVDI-19. *Coronaviruses*, *2*(2), 516–520. doi:10.2174/2666796701999201005212801

Chapter 13
The Constraints and Obstacles of Social Media Entrepreneurship Powered by AI

Sheneen Hossain
BRAC University, Bangladesh

EXECUTIVE SUMMARY

The emergence of globalization has changed the entire direction of entrepreneurship and business structure. In today's world, technology has become a significant part of our everyday lives, which is impacting various sectors and education. However, this advantage has caused an emerging, challenging, set of constraints and obstacles that future entrepreneurs must navigate. The significance of this proposal is to outlay the content and scope of the chapter, which will help to explore all the significant limitations and challenges faced by social media entrepreneurship, which are AI-driven. This chapter will also portray the impact of these challenges and constraints on the business strategies and success of AI-powered social media entrepreneurship. It primarily targets educators, policymakers concerned with ethical and legal issues related to AI in social media, students of e-business, and anyone interested in technology and entrepreneurship. Alongside this, all the ethical concerns related to Al in social media and the recommendations to mitigate these limitations are discussed.

INTRODUCTION

In today's world, AI generated chats and personalized advertising in social media. The entrepreneurs are getting more empowered in the business landscape however, as more fierce competition arises in this area The businesses, who are relying on these technological features are facing several obstacles and constraints every day. For this reason, this research aims to provide proper insights into the challenges and upcoming opportunities that are inherent in leveraging these new AI technologies for the business growth in the revolutionary realm of social media.

Artificial intelligence (AI) has brought about a revolutionary change in social media entrepreneurship. There is an increasing need to comprehend the limitations and challenges that come with this junction

DOI: 10.4018/979-8-3693-1781-5.ch013

as business owners use AI technology to optimize strategy and engage audiences. In order to provide insights into the changing scene, this review of the literature attempts to summarize the body of research on the difficulties faced by social media entrepreneurs that use AI.

Besides, a comprehensive review of several that hide lighted in the current state of the AI among the social media entrepreneurs are discussed in this research. It also includes several insides above successful implementation, rising trains and notable studies. It will set the foundation for identifying the gaps and obstacles in the existing knowledge base.

The use of AI into social media entrepreneurship has entirely transformed the business landscape by offering immense opportunities, as well as many complex cities. This study introduces the research focus by emphasizing the necessity to analyze and understand different sorts of constraints and obstacles, faced by the interpreters every day in this evolving aspect of the business.

LITERATURE REVIEW

The industrial revolution is entering a new phase, which we are living in now. Although the third revolution concentrated on the use of computers in manufacturing, the new paradigm known as Industry 4.0 is the result of technical advancements and future models that provide automated and fully digitalized production processes as well as intelligent systems (Muhuri et al., 2019). Industry 4.0 is the transition from a manufacturing paradigm in which machines just operationalize processes to digital manufacturing, in which machines are able to communicate, self-monitor, and work together on their own (Oztemel and Gursev, 2018). Artificial intelligence (AI) is a major component of this new revolution. It is simply intelligence displayed by machines. Or, to put it in academic terms, the study of how complex problems are solved and tasks carried out by digital computers and algorithms that ordinarily require or surpass the capacity for human intelligence, reasoning, and prediction needed to adjust to changing conditions. Since computer scientist John McCarthy initially defined AI more than 60 years ago, when he defined it as "the science and engineering of making intelligent machines" (Andersen, 2002; McCarthy, 1958), the term has changed. But in order to fully implement this revolution, a company's organizational structure must also alter (Manesh et al., 2021). For instance, a resurgence of human labor is occurring in some of the most automated industries as a result of the integration of AI processes. Artificial intelligence (AI) often frees up time, creativity, and human capital, allowing individuals to operate in a less automated and more human way. People can achieve more and behave with superhuman ability thanks to AI, which gives them strong tools. AI has the ability to re-humanize labor in this way, allowing us to spend more time being human instead of operating like robots (Daugherty and Wilson, 2018).

Attention has been drawn to the moral implications of AI-powered social media businesses. Scholars (Diakopoulos, 2016; Chouldechova, 2017) talk about the possible biases that algorithms may have and emphasize the value of ongoing audits and mitigation initiatives. Algorithmic decision-making must be committed to justice, accountability, and openness in order to address ethical problems.

On the other hand, Facebook experienced significant algorithmic changes aimed at prioritizing user-generated content over brand or publisher content in users' news feeds. This impacted the reach and visibility of content for businesses and entrepreneurs relying on the platform for audience engagement. For this issue, Facebook toughened its data access guidelines and improved user privacy settings in response to privacy concerns. The granularity of individualized suggestions was limited when entrepreneurs had to restructure their AI systems to rely on aggregated and anonymized data.

To put it succinctly, the primary problem for the future is to balance the benefits of AI technologies—such as increased productivity and new opportunities—with the risks—such as job losses and widening wealth disparities (Makridakis, 2017). AI may have both advantageous and harmful effects on society as a whole. In this case, entrepreneurs and the manner in which they might leverage these technologies will be crucial. Academic arguments around AI continue to be populated by a "green field" of divergent discoveries, scenarios, and possible methods (Levesque and Stephan, 2020). In order to provide possible avenues for future study, we thus want to conduct a thorough literature analysis on the subject of the interaction between AI and entrepreneurship.

Positive Aspects of the Social Media Entrepreneurship Powered by AI

As the world of digital marketing is rapidly evolving, artificial intelligence will play a significant role in the transformation era. For instance, AI automated social media posts are getting very popular among current social media entrepreneurs as most of them are trying to stand out among the fierce competition. Besides, it is quite easy and less time-consuming to attract the desired audiences and enhance their engagement. These AI-generated posts can be modified to target specific segments of customers by developing personalized content for them to resonate. So it is observed that AI is making a revolutionary change where digital marketers are being able to create content and interact with customers for which it has become an essential tool for digital marketers.

Recently it has been seen that AI tools are assisting to manage the lifecycle of content in social media better by creating the desired post which can be most likely to be trade and light. It is seen that these types of posts are becoming more relevant and AI is easily able to identify the latest trends to create and deliver to the right audience. AI Technology has been enabling businesses to properly oversee and analyze social media conversation at a high skill which is known as social listening. By using the NPL or natural language processing AI algorithms are able to easily identify the users' sentiments, trends and opinions in order to analyze them to come with personalized content.

Besides, AI-generated social media has proved that it can ensure optimal content delivery by providing custom content to a specific audience. As a result, more people are getting resonate with the content which have increased engagement. It also identifies the most convenient possible time to publish a post and delivery to the right moment when it will be most likely to be attracted by the audience. This tool has also created innovations like Jackpot style posts that can resemble a human conversation which are designed to be more controversial and for all structure than the traditional (Treiblmaier, 2018).

Besides, it is also observed that the most renowned OT platform Netflix employees, the aspects of artificial intelligence, are ways to enhance their user experiences by providing personalized content recommendation. This platform try to use the advanced aspects of learning algorithms to analyze and understand the preferences, behavior, and history of the user so they can recommend their personalized contents. For instance, the company tried to use collaborative algorithms of filtering to look in the contest, based on the users' interest with their similar viewing histories. If they observe two of the people have similar type of taste, and one of them has watched a significant show, that algorithm tries to suggest that show for the user as well.

For enterprises who depend on AI-driven initiatives, the ever-changing algorithmic landscape of social media platforms presents a formidable obstacle. In light of these developments, scholars (Li et al., 2019; Kim & Park, 2020) emphasize the significance of flexibility. Studies indicate that to sustain efficacy in content distribution and user engagement, algorithmic flexibility, quick modifications, and ongoing monitoring are essential.

Moreover, it is seen that there is a certain growth of the use of AI power chat boats to handle the customer enquiries and interaction on Defense social media platforms has become significantly high. Because rather than human beings chatbots are becoming more quick and efficient to handle the routine enquiry which has freed up the human representative customer service to focus on more complicated issues. It also has helped the business to create more inclusive social media campaigns through analyzing the data by using demographic and preference.

Another unique aspect is that today AI can create new content just by detecting the keywords and phrases. If a person can include the keywords in the post the algorithms the AI will be able to detect and deliver the contents according to the customer's preference. This is one way the post is customized to be published at the right time. So it doesn't have to be published too late or too early, it is published at the right time to increase engagement to a maximum level. With the rapid growth of digital marketing, it is seen there is a requirement for robust fraudulent detection and brand safety measures. Here AI algorithms play a very significant role in identifying mitigated fraudulent activities on the platforms of social media. Through analyzing several patterns, behaviors and matrix of engagement the AI algorithms are effectively able to detect fake accounts, fraud activity and suspicious rates of click-through. It also helps the entrepreneurs to ensure that there ad campaigns are real and reaching to real users and not falling victim to any sort of fraudulent practice

AI and Aspects of Entrepreneurship

The foundation of any Industry 4.0 technology paradigm is AI. According to Lasi et al. (2014), it is utilized in smart factories, which are completely automated manufacturing systems that mostly function without the need for human involvement because of the generation, transmission, and analysis of the flowing data needed to carry out necessary production activities. With regard to scheduling interventions for the automated machinery, designing operational workflows, managing the quality of outputs, and automatically programming and carrying out maintenance tasks, artificial intelligence (AI) upholds intelligent control over the entire system (Meziane et al., 2014; Murray, 1999). Similar to this, artificial intelligence (AI) is essential to the Internet of things (IoT), which is a vast, interconnected system of physical objects that are able to communicate with one another, interact, and be controlled or seen from a distance (Ashton, 2009). AI connects the software languages that IoT devices impose by processing and transforming massive amounts of data to provide valuable results (Ahmad et al., 2021). And last, blockchain—a decentralized ledger that securely and openly maintains records of digital assets—is combined with AI (Treiblmaier, 2018). Because AI is data-driven, meaning it needs data to learn and make judgments, this combination enables AI to operate on digitally signed, reliable, and safely shared data in a decentralized ledger, producing more reliable and trustworthy results (Kuhnle et al., 2018). Even though AI presents a huge opportunity for social media marketing among the entrepreneurs it also raises questions for maintaining the ethical considerations and overcoming the challenges. As nowadays AI concerns data security and algorithm bias are some issues that entrepreneurs working with social media platforms need to address while implementing the AI-driven strategies. Today it has become very crucial to ensure the transparency and accountability for using AI algorithms to avoid any short of inconvenient consequences or illegal practices. They also maintain a right balance between Privacy and personal space of the customers in maintaining their trust and loyalty.

Rise of AI-Powered Startups

Agile startups may compete by structuring and building their organizations around artificial intelligence (AI) in response to the transformation difficulties faced by major corporations. Thus, by creating an AI factory instead of undergoing a difficult transition, AI-powered firms may more effectively employ AI at scale. Companies will be specifically developed around digitalization and AI technology once a well-organized structure for managing AI capabilities is established. In this instance, AI becomes the primary engine driving the company's expansion rather than a supplementary enabler. AI-powered firms need to invest a lot of money in developing their AI factories, building their AI skills, and managing the risks associated with AI. In the firms they invest in, venture capitalists (VCs) perform several functions, such as development, information intermediation, monitoring, and strategy analysis (Hsu et al. 2014). They keep an eye on their investments through site visits, board memberships, and, in dire situations, the replacement of CEOs and other executive team members (Gorman and Sahlman 1989). Especially between the companies they invest in, venture capitalists (VCs) can act as an information intermediary and may be able to assist in the selection of R&D partners. (Reuer and Devarakonda 2017). According to Gorman and Sahlman (1989), they also help businesses by helping to attract managers, raise more capital, and provide strategy analysis and development consultancy. Venture capital (VC) investment provides crucial financial resources needed for constructing the AI factory and overseeing AI procedures in the context of AI-powered companies. Furthermore, one of the most significant challenges confronting AI-powered firms that are growing internationally is political risk. Thus, VCs' proficiency in handling political risk is particularly crucial. Venture capitalists (VCs) may be of great assistance to AI-powered firms as they establish strong governance structures to address various legal and ethical concerns associated with AI and large data. As a matchmaker for strategic agreements, VCs can, under certain conditions, assist in lowering political risk. Venture capital (VC) investment provides crucial financial resources needed for constructing the AI factory and overseeing AI procedures in the context of AI-powered companies. Furthermore, one of the most significant challenges confronting AI-powered firms that are growing internationally is political risk. Thus, VCs' proficiency in handling political risk becomes especially crucial. Venture capitalists (VCs) may be of great assistance to AI-powered firms as they establish strong governance structures to address various legal and ethical concerns linked to AI and large data. As a matchmaker for strategic agreements, VCs can, under certain conditions, assist in lowering political risk.

RESEARCH METHODOLOGY

By using the secondary research method this study analyzes the ever-changing aspects of using AI tools in the social platforms by the entrepreneurs. The proper discussion of the methodology, data collection techniques and justification for this research in this section.

The study begins with an extensive analysis with the literature with the aim of getting a deeper understanding of the current condition of AI technologies that are used in the social media platforms by entrepreneurs along with the present state of social media entrepreneurship. A summary of literature of the topic which portrays the data which form the foundation of the study. Besides in-depth analysis of 3 case studies, and 12 papers that addressed the topics were discussed in this project. This comprehensive evaluation of the papers help the resource and their remainder of the studies, limitation along with the areas that require more research.

Alongside the research design included analysis of different reports of young entrepreneurs who actively use the social media platforms through AI technology. This qualitative method also helped to reach the research by providing some practical accounts of the entrepreneurs involved in using AI technology in social media. This stage tends to offer. The research is a strong foundation for the next data and analysis through the combination of the results of several investigations.

Research Design

For conducting the study it is crucial for proper selection data collection methods regarding the study during the research process as it states, the way the data will be gathered for the study. Even though there are several additional choices that are required to be made, which are linked with each other. For this reason, we have chosen qualitative research design for the study in order to get proper results through several reports and research papers.

RESEARCH OBJECTIVES

The objective for the qualitative research is to acquire a detailed understanding of all the obstacles and constraints that the social media entrepreneurs that use AI technology. So based on the research, we try to find different perceptions regarding the entrepreneurs who use AI technology in social media platforms for business.

DATA ANALYSIS

For this research quality methodologies will be employed to analyze the data that are obtained from the annual reports and other research papers. In order to find a recurring theme and patterns among these secondary thematic, analyze where used. By using them, it was possible to identify some very significant themes and insights from the reports that many entrepreneurs can relate to. Besides, it also aids the creation of a clear image of the difficulties, challenges, solutions, and prospective areas of expansion for the entrepreneurs who were involved in using technology in the social media platforms.

FINDINGS

The study will help to know about the way social media is gradually impairing the entrepreneurs through the features of AI technology in their business. Most of the findings were gathered from several annual reports, case study and research papers by in-depth analysis. Some of them are discussed below.

AI POWERED STARTUPS

Case Overview of OpenAI Inc.

The non-profit OpenAI Inc. and the for-profit OpenAI LP together form OpenAI, a research laboratory. The goal of its founding was to advance digital intelligence for the good of humankind. GPT-3 (Generative Pre-trained Transformer 3) is the most recent and well-known artificial intelligence model that OpenAI has created. With its ability to comprehend and produce text that resembles that of a person, GPT-3 is a language model that may be used for a wide range of natural language processing applications. The technology developed by OpenAI finds use in chatbots, content production, natural language comprehension, text generation, and other areas. The business works with a range of sectors or other business entities to enhance current procedures and incorporate AI technologies where it is feasible.

Certain organizations such as OpenAI actively supports the larger AI community, its influence goes much beyond its own initiatives. Through the development of an API (Application Programming Interface), OpenAI has made it possible for companies to incorporate its language models into their apps, creating new avenues for the interpretation and production of natural language. Customer service, content production, programming, healthcare, and education are just a few of the businesses that stand to gain significantly from this. Businesses may use AI technology to create cutting-edge products, automate and improve communication processes, and simplify challenging activities. OpenAI's language models, for instance, may be used to build chatbots and virtual assistants for customer service in any other social media platforms of certain business such as; Daraz, Amazon, etc. that can comprehend and answer user questions with very high accuracy. This enriches the user experience overall and boosts the effectiveness of customer support. Certain AI models facilitate content creation by helping authors and artists produce creative pieces, articles, and even little bits of code. This opens up new avenues for creative expression and speeds up the process of creating material. Moreover, AI has also brought immense efficiency in the health care sector, models may help with patient report generation, research assistance, and medical literature analysis in the healthcare industry. Decision-making and medical progress can benefit greatly from the capacity to glean insights from massive volumes of textual data. Gradually AI technology may be used into e-learning platforms to offer tailored and interactive educational experiences. In addition to producing instructional materials and offering comments on written projects, the models can assist students in comprehending difficult ideas.

To summarize, companies in several industries keep investigating the possibilities of artificial intelligence. Certain AI building organizations are committed to making sure AI is created and used properly, as seen by its commitment to ethical concerns, openness, and cooperation. The impact that AI has on other companies goes beyond technology; it also touches on the moral parameters that govern the use of AI, highlighting the significance of coordinating AI developments with society norms. All things considered, OpenAI Inc. is a leader in responsible AI innovation, bringing about constructive change and cultivating a future in which artificial intelligence is beneficial to all people.

Case Overview of Cyber Inc. Using AI for Video Courses

A renowned IT tech service, known as Cyber Inc is using AI for content creation with the help of a developed AI module which they named Syntheisa AI. This AI video creation platform tends to generate videos for several online courses. This company tried to quickly scale up their content creation and expand their reach globally through creating videos in multiple languages. This platform aims to assist businesses by optimizing the social media strategies through utilizing the advanced algorithms of artificial intelligence.

Cyber Inc analyzes the engagement, data and traits of the user by evaluating the contents, videos, format and timings of social media videos, in order to maximize the reach and impact of the businesses. It also is using machine learning algorithms to segment the audience based on their likings, demographics, and preferences. This has helped the company to tailor their message to the targeted audience more effectively. Also, by using the AI technology, the company is continuously being able to analyze the performance of several advertising campaigns by adjusting the parameters targets, and add creatives in real time in order to improve the rates of conversion and minimize costing.

However, the company is going through significant challenges to add up quickly with the algorithmic change on the social media platforms every day. For this reason, the company's IT team is gone continuously, investing their time to monitor and update the features of the technology in order to share the Platform compatibility with the evolving algorithms of their other competitors. Also, they have to prioritize the measures of data privacy of their customers for their. They are trying to automate and aggregate the personal data in order to ensure compliance and follow the protection regulations.

Case Overview: Using of AI for Personalized Recommendation by Hoichoi

Hoichoi is known for its renowned platform of online streaming with excellent marketing in the South Asian region. One thing that makes the company stand out is its use of AI for personalization. Here AI algorithms are used to gather the preferences and likings of the subscribers through these trade data to recommend the movies or series that they would like to watch and even promote them in their social media accounts.

This platform uses the algorithm of collaborative filtering for recommending the movies and series, based on the preferences of the users by using similar viewing histories. Even if two users have a similar kind of taste in a particular show, the algorithm might suggest that show to the user. Also, Hoichoi uses the models of the learning to enhance the accuracy of the recommendation in both the platform and social media channels. This AI developed models of the learning are able to detect the complex patterns and relationships among the large data which helps them to improve the suggestions of contents precisely.

Even though it can be seen that there might be some concerns of ethical AI biases which might result in impacting negatively among the users. For instance, many hidden and personal data of the customers may provoke a crucial concern. For this the platform strives to regularly refine and audit the algorithms to reduce the bias and promote transparency in using the AI features.

DISCUSSION

- **Constant Algorithm Changes:** Platforms routinely adjust their algorithms, affecting content exposure and reach as it can be highlighted from the case study of OpenAI Inc.
- **Algorithmic Bias:** AI-driven algorithms may accidentally favor certain material over others, resulting in biased exposure.

Table 1. Literature review on the constraints and obstacles of social media entrepreneurship powered by AI

Authors	Title	Keywords	Context
Beghetto, R. A. (2023)	A new horizon for possibility thinking: A conceptual case study of Human × AI collaboration	• Possibility Thinking • OpenAI	Tis study analyzes the proper collaboration of PT. The recent advances in AI can be utilized effectively by using several examples.
Kaur (2023)	10 Real-Life AI Marketing Examples and Use Cases	• Data Privacy • AI Algorithms	Cber Inc IT service uses AI technology for content creation, where they try to generate videos for online stations in multiple languages by using AI algorithms.
Sanzida Akter, (2023)	Bengali Movie Recommendation System using K Nearest Neighbor and Cosine Similarity	• Automated Recommendations. • Personalized Contents	I the first-paced world, online streaming platforms have become a main source of entertainment. It is seen in the South Asian region Hoichoi has become the most viewed platform among the participants where it became quite popular for the automated recommendations in the apps and social media platforms.
Pranab K. Muhuri Amit K. Shukla Ajith Abraham (2019)	Industry 4.0: A bibliometric analysis and detailed overview	• Bibliometric analysis • Machine learning	Tis study discussed the different performance metrics driven by AI which are used to analyze the different aspects of social media channels for business purposes. It also talks about the industrial revolution and how most of the promotional aspects of business are dependent on online social media platforms.
Manesh et al. (2021)	Organizing a sustainable smart urban ecosystem: Perspectives and insights from a bibliometric analysis and literature review	• Urban sustainability • Smart urban ecosystem	Te study analyzed the approaches that should be embraced running a smart urban ecosystem where most of the aspects of business are operated by ai technology.
Daugherty and Wilson (2018).	Collaborative intelligence: Humans and AI are joining forces	• Collaboration • AI intelligence	Te article talks about the core factors of artificial intelligence where it plays an important role to boost up our analytic and decision making capabilities. The collaborative support of AI in the operational factors of business has made the goals to be achieved more effectively and efficiently
Makridakis(2017)	The forthcoming Artificial Intelligence (AI) revolution: Its impact on society and firms	• Digital revolution • Global competition	Tis study tried to observe and identified AI has significant influence on leading to highly integrated organizations where they work with decision making by using big data and algorithms.
Treiblmaier (2018)	The impact of the blockchain on the supply chain: A theory-based research framework and a call for action	• Gamification • Theory building	Hre the study discusses the several theories that can be used through the AI tools to analyze the blockchain of businesses.

Table 1. Continued

Authors	Title	Keywords	Context
Ashton (2009)	That 'internet of things' thing	• Empowering computers	Te article discusses that how the AI technologies are collecting the information to the people from the internet and coming out with solutions by processing which business are now being able to use in their various segments of operation
Kuhnle et al. (2018)	Multiplex influence maximization in online social networks with heterogeneous diffusion models	• Multiplexing • Computational modeling	Tis paper studies the impact of maximization problem oh\f multiplex on propagation of using AI algorithms. Here it tries to portray how heterogeneous models are used to function the social platforms.
Reuer and Devarakonda (2017)	Partner selection in R&D collaborations: Effects of affiliations with venture capitalists	• R&D partner selection • Venture capitalists • Entrepreneurial ventures	Hre the paper demonstrates how different operations of an organization are. AI has also have the capability enable partnerships between entrepreneurial Ventures The knowledge of each other technological resources
Levesque and Stephan .(2020)	It's time we talk about time in entrepreneurship. Entrepreneurship Theory and Practice	• Time perspective • Time allocation • Entrepreneurship	Te research focuses on two aspects of entrepreneurship which are time management and perspective.
Vanya Shrivastava (2023)	Skilled Resilience: Revitalizing Asian American and Pacific Islander Entrepreneurship Through AI-Driven Social Media Marketing Techniques	• Cultural sensibility tools • Small Business • AI Driven Marketing Strategies	Tis study discusses about the there beneficial marketing strategies which are AI driven where the entrepreneurs will be able to continuously evaluate monitor and behavior of the purchase pattern of the targeted audiences
Hossain, S.F.A., Nurunnabi, M., Hussain, K. and Shan, X.	Smartphone-based m-shopping behavior and innovative entrepreneurial tendency among women in emerging Asia	• Women entrepreneurship • Asia • Emerging Nations	Tis article discusses about the impacts of using smartphone for expanding entrepreneurial opportunity.
Guglielmo Giuggioli and Massimiliano Matteo Pellegrini (2022)	Artificial intelligence as an enabler for entrepreneurs: a systematic literature review and an agenda for future research	• Deep learning • Technology • Innovation	Te Purpose of this article to understand how artificial intelligence benefits the entrepreneurs. The study proves there are major consequences for entrepreneurship in general and benefit entrepreneurs in their operations and performances.

- **Understanding Complex Algorithms:** Entrepreneurs must constantly research and change methods to match with algorithmic preferences or like many businesses the entity is opted towards collapse or burned out.
- **Risks to Data Security:** Handling massive volumes of user data need comprehensive security measures to avoid breaches and retain confidence.
- **Compliance with developing data protection rules** (e.g., GDPR, CCPA) necessitates continual attention and resources.
- **Ethical Data Usage:** It is critical to ensure the ethical treatment of user data while employing AI for targeting and customisation.

- **Overwhelming content volume** limits exposure and engagement for new businesses as many new entities do not have necessary resources or expertise to maintain these contents consistently.
- **Quality vs. Quantity:** Finding a happy medium between providing high-quality content and meeting the demand for regular updates is difficult.
- **AI-Generated material:** Using AI to create material raises concerns about originality, authenticity, and audience reaction.
- **Changes in Platform Algorithms**: Algorithm changes can have a major influence on engagement numbers, making consistency challenging.
- **Building true Relationships:** It might be difficult to maintain true ties with an audience in the middle of automation resulting in business to fail in meeting necessary consumer wants and demands.
- **Balancing Automation and Human Interaction:** Finding the perfect balance in engagement between AI-powered automation and personal touch is often difficult, likely resulting in the business to incur high levels of expenditures.
- **Rapid Technological Evolution:** Keeping up with AI developments and incorporating them into plans necessitates ongoing learning is difficult as well as resource captivating.
- **Allocation of Resources:** Investing in the newest AI tools and technology can be pricey, providing a barrier for smaller companies.
- **Upgrading abilities:** To remain competitive in a changing world, entrepreneurs must continually improve their AI-related abilities which will lead them to gain competitive edge in the long run.
- **Complexity of ROI Measurement:** Because of various variables, determining the real returns on AI-powered social media activities can be difficult.
- **Monetization Strategies:** It might be difficult to identify and implement successful monetization strategies based on AI-generated insights and researches show that the perfect tool in regards to AI is still not effective.
- **Value Demonstration:** Communicating the value proposition of artificial intelligence-powered social media campaigns to potential investors or clients might be difficult, if the target audience is technologically challenged.
- **Concerns about intellectual property:** Issues about ownership and usage rights of AI-generated material require clarification and a legal framework.
- **Ethical AI Usage:** It is vital for brand reputation to ensure ethical AI practices in content generation, targeting, and engagement methods.
- **Regulatory Compliance:** Navigating diverse legal frameworks and remaining in compliance with AI-specific legislation is an ongoing problem.
- **Intense Competition:** As AI-powered techniques proliferate, competition intensifies, necessitating novel approaches to stand out.
- **Brand Differentiation:** Creating a distinct brand identity in the middle of AI-driven content saturation is a huge challenge.
- **Adapting to Changes in Competitor Strategies:** Constantly developing competitor strategies need nimble adaptation for sustainable growth.
- **Overdependence on the policies of the platforms:** Entrepreneurs of social media, who rely on AI technological aspects, are subject to all the changes and policies of the platform. They are currently operating on. Over almost every day there are certain changes in the algorithm content,

guide, lines and policies that can impact on the effectiveness of the entrepreneurs, who strategies are driven by the AI aspects.

- **Convincing people to embrace AI-powered interactions** and content may necessitate efforts to develop trust and openness.
- Some people may be **resistant to automated interactions,** preferring human-driven contact.
- **Educating Users:** Informing the audience about the advantages and drawbacks of AI-powered social media businesses.
- **Gaining user trust:** by going through several cases, it was identified that manufactures influences the user trust in the AI powered social media entrepreneurship where they had to the communication transparency, and the perception of the user for data usage, and taking proper for permission to utilize their personal data for giving them better service and products

To address these issues, a comprehensive solution combining technological competence, strategic planning, ethical concerns, and continual adaptation is required. To compete in this dynamic field, entrepreneurs exploring the convergence of AI and social media must be nimble, ethical, and imaginative.

RECOMMENDATIONS

This comprehensive study tried to contribute by providing important insights about the growing field of AI power, social media, and entrepreneurship by offering some practical recommendation of case studies of different startup businesses to learn about the way they are navigating the challenges. Despite all these obstacles, social media entrepreneurship is mobilized by AI presence and new media opportunities for the new businesses to efficiently grow and come up with more innovative tactics. And the startups who are able to effectively overcome the obstacles sustainably stand to benefit from the positive aspects offered by the AI technology in the landscape of social media. In order to address all the obstacles and challenges of social media internship that uses AI, a business needs to use several approaches that are multifaceted like business strategies, ethical concepts and technology. Some of the effective ways that can help to overcome the current identified challenges of AI in social media platform are mentioned below:

- **Keeping continuous monitoring and adjustment:** the entrepreneurs who uses AI aspects in the social media, should try to regularly monitor the changes in the algorithm factors on the social media platforms. Besides, they should try to develop a dynamic system which can easily add up to the upcoming modifications by ensuring all the other AI algorithms remain effective.
- **Practice of transparent data:** in order to insure the concern of data previously the businesses that use AI technology should keep clear communication on how the user data are collected, stored and utilized. Through implementing the transparent practice of data collection and usage will build and sustain the user trust.
- **Considerations of ethical aspects:** To maintain all the rules and regulations the innovations should properly observe and refine their AI algorithms to minimize any sort of bias. Through proper in like drivers training, data said, and assessment fairly can ensure ethical AI practices.
- **Effective investments:** entrepreneurs should try to invest in solutions of scalable AI technologies that have that ability to grow with the business. For instance, they can explore the cloud base ser-

vice of AI in order to reduce the initial cost of infrastructure by considering collaborative ventures in order to share development expenses.

- **Enhancing expertises:** through establishing different programs of training in order to expand the expertise of technical support of the team. Also, by encouraging continuous learning in order to adapt with the advancement of AI technologies that are used in slow media platforms can be quite useful for keeping the entrepreneurs business sustainable.
- **Advancing technologies rapidly:** through investment of agile methodologies of development, in order to get along with the technological changes quickly can be a significant advantage for the AI powered pay underproduce in social media. And they can foster a culture of innovation where they encourage experimentation with the technologies that are emerging from AI.
- **Unique Value Proposition:** Offer a distinct value proposition to set your company apart from competitors. Stay ahead of the competition by concentrating on specialized markets or certain consumer groups and by consistently innovating.
- **Active Adherence:** Keep up with the latest developments in AI-related legislation. Make a proactive effort to ensure that all current and future rules are followed, and work with regulatory organizations to support ethical AI research.
- **Diversification Strategies:** Investigate a variety of channels in order to diversify your reliance on social media platforms. Be ready to modify tactics in accordance with each platform's regulations and keep your approach flexible.
- **Updating Analytics:** Investing in sophisticated analytics can help you better understand consumer preferences and behavior. Refine recommendation algorithms continuously to deliver more precise and customized content recommendations.

CONCLUSION

In summary, the complex world of social media entrepreneurship, driven by artificial intelligence's revolutionary potential, offers a vibrant yet difficult environment for would-be business owners. This study has examined the many limitations and challenges that are peculiar to this developing field. The combination of social media and AI business is a complex ecosystem that needs careful analysis and strategic navigation due to algorithmic biases, privacy issues, technology constraints, and the always changing socio-cultural dynamics. Upon considering the results of this investigation, it is apparent that achieving success in this field necessitates not only technical proficiency but also a profound comprehension of ethical considerations, flexibility in response to swift technological progress, and a sophisticated analysis of the socio-economic ramifications of AI-supported endeavors.

As business owners continue to reshape and transform the digital environment, they must continue to be aware of the issues raised in this study and use them as a starting point to plot a path towards an AI-powered future for social media entrepreneurship that is more ethically sound, inclusive, and sustainable. To conclude the research overall try to discuss the simplifications for the entrepreneurs, researchers and policy makers about the way they can overcome all that identify challenges and obstacles that they have to face using AI technologies in the social media platforms. Also, the research tries to identify some suggestions that can be used for future research for further advance understanding in this domain.

REFERENCES

Aboulilah, H. M. A. E., Hossain, S. F. A., Vuong, B. N., & Jebril, T. (2022). Exploring the Relationship between WeChat Usage and E-purchase Intention During the COVID-19 Pandemic Among University Students in China. *SAGE Open*, *12*(4). doi:10.1177/21582440221139447 PMID:36466966

Ashton, K. (2009). That 'internet of things' thing. *RFID Journal, 22*(7), 97-114.

Beghetto, R. A. (2023). A new horizon for possibility thinking: A conceptual case study of Human × AI collaboration. *Possibility Studies & Society*, *1*(3), 324–341. doi:10.1177/27538699231160136

Chouldechova, A. (2017). Fair prediction with disparate impact: A study of bias in recidivism prediction instruments. *Big Data*, *5*(2), 153–163. doi:10.1089/big.2016.0047 PMID:28632438

Diakopoulos, N. (2016). Accountability in algorithmic decision making. *Communications of the ACM*, *59*(2), 56–62. doi:10.1145/2844110

Emmanuel, C. P., Qin, S., Hossain, S. F. A., & Hussain, K. (2022). Factors influencing social-media-based entrepreneurship prospect among female students in China. *Heliyon*, *8*(12), e12041. doi:10.1016/j.heliyon.2022.e12041 PMID:36483305

Hossain, S. F. A., Nurunnabi, M., Hussain, K., & Saha, S. K. (2019). Effects of variety-seeking intention by mobile phone usage on university students' academic performance. *Cogent Education*, *6*(1), 1574692. doi:10.1080/2331186X.2019.1574692

Hossain, S. F. A., Nurunnabi, M., Hussain, K., & Shan, X. (2020). Smartphone-based m-shopping behavior and innovative entrepreneurial tendency among women in emerging Asia. *International Journal of Gender and Entrepreneurship*, *12*(2), 173–189. doi:10.1108/IJGE-03-2019-0054

Hossain, S. F. A., Shan, X., Musa, M., & Rahman, P. (2023). Social media and increased venture creation tendency with innovative ideas: the case of female students in Asia. In *Research Anthology on Applying Social Networking Strategies to Classrooms and Libraries* (pp. 1716–1731). IGI Global.

Hossain, S. F. A., Shan, X., Nurunnabi, M., Tushar, H., Mohsin, A. K. M., & Ahsan, F. T. (2021). Opportunities and challenges of m-learning during the COVID-19 pandemic: A mixed methodology approach. *E-Collaboration Technologies and Strategies for Competitive Advantage Amid Challenging Times*, 210-227.

Hossain, S. F. A., Xi, Z., Nurunnabi, M., & Hussain, K. (2020). Ubiquitous role of social networking in driving M-Commerce: Evaluating the use of mobile phones for online shopping and payment in the context of trust. *SAGE Open*, *10*(3). doi:10.1177/2158244020939536

Kaur, F. P. (2023). *10 creative AI marketing examples and use cases.* Mailmodo. Available at: https://www.mailmodo.com/guides/ai-in-marketing-examples/

Kuhnle, A., Alim, M. A., Li, X., Zhang, H., & Thai, M. T. (2018). Multiplex influence maximization in online social networks with heterogeneous diffusion models. *IEEE Transactions on Computational Social Systems*, *5*(2), 418–429. doi:10.1109/TCSS.2018.2813262

Lévesque, M., & Stephan, U. (2020). It's time we talk about time in entrepreneurship. *Entrepreneurship Theory and Practice*, *44*(2), 163–184. doi:10.1177/1042258719839711

Makridakis, S. (2017). The forthcoming Artificial Intelligence (AI) revolution: Its impact on society and firms. *Futures*, *90*, 90. doi:10.1016/j.futures.2017.03.006

Mohsin, A. K. M., Hongzhen, L., & Hossain, S. F. A. (2021). Impact of COVID-19 pandemic on consumer economy: Countermeasures analysis. *SAGE Open*, *11*(2). doi:10.1177/21582440211008875

Muhuri, P. K., Shukla, A. K., & Abraham, A. (2019). Industry 4.0: A Bibliometric analysis and detailed overview. *Engineering Applications of Artificial Intelligence*, *78*, 218–235. doi:10.1016/j.engappai.2018.11.007

Oztemel, E., & Gursev, S. (2020). Literature review of Industry 4.0 and related technologies. *Journal of Intelligent Manufacturing*, *31*(1), 127–182. doi:10.1007/s10845-018-1433-8

Palumbo, R., Manesh, M. F., Pellegrini, M. M., Caputo, A., & Flamini, G. (2021). Organizing a sustainable smart urban ecosystem: Perspectives and insights from a bibliometric analysis and literature review. *Journal of Cleaner Production*, *297*, 126622. doi:10.1016/j.jclepro.2021.126622

Reuer, J. J., & Devarakonda, R. (2017). Partner selection in R&D collaborations: Effects of affiliations with venture capitalists. *Organization Science*, *28*(3), 574–595. doi:10.1287/orsc.2017.1124

Sanzida Akter Department of computer science and Engineering. (2023) .*Bengali movie recommendation system using k nearest neighbor and cosine similarity: Proceedings of the 2023 9th International Conference on Computer Technology Applications, ACM Other conferences*. Available at: https://dl.acm.org/doi/abs/10.1145/3605423.3605432

ShrivastavaV.ResilienceS. (2023). Revitalizing Asian American and Pacific Islander Entrepreneurship Through AI-Driven Social Media Marketing Techniques. https://ssrn.com/abstract=4507541 doi:10.2139/ssrn.4507541

Treiblmaier, H. (2018). The impact of the blockchain on the supply chain: A theory-based research framework and a call for action. *Supply Chain Management*, *23*(6), 545–549. doi:10.1108/SCM-01-2018-0029

Vuong, B. N., Tushar, H., & Hossain, S. F. A. (2023). The effect of social support on job performance through organizational commitment and innovative work behavior: Does innovative climate matter? *Asia-Pacific Journal of Business Administration*, *15*(5), 832–854. doi:10.1108/APJBA-06-2021-0256

Wilson, H. J., & Daugherty, P. R. (2018). Collaborative intelligence: Humans and AI are joining forces. *Harvard Business Review*, *96*(4), 114–123.

Chapter 14
The Future of Social Media Entrepreneurship in Business for Women Entrepreneurs

Shafiqua Nawar
BRAC University, Bangladesh

Marzia Zaman
BRAC University, Bangladesh

Tasnim Binte Zahir
BRAC University, Bangladesh

Md. Shadman Rahman Khan
McMaster University, Canada

Md. Sajid Shariar
Coventry University, London, UK

EXECUTIVE SUMMARY

This research explores how social media transforms women's entrepreneurship, examining its impact on networking, information gathering, and crowdfunding. Assessing advantages, disadvantages, and global potential, it addresses challenges and growth strategies. Acknowledging rapid social media growth, especially on platforms like Facebook and Instagram, the study delves into technology's role, emphasizing underdeveloped countries. It investigates challenges for rural women, proposing strategies for business expansion. The study emphasizes the future of social media entrepreneurship for women, highlighting creativity, productivity, and overcoming societal barriers. Practical applications include guidance for female entrepreneurs, aiding organizations in promoting women in business. The mixed-methods approach, despite limitations, contributes valuable insights to the evolving field.

DOI: 10.4018/979-8-3693-1781-5.ch014

INTRODUCTION

In the last ten years, social media's (SM) explosive expansion has changed the face of entrepreneurship (Troise, Dana, Tani, & Lee, 2022). Social media platforms, including Instagram, LinkedIn, and Facebook, have revolutionized the way entrepreneurs operate by encouraging creativity, transparency, and idea management (Troise et al., 2022). They promote the development of relationships, strengthen communication, and boost productivity in the workplace. Through its ability to link entrepreneurs with wider networks, social media (SM) fosters emotional attachments, increases creativity, and enhances business chances (Troise et al., 2022). Creating valuable development towards economy and job creation, the number of business women are increasing vastly in this current era. (Alhakimi & Albashiri, 2023) due to many facilities of social media and the future of social media entrepreneurship for women is promising, driven by evolving platforms that offer accessibility, flexibility, cost-effective marketing, and global reach(Rahman, Hasan, Chandra Deb, Rahman, & Kabir, 2023).Women entrepreneurs on platforms like Facebook are breaking stereotypes and empowering others.(Rahman et al., 2023). Furthermore, through the creation of jobs, women entrepreneurs contribute significantly to economic growth (Hossain, Nurunnabi, Hussain, & Saha, 2019). Studies have indicated that those who use digital technology and participate in a variety of online activities have both advantages and disadvantages (Olsson & Bernhard, 2021a). It is well known that social media platforms have a worldwide potential for empowering women entrepreneurs. Findings show that starting a social media-based business involves very little infrastructure, very little funding, and just rudimentary technological knowledge (Rahman et al., 2023). Furthermore, because to recent technology advancements, individuals have access to the internet (Emmanuel, Qin, Hossain, & Hussain, 2022) and other communication tools even in remote regions (Rahman et al., 2023) and additionally, social media has a big impact on entrepreneurship as it gives female entrepreneurs a rare chance to increase their information exposure (Troise et al., 2022). This makes it easier for people to perform social media entrepreneurship in both rural and metropolitan locations (Mohsin, Hongzhen, & Hossain, 2021). Therefore, women may finally realize their long-held dream of transitioning from traditional economic activities—especially home-based farming—to a fully functional corporate structure through this type of business opportunity(Rahman et al., 2023). Again, women's business owners and organizations may encourage transparency with the use of social media. These platforms have the potential to improve organizational idea capture (Hossain, Nurunnabi, Hussain, & Shan, 2020) and management procedures as well as speed up and improve the efficacy of innovation processes (Troise et al., 2022) .To sell, attract, engage, and communicate with clients, women in this business just manage a Facebook page. They only require a smartphone or laptop with an internet connection in this respect(Rahman et al., 2023). Specifically, some academics claim that these platforms generate a number of advantages related to learning and knowledge management that might enhance organizational performance. Early challenges and shortcomings faced by female entrepreneurs can be surmounted because to social media's openness and connectedness (Troise et al., 2022). This research paper will explore how social media is transforming the landscape for female entrepreneurs. Additionally, it will examine the advantages of social media on networking and information collecting(Olanrewaju, Hossain, Whiteside, & Mercieca, 2020) as well as how social media helps in boosting innovation and company performance through cutting cost and maximizing efficacy in various operations. It seeks to assess social media's capacity to empower women and to understand the challenges and opportunities that face female digital entrepreneurs. It also looks at how social media is revolutionizing the business landscape for women-owned small businesses (Alhakimi & Albashiri, 2023) and how to overcome societal, cultural, financial, and educational barriers.

LITERATURE REVIEW

The Empowering Role of Social Media in Women's Entrepreneurship

The amount of people utilizing messaging applications and social media platforms worldwide is rapidly increasing. Facebook and WhatsApp, the two most popular online communication networks, claimed 1.65 billion active users combined in 2016 and more than one billion users overall, according to Statista. (Jose, 2018). Social media enhances an organization's entrepreneurial mindset, fostering innovation, proactiveness, and risk-taking (Parveen, Jaafar, & Ainin, 2016) and for achieving entrepreneurial success, social network is considered to be important tool (Wafeq et al., 2019) and specially, women have a platform to share their knowledge with a large audience through social media platforms (Naudin & Patel, 2019). Women's entrepreneurship has the potential to be a catalyst for social and economic growth for women as well as the economies of many developing countries, given this level of empowerment (Simba, Martins Ogundana, Braune, & Dana, 2023). Social media-based entrepreneurship requires minimal capital and technical know-how, making it accessible to a lot of women with limited income and education (Vuong, Tushar, & Hossain, 2023) and with increased internet access in both rural and urban areas, women can transition from traditional economic activities to social media entrepreneurship, creating new business opportunities (Rahman et al., 2023). The study claims that social networking sites (SNS) are essential to the operations of female entrepreneurs because they allow them to take full use of their networks for prospecting, engaging, and building relationships with stakeholders(Lichy, Farquhar, & Kachour, 2021) and the results demonstrate that women entrepreneurs must continuously acquire new skills and assist the growth of their companies if they are to fully capitalise on the opportunities presented by digitalization and keep a competitive advantage. This is especially true in terms of social media usage and proficiency(Olsson & Bernhard, 2021a). Additionally, it has been demonstrated that the affordances of SM allow women entrepreneurs to build up social capital, which is generated in a new way through SM. This social capital helps with resource mobilization, resource identification and allocation, knowledge gathering, entrepreneurship success, and opportunity recognition and monetization(Olanrewaju et al., 2020). Using social media for entrepreneurial marketing is becoming more and more important as a way to achieve psychological empowerment through female business (Chakraborty & Biswal, 2023a) and the activity of female entrepreneurs on social media has increased noticeably. Extensive data analysis confirms the significant influence that social media use has on female entrepreneurs' aspirations to pursue digital entrepreneurship, which in turn affects their confidence (Chakraborty & Biswal, 2023a).). Research has shown that social media may be an effective tool for increasing market shares and customer connections, e-commerce growth in developing nations, and the sustainability and credibility of SMEs by providing effective avenues for communication (Secundo, Del Vecchio, & Mele, 2021). The choice to launch social commerce was mostly driven by pull factors. Facebook's beneficial qualities have enabled women to build consumer networks, employ free natural marketing tools, and develop a positive mindset towards entrepreneurship(Brahem & Boussema, 2023). Adoption of social media is a potential way for these female entrepreneurs to get over obstacles and take use of all the advantages these online platforms have to offer(Alhakimi & Albashiri, 2023). Firstly, social media platforms make it possible to implement marketing techniques at a minimal cost.(Alhakimi & Albashiri, 2023). The growing popularity of social media channels among female entrepreneurs with small and medium-sized enterprises (SMEs) can be attributed to factors like affordability, speed, user-friendliness, and the customised communication experience. The internet penetration rate has been impacted by elements like network coverage, high-speed internet accessibility, and reasonably priced network plans (Jose, 2018).Secondly, the use of social media presents a distinctive prospect for female entrepreneurs to establish and cultivate significant networks with clients and industry luminaries, therefore fostering an encouraging environment for information exchange, cooperation, and coaching and finally, social media gives women company owners the ability to build their own brands, express themselves, show off their knowledge, participate in focused networking, and accelerate the expansion of their companies (Alhakimi & Albashiri, 2023). As a result, the study comes to the conclusion that social media utilization benefits businesses greatly. Lower costs, better customer service, and simpler information availability are the outcomes (Parveen et al., 2016) Alongside, social media encourages communication in both directions, lowers the expense of advertising, and improves customer service by giving users instant access to information (Parveen et al., 2016).Brand perceptions may be influenced by entrepreneurs by persistent activity, focused conversations, and successful involvement on social media sites like Facebook. However, active customers also support business owners by recommending products and/or sharing their positive product experiences, which helps to influence other customers' decisions to buy. Research indicates that over one-third of internet users provide product and service reviews, share their thoughts on a regular basis, contribute to the development of online content, and take part in activities that have influence (Turan & Kara, 2018a). It also fortifies an organization's spirit of entrepreneurship, encouraging creativity and initiative. This suggests that utilizing social media promotes a more adaptive and flexible organizational style (Parveen et al., 2016). Using social media on the internet has a lot of potential advantages for entrepreneurs looking to build networks and partnerships such as a strong social media presence also helps to create synergy through integrated marketing communication and improves the efficacy of traditional marketing initiatives (Turan & Kara, 2018a). Women are more likely to use social media (SM) for business purposes when influenced by external factors like friends and family. SM can provide equitable and widespread chances for women to work from home with limited time and resources. Due to these reasons, it is seen that a large number of educated and talented women are now improving their families' and countries' economies.(Fatima & Ali, 2023). According to research, family income may be impacted by social media entrepreneurship, which supports sustainable development. Entrepreneurship is crucial for fostering economic growth and development on a local and national level. This is especially true for women. This is particularly important in economies where women are starting their own businesses at a very young age (Rahman et al., 2023). Keeping track of social media trends and market demand; managing client relationships and communication; ease of running a home-based business; product marketing and advertising, and company visibility; business extension and no-travel cost are the reasons of using social media (Fatima & Ali, 2023). Again, women may generate revenue through social media entrepreneurship, even those in rural locations, since they can utilize these platforms to purchase and sell goods. This reduces the disparity in income that exists between women in rural and urban locations (Rahman et al., 2023). As a means of achieving psychological empowerment through female entrepreneurship, social media usage is becoming increasingly crucial for entrepreneurial marketing, and the amount of time that female entrepreneurs spend on social media has grown dramatically (Chakraborty & Biswal, 2023b).According to data study, social media use has a major impact on female entrepreneurs' intentions to pursue digital entrepreneurship, which in turn influences their psychological independence(Chakraborty & Biswal, 2023b) .Thus, social media entrepreneurship has become a powerful force for change, especially for female entrepreneurs, and it has significant effects on sustainable development.

Challenges and Barriers for Women Entrepreneurs

The development of social media applications in particular has undoubtedly fundamentally altered how individuals interact and share content across a wide range of previously unreachable and scattered social communities and networks. New approaches of gathering, watching, analysing, and visualizing social media discussions and interactions have also created new problems and directions for study (Ketonen-Oksi, Jussila, & Kärkkäinen, 2016). Empirical evidence indicates that female entrepreneurs around the area have comparable pressing concerns that require attention (Ameen & Willis, 2016). In industrialized nations, female entrepreneurs require moral support; in poor nations, however, they require financial help in order to enhance their company success. Moore (1997) posits that women become entrepreneurs due to three factors: the corporate glass ceiling, a desire for challenge and self-determination, and a desire to combine work and family duties (Jose, 2018). The findings indicate that female entrepreneurs prioritise the counsel and support of their social network more highly, which positively affects their desire to take advantage of chances (Emami, Ashourizadeh, & Packard, 2023) and through entrepreneurship, they are able to maintain the social fibre of the family and have an additional source of income and simpler interactions(Lichy et al., 2021). Some of the difficulties associated with digitization that the female entrepreneurs bring up include a lack of resources, the ongoing requirement to acquire new abilities, digital stress or even burnout because of the expectations from both internal and external sources to be active online, and the upkeep and monitoring of social media platforms (Olsson & Bernhard, 2021a). Mobile phone use, which is available to women in these nations, has the ability to get over some of these obstacles and encourage female entrepreneurship.(Ameen & Willis, 2016). This has created a plethora of options for companies wishing to use social media data for innovation or new service pursuits (Aboulilah, Hossain, Vuong, & Jebril, 2022). For example, organisations may now use advanced social media analytics tools and analytical approaches to access real-time data and extract meaningful patterns and information about, say, customer behaviour (Ketonen-Oksi et al., 2016). There are a lot of significant gender gaps in women's entrepreneurship(Ameen & Willis, 2016). These differences include those in educational possibilities, where men are given greater attention and training when it comes to launching enterprises. Because there aren't many official financial institutions that serve them, women have less access to financial help and business education (Ameen & Willis, 2016). Significant barriers are presented by women's obligations to their families and the unsupportive character of some family structures. The lack of encouragement and support from male family members exacerbates these issues. Women company owners throughout the world frequently struggle to strike a balance between their personal and professional lives (Lichy et al., 2021). Furthermore, the uptake of ICTs is still slow, particularly in small and medium establishments. By giving women easier access to information, less training requirements, a lower initial investment, and the flexibility of working from home, social media entrepreneurship offers a method to overcome these numerous obstacles. The COVID-19 epidemic has expedited women who have lost their careers' adoption of social media business. Social media platforms facilitate their ability to establish connections with prospective clients, participate in reciprocal dialogues, and efficiently market their products and services (Rahman et al., 2023). Social networks were crucial in helping female entrepreneurs obtain resources and have the confidence to break through hurdles to their company initiatives based on their gender (Muzaffar, 2023). Social media entrepreneurship is essential to reaching sustainable development objectives because it promotes gender equality, lowers poverty and inequality, creates jobs, and helps marginalized groups—women and minorities, in particular—by producing jobs(Rahman et al., 2023) because women's labour force participation is directly correlated with GDP growth, women's entrepreneurship is a major factor in Bangladesh's economic and social development(Olsson & Bernhard, 2021a). Due in large part to their involvement in social media entrepreneurship, the number of women entrepreneurs in the nation has increased significantly.

Design Methodology

Using a mixed-methods approach, this study examines the ever-changing field of social media entrepreneurship, concentrating on female entrepreneurs. We provide the methodology, data collection techniques, and justification for this approach in this section.

This study starts with an extensive analysis of the existing literature with the goal to obtain a thorough understanding of the present state of social media entrepreneurship, especially for women entrepreneurs. A summary of the literature on the subject, which drew data and perspectives from credible sources, forms the basis for this study. We performed an in-depth examination of 22 scholarly papers that addressed the topics addressed in this project. This comprehensive evaluation serves as both a resource and a reminder of the study's limitations and areas requiring more research. (Lee & Hallak, 2020a)

Furthermore, the research design includes in-depth interviews with eight female entrepreneurs who actively use social media platforms for commercial purposes. This qualitative method enriches the research by providing firsthand accounts of female entrepreneurs involved in social media entrepreneurship. These interviews were carefully planned to capture a wide range of experiences and viewpoints on social media business. This stage seeks to offer a strong foundation for the next data gathering and analysis by combining the results of several investigations.

Research Design

The selection regarding research approach is crucial in the research design process as it dictates how pertinent data will be gathered for the study. (Olsson & Bernhard, 2021b)However, there are many additional choices that need to be made which are connected to each other. (Jilcha Sileyew, 2020) We have chosen qualitative research design for our study to get proper results through our structured interviews.

Research Objective

The primary objective of this qualitative research is to gain a detailed understanding of obstacles, strategies, and opportunities in social media platforms. Usually, we find some different perceptions regarding social media that relates to their business.

Primary Data Collection

The primary data collection method is served by arranging structured interviews. Eight female entrepreneurs who regularly use social media platforms for commercial purposes were interviewed in-depth to gather primary data in addition to the literature study. The qualitative research approach was selected

Table 1.

SL	Time of Interview	Years of Operation	Profile of Business	Ownership Status
R1	5 September 2023	2 years	Makeup Studio or salon	Sole owner
R2	18 September,2023	3 years	Retail jewelry and fashion	Sole owner
R3	25 September, 2023	4 years	Craft studio	Sole owner
R4	10 October, 2023	7 years	Fashion boutique	Sole owner
R5	19 October, 2023	4 years	Online clothing retail	Sole owner
R6	23 October, 2023	3 years	Shopping and retail	Sole Owner
R7	26 October,2023	2 years	Pre-Order business	Sole owner
R8	29 October, 2023	2 years	Hair oil business	Sole owner

to yield rich and illuminating data, presenting first-hand narratives and individual experiences of these business owners (Jilcha Sileyew, 2020).

The necessity to delve deeply into the nuances of social media entrepreneurship drove the selection of in-depth interviews. Open-ended questions during interviews let participants talk about their entrepreneurial experiences, difficulties, and solutions in their own words. These stories offer an insightful viewpoint that enhances the quantitative information found in the literature (Turan & Kara, 2018b).

Participant Selection

The participants were carefully chosen with the goal of guaranteeing variety and representation from various business scales and industries. The eight female business owners who were selected for this research provide a range of perspectives on the social media entrepreneurship landscape. Their combined backgrounds include influencer marketing, e-commerce, and service-oriented companies. The backgrounds and experiences of the participants vary which adds to a deeper and more comprehensive grasp of the topic (Olsson & Bernhard, 2021b).

Interview Protocol

We created a structured interview questionnaire with planned questions. Make sure the questions are clear, brief, and relevant to the research objectives. To ensure consistency throughout interviews, the interview method will be standardized.

Data Analysis

Qualitative research methodologies will be employed to analyze the data obtained from interviews. To find recurring themes and patterns in the participants' responses, thematic analysis will be used. Using this method, it is possible to identify important themes and insights from the stories that the female entrepreneurs relate. It also aids in the creation of a thorough image of the difficulties, solutions, and prospective areas of expansion for women involved in social media entrepreneurship.

Trustworthiness

To maintain the study's legitimacy, strict data management and documentation procedures would be followed. To improve the dependability and confirmability of the results, peer debriefing and member verification may be used.

Ethical Considerations

Throughout the research procedure, ethical concerns were addressed. Everyone who participated gave their informed consent, confirming that they understood the objective of the study and how their information would be managed. Furthermore, measures were implemented to guarantee the participants' identity and confidentiality, given that certain information disclosed during the interviews can be delicate.

In summary, it is anticipated that this mixed-methods approach will offer a comprehensive and nuanced understanding of the topic, identifying opportunities, problems, and possible future approaches. The findings and discussions based on the mixed-methods research technique described in this part will be presented in the upcoming sections of this study.

Findings

The current study helps us to know about how social media is empowering women in their business. Their experiences are being shared in quotes below as per some questions which we have taken in our in-depth interview.

1. How did you start your business and what motivated you to become an entrepreneur?

By collecting overall respondents, we got some common entrepreneurial behavior i.e., "Financial Independency" (R1) (R4) (R6) (R5), "educational background or curiosity" (R7) (R2) and "self- satisfaction or hobby" (R8) (R3). These all things were possible to implement because of social media factors. This behavior was observed in depth interview, the quotes are written below:

I started my business in June last year and my motivation to become an entrepreneur was written by a combination of my educational background, which is marketing. (R7)

It was Covid 19. From my very childhood, I wanted to do something. I heard that online Chinese products were very famous at that time....... Now, I am doing great, my monthly revenues are way too much to cover my expenses. (R2)

Since, some of the respondents clearly depicts that they have started their business for financial independency and got motivated by their family, the quotes are shown below:

My children motivated me to be independent...and to look after them. (R4)

I want to help my family with my own earnings so that we can live a better life ahead. (R1)

2. Can you tell me how you use social media for your business?

Which Platforms Do You Use, and Why?

Several respondents said that they have used social media like Facebook and Instagram for better reach. They believed that most of the audience were from these two platforms. And these platforms help them with their better subscription plans which are emphasized below with quotes:

Since, I am makeup artist…I must make reels every day. These reels are the most showing item of these platforms from which I got my targeted audience. (R1)

I have used Instagram to reach people by creating awareness of using home DIY for hair fall.... After that, I got huge responses of order (R8)

I use Facebook and Instagram...due to its extensive reach and popularity in our target market.... You know that Facebook allows us to create a big response and showcase our products and interact with our potential customers directly and it offers Instagram for sharing. (R7)

Again, with one respondent, we got different views. That is, Pinterest and TikTok's are being used to attract customers. The quotes are given below:

She mostly utilizes Instagram and Facebook, with occasionally use of TikTok. She utilizes Pinterest to generate ideas. She has joined a few Facebook groups where she advertises her items. (R3)

3. Have you found social media helpful for connecting with customers and growing your business? Can you share examples?

Many respondents agreed that social media helped them to increase their customers and was responsible for their exposure. They believed that online marketing is way too friendly and cheap than physical marketing due to the influencers in social media. Some quotes are depicted below showing how social media helped all of them to secure a good position in the online marketplace.

My company only conducts business online. Whenever any influencers would post the review of my business regarding the oil, followers of influencers would reach out to me to get the product. (R8)

I used to check everyday the recent trends of accessories so that I could bring customer demands products (R7)

People used to recommend my page in various groups through which I got great exposure in social media. (R5)

Moreover, many respondents believe that their communication with customers became easy as a result they had a very good bonding relationship. There are reviews options on social media helped them to maintain these bonds, some quotes are given below:

Yes. People appreciate my work and I made sure to keep good conversation with the customers. Recently, one of my customers before taking an appointment she appreciated my work and said will soon book for her wedding. This type of thing encourages me a lot. (R1)

Yes, it's been useful; we engage with customers through posts and messages. We have loyal customers who always post reviews of our products in our groups and pages. (R2)

4. How has social media influenced your ability to gather information or ideas for your business?

Maximum respondents have talked about that they have used the ideas of "sending PRs to the influencers" (R2) (R8). Also, many of them got "inspiration from different pages" (R6) (R3) which are depicted through quotes below:

Different pages worked as an inspiration for me to designing the clothes......Collaborating with influencers increased my sales too. (R6)

I didn't pay anyone to provide positive product reviews...... I have also told them to provide feedback if this worked. Gradually, I noticed over time that when people learned about my company, a small number of influential people even approached me to send oil as PR. They regularly use this oil for themselves as well, not just for promotion. (R8)

On the other hand, some of them talked about the trend analysis of online market and different marketing tools they have been acquainted with are depicted in the quotes below:

Social media has been a valuable tool for gathering information. I use it to stay updated on the market targeting, target market trends, gather feedback from customers and monitor our competitors. This helps me to make informed decisions and product selection and marketing strategies. Productivity increased through using chatbots to answer questions of customers and provide a seamless shopping experience which improved customer satisfaction. (R7)

I performed some trend analysis of the Facebook posts and then changed the business patterns. (R2)

I usually conduct extensive research on textiles for apparel from various regions of India.... My primary method of information collecting, in addition to using articles from other websites and Pinterest. (R5)

There was one incident when people were into polaroid cameras and after knowing that from various Facebook groups, I introduced polaroid camera in her business page. (R8)

5. Have you faced any challenges while using social media for your business? How did you overcome them?

Almost all the respondents have mentioned that they have faced challenges while using social media. But they have also overcome these challenges with different tactics which are given in quotes below:

Most of the cases some unwanted and creepy texts or comments can be seen in my posts or videos. I usually blocked those accounts and daily I checked my followers list which accounts are new to Facebook. (R1)

I have faced harassment on Facebook Lives. (R5)

Moreover, some of the respondents faced some competitions and fraudulent activities in their page which are given in the quotes below:

When we initially started with Shein products, I faced intense competition from numerous similar businesses in Bangladesh. To address this, I have shifted our focus to niche Japanese skincare products, which had less competition. This strategic pivot allowed me to stand out and generate better profits. (R7)

The biggest challenge is for me differentiating real clients from fake ones. Customers sometimes place orders for things, but they never receive them when they are delivered. Occasionally, when I upload photos, someone else uses those images on their page. To overcome those, I have received advance payment via Bkash so that I can understand the actual customer. (R3)

6. How has the COVID-19 pandemic impacted your business and your use of social media?

In our in-depth interview, most respondents didn't start their business before the pandemic. But some of them had faced some problem which depicted below in quotes:

In Covid-19, as I was a makeup artist, people were scared to come to my studio, and I was unable to move into their place. Thus, my business didn't go well then. (R1)

Delivery companies were off for some days. I faced difficulties in collecting raw materials for my clothes. (R5)

I had to stop my business for five or six months since raw materials were not available at that time. (R3)

7. What strategies or support have you found effective in using social media for business growth.

Many respondents shared with us that they have followed some strategies in using social media which led their growth of business very fast depicts in quotes below:

I believe that engaging with the community helps my business to grow properly. Also, giving training on digital literacy would help people to rise more in this business. (R7)

Page boosting regularly helps my business to grow in a faster way. (R5)

I personally prefer Search Engine Optimization (SE0) for special searching keywords for my page helps me to be well known among the audience. (R4)

I maintain social media algorithms to post my products pictures to get targeted audience. (R3)

8. In your opinion, how does social media empower women in business and provide financial independence?

Different respondents have told us their own perception that how they think about financial independency quoted below:

I believe that social media opens several opportunities for women like anyone can work from home. It increases financial independence. (R1)

Due to social media, we can connect with people globally and get positive responses. For this encouragement of our works, we could work more and can know the importance of financial independency. (R2)

Numerous tools are helpful for boosting my page and as a result I feel that these tools encourage women to start their business. (R5)

Literature Review on Social Media Entrepreneurship for Women

see Table 2.

ANALYSIS

As part of the study, in-depth interviews with female entrepreneurs were conducted to find out more about their motivations and histories, as well as how they use social media to interact with clients, get information, get over challenges, and create growth plans. We will look at the key concepts and implications of this analysis's findings.

1. **Reasons for Pursuing Entrepreneurship:** The report indicates that the primary motivators for female entrepreneurs to choose self-employment are their hobbies, educational background, and need for personal fulfilment. A common topic among the respondents was financial freedom, indicating that more and more women are resorting to business to achieve economic emancipation.

The study's findings highlight how important it is to recognize and assist women to pursue careers in entrepreneurship.

2. **Social Media Usage:** The study's entrepreneurs mainly advertise their companies on Facebook and Instagram, among other social media sites. These platforms have a wide audience, easy-to-use subscription options, and a welcoming atmosphere for product displays and customer interactions.

Table 2.

Author(s)	Context	Methodology	Key Findings
(Secundo et al., 2021)	This study examines how social media affects entrepreneurship, synthesizing previous research, addressing current findings, and recommending future research options.	Studied 159 Scopus articles via systematic review. Analyzed 69 scholarly articles in relevant fields.	- Research underscores social media's vital role in entrepreneurship, particularly in digital business, for identifying opportunities and improving outcomes.
(Troise et al., 2022)	This study aims to explore the relationship between social media usage (SMU) and start-ups' entrepreneurial opportunities and orientation (EO).	Used PLS-SEM for hypothesis testing.	According to the study, SMU has a significant beneficial influence on EOP but no effect on startups' EO. It's interesting to see that SMU has a greater effect on EOP than EO does.
(Olanrewaju et al., 2020)	Social media greatly impacts entrepreneurship by boosting networking, information search, crowdfunding, and innovation, benefiting business performance and future applications and research.	Gathered data from databases using specific keywords in English-language journal papers. Developed an integrated framework by analyzing 160 papers in the field.	This study highlights social media's impact on entrepreneurial behavior, emphasizing innovation over firm performance. It identifies cultural and contextual factors influencing adoption, paving the way for future research.
(Alhakimi & Albashiri, 2023)	This study aims to assess the variables associated with women-owned small enterprises' (ESBs') usage of social media.	Collected data from 101 Yemeni women entrepreneurs using a standardized survey, then analyzed it with descriptive statistics.	The findings confirm that Yemeni women entrepreneurs widely utilize social media, particularly for marketing, promotion, and communication. The adoption is influenced by non-technical factors such as management mindset, in addition to technical barriers like cost.
(Emami et al., 2023)	This study looks at how aspiring entrepreneurs use their social networks during difficult times, taking gender disparities into account. To understand these differences, it employs social support and gender schema theories.	Science and Technology Parks provided two-stage primary survey data to the authors for potential entrepreneurs during the pandemic.	Results show that female entrepreneurs rely more on social network direction and encouragement, positively affecting their intent to seize opportunities. Men also experience this impact, though less strongly. Potential female entrepreneurs are more discouraged by the perceived challenging environment.
(Lichy et al., 2021)	This study explores how women entrepreneurs in Lebanon use social networking sites to promote their businesses, aiming to gain insights into marketing practices in the Middle East and North Africa (MENA).	This study uses a two-phase methodology, involving expert business commentators and digital qualitative data collection,	The study highlights the importance of social networking sites (SNS) for female entrepreneurs. SNS helps them prospect, communicate, and build connections with stakeholders. It also serves as a second source of income, supporting family social cohesion.
(Ketonen-Oksi et al., 2016)	This study aims to present a coherent picture of the state of knowledge on value creation and business strategies based on social media.	A systematic review of scholarly journal articles from 2005 to 2014 followed Fink's (2005) process model. The study was built upon the theoretical framework of service-dominant logic.	This study delves into the social media mechanisms shaping value networks and their impacts on business models.
(Turan & Kara, 2018a)	Entrepreneurs in emerging markets rely on social media for cost-effective communication and accessing vital resources. This study explores their reasons and expected benefits.	This study analyzed entrepreneurs' online social media trends with data from 368 organizations, using questionnaires and interviews, and validated the conceptual model with CFA and SEM.	Data analysis reveals that a significant portion of the variance in entrepreneurs' intent to use online social media is associated with perceptions of effort, performance expectations, and social pressures. All tested hypotheses in the study were confirmed.
(Brahem & Boussema, 2023)	This study explores why Tunisian women use Facebook for their businesses and what drives them, considering personal, technological, and institutional factors.	The methodology used in this study involved conducting semi-structured interviews with 24 women entrepreneurs. They employed a qualitative approach to investigate the precursors of entrepreneurship in the digital age.	The study affirms that social media empowers women in entrepreneurship, particularly through Facebook's free marketing tools and positive outlook. However, transitioning to a formal structure remains a challenge as women aim for business expansion.
(Naudin & Patel, 2019)	This article investigates how female cultural entrepreneurs use Twitter to establish their expertise and professional identity in the face of gender disparities in the cultural sector.	Researchers performed online ethnography by studying six female entrepreneurs' Twitter (X) activities in Cultural and Creative Industries (CCIs) over 3 to 5 years (2010–2015). Selection was based on their active professional engagement and work-related Twitter (X) posts.	Female CCIs (Cultural and Creative Industries) entrepreneurs on Twitter (X) use an approach aligning with feminism, blending personal and professional aspects. They demonstrate expertise through engagement and strategic hashtag use, emphasizing the need for deeper exploration of their online roles and 'entangled' expertise.

Table 2. Continued

Author(s)	Context	Methodology	Key Findings
(Simba et al., 2023)	This research focuses on the underexplored area of communal financing's impact on female entrepreneurs in developing countries. It aims to understand how communal funding processes affect women business owners in these regions.	Field research in Lagos, Nigeria, engaged 75 women entrepreneurs, sampled from associations and snowballing. Using qualitative interactionism, the study delved into capital acquisition in a gender-role-centric society.	Female entrepreneurs encounter gender bias, with 25% facing lengthy loan approval delays. Approximately 25% find the application process burdensome, and nearly 45% avoid formal financing due to concerns like embarrassment and high interest rates. 'Ajo,' a communal financing system, strongly influences their entrepreneurial paths, with 87% relying on it to start their businesses.
(Rahman et al., 2023)	The research explores the impact of rural female engagement in entrepreneurial activities via social media on sustainable development within Bangladesh	The study gathered 376 responses from online apparel store owners using simple random sampling. Data analysis involved PLS-SEM with Smart PLS 3.3v software, applying a quantitative research framework to evaluate the conceptual model.	The study demonstrates that women's involvement in social media entrepreneurship enhances sustainable development in Bangladesh's online clothing businesses, creating rural job opportunities and increasing women's household contributions.
(Saner & Yiu, 2019)	The goal of this essay is to evaluate Jamaica's progress in terms of the financial empowerment of women, female entrepreneurship, and its advancement of strategies in support of the growth of women's entrepreneurship.	This study combines literature review, database analysis, and index cross-referencing to assess female entrepreneurship in Jamaica and its relationship with the country's economic growth and business environment.	Jamaican women, more educated but hindered by traditional roles, face workforce challenges. The study analyzes legislation and budget allocations favoring female entrepreneurship for more inclusive growth and provides government support recommendations.
(Parveen et al., 2016)	This study aims to look into how social media use affects an organization's performance and entrepreneurial orientation. It is based on the framework of value chain theory.	174 organizations in total answered the questionnaire.	According to the study's findings, using social media significantly improves the efficiency of an organization in terms of cost savings, greater customer interactions, and information accessibility.
(Muzaffar, 2023)	This study examines how COVID-19 disrupted gender norms in urban Turkish entrepreneurship, enabling some women to start businesses. It also explores how female entrepreneurs used their social networks to overcome gender-related barriers during the pandemic.	In-depth semistructured interviews were used in this study to investigate the research questions.	The results show that, during the COVID crisis in urban Turkey, female participants saw an opportunity to challenge gender stereotypes in entrepreneurship and start their businesses. Social networks played a crucial role in helping them access resources and overcome gender-based obstacles to business success.
(Chakraborty & Biswal, 2023b)	The main agenda of this research is to find the effects of social media on women entrepreneur goals in their digital entrepreneurship and physical empowerment	This study combines the Stimulus-Organism-Response framework with the Uses and Satisfaction Theory to understand the importance of social media for female entrepreneurship. It assesses internal consistency with Cronbach's alpha, confirms uni-dimensionality with exploratory factor analysis, and tests the theory using structural equation modeling.	Data analysis reveals that social media engagement has a considerable impact on female entrepreneurs' intentions to engage in digital entrepreneurship, which also has an impact on their psychological empowerment.
(Fatima & Ali, 2023)	This research investigation evaluates how women entrepreneurs operating small and micro businesses (MSEs) use social media for client interactions as it compares the favorable effects associated with social media and its impact on business success with traditional media outlets.	Based on interviews with businesswomen	Businesswomen use social media for promotion but often lack proficiency. External factors like family and friends influence their decision. Effective social media usage can boost sales and consumer engagement alongside traditional marketing techniques.
(Wafeq et al., 2019)	Afghanistan's volatile environment presents significant challenges for entrepreneurs, particularly female business owners. This essay explores the connection between marketing and the confidence of Afghan women entrepreneurs in their business success.	For this study, primary data gathering was employed. A telephone study was conducted with 248 female entrepreneurs from five Afghan provinces.	Findings show that marketing activities and a marketing-focused approach have a favorable and significant impact on the optimism of female Afghan entrepreneurs. However, the perceived success of the business endeavor is unaffected by independence and outward orientation.
(Jose, 2018)	The paper aims to investigate how female entrepreneurs strategically utilize chat apps and social media to market their enterprises.	This study employed qualitative research due to limited data on women's entrepreneurship in the Middle East. It consisted of 20 in-depth interviews with immigrant women entrepreneurs in the UAE	Foreign women entrepreneurs in the article use chat apps and social media for business promotion. WhatsApp is for direct marketing, Facebook for branding. Combining digital and traditional methods is common, with digital tools being more effective.

Table 2. Continued

Author(s)	Context	Methodology	Key Findings
(Ameen & Willis, 2016)	The benefits of using mobile phone for Arab women is the main goal of the paper. Examining novel approaches to reduce the gender disparity in entrepreneurship in these nations is the aim of this study.	In-depth analysis of the existing literature and recent reports on women's entrepreneurship and on the adoption and use of mobile phones in Arab countries.	The study suggests that Arab women entrepreneurs find mobile phone use appealing. However, they have untapped potential in harnessing mobile technology beyond basic applications. Mobile phones can address obstacles these entrepreneurs face.
(Blanco-Gonzalez-Tejero & Cano-Marin, 2023)	The main goal is to increase global awareness of women's roles in family enterprises and entrepreneurship. It assesses their influence and empowerment through user-generated content on Twitter.	The research is carried out from a quantitative and qualitative perspective through the evaluation of UGC from the social platform Twitter	The generated material had a positive correlation with women leaders and entrepreneurs. The frequency and topics of tweets, mainly addressing women's workplace challenges, showed an increasing trend.
(Olsson & Bernhard, 2021a)	Using data from studies on women entrepreneurs, digitalization, and digital skills, this study investigates how female small business owners embrace digitalization and develop social media competencies for their profession.	Qualitative approaches were used, such as observations of the digital presence of the 11 women entrepreneurs in nine small enterprises and a total of 13 in-depth interviews conducted in two parts in 2017 and 2019.	Female business owners adapt to the digital age through self-improvement, hiring digitally skilled workers, and emphasizing lifelong learning, particularly in social media. Resources are limited, digital stress is prevalent, and work-life balance is challenging, with minimal online gender stereotyping.

This platform's flexibility and agility demonstrate how social media is a dynamic tool for business marketing.

The report also emphasizes how critical it is to use social media to keep solid client relationships. Easy feedback channels and communication are important for building a devoted clientele, according to respondents. This highlights how social media helps a firm create a community and cultivate client loyalty.

4. **Knowledge and Idea Gathering**: To get ideas and knowledge for their company, female entrepreneurs turn to social media. Social media is a great tool for learning about consumer preferences, competitive landscape, and market dynamics (Turan & Kara, 2018a). This suggests that social media is being actively used by female entrepreneurs as a source of business intelligence.

According to the report, female entrepreneurs are skilled at generating ideas and analyzing trends on social media, which demonstrates their adaptability to changes in the market.

6. **COVID-19 Pandemic Impact:** Certain entrepreneurs encountered challenges as a result of limitations and disturbances in the supply chain, but others adjusted to the evolving situation. The pandemic emphasizes the value of adaptability and perseverance in enterprise, as well as the necessity of utilizing social media and e-commerce to their fullest amid trying circumstances.
7. **Business Growth Strategies:** The study shows the different approaches taken by female entrepreneurs to use social media to grow their businesses. These tactics include SEO, algorithm optimization, page boosting, and community involvement. These strategies highlight the need of strategic planning in utilizing social media for business success and are in line with the best practices of digital marketing(Olsson & Bernhard, 2021a).
8. **Empowerment and Financial Independence**: Study participants discuss how social media contributes to women's increased financial independence and influence in the workplace. It is believed that social media plays a key role in women's capacity to work from home, interact with a global

audience, and become financially independent. Women gain mental satisfaction being financial independency using social media. Since social media has various tools it helps us as a woman to explore more and have sense of accomplishments It helps women overcome traditional barriers and enter a wider market, realizing their aspirations of becoming business owners(Lee & Hallak, 2020b).

CONCLUSION

This study paper's findings demonstrate the significant influence of social media for female entrepreneurship. Social media platforms are now essential for promoting a feeling of community, connecting business owners with clients, and accelerating business growth. A growing number of female business owners are driven to become financially independent and utilize social media as a tool to do it.

The report emphasizes how critical it is to identify and support the factors that inspire women to start their own businesses. It also highlights the importance of flexible tactics, strong approaches to problems, and the possibility of ongoing learning and market adjustment. Against the backdrop of the COVID-19 pandemic, female businesses have proven they can use digital tools to overcome unpredictable situations.

REFERENCES

Aboulilah, H. M. A. E., Hossain, S. F. A., Vuong, B. N., & Jebril, T. (2022). Exploring the Relationship between WeChat Usage and E-purchase Intention During the COVID-19 Pandemic Among University Students in China. *SAGE Open*, *12*(4). doi:10.1177/21582440221139447 PMID:36466966

Alhakimi, W., & Albashiri, S. (2023). *Social media adoption by women entrepreneurial small businesses*. Asia Pacific Journal of Innovation and Entrepreneurship. doi:10.1108/APJIE-03-2023-0060

Ameen, N. A., & Willis, R. (2016). The use of mobile phones to support women's entrepreneurship in the Arab countries. *International Journal of Gender and Entrepreneurship*, *8*(4), 424–445. doi:10.1108/IJGE-10-2015-0037

Blanco-Gonzalez-Tejero, C., & Cano-Marin, E. (2023). Empowerment of women's entrepreneurship in family business through Twitter. *Journal of Family Business Management*, *13*(3), 607–625. doi:10.1108/JFBM-04-2022-0050

Brahem, M., & Boussema, S. (2023). Social media entrepreneurship as an opportunity for women: The case of Facebook-commerce. *International Journal of Entrepreneurship and Innovation*, *24*(3), 191–201. doi:10.1177/14657503211066010

Chakraborty, U., & Biswal, S. K. (2023). Impact of social media participation on female entrepreneurs towards their digital entrepreneurship intention and psychological empowerment. *Journal of Research in Marketing and Entrepreneurship*. doi:10.1108/JRME-03-2021-0028

Emami, A., Ashourizadeh, S., & Packard, M. D. (2023). The impact of social network support on opportunity intention among prospective male and female entrepreneurs during 2019-nCov pandemic. *International Journal of Entrepreneurial Behaviour & Research*, *29*(11), 132–169. doi:10.1108/IJEBR-03-2022-0223

Emmanuel, C. P., Qin, S., Hossain, S. F., & Hussain, K. (2022). Factors influencing social-media-based entrepreneurship prospect among female students in China. *Heliyon*, *8*(12), e12041. Advance online publication. doi:10.1016/j.heliyon.2022.e12041 PMID:36483305

Emmanuel, C. P., Qin, S., Hossain, S. F. A., & Hussain, K. (2022). Factors influencing social-media-based entrepreneurship prospect among female students in China. *Heliyon*, *8*(12), e12041. doi:10.1016/j.heliyon.2022.e12041 PMID:36483305

Fatima, N., & Ali, R. (2023). How businesswomen engage customers on social media? *Spanish Journal of Marketing - ESIC*, *27*(2), 221–240. doi:10.1108/SJME-09-2021-0172

Hossain, S. F. A., Nurunnabi, M., Hussain, K., & Saha, S. K. (2019). Effects of variety-seeking intention by mobile phone usage on university students' academic performance. *Cogent Education*, *6*(1), 1574692. doi:10.1080/2331186X.2019.1574692

Hossain, S. F. A., Nurunnabi, M., Hussain, K., Saha, S. K., & Wang, S. (2019). Effects of variety-seeking intention by mobile phone usage on university students' academic performance. *Cogent Education*, *6*(1), 1574692. Advance online publication. doi:10.1080/2331186X.2019.1574692

Hossain, S. F. A., Nurunnabi, M., Hussain, K., & Shan, X. (2020). Smartphone-based m-shopping behavior and innovative entrepreneurial tendency among women in emerging Asia. *International Journal of Gender and Entrepreneurship*, *12*(2), 173–189. doi:10.1108/IJGE-03-2019-0054

Hossain, S. F. A., Nurunnabi, M., Hussain, K., & Shan, X. (2020). *Smartphone-based M-shopping behavior and innovative entrepreneurial tendency among women in emerging Asia*. Retrieved from https://www.emerald.com/insight/content/doi/10.1108/IJGE-03-2019-0054/full/html

Jilcha Sileyew, K. (2020). Research Design and Methodology. In E. Abu-Taieh, A. El Mouatasim, & I. H. Al Hadid (Eds.), *Cyberspace*. IntechOpen. doi:10.5772/intechopen.85731

Jose, S. (2018). Strategic use of digital promotion strategies among female emigrant entrepreneurs in UAE. *International Journal of Emerging Markets*, *13*(6), 1699–1718. doi:10.1108/IJoEM-10-2016-0268

Ketonen-Oksi, S., Jussila, J. J., & Kärkkäinen, H. (2016). Social media based value creation and business models. *Industrial Management & Data Systems*, *116*(8), 1820–1838. doi:10.1108/IMDS-05-2015-0199

Lee, C., & Hallak, R. (2020). Investigating the effects of offline and online social capital on tourism SME performance: A mixed-methods study of New Zealand entrepreneurs. *Tourism Management*, *80*, 104128. doi:10.1016/j.tourman.2020.104128

Lichy, J., Farquhar, J. D., & Kachour, M. (2021). Entrepreneurship via social networks – "connected woman" in Lebanon. *Qualitative Market Research*, *24*(4), 426–448. doi:10.1108/QMR-01-2020-0004

Mohsin, A., Hongzhen, L., & Hossain, S. F. A. (2021). Impact of COVID-19 Pandemic on Consumer Economy: Countermeasures Analysis. *SAGE Open*, *11*(2). doi:10.1177/21582440211008875

Muzaffar, H. (2023). Pandemic silver lining: How the COVID-19 pandemic helped women to beat the "gender stereotypes pandemic" in entrepreneurship. *Gender in Management*, *38*(1), 76–92. doi:10.1108/GM-10-2021-0316

Naudin, A., & Patel, K. (2019). Entangled expertise: Women's use of social media in entrepreneurial work. *European Journal of Cultural Studies*, *22*(5–6), 511–527. doi:10.1177/1367549417743037

Olanrewaju, A.-S. T., Hossain, M. A., Whiteside, N., & Mercieca, P. (2020). Social media and entrepreneurship research: A literature review. *International Journal of Information Management*, *50*, 90–110. doi:10.1016/j.ijinfomgt.2019.05.011

Olsson, A. K., & Bernhard, I. (2021). Keeping up the pace of digitalization in small businesses–Women entrepreneurs' knowledge and use of social media. *International Journal of Entrepreneurial Behaviour & Research*, *27*(2), 378–396. doi:10.1108/IJEBR-10-2019-0615

Parveen, F., Jaafar, N. I., & Ainin, S. (2016). Social media's impact on organizational performance and entrepreneurial orientation in organizations. *Management Decision*, *54*(9), 2208–2234. doi:10.1108/MD-08-2015-0336

Rahman, M. M., Hasan, M. J., Chandra Deb, B., Rahman, M. S., & Kabir, A. S. (2023). The effect of social media entrepreneurship on sustainable development: Evidence from online clothing shops in Bangladesh. *Heliyon*, *9*(9), e19397. doi:10.1016/j.heliyon.2023.e19397 PMID:37662716

Saner, R., & Yiu, L. (2019). Jamaica's development of women entrepreneurship: Challenges and opportunities. *Public Administration and Policy*, *22*(2), 152–172. doi:10.1108/PAP-09-2019-0023

Secundo, G., Del Vecchio, P., & Mele, G. (2021). Social media for entrepreneurship: Myth or reality? A structured literature review and a future research agenda. *International Journal of Entrepreneurial Behaviour & Research*, *27*(1), 149–177. doi:10.1108/IJEBR-07-2020-0453

Simba, A., Martins Ogundana, O., Braune, E., & Dana, L. (2023). Community financing in entrepreneurship: A focus on women entrepreneurs in the developing world. *Journal of Business Research*, *163*, 113962. doi:10.1016/j.jbusres.2023.113962

Troise, C., Dana, L. P., Tani, M., & Lee, K. Y. (2022). Social media and entrepreneurship: Exploring the impact of social media use of start-ups on their entrepreneurial orientation and opportunities. *Journal of Small Business and Enterprise Development*, *29*(1), 47–73. doi:10.1108/JSBED-01-2021-0041

Turan, M., & Kara, A. (2018). Online social media usage behavior of entrepreneurs in an emerging market: Reasons, expected benefits and intentions. *Journal of Research in Marketing and Entrepreneurship*, *20*(2), 273–291. doi:10.1108/JRME-09-2016-0034

Vuong, B. N., Tushar, H., & Hossain, S. F. A. (2022). *The effect of social support on job performance through organizational commitment and innovative work behavior: Does innovative climate matter?* Retrieved from https://www.emerald.com/insight/content/doi/10.1108/APJBA-06-2021-0256/full/html

Vuong, B. N., Tushar, H., & Hossain, S. F. A. (2023). The effect of social support on job performance through organizational commitment and innovative work behavior: Does innovative climate matter? *Asia-Pacific Journal of Business Administration*, *15*(5), 832–854. doi:10.1108/APJBA-06-2021-0256

Wafeq, M., Al Serhan, O., Catherine Gleason, K., Dasanayaka, S. W. S. B., Houjeir, R., & Al Sakka, M. (2019). Marketing management and optimism of Afghan female entrepreneurs. *Journal of Entrepreneurship in Emerging Economies*, *11*(3), 436–463. doi:10.1108/JEEE-02-2018-0020

Chapter 15
The Role of Social Media Entrepreneurship in Overcoming Possible Obstacles

Rezuana Tabassum
BRAC University, Bangladesh

Sayada Mollika
https://orcid.org/0009-0005-9826-4980
BRAC University, Bangladesh

Md. Ahsanul Islam Saqlain
BRAC University, Bangladesh

Md. Ikramul Haque
BRAC University, Bangladesh

Abdullah Al Fahim
BRAC University, Bangladesh

Amreen Azam
Swinburne University of Technology, Australia

EXECUTIVE SUMMARY

This systematic literature review comprises pertinent and reviewed research chapters. It provides an all-encompassing synopsis of recent advancements in social media entrepreneurship, enabling organizations to gain fresh insights into brand recognition, promotional tactics, customer involvement, conduct, and allegiance, in addition to the utilization of social media to generate prospects. A single chapter comprises multiple sections, each of which was authored by a different researcher and edited by an authority in the field of study. Each individual section is self-contained, yet they are unified by a common research study topic. The objective of this publication is to present a comprehensive summary of the most recent research endeavours undertaken by authors from around the world and to pave the way for additional innovative developments.

DOI: 10.4018/979-8-3693-1781-5.ch015

1. INTRODUCTION

The ubiquitous presence and impact of social media platforms have profoundly altered the landscape of contemporary entrepreneurship. In navigating the intricacies of the digital era, social media entrepreneurship arises as a dynamic catalyst that promotes innovation, interconnectedness, and novel avenues to achieve prosperity. Nevertheless, entrepreneurs encounter formidable obstacles that must be overcome in order to thrive in this rapidly growing ecosystem. Social media, as exemplified by platforms such as Facebook, Instagram, TikTok, and WhatsApp, possesses a pervasive and all-encompassing influence that caters to a diverse and extensive user demographic. Entrepreneurs often utilize social media as a strategic instrument when confronted with a multitude of obstacles in the sales domain. Beyond sales, this application ranges from comprehending customer behaviour and obtaining capital for venture advancement to sustaining continuous customer relationships after a business launch (De Zubielqui & Jones, 2020; Cheng & Shiu, 2019;). In addition, social media platforms facilitate the efficient administration of offline and online connections for business owners, thus enhancing relational dynamics as a whole (Thomas et al., 2020; Smith et al., 2017; Wang et al., 2019). It is exceedingly challenging for entrepreneurs, especially those with limited resources, to survive in today's globalized and extremely competitive business market. Even more challenging is making the case for early-stage new ventures. According to Creswell and Creswell (2017), startups often do not have a large marketing budget.

The purpose of this chapter is to examine the role of social media entrepreneurship in addressing and overcoming obstacles related to Brand Awareness, Marketing Strategies, Consumer Engagement, Behavior and Loyalty, utilizing social media for Success, crafting opportunities, social media criticisms and unfavorable outcomes. We hope to give insights that will empower businesses and researchers alike by evaluating real-world instances, developing trends, and new techniques. Our goal is to offer insights beneficial for entrepreneurs facing obstacles in operating their businesses on social media and to highlight the adaptive tactics that allow entrepreneurs to thrive in the face of adversity.

2. METHODOLOGY OF THE RESEARCH

The methodology used to conduct this chapter is SLR (Systematic Literature Review). Moreover, several procedures suggested by diverse studies have been adapted to organize search procedures (Silaban et al., 2022), quality assessment (QA) (Okoli & Schabram, 2010), and scoring articles (Kitchenham et al., 2009)

2.1. Research Questions

The following research questions were formulated for this research.

RQ1: How do social media entrepreneurs leverage consumer behaviors on platforms like Facebook, Instagram, TikTok, YouTube, Twitter, and WhatsApp to enhance product/service visibility?

RQ2: What strategies do social media entrepreneurs employ to grow and maintain a loyal customer base, particularly through trendy online platforms?

RQ3: How do entrepreneurs utilize algorithms and features on social media platforms (e.g., Facebook, Instagram, TikTok, YouTube, Twitter, WhatsApp) to enhance their business visibility and engagement?

RQ4: What are the strategies employed by social media entrepreneurs to address criticism, especially in relation to accusations of creating false-positive reviews for their products?

2.2. Search Procedure

This research aims to explore the field of social media entrepreneurship and assess its effectiveness in overcoming obstacles and promoting achievement. This research strategically evaluates strategies for improving product awareness, fostering customer loyalty, managing unfavourable branding and criticism, and enhancing public relations. The study makes use of popular search engines like EBSCOhost (Business Source Premier) by Brac University, Google Scholar, ResearchGate, Science Direct, SpringerLink, Wiley Online Library, JSTOR, Scopus, Elsevier, Emerald Insight, and Web of Science, to extract data in the timeframe of November 3rd-25th, 2023. Articles filtered by search terms such as "SME Branding on Social Media", "Social Media Success and User Engagement", "Challenges in Social Media Business", "Digital Marketing: ROI", "Customer Acquisition Best practices", "Entrepreneurial Resilience and Customer Loyalty", "E-commerce Opportunities". Table (Will be added) displays the results of the search method. The objective is to extract beneficial insight that is pertinent to the ever-changing social media entrepreneurship scene.

Figure 1. Search procedure adapted from Silaban (2022)

2.3. Study Selection

For this research, initially, 775 results have been found. However, to assess further and select the most relevant literature, preliminarily the following cited study selection procedure has been applied. Here, the eliminations are based on

- redundant works and publications.
- the title of the research article
- articles written in other languages but English are excluded
- articles published before 2019 are excluded.

2.4 Inclusion Criteria

In this stage, the criteria for research article inclusion are stated implicitly as it is important for further assessments (Silaban et al., 2022). This literature review's inclusion criteria include,

- research articles that have been published in highly regarded academic journals and are indexed by reputable databases such as Scopus and others mentioned previously
- publication date between January 2019 to October 2023
- articles related to SME Branding on Social Media, Social Media Success and User Engagement, Challenges in Social Media Entrepreneurship, Overcoming Obstacles in SME Digital Marketing: ROI, Customer Acquisition Best Practices, Entrepreneurial Resilience and Customer Loyalty, and E-commerce Opportunities.

Thus, the table (1.1) displays the results of the search method.

2.5 Quality Assessment

According to Kitchanham et al. (2009), in any systematic literature review, QA needs to be made mandatory with special consideration (as cited in Yang et al., 2021). For this research, there are some explicit criteria to judge which articles have the quality to be included in the review synthesis (Okoli & Schabram, 2010).

QA1: Does the research article connect social media platforms with business entrepreneurship?

QA2: Does the study offer insights beneficial for entrepreneurs facing obstacles in operating their businesses on social media?

QA3: Does the study include primary data?

Okoli and Schabram (2010) stated that prior to inclusion, articles need to be scored for their quality which will help to eliminate articles that are deficient in quality. The scoring process we have adapted is,

- Y (YES)= 1 (If the article includes what is required as per each mentioned QA)
- P (Partial)=.5 (If the article partially includes what is required as per each mentioned QA)
- N (No)= 0 (If the article does not include what is required as per each mentioned QA) (Kitchenham et al., 2009)

Here, after rating based on QAs, each of the research articles has to get a minimum of total 1.5 to be included in the discussion section. Articles that scored less than 1.5 are excluded. The process is given below in Table 1.2

2.6 Data Collection

see table 1.

Table 1. Systematic literature review

Paper ID	Author & Date	Objective	Methodology	Findings
1	Junaidi (2022)	To investigate the impact of Instagram stories, Instagram posts, and Instagram Reels on the brand awareness of the Muslim clothing brand Zombasic.	Data was gathered from online questionnaires which included a total population of 236,000 followers. A sample of 100 respondents met the requirements of active users of Instagram following the Zombasic Instagram account. Multiple linear regression analysis with Instagram features as independent variables and brand awareness as the dependent variable	Instagram stories and reels have a positive effect on building brand awareness and fostering promising engagement. Zombasic employs a unique approach to portraying products with a premium impression, instigating a need for affordable premium products among customers. The brand focuses on building a community based on the Islamic Syariah lifestyle, establishing trust and respect through Instagram activities. Zombasic's use of Instagram for sales is preferred over traditional marketing due to its effectiveness in promoting brand awareness.
2	Volkova et al. (2020)	To analyze LEGO brand communication for children in social media, specifically focusing on aspects such as consumer behavior, social media platforms, and the impact on loyalty.	The research began by categorizing different age groups of children based on personality standards. The study analyzed consumer intention, interest, and loyalty toward LEGO toys, referencing previous studies. Social media platforms were then selected for analysis. The study examined LEGO's community on its social network, YouTube channels, Facebook, Instagram, Twitter, and Pinterest. The approach was to understand customer behaviour and foster a mutual bond based on different behavioral patterns.	LEGO created a community on its social network for consumers to share and post their designs, building loyalty YouTube channels were used to promote products, with influencers discussing advantages, disadvantages, and new suggestions regularly. Facebook was utilized for daily articles, surveys, and contests to align with customer interests. Instagram featured pictures and videos of new and upcoming products. LEGO planned to extend brand awareness on less popular platforms like Twitter and Pinterest. LEGO positioned content based on customer behavioral patterns, recognizing parents as parallel audiences. Social media engagements helped LEGO entrepreneurs increase sales, brand awareness, and visibility, especially through innovative communication and the use of famous characters.
3	Rathnayake and Lakshika (2023)	To investigate the influence of influencer's credibility on the purchase intention of beauty products in Sri Lanka.	A survey was conducted with 150 Instagram users aged 18-34 in Colombo, Sri Lanka. Single and multiple regression analyses were used to test the conceptual model.	Purchase intention in Sri Lanka is influenced by Instagram influencers, with a positive correlation. - Consumers prefer physically attractive influencers for buying dermatology products. -Social media influencers are preferred opinion leaders for expressing and representing a brand. - Beauty products, foods, and services presented with influencers on social media are likely to secure more sales, brand engagements, and awareness compared to traditional local marketing.

Table 1. Continued

Paper ID	Author & Date	Objective	Methodology	Findings
4	Gesmundo et al. (2022)	To examine the influence of brand awareness and brand recall on millennial purchasing intentions using TikTok as a marketing platform. The study aims to understand the impact of TikTok on brand promotion and its role in shaping consumer behavior among millennials.	Descriptive causal analysis. The research involved polling millennials aged 25 to 40 in the Philippines' National Capital Region (NCR) through Google Forms. Data analysis employed techniques such as frequency and percentage distribution, mean and standard deviation as well as Partial Least Squares Structural Equation Modeling.	TikTok is not only used for recreational purposes but also for promotional activities for brand awareness. - TikTok has a significant influence on marketing products through cross-promotion, contributing to increased sales and brand visibility due to its growing user base. - Brand recall on TikTok among millennials is found to be low, indicating users struggle to remember brands seen on the platform. - There is a direct relationship between brand awareness on TikTok and purchase intentions, emphasizing the importance of regular brand promotion on the platform for maintaining consumer interest and communication at a cost-effective rate.
5	Ghoshal (2019)	To determine the significance and efficacy of social media as a marketing and promotional tool. Assess the influence of social media on purchasing decisions and investigate gender prejudices. Examine the gap between client expectations and social media performance.	Descriptive research method. Used a questionnaire divided into two parts: Part I (demographic information and use patterns) and Part II (influence of social media on purchasing decisions and expectations). Conducted a pilot survey with five respondents from each age group through Google Docs.	The study revealed several noteworthy findings. Firstly, it discovered that the effectiveness of social media platforms (Facebook, Instagram, Twitter) for business acceleration is not contingent on user density but rather on the quality of content, emphasizing the importance of useful and entertaining information. Additionally, the research identified a gap between consumer trust and brand offerings on social media, indicating a need for brands to align their online presence with their promises. The study suggested that brands should actively communicate their presence through engaging content, tweets, and be conscious of their commitments to foster long-lasting customer relationships and brand visibility. Furthermore, it emphasized that physical-only presence might not suffice for brands in the long run, underlining the significance of an online presence for effectiveness, visibility, activities, loyalty, and sales. The study provided practical advice for firms to enhance engagement and promote products on social media, emphasizing the creation of appealing and customer-centric content and behaving online as they would in person.
6	Suariedewi and Wulandari (2023)	Determine the influence of social media quality and brand awareness on purchasing decisions, with brand image as a moderator.	Purposive sampling method, questionnaire instrument for data collection, 100 respondents, surveyed Endek consumers in Denpasar City, Partial Least Squares (PLS) technique used for analysis.	Social media (Facebook, Instagram, and Tiktok), presence impacts consumer impression.- Brand dominance increases with consumer knowledge. - Brand image is crucial for a brand's reputation. - Maintaining a positive brand image positively affects buying decisions. - Companies need a prominent social media presence for trust and awareness.

Table 1. Continued

Paper ID	Author & Date	Objective	Methodology	Findings
7	Harrasi et al. (2022)	The study aims to investigate how social media usage contributes to addressing entrepreneurship challenges faced by young entrepreneurs in the Sultanate of Oman, testing the hypothesis that social media plays a significant role in overcoming these challenges.	Uses a survey translated into Arabic to hear from entrepreneurs registered with the Public Authority for SME Development. A small test conducted with 30 people to make sure the survey is reliable and fixed any issues. The Sample size is 174 entrepreneurs, with participants' to conduct the research	The study reveals that entrepreneurs face challenges such as a lack of entrepreneurial skills, limited industry contacts, and restricted access to technology, with social media proving to be a significant solution. There is a positive correlation between social media engagement and overcoming challenges related to intense competition, market fluctuations, and product-related issues. Entrepreneurs find success in enhancing managerial skills, self-confidence, and work-life balance through increased use of social media platforms. Gender differences indicate that female entrepreneurs, particularly in Oman, benefit more from social media in achieving work-life balance and acquiring managerial skills. WhatsApp (45%), Instagram (26.9%), Snapchat, and Twitter emerge as the most frequently used social media platforms. Additionally, there is a positive relationship between social media engagement and accessing modern technology, better market understanding, and overcoming competition through increased likes or followers on social media platforms
8	Lose and Eze (2023)	To explore virtual small business entrepreneurship opportunities in a selected rural community in the Eastern Cape, with the aim of informing recent graduates about potential business ventures to contribute to addressing unemployment challenges.	Conducted 60 interviews with entrepreneurs in a selected mall in a township in the Eastern Cape using purposive sampling. Analyzed results using Atlas.ti. Sequentially analyzed results from Phase 1 to guide in-depth interviews with the same entrepreneurs, aiming to gather more information and make a comprehensive exploration of identified matters.	The study conducted in a South African township sheds light on challenges faced by small business entrepreneurs, including power cuts, lack of finance for digital systems, and a deficit in digital marketing skills. The identified obstacles present opportunities for entrepreneurial initiatives. Entrepreneurs can address the issue of power cuts by supplying alternative power sources like solar or generators. The lack of digital marketing skills opens doors for infopreneurship or digital marketing services. Another avenue lies in retailing digital infrastructure, including wifi and IT gadgets. Entrepreneurs can fill the knowledge gap by offering ICT education and training. To overcome financial hurdles for digital implementations, microfinancing models tailored for digital ventures can be developed. Business development consulting services become crucial in guiding businesses through digital transformation. In summary, the study underscores how challenges in the small business sector can be transformed into entrepreneurial opportunities, showcasing the adaptability needed in the digital age.
9	Lamba and Jain (2022)	Explore how digital entrepreneurs overcome challenges during the early stages of their startups during the COVID-19 pandemic.	Selected 24 digital businesses (southern and western India; < 2 years old). Conducted semi-structured video interviews, transcribed them, and applied manual thematic analysis. Used a design thinking approach for iterative divergent and convergent thinking.	The study outlines key challenges faced by small and medium-sized digital businesses (SMEs) and proposes solutions.

Table 1. Continued

Paper ID	Author & Date	Objective	Methodology	Findings
10	Adula and Kant (2023)	Investigate the primary challenges faced by active female entrepreneurs, analyze the main obstacles encountered by aspiring female business owners, and explore the perspectives of non-operating female entrepreneurs on the challenges they perceive.	The study employed a qualitative research design, utilizing an interpretative phenomenological approach to understand the lived experiences A deliberate sampling technique was employed to select participants, including active and potential female entrepreneurs, government officials, a women's issues specialist, and a representative from micro and small businesses. Personal interviews conducted in Amharic and Afaan Oromo were the primary method of data collection.	The study focused on challenges faced by female entrepreneurs in Bule Hora town, highlighting obstacles and solutions.-Six female entrepreneurs were interviewed, revealing common difficulties like financial constraints and workplace challenges. Many struggled to secure sufficient funds, often resorting to borrowing from institutions like Oromia Credit Saving Association (OSCO).-Issues with loan terms being changed without consent caused stress and hindered business growth.-Workplace problems were prevalent, particularly impacting female entrepreneurs in the service industry.-Training difficulties were noted, with caregiving responsibilities and societal expectations adding to the complexity.-Money was identified as a crucial factor in business growth, emphasizing challenges in accessing working capital and financial resources.-Social media entrepreneurship was suggested as a potential solution to mitigate obstacles, providing a platform for networking, business promotion, and resource access.
11	Boshmaf (2023)	The purpose of this study is to look into the elements that have influenced women entrepreneurs to use social media to run their firms. Furthermore, it investigates how social media has influenced and affected the enterprises of women entrepreneurs, as well as the social changes in their lives brought about by using social media for commercial objectives	The study employs a qualitative-inductive technique and semi-structured interviews with 30 female entrepreneurs from various industries in Jordan's three major cities.	The study underscores the vital role of Facebook and Instagram in empowering Jordanian women entrepreneurs, particularly those aged 20-29. Social media serves as a cost-effective marketing platform, allowing women to showcase and sell products, fostering financial independence. Flexibility enables them to balance entrepreneurship with domestic responsibilities. Challenges include complex registration processes and high fees, discouraging official registration. Recommendations include streamlining registration, reducing fees, and establishing support centers for training and information on legal and technical aspects. Overall, social media acts as a transformative force, enabling women to overcome obstacles and pursue entrepreneurship independently.
12	Khalid and Allioui, (2023)	To examine the impact of social media on female micro entrepreneurs in developing countries and its potential for alleviating poverty.	Desk research and a comparative approach were combined. Desk research is gathering and analyzing existing secondary data. A comparative approach entails examining current case studies from various emerging countries.	Social media, including platforms like Facebook and Instagram, plays a crucial role in empowering women entrepreneurs by offering a cost-effective and powerful way to market their businesses. It provides a support network, especially important for those facing isolation, and facilitates networking and collaboration. The studies highlight the positive impact of technology adoption, particularly through social media, in mitigating obstacles faced by women entrepreneurs. Interviews underscore the effectiveness of platforms like WhatsApp and Facebook in advertising products and attracting customers. Despite challenges like a lack of access to technology and digital skills, social media emerges as a powerful tool for women-led microenterprises, fostering economic development and contributing to poverty alleviation.

Table 1. Continued

Paper ID	Author & Date	Objective	Methodology	Findings
13	Sawy and Bögenhold (2022)	To address the less-explored dark and negative consequences of entrepreneurial use of social media, advising practitioners on balancing pros and cons in their business and marketing strategies.	Qualitative interviews with a focus on the mixed experiences of micro-entrepreneurs on social media. The theoretical framework of Baccarella et al. (2018) was used and adapted for the classification of reported experiences.	The text explores the dual impact of social media on micro-entrepreneurs, highlighting both its advantages and challenges. For micro-business owners in Austria, especially in rural areas like Carinthia, social media offers opportunities for business growth but demands effective time management due to the multitasking nature of their roles. The study emphasizes the significance of a strong online presence for success. However, it underscores the time-consuming aspect of social media use, affecting micro-entrepreneurs engagement. Reputation concerns on social media are less prominent in regions like Carinthia, attributed to robust offline networks. The text also discusses strategies, such as identity creation and self-regulation, employed by micro-entrepreneurs to mitigate negative experiences on social media. Overall, the role of social media in entrepreneurship is portrayed as intricate, demanding a balance between benefits and challenges, with a focus on effective time management, identity separation, and online interaction.
14	Alzoubi et al. (2022).	The primary goal of the research is to analyze the influence of Beacon technology implementations on Customer Loyalty as measured by Customer Satisfaction at Global Village in Dubai.	In this quantitative study, the impact of Beacon technology applications on Customer Loyalty through Customer Satisfaction at Global Village in Dubai was rigorously examined using ANOVA, regression, and correlation analyses.	The key results of the study are: Customer Loyalty is immediately and positively influenced by proximity marketing, loyalty programs, in-store navigation, and real-time marketing. Customer Satisfaction is highly influenced by beacon technology implementations (r = 0.578, p 0.05), reinforcing customer loyalty. Customer Loyalty is indirectly affected by the adoption intention of BLE Technology due to its beneficial influence on Customer Satisfaction. Businesses in dynamic situations may explore employing Beacon technology to boost consumer engagement, satisfaction, and long-term loyalty.
15	Kamkankaew et al.(2022)	The primary objective of this paper is to provide an enlightening and logical analysis of the various aspects related to customer behavior and digital marketing.	Qualitative review and analysis of studies, articles, and other sources to find information about the topics that have been chosen.	The study results show three factors that affect businesses' digital marketing: how well inbound marketing works, the benefits of e-commerce, and the popularity of well-known social networks. The study also shows different digital advertising strategies that brands use to get their customers' attention. Remarketing, mobile marketing, social media posts, a responsive website, email and content marketing, and location-based marketing are just a few of the things that can be used. It was found that a complete digital marketing plan should be made that targets specific products and audiences, tracks the customer's journey through all digital marketing touchpoints, and builds value with the customer.

Table 1. Continued

Paper ID	Author & Date	Objective	Methodology	Findings
16	Sahai et al.(2019)	The paper seeks to investigate the factors that affect consumers' loyalty to online fashion brands as well as the strategies that work best to win over new customers.	Mix-method research with qualitative interviews and quantitative survey.	As indicated by strong Cronbach's alpha values (range from 0.796 to 0.979), the study findings show outstanding reliability for service quality, service trust, trendy communication tactics, brand image, individualized emotional connection, and website distinction. However, responsiveness had a lower alpha score (0.611), indicating that it is adequate but might be improved. The study emphasizes the relevance of trendy communication methods, brand image, emotional connection, responsiveness, differentiation strategies, website difference, and consumer loyalty in determining consumer perceptions and loyalty.
17	Hawkins and Hoon, (2019).	The study aimed to assess the impact of CRM, brand loyalty, and customer satisfaction on customer retention in a small service-based firm.	The research employed qualitative interviews.	The results of the study reveal that positive communication and emotional investment are significant determinants in fostering enduring consumer relationships within a small service-oriented organization. As a result of meeting customers' expectations, customer satisfaction has emerged as a crucial factor in determining customer loyalty and recurrent business. The significance of establishing trust through profound emotive connections was emphasized as critical for retaining customers. It was determined that quality assurance, accomplished by increasing customer satisfaction and ensuring accountability, is a crucial tactic for promoting favorable customer perceptions and recovering from service failures. In its entirety, the research highlights the interrelated importance of emotional investment, customer satisfaction, trust, and quality assurance in influencing the dynamics of customer retention for small service-oriented organizations.
18	Muangmee, (2021)	The goal of this study was to look into and examine how start-up businesses, especially those in the food and fashion industries, use Facebook advertising. The main goal was to figure out how this kind of tool could improve interactions with new and possible customers, form relationships with clients stronger, and help the business grow as a whole.	The quantitative study utilised a survey methodology to gather information from 225 start-up companies operating in the culinary and fashion industries. Using SmartPLS, a statistical instrument for structural equation modeling, the data were analyzed. Facebook's marketing capabilities, Potential customer engagement, page updates, and page authority were the primary variables under investigation.	Facebook advertising factors affecting start-up brand loyalty and growth: 1. Potential customer engagement 2. Facebook's marketing capabilities 3. Page Authority 4. Regular Page Updates Prominent Mediation Effects: Partial Mediation: The relationship between Facebook's marketing capabilities and sustainable brand loyalty and growth is partially mediated by potential customer engagement and Facebook page changes. Full Mediation: Facebook promotional strategies fully mediate the relationship between brand loyalty and growth for start-up enterprises. Implications The study highlights the advantages of using Facebook as a marketing tool for start-ups. Brand loyalty and growth depend on increasing customer involvement, using Facebook's marketing tools, maintaining page authority, and updating the page regularly.
19.	Wang Yang (2020)	To understand how social media platforms are used to build dialogic relationships with the public to work on different issues.	The study analyzed Twitter pages of Fortune 500 companies and top 100 nonprofit organizations, and total 6678 tweets to focus on their dialogic communication features and statistical tests were conducted as well.	It was found that organizations pay more attention to build up public engagement by posting contents on social media and Twitter was the highlight as it is used by more than 84% of business for its features

Table 1. Continued

Paper ID	Author & Date	Objective	Methodology	Findings
20.	Dunn and Grimes (2022)	To investigate how companies can effectively respond to NUGC on social media, focusing on quick and symmetric responses to maintain CSR perceptions and organizational legitimacy.	The study involved 660 UK adult participants randomly assigned to six groups based on socio-demographic profiles, with a 50-50 gender ratio and 18-65+ years of age.	The study reveals that speed and symmetry of response are crucial for mitigating negative effects of NUGC on a company's CSR post on social media, suggesting an integrated approach.
21.	Li et al. (2022)	The study explores the link between social media criticisms and earnings management, evaluating the influence on ethical performance, negative content, financial market, and financial reporting quality.	The study examined criticisms on earnings management in firms using a difference-in-differences approach and change specification. Data was collected from Guba EastMoney, China's largest stock board, and analyzed using Baidu Brain	The study revealed that negative postings on stock boards can promote earnings management, but not necessarily deteriorate internal governance or operating performance, suggesting that addressing the negative influence of social media on corporate governance is crucial for academics, practitioners, and policymakers.
22.	Nobi et al. (2023)	The study examines how website design, features, and social media advertising affect Bangladeshi consumers' purchases decisions. The study seeks to confirm hypotheses and understand the complex network of individual, social, psychological, cultural, and environmental factors that affect consumer behaviour.	The quantitative study examined 244 respondents. The majority of respondents were male (57.4%), between 18 and 20 (63.1%), had BSc/BA degrees (42.6%), and worked in the private sector (48.4%).	Key findings of the study Website design, features, and social media affect 42.9% of purchases. 42.6% are motivated by time savings. Website features/ design impact (55.2%) more than social media. 53.5% believe social media benefits youth. ANOVA shows a strong correlation between social media, website design, and purchase frequency. Purchase Intention: Social media boosts purchase intention by 42.9%. Social media features/designs boost purchase intention by 55.2%.

3. RESULTS

The tables mentioned above summarize the entire SLR, including the research results and QA provided in Table 1.2, in this section of the discussion.

3.1 Search Result

Following significant research, the authors arrived at a conclusion and analyzed 22 scholarly articles that best synthesized the required research information and citations. The papers in Table 1.1 were mostly obtained from various electronic databases. The procedure was repeated throughout the research process. It includes information on the author, the year of publication, the primary research objectives, the technique used, and the findings of each and every selected paper. the chosen paper has been widely published in prestigious journals.

3.2 Quality Evaluation of the Papers

The research assessed QA using a scoring approach that is detailed in Table 1.2. Furthermore, it was carried out based on the three questions provided in Section 2.5. As previously stated, the publications that failed the quality evaluation test were not included in the analysis. The papers that were chosen received at least 1.5 out of 3, as detailed in Table 1.2. However, the majority of the papers received a minimum of 3 and the lowest among them still scored 2 > 1.5.

Table 2. Quality assessment

Paper ID	QA1	QA2	QA3	Score
1	Yes	Yes	Yes	3
2	Yes	Yes	No	2
3	Yes	Yes	Yes	3
4	Yes	Yes	Yes	3
5	Yes	Yes	Yes	3
6	Yes	Yes	Yes	3
7	Yes	Yes	Yes	3
8	Partial	Yes	Yes	2.5
9	Yes	Yes	Yes	3
10	Partial	Yes	Yes	2.5
11	Yes	Yes	Yes	3
12	Yes	Yes	No	2
13	Yes	Yes	Yes	3
14	Yes	Yes	Yes	3
15	Yes	Yes	No	2
16	Yes	Yes	Yes	3
17	Yes	Yes	Yes	3
18	Yes	Yes	Yes	3
19	Partial	Yes	Yes	2.5
20	Yes	Yes	Yes	3
21	Yes	Yes	Yes	3
22	Yes	Yes	Yes	3

3.3 Discussion

3.3.1 Brand Awareness and Marketing Strategies

According to Volkova et al., entrepreneurs encounter major obstacles when attempting to build brand awareness through conventional channels like billboards (2020). Suariedewi and Wulandari (2023), however, highlight social media's role in removing obstacles related to conventional methods and shed light on the revolutionary impact it has on consumers' perceptions of brands. Safitri (2022) provides an example of how to leverage multiple platforms to promote brand awareness through social media. Zombasic uses Instagram to strategically present its products, giving the impression that they are more expensive than they actually are. Their emphasis on the Syariah-based lifestyle of Islam is in line with this strategy, which promotes consumer respect and trust. The expressive and reliable appeal created by Instagram marketing initiatives fosters enduring relationships with clients and steady revenue growth.

In a similar vein, Volkova et al. (2020) highlight LEGO's skillful use of Instagram and Facebook to foster and preserve brand loyalty. LEGO uses Facebook to engage customers with articles, polls, and competitions that are relevant to their interests, and Instagram to visually showcase new products. This clever use of social media increases sales as well as brand visibility and awareness. As discussed by Volkova et al. (2020), LEGO's creative strategy of using well-known characters as toy models highlights the shortcomings of conventional marketing techniques and highlights the effectiveness of social media in quickly promoting unique products through influencers and opinion leaders.

Having a closer look at TikTok, Gesmundo et al. (2022) demonstrates how the platform is evolving from a purely recreational app to a potent tool for raising brand awareness and promotion. TikTok's impact on cross-promotion ease is apparent, given its millions of active users. Purchase intention and brand awareness on TikTok are positively correlated, suggesting that the platform may have an influence on consumer choices. In order to effectively engage with a large audience, the study suggests regular promotion on TikTok. This further demonstrates the cost-effectiveness of social media in influencing purchasing decisions and building brand awareness.

In conclusion, the studies under review collectively demonstrate the revolutionary impact of social media on brand awareness, giving business owners adaptable instruments to get past conventional obstacles and build genuine relationships with customers.

3.3.2 Consumer Engagement and Behavior

Suariedewi and Wulandari (2023) emphasize the importance of brand image in influencing consumer purchasing decisions. Their research emphasizes the evolution of consumer engagement enabled by social media, emphasizing the importance of companies establishing a robust presence and regular communication in order to position themselves as influential opinion leaders. As a result, brand trust and awareness grow. Suariedewi and Wulandari (2023) identified strategies such as posting informative content, sharing anecdotal stories, using engaging formats such as reels and stories for new products, and leveraging TikTok influencers.

Similarly, Safitri (2022) demonstrates the effectiveness of creating communities on social platforms that are tailored to specific customers. The focus on the Islamic lifestyle has contributed to Zombasic's success in engaging and building a community on Instagram. Zombasic builds trust and respect within the Islamic community by aligning their content with Shariah-based principles, positively influencing consumer behavior.

Volkova et al. (2020) investigated LEGO's innovative approach to community-building on social networks, which involves encouraging consumers to share their LEGO designs. This strategy not only fosters a sense of belonging but also uses user-generated content to promote the brand. YouTube channels featuring influencers help to maintain interest and loyalty by providing regular insights into product benefits, drawbacks, and new suggestions.

Ghoshal (2019) highlights a potential disconnect between consumer trust and a brand's social media offerings. To ensure long-term customer retention and visibility, the study advocates for brands to actively communicate their presence through content, tweets, and keeping promises. This emphasizes the significance of having a consistent online and offline brand presence.

Rathnayake and Lakshika (2023) expand on this by emphasizing the influential role of social media influencers in shaping consumer perceptions, particularly in industries such as dermatology products. Consumers prefer attractive influencers, viewing them as opinion leaders who influence purchasing decisions. The study emphasizes the efficacy of social media influencers in creating long-lasting impressions and influencing brand engagement, awareness, and sales, which outperforms traditional local marketing approaches.

Finally, these studies illuminate the multifaceted impact of social media on consumer engagement, brand image, and purchasing decisions across various industries, providing valuable insights for businesses looking to effectively leverage these platforms.

3.3.3 Navigating Digital Waves: Crafting Loyalty in the Social Media Realm

Sahai et al. (2019) stresses the importance of managing client experiences, which include both physical and emotional aspects, in the pursuit of organizational loyalty. Key challenges are identified and strategic solutions are proposed in the study:

Concern for Customer Satisfaction Centers on a Possible Deterioration in Service Quality. The solution is to make improving the quality of service a top priority so that customers are satisfied. Additionally, the research shows that there has to be more effort put into building trust with consumers. The solution is to put plans in place to increase trust so that relationships can last. Finally, a lower alpha of 0.611 in responsiveness reveals a crucial area for improving overall customer service, which presents a challenge. The solution is to fix the responsiveness problems so that you can quickly meet your customers' expectations. Providing reliable and high-quality services, gaining clients' trust, and becoming more responsive are the main points of the strategy put forth by Sahai et al. In line with the overarching objective of increasing organizational loyalty, this all-encompassing strategy seeks to produce a dependable and pleasant customer experience.

In their study, Kamkankaew et al. (2022) highlight three significant discoveries in the field of digital marketing: the efficacy of inbound marketing, the benefits of e-commerce, and the persistent impact of social networks. The study highlights the importance of employing various digital advertising strategies and emphasizes the necessity of a customized and all-encompassing digital marketing plan. This strategy, which concentrates on particular products and target demographics, places importance on monitoring the customer's progression in order to establish long-lasting value.

Hawkins and Hoon's 2019 study looked at how small service-based businesses maintain customers. Participants drew attention to important themes: "Engagement & Communication" talked about how feelings and good interactions are important for long-term relationships. "Satisfaction is Invaluable" emphasized that loyalty was based on meeting expectations. "Trust" turned out to be very important, affecting commitment and repeat purchases. "Quality Assurance" made it clear how important it is to keep service standards high. All of these things are very important for small service-based businesses because they build loyalty and make sure they succeed.

Nobi et al. (2023) revealed crucial findings regarding consumer buying patterns in Bangladesh. The study emphasized the substantial impact of website design, features, and social media advertising on purchasing decisions, particularly in relation to the desire to save time. Significantly, the influence of website features and design was more pronounced than that of social media advertising. The research emphasized the favorable influence of social media advertising on the youth in Bangladesh, revealing a robust correlation between its advantages, website layout, and the frequency of customer acquisitions. Furthermore, it was discovered that social media advertising has a positive impact on the intention to make purchases, with its distinctive features and designs playing a crucial role. To summarize, the results confirmed the positive influence of social media marketing on the buying habits of young individuals in Bangladesh. The study illuminated these dynamics and suggested the existence of supplementary variables, such as individual, social, psychological, cultural, and environmental factors, that contribute to a more comprehensive comprehension of the influences on consumer behavior in website design and social media marketing.

Muangmee (2021) employed a quantitative methodology to examine the intricacies of Facebook advertising across 225 companies operating in the Thai food and fashion sectors. The research underscored the adverse effects that investments, promotional campaigns, and Facebook page authority had on both brand loyalty and growth. On the other hand, favorable results were noted with regards to heightened awareness of the brand, intrigue from potential clients, and the particularly advantageous impact of Facebook Marketing Functionalities. The adverse consequences underscore the necessity for an intricate and purposeful approach in Facebook advertising. Consistent with more extensive understandings in the realm of digital marketing, the research emphasizes the critical significance of engaging potential customers. This report provides significant recommendations for small enterprises operating in Thailand, underscoring the need for customized approaches, proactive user involvement, and a sophisticated comprehension of fluctuating effects in order to cultivate brand allegiance and enduring expansion via the platform.

The study carried out in Dubai's Global Village by Alzoubi et al. (2022) provides valuable insight into how Beacon technology, and specifically proximity marketing, significantly influences consumer actions. The study highlights the importance of important factors, one of which is proximity marketing, which has a significant impact on the participants.Customers are more loyal to businesses that use proximity marketing, loyalty programs, in-store navigation, and real-time marketing, according to the study. Among the most important factors, location marketing stands out, while in-store navigation, real-time marketing, and loyalty programs follow closely behind. A key finding of the study is that customer loyalty is positively affected by Beacon technology due to its versatile applications. Businesses in Global Village can use the insights it provides to improve customer engagement and loyalty through the use of Beacon technology. The study also notes that BLE technology adoption can increase customer happiness and loyalty. Businesses in Dubai can benefit greatly from these findings, which highlight the ever-changing impact of Beacon technology on customer behavior and call for a strategic approach to boost engagement and loyalty in this dynamic market.

3.3.4 Harnessing Social Media for Entrepreneurial Success

According to Harrasi (2022), entrepreneurs in Oman face various challenges, including a lack of knowledge in entrepreneurial skills, intense competition, fluctuating market conditions, restricted access to technology and limited industry contacts. However, the findings reveal that engagement with social media, especially platforms like WhatsApp, Instagram, and Twitter, serves as a valuable tool for overcoming these challenges. The positive correlation between social media access and usage of modern technology, understanding market conditions, and reducing the impact of heavy competition is emphasized which highlights the transformative impact of social media on SMEs. The study suggests that number of likes or followers on business-related social media platforms is identified as crucial in addressing challenges and fostering networks that underline the importance of social media in the entrepreneurial context.

Similarly, Lamba & Jain (2022) talk about how important social media is to build a support network for advice and credibility, act quickly to keep things from becoming obsolete, keep learning new software skills, have a positive impact on the community for economic growth as well as have a strong system for managing processes. It is emphasized that resilience is a good way to adapt to a competitive environment. To get through these problems, entrepreneurs should use design thinking. The study highlights how important the digital world is in today's world by suggesting that insights could be useful for startups that aren't digital.

In addition to the Omani context, the South African township study (Lose & Eze, 2023), research identifies obstacles such as power cuts, lack of finance for digital systems, and a deficit in digital marketing skills. Entrepreneurs in this context are encouraged to view these challenges as opportunities, leveraging social media for solutions. For instance, the study suggests addressing power cuts by supplying alternative power sources like solar or generators and filling the knowledge gap by offering ICT education and training. This exemplifies the adaptability required in the digital age, where social media emerges as a powerful ally in transforming challenges into entrepreneurial opportunities. The study suggests that to overcome financial hurdles for digital implementations, microfinancing models tailored for digital businesses can be developed. Serving as a middleman in the digital value chain is an opportunity to counter the compromise on product quality. Moreover, by understanding the local market's limitations, entrepreneurs can specialize in local marketing for digital products. In conclusion, the study asserts that entrepreneurs in the field of international marketing for digital products are necessary to bridge gaps with international suppliers.

3.3.5 Converting Obstacles into Possibilities: The Entrepreneurial Environment

Adula and Kant's (2023) study illuminated the challenges faced by female entrepreneurs in Bule Hora town, which bear similarities to the financial constraints and workplace problems encountered by their Omani counterparts. These entrepreneurs turn to groups like the Oromia Credit Saving Association (OSCO) for loans when they are unable to obtain sufficient funds on their own. However, the study does emphasize how crucial social media entrepreneurship is to address these problems. Adula and Kant (2023) claim that the outcomes also show how social media can be used as a platform for networking, promoting goods and services, and gaining access to information and resources.

Similarly, Khalid and Allioui (2023) stated that in the digital age, these social platforms offer a cost-effective and powerful means for entrepreneurs to market their businesses, connect with customers, reach a wider audience and provide significant business value at a low cost, allowing entrepreneurs to engage in business networking, crowdfunding, and accessing updated information to promote their ventures. The study also highlights how social media facilitates networking and collaboration among women entrepreneurs, providing a support network crucial for those who may face isolation and limited access to traditional business networks. Interviews featured in the research emphasize the role of platforms like WhatsApp and Facebook in advertising products and attracting customers, demonstrating the power of social media in boosting businesses.

Moreover, Boshmaf (2023) in his research on Jordanian female entrepreneurs provides a detailed perspective on the role of social media in empowering entrepreneurs. This study sheds light on the problems and opportunities experienced by Jordanian women entrepreneurs, especially when it comes to harnessing social media for empowerment. It demonstrates that women entrepreneurs, predominantly between the ages of 20 and 29, use social media, particularly Facebook, to sell their products, share information, and conduct sales. This not only answers the issues raised by complicated registration procedures and costly fees, but it also adds to financial independence. For these women, social media is a low-cost platform for promoting products, recruiting new customers, and running enterprises from the comfort of their own homes. The study emphasizes social media's disruptive impact on the entrepreneurial situation, providing individuals with a platform to negotiate problems and pursue possibilities, thereby breaking established gender roles and prejudices (Boshmaf, 2023).

Furthermore, Sawy & Bögenhold's (2022) exploration of the experiences of micro-entrepreneurs in Austria further contributes to the discussion on social media's role in entrepreneurship. The study highlights the dual nature of social media, presenting both positive opportunities for business growth and challenges such as time management and potential negative impacts on personal identity. In rural areas like Carinthia, where a strong online presence becomes crucial for business success, micro-entrepreneurs struggle with the time-consuming nature of social media use. However, the study also points out that concerns about reputation damage through social media are less significant due to strong offline networks. Micro-entrepreneurs employ strategies such as identity creation and self-regulation to mitigate negative experiences on social media, emphasizing the need for a balance between the benefits and challenges of social media use.

3.3.6 Social Media for Addressing Criticisms and Unintended Results

Social media, for its dark side, does put companies under pressure when faced criticism over their legitimacy, CSR activities, earnings management in a manner of NUGC (negative user generated content). Now, it is important for companies to address these criticisms otherwise they will not sustain its credibility, stakeholder support, secure long-term developments, lose financial credibility, force managers to behave unethically and remain scarce for a "goodwill buffer" when facing adverse situations. If the stakeholders have poor perceptions towards a company's activities such as CSR, financial reporting, and overall legitimacy, will indeed hamper the existing reputations and future prospects of the company. However, on the good side, social media does help in changing these criticisms into positive views. For example, using social media platforms such as Twitter to build dialogic relationships, which is for negotiating or exchanging opinions or ideas with the public, to retain good stakeholder relationships (Wang & Yang, 2020). This is important since a positive relationship has been found between discretionary questionable activities such as opportunistic earnings management among managers and negative fundamental postings on social media. An example of this can be the Enron scandal caught in 2001 where the messages posted on Yahoo questioned the company's accounting data but before that in 1997, investors warned about investing in Enron's stocks. (Li et al., 2022). For companies to escape such wrongdoings and criticism, dialogic relationships must be established effectively by being quick and symmetrical in responding to the audience. As per the study on how social media may help in mitigating NUGC, high symmetry in responses is preferred when combined with factors such as the speed of making those responses. This denotes that only ensuring symmetry or quick response will ensure partial mitigation but the culmination of both fast and symmetrical responses is the key to fully mitigating criticism and concerns over companies' activities (Dunn & Grimes, 2022).

4. CONCLUSION

Finally, this systematic review sheds light on the critical role of social media entrepreneurship in navigating and overcoming potential obstacles. The synthesis of existing research emphasizes the multifaceted nature of the challenges that entrepreneurs face in the social media landscape. The findings show how entrepreneurial initiatives can use social media platforms to overcome obstacles, foster innovation, and grow resilient businesses. This review provides a comprehensive understanding of the dynamic interplay between entrepreneurship and social media in overcoming barriers by exploring diverse strategies and approaches used by social media entrepreneurs. In the future, the insights gained from this synthesis will serve as a valuable foundation for future research and practical applications, providing a roadmap for entrepreneurs to fully leverage the potential of social media in overcoming obstacles and achieving long-term success in the digital age.

4.1 Limitation and Further Research Scope

Regardless of the significant insights gained from the studies reviewed, it is critical to recognize the limits of the research presented in this chapter. The context-specific character of some findings, as well as the rapidly expanding social media ecosystem, make generalizing conclusions across varied entrepreneurial situations difficult. Furthermore, external factors such as changes in social media algorithms and user behaviors may alter the validity and applicability of the findings over time.

The investigation of social media entrepreneurship and its impact on overcoming difficulties is a fluid field that begs additional investigation. Future research could focus on the shifting techniques used by businesses to negotiate the constantly changing algorithms and features of popular social media platforms. Furthermore, a more nuanced knowledge of how influencers effect consumer behavior and contribute to brand loyalty would provide significant insights to the marketing landscape.

Exploring the impact of social media in addressing specific difficulties encountered by businesses in various industry or geographical locations could give entrepreneurs with focused solutions. Furthermore, researching the ethical concerns and potential hazards linked with influencer-driven marketing methods may provide a more nuanced view on the intricacies of this developing area. In essence, the scope for future research lies in unraveling the complexities of social media entrepreneurship, comprehending its implications in various contexts, and developing strategic frameworks to assist businesses in harnessing the full potential of digital platforms for long-term success.

REFERENCES

Aboulilah, H. M. E., Hossain, S. F. A., Vương, B. N., & Jebril, T. (2022). Exploring the Relationship between WeChat Usage and E-purchase Intention During the COVID-19 Pandemic Among University Students in China. *SAGE Open*, *12*(4). doi:10.1177/21582440221139447 PMID:36466966

Boshmaf, H. (2023). Jordanian women entrepreneurs and the role of social media: The road to Empowerment. *Dirasat: Human and Social Sciences*, *50*(3), 139–152. doi:10.35516/hum.v50i3.5402

C. (2021). Effects of Facebook advertising on sustainable brand loyalty and growth: case of Thai start-up businesses. *Transnational Corporations Review*, 1-12. doi:10.1080/19186444.2021.1986340

Cheng, C. C., & Shiu, E. C. (2019). How to enhance SMEs customer involvement using social media: The role of Social CRM. *International Small Business Journal*, *37*(1), 22–42. doi:10.1177/0266242618774831

Creswell, J. W., & Creswell, J. D. (2017). *Research design: Qualitative, quantitative, and mixed methods approaches*. Sage publications.

De Zubielqui, G. C., & Jones, J. (2020). How and when social media affects innovation in start-ups. A moderated mediation model. *Industrial Marketing Management*, *85*, 209–220. doi:10.1016/j.indmarman.2019.11.006

Dunn, K., & Grimes, A. (2022). Speed and symmetry: Developing effective organisational responses to social media criticism of CSR. *Computers in Human Behavior*, *134*, 107336. doi:10.1016/j.chb.2022.107336

Emmanuel, C. P., Qin, S., Hossain, S. F. A., & Hussain, K. (2021). Factors influencing social-media-based entrepreneurship prospect among female students in China. *Heliyon*, *8*(12), e12041. Advance online publication. doi:10.1016/j.heliyon.2022.e12041 PMID:36483305

Harrasi, N. A., Hakro, A. N., Srinavasan, V., Christina, B., & Jabri, M. A. (2022). Social Media and Entrepreneurship Challenges in the Sultanate of Oman. *Hong Kong Journal of Social Sciences*, *58*, 765–776.

HawkinsD. L.HoonS. (2019). The impact of customer retention strategies and the survival of small service-based businesses. *Available at* SSRN 3445173. doi:10.2139/ssrn.3445173

Hossain, S. F. A. (2019). Social networking and its role in media entrepreneurship. *Journal of Media Management and Entrepreneurship*, *1*(1), 73–86. doi:10.4018/JMME.2019010105

Hossain, S. F. A., Nurunnabi, M., Hussain, K., & Saha, S. K. (2019). Effects of variety-seeking intention by mobile phone usage on university students' academic performance. *Cogent Education*, *6*(1), 1574692. doi:10.1080/2331186X.2019.1574692

Hossain, S. F. A., Nurunnabi, M., Hussain, K., & Xu, S. (2020). Smartphone-based m-shopping behavior and innovative entrepreneurial tendency among women in emerging Asia. *International Journal of Gender and Entrepreneurship*, *12*(2), 173–189. doi:10.1108/IJGE-03-2019-0054

Hossain, S. F. A., Xu, S., Musa, M., & Rahman, P. (2022). Social media and Increased venture creation tendency with innovative ideas. In IGI Global eBooks (pp. 1716–1731). doi:10.4018/978-1-6684-7123-4.ch093

Hossain, S. F. A., Xu, S., Nurunnabi, M., Tushar, H., Mohsin, A. K. M., & Ahsan, F. T. (2021). Opportunities and Challenges of M-Learning during the COVID-19 Pandemic. In Advances in social networking and online communities book series (pp. 210–227). doi:10.4018/978-1-7998-7764-6.ch007

Hossain, S. F. A., Zhao, X., Nurunnabi, M., & Hussain, K. (2020). Ubiquitous role of social networking in driving M-Commerce: Evaluating the use of mobile phones for online shopping and payment in the context of trust. *SAGE Open*, *10*(3). doi:10.1177/2158244020939536

Kamkankaew, P., Sribenjachot, S., Wongmahatlek, J., Phattarowas, V., & Khumwongpin, S. (2022). Reconsidering the Mystery of Digital Marketing Strategy in the Technological Environment: Opportunities and Challenges in Digital Consumer Behavior. *International Journal of Sociologies and Anthropologies Science Reviews*, *2*(4), 43–60. doi:10.14456/jsasr.2022.29

Khalid, C., & Allioui, S. (2023). Empowering female entrepreneurs in developing countries: A comparative case study on the impact of social media on microenterprises and poverty alleviation. *International May Conference on Strategic Management, 19*(1), 242-251.

Kitchenham, B., Brereton, O. P., Budgen, D., Turner, M., Bailey, J., & Linkman, S. (2009). Systematic literature reviews in software engineering – A systematic literature review. *Information and Software Technology*, *51*(1), 7–15. doi:10.1016/j.infsof.2008.09.009

Lamba, P. S., & Jain, N. R. (2022). Overcoming challenges faced by digital entrepreneurs: A design thinking approach. *Development and Learning in Organizations*, *36*(6), 12–14. doi:10.1108/DLO-11-2021-0195

Li, Y., Zhang, W., Urquhart, A., & Wang, P. (2022). The unintended consequence of social media criticisms: An earnings management perspective. *European Journal of Finance*, *29*(1), 33–57. doi:10.1080/1351847X.2022.2097885

Lose, T., & Eze, I. F. (2023). Virtual small business entrepreneurship opportunities. *Eureka: Social and Humanities, 4*, 13–19. https://doi.org/ doi:10.21303/2504-5571.2023.002912

Mohsin, A. K. M., Lei, H., & Hossain, S. F. A. (2021). Impact of COVID-19 Pandemic on Consumer Economy: Countermeasures analysis. *SAGE Open*, *11*(2). doi:10.1177/21582440211008875

Muangmee, A. (2023). Focused Group Interview Literature Review of Challenges Ethiopian Female Entrepreneurs Face in their Business Ventures. *International Journal of Social Science Management and Economics Research*, *01*(03), 36–47. doi:10.61421/IJSSMER.2023.1303

Nobi. (2023). Impact of Social Media Advertising on Buying Decision of Young Group of Consumers in Bangladesh: A Study Dhaka City. *Studies of Applied Economics, 41*(2). doi:10.25115/sae.v41i2.9105

Öberg, C. (2019). The role of business networks for innovation. *Journal of Innovation & Knowledge*, *4*(2), 124–128. doi:10.1016/j.jik.2017.10.001

OkoliC.SchabramK. (2010). A Guide to conducting a Systematic Literature Review of Information Systems Research. *Social Science Research Network*. doi:10.2139/ssrn.1954824

Sahai, S., Goel, R., Venaik, A., & Garg, V. (2019). Impact of digital commerce on fashion industry to gain customer loyalty. *International Journal of Engineering and Advanced Technology*, *8*(5), 730–740.

Silaban, P. H., Chen, W., & Silalahi, A. D. K. (2022). The use of social media by entrepreneurial and small firms: systematic literature review. *2022 International Conference on Decision Aid Sciences and Applications (DASA)*, 947–952. 10.1109/DASA54658.2022.9765244

Smith, L., Liang, Q., James, P., & Lin, W. (2017). Assessing the utility of social media as a data source for flood risk management using a real-time modelling framework. *Journal of Flood Risk Management*, *10*(3), 370–380. doi:10.1111/jfr3.12154

Thomas, L., Orme, E., & Kerrigan, F. (2020). Student loneliness: The role of social media through life transitions. *Computers & Education*, *146*, 103754. doi:10.1016/j.compedu.2019.103754

Vương, B. N., Tushar, H., & Hossain, S. F. A. (2022). The effect of social support on job performance through organizational commitment and innovative work behavior: Does innovative climate matter? *Asia-Pacific Journal of Business Administration*. Advance online publication. doi:10.1108/APJBA-06-2021-0256

Wang, Y., McKee, M., Torbica, A., & Stuckler, D. (2019). Systematic literature review on the spread of health-related misinformation on social media. *Social Science & Medicine*, *240*, 112552. doi:10.1016/j.socscimed.2019.112552 PMID:31561111

Wang, Y., & Yang, Y. (2020). Dialogic communication on social media: How organizations use Twitter to build dialogic relationships with their publics. *Computers in Human Behavior*, *104*, 106183. doi:10.1016/j.chb.2019.106183

Yang, L., Zhang, H., Shen, H., Huang, X., Zhou, X., Rong, G., & Dong, S. (2021). Quality Assessment in Systematic Literature Reviews: A Software Engineering Perspective. *Information and Software Technology*, *130*, 106397. doi:10.1016/j.infsof.2020.106397

Chapter 16
How Social Media Entrepreneurship Can Boost Business in the Future

Mithila Zaman Priasa
BRAC University, Bangladesh

Rashidul Hasan Mahim
BRAC University, Bangladesh

Jotirmoyee Prodhan
BRAC University, Bangladesh

Tanzila Akther
BRAC University, Bangladesh

Tanzid Morshed
https://orcid.org/0009-0001-5099-9751
BRAC University, Bangladesh

Fatima Tuz Juhana
BRAC University, Bangladesh

EXECUTIVE SUMMARY

This chapter uses a thorough study method to examine the revolutionary power of the social media business. Part of the plan for the study is to do a complete literature review that includes books, papers, journals, and Google Scholar documentation. Sites like Facebook and Statista are also used for their data and cases in the study. During the study process, strict academic standards are applied to ensure the results are real and accurate. Data can come from many places, like business records, scholarly publications, and social networking sites. There are quantifiable and qualitative ways to look at data to find meaningful trends, patterns, and insights. The study results are given in a short form and are backed up by relevant data and figures. The last part of the chapter talks about what this study means for business and social media creators in the future.

DOI: 10.4018/979-8-3693-1781-5.ch016

INTRODUCTION

In today's age of digital interconnectivity and constantly changing market dynamics, the integration of social media with entrepreneurial pursuits has sparked a significant transformation in corporate strategies and opportunities for growth. The complex interaction between social media platforms and entrepreneurial endeavors has restructured the business environment and ushered in a transformative era of connectivity and innovation. From the early days of Internet networking to the current domination of global social media giants such as Facebook, Instagram, Twitter, and LinkedIn, the development and incorporation of social media entrepreneurship have become crucial factors in influencing the future direction of commerce (Hossain et al., 2023). This study thoroughly investigates the role of social media entrepreneurship in driving future business growth. This study seeks to shed light on the various ways social media entrepreneurship is expected to go and redefine corporate growth paradigms in the near future. This study article attempts to explore the various aspects of social media entrepreneurship and its crucial function in enhancing business expansion. This study aims to thoroughly understand how social media entrepreneurship drives business expansion, innovation, and sustained success in the future. It analyzes historical foundations, examines the impact on entrepreneurial strategies, discusses the advantages and challenges, and predicts future trends.

LITERATURE REVIEW

How Entrepreneurs Use Social Media

The present study examines how entrepreneurs use social media sites for marketing, including Facebook, Twitter, YouTube, and LinkedIn. How may these platforms market products and services, engage customers, and boost brand visibility?

Social media marketing has grown in popularity. This strategy has several advantages and drawbacks that should be considered. Social media marketing may reach a large audience, which is a significant benefit. Businesses can get and engage billions of active users across platforms. As this study shows, social media marketing is cost-effective, rich, participatory, and able to produce meaningful feedback. Several research problems are also acknowledged in this work. The study's time investment, possibly unfavorable remarks, privacy issues, and measurement complexity are among these obstacles.

This section discusses field-specific best practices and suggestions. Experts undertook significant study and analysis to establish these practices and recommendations. These Entrepreneurial social media marketing tactics are thoroughly examined in this research. It provides crucial social media optimization tips. These suggestions include setting clear goals, carefully choosing platforms, creating high-quality content, engaging with the target audience, and tracking results. (The Evolution of Social Media as a Marketing Tool for Entrepreneurs - ProQuest, n.d.)

Social Media Marketing Trends

A thorough social media marketing report begins with this paper. The paper seeks to illuminate social media marketing trends. This research is based on a comprehensive poll of expert marketers. This research analyzes the answers of thousands of industry professionals to illustrate the current status of social media marketing and provides tips for marketers looking to improve their strategy. The report covers organic, video, and social ads.

The analysis shows Facebook's decline, TikTok's rise, and advertisers' love of YouTube. These prominent social media networks serve different objectives and audiences.

This website emphasizes the need for a well-developed and current social media strategy and plans for businesses. The study helps marketers discover new ideas, learn from successful techniques, and avoid social media mistakes.

Report author Michael Stelzner is introduced on the webpage. Michael Stelzner founded Social Media Examiner, a popular online forum for social media marketing advice. Besides his main interests, he does additional scholarly work. These include presenting a podcast to share expertise and facilitate discussions. He also organizes a conference for specialists and fans to share ideas. Finally, his writings have expanded the literature and scholarly conversation on the issue. (Stelzner, 2023)

EVOLUTION OF SOCIAL MEDIA ENTREPRENEURSHIP

The Origin of Social Media

A combination of technological advancements and the innate human need to communicate has driven the expansion of social media. This is a story about making and keeping large-scale human ties. Less than a generation has passed since social media first emerged as a means of immediate electronic information sharing; now, it serves as a virtual community, a marketplace, and an essential marketing instrument for the modern marketing mix. Traditional modes of textual communication were the genesis of social media. Handwritten letters were the first form of long-distance communication. Even the most basic kind of mail transport started as far back as 550 B.C.E., and during the centuries that followed, it became more efficient and expanded. With the invention of the telegraph in 1792, long-distance personal messages could be sent far more quickly than with a horse and rider. Even though telegraph messages were brief, they were a game-changer for communicating information and news. Many others even go so far as to say that the invention of the telegraph was the exact moment when social media first emerged. In 1865, a new method of speedy mail delivery was introduced with the invention of the pneumatic post. Despite its waning appeal outside of drive-through banking, the pneumatic post—which transports capsules via subterranean pressurized air tubes—is still used today. The invention of the telephone in 1890 and the radio in 1891 were two significant technological advances in the last decade of the nineteenth century. A first for humankind, the invention of the telephone and the radio allowed instantaneous transmission of messages across enormous distances. Despite the fact that both technologies have evolved significantly since their inception, they are both being used today.

Social Media in the 20th Century

In the early 20th century, both technology and social media started to advance at a rapid pace. The concept of interconnected computer networks emerged in the 1940s when the first supercomputers were built. This work eventually led to what is now known as the World Wide Web and the Internet.

Figure 1.

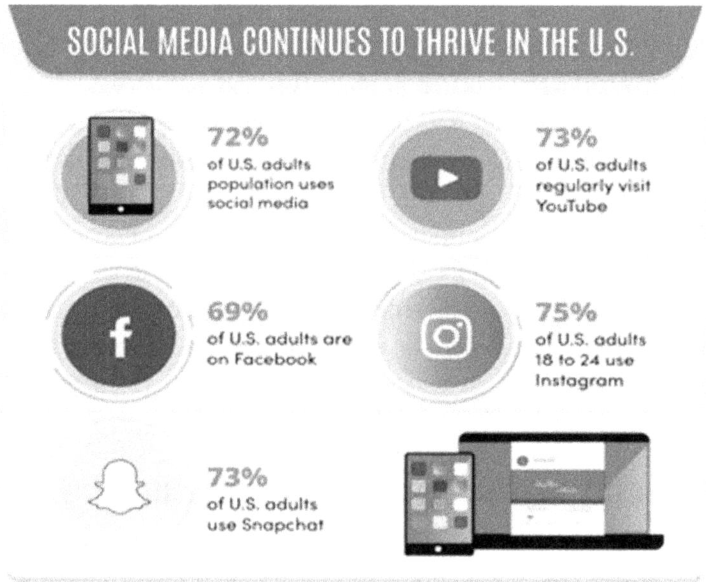

Now in the present generation, social media is beneficial for entrepreneurs because it is connected with entrepreneurial intuition, entrepreneurial alertness, entrepreneurial turn which help to maintain the sustainability of SMEs.

In the 1960s, companies like CompuServe created the first versions of what would later be known as the Internet. During this time, people also began developing the earliest electronic communication. With the advancement of networking technology in the 1970s, UseNet enabled users to connect via digital bulletin board systems and virtual newsletters in 1979. Modern forms of social media started to emerge just before the century came to a close. Launched in 1997, Six Degrees was the first well-known social media site. It lets people create profiles and connect with others. A social media phenomenon that has endured since its inception, user-generated content (UGC) blogs first gained traction in 1999. Near the

Figure 2.

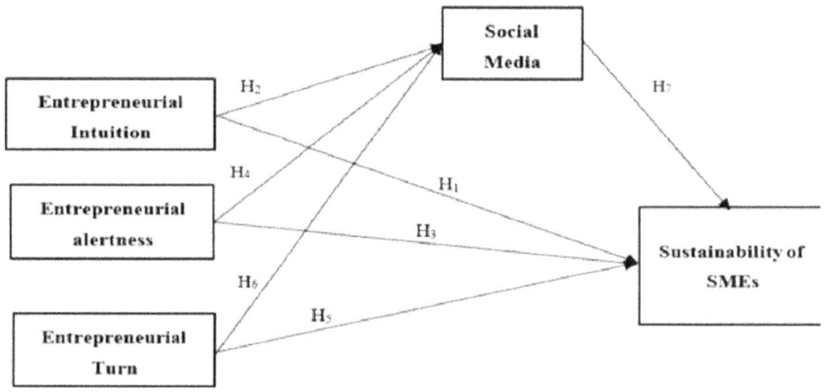

Figure 3.

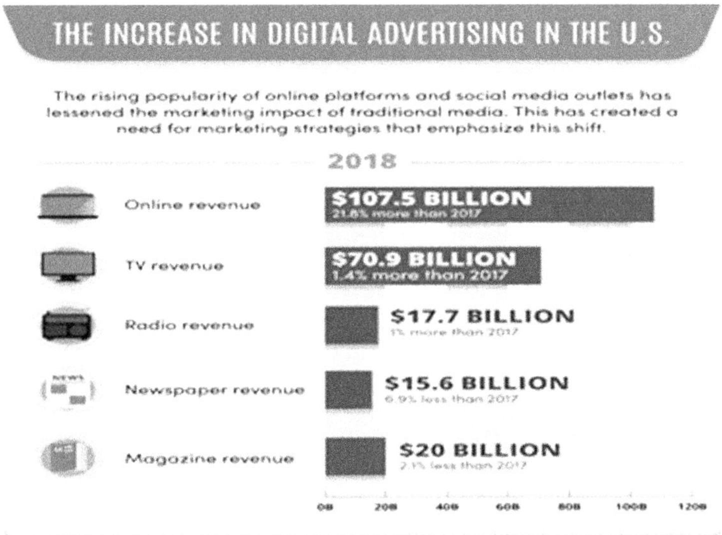

turn of the last century, service providers like America Online also debuted immensely successful IM applications. The prevalence of personal computers and the sophistication of social media had increased by the 1980s. Internet relay conversations (IRCs) were popular throughout the '80s and '90s after their initial use in 1988.(Vương et al., 2022)

In 1997, following the first social networking patent application by Six Degrees founder Andrew Weinreich—sometimes referred to as the "father of social networking"—the first genuine social media platform went live. He elaborated on "a networking database containing a plurality of records for different individuals, in which individuals are connected in the database by defined relationships."

According to Weinrich, the "six degrees of separation" theory—which states that there are no more than six connections between any two people on Earth—inspired the first social media website's name. The original concept behind Six Degrees laid the groundwork for the subsequent fast development of social media, even though the site itself did not endure long, ceasing operations in 2001.

Historical Progression

Nevertheless, Facebook's introduction in 2004 was the catalyst for the social media revolution. After quickly gaining traction on college campuses, Facebook went global and sparked a social media revolution.

Global Growth Trends

There has been a meteoric rise in the number of social media sites. In its early years, Facebook had a few million users; now, that number has ballooned to billions throughout the globe. This pattern in growth can be better seen with graphs that show user growth, engagement data, or even charts that compare platforms.

Example: In 2022, Facebook reported having 2.89 billion monthly active users worldwide, demonstrating its unprecedented growth and influence.

Figure 4.

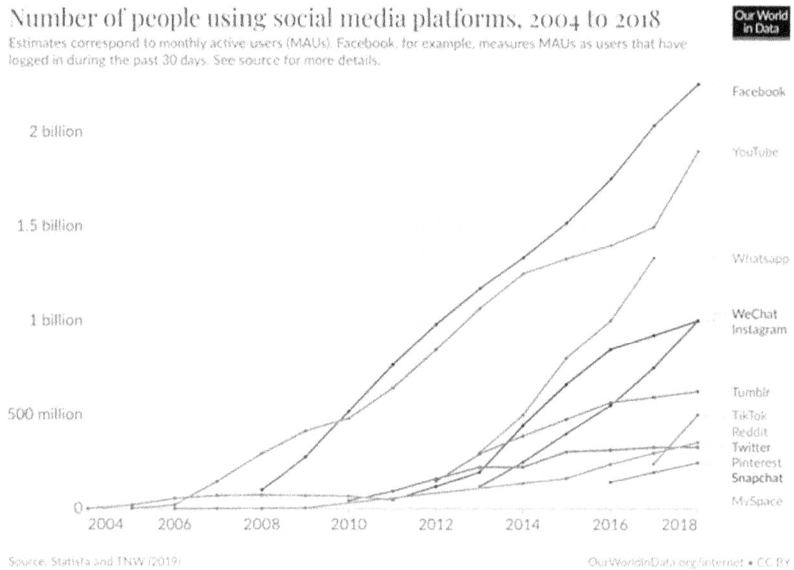

With the rise of smartphones and better internet connectivity, people were able to access and engage with social media sites instantly, contributing to their growth.

Impact of Social Media Platforms on Entrepreneurship

The once-exclusive world of building a strong online presence has become more accessible to businesses of all sizes thanks to social media platforms, which have given them unprecedented access to a worldwide customer base. Businesses of all sizes are able to connect with consumers all over the globe thanks to these channels, which were once only accessible to multinational conglomerates. Think about how Instagram has changed the game for freelancers and small businesses; it does not care about where you are or what you sell. Its visually immersive interface gave small businesses a leg up, letting them show off their wares to a global audience that knew nothing about boundaries, which in turn increased sales and brand awareness like never before.

Without social media it's impossible to see business growth in a business now. Because the audience insights, competitors' analysis are interconnected with these factors. Not only these but also content performance analysis is one of the major factors which cannot be done without social media.

In addition, businesses can communicate with their target audience and build brand identification using social media platforms directly and cost-effectively. The creative use of YouTube in the "Dove Real Beauty" campaign is a prime example of how these platforms can boost brand awareness and sales by sparking important discussions about global issues like beauty standards. This new way of thinking about marketing has completely changed the game, opening up previously unimaginable communication channels between brands and their customers.

With the rise of social media influencers, brands now have new ways to connect with consumers through endorsements and partnerships, further revolutionizing marketing. Partnerships with prominent

Figure 5.

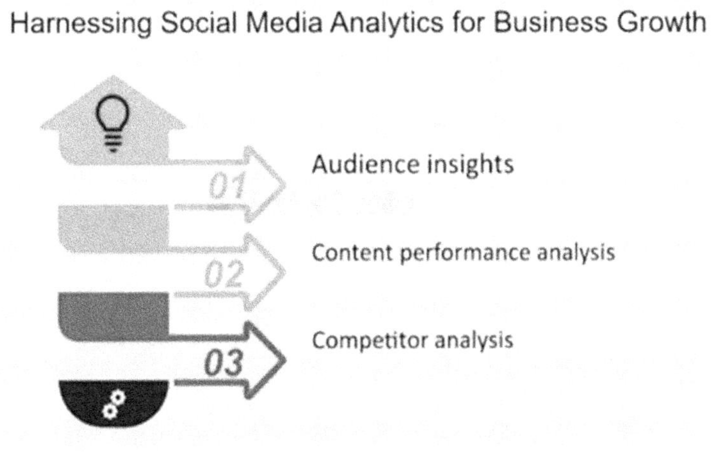

personalities significantly increased brand recognition and revenue for Daniel Wellington, and influencer marketing on platforms like Instagram played a significant role in his ascent to fame.

A slew of new business tactics are coming in response to social media tech developments like data analytics, AR/VR, and AI-driven customization. These innovations are changing how companies interact with customers by providing personalized experiences and altering buying habits through targeted ads, user-generated content, and reviews.

These changes have made social media a place where businesses can grow and innovate. Here, companies of all sizes can find their way and make the most of these resources to tell stories that resonate, build lasting relationships, and achieve long-term success in a cutthroat industry.

Figure 6.

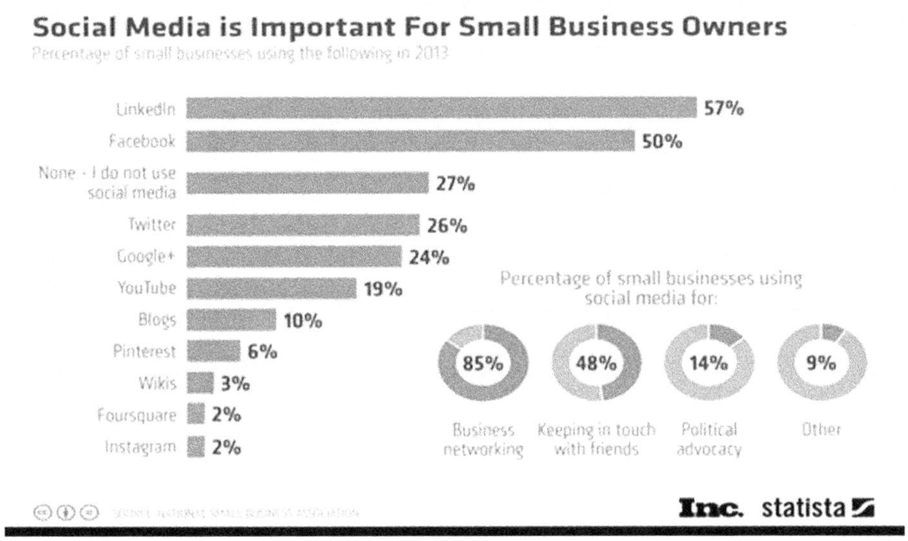

Figure 7.

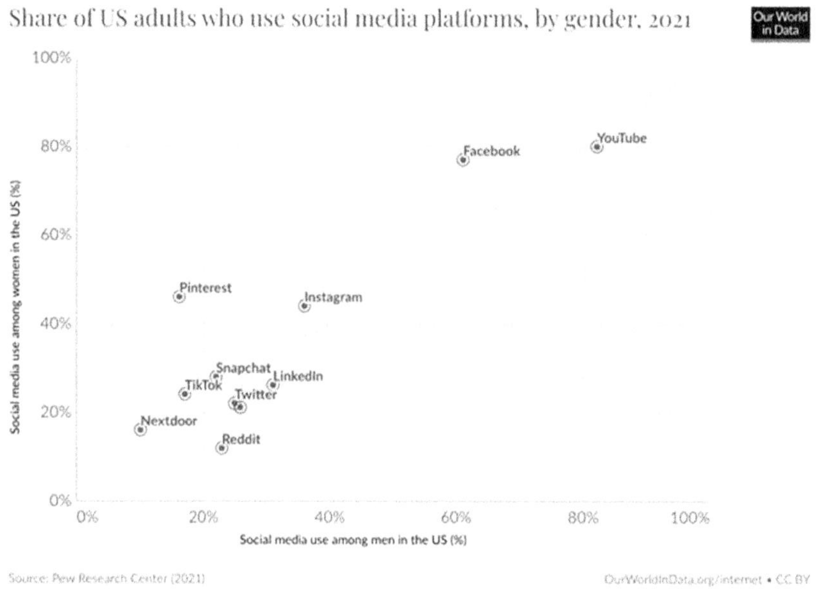

Overall, the rise of social media entrepreneurship is changing the face of contemporary business. The historical history of social media exhibits an unparalleled growth trajectory, from its humble beginnings with platforms like Six Degrees to Facebook's worldwide dominance and beyond. In today's increasingly digital environment, this transformation has completely transformed the way businesses interact, engage, and succeed. Thanks to the reach, accessibility, and cost-effective marketing channels offered

Figure 8.

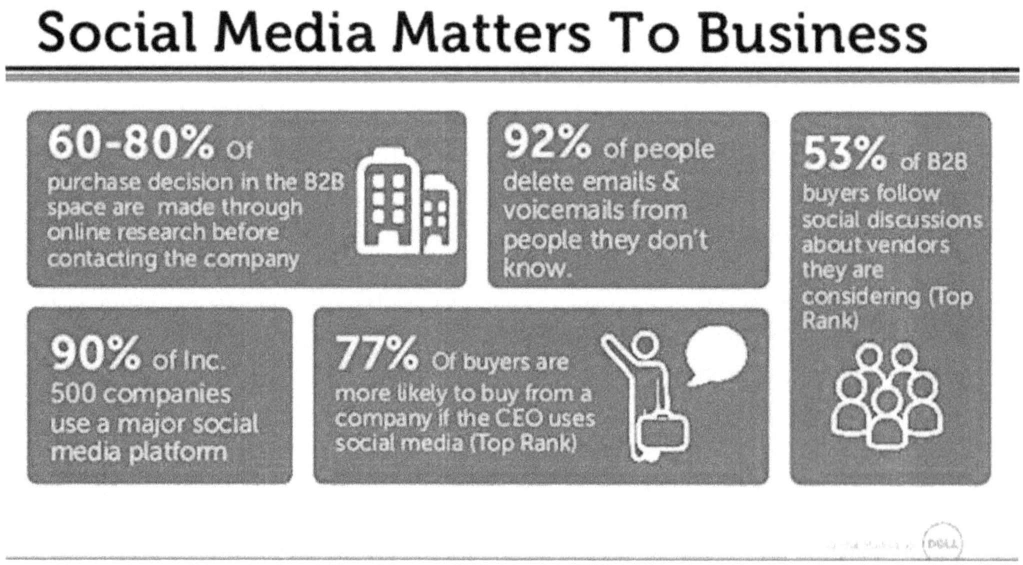

by social media platforms, businesses of all sizes are now able to establish a brand presence and connect with a global audience. The rise of influencer marketing and other digital advancements like artificial intelligence (AI), augmented reality (AR), virtual reality (VR), and data analytics have increased the influence of social media on both consumer habits and business tactics. Constant innovation and game-changing expansion in the corporate world are in store for the future of social media entrepreneurship, notwithstanding obstacles like privacy worries and algorithmic changes.

Case Studies and Examples

The evolving and dynamic field of entrepreneurship is increasingly influenced by the role of social media, which holds great potential for boosting business prospects in the future. This section of the research paper derives insights from three primary sources to elucidate the significant role of social media entrepreneurship in shaping business landscapes and entrepreneurial endeavors, particularly within developing nations and among the younger generation. Much focus has been paid to the role of social media as an entrepreneur in recent years. Some researchers have examined how social media sites have helped businesses grow and succeed. Entrepreneurs have been able to reach more people and build their brands thanks to social media, which makes contact and marketing easy and cheap.

The study showed how important social media is in developing countries, especially for teaching people how to be entrepreneurs (EE) and how that affects people's long-term plans to become entrepreneurs (SEIs). In their paper, the writers stress how crucial social media sites are evolving to help business graduates in these areas learn how to be entrepreneurs. Prospective entrepreneurs in developing nations can cultivate intentions that align with enduring environmental and social objectives and augment their comprehension of sustainable business practices through social media (El-Gohary et al., 2023). This study shows that more and more people are realizing how important social media is to entrepreneurs and how it can help these countries improve in a way that lasts. This study's research is mostly about how social media can be used in Pakistani colleges' entrepreneurial education (EE). The findings of this study shed light on the positive effects of this integration on students' attitudes toward sustainable entrepreneurship (ATSE) and, subsequently, their entrepreneurial intentions. The observed phenomenon exemplifies a prevailing pattern wherein youthful entrepreneurs in emerging economies harness the power of social media platforms to establish and grow their enterprises, effectively circumventing conventional obstacles associated with market entry.

The present study aims to delve into social media's moderating and mediating effects in the context of the relationship between ATSE (Academic Task Self-Efficacy) and SEIs (Student Engagement Indicators). Specifically, we examine how social media may influence or moderate this relationship. This study's findings indicate a positive correlation between increased engagement with social media and strengthening the relationship in question. This suggests that social media plays a significant role within the entrepreneurial ecosystem. This perspective follows the overarching perspective of the fourth industrial revolution, wherein digital platforms such as social media fundamentally alter the dynamics of markets and create new avenues for entrepreneurial pursuits.

The research paper titled "Role of Social Media and E-Commerce for Graduates' Entrepreneurial Intention in a Developing Country: The Influence of Social Media and E-Commerce Adoption (SMEA)" presents a comprehensive analysis of the impact of social media and e-commerce adoption on entrepreneurial intentions of graduates in a developing country. The study offers valuable insights into the practical implications of these factors in shaping entrepreneurial aspirations within the specific context of Malaysia and Pakistan (Shi et al., 2022). The present analysis showcases case studies from Malaysia, which effectively illustrate the noteworthy impact of social media in generating fresh business prospects and cultivating a conducive atmosphere for entrepreneurial endeavors among recent graduates.

In the study titled "The Examination of Factors Influencing Saudi Small Businesses' Social Media Adoption by Using UTAUT Model," the researchers delve into the impact of social media adoption on small businesses, with a specific emphasis on those operated by student entrepreneurs (Humaid & Ibrahim, 2019). The present study highlights the considerable potential of social media platforms in terms of their cost-effectiveness and efficacy in reaching specific target markets and fostering brand awareness, particularly for aspiring entrepreneurs in their early stages of development.

The implications and future directions of the present study are paramount in advancing our understanding of the subject matter. The findings of this research shed light on various aspects that warrant further investigation and exploration. Firstly, the implications of educational integration pertain to integrating social media platforms into entrepreneurial education. This integration can significantly augment students' entrepreneurial intentions and capabilities. In order to adequately prepare students for the demands of the digital age, educational institutions must incorporate social media strategies into their curricula.

In light of the imperative of educational integration, it is crucial to acknowledge the necessity for policy and support mechanisms that duly acknowledge the inherent potential of social media platforms in cultivating entrepreneurial endeavors. This is particularly pertinent in the context of developing nations. It is imperative that governments and educational institutions actively promote and support the development of social media literacy and utilization among individuals with entrepreneurial aspirations. By doing so, they can foster an environment conducive to entrepreneurship's growth and success.(Hossain et al., 2020)

In addition, it is recommended that future investigations prioritize implementing longitudinal studies to ascertain how students' involvement with social media platforms manifests in tangible entrepreneurial undertakings and their subsequent achievements. The investigation of the long-term effects of social media on entrepreneurship would yield significant insights of great value. In order to achieve a thorough comprehension of the impact of social media on entrepreneurship, it is imperative to incorporate a wide array of demographic variables and geographic locations in forthcoming research endeavors. This proposed methodology aims to elucidate the impact of social media on entrepreneurial activities within diverse settings and across heterogeneous demographic cohorts.

The phenomenon of social media entrepreneurship has emerged as a dynamic and influential avenue for enhancing business prospects, particularly in developing countries. The significance of its integration with entrepreneurial education and its role in moderating and mediating entrepreneurial intentions highlights its importance within the present and future business environment. The case studies conducted in Pakistan and Malaysia provide valuable insights into the phenomenon under investigation, shedding light on the importance of educational integration and supportive policies in effectively leveraging the vast potential of social media for entrepreneurial purposes.

Benefits of Social Media Entrepreneurship for Businesses

In the digital world we live in now, social media has become an essential tool for companies of all kinds. A phenomenon, social media entrepreneurship has fundamentally altered how businesses function and interact with their clientele. Social media entrepreneurship offers many benefits, enabling businesses to connect with their target audience, enhance brand visibility, and implement cost-effective marketing strategies. This article delves into the key advantages of social media entrepreneurship, exploring how businesses can leverage these platforms to achieve their goals and gain a competitive edge.

Increased Brand Visibility and Awareness

Social media entrepreneurship is vital to global business. This method boosts brand presence and audience awareness, among other benefits. According to Statista, 55% of worldwide industry professionals consider increased exposure the most significant benefit of using social media for marketing. The first issue is the necessity of education research. Research matters. Recent data shows that marketers worldwide use Facebook, Instagram, and LinkedIn.

Research by researchers and experts shows that increased brand visibility and awareness can seriously affect firms. Increased visibility boosts website traffic, lead creation, and client loyalty. First, brand presence can boost website visitors—online traffic increases when a brand is well-known among its target demographic. Brand presence has boosted interest and curiosity, resulting in this traffic. So, businesses may expect more website visitors, which can lead to more. (Benefits of Social Media Marketing Worldwide 2023 | Statista, 2023)

Research shows that increasing brand presence and awareness can benefit firms. One result is increased brand platform traffic. Traffic increased due to brand recognition and familiarity among potential customers. Improved brand exposure increases the possibility of attracting and engaging potential customers interested in the brand's offerings, which can lead to lead generation. Increased brand recognition and exposure boost fan loyalty. Strong brand identification and continuous value delivery build customer loyalty. Overall, investing in brand exposure and awareness methods can benefit SCORE. It was found that 77% of small businesses use social media to boost brand recognition, expedite customer service, and double revenue. (Peek, 2023)

Recently, social media marketing has become popular worldwide. This study examines the global acceptance and use of social media for marketing. Current trends and statistics are examined in this study.

Influencer marketing has grown in efficacy due to clients' increased demand for informed, authentic, honest, and transparent advertising.

Social media entrepreneurship has many benefits, but marketing initiatives require an intentional approach. Passive and active approaches are considered. The former strategy uses user-generated material to enhance communication between existing and future clients. This method uses genuine encounters to create organic advertising. However, the active method requires intentionally using tactics and organizations committed to marketing campaign planning and implementation. This investigation begins with defining the question or goal.

Enhanced Customer Engagement and Interaction

Social media entrepreneurship is vital to global business. This technology boosts customer engagement and interaction, among other benefits. Springer studied social media client involvement and its drivers. This study found that contentment, good emotions, and trust affect consumer engagement. The study found no substantial effect of commitment on social media customer engagement. The provided graph illustrates the distribution of medium and large businesses based on the proportion of their total marketing budget allocated to social media platforms such as Twitter, Instagram, Facebook, Pinterest, and LinkedIn. The objective behind this allocation is to foster increased customer engagement.

Figure 9.

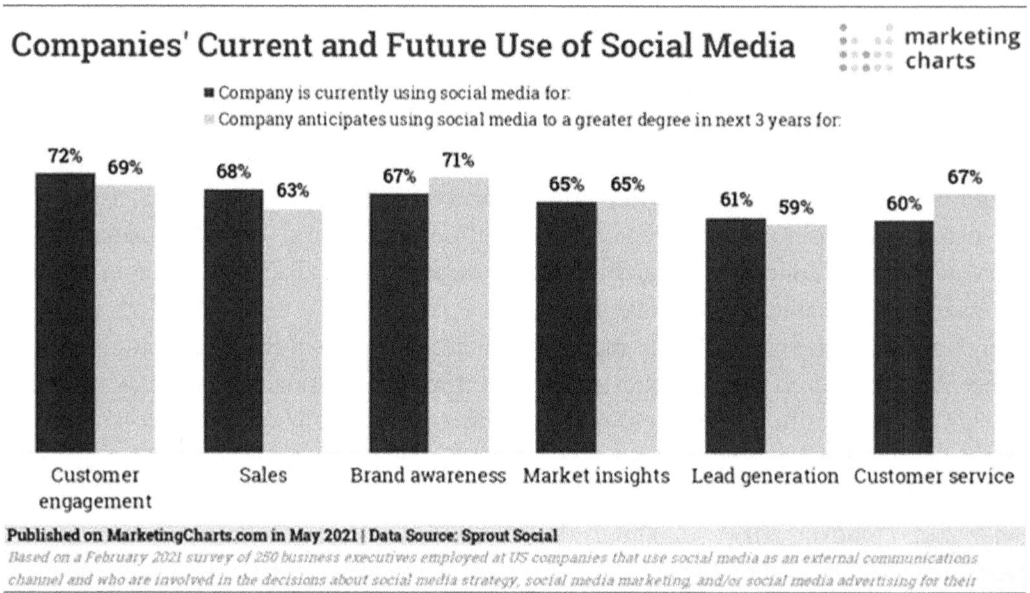

The provided graph illustrates the distribution of medium and large businesses based on the proportion of their total marketing budget allocated to social media platforms such as Twitter, Instagram, Facebook, Pinterest, and LinkedIn. The objective behind this allocation is to foster increased customer engagement.

According to a recent report, 80% of firms use social media to communicate with customers. Additionally, 72% of consumers are more likely to trust a firm that engages with them on social media. The social media business has several benefits. First, it helps businesses build brand awareness and familiarity among their target audience. Entrepreneurs may promote their goods and services on social media, gaining clients. Second, social media entrepreneurship generates leads and sales. Effective social media marketing may help businesses contact more clients and turn them into buyers. This may boost company growth and profitability.

Additionally, social media networks are helpful for customer support. Entrepreneurs can quickly respond to consumer queries, complaints, and difficulties, increasing customer satisfaction and loyalty. Direct and engaging connection with consumers improves brand image and develops the entrepreneur-customer relationship. Social media entrepreneurship also helps get client feedback. Social networking lets entrepreneurs obtain client feedback and recommendations. Customer input may improve goods and services, boost corporate development, and improve customer experiences. Social media entrepreneurs may also do market research. Businesses may learn about customer preferences, trends, and competition by monitoring and analyzing social media interactions. (Stelzner, 2023). This data may help businesses make intelligent decisions and remain ahead.

Many businesses nowadays have successfully used social media to communicate with their customers. These examples demonstrate social media's consumer engagement success.

Overall, social media entrepreneurship may help firms achieve their goals. Social media allows companies to actively communicate with their customers, building strong and lasting relationships. This involvement builds trust and loyalty with consumers and gives organizations vital information into their preferences, wants, and expectations. Businesses may use this information to make educated choices and personalize their goods and services to their target audience. This improved awareness of client preferences may boost customer happiness, brand loyalty, and company success.

Cost-Effective Marketing Strategies

Social media entrepreneurship is vital to global business. This technique offers several benefits, including cost-effective marketing tactics. According to Forbes, social media marketing is a cost-effective way for small companies and startups to spread information. This strategy might reach millions, boosting their message.

Social media marketing budgets are of interest. This research examines how social media marketing strategies allocate funds. The goal is to find the best budget allocation method to maximize. Numerous experts have shown that social media marketing is an excellent and cost-effective way for firms to reach a large and diversified audience. Social media platforms allow firms to market their goods and services, spread information, and build brand recognition while reducing costs. This strategy has been effective because it lets companies harness social media's massive user base to increase their reach and influence. Thus, social media marketing is essential. Adobe found that social media marketing may boost a company's brand, internet traffic, and revenue thrice. Social media marketing methods increase exposure and reach, which is their main benefit. Additionally, website traffic and lead generation increase. Statista found that 43% of marketers prioritize social media. The report shows that 63% of marketers are B2C, and 37% are B2B. (The Executive Headlines - Top Business Magazine & News Headlines Sources, n.d.).

These statistics show marketing industry duties and market sectors. As of January 2023, the graph below shows the main benefits of worldwide social media marketing. This study examines social media marketing's main advantages. Social media marketing promotes goods, services, and brands on social media. Its ability to reach a vast and diversified audience has made this kind of marketing successful in recent years.

In conclusion, social media entrepreneurship is vital to global business. This phenomenon has several benefits, including cost-effective marketing. Social media marketing is a cost-effective way for companies to reach a large audience, increase brand recognition, drive website traffic, and improve sales. Social media marketing has two major approaches: passive and active. Experienced and fresh professionals agree that the active approach requires particular methods or teams to build and execute practical marketing initiatives.

Access to Targeted Audience and Market Segmentation

Social media entrepreneurship has become a vital element in the global economic environment. This instrument offers several benefits, including the capacity to target a particular audience and efficiently segment the market into various groups. A research done by Hootsuite revealed that social media platforms provide companies with the means to target specific demographics and interests precisely, streamlining the process of reaching the intended audience.

Organizations dedicate a minimum of 11% of their total marketing expenditure on social media sites like Twitter, Instagram, Facebook, Pinterest, and LinkedIn to promote more customer involvement. (Troise et al., 2021) The subject of concern is the distribution of financial resources to promote products or services via social media platforms. This field of research examines explicitly the allocation of financial resources to enhance the promotion of businesses or services across different social media platforms. The goal is to ascertain the optimal and streamlined method for allocating resources. Social media platforms allow companies to target specific demographics and interests precisely, making it easier to reach the right audience.

Forbes, a reliable source, suggests that social media marketing may be a cost-effective approach for small firms and startups to distribute information about their brand effectively. This strategy has the capacity to reach a significant audience, perhaps up to millions, thereby enhancing the influence of their message. According to the statistics presented by Statista, a substantial percentage of marketers, precisely 43%, consider social media to be their main area of concentration. Furthermore, the report indicates that 63% of marketers are active in business-to-consumer (B2C) marketing operations, while the remaining 37% are engaged in business-to-business (B2B) marketing undertakings. (McLachlan, 2023)

These data provide insight into the allocation of duties and market divisions within the marketing field. The graph below depicts the key benefits of using social media for worldwide marketing efforts, especially as of January 2023.

The current epoch is seeing a notable transformation in the marketing domain, with social media emerging as a potent instrument for firms to establish connections with their intended audience. The

Figure 10.

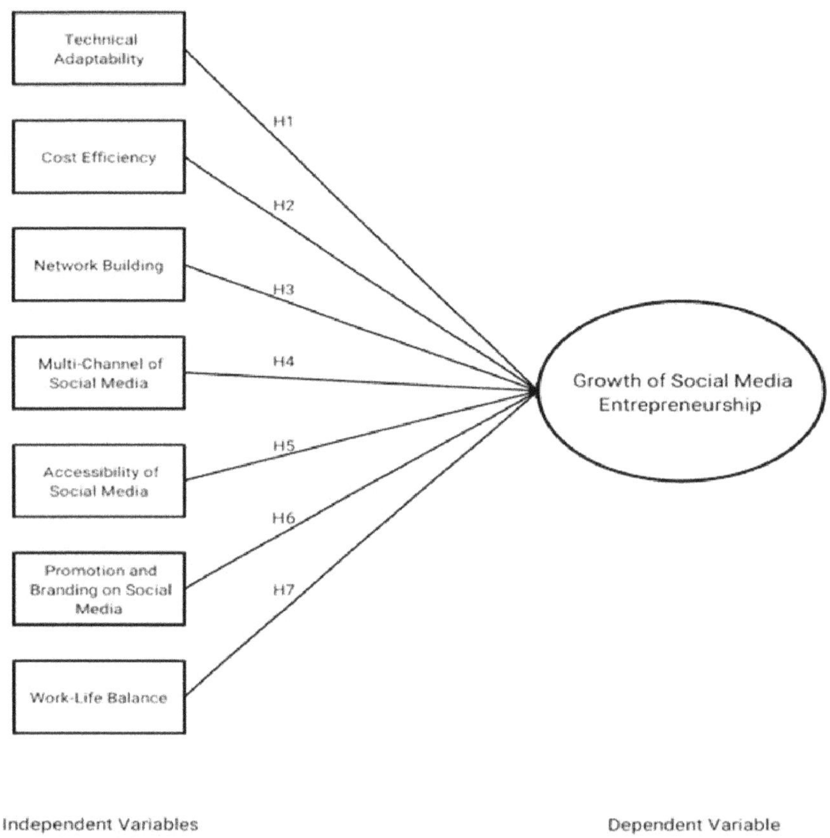

popularity of social media marketing has surged owing to its many advantages, which have transformed the methods organizations use to advertise their goods and services.

Ultimately, it is evident that social media entrepreneurship has become an essential element in the worldwide commercial environment. This phenomenon has resulted in several benefits, including the capacity to effectively contact and interact with particular target groups and the chance to adopt efficient market segmentation strategies. Social media platforms enable companies to target specific demographics and interests precisely, therefore streamlining the process of reaching the intended audience successfully. Social media marketing has become hugely beneficial for small companies and startups to distribute information about their brand effectively. This strategy provides a cost-efficient method to quickly reach a large audience, possibly millions of people, enhancing the influence of their message.

Challenges and Consideration

Social media is essential for businesses and organizations because it has many benefits. (Briones et al., 2011), but it also comes with several challenges and considerations:

First of all, concerns about privacy and data protection are big problems for people who want to start their own social media business. Cyberattackers often go after social media sites, which can lead to information breaches and the release of private user information. It can be hard to keep up with privacy rules that are constantly changing worldwide, like GDPR and CCPA, which means that user data needs to be handled carefully. Then, worries about misuse of information or poor handling can hurt trust between enterprises and their customers, which can hurt the brand's image. Also, ads, analytics, or other features run on outside applications or platforms could open up more security holes. They use strong data security measures like encryption and secure storage methods to keep user information safe. Ensure data usage rules are clear, get user permission, and provide straightforward ways to opt in or out. Always know the latest privacy rules worldwide and follow them precisely to avoid legal trouble. Do security audits and reviews regularly to find and fix holes immediately. To create trust and comfort customers about their privacy, teach customers about the steps that are in place to protect their data. Social media sites have evolved how people talk to each other and work together and have also created new ways to network (de Reuver et al., 2018). Social media has been shown to be suitable for entrepreneurs (Nah & Saxton, 2013). Taking care of data security and privacy issues is essential for social media businesses to grow in a way that does not hurt user trust or break the rules as they change.

Secondly, algorithm changes and how platforms work pose big problems and things to consider for social media entrepreneurs. Social media sites often change formulas, affecting how visible, reachable, and engaging content is. When algorithms change, organic reach often goes down. This makes it difficult for businesses to reach their audience without spending money on ads. Then, businesses must always change their approach to content to keep up with how platform analytics and user tastes change. It can take a lot of time and resources to keep up with changes to algorithms and make changes to tactics. Spreading business across several platforms can lessen the effect of algorithm changes on the whole business. People have said that social media is beneficial for business people because it helps them in many ways (Olanrewaju et al., 2020). It is essential to make flexible content strategies that can quickly change to fit changes in algorithms and user trends. Paid ads can help compensate for the loss of organic reach caused by algorithm changes. Also, getting community members to connect and engage with each other can help the content get noticed even when algorithms change. Monitoring analytics and platform data regularly is important to understand how algorithm changes affect strategies and make changes as needed. Lastly, to keep up with the rapid development of social media systems and grow business in the long term, businesses need to handle these challenges and think ahead of time.

Thirdly, managing your online image and talking to people during a crisis is essential to being a social media entrepreneur. They also come with a particular set of difficulties and considerations. Because social media allows real-time feedback, responding quickly and effectively to negative comments or problems can take time. Crisis or harmful content may quickly go viral, which could hurt the brand's image if it needs to be dealt with quickly and correctly. Because social media is always active, it must be constantly watched to quickly deal with image crises or threats. Different sites have different audiences and ways of working, so crisis communication plans need to be different for each. Few barriers exist in businesses using it for content marketing and sharing stories (Pulizzi, 2012). Brands of all sizes can communicate with customers on social media these days (Pulizzi, 2012). Make sure to have clear rules and procedures for handling emergencies or negative feedback so that users can respond quickly and consistently. Keep an eye on company mentions, comments, and sentiments on social media regularly to spot problems before they get worse. Anyone who gets negative feedback or a crisis should respond quickly and honestly, recognizing the problem and giving solutions or more information. Teach team members how to communicate in a crisis and what to do in different situations so they can do a good job when things get tough. Build a strong, favorable online profile through regular engagement and good content. This can help you handle problems when they come up. Also, look back at past crises or cases of negative feedback to learn how to handle crises better in the future. Managing online reputation and handling a problem on social media is very important for keeping a good brand image and building trust with the audience, which is very important for lasting achievement in global business.

To make use of social media, a successful entrepreneur needs to deal with these issues and challenges while also taking advantage of the vast market reach and growth potential on a global level.

Emerging Technologies in Social Media Entrepreneurship

- Blockchain for social media transactions: Blockchain technology is an advanced technology mechanism. Through this chain, very transparent data and information are shared. It is like a lodger where most corpocracy's transactions are recorded. It automatically stores data and keeps a record of every financial transaction (Hayes, 2023). For example, Brave browser, using this browser it utilizes the micropayment of viewers who choose to view ads. It creates more clear financial transactions with the users and content creators. It is using blockchain technology for social media transactions.
- Artificial intelligence and chatbot: Chatbots in social media are generated by AI, where customers can frequently ask questions and get replies quickly. They can experience real-time communication. Social media platforms like Facebook and Instagram largely use these platforms to provide automated customer support, virtual assistance, online personalization, and critical insights into customers by recording the data they accumulate. It saves time for both customers and entrepreneurs (Talkative, 2022). For example, ManyChat is a platform that uses this AI in Facebook Messenger to increase customer engagement.
- User-generated content: Social media entrepreneurs use user-generated content to increase engagement and acquisitions. User-generated content, or UGC, influences customers to make videos, audio, visuals, or photos and share them on social media. When any customer posts any video or image regarding a business page, it works like a review for the potential customers. According

Figure 11. UGC ratios

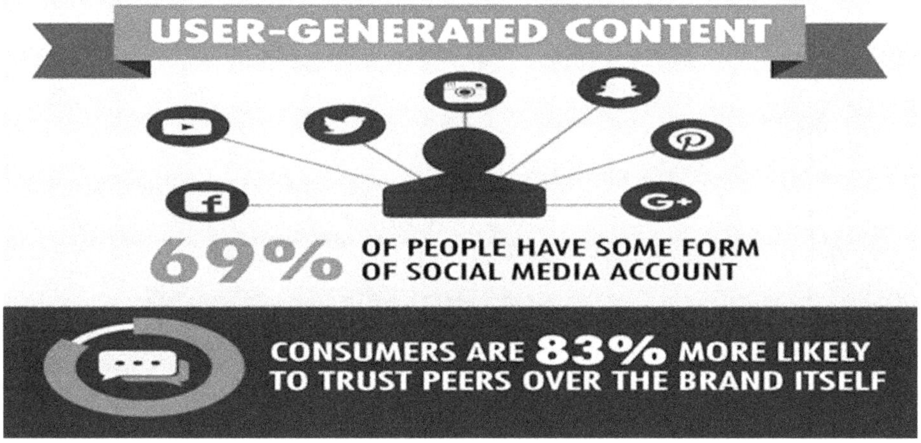

to statistics, 45% of customers purchase a product by watching its reviews on social media. For example, YouTube shorts, Facebook or Instagram shorts, etc, are the most common forms of UGC. Other forms of UGC include social posts, reviews, blogs, referrals, conferences, webinars, etc.

Prediction for the Role of Social Media in Business Growth

Social media will play a role and prove its worth to continue the pace of business growth. From promoting to engaging customers, it helps create a long-term, belong-term pact.

- Audience engagement and brand building: Posting one video on social media gives access to all the global audience to know about the product. Social media has become a suitable platform for grabbing the target audience's attention. Many companies have become very successful using social media marketing. It builds a strong brand identity around the globe. For example, Nike runs over 300 social media platforms. We will find different social media platforms like Nike football, Nike cricket, Nike swim, etc. Their social media strategy helped them engage with the target audience (Deren, 2023).
- Influencer marketing evolution: Nowadays, as a generation, we quickly become influenced by known or famous figures. Influencing marketing has become so famous that it is expected to have an industry value of $21.1 billion in 2023. Also, globally, 83% of firms now believe in the effectiveness of influencer marketing. Now, firms are also creating a budget for influencing marketing. 67% of the firms are adapting social media and creating budgeting for influencing marketing. For example, Fashion Nova is a clothing brand famous for influencing marketing (Geyser, 2024).
- Data-driven decision: Social media options like Facebook insights and Twitter analytics provide entrepreneurs with information about customer engagement. It helps gather information about customers' preferences, trends, buying patterns, acquisition and engagement rates, etc. This helps entrepreneurs to gather more information and make strategies accordingly.

Figure 12. Crowdfunding phases

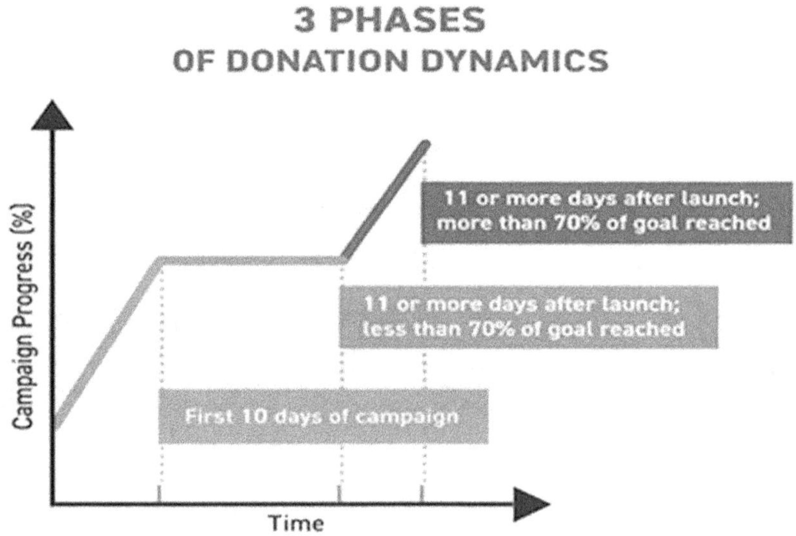

Potential innovations and transformation in entrepreneurial strategies.

We all know what Airbnb has done through social media platforms. It has developed different business models and strategies to connect with more stakeholders. Also, platforms like Kickstarter and Indiegogo are famous for crowdsourcing. It is an entirely new addition to social media. Crowdfunding is the funding system where entrepreneurs collect funds from different donors. Social media platforms are very famous for this. Crowdfunding can occur through profit or non-profit motives. Some donors may demand company shares or ownership, or some may donate with a nonprofit demand (Magelssen, 2022). Additionally, entrepreneurs can work virtually in remote areas via Zoom, Slack, Asana, etc.

CONCLUSION

In conclusion, the interdependent connection between social media and entrepreneurship serves as a crucial catalyst in transforming the structure of contemporary companies. The progression of social media platforms from basic networking spaces to versatile worldwide hubs has transformed the entrepreneurial landscape, providing enterprises with unprecedented prospects for expansion, creativity, and market entry. From a historical perspective, it is clear that social media entrepreneurship has made access to audiences and markets more democratic. This has allowed enterprises of different sizes to build their online presence and interact with global audiences (Aboulilah et al., 2022; Hossain et al., 2023). The deliberate incorporation of social media has provided businesses with opportunities to enhance brand exposure, cultivate genuine customer engagements, and implement economic marketing tactics, as demonstrated by successful initiatives like the "Dove Real Beauty" campaign and the emergence of influencer marketing. Nevertheless, within the realm of possibilities, there are obstacles to overcome, such as privacy-related issues, algorithm changes, and the urgent requirement for skillful crisis communication. In the future, we can expect a landscape shaped by advanced technologies such as AI-driven personalization, augmented reality, and data analytics. These technologies will provide new opportunities for entrepreneurial initiatives. As businesses negotiate this rapidly changing landscape, it is confident that social media entrepreneurship will remain a crucial force, driving business growth, innovation, and ongoing relevance in the always-evolving digital realm.

REFERENCES

Aboulilah, H. M. A. E., Hossain, S. F. A., Vuong, B. N., & Jebril, T. (2022). Exploring the Relationship between WeChat Usage and E-purchase Intention During the COVID-19 Pandemic Among University Students in China. *SAGE Open*, *12*(4). doi:10.1177/21582440221139447 PMID:36466966

Briones, R. L., Kuch, B., Liu, B. F., & Jin, Y. (2011). Keeping up with the digital age: How the American Red Cross uses social media to build relationships. *Public Relations Review*, *37*(1), 37–43. doi:10.1016/j.pubrev.2010.12.006

Chatbots, S. M. (2023, September 15). How to Automate Your Messaging Channels. *Talkative*. https://gettalkative.com/info/social-media-chatbots#1

Cristhyan. (1970, September 9). *The History of Social Media Marketing: The Past & Future of a Business Revolution*. Digital Marketing Agency. https://codedesign.org/en/history-social-media-marketing-past-future-business-revolution

De Reuver, M., Sørensen, C., & Basole, R. C. (2018). The digital platform: A research agenda. *Journal of Information Technology*, *33*(2), 124–135. doi:10.1057/s41265-016-0033-3

Dereń, K., & Dereń, K. (2023, July 3). *How Effective is Nike's Social Media Strategy? | Brand24*. Brand24 Blog. https://brand24.com/blog/nike-social-media-strategy/

El-Gohary, H., Sultan, F., Alam, S., Abbas, M., & Muhammad, S. (2023). Shaping Sustainable Entrepreneurial Intentions among Business Graduates in Developing Countries through Social Media Adoption: A Moderating-Mediated Mechanism in Pakistan. *Sustainability (Basel)*, *15*(3), 2489. doi:10.3390/su15032489

Emmanuel, C. P., Qin, S., Hossain, S. F. A., & Hussain, K. (2022). Factors influencing social-media-based entrepreneurship prospect among female students in China. *Heliyon*, *8*(12), e12041. doi:10.1016/j.heliyon.2022.e12041 PMID:36483305

Geyser, W. (2024, January 30). *What is Influencer Marketing? – The Ultimate Guide for 2024*. Influencer Marketing Hub, Retrieved from https://influencermarketinghub.com/influencer-marketing/

Hayes, A. (2023, April 23). *Blockchain Facts: What is it, how does it work, and how can it be used*? Investopedia. https://www.investopedia.com/terms/b/blockchain.asp

Hossain, S. F. A., Nurunnabi, M., Hussain, K., & Shan, X. (2020). Smartphone-based m-shopping behavior and innovative entrepreneurial tendency among women in emerging Asia. *International Journal of Gender and Entrepreneurship*, *12*(2), 173–189. doi:10.1108/IJGE-03-2019-0054

Hossain, S. F. A., Nurunnabi, M., Hussain, K., & Xu, S. (2020, February 22). Smartphone-based m-shopping behavior and innovative entrepreneurial tendency among women in emerging Asia. *International Journal of Gender and Entrepreneurship, 12*(2), 173–189. Advance online publication. doi:10.1108/IJGE-03-2019-0054

Hossain, S. F. A., Shan, X., Musa, M., & Rahman, P. (2023). Social media and increased venture creation tendency with innovative ideas: the case of female students in Asia. In *Research Anthology on Applying Social Networking Strategies to Classrooms and Libraries* (pp. 1716–1731). IGI Global.

Hossain, S. F. A., Shan, X., Nurunnabi, M., Tushar, H., Mohsin, A. K. M., & Ahsan, F. T. (2021). Opportunities and challenges of m-learning during the COVID-19 pandemic: A mixed methodology approach. *E-Collaboration Technologies and Strategies for Competitive Advantage Amid Challenging Times*, 210-227.

Humaid, A. B., & Ibrahim, Y. M. (2019). The examination of factors influencing Saudi small businesses' social media adoption by using the UTAUT model. *International Journal of Business Administration, 10*(2), 96. doi:10.5430/ijba.v10n2p96

Lile, S. (2023, August 4). *Complete history of social media: Then and now*. Small Business Trends. https://smallbiztrends.com/2023/08/history-of-social-media.html

Madams. (2023, October 30). *The evolution of social media: How did it begin, and where could it go next?* Maryville University Online. https://online.maryville.edu/blog/evolution-social-media/#history

Myers, D. (2023, January 16). 4 Great Examples of User-Generated Content (UGC). *Digital Marketing Institute*. https://digitalmarketinginstitute.com/blog/how-to-use-user-generated-content-ugc-with-4-great-examples

Nah, S., & Saxton, G. D. (2013). Modeling the adoption and use of social media by nonprofit organizations. *New Media & Society, 15*(2), 294–313. doi:10.1177/1461444812452411

Olanrewaju, A. T., Hossain, M. A., Whiteside, N., & Mercieca, P. (2020). *Social media and entrepreneurship research: A literature review. International Journal of Information Management*. https://www.researchgate.net/publication/338970287_Social_media_and_entrepreneurship_research_A_literature_review

Ortiz-Ospina, E., & Roser, M. (2023, November 23). *The rise of Social Media*. Our World in Data. https://ourworldindata.org/rise-of-social-media

Pulizzi, J. (2012). The rise of storytelling as the new marketing. *Publishing Research Quarterly, 28*(2), 116–123. doi:10.1007/s12109-012-9264-5

Shi, J., Nyedu, D. S. K., Huang, L., & Lovia, B. S. (2022). Graduates' Entrepreneurial Intention in a Developing Country: The Influence of Social Media and E-commerce Adoption (SMEA) and its Antecedents. *Information Development*. Advance online publication. doi:10.1177/02666669211073457

Study explores social media's influence on crowdfunding campaigns. (n.d.). News Center. https://news.utdallas.edu/business-management/social-media-crowdfunding-2022/

Team, A. (2023, January 31). *The Impact of Social Media on Entrepreneurship*. AIContentfy. Retrieved from https://aicontentfy.com/en/blog/impact-of-social-media-on-entrepreneurship

The history of social media and its impact on business - researchgate. (n.d.). https://www.researchgate.net/publication/303216233_The_history_of_social_media_and_its_impact_on_business

Vương, B. N., Tushar, H., & Hossain, S. F. A. (2022, June 16). The effect of social support on job performance through organizational commitment and innovative work behavior: Does innovative climate matter? *Asia-Pacific Journal of Business Administration*. Advance online publication. doi:10.1108/APJBA-06-2021-0256

Compilation of References

A Quickbite Trendsetter - The Prestige Magazine. (2023, January 25). https://theprestige.global/a-quickbite-trendsetter

Aaker, D. A. (1991). *Managing Brand Equity: Capitalizing on the value of a brand name*. The Free Press.

Abbas, J. (2020). Impact of total quality management on corporate green performance through the mediating role of corporate social responsibility. *Journal of Cleaner Production*, *242*, 118458. doi:10.1016/j.jclepro.2019.118458

Abdullah, M. (2020, June 12). Bangladesh globally ranks 10th on daily increase in Covid-19 cases. *Dhaka Tribune*. Retrieved from https://www.dhakatribune.com/bangladesh/2020/06/12/bangladesh-ranks-10th-globallyon-daily-increase-in-covid-19-cases

Aboulilah, H. M. E., Hossain, S. F. A., Vương, B. N., & Jebril, T. (2022). Exploring the Relationship between WeChat Usage and E-purchase Intention During the COVID-19 Pandemic Among University Students in China. *SAGE Open*, *12*(4). doi:10.1177/21582440221139447 PMID:36466966

Acharya, A., Mukherjee, S., Bhattacharjee, A. K., Datta, D., & Deyasi, A. (2022). COVID-19: will it be a game changer in higher education in India? *Data Science for COVID-19*, *2*(1), 611-629. doi:10.1016/B978-0-323-90769-9.00034-7

Adams, D. M., Nelson, R. E., & Todd, P. (1992). Perceived usefulness, ease of use, and usage of information technology: A replication. *Management Information Systems Quarterly*, *16*(2), 227. doi:10.2307/249577

Adhi, R., & Yunus, U. (2021). The Meaning of Coffee for Barista in Speciality Coffee Shop in Indonesia. *Journal of Creative Communications*, *17*(1), 097325862110058. doi:10.1177/09732586211005880

Adi, S., Heripracoyo, S., & Simamora, B. H. (2021). Potential used of social media/mobile phone to support promotion and marketing in the rural tourism destination. *Proc Int Conf Ind Eng Oper Manag*, 3370-3379. 10.46254/AN11.20210609

Ads, R. R. (2023, July 22). *Waffle Bae Best Neon Sign Company in Bangladesh*. Best Advertising Agency in Bangladesh. https://redroseadbd.com/best-neon-sign-company-in-bangladesh/

Agrawal, A., Gans, J., & Goldfarb, A. (2020). How to win with machine learning. *Harvard Business Review*.

Agusiady, R., Saepudin, D., & Aripin, Z. (2024). The Influence of Social Media Communication on Consumer Perceptions of Brands and Purchase Intentions in the Pandemic and Post-Pandemic Era: An Analytical Study. *Journal of Economics, Accounting, Business, Management, Engineering and Society*, *2*(1), 16–30.

Ahmed, N., Monzur, H., & Iqbal, H. (2017). Women Entrepreneurs in SMEs: Bangladesh Perspective. *Journal of Business and Entrepreneurship*, *15*(3), 112–125.

Alhakimi, W., & Albashiri, S. (2023). *Social media adoption by women entrepreneurial small businesses*. Asia Pacific Journal of Innovation and Entrepreneurship. doi:10.1108/APJIE-03-2023-0060

Ali, A. (2022). Battle of Deep Fakes: Artificial Intelligence Set to Become a Major Threat to the Individual and National Security. *2022 International Conference on Cyber Resilience (ICCR)*, 1–5. 10.1109/ICCR56254.2022.9995821

Ali, H., & Omar, M. A. A. (2022). The effects of influencer marketing on overall brand equity through brand awareness and customer brand engagement. *International Journal of Data and Network Science*, *6*(6), 651–658. doi:10.5267/j.ijdns.2022.4.007

Allam, Z., & Allam, Z. (2020). Digital urban networks and social media. *Cities and the digital revolution: Aligning technology and humanity*, 61-83.

AlWahashi & Medjedel. (2022). Impact of CSR on brand equity in the wake of Covid-19 Pandemic: Special Reference To The STC Saudi Arabia. *International Journal of Management & IT A Refereed Research, 13*(2), 15-27. Available at: https://www.globusjournal.com/wp-content/uploads/2022/05/GMIT-132-JJ22-Abdulwahab- Saleh-AlWahashi.pdf

Amatulli, C., De Angelis, M., Sestino, A., & Guido, G. (2021). Omnichannel shopping experiences for fast fashion and luxury brands: An exploratory study. In *Developing Successful Global Strategies for Marketing Luxury Brands* (pp. 22–43). IGI Global. doi:10.4018/978-1-7998-5882-9.ch002

Ameen, N. A., & Willis, R. (2016). The use of mobile phones to support women's entrepreneurship in the Arab countries. *International Journal of Gender and Entrepreneurship*, *8*(4), 424–445. doi:10.1108/IJGE-10-2015-0037

Anastasya, Misjedi, Gunawan, Leo, & Tunjungsari. (2022). The Impact of Storytelling Marketing on Brand Equity and Purchase Decisions on Shopee During Pandemic Covid-19. Advances in Social Science, Education and Humanities Research, 4-21.

Anderson, J. (2020, January 13). *What is Your "Green Leadership Style"?* Retrieved from Planteria website: https://www.planteriagroup.com/blog/what-is-your-green-leadership-style/

Arora, A. K., & Srinivasan, R. (2020). Impact of pandemic COVID-19 on the teaching – learning process: A study of higher education teachers. *Prabandhan: Indian Journal of Management*, *13*(4), 1–13. doi:10.17010/pijom/2020/v13i4/151825

Ashraf, S. N., & Singh, A. K. (2022). Implications of appropriate technology and farm inputs in the agricultural sector of Gujarat: Empirical analysis based on primary data. *Agricultural Economics Research Review*, *35*(2), 59–77. doi:10.5958/0974-0279.2022.00031.3

Ashton, K. (2009). That 'internet of things' thing. *RFID Journal, 22*(7), 97-114.

Atamanchuk, Z. A. (2019). Digital transformations in international tourism as a factor of economic. *Strategic priorities of the transformation of the economy in conditions of digitalization: Materials of the International Scientific and Practical Conference, Zaporizhzhia.* Zaporizhia Polytechnic National University.

Azmi, F. M., Khan, H. N., & Azmi, A. M. (2022). The impact of virtual learning on students' educational behavior and pervasiveness of depression among university students due to the COVID-19 pandemic. *Globalization and Health*, *18*(70), 1–9. doi:10.1186/s12992-022-00863-z PMID:35836278

Babu, K. E. K. (2021). Artificial intelligence in Bangladesh, its applications in different sectors and relevant challenges for the government: An analysis. *International Journal of Public Law and Policy*, *7*(4), 319–333. doi:10.1504/IJPLAP.2021.118891

Bandura, A. (1999). A social cognitive theory of personality. In L. Pervin & O. John (Eds.), *Handbook of personality* (2nd ed., pp. 154–196). Guilford Publications.

Bangladesh - eCommerce. (n.d.). Retrieved from https://www.trade.gov/country-commercial-guides/bangladesh-ecommerce

Bangladesh's sweets businesses thriving with a market worth Tk20,000 crore. (2021, June 1). The Business Standard. https://www.tbsnews.net/supplement/bangladeshs-sweets-businesses-thriving-market-worth-tk20000-crore-254023

Bansal, M. (2023). Multidimensional impact of COVID-19 on the Indian education sector. *Management and Labour Studies*, *48*(2), 214–223. doi:10.1177/0258042X211069509

Bast, F. (2021). Perception of online learning among students from India set against the pandemic. *Frontiers in Education*, *6*(1), 1–8. doi:10.3389/feduc.2021.705013

Beghetto, R. A. (2023). A new horizon for possibility thinking: A conceptual case study of Human × AI collaboration. *Possibility Studies & Society*, *1*(3), 324–341. doi:10.1177/27538699231160136

Benoit-Moreau, F., & Parguel, B. (2011). Building brand equity with environmental communication: An empirical investigation in France. *EuroMed Journal of Business*, *6*(1), 100–116. doi:10.1108/14502191111130334

Berry, L. L. (2002). Relationship Marketing of Services Perspectives from 1983 and 2000. *Journal of Relationship Marketing*, *1*(1), 59–77. doi:10.1300/J366v01n01_05

Bessis, N., & Dobre, C. (Eds.). (2014). *Big data and internet of things: A roadmap for smart environments* (Vol. 546). Springer. doi:10.1007/978-3-319-05029-4

Bilgihan, Ö., Öztürk, Y., Okumus, F. & Surcu, A. (2019). Brand awareness, image, physical quality and employee behavior as building blocks of customer-based brand equity (CBBE): Consequences in the hotel context. *Journal of Hospitality and Tourism Management, 40*, 114–124. doi:10.1016/j.jhtm.2019.07.002

Blanco-Gonzalez-Tejero, C., & Cano-Marin, E. (2023). Empowerment of women's entrepreneurship in family business through Twitter. *Journal of Family Business Management*, *13*(3), 607–625. doi:10.1108/JFBM-04-2022-0050

Borovets, R., & Kit, Y. (2018). Advertising of the company's activities via the Internet. *Information, communication, society: Materials of the 7th International Scientific Conference ICS-2018*. Lviv: Publishing House of Lviv Polytechnic.

Boshmaf, H. (2023). Jordanian women entrepreneurs and the role of social media: The road to Empowerment. *Dirasat: Human and Social Sciences*, *50*(3), 139–152. doi:10.35516/hum.v50i3.5402

Boyd, C. (2010). *How Spotify Recommends Your New Favorite Artist*. Medium.

Boyko, V., Osadchiy, A., & Boyko, L. (2021). Social networks are a promising direction of business promotion in entrepreneurial activity. *KhNTU Bulletin, 2*(77), 178-185.

Brahem, M., & Boussema, S. (2023). Social media entrepreneurship as an opportunity for women: The case of Facebook-commerce. *International Journal of Entrepreneurship and Innovation*, *24*(3), 191–201. doi:10.1177/14657503211066010

Brehm, J. W. (1966). *A theory of psychological reactance*. Academic Press.

Brei, V. A. (2020). Machine learning in marketing: Overview, learning strategies, applications, and future developments. *Foundations and Trends in Marketing*, *14*(3), 173–236. doi:10.1561/1700000065

Briones, R. L., Kuch, B., Liu, B. F., & Jin, Y. (2011). Keeping up with the digital age: How the American Red Cross uses social media to build relationships. *Public Relations Review*, *37*(1), 37–43. doi:10.1016/j.pubrev.2010.12.006

Bruun, E. P. G., & Duka, A. (2018). Artificial intelligence, jobs and the future of work: Racing with the machines. *Basic Income Studies*, *13*(2). Advance online publication. doi:10.1515/bis-2018-0018

Buljan, B., & Miočić, B. K. (2021, June). Youth Entrepreneurship in Rural Areas–Reflection on Croatia. *Proceedings of FEB Zagreb International Odyssey Conference on Economics and Business*, 3, 196-212.

Burt, S. (2000). The strategic role of retail brands in British grocery retailing. *European Journal of Marketing*, *34*(8), 875–890. doi:10.1108/03090560010331351

C. (2021). Effects of Facebook advertising on sustainable brand loyalty and growth: case of Thai start-up businesses. *Transnational Corporations Review*, 1-12. doi:10.1080/19186444.2021.1986340

Campbell, C., Sands, S., Ferraro, C., Tsao, H. Y., & Mavrommatis, A. (2020). From data to action: How marketers can leverage AI. *Business Horizons*, *63*(2), 227–243. doi:10.1016/j.bushor.2019.12.002

Carbonara, E., & Tagliaventi, M. R. (2023). *Smes in the digital era: Opportunities and challenges of the digital single market*. Edward Elgar Publishing. doi:10.4337/9781803921648

CDP gives Unilever triple "A" for sustainability leadership. (n.d.). Retrieved from Unilever website: https://www.unilever.com/news/news-search/2020/cdp-gives-unilever-triple-a-for-sustainability-le adership/

Cesaroni, F. M., Demartini, P., & Paoloni, P. (2017). Women in business and social media: Implications for female entrepreneurship in emerging countries. *African Journal of Business Management*, *11*(14), 316–326. doi:10.5897/AJBM2017.8281

Chahal, J., & Rani, N. (2022). Exploring the acceptance for e-learning among higher education students in India: Combining technology acceptance model with external variables. *Journal of Computing in Higher Education*, *34*(1), 844–867. doi:10.1007/s12528-022-09327-0 PMID:35668837

Chakraborty, U., & Biswal, S. K. (2023). Impact of social media participation on female entrepreneurs towards their digital entrepreneurship intention and psychological empowerment. *Journal of Research in Marketing and Entrepreneurship*. doi:10.1108/JRME-03-2021-0028

Chan, A., Suryadipura, D., & Novel, N. J. A. (2022). Brand Element: Exploring the Effect on City Branding. *International Journal of Professional Business Review*, *7*(4), e0750. doi:10.26668/businessreview/2022.v7i4.e750

Chang, R.-D., Zuo, J., Zhao, Z.-Y., Zillante, G., Gan, X.-L., & Soebarto, V. (2017). Evolving theories of sustainability and firms: History, future directions and implications for renewable energy research. *Renewable & Sustainable Energy Reviews*, *72*, 48–56. doi:10.1016/j.rser.2017.01.029

Chatbots, S. M. (2023, September 15). How to Automate Your Messaging Channels. *Talkative*. https://gettalkative.com/info/social-media-chatbots#1

Cheng, C. C., & Shiu, E. C. (2019). How to enhance SMEs customer involvement using social media: The role of Social CRM. *International Small Business Journal*, *37*(1), 22–42. doi:10.1177/0266242618774831

Chen, Y. S., & Chang, C. H. (2013). The determinants of green product development performance: Green dynamic capabilities, green transformational leadership, and green creativity. *Journal of Business Ethics*, *116*(1), 107–119. doi:10.1007/s10551-012-1452-x

Chouldechova, A. (2017). Fair prediction with disparate impact: A study of bias in recidivism prediction instruments. *Big Data*, *5*(2), 153–163. doi:10.1089/big.2016.0047 PMID:28632438

Chowdhury, A. R. (2023, June 5). More roads are not the answer to Bangladesh's traffic problem. *The Daily Star*. Retrieved from https://www.thedailystar.net

Chowdhury, J. (2023, August 28). Do our sweets have sweeter potential in the global market? *The Business Standard*. https://www.tbsnews.net/economy/do-our-sweets-have-sweeter-potential-global-market-689978

Chowdhury, M. H., & Chowdhury, M. H. (2021, October 5). *Extreme heat bakes 25 Dhaka neighbourhoods as climate warms up: study*. Retrieved from https://bdnews24.com/environment/extreme-heat-bakes-25-dhaka-neighbourhoods-as-climate-warms-up-study

Chowdhury, S., & Rabbani, G. (2013). Policies and institutional supports for women entrepreneurship development in Bangladesh: Achievements and challenges. *International Journal of Research in Business and Social Science, 2*(1), 31-39.

Çiçek, B. (2018). Social Media Entrepreneurship. *İçtimaiyat Sosyal Bilimler Dergisi, 2*(1), 10-17.

Corbo, L., Costa, S., & Dabi, M. (2022). The evolving role of artificial intelligence in marketing: A review and research agenda. *Journal of Business Research, 128*(March), 187–203.

Corrigan, H. B., Craciun, G., & Powell, A. M. (2014). Case study consumer analytics to make marketing decisions. *Marketing Education Review, 24*(2), 159–165. doi:10.2753/MER1052-8008240206

cosmetics design-europe.com. (n.d.). *Unilever's new pigment to help recycling of plastic packaging*. Retrieved from cosmeticsdesign-europe.com website: https://www.cosmeticsdesign-europe.com/Article/2019/05/29/Unilever-s-new-pigment-to-help-re cycling-of-plastic-packaging?utm_source=copyright&utm_medium=OnSite&utm_campaign=copyright

Creswell, J. W., & Creswell, J. D. (2017). *Research design: Qualitative, quantitative, and mixed methods approaches*. Sage publications.

Cristhyan. (1970, September 9). *The History of Social Media Marketing: The Past & Future of a Business Revolution*. Digital Marketing Agency. https://codedesign.org/en/history-social-media-marketing-past-future-business-revolution

Crossman, J. (2011). Environmental and spiritual leadership: Tracing the synergies from an organizational perspective. *Journal of Business Ethics, 103*(4), 553–565. doi:10.1007/s10551-011-0880-3

Csikszentmihalyi, M. (1990). *Flow*. Harper & Row.

Cuccurullo, C., Aria, M., & Sarto, F. (2016). Foundations and trends in performance management. A twenty-five years bibliometric analysis in business and public administration domains. *Scientometrics, 108*(2), 595–611. doi:10.1007/s11192-016-1948-8

Cyrine, B.-H., Mario, T., Troise, C., & Yablonsky, S. A. (2022). New technologies and entrepreneurship: Exploring entrepreneurial behavior in the digital transformation era. *International Journal of Entrepreneurial Behaviour & Research, 28*(5), 1129–1137. Advance online publication. doi:10.1108/IJEBR-08-2022-999

Da Silva, L., Soltovski, R., Pontes, J., Treinta, F. T., Leitão, P., Mosconi, E., Resende, L. M., & Yoshino, R. T. (2022). Human resources management 4.0: Literature review and trends. *Computers & Industrial Engineering, 168*, 108111. doi:10.1016/j.cie.2022.108111

Das, P. K. (2021). Impact of pandemic Covid-19 on higher education-Indian context. *Universal Journal of Business and Management, 1*(1), 13–21. doi:10.31586/ujbm.2021.010102

Datskevich, N. O. (2016). The dialectic of interaction between the social responsibility of entrepreneurship and the social capital of society. *Efficient Economy,* (7), 1-4.

Davenport, T. H., Dalle Mule, L., & Lucker, J. (2011). Know what your customers want before they do. *Harvard Business Review, 89*(12), 84–92.

Davenport, T. H., & Ronanki, R. (2018). Artificial intelligence for the real world. *Harvard Business Review, 96*(1), 108–116.

Davenport, T., Guha, A., Grewal, D., & Bressgott, T. (2020). How artificial intelligence will change the future of marketing. *Journal of the Academy of Marketing Science*, *48*(1), 24–42. doi:10.1007/s11747-019-00696-0

Davis, F. D. (1986). *A Technology Acceptance Model for Empirically Testing New End-User Information Systems: Theory and Results*. Sloan School of Management, Massachusetts Institute of Technology.

Dayal, S. (2023). Online education and its effects on teachers during COVID-19 – a case study from India. *PLoS One*, *18*(3), 1–15. doi:10.1371/journal.pone.0282287 PMID:36862704

de Cosmo, L. M., Piper, L., & Di Vittorio, A. (2021). The role of attitude toward chatbots and privacy concerns the relationship between attitude toward mobile advertising and behavioral intent to use chatbots. *Italian Journal of Marketing*, *1*(1-2), 83–102. doi:10.1007/s43039-021-00020-1

De Mauro, A., Greco, M., & Grimaldi, M. (2015, February). What is big data? A consensual definition and a review of key research topics. In AIP conference proceedings (Vol. 1644, No. 1, pp. 97–104). American Institute of Physics.

De Mauro, A., Greco, M., Grimaldi, M., & Ritala, P. (2018). Human resources for Big Data professions: A systematic classification of job roles and required skill sets. *Information Processing & Management*, *54*(5), 807–817. doi:10.1016/j.ipm.2017.05.004

De Mauro, A., Sestino, A., & Bacconi, A. (2022). Machine learning and artificial intelligence use in marketing: A general taxonomy. *Ital. J. Mark.*, *2022*(4), 439–457. doi:10.1007/s43039-022-00057-w

De Reuver, M., Sørensen, C., & Basole, R. C. (2018). The digital platform: A research agenda. *Journal of Information Technology*, *33*(2), 124–135. doi:10.1057/s41265-016-0033-3

De Vita, L., Mari, M., & Poggesi, S. (2014). Women entrepreneurs in and from developing countries: Evidences from the literature. *European Management Journal*, *32*(3), 451–460. doi:10.1016/j.emj.2013.07.009

De Zubielqui, G. C., & Jones, J. (2020). How and when social media affects innovation in start-ups. A moderated mediation model. *Industrial Marketing Management*, *85*, 209–220. doi:10.1016/j.indmarman.2019.11.006

Dedehayir, O., & Steinert, M. (2016). The hype cycle model: A review and future directions. *Technological Forecasting and Social Change*, *108*, 28–41. doi:10.1016/j.techfore.2016.04.005

Deka, P. K. (2021). Factors influencing student engagement in online learning during the COVID-19 pandemic period in India. *Journal of Management in Practice*, *6*(1), 1–16.

DeLone, W. H., & McLean, E. R. (1992). Information Systems Success: The quest for the dependent variable. *Information Systems Research*, *3*(1), 60–95. doi:10.1287/isre.3.1.60

Demydchuk, L. B., & Sapozhnyk, D. I. (2021). Influence of social networks on business development. Academic Press.

Dereń, K., & Dereń, K. (2023, July 3). *How Effective is Nike's Social Media Strategy? | Brand24*. Brand24 Blog. https://brand24.com/blog/nike-social-media-strategy/

Derkach, N. (2023). How much Ukrainians spent on online purchases in 2023. *PAYSPACE*. https://psm7.com/ru/e-commerce/skolko-ukraincy-potratili-na-online-pokupki-v-2023-godu.html

Dhaka's Street Food Vendors to Survive during Pandemic. (n.d.). Retrieved January 8, 2024, from https://www.changemag-diinsider.com/blog/struggles-of-dhaka-s-street-food-vendors-to-survive-during-pandemic

Diakopoulos, N. (2016). Accountability in algorithmic decision making. *Communications of the ACM*, *59*(2), 56–62. doi:10.1145/2844110

Dlamini, R., & Ndzinisa, R. (2020). Universities trailing behind: Unquestioned epistemological foundations constraining the transition to online instructional delivery and learning. *South African Journal of Higher Education, 34*(6), 52–64. doi:10.20853/34-6-4073

Drinkwater, M. (2009). 'We are also Human': identity and power in gender relations. Rights-based approaches to development: Exploring the potential and pitfalls. Kumarian Press.

Duan, Y., Edwards, J. S., & Dwivedi, Y. K. (2019). Artificial intelligence for decision making in the era of Big Data—Evolution, challenges and research agenda. *International Journal of Information Management, 48*(February), 63–71. doi:10.1016/j.ijinfomgt.2019.01.021

Duggal, S. (2022). Factors impacting acceptance of e-learning in India: Learners' perspective. *Asian Association of Open University Journal, 17*(2), 101–119. doi:10.1108/AAOUJ-01-2022-0010

Dunn, K., & Grimes, A. (2022). Speed and symmetry: Developing effective organisational responses to social media criticism of CSR. *Computers in Human Behavior, 134*, 107336. doi:10.1016/j.chb.2022.107336

Eachempati, P., Srivastava, P. R., & Zhang, Z. J. (2021). Gauging opinions about the COVID-19: A multi-channel social media approach. *Enterprise Information Systems, 15*(6), 794–828. doi:10.1080/17517575.2020.1856418

El-Gohary, H., Sultan, F., Alam, S., Abbas, M., & Muhammad, S. (2023). Shaping Sustainable Entrepreneurial Intentions among Business Graduates in Developing Countries through Social Media Adoption: A Moderating-Mediated Mechanism in Pakistan. *Sustainability (Basel), 15*(3), 2489. doi:10.3390/su15032489

Elliott, V. (2018). Thinking about the coding process in qualitative data analysis. *The Qualitative Report, 23*(11), 2850–2861. doi:10.46743/2160-3715/2018.3560

Emami, A., Ashourizadeh, S., & Packard, M. D. (2023). The impact of social network support on opportunity intention among prospective male and female entrepreneurs during 2019-nCov pandemic. *International Journal of Entrepreneurial Behaviour & Research, 29*(11), 132–169. doi:10.1108/IJEBR-03-2022-0223

Emmanuel, C. P., Qin, S., Hossain, S. F. A., & Hussain, K. (2022). Factors influencing social-media-based entrepreneurship prospect among female students in China. *Heliyon, 8*(12), e12041. doi:10.1016/j.heliyon.2022.e12041 PMID:36483305

Erevelles, S., Fukawa, N., & Swayne, L. (2016). Big Data consumer analytics and the transformation of marketing. *Journal of Business Research, 69*(2), 897–904. doi:10.1016/j.jbusres.2015.07.001

Evans, J., O'Brien, J., & Ch Ng, B. (2018). Towards a geography of informal transport: Mobility, infrastructure and urban sustainability from the back of a motorbike. *Transactions of the Institute of British Geographers, 43*(4), 674–688. doi:10.1111/tran.12239

FACT MR. (2022). *Coffee Machine Market Outlook*. Available at: https://www.factmr.com/report/2452/coffee-machine-market

Fatima, N., & Ali, R. (2023). How businesswomen engage customers on social media? *Spanish Journal of Marketing - ESIC, 27*(2), 221–240. doi:10.1108/SJME-09-2021-0172

Filieri, L., Lin, S., Antone, E., & Chatzopoulou, P. (2019). 'Cultural approach to brand equity: The role of brand mianzi and brand popularity in China'. *Journal of Brand Management, 26*(4), 376–394. doi:10.1057/s41262-018-0137-x

Fleming, P. (2019). Robots and organization studies: Why robots might not want to steal your job. *Organization Studies, 40*(1), 23–38. doi:10.1177/0170840618765568

Food for the Cities: Street foods. (n.d.). https://www.fao.org/fcit/food-processing/street-foods/en/

Ford, J., Jain, V., Wadhwani, K., & Gupta, D. G. (2023). *AI advertising: An overview and guidelines*. Retrieved February 11, 2019 from https://www.sltrib.com/news/business/2019/02/01/doorbells-have-eyes/

Foroudi, P., Jin, Z., Gupta, S., Foroudi, M. M., & Kitchen, P. J. (2018). Perceptional components of brand equity: Configuring the Symmetrical and Asymmetrical Paths to brand loyalty and brand purchase intention. *Journal of Business Research, 89*, 462–474. doi:10.1016/j.jbusres.2018.01.031

French, K. (2018). *Your new best friend: AI chatbot*. Retrieved February 13, 2019 from https://futurism.com/ai-chatbot-meaningful-conversation

Fuentes-Fuentes, M. D. M., Bojica, A. M., & Ruiz-Arroyo, M. (2015). Entrepreneurial orientation and knowledge acquisition: Effects on performance in the specific context of women-owned firms. *The International Entrepreneurship and Management Journal, 11*(3), 695–717. doi:10.1007/s11365-014-0336-1

Galushka, Z. (2013). The phenomenon of social entrepreneurship: Concepts and prospects for development in Ukraine. *Bulletin of Taras Shevchenko Kyiv National University Economics*, (148), 15–17.

Gans, J., Agrawal, A., & Goldfarb, A. (2017). How AI will change strategy: A thought experiment. *Harvard Business Review Online*. Retrieved February 11, 2019 from https://hbr.org/product/how-ai-will-change-strategy-a-thought-experiment/H03XDI-PDF-ENG

Gartner, W. I., & Ruzzier, M. K. (2021). 'Tourism destination brand equity dimensions: Renewal versus repeat market'. *Journal of Travel Research, 50*(5), 471–481. doi:10.1177/0047287510379157

Gaudin, S. (2016). *At stitch fix, data scientists and a.I. become personal stylists*. Retrieved February 11, 2019 from https://www.computerworld.com/article/3067264/artificial-intelligence/at-stitch-fix-data-scientists-and-ai-become-personal-stylists.html

Geyser, W. (2024, January 30). *What is Influencer Marketing? – The Ultimate Guide for 2024*. Influencer Marketing Hub, Retrieved from https://influencermarketinghub.com/influencer-marketing/

Gigauri, I. (2020). Effects of Covid-19 on Human Resource Management from the Perspective of Digitalization and Work-life-balance. *International Journal of Innovative Technologies in Economy, 4*(31), 1–10. doi:10.31435/rsglobal_ijite/30092020/7148

Giuggioli, G., & Pellegrini, M. M. (2022). Artificial intelligence as an enabler for entrepreneurs: A systematic literature review and an agenda for future research. *International Journal of Entrepreneurial Behaviour & Research, 29*(4), 816–837. doi:10.1108/IJEBR-05-2021-0426

Global experts rank Unilever No.1 for sustainability leadership. (n.d.). Retrieved December 20, 2022, from Unilever website: https://www.unilever.com/news/news-search/2020/global-experts-rank-unilever-no1-for-sustaina bility-leadership/

Golob, U., Burghausen, M., Kernstock, J., & Davies, M. A. P. (2022). Brand management and sustainability: Exploring potential for the transformative power of brands. *Journal of Brand Management, 29*(6), 513–519. doi:10.1057/s41262-022-00293-7

Google Trend. (2023). *Google trends*. https://trends.google.com/trends/explore?geo=BD&q=uber&hl=en

Gopal, R., Singh, V., & Aggarwal, A. (2021). Impact of online classes on the satisfaction and performance of students during the pandemic period of COVID 19. *Education and Information Technologies, 26*(1), 6923–6947. doi:10.1007/s10639-021-10523-1 PMID:33903795

Goswami, M. P., Thanvi, J., & Padhi, S. R. (2021). Impact of online learning in India: A survey of university students during the COVID-19 crisis. *Asian Journal for Public Opinion Research, 9*(4), 331–351. doi:10.15206/ajpor.2021.9.4.331

Grover, S., & Mathew, L. (2022). Exploring the digital revolution in education in India during COVID-19 pandemic. *International Journal of Social Quality*, *12*(2), 51–71. doi:10.3167/IJSQ.2022.120204

GSMA. (2022). *GSMA Gender Gap*. Retrieved from: https://www.gsma.com/r/gender-gap/

Guda, H., & Subramanian, U. (2019). Your uber is arriving: Managing on-demand workers through surge pricing, forecast communication, and worker incentives. *Management Science*, *65*(5), 1995–2014. doi:10.1287/mnsc.2018.3050

Gudz, G. O. (2016). Information systems and technologies in insurance protection of agrarian entrepreneurship. *Accounting and Finance*, (2), 95–103.

Guliyev Seymur, M. (2022). Factors Influencing Brand Equity of Food Componies in Azerbaijan'. Marketing. *Advertising and Branding Journal*, *15*(1), 16–30.

Gustafsson, V., & Khan, M. S. (2017). Monetising blogs: Enterprising behaviour, co-creation of opportunities and social media entrepreneurship. *Journal of Business Venturing Insights*, *7*, 26–31. doi:10.1016/j.jbvi.2017.01.002

Habib, K. R. (2016). Understanding Challenges Faced By Street Food Vendors to Maintain Street Food Hygiene in Dhaka City. *Journal of Food and Nutrition Sciences*, *4*(4), 78–85. doi:10.11648/j.jfns.20160404.11

Haleem, A., Javaid, M., Qadri, M. A., Singh, R. P., & Suman, R. (2022). Artificial intelligence (AI) applications for marketing: A literature-based study. *International Journal of Intelligent Networks*, *3*, 119–132. doi:10.1016/j.ijin.2022.08.005

Hansen, A. (2016). Driving development? The problems and promises of the car in Vietnam. *Journal of Contemporary Asia*, *46*(4), 551–569. doi:10.1080/00472336.2016.1151916

Harkusha, S. A. (2020). Taxation of activities in social networks. *Eastern Europe: Economics. Business and Management.*, *2*(25), 340–345.

Harrasi, N. A., Hakro, A. N., Srinavasan, V., Christina, B., & Jabri, M. A. (2022). Social Media and Entrepreneurship Challenges in the Sultanate of Oman. *Hong Kong Journal of Social Sciences*, *58*, 765–776.

Harriet, T. (2016). *Lowe's introduces LoweBot, a new autonomous in-store robot.* CNBC. https://www.statista.com/outlook/dmo/digital-advertising/social-media-advertising/worldwide

Harun, S. A., Fauzi, M. A., Kasim, N. M., & Wider, W. (2022). Determinants of Energy Efficient Appliances among Malaysian Households: Roles of Theory of Planned Behavior, Social Interaction and Appliance Quality. *Asian Economic and Financial Review*, *12*(3), 212–226. doi:10.55493/5002.v12i3.4463

Hassan, I. (2022, December 7). Hospitality and the restaurant sectors grows 58% in 11 years. *Dhaka Tribune*. https://www.dhakatribune.com/business/279949/hospitality-and-the-restaurant-sectors-grows-58%25

HawkinsD. L.HoonS. (2019). The impact of customer retention strategies and the survival of small service-based businesses. *Available at* SSRN 3445173. doi:10.2139/ssrn.3445173

Hayes, A. (2023, April 23). *Blockchain Facts: What is it, how does it work, and how can it be used*? Investopedia. https://www.investopedia.com/terms/b/blockchain.asp

Hechevarría, D., Bullough, A., Brush, C., & Edelman, L. (2019). High-growth women's entrepreneurship: Fueling social and economic development. *Journal of Small Business Management*, *57*(1), 5–13. doi:10.1111/jsbm.12503

Heiko, T. (2020). Priorities for the development of entrepreneurship in Ukraine in the conditions of the COVID-19 pandemic and in the post-quarantine period. *Bulletin of Socio-Economic Research,* *2*(73), 62-71.

Hinton, P. R., McMurray, I., & Brownlow, C. (2014). *SPSS explained (2nd ed.)*. Routledge. doi:10.4324/9781315797298

Hossain, S. F. A. M. N. (2019). Effects of variety-seeking intention by mobile phone usage on university students' academic performance. In Cogent Education (Vol. 6, pp. 1-18). Academic Press.

Hossain, S. F. A., Nurunnabi, M., Hussain, K., & Shan, X. (2020). *Smartphone-based M-shopping behavior and innovative entrepreneurial tendency among women in emerging Asia.* Retrieved from https://www.emerald.com/insight/content/doi/10.1108/IJGE-03-2019-0054/full/html

Hossain, S. F. A., Shan, X., Nurunnabi, M., Tushar, H., Mohsin, A. K. M., & Ahsan, F. T. (2021). Opportunities and challenges of m-learning during the COVID-19 pandemic: A mixed methodology approach. *E-Collaboration Technologies and Strategies for Competitive Advantage Amid Challenging Times*, 210-227.

Hossain, S. F. A., Xu, S., Musa, M., & Rahman, P. (2022). Social media and Increased venture creation tendency with innovative ideas. In IGI Global eBooks (pp. 1716–1731). doi:10.4018/978-1-6684-7123-4.ch093

Hossain, S. F. A., Xu, S., Nurunnabi, M., Tushar, H., Mohsin, A. K. M., & Ahsan, F. T. (2021). Opportunities and Challenges of M-Learning During the COVID-19 Pandemic. In E-Collaboration Technologies and Strategies for Competitive Advantage Amid Challenging Times (pp. 210–227). doi:10.4018/978-1-7998-7764-6.ch007

Hossain, S. F. A. (2019). Social networking and its role in media entrepreneurship. *Journal of Media Management and Entrepreneurship*, *1*(1), 73–86. doi:10.4018/JMME.2019010105

Hossain, S. F. A., Nurunnabi, M., Hussain, K., & Saha, S. K. (2019). Effects of variety-seeking intention by mobile phone usage on university students' academic performance. *Cogent Education*, *6*(1), 1574692. doi:10.1080/2331186X.2019.1574692

Hossain, S. F. A., Nurunnabi, M., Hussain, K., & Xu, S. (2020). Smartphone-based m-shopping behavior and innovative entrepreneurial tendency among women in emerging Asia. *International Journal of Gender and Entrepreneurship*, *12*(2), 173–189. doi:10.1108/IJGE-03-2019-0054

Hossain, S. F. A., Shan, X., Musa, M., & Rahman, P. (2023). Social media and increased venture creation tendency with innovative ideas: the case of female students in Asia. In *Research Anthology on Applying Social Networking Strategies to Classrooms and Libraries* (pp. 1716–1731). IGI Global.

Hossain, S. F. A., Zhao, X., Nurunnabi, M., & Hussain, K. (2020). Ubiquitous role of social networking in driving M-Commerce: Evaluating the use of mobile phones for online shopping and payment in the context of trust. *SAGE Open*, *10*(3). doi:10.1177/2158244020939536

Hrytsaenko, M. I. (2017). Social capital in the formation of the entrepreneurial network of the agrarian sphere of Ukraine. *Economy of Agro-Industrial Complex, 5,* 58-64.

Hrytsaenko, M. I. (2020). The place of social capital in the development of self-regulation of entrepreneurial activity. Academic Press.

Huang, M. H., & Rust, R. T. (2021). A strategic framework for artificial intelligence in marketing. *Journal of the Academy of Marketing Science*, *49*(1), 30–50. doi:10.1007/s11747-020-00749-9

Humaid, A. B., & Ibrahim, Y. M. (2019). The examination of factors influencing Saudi small businesses' social media adoption by using the UTAUT model. *International Journal of Business Administration*, *10*(2), 96. doi:10.5430/ijba.v10n2p96

Husain, R., Ahmad, A., Khan, B. M., & Khalil, O. (2022). The role of status consumption and brand equity: A comparative study of the marketing of Indian luxury brands by traditional and social-media. *Journal of Management and Sustainability*, *16*(4), 67–80.

ICO. (2022). *Monthly Coffee Market Report (2021/22).* Available at: https://www.ico.org/Market-Report-21-22-e.asp

Iglesias, O., & Ind, N. (2020). Towards a theory of conscientious corporate brand co-creation: The next key challenge in brand management. *Journal of Brand Management*, *27*(6), 710–720. Advance online publication. doi:10.1057/s41262-020-00205-7

Improving the level of SEO in Ukraine. (2016). https://seosolution.ua/blog/infographics/internet-trade.html

Intelligence, M. (2022). *Coffee machine market - growth, trends, covid-19 impact, and forecasts (2022 - 2027).* Available at: https://www.mordorintelligence.com/industry-reports/global-coffee-machine-market

IslamN. (2020) Women Empowerment through Entrepreneurship Development in Bangladesh: A Multivariate Analysis. *International Journal of Management, 11*(10). https://ssrn.com/abstract=3734569

Jena, P. K. (2020). Online learning during lockdown period for COVID-19 in India. *International Journal of Multidisciplinary Education Research*, *9*(5), 82–91. doi:10.31235/osf.io/qu38b

Jha, A. (2023). Immersive Marketing on Metaverse: Development of Metrics for Performance Analysis and Security-Related Challenges. In P. Pires, J. Santos, I. Pereira, & A. Torres (Eds.), Confronting Security and Privacy Challenges in Digital Marketing (pp. 267-289). IGI Global. doi:10.4018/978-1-6684-8958-1.ch013

Jha, A., & Jha, A. (2022). Data Encryption Dispute Resolutions under Intermediary Guidelines of Information Technology Act Challenges and Future Framework. *DESIDOC Journal of Library and Information Technology*, *42*(3), 201–207. doi:10.14429/djlit.42.3.17869

Jia, J., Liu, H., Chin, T., & Hu, D. (2018). The Continuous Mediating Effects of GHRM on Employees' Green Passion via Transformational Leadership and Green Creativity. *Sustainability (Basel)*, *10*(9), 3237. doi:10.3390/su10093237

Jilcha Sileyew, K. (2020). Research Design and Methodology. In E. Abu-Taieh, A. El Mouatasim, & I. H. Al Hadid (Eds.), *Cyberspace*. IntechOpen. doi:10.5772/intechopen.85731

Jin, D., Melewar, T.C., Foroudi, P., & Zhong, Z.Y. (2020). An assessment of brand experience knowledge literature: using bibliometric data to identify future research direction. *International Journal of Management Reviews, 22*(3), 287-317.

Jordan, M. I., & Mitchell, T. M. (2015). Machine learning: Trends, perspectives, and prospects. *Science*, *349*(6245), 255–260. doi:10.1126/science.aaa8415 PMID:26185243

Jose, S. (2018). Strategic use of digital promotion strategies among female emigrant entrepreneurs in UAE. *International Journal of Emerging Markets*, *13*(6), 1699–1718. doi:10.1108/IJoEM-10-2016-0268

Joshi, A., Vinay, M., & Bhaskar, P. (2020). Online teaching amidst COVID-19 in India: An outlook. *Asian Journal of Distance Education*, *15*(2), 105–111.

Julius, Z. (2021). *At home barista experience was one of the key coffee culture trends in 2021.* International Communicafe. Available at: https://www.comunicaffe.com/at-home-barista- experience-one-of-the-key-coffee-trends-of-2021/

Jyoti, B., & Singh, A. K. (2023). Does digitalization have a causal relationship with economic development? an experience from a country-wise panel data statistical analysis. In R. Sine Nazlı & G. Sari (Eds.), Handbook of Research on Perspectives on Society and Technology Addiction (pp. 34-61). IGI Global. doi:10.4018/978-1-6684-8397-8.ch003

Jyoti, B., Singh, A. K., & Ashraf, S. N. (2023). Appropriate technologies and their implications in the agricultural sector. In P. H. Alex Khang (Ed.), *Advanced Technologies and AI-Equipped IoT Applications in High-Tech Agriculture* (pp. 65–87). IGI Global. doi:10.4018/978-1-6684-9231-4.ch004

Kadam, A., & Ayarekar, S. (2014). Impact of Social Media on Entrepreneurship and Entrepreneurial Performance: Special Reference to Small and Medium Scale Enterprises. *SIES Journal of Management, 10*(1).

Kalia, P., Behal, B., Kaur, K., & Mehta, D. (2024). Impact of COVID-19 on education in India: Stakeholders' voice. *Benchmarking*, *31*(1), 243–264. doi:10.1108/BIJ-11-2021-0665

Kamkankaew, P., Sribenjachot, S., Wongmahatlek, J., Phattarowas, V., & Khumwongpin, S. (2022). Reconsidering the Mystery of Digital Marketing Strategy in the Technological Environment: Opportunities and Challenges in Digital Consumer Behavior. *International Journal of Sociologies and Anthropologies Science Reviews*, *2*(4), 43–60. doi:10.14456/jsasr.2022.29

Kampa, R. K. (2023). Combining technology readiness and acceptance model for investigating the acceptance of m-learning in higher education in India. *Asian Association of Open Universities Journal*, *18*(2), 105–120. doi:10.1108/AAOUJ-10-2022-0149

Kapustina, K. (2020, December 29). The corona virus has spurred the development of online commerce in Ukraine. *Today.* https://economics.segodnya.ua/economics/business/cifra-dnya-ukraincy-podseli-na-internet-shoping-skolko-tratim-v-seti-1497960.html

Kashive, N., & Khanna, V. T. (2022). Emerging HR analytics role in a crisis: An analysis of LinkedIn data. *Competitiveness Review*.

Katz, E., Blumler, J. G., & Gurevitch, M. (1973). Uses and Gratifications Research. *Public Opinion Quarterly*, *37*(4), 509–523. doi:10.1086/268109

Kaur, F. P. (2023). *10 creative AI marketing examples and use cases.* Mailmodo. Available at: https://www.mailmodo.com/guides/ai-in-marketing-examples/

Kazak, A. S. (2021). Factor assessment of the influence of social networks on the economic efficiency of entrepreneurial activity. Academic Press.

Keller, K. L. (1993). Conceptualizing, Measuring and Managing Customer Based Brand Equity. *Journal of Marketing*, *57*(1), 1–22. doi:10.1177/002224299305700101

Keller, K. L. (2003). Brand synthesis: The multidimensionality of brand knowledge. *The Journal of Consumer Research*, *29*(4), 595–600. doi:10.1086/346254

Keller, K. L., & Lehman, D. R. (2006). Brands and Branding: Research Findings and Future Priorities. *Marketing Science*, *25*(6), 740–759. doi:10.1287/mksc.1050.0153

Kemper, J. A., & Ballantine, P. W. (2019). What do we mean by sustainability marketing? *Journal of Marketing Management*, *35*(3–4), 277–309. doi:10.1080/0267257X.2019.1573845

Ketonen-Oksi, S., Jussila, J. J., & Kärkkäinen, H. (2016). Social media based value creation and business models. *Industrial Management & Data Systems*, *116*(8), 1820–1838. doi:10.1108/IMDS-05-2015-0199

Khadim, R. A., Hanan, M., Arshad, A., Saleem, N., & Khadim, N. (2018). Revisiting antecedents of brand loyalty: Impact of perceived social media communication with brand trust and brand equity as mediators. *Academy of Strategic Management Journal*, *17*(1), 1–14.

Khairunisa, M., & Kusuma, N. (2021, July 9). *How Unilever Transforms Its Business with Unilever Sustainable Living Plan.* Retrieved from Green Network Asia website: https://greennetwork.asia/news/how-unilever-transforms-its-business-with-unilever-sustainable-li ving-plan/

Khalid, C., & Allioui, S. (2023). Empowering female entrepreneurs in developing countries: A comparative case study on the impact of social media on microenterprises and poverty alleviation. *International May Conference on Strategic Management, 19*(1), 242-251.

Khan, M. J. (2022). *Social media marketing* [Master's thesis]. Centria University of Applied Sciences. https://www.theseus.fi/handle/10024/780131

Khan, H. M. (2021). The Role of LinkedIn Profile on Hiring Preference: Evidence from Bangladeshi Employers. Asian Journal of Economics. *Business and Accounting*, *21*(18), 42–56.

Khan, M. A., Vivek, V., Nabi, M. K., Khojah, M., & Tahir, M. (2021). Students' perception towards e-learning during COVID-19 pandemic in India: An empirical study. *Sustainability (Basel)*, *13*(1), 1–14. doi:10.3390/su13010057

Khokhar, P., & Chitsimran. (2019). Evolution Of Artificial Intelligence In Marketing, Comparison With Traditional Marketing. *Our Heritage*, *67*(5), 375–389.

Khymitsa, N., & Sekanova, A. (2018). Advertising and information presentation of PJSC "Myronivskyi Hliboprodukt" in social networks. *Information Communication and Society*, *1*, 77.

Kim, T.-Y., Liden, R. C., Kim, S.-P., & Lee, D.-R. (2015). The interplay between follower core self-evaluation and transformational leadership: Effects on employee outcomes. *Journal of Business and Psychology*, *30*(2), 345–355. doi:10.1007/s10869-014-9364-7

Kitchenham, B., Brereton, O. P., Budgen, D., Turner, M., Bailey, J., & Linkman, S. (2009). Systematic literature reviews in software engineering – A systematic literature review. *Information and Software Technology*, *51*(1), 7–15. doi:10.1016/j.infsof.2008.09.009

Kohlegger, M., Maier, R., & Thalmann, S. (2009). Understanding maturity models results of a structured content analysis. *Proceedings of IKNOW '09 and ISEMANTICS '09*, 51–61.

Kornetsky, A. O., & Ishakov, E. Sh. (2016). Alternative social networks: Business model and entrepreneurship. *Scientific Bulletin of Kherson State University. Ser. Economic Sciences*, 19(1), 95–99.

Kornukh, O. V., & Makhanko, L. V. (2014). Startup as a progressive form of innovative entrepreneurship. *Investments: Practice and Experience*, (23), 26-30.

Korotich, O. B., Orel, Yu. L., & Ryabichko, O. V. (2010). Entrepreneurship as a socio-economic phenomenon. *Theory and Practice of Public Administration*, (4), 211-216.

Kotler, P., Kartajaya, H., & Setiawan, I. (2021). *Marketing 5.0: Technology for humanity*. Wiley.

Kotler, P., & Keller, K. L. (2006). *Marketing Management (12th ed.)*. Prentice-Hall.

Kozlovskyi, S. V., & Tanasienko, O. I. (2019). The paradigm of social entrepreneurship. Academic Press.

Kuhnle, A., Alim, M. A., Li, X., Zhang, H., & Thai, M. T. (2018). Multiplex influence maximization in online social networks with heterogeneous diffusion models. *IEEE Transactions on Computational Social Systems*, *5*(2), 418–429. doi:10.1109/TCSS.2018.2813262

Kulikova, N. O. (2022). *Electronic technologies and development of entrepreneurship*. Symi.

Kumar, V., Rajan, B., Venkatesan, R., & Lecinski, J. (2019). Understanding the role of artificial intelligence in personalized engagement marketing. *California Management Review*, *61*(4), 135–155. doi:10.1177/0008125619859317

Kundu, A., & Kundu, S. (2022). Online education in India, an insight into the future: From the students' experience during the lockdown for COVID-19. *Towards Excellence*, *14*(2), 292–305. doi:10.37867/TE140227

Kurachi, Y., Narukawa, S., & Hara, H. (2018). AI chatbot to realize sophistication of consumer contact points. *Fujitsu Scientific and Technical Journal*, *54*(3), 2–8.

Lamach, M. W. (2017, October 27). *How Our Company Connected Our Strategy to Sustainability Goals.* Retrieved from Harvard Business Review website: https://hbr.org/2017/10/how-our-company-connected-our-strategy-to-sustainability-goals

Lamba, P. S., & Jain, N. R. (2022). Overcoming challenges faced by digital entrepreneurs: A design thinking approach. *Development and Learning in Organizations*, *36*(6), 12–14. doi:10.1108/DLO-11-2021-0195

Lebiedieva, Z. (2023). *ESP Writing as a Practical Mean of Cultural Communication Between Ukrainian Music Teachers and Chinese Students. In Cases on Error Analysis in Foreign Language Technical Writing*. IGI Global. doi:10.4018/978-1-6684-6222-5.ch008

Lee, C. T., Pan, L., & Hsieh, S. H. (2021). Artificial intelligent chatbots as brand promoters: A two-stage structural equation modeling-artificial neural network approach. *Internet Research*, *32*(4), 1329–1356. doi:10.1108/INTR-01-2021-0030

Lee, C., & Hallak, R. (2020). Investigating the effects of offline and online social capital on tourism SME performance: A mixed-methods study of New Zealand entrepreneurs. *Tourism Management*, *80*, 104128. doi:10.1016/j.tourman.2020.104128

Lee, J. E., Goh, M. L., & Noor, M. N. B. M. (2019). Understanding purchase intention of university students towards skin care products. *PSU Research Review.*, *3*(3), 161–178. doi:10.1108/PRR-11-2018-0031

Lee, M. H., Lin, C., Lin, C. K., & Lu, W. Y. (2014). Moderating effect of institutional responsiveness on the relationship between green leadership and green competitiveness. *Social Behavior and Personality*, *42*(9), 1483–1494. doi:10.2224/sbp.2014.42.9.1483

Lévesque, M., & Stephan, U. (2020). It's time we talk about time in entrepreneurship. *Entrepreneurship Theory and Practice*, *44*(2), 163–184. doi:10.1177/1042258719839711

Lichy, J., Farquhar, J. D., & Kachour, M. (2021). Entrepreneurship via social networks – "connected woman" in Lebanon. *Qualitative Market Research*, *24*(4), 426–448. doi:10.1108/QMR-01-2020-0004

Lifebuoy, P. (2020, May 7). *Unilever Marks Sustainable Living Plan's 10th Year; New "Compass" to Guide Further Progress*. Retrieved from Sustainable Brands website: https://sustainablebrands.com/read/leadership/unilever-marks-sustainable-living-plan-s-10th-year -new-compass-to-guide-further-progress

Lile, S. (2023, August 4). *Complete history of social media: Then and now*. Small Business Trends. https://smallbiztrends.com/2023/08/history-of-social-media.html

Lipkin, J. (2015). *Sieving through the data to find the person: HR's imperative for balancing big data with people centricity*. Academic Press.

Litvine, D., & Wüstenhagen, R. (2011). Helping "light green" consumers walk the talk: Results of a behavioural intervention survey in the Swiss electricity market. *Ecological Economics*, *70*(3), 462–474. doi:10.1016/j.ecolecon.2010.10.005

Liu, Y., & Li, Z. (2021, December 1). *Application analysis of artificial intelligence technology in brand Marketing Strategy*. Retrieved from https://ieeexplore.ieee.org/stamp/stamp.jsp?tp=&arnumber=9759931

Li, W., Bhutto, T. A., Xuhui, W., Maitlo, Q., Zafar, A. U., & Ahmed Bhutto, N. (2020). Unlocking employees' green creativity: The effects of green transformational leadership, green intrinsic, and extrinsic motivation. *Journal of Cleaner Production*, *255*, 120229. doi:10.1016/j.jclepro.2020.120229

Li, Y., Zhang, W., Urquhart, A., & Wang, P. (2022). The unintended consequence of social media criticisms: An earnings management perspective. *European Journal of Finance*, *29*(1), 33–57. doi:10.1080/1351847X.2022.2097885

Lockee, B. B. (2022). Online education in the post-COVID era. *Nature Electronics*, *4*(1), 5–6. doi:10.1038/s41928-020-00534-0

Long, S. (2022, October 14). *The Benefits of Active Leadership in Sustainability*. Retrieved from Green Business Bureau website: https://greenbusinessbureau.com/topics/green-culture/the-benefits-of-active-leadership-in-sustain ability/

Lose, T., & Eze, I. F. (2023). Virtual small business entrepreneurship opportunities. *Eureka: Social and Humanities, 4*, 13–19. https://doi.org/ doi:10.21303/2504-5571.2023.002912

Luis, V., Casaló, L. V., Flavián, C., & Ibáñez-Sánchez, S. (2021). Be creative, my friend! Engaging users on Instagram by promoting positive emotions. *Journal of Business Research*, *130*, 416–425. doi:10.1016/j.jbusres.2020.02.014

Lumpkin, G. T., & Dess, G. G. (1996). Clarifying the entrepreneurial orientation construct and linking it to performance. *Academy of Management Review*, *21*(1), 135–172. doi:10.2307/258632

Madams. (2023, October 30). *The evolution of social media: How did it begin, and where could it go next?* Maryville University Online. https://online.maryville.edu/blog/evolution-social-media/#history

Makridakis, S. (2017). The forthcoming Artificial Intelligence (AI) revolution: Its impact on society and firms. *Futures*, *90*, 90. doi:10.1016/j.futures.2017.03.006

Ma, L., & Sun, B. (2020). Machine learning and AI in marketing – Connecting computing power to human insights. *International Journal of Research in Marketing*, *37*(3), 481–504. doi:10.1016/j.ijresmar.2020.04.005

Mamun, M. Z., & Haq, M. R. (2023). Urban Women Entrepreneurship Development in Bangladesh: Challenges and Preparations. *International Journal of Research and Innovation in Social Science*, *7*(7), 129–149. doi:10.47772/IJRISS.2023.70709

Mangushev, D. V., & Pikhtin, A. V. (2021). Application of digital marketing tools to increase the efficiency of business activities. *Modern Economics.*, *30*, 147–152. doi:10.31521/modecon.V30(2021)-23

Mariani, M., & Fosso Wamba, S. (2020). Exploring how consumer goods companies innovate in the digital age: The role of big data analytics companies. *Journal of Business Research*, *121*, 338–352. doi:10.1016/j.jbusres.2020.09.012

Marques, C., Silva, R. V., Davcik, N. S., & Faria, R. T. (2020). The role of brand equity in a new rebranding strategy of a private label brand. *Journal of Business Research*, *117*, 497–507. doi:10.1016/j.jbusres.2020.06.022

Marr, B. (2016). *Big data in practice: How 45 successful companies used big data analytics to deliver extraordinary results*. Wiley. doi:10.1002/9781119278825

Martín, A. V. D., & Ramos, J. M. L. (2022). DEIFD framework: Evaluation of digital education deployment in India in the midst of Covid-19 pandemic. *Social Sciences & Humanities Open*, *6*(1), 1–11. doi:10.1016/j.ssaho.2022.100281

Martín-Rojas, R., Garrido-Moreno, A., & García-Morales, V. J. (2020). Fostering Corporate Entrepreneurship with the use of social media tools. *Journal of Business Research*, *112*, 396–412. doi:10.1016/j.jbusres.2019.11.072

Mayring, P. (2008). *Qualitative Inhaltsanalyse*. Beltz Deutscher Studien Verlag.

Mehmet, S., & Mohamed, Y. C. (2022). An Examination of the Effect of Social Media Marketing on Customer Based Brand Equity. *Journal of Business Research*, *69*(12), 5833–5841.

Mihailina, T., & Bevzyuk, K. (2019). Problems of using objects of inttllectual property rights during business activities in social networks. Economic and Law Paradigm of Modern Society, 81.

Miklosik, A., & Evans, N. (2020). Impact of big data and machine learning on digital transformation in marketing: A literature review. *IEEE Access : Practical Innovations, Open Solutions*, *8*, 101284–101292. doi:10.1109/ACCESS.2020.2998754

Miklosik, A., Kuchta, M., Evans, N., & Zak, S. (2019). Towards the adoption of machine learning-based analytical tools in digital marketing. *IEEE Access : Practical Innovations, Open Solutions*, *7*, 85705–85718. doi:10.1109/ACCESS.2019.2924425

Miliue, D. (2021). *How is the home espresso machine market evolving?* Coffee Roasters and Plant. Available at: https://perfectdailygrind.com/2022/04/home-espresso-machine-evolution/

MishraA. (2022). Retrieved from https://www.researchgate.net/publication/357705863_Role_of_Artificial_Intelligence_in_Social_Media_Marketing

Mittal, S., & Dhar, R. L. (2016). Effect of green transformational leadership on green creativity: A study of tourist hotels. *Tourism Management*, *57*, 18–127. doi:10.1016/j.tourman.2016.05.007

Mohsin, A. K. M., Lei, H., & Hossain, S. F. A. (2021). Impact of COVID-19 Pandemic on Consumer Economy: Countermeasures analysis. *SAGE Open*, *11*(2). doi:10.1177/21582440211008875

Mozumdar, L., Hagelaar, G., van der Velde, G., & Omta, S. W. F. (2020). Determinants of the business performance of women entrepreneurs in the developing world context. *J*, *3*(2), 17.

Mozumdar, L., Farid, K. S., & Sarma, P. K. (2017). Relevance of social capital in women s business performance in Bangladesh. *Journal of the Bangladesh Agricultural University*, *15*(1), 87–94. doi:10.3329/jbau.v15i1.33533

Mozumdar, L., Materia, V. C., Hagelaar, G., Islam, M. A., van der Velde, G., & Omta, S. W. F. (2022). Contextuality of Entrepreneurial Orientation and Business Performance: The Case of Women Entrepreneurs in Bangladesh. *Journal of Entrepreneurship and Innovation in Emerging Economies*, *8*(1), 94–120. doi:10.1177/23939575211062433

Mozumder, N. A. (2018). A multilevel trust-based model of ethical public leadership. *Journal of Business Ethics*, *153*(1), 167–184. doi:10.1007/s10551-016-3341-1

Muangmee, A. (2023). Focused Group Interview Literature Review of Challenges Ethiopian Female Entrepreneurs Face in their Business Ventures. *International Journal of Social Science Management and Economics Research*, *01*(03), 36–47. doi:10.61421/IJSSMER.2023.1303

Muhuri, P. K., Shukla, A. K., & Abraham, A. (2019). Industry 4.0: A Bibliometric analysis and detailed overview. *Engineering Applications of Artificial Intelligence*, *78*, 218–235. doi:10.1016/j.engappai.2018.11.007

Murgai, A. (2018). Transforming digital marketing with artificial intelligence. *Int J Latest Technol Eng Manag Appl Sci*, *7*(4), 259–262.

Muthuprasad, T., Aiswarya, S., Aditya, K. S., & Jha, G. K. (2021). Students' perception and preference for online education in India during COVID – 19 pandemic. *Social Sciences & Humanities Open*, *3*(1), 1–11. doi:10.1016/j.ssaho.2020.100101 PMID:34173507

Muyanja, C., Nayiga, L., Brenda, N., & Nasinyama, G. (2011, October). Practices, knowledge and risk factors of street food vendors in Uganda. *Food Control*, *22*(10), 1551–1558. doi:10.1016/j.foodcont.2011.01.016

Muzaffar, A. T., Huq, I., & Mallik, B. A. (2009, February 18). Entrepreneurs of the Streets: An Analytical Work on the Street Food Vendors of Dhaka City. *International Journal of Business and Management*, *4*(2). Advance online publication. doi:10.5539/ijbm.v4n2p80

Muzaffar, H. (2023). Pandemic silver lining: How the COVID-19 pandemic helped women to beat the "gender stereotypes pandemic" in entrepreneurship. *Gender in Management*, *38*(1), 76–92. doi:10.1108/GM-10-2021-0316

Myers, D. (2023, January 16). 4 Great Examples of User-Generated Content (UGC). *Digital Marketing Institute*. https://digitalmarketinginstitute.com/blog/how-to-use-user-generated-content-ugc-with-4-great-examples

Nah, S., & Saxton, G. D. (2013). Modeling the adoption and use of social media by nonprofit organizations. *New Media & Society*, *15*(2), 294–313. doi:10.1177/1461444812452411

Nakara, W. A., Benmoussa, F. Z., & Jaouen, A. (2012). Entrepreneurship and social media marketing: Evidence from French small business. *International Journal of Entrepreneurship and Small Business*, *16*(4), 386–405. doi:10.1504/IJESB.2012.047608

Nambiar, D. (2020). The impact of online learning during COVID-19: Students' and teachers' perspective. *International Journal of Indian Psychology*, *8*(2), 783–793. doi:10.25215/0802.094

Naudin, A., & Patel, K. (2019). Entangled expertise: Women's use of social media in entrepreneurial work. *European Journal of Cultural Studies*, *22*(5–6), 511–527. doi:10.1177/1367549417743037

Navaneeth, M. S., & Ismail, S. (2022). How inclusive is online education in India: Lessons from pandemic. In *Socioeconomic inclusion during an era of online education, Manuel, B. G. (Edt.)* (pp. 135–155). IGI Global. doi:10.4018/978-1-6684-4364-4.ch007

NCA. (2022). *The National Coffee Data Trends Market Research Series - the "Atlas of American Coffee"*. Retrieved from: https://www.ncausa.org/Research-Trends/Market-Research/NCDT

Nedra, B. A., Hadhri, W., & Mezrani, M. (2019). Determinants of customers' intentions to use hedonic networks: The case of Instagram. *Journal of Retailing and Consumer Services*, *46*, 21–32. doi:10.1016/j.jretconser.2018.09.001

Nguyen, B., & Simkin, L. (2017). The Internet of Things (IoT) and marketing : The state of play, future trends and the implications for marketing. *Journal of Marketing Management*, *33*(1–2), 1–6. doi:10.1080/0267257X.2016.1257542

Nguyen, C. Q., Luu, C., & Hang, T. D. (2018). Factors affecting consumer-based brand equity of Vietnamese pharmaceutical companies. *Dalat University Journal of Science.*, *8*(1S, 1s), 145–157. doi:10.37569/DalatUniversity.8.1S.432(2018)

Nikou, S., Brännback, M. E., Orrensalo, T. P., & Widén, G. (2020). Social media and entrepreneurship: exploring the role of digital source selection and information literacy. *Understanding Social Media and Entrepreneurship*, 29-46.

Nizame, F. A., Alam, M. U., Masud, A. A., Shoab, A. K., Opel, A., Islam, M. K., Luby, S. P., & Unicomb, L. (2019, September 4). Hygiene in Restaurants and among Street Food Vendors in Bangladesh. *The American Journal of Tropical Medicine and Hygiene*, *101*(3), 566–575. doi:10.4269/ajtmh.18-0896 PMID:31333161

Nobi. (2023). Impact of Social Media Advertising on Buying Decision of Young Group of Consumers in Bangladesh: A Study Dhaka City. *Studies of Applied Economics, 41*(2). doi:10.25115/sae.v41i2.9105

NorströmL.IslindA.SnisU. (2020). Retrieved from https://www.researchgate.net/publication/342421823_Algorithmic_Work_The_Impact_of_Algorithms_on_Work_with_Social_Media

Nyawo, T., Kesa, H., & Onyenweaku, E. (2021, April 30). *Food Safety and Hygiene: Knowledge, Attitude and Practices among Food Handlers*. doi:10.46222/ajhtl.19770720.117

Obeidat, B. Y. (2012). The Relationship between Human Resource Information System (HRIS) Functions and Human Resource Management (HRM) Functionalities. *Journal of Management Research*, *4*(4). Advance online publication. doi:10.5296/jmr.v4i4.2262

Öberg, C. (2019). The role of business networks for innovation. *Journal of Innovation & Knowledge*, *4*(2), 124–128. doi:10.1016/j.jik.2017.10.001

Obschonka, M., & Audretsch, D. B. (2019). Artificial intelligence and big data in entrepreneurship: A new era has begun. *Small Business Economics*, *55*(3), 529–539. doi:10.1007/s11187-019-00202-4

Ognevyuk, G. (2016). Peculiarities of using intellectual property objects in social networks. *Entrepreneurship, Economy and Law*, (7), 21-25.

OkoliC.SchabramK. (2010). A Guide to conducting a Systematic Literature Review of Information Systems Research. *Social Science Research Network*. doi:10.2139/ssrn.1954824

Olanrewaju, A. S. T., Hossain, M. A., Whiteside, N., & Mercieca, P. (2020). Social media and entrepreneurship research: A literature review. *International Journal of Information Management*, *50*, 90–110. doi:10.1016/j.ijinfomgt.2019.05.011

Olanrewaju, A. T., Hossain, M. A., Whiteside, N., & Mercieca, P. (2020). *Social media and entrepreneurship research: A literature review. International Journal of Information Management*. https://www.researchgate.net/publication/338970287_Social_media_and_entrepreneurship_research_A_literature_review

Oliver, D., Lara-Rodríguez, K., Rojas Contreras, G., & Duque, E. J. (2019). Discovering emerging research topics for brand personality: A bibliometric analysis. *Australasian Marketing Journal*, *27*(4), 261–272. doi:10.1016/j.ausmj.2019.06.002

Olsson, A. K., & Bernhard, I. (2021). Keeping up the pace of digitalization in small businesses–Women entrepreneurs' knowledge and use of social media. *International Journal of Entrepreneurial Behaviour & Research*, *27*(2), 378–396. doi:10.1108/IJEBR-10-2019-0615

Omelchuk, N. (2020). How much Ukrainians spent on online purchases. *PAYSPACE*. https://psm7.com/ru/e-commerce/itogi-goda-skolko-potratili-ukraincy-na-pokupki-v-internete-v-2020.html

Ortiz-Ospina, E., & Roser, M. (2023, November 23). *The rise of Social Media*. Our World in Data. https://ourworldindata.org/rise-of-social-media

Osisanwo, F. Y., Akinsola, J. E. T., Awodele, O., Hinmikaiye, J. O., Olakanmi, O., & Akinjobi, J. (2017). Supervised machine learning algorithms: Classification and comparison. *International Journal of Computer Trends and Technology*, *48*(3), 128–138. doi:10.14445/22312803/IJCTT-V48P126

Oztemel, E., & Gursev, S. (2020). Literature review of Industry 4.0 and related technologies. *Journal of Intelligent Manufacturing*, *31*(1), 127–182. doi:10.1007/s10845-018-1433-8

Packalén, S. (2010). Culture and sustainability. *Corporate Social Responsibility and Environmental Management*, *17*(2), 118–121. doi:10.1002/csr.236

Palumbo, R., Manesh, M. F., Pellegrini, M. M., Caputo, A., & Flamini, G. (2021). Organizing a sustainable smart urban ecosystem: Perspectives and insights from a bibliometric analysis and literature review. *Journal of Cleaner Production*, *297*, 126622. doi:10.1016/j.jclepro.2021.126622

Palvia, S., Aeron, P., Gupta, P., Mahapatra, D., Parida, R., Rosner, R., & Sindhi, S. (2018). Online education: Worldwide status, challenges, trends, and implications. *Journal of Global Information Technology Management*, *21*(4), 233–241. doi:10.1080/1097198X.2018.1542262

Pangesti, V. N. (2022). Credible Online Reviews of Skincare Products on Brand Equity and Its Impact on Purchase Intention. *International Conference on Industrial and Systems Engineering, Technology, Innovation, and Management (ICISETIM),* 20-29.

Pappu, R., Quester, P., & Cooksey, R. (2005). Consumer-based brand equity: Improving the measurement empirical evidence. *Journal of Product and Brand Management, 14*(3), 143–154. doi:10.1108/10610420510601012

Parveen, F., Jaafar, N. I., & Ainin, S. (2016). Social media's impact on organizational performance and entrepreneurial orientation in organizations. *Management Decision, 54*(9), 2208–2234. doi:10.1108/MD-08-2015-0336

Paulraj, M. P., Majid, M. S. A., Yaacob, S., & Zin, M. Z. M. (2008, December). Motorbike engine faults diagnosing system using neural network. In *2008 International Conference on Electronic Design* (pp. 1-6). IEEE. 10.1109/ICED.2008.4786641

Păvăloaia, V. D., Anastasiei, I. D., & Fotache, D. (2020). Social media and e-mail marketing campaigns: Symmetry versus convergence. *Symmetry, 12*(12), 1940. doi:10.3390/sym12121940

Perifanis, N., & Kitsios, F. (2023). Investigating the Influence of Artificial intelligence on business Value in the digital Era of Strategy: a literature review. *Information, 14*(2), 85. doi:10.3390/info14020085

Petty, R. E., & Cacioppo, J. T. (1986). The Elaboration Likelihood Model of Persuasion. *Advances in Experimental Social Psychology, 19*, 123–205. doi:10.1016/S0065-2601(08)60214-2

Phoemphon, S., So-In, C., & Niyato, D. T. (2018). A hybrid model using fuzzy logic and an extreme learning machine with vector particle swarm optimization for wireless sensor network localization. *Applied Soft Computing, 65*, 101–120. doi:10.1016/j.asoc.2018.01.004

Power, B. (2017). How Harley-Davidson used artificial intelligence to increase New York sales leads by 2,930%. *Harvard Business Review.* https://hbr.org/2017/05/how-harley-davidson-used-predictive-analytics-to-increase-new-york-sales-leads-by-2930

Prasad, K., Tomar, A. S., De, T., & Soni, H. (2022). A Conceptual Model for Building the Relationship Between Augmented Reality, Experiential Marketing & Brand Equity. *International Journal of Professional Business Review, 7*(6), e01030. doi:10.26668/businessreview/2022.v7i6.1030

Pulizzi, J. (2012). The rise of storytelling as the new marketing. *Publishing Research Quarterly, 28*(2), 116–123. doi:10.1007/s12109-012-9264-5

Puntoni, S., Reczek, R., Giesler, M., & Botti, S. (2020). Consumers and Artificial Intelligence: An Experiential Perspective. *Journal of Marketing, 85*(1), 131–151. Advance online publication. doi:10.1177/0022242920953847

Rafi, T. (2022, June 9). *Why sustainability is crucial for corporate strategy.* Retrieved from World Economic Forum website: https://www.weforum.org/agenda/2022/06/why-sustainability-is-crucial-for-corporate-strategy/

Rahim, S. A., Islam, S. M. S., & Bepari, S. P. (2018). A contextual study on the development of women entrepreneurs in Bangladesh. *Global Journal of Entrepreneurship, 3*(1). https://link.gale.com/apps/doc/A613341443/AONE?u=anon~b51a2dff&sid=googleScholar&xid=919e2b15

Rahman, S. (2023). Women Making a Mark in Digital Space. *The Daily Star.* Retrieved from https://www.thedailystar.net/business/economy/news/women-making-mark-digital-space-2977961

Rahman, A. (2021). Using students' experience to derive effectiveness of COVID-19-lockdown-induced emergency online learning at undergraduate level: Evidence from Assam, India. *Higher Education for the Future, 8*(1), 71–89. doi:10.1177/2347631120980549

Rahman, M. M., Hasan, M. J., Deb, B. C., Rahman, M. S., & Kabir, A. S. (2023). The effect of social media entrepreneurship on sustainable development: Evidence from online clothing shops in Bangladesh. *Heliyon*, *9*(9), e19397. doi:10.1016/j.heliyon.2023.e19397 PMID:37662716

Raidah, N. (2023, July 16). Waffle-Up: worth the fuss? The Daily Star. https://www.thedailystar.net/shout/news/waffle-worth-the-fuss-3193591

Rajhans, V., Memon, U., Patil, V., & Goyal, A. (2020). Impact of COVID – 19 on academic activities and way forward in Indian optometry. *Journal of Optometry*, *13*(1), 216–226. doi:10.1016/j.optom.2020.06.002 PMID:32703749

Ramane, D. V., Devare, U. K., & Kapatkar, M. V. (2021). The impact of online learning on learners' education and health. *The Online Journal of Distance Education and e-Learning : TOJDEL*, *9*(2), 303–309.

Rani, S., & Bhattacharya, S. (2022). A descriptive study to assess the impact and perception of online classes on student community pan India during COVID-19. *The Journal of Communicable Diseases*, *1*(1), 9–14. doi:10.24321/0019.5138.202202

Reisach, U. (2021). The responsibility of social media in times of societal and political manipulation. *European Journal of Operational Research*, *291*(3), 906–917. doi:10.1016/j.ejor.2020.09.020 PMID:32982027

Ren, S., Tang, G., & Jackson, S. E. (2017). Green human resource management research in emergence: A review and future directions. *Asia Pacific Journal of Management*, *2*, 1–35.

Reuer, J. J., & Devarakonda, R. (2017). Partner selection in R&D collaborations: Effects of affiliations with venture capitalists. *Organization Science*, *28*(3), 574–595. doi:10.1287/orsc.2017.1124

Rifi, A., & Mostafa, R. B. (2021). Brand credibility and customer-based brand equity: A service recovery perspective. *Journal of Financial Services Marketing*, *27*(1), 1–16. doi:10.1057/s41264-021-00097-x

Roeckelein, J. E. (2006). *Elsevier's Dictionary of Psychological Theories*. Retrieved from http://ci.nii.ac.jp/ncid/BA7675599X

Romanyshyn, S. B., & Greskiv, I. R. (2015). Peculiarities of marketing activities in social networks. *Bulletin of the Lviv Polytechnic National University,* (819), 183-188.

Roskosa, A., & Stukalina, Y. (2022). *Exploring Brand Equity-Related Factors in Higher Education*. Rural Environment, Education and Personality. Available at https://llufb.llu.lv/conference/REEP/2022/Latvia_REEP_2022_proceedings_No15_online-27- 34.pdf doi:10.22616/REEP.2022.15.003

Roy, D. G., Battacharya, S., & Mukherjee, S. (2020). Qualitative explorations into customer-based brand equity (CBBE) for medical tourism in India. *The Qualitative Report*, *23*(10), 2422–2452.

Roy, S., & Brown, S. (2022). Higher education in India in the time of pandemic, sans a learning management system. *AERA Open*, *8*(1), 23–37. doi:10.1177/23328584211069527

Rungsrisawat, S., & Sirinapatpokin, S. (2019). Impact of brand equity on consumer purchase intent. *Utopía y Praxis Latinoamericana*, *24*(6), 360–369.

SadikuM.AshaoluT.MajebiA.MusaS. (2021). Retrieved from https://www.researchgate.net/publication/368060163_Artificial_Intelligence_in_Social_Media

Sahai, S., Goel, R., Venaik, A., & Garg, V. (2019). Impact of digital commerce on fashion industry to gain customer loyalty. *International Journal of Engineering and Advanced Technology*, *8*(5), 730–740.

Sahoo, M. B. (2019). People Analytics and Disruptive Technologies are Transforming Human Resources Roles. *Southwestern Business Administration Journal*, *18*(1), 4.

Saner, R., & Yiu, L. (2019). Jamaica's development of women entrepreneurship: Challenges and opportunities. *Public Administration and Policy*, *22*(2), 152–172. doi:10.1108/PAP-09-2019-0023

Sanzida Akter Department of computer science and Engineering. (2023) .*Bengali movie recommendation system using k nearest neighbor and cosine similarity: Proceedings of the 2023 9th International Conference on Computer Technology Applications, ACM Other conferences*. Available at: https://dl.acm.org/doi/abs/10.1145/3605423.3605432

Saxena, M., Bagga, T., & Gupta, S. 2021, January. Hr during covid-19 era: Study on recent HR transformations through technological tools and trends. In *2021 11th International Conference on Cloud Computing, Data Science & Engineering (Confluence)* (pp. 110-113). IEEE.

SchererM. U. (2021, March 8). *About*. HeinOnline. https://heinonline.org/HOL/LandingPage?handle=hein.journals%2Fhjlt29&div=15&id=&page=

Schjoedt, L., Brännback, M. E., & Carsrud, A. L. (2020). *Understanding Social Media and Entrepreneurship*. Springer. doi:10.1007/978-3-030-43453-3

Secundo, G., Del Vecchio, P., & Mele, G. (2021). Social media for entrepreneurship: Myth or reality? A structured literature review and a future research agenda. *International Journal of Entrepreneurial Behaviour & Research*, *27*(1), 149–177. doi:10.1108/IJEBR-07-2020-0453

Sengupta, S. (2022). Possibilities and challenges of online education in India during the COVDI-19 pandemic. *International Journal of Web-Based Learning and Teaching Technologies*, *17*(4), 1–11. doi:10.4018/IJWLTT.285567

Seo, E. J., & Park, J. W. (2019). A study on the effects of social media marketing activities on brand equity and customer response in the airline industry. *Journal of Air Transport Management*, *6*(6), 36–41.

Sestino, A., & De Mauro, A. (2021). Leveraging Artificial Intelligence in Business: Implications, Applications and Methods. *Technology Analysis and Strategic Management*, 1–14.

Sestino, A., Prete, M. I., Piper, L., & Guido, G. (2020). Internet of Things and Big Data as enablers for business digitalization strategies. *Technovation*, *98*, 102173. doi:10.1016/j.technovation.2020.102173

SFA, X. S. (n.d.). *Social Media and Increased Venture Creation Tendency With Innovative Ideas: The Case of Female Students in Asia*. Academic Press.

Shamaileh, N. A., Eldahamsheh, M. M., Alneimat, S., Istaiteyeh, R., Azzam, I. A., & Al-Hawary, S. I. S. (2023). The effects of smart human resources 4.0 on employee job effectiveness: The mediating role of employee job satisfaction. *International Journal of Data and Network Science*, *7*(2), 801–808. doi:10.5267/j.ijdns.2023.1.009

Shamim, S., Cang, S., Yu, H., & Li, Y. (2016). *Management Approaches for Industry 4.0: A human resource management perspective*. IEEE. doi:10.1109/CEC.2016.7748365

Shankar, V. (2018). How Artificial Intelligence (AI) Is Reshaping Retailing. *Journal of Retailing*, *94*(4), 6–9. doi:10.1016/S0022-4359(18)30076-9

Sharma, B. (2021). Online classes experience among students during lockdown. *The online Journal of Distance and e-Learning*, *9*(2), 247-254.

Sharma, R. (2019). Consumer-Based Brand Equity: Does Country of Origin (COO) Matter to Generation Z Consumers? *South Asian Journal of Management*, *26*(1), 136–150.

Sheth, J., & Kellstadt, C. H. (2021). Next frontiers of research in data driven marketing: Will techniques keep up with data tsunami? *Journal of Business Research*, *125*, 780–784. doi:10.1016/j.jbusres.2020.04.050

Shi, J., Nyedu, D. S. K., Huang, L., & Lovia, B. S. (2022). Graduates' Entrepreneurial Intention in a Developing Country: The Influence of Social Media and E-commerce Adoption (SMEA) and its Antecedents. *Information Development*. Advance online publication. doi:10.1177/02666669211073457

Shpykulyak, O. G., & Hrytsaenko, M. I. (2019). Intellectual model of social capital: concepts of institutionalization. *Cooperation,* 186-196.

ShrivastavaV.ResilienceS. (2023). Revitalizing Asian American and Pacific Islander Entrepreneurship Through AI-Driven Social Media Marketing Techniques. https://ssrn.com/abstract=4507541 doi:10.2139/ssrn.4507541

Siddiqui, K. (2022). *Celebrity Endorsement, Brand Equity, and Green Cosmetics Purchase Intention Among Chinese Youth*. Academic Press.

Sierra, K., Markovic, S., Singh, J. V., & Iglesias, O. (2019). Do customer perceptions of corporate services brand ethicality improve brand equity? Considering the roles of brand heritage, brand image, and recognition benefits. *Journal of Business Ethics*, *154*(2), 441–459. doi:10.1007/s10551-017-3455-0

Silaban, P. H., Chen, W., & Silalahi, A. D. K. (2022). The use of social media by entrepreneurial and small firms: systematic literature review. *2022 International Conference on Decision Aid Sciences and Applications (DASA)*, 947–952. 10.1109/DASA54658.2022.9765244

Simba, A., Martins Ogundana, O., Braune, E., & Dana, L. (2023). Community financing in entrepreneurship: A focus on women entrepreneurs in the developing world. *Journal of Business Research*, *163*, 113962. doi:10.1016/j.jbusres.2023.113962

Singh, A. K., & Ashraf, S. N. (2019). Viability of Bayh-Dole Act of USA in context of India: critical evidence from review of literature. *JNNCE Journal of Engineering & Management, 3*(1), 7-22. http://jjem.jnnce.ac.in/article/JJEM030102.pdf

Singh, A. K., & Jyoti, B. (2023a). Empirical evidence from different income group countries on the interdependency between digitalization and economic development. In 5G, Artificial Intelligence, and Next Generation Internet of Things: Digital Innovation for Green and Sustainable Economies (pp. 44-85). IGI Global. doi:10.4018/978-1-6684-8634-4.ch003

Singh, A. K., Kumar, S., & Jyoti, B. (2022). Impact of the COVID-19 on food security and sustainable development goals in India: Evidence from existing literature. *GNOSI: An Interdisciplinary Journal of Human Theory and Praxis, 5*(2), 94-109. http://gnosijournal.com/index.php/gnosi/article/view/196/225

Singh, S. (2020). An analysis of factors responsible for the rapid growth of e-learning in India. *Palarch's Journal of Archaeology of Egypt/Egyptology*, *17*(12), 1454-1466.

Singh, A. K. (2023). Relative performance of entrepreneurship ecosystem for selected countries using a composite Z-score technique of index estimation. *Eurasian Journal of Management & Social Sciences*, *4*(2), 1–32. doi:10.23918/ejmss.V4i2p1

Singh, A. K., Ashraf, S. N., & Arya, A. (2019). Estimating factors affecting technical efficiency in Indian manufacturing sector. *Eurasian Journal of Business and Economics*, *12*(24), 65–86. doi:10.17015/ejbe.2019.024.04

Singh, A. K., Ashraf, S. N., Sharma, S. K., & Kumar, S. (2023). Factors affecting farm income and climate adaptation strategies in the farming sector of Gujarat state of India. In B. J. Sadhik, J. Adewole, A. Yeneneh, & L. Abidoye (Eds.), *Opportunities and Challenges in Climate-Friendly Clean Water and Energy Technologies* (pp. 122–147). IGI Global. doi:10.4018/978-1-6684-7303-0.ch006

Singh, A. K., & Jyoti, B. (2020). Factors affecting firm's annual turnover in selected manufacturing industries of India: An empirical study. *Business Perspectives and Research*, *2*(3), 33–59. doi:10.38157/business-perspective-review.v2i3.206

Singh, A. K., & Jyoti, B. (2023b). Does digitalization have a bi-directional causal relationship with the entrepreneurship ecosystem? Evidence from a country-wise panel data analysis. In R. Yanamandra & L. Indiran (Eds.), *Handbook of Research on Designing Sustainable Strategies to Develop Entrepreneurial Intention* (pp. 178–172). IGI Global. doi:10.4018/978-1-6684-8781-5.ch007

Singh, A. K., & Jyoti, B. (2023c). *Impact of digitalization on global sustainable development across countries*. Green and Low-carbon Economy. doi:10.47852/bonviewGLCE32021482

Singh, A. K., & Kumar, S. (2021). Assessing the performance and factors affecting industrial development in Indian states: An empirical analysis. *Journal of Social Economics Research*, *8*(2), 135–154. doi:10.18488/journal.35.2021.82.135.154

Singh, A. K., & Kumar, S. (2022). Expert's perception on technology transfer and commercialization, and intellectual property rights in India: Evidence from selected research organizations. *Journal of Management, Economics, and Industrial Organization*, *6*(1), 1–33. doi:10.31039/jomeino.2022.6.1.1

Singh, A. K., Singh, B., & Ashraf, S. N. (2020). Implications of intellectual property protection, and science and technological development in the manufacturing sector in selected economies. *Journal of Advocacy. Research in Education*, *7*(1), 16–35. https://oaji.net/articles/2021/1704-1615668997.pdf

Singh, A. K., & Singh, S. (2024). A case study from kanpur nagar, uttar pradesh for assessing the economic value of water and its determinants. In A. Karmaoui (Ed.), *Water-Soil-Plant-Animal Nexus in the Era of Climate Change* (pp. 212–242). IGI Global. doi:10.4018/978-1-6684-9838-5.ch010

Singh, A., Varghese, L. M., Yadav, R. D., & Mahajan, R. (2020). A pollution reducing enzymatic deinking approach for recycling of mixed office waste paper. *Environmental Science and Pollution Research International*, *27*(36), 45814–45823. doi:10.1007/s11356-020-10440-9 PMID:32803575

Singh, K., Hasan, M., & Rajendran, R. P. (2023). Opportunities and Challenges of AI/ML in Finance. *The Impact of AI Innovation on Financial Sectors in the Era of Industry*, *5*(0), 238–260.

Sirimanne, S. N., & Adhikari, R. (2023, March 8). *How to unlock women's potential in the digital economy*. UNCTAD.

Sivathanu, B., & Pillai, R. (2018). Smart HR 4.0 – how industry 4.0 is disrupting HR. *Human Resource Management International Digest*, *26*(4), 7–11. doi:10.1108/HRMID-04-2018-0059

Sk, M. S. (2021). Impact of COVID-19 on e-learning at higher education in India. *Towards Excellence*, *13*(1), 184–191.

Smal, V., & Kokot, V. (2017). What you should know about social entrepreneurship [Guide]. Academic Press.

Smith, L., Liang, Q., James, P., & Lin, W. (2017). Assessing the utility of social media as a data source for flood risk management using a real-time modelling framework. *Journal of Flood Risk Management*, *10*(3), 370–380. doi:10.1111/jfr3.12154

Song, W., & Yu, H. (2018). Green innovation strategy and green innovation: The roles of green creativity and green organizational identity. *Corporate Social Responsibility and Environmental Management*, *25*(2), 135–150. doi:10.1002/csr.1445

Sozer, E. G., & Civelek, M. E. (2018). The Effect of Perceived Benefit on Consumer Based Brand Equity in Online Shopping Context. *Ege Academic Review*, *18*(4), 711–725.

Sreeraj, R. N., Joy, S., Lijisha, P. V., & Senthilkumar, T. (2021). A study to assess the impact of online learning among school children in Kerala. *Medicon Medical Sciences*, *1*(2), 29–34.

Srinidhi, S., Vezhaventhan, D., Shoba, J. K. S., Kirubagaran, K., Karthikheyan, T. C., & Gopalan, K. R. (2022). Effect Of Online Education on Elementary Education in India *Journal for Educators. Teachers and Trainers*, *13*(2), 76–88.

Stalidis, G., Karapistolis, D., & Vafeiadis, A. (2015). Marketing Decision Support Using Artificial Intelligence and Knowledge Modeling: Application to Tourist Destination Management. *Procedia: Social and Behavioral Sciences*, *175*, 106–113. doi:10.1016/j.sbspro.2015.01.1180

Struggles of Dhaka's Street food Vendors to Survive During Pandemic. (n.d.). Retrieved January 8, 2024, from https://www.changemag-diinsider.com/blog/struggles-of-dhaka-s-street-food-vendors-to-survive-during-pandemic

Study explores social media's influence on crowdfunding campaigns. (n.d.). News Center. https://news.utdallas.edu/business-management/social-media-crowdfunding-2022/

Stukalina, Y., & Pavlyuk, D. (2021). Using customer-based brand equity model in the higher education context: simulating the current university's brand. *Business, Management and Economics Engineering, 2*(11), 278-288.

Sukumar, A., Jafari-Sadeghi, V., & Xu, Z. (2021). The influences of social media on Chinese start-up stage entrepreneurship. *World Review of Entrepreneurship, Management and Sustainable Development*, *17*(5), 559–578. doi:10.1504/WREMSD.2021.117442

Sumardi, A. (2018). Brand Equity: Anticedents Consumer Responses. *Media Riset Bisnis & Manajemen.*, *18*(2), 100–110. doi:10.25105/mrbm.v18i2.5002

Supply chain outsourcing vs in-house - an honest comparison. (2022, March 9). Young Foodies. https://youngfoodies.co.uk/supply-chain-outsourcing-vs-in-house-an-honest-comparison

Surugiu, M. R., & Surugiu, C. (2015). Heritage tourism entrepreneurship and social media: Opportunities and challenges. *Procedia: Social and Behavioral Sciences*, *188*, 74–81. doi:10.1016/j.sbspro.2015.03.340

Szirmai, A., Naudé, W., & Goedhuys, M. (Eds.). (2011). *Entrepreneurship, innovation, and economic development*. Oxford University Press. doi:10.1093/acprof:oso/9780199596515.001.0001

Tadesse, S., & Muluye, W. (2020). The impact of COVID-19 pandemic on education system in developing countries: A review. *Open Journal of Social Sciences*, *8*(1), 159–170. doi:10.4236/jss.2020.810011

Tan, B., Pan, S., & Zuo, M. (2011). *Attaining and enacting green leadership: Insights from the green IT initiatives of China Mobile*. Academic Press.

Tang, G., Chen, Y., Jiang, Y., Paillé, P., & Jia, J. (2018). Green human resource management practices: Scale development and validity. *Asia Pacific Journal of Human Resources*, *56*(1), 31–55. doi:10.1111/1744-7941.12147

Tannady, H. (2022). Ideal Self-Congruence: Its Impacts on Customer Love and Loyalty to Luxury Brands in Indonesia. *International Journal of Professional Business Review*, *7*(6), e0769. doi:10.26668/businessreview/2022.v7i6.e769

Tareq, Homsi, Said, & Frehait. (2021). Role of Big Data in Increasing Brand Equity within Pharmaceutical Industry. *Academy of Entrepreneurship Journal*, *28*(1), 7–13.

Team, A. (2023, January 31). *The Impact of Social Media on Entrepreneurship*. AIContentfy. Retrieved from https://aicontentfy.com/en/blog/impact-of-social-media-on-entrepreneurship

The Daily Star. (n.d.). *The Daily Star – Leading English Daily among Bangladesh Newspapers*. Retrieved from https://www.thedailystar.net/

The Financial Express. (2022, March 31). Gulshan, Banani, Baridhara residents to pay increased holding tax from July. *The Financial Express*. Retrieved from https://thefinancialexpress.com.bd

The history of social media and its impact on business - researchgate. (n.d.). https://www.researchgate.net/publication/303216233_The_history_of_social_media_and_its_impact_on_business

The Street Food Initiative in Khulna | Improving food safety in Bangladesh | FAO. (n.d.). https://www.fao.org/in-action/food-safety-bangladesh/news/detail/en/c/411752/

Thomas, L., Orme, E., & Kerrigan, F. (2020). Student loneliness: The role of social media through life transitions. *Computers & Education*, *146*, 103754. doi:10.1016/j.compedu.2019.103754

Tradingeconomics.com. (2019). Available at: https://tradingeconomics.com/bangladesh/consumer-spending

Treiblmaier, H. (2018). The impact of the blockchain on the supply chain: A theory-based research framework and a call for action. *Supply Chain Management*, *23*(6), 545–549. doi:10.1108/SCM-01-2018-0029

Troise, C., Dana, L. P., Tani, M., & Lee, K. Y. (2022). Social media and entrepreneurship: Exploring the impact of social media use of start-ups on their entrepreneurial orientation and opportunities. *Journal of Small Business and Enterprise Development*, *29*(1), 47–73. doi:10.1108/JSBED-01-2021-0041

Turan, M., & Kara, A. (2018). Online social media usage behavior of entrepreneurs in an emerging market: Reasons, expected benefits and intentions. *Journal of Research in Marketing and Entrepreneurship*, *20*(2), 273–291. doi:10.1108/JRME-09-2016-0034

Ugolkova, O. Z. (2021). Digital marketing and social networks. *Management and Entrepreneurship in Ukraine: Stages of Formation and Development Problems, 3*(1), 146-152.

Unilever. (2020, August 13). *Global experts rank Unilever No.1 for sustainability leadership*. Retrieved from Unilever website: https://www.unilever.com/news/news-search/2020/global-experts-rank-unilever-no1-for-sustainab ility-leadership/

Upadhyay, N., Upadhyay, S., & Dwivedi, Y. K. (2021). Theorizing artificial intelligence acceptance and digital entrepreneurship model. *International Journal of Entrepreneurial Behaviour & Research*, *28*(5), 1138–1166. doi:10.1108/IJEBR-01-2021-0052

Uz Zaman, A. H., & Islam, M. J. (2011). Small and medium enterprises development in Bangladesh: Problems and prospects. *ASA University Review*, *5*(1), 145–160.

Uzir, M. U. H., Al Halbusi, H., Lim, R., Jerin, I., Hamid, A. B. A., Ramayah, T., & Haque, A. (2021). Applied Artificial Intelligence and user satisfaction: Smartwatch usage for healthcare in Bangladesh during COVID-19. *Technology in Society*, *67*, 101780. doi:10.1016/j.techsoc.2021.101780 PMID:34697510

Varyani, H., & Navaneeth, M. S. (2022). The past, present and future of e-learning: In India. *International Journal of Policy Sciences and Law*, *1*(1), 99–118.

Vivarelli, M. (2012). *Innovation, employment and skills in advanced and developing countries: A survey of the literature*. Academic Press.

Voola, R., Bandyopadhyay, C., Azmat, F., Ray, S., & Nayak, L. (2022). How are consumer behavior and marketing strategy researchers incorporating the SDGs? A review and opportunities for future research. *Australasian Marketing Journal*, *30*(2), 119–130. doi:10.1177/14413582221079431

Vuong, B. N., Tushar, H., & Hossain, S. F. A. (2022). *The effect of social support on job performance through organizational commitment and innovative work behavior: Does innovative climate matter?* Retrieved from https://www.emerald.com/insight/content/doi/10.1108/APJBA-06-2021-0256/full/html

Vương, B. N., Tushar, H., & Hossain, S. F. A. (2022). The effect of social support on job performance through organizational commitment and innovative work behavior: Does innovative climate matter? *Asia-Pacific Journal of Business Administration*. Advance online publication. doi:10.1108/APJBA-06-2021-0256

Vytvytska, O., Suvorova, S., & Koryugin, A. (2022). The influence of digital marketing on the development of entrepreneurship in the conditions of war. *Economy and Society*, (40), 1–7.

Wach, K., Duong, C. D., Ejdys, J., Kazlauskaitė, R., Korzynski, P., Mazurek, G., Paliszkiewicz, J., & Ziemba, E. (2023, June). 'The Dark Side of Generative Artificial Intelligence: A Critical Analysis of Controversies and Risks of ChatGPT'. *Entrepreneurial Business and Economics Review*, *11*(2), 7–30. eber.uek.krakow.pl. doi:10.15678/EBER.2023.110201

Wafeq, M., Al Serhan, O., Catherine Gleason, K., Dasanayaka, S. W. S. B., Houjeir, R., & Al Sakka, M. (2019). Marketing management and optimism of Afghan female entrepreneurs. *Journal of Entrepreneurship in Emerging Economies*, *11*(3), 436–463. doi:10.1108/JEEE-02-2018-0020

Waffle Up: A bistro trendsetter. (n.d.). The Financial Express. https://thefinancialexpress.com.bd/lifestyle/others/waffle-up-a-bistro-trendsetter-1661320894

WaffleUp. Square is the new heart. (2022, June 10). *The Business Standard*. https://www.tbsnews.net/features/food/waffleup-square-new-heart-437010

Wallsten, S. J., & Rhyan, C. (2014). Social media and entrepreneurship: The case of food trucks. *Technology Policy Institute: Selected Works*, *1*, 1–12.

Wang, Y., McKee, M., Torbica, A., & Stuckler, D. (2019). Systematic literature review on the spread of health-related misinformation on social media. *Social Science & Medicine*, *240*, 112552. doi:10.1016/j.socscimed.2019.112552 PMID:31561111

Wang, Y., & Yang, Y. (2020). Dialogic communication on social media: How organizations use Twitter to build dialogic relationships with their publics. *Computers in Human Behavior*, *104*, 106183. doi:10.1016/j.chb.2019.106183

Wang, Z. R., & Marjerison, R. K. (2019). Factors Influencing Consumers' Purchase Intentions Towards Made to-Order Tea Drinks in China. *International Journal of Food and Beverage Manufacturing and Business Models.*, *4*(2), 29–52. doi:10.4018/IJFBMBM.2019070103

Wilson, H. J., & Daugherty, P. R. (2018). Collaborative intelligence: Humans and AI are joining forces. *Harvard Business Review*, *96*(4), 114–123.

Witte, K. (1992). Putting the fear back into fear appeals: The extended parallel process model. *Communication Monographs*, *59*(4), 329–349. doi:10.1080/03637759209376276

Wright, L. T., Robin, R., Stone, M., & Aravopoulou, D. E. (2019). Adoption of big data technology for innovation in B2B marketing. *Journal of Business-To-Business Marketing*, *26*(3-4), 281–293. doi:10.1080/1051712X.2019.1611082

Wu, Y., & Song, D. (2019). Gratifications for social media use in entrepreneurship courses: Learners' perspective. *Frontiers in Psychology*, *10*, 1270. doi:10.3389/fpsyg.2019.01270 PMID:31214081

Xie, C., Bagozzi, R. P., & Grønhaug, K. (2015). The role of moral emotions and individual differences in consumer responses to corporate green and non-green actions. *Journal of the Academy of Marketing Science*, *43*(3), 333–356. doi:10.1007/s11747-014-0394-5

Xu, L.Q., Wang, K.Y., Ma, C.G., & Zhang, X.F. (2020). Business intelligence in online customer textual reviews: Understanding consumer perceptions and influential factors. *International Journal of Information Management, 37*(6), 673-683.

Yadav, A. K. (2021). Impact of online teaching on students' education and health in India during the pandemic of COVDI-19. *Coronaviruses*, *2*(2), 516–520. doi:10.2174/2666796701999201005212801

Yang, D., Sonmez, M., Gonzalez, M., Liu, Y., & Yoder, C. Y. (2019). Consumer-based brand equity and consumer-based brand performance: Evidence from smartphone brands in the USA. *Journal of Brand Management*, *26*(6), 717–732. doi:10.1057/s41262-019-00154-w

Yang, L., Zhang, H., Shen, H., Huang, X., Zhou, X., Rong, G., & Dong, S. (2021). Quality Assessment in Systematic Literature Reviews: A Software Engineering Perspective. *Information and Software Technology*, *130*, 106397. doi:10.1016/j.infsof.2020.106397

Yarmolyuk, O. Ya., Fisun, Yu. V., & Shapovalova, A. A. (2020). Social networks as a modern promotion tool. *Entrepreneurship and Innovation, 11*(2), 62-65. doi:10.37320/2415-3583/11.28

Yong, J. Y., Yusliza, M. Y., & Fawehinmi, O. O. (2020). Green human resource management: A systematic literature review from 2007 to 2019. *Benchmarking*, *27*(7), 2005–2027. doi:10.1108/BIJ-12-2018-0438

Yoo, B., & Donthu, N. (2021). Developing a Scale to Measure the Perceived Quality of an Online Shopping Mall. *Quarterly Journal of Electronic Commerce*, *2*(1), 31–47.

Yuri, B. (2021). *Transformation of business sustainability strategies of FMCG companies in the 21st century on the examples of Unilever and L'Oréal* [Master's Thesis]. Retrieved from https://dspace.spbu.ru/bitstream/11701/32242/1/MT_Ksenia_Koreneva_GSOM.pdf

Yuskiv, N. O. (2021). Legal problems of electronic commerce in social. *European integration changes in the legislation of Ukraine*, 127.

Yusoff, Y. B., Anwar, I. F. B., Rahayu, S. B., Lajin, N. F. B. M., & Ridzwan, M. B. (2023). A Review on Integrating Emotional Intelligence with Artificial Intelligence in Social Media Marketing Among Entrepreneurs. *Journal of Contemporary Social Science and Education Studies*, *3*(2), 44–50. https://www.researchgate.net/publication/373840570_Journal_of_Contemporary_Social_Science_and_Education_Studies_A_Review_on_Integrating_Emotional_Intelligence_with_Artificial_Intelligence_in_Social_Media_Marketing_Among_Entrepreneurs

Zapanta, T. (2023, February 28). *The impact of AI on business*. Microsourcing. Retrieved from https://www.microsourcing.com/learn/blog/the-impact-of-ai-on-business/

Zeithaml, V. A. (1988). Consumer Perceptions of Price, Quality and Value: A Means-End Model and Synthesis of Evidence. *Journal of Marketing, 52*(3), 2-22. Available at: https://www.lucintel.com/Malaysia/opportunities-for-the-coffee-maker.aspx

Zhai, Al Mamun, Hayat, Salamah, Low, & Ali. (2022). Brand equity trend analysis for fashion brands (2001-2021). *The Journal of Psychology*, *13*(1), 238–255.

Zhurylo, V. V. (2020). Influence marketing as a communication tool for product promotion in social Internet networks. *Entrepreneurship and Innovation*, *11*(2), 29-36.

Zia, Younus, & Mirza. (2021). Investigating the Impact of Brand Image and Brand Loyalty on Brand Equity: the Mediating Role of Brand Awareness. *International Journal of Innovation, Creativity and Change, 15*(2), 91–106.

Zientara, P., & Zamojska, A. (2016). Green organizational climates and employee pro-environmental behavior in the behavior in the hotel industry. *Journal of Sustainable Tourism*, *1*, 1–18.

Zollo, L., Filieri, R., Rialti, R., & Yoon, S. (2020). Unpacking the relationship between social media marketing and brand equity: The mediating role of consumers' benefits and experience. *Journal of Business Research*, *11*(7), 256–267. doi:10.1016/j.jbusres.2020.05.001

About the Contributors

Syed Far Abid Hossain, Dr., is currently working as an Assistant Professor at BRAC Business School, BRAC University. He has obtained PhD in Management Science from the School of Management (AACSB Accredited), Xi'an Jiaotong University, PRC. He holds an MBA (Management) degree from the University of Sunderland, UK and a BBA (Marketing) degree from Dhaka University. Dr. Abid authored 55+ academic journal articles, conference papers and book chapters in internationally recognized, peer reviewed and well-indexed Journals (ISI, Scopus, SSCI, SCIE, ABDC, ESCI, EI) from Elsevier, Springer, SAGE, Taylor and Francis, Frontiers, Science Direct, Emerald, MDPI and IGI global. Dr. Abid has published numerous book chapters and conference proceedings with famous publishers like Springer Nature and IGI global. His research interests include AI, market turbulence, academic performance, education psychology, education management, technology in education, women entrepreneurship, innovation and media entrepreneurship. Apart from his current roles at BRAC Business School, Dr. Abid served as a reviewer of 45 famous journals from reputed publishers including Elsevier, Wiley, Springer, SAGE, IGI Global, etc.

* * *

Faiza Tanaz Ahsan is a research assistant. She completed her MSc from the University of Nottingham in Economic Development and Policy Analysis in 2023. She is currently working as a Student Mentor at an NGO named IntoUniversity in the United Kingdom. Her research interests lie in field experiments in developing countries, policy measures, addressing gender gaps in various contexts, women empowerment and the financial sector.

Rahma Akhter, a distinguished Senior Lecturer at the Business School of BRAC University, stands as an accomplished scholar with a fervent commitment to academic and research pursuits. Currently pursuing a Doctor of Philosophy (PhD) program at Xi'an Jiaotong University, she has chosen to further enrich her expertise at one of China's renowned institutions celebrated for its academic prowess and impactful research contributions. Her scholarly journey is characterized by a profound passion for research, reflected in her noteworthy publications in esteemed journals. Her research endeavors span a diverse range of topics, including the integration of destination branding and supply chain management opportunities, as well as investigations into tourism, consumer behavior, branding, and the socio-cultural factors influencing entrepreneurial activities.

Tanzila Akther is an aspiring student enrolled at BRAC University in Bangladesh, passionately navigating the realms of Finance, Banking, Insurance, and Marketing through a dual major pursuit. Tanzila's journey illuminates a path where academic excellence converges with a fervor for empowering both academic peers and the broader community through the exploration of new ideas and research avenues.

Tazrian Binte Ansar is a final year undergraduate BBA student at BRAC University. They have majored in Marketing, and their keen interest in Information Technology further led them to pursue a minor in Management Information Systems. They had been actively involved in the Marketing and Public Relations department for the university's Business Club, BIZBEE, resigning from their Assistant Director position in June of 2023. Currently, they are involved in their department as a Student Tutor, supervising students and aiding faculties. In their free time, they indulge themselves in art, film, and music. They are also very passionate about research and aspire to pursue a Master's in Marketing abroad after completing their Bachelor's.

Amreen Azam is a second-year student at Swinburne University of Science and Technology as of 2023. She has a strong desire to study and explore. She was employed at NNO (National Newspaper Olympiad) as the head of human resources. She presently works as a crew member at McDonald's, where she completed her internship.

Abdullah Al Fahim is currently enrolled in the Bachelor of Business Administration program at Brac University. He is a final-year student and is doing his internship at bKash Limited as a bnext intern. He is interested in the corporate sector to help his career flourish.

Sarika Faisal is a research assistant at BBS, BRAC University.

Meenakshi Gupta is working as an Assistant Professor in the School of Economics, at Shri Mata Vaishno Devi University, Katra. She has teaching and research experience of almost 16 years. She has been a part of many academic and non- academic committees of the university since 2007. Her main areas of interest are Agricultural Economics, Environmental Economics and Development Economics. Her research work has been published in various national and international journals. She has contributed to various books also. She has also presented various articles at National and International Conferences. She is also awarded with many prestigious national and international awards. She is a life Member of Indian Economic Association, Indian Society of Agri- business and Management, Indian Society of Agricultural Economics, TIES, AERA, etc.

Md. Ikramul Haque is a third-year undergraduate student at Brac University pursuing a Bachelor of Business Administration degree. He appreciates fitness and enjoys fitness-related stuff and informally promotes them on social media. He has a strong interest in managing tasks and participates actively in the Business Club at Brac University's Organizing and Managing Department (BIZ BEE). In addition, he has an interest in entrepreneurship and aspires to run a small business independently.

Wong Chee Hoo received a PhD in marketing from Universiti Putra Malaysia's Graduate School of Management in 2012. He had worked in the advertising industry for more than two decades, lastly at one of Malaysia's largest media companies. The past four years have seen him serve as an associate professor at INTI International University Malaysia. He is an associate managing editor for the Journal of Business and Social Sciences, where he provides peer reviews of manuscripts (JoBSS). His research interests lie in the areas of sustainable marketing, brand strategy, and consumer intent.

Amaresh Jha is an experienced media professional: has been a Senior Producer with Zee News, News Express, TV9, India News, and India TV and has also produced news for DD News. Amaresh has previously taught at Amity University (where he led the UG Program at Amity School of Communication) and Galgotias University. Apart from his work as a multimedia professional, Amaresh's previous teaching includes courses on the web journalism, data journalism, multimedia storytelling, television production, digital media production, and communication research- among other things. Amaresh is a reviewer and article editor of reputed journals published by SAGE and CG Network, USA.

Fatima Tuz Juhana, a student at BRAC University in Bangladesh, passionately seeks a minor in Computer Information Systems and a major in Human Resources Management. She is known for her insatiable interest and drive for understanding, Fatima stands as a beacon of motivation, directing the charge in research efforts while promoting and encouraging fellow learners to explore their educational potential.

Md. Shadman Khan is a student of McMaster University in my final year of Honours Economics Specialist undergraduate program.

Nadezhda Anatolievna Lebedeva is a Doctor of Philosophy in the field of Cultural Studies, professor of International Personnel Academy (Germany) and a full member of the Eurasian Academy of Television and Radio. She worked at the Kherson State Agrarian University in Ukraine as the Head department of Humanitarian Disciplines Chair. Currently, Nadezhda Lebedeva is the Chairwoman of the Editorial Board of the international scientific project "Scientific Forum". She also the Main Editor of the international journal "Universum: Philology & Arts", a reviewer and member of the editorial board of scientific collections of international conferences and scientific journals ("Journal of Social, Humanity, and Education", "Journal of Sustainable Tourism and Entrepreneurship" - Indonesia), the author of more than a hundred publications, including Scopus, has recommendations and certificates of honour for successful scientific activity). Experienced in project cinematography management and developed lecture courses in a foreign language for students of state administration. Also she led ESP classes for future architectures and hydraulic engineering and water resources students. N. Lebedeva graduated from the Kherson State Pedagogical Institute in 1996. After graduating from the post-graduate course at the Kherson State University, became a lecturer at the History of World Culture and Literature Department of the Foreign Languages Faculty in Kherson State University. In June 2008 was enrolled in the doctoral program of the Interregional Academy of Personnel Management in Kyiv, specializing in Cultural Studies. She was awarded the medal "For Civil Courage" of the Afghan Veterans' Ukrainian Union for the book "My Afghan" by Nikolay Vishnyak". Participation in the creation of documentary films and scientific articles is marked by her membership in the Eurasian Academy of Television and Radio (November 2012). The monograph "Cultural Aspect of Alexander Elagin's Creativeness" was awarded by the 1st prize in a scientific direction "Cultural Studies" and she became the winner of the competition for educational projects "Interclover – 2017" in the nomination – "Research Project". N. Lebedeva also was invited to be a member of the Ukrainian Assembly of Doctors of Sciences in the

Field of State Administration (February 2018). Scope of her scientific interests: state administration, regional development, philosophy, pedagogy, Russian, Ukrainian and English philology, cultural studies and ethnology.

Rashidul Hasan Mahim, a dedicated student at BRAC University in Bangladesh, passionately pursues a dual major in Computer Information Systems and Human Resources Management. Known for his insatiable curiosity and drive for knowledge, Rashidul stands as a beacon of inspiration, leading the charge in research endeavors while nurturing and encouraging fellow students to explore their academic potential.

Sayada Mollika graduated from BRAC University with a Bachelor of Arts in English, concentrating in ELT and Applied Linguistics in 2021. At BRAC University, where she is presently enrolled in the Master of Arts in English program, she is employed as a Teaching Assistant in the Department of English and Humanities. She was a YouTube content creator and a beginner-level WordPress developer from 2017 to 2019. Her entrepreneurial endeavors included crafting and selling handmade artificial flowers online. Sayada Mollika's diverse experiences reflect her multifaceted skills, as does her keen interest in online entrepreneurship. Her research interests include teaching English as a foreign and second language, the integration of technological gadgets and AI assistance in English teaching, syllabus and materials design, barriers to ESOL learners mastering English in urban and rural contexts, tailored English for the hotel and tourism industry, English for business professionals, The art of sophisticated language and persuasion in business, English education policy and practice and ELT in religious seminaries.

Tanzid Morshed, a diligent student enrolled at BRAC University in Bangladesh, ambitiously delves into the realms of Computer Information Systems and Marketing. Tanzid's influence echoes through his unwavering dedication to both personal growth and societal betterment, painting a portrait of a student leader and an advocate for positive change. Tanzid Morshed is a dedicated student currently pursuing a double major in Marketing and Computer Information Management at Brac Business School, Brac University. Alongside his academic pursuits, he actively engages in entrepreneurial endeavors through Facebook Marketplace. As the Director of the Brac University Entrepreneurship Forum (BUEDF), Tanzid is committed to fostering a spirit of innovation and entrepreneurship within his university community. While he has yet to publish research, his strong interest in the field and his role in BUEDF showcase his passion for contributing to the world of business and technology. In his free time, Tanzid indulges in his love for exploration, traveling to new places, and savoring diverse cuisines. He also dedicates his leisure hours to tasks such as page management, post writing, and market research for his business, demonstrating his proactive approach to learning and growth.

Shafiqua Nawar, born on February 28, 2001, in Dhaka, Bangladesh, is a student at BRAC University's BRAC Business School. Notable achievements include securing 3rd place in the COVID-19 Combatants Unification Competition and contributing to a research paper presented at the 2nd International Conference on Aviation Future. Shafiqua has served as a Student Tutor, Director at the Business and Economics Forum, and a Subject Matter Specialist at Emerging Study Bangladesh Ltd. Beyond academics, she is passionate about case solving, research, content writing, sketching, and singing. Guided by the motto "Consistency is the key to success," Shafiqua aspires to create positive societal change through impactful research.

Zeun Tafsir Nova, born on December 6, 2000, in Tangail grew up in a family where everyone was so passionate about educational excellence. Zeun attended Bindubasini government girls high school where she was a captain of the cultural club. Academic: Zeun pursued her undergraduate studies at Brac University, majoring in Marketing. Vision for the future: Zeun aims to achieve skills related to her majoring subject.

Mithila Zaman Priasa is currently an undergraduate student studying at BRAC university in BBS department. She is major in Marketing and HR .She has always been interested in research work and she has contributed in research activities under her supervisors. She aims to provide solutions for the society through active research work.

Jotirmoyee Prodhan is a passionate and driven undergraduate student with a keen interest in research and English Language Teaching (ELT). Having pursued a major in linguistics and (ELT), Jotirmoyee Prodhan quickly distinguished her through academic excellence and a fervent commitment to exploring the realm of language education. Beyond the classroom, Jotirmoyee has actively contributed to the ELT community through hands-on experiences, including volunteer work in local language programs and collaborations with educators to enhance language teaching methodologies as well as research work.

Proma Quadir, a dynamic BBA senior at BRAC Business School, BRAC University, is blending her Marketing major with a minor in Computer Information Management (CIM). Beyond academics, she serves as a student tutor (undergraduate Teaching Assistant), assisting her faculties, enhancing student learning experiences and bringing her expertise to her peers. Actively engaged in extracurriculars, Proma serves as the Assistant Director of the Marketing and Public Relations department for the BRAC University Business Club (BIZ BEE). She previously held the position of Executive of Strategic Partnership for Hult Prize at BRAC University 2023 and contributed as a Campus Ambassador for 10 Minute School. Passionate about art, film, music, table tennis, and basketball, she finds joy in diverse interests. Proma's journey reflects her commitment to academic excellence and a vibrant campus life.

Md. Ahsanul Islam Saqlain is a third-year undergraduate in the Bachelor of Business Administration program at Brac University. He was an SEO content writer for Best Seo BD for a time, and he is presently involved with the Brac University Business Club's Research and Publication Department (BIZ BEE). He has a strong interest in entrepreneurship and manages his own eSports hub.

Sandeep Kumar Sharma is working as an Assistant Professor (Linguistic) in the in the School of Liberal Arts & Management, DIT University, Dehradun, Uttarakhand. He received his PhD in Linguistic from IIT Patna. He has research interest in climate and social linguistic, and role of linguistic in HEIs.

Ajay K. Singh is working as an Associate Professor (Research) in the Department of Humanities and Social Science, Graphic Era (Deemed to be University) Dehradun. He has worked as Assistant Professor (Economics) in the School of Liberal Arts & Management, DIT University Dehradun for 6 years. He did Post-Doctorate Research with EDI of India, Ahmedabad, Gujarat (India). He received MPhil (Economics) from DAVV Indore (India), and PhD (Economics) from IIT Indore (India. He has published several research papers in the diversified area such as climate change, agricultural productivity, assessment of food security; estimation of GFSI, development of environmental sustainability index (ESI) and its association with socio-economic indicators; measurement and determinants of entrepreneurship ecosystem, and dimension of sustainable development and its interlinkages with economic development.

Santosh Singh is working as an Assistant Professor (English) in the in the School of Liberal Arts & Management, DIT University, Dehradun, Uttarakhand. He received his PhD in English Literature from Gurukul Kangri Vishwavidyalaya, Haridwar in 2015, and MA in English Literature and BA from HNB Garhwal University. He is having more than 22 years' experience in industry and teaching. His research interest lies in Indian Street theatre, Postcolonial Studies, Folk Studies and Indian Writing in English. He has published many research papers and book chapters in his credit in nationally and internationally reputed journals. He has also experience working as Assistant Professor at Raffles University Neemrana, Rajasthan and Uttaranchal University, Dehradun, Uttarakhand.

Rezuana Tabassum completed her Bachelor of Arts in English from BRAC University in 2022 with two majors, 'ELT and Applied linguistics' and 'Human Resource Management'. She is currently pursuing her Master of Arts in English from BRAC University as well. She is working there as a Teaching Assistant in the English and Humanities Department. Her research interest includes various sectors related to English as well as the business sector.

Nuzhat Tanisha is a 4th Year Student majoring in finance in the Bachelor in Business Administration Department of BRAC University. She is also the Assistant Director of the Research and Publications department in the University's Business Club (BIZBEE). She is a student tutor and Freshmen advisor for her department helping her peers navigate the complexities of the degree. She aims to get her CFA degree after completing her Bachelors.

Tasnim Binte Zahir is a student of BRAC University doing major in CIM(Computer information management) and minor in accounting. Moreover, Tasnim is currently playing roles both as a student tutor and a FYAT mentor at BRAC university where she assists students with their studies and faculties with their paper work.

Marzia Zaman is about to complete her graduation from BRAC University, Dhaka, Bangladesh. She is currently working as a student tutor in her school, pursuing double majors in Finance and CIM(Computer Information Management). Marzia's research interests are in technology-driven domains and social enterprises. Marzia is keen to contribute to innovative and socially impactful solutions through research.

Index

A

B

C

D

E

F

G

H

I

L

M

N

O

P

R

S

T

U

W

www.ingramcontent.com/pod-product-compliance
Lightning Source LLC
LaVergne TN
LVHW080639011026
849160LV00014B/1260